Wilhard Becker

Du kannst deine Wut in Stärke verwandeln

Textausgabe

Verlag Ernst Kaufmann

2. Auflage 1990
© 1989 by Verlag Ernst Kaufmann, Lahr · Alle Rechte vorbehalten
Hergestellt bei Studio-Druck, Nürtingen-Raidwangen · Gestaltung: JAC
ISBN 3-7806-2192-4

Aggressionen sind „in". Sie sind heute fast zu einem Gütezeichen für Echtheit geworden. Tatsächlich sind sie ein notwendiges Signal einer inneren Störung.

Es gibt verschiedene Möglichkeiten, mit Aggressionen umzugehen. Ich kann meine Wut ausagieren – um mich schlagen und meine Umwelt dafür verantwortlich machen.

Ich kann aber auch meine Wut anschauen, wenn sie mich „gepackt" hat, und überlegen, was ich tun will, um die Situation zu verändern.

Habe ich Wut – oder hat die Wut mich?

Benutze ich die Steine, die mir andere in den Weg gelegt haben, um sie ihnen wieder an den Kopf zu werfen, oder verwende ich sie als Baumaterial für eine neue Wegstrecke?

Das erste ist spontaner und üblicher, das zweite erfordert Arbeit und Überlegung. Ich kenne Aggressionen; ich kenne Wut – Stinkwut und ohnmächtige Wut.

Ich bin wütend, wenn man mir das Wort abschneidet und mich nicht ausreden läßt.

Ich bin stinkwütend, wenn mir jemand in meinen geparkten Wagen fährt und heimlich abhaut.

Ich fühle mich ohnmächtig wütend angesichts der Zerstörung unserer Umwelt und der Unfähigkeit, dem Einhalt zu gebieten.

Die gleiche Wut erlebt der Arbeiter, dessen Arbeitsplatz wegrationalisiert wird, ebenso wie der Arbeitgeber, der zu Tarifabschlüssen gezwungen wird, die seinen Betrieb ruinieren, oder der Abiturient, der trotz seiner guten Abschlußnote keine Chance auf einen Studienplatz hat. Wut entwickelt sich sowohl bei Demonstrationen, die auf eine Polizeikette treffen, als auch bei Polizisten, die als „Bullen" beschimpft werden, wenn sie ihrer Pflicht nachkommen. Es gibt die kleine Wut und die große Wut – eine Wut, die alles kaputtmachen möchte, und die Wut, sich am liebsten selbst umzubringen. Manche schreien, andere weinen vor Wut. Man kann seine Wut auch hinunterschlucken oder mit Arbeit betäuben; man kann krank werden vor Wut oder andere krankenhausreif schlagen!

(Man kann über ein Buch wie dieses wütend werden oder dem Autor einen entsprechenden Brief schreiben!)

Wut ist ein Gefühl, das jeder schon kennenlernt, lange bevor er es beim Namen nennen kann. Der erste Schrei, mit dem wir bei unserer Geburt diese Welt begrüßen, war vielleicht schon ein Wutschrei! Strapaziös genug ist die Prozedur jedenfalls, durch die wir ans Licht der Welt kommen.

Später, in den Trotzphasen, sind nicht nur die Kinder wütend, sondern manchmal auch die Eltern, wenn sie bis zur „Weißglut" gereizt werden.

Das Gefühl der Wut begleitet uns recht zuverlässig durch alle Entwicklungsstufen unserer Kinder- und Jugendzeit. Auch in den engsten freundschaftlichen Beziehungen bleiben wir nicht von Wut verschont – und selbst in der Ehe können wir die ganze Skala der Wutgefühle erleben.

Wie entsteht Wut? Was spielt sich in uns ab, wenn wir wütend werden?

Manche erleben dieses Gefühl wie einen unerträglichen inneren Druck, der sie rasend macht. Tatsächlich stammt das Wort Wut aus dem Althochdeutschen „wuot" und heißt „Raserei". Ganz ähnlich kling das Wort Mut. Es leitet sich aus dem althochdeutschen Wort „muot" ab, das ursprünglich „Kraft des Denkens, Empfindens und Wollens" bedeutet.

Es gehört tatsächlich Mut dazu, mit der Wut so umzugehen, daß daraus kein Unheil entsteht und die gestaute Energie konstruktiv eingesetzt werden kann.

Wut oder Mut? An dieser Frage wird sich die Kraft und Qualität unseres Lebens und vielleicht sogar das Überleben der Menschheit entscheiden!

Wie Wut entsteht

Ein Aggressionsmodell

Wut entsteht, wenn natürliche Bedürfnisse und Wünsche unterdrückt werden. Diese Unterdrückung kann schon in der Kinderstube beginnen. Ein autoritärer Erziehungsstil führt dann zur ersten Begegnung mit Macht. Macht erzeugt Ohnmacht; Ohnmacht wird zur ohnmächtigen Wut.
 Von Anfang unseres Lebens an haben wir es mit Menschen zu tun, die stärker sind als wir — die mehr wissen und mehr können. Liebevoll oder streng wird uns gezeigt, was für uns richtig und was verkehrt ist — was wir tun dürfen und was wir lassen sollen. Wir erleben die „Großen", auch wenn sie uns sehr lieben, als mächtig.
 Wir werden in Machtverhältnisse hineingeboren. Unser Leben ist eine ständige Auseinandersetzung mit diesen Verhältnissen. Dabei pendeln wir hin und her zwischen Anpassung und Widerstand, zwischen Unterdrücken und Unterdrücktwerden.

Diese Erfahrung gilt nicht nur für den persönlich-familiären Bereich, sondern auch für die Auseinandersetzung mit den kollektiven Machtverhältnissen unserer Gesellschaft.
Der einzelne ist immer wieder vor die Entscheidung gestellt, ob er sich den gegebenen Verhältnissen unterordnet und sein Leben von außen bestimmen läßt oder ob er Kräfte entwickelt, mit denen er sich einen eigenen Lebensraum schafft. Jedes Kollektiv hat die Tendenz, das Individuelle und Persönliche einzuebnen. Eigenständige Persönlichkeiten stören die Gesellschaft. Sie stören besonders diejenigen, die das Sagen haben. Wer oben ist, will oben bleiben und regieren. Der Unterlegene möchte gern nach oben kommen.

Überall, wo Menschen miteinander leben, findet ein ständiger Kampf statt. Gekämpft wird auf unterschiedliche Weise: durch Flüchten oder Angreifen, sich Durchsetzen und andere Zurücksetzen, mit List und Tücke, teils offen, teils versteckt. Schwer zu durchschauen sind die subtilen und getarnten Formen der Machtausübung, die aber gerade darum eine besondere Hilflosigkeit und Wut auslösen.
 Die folgenden Beispiele können diese Situation veranschaulichen:

Es gibt den Terror der Schwachen. Hier wird vielleicht eine Krankheit benutzt, um den anderen in Schach zu halten. „Nimm bitte Rücksicht auf meine Migräne, oder meine schwachen Nerven, oder meine Überarbeitung."

Man kann auch auf der Klaviatur der Gefühle spielen, um Druck auszuüben: „Wenn du das tust, bin ich aber traurig." „Nach allem, was ich für dich getan habe, kannst du mir das doch nicht antun."

Es gibt auch eine angemaßte Verantwortung, die den anderen unmündig hält und damit versteckt Macht ausübt. „Ich will ja nur das Beste für dich." „Ich mache mir deinetwegen Sorgen" usw.

Wer seine Krankheit und Schwächen als Waffe einsetzt, überlebt meistens den Gesunden! Mit „liebevoller" Verantwortung kann ich den anderen ersticken.

Gegen solche scheinbar guten Motive kann man sich nur schwer zur Wehr setzen. Man fühlt sich zwar ohnmächtig, aber moralisch nicht berechtigt, wütend zu werden.

Im Kampf um die Macht versucht jeder nach „oben" zu kommen. Obensein bedeutet aber immer, daß andere unten sind! Siegersein und Obensein bürgt nicht in jedem Fall für Qualität. Der Schlaue und Raffinierte, der oben ist, ist nicht immer auch der Beste. Dasselbe gilt für die umgekehrte Situation. Untensein und Verlieren ist noch lange kein Beweis für Minderwertigkeit.

Der Kampf um die Macht kennzeichnet das menschliche Leben und ist ein wichtiger Motor für die Entwicklung auf vielen Gebieten. Aber nicht immer verlaufen Entwicklungen positiv. Im Kampf gegen die Naturmächte hat der Mensch scheinbar gewonnen. Heute jedoch beginnt sich dieser Sieg in manchen Bereichen gegen uns zu wenden. Die Macht als gewaltsame Unterdrückung bewirkt auf Dauer keinen Frieden und keine gesunde Atmosphäre – auch nicht im Umgang mit der uns umgebenden Natur.

Jeder hat seine eigene Geschichte mit der Macht. Wir liefern uns Kraftproben nicht nur in Familie und Beruf, sondern in allen gesellschaftlichen Bereichen. Harmonie und Gleichheit, friedliches Zusammenleben und Zusammenarbeiten sind meist nicht von langer Dauer. Immer wieder entstehen zwangsläufig Differenzen – immer wieder gibt es Große, die bestimmen, und Kleine, die bestimmt werden.

Schon als Kinder haben wir das entdeckt und unterschiedlich darauf reagiert: entweder brav und gehorsam oder trotzig und unangepaßt. In jeder Lebensstufe hatten wir uns mit Machtverhältnissen auseinanderzusetzen. Jeder entwickelte dabei seine eigene Strategie.

Zunächst erleben wir die körperliche Überlegenheit der Eltern und älteren Geschwister. Später kann uns größere Intelligenz und „Schlagfertigkeit" anderer das Gefühl geben, ohnmächtig zu sein.

Dann lernen wir die Macht der Institutionen kennen. Wir sammeln unsere Erfahrungen in Gruppen, Verbänden und staatlichen Einrichtungen. Die Schule mit ihren eigenen Gesetzmäßigkeiten hält uns für viele Jahre in Schach. Solange wir den Anforderungen entsprechen, spüren wir nicht viel von unserer Ohnmacht. Wer aber an den Rand gerät, leistungsmäßig oder disziplinarisch, kann Ohnmacht und ohnmächtige Wut erleben. Die Begegnung mit der Ordnungsmacht, sei es in Gestalt eines Lehrerkollegiums oder später mit anderen staatlichen Ordnungen, zeigt uns die Grenzen unserer Eigenmächtigkeit. Wir müssen uns fügen, leiden oder zu Rebellen werden.

Häufiger und vielleicht schlimmer sind aber die inneren Verletzungen, die wir als Unterlegene abbekommen. Große Leute können uns kränken, demütigen und abhängig machen.

Viele leiden unter den seelischen Wunden ihrer Kindheit und schaffen es nicht, ihr Ohnmachtsgefühl zu überwinden. Sie finden dafür Ausdrücke wie Minderwertigkeitskomplexe oder Selbstunsicherheit. Ihr Leben bleibt unter dem Niveau, das sie eigentlich ihren Gaben entsprechend haben könnten. Die Wut über ihr Unterdrücktsein und über die ihnen zugefügten Kränkungen bleibt sehr oft unbewußt. Die Energie dieser unterdrückten Aggressionen bleibt demzufolge auch unverfügbar. Häufig beeinflußt auch die Macht der Zahl unser Leben. Das beginnt schon in der Kindheit. Wenn die Bande, mit der wir in Fehde lagen, mehr Mitglieder hatte als unsere Clique, bekamen wir es mit der Angst zu tun.

Zahlen gewinnen auch Macht, wenn es ums Geld geht. Abhängigkeitsgefühle kennen viele von Kindheit an, wenn sie ans „Zahlen" denken! Macht und Ohnmacht im Verhältnis zum Geld spielt in unserem Gefühl oft eine große Rolle.

Auch in der Demokratie gilt die Macht der Zahl: die Zahl der Wählerstimmen. Wer die Mehrheit hat, sitzt oben. Die Minderheiten sitzen in der Opposition. Noch schlimmer sind die dran, denen es nicht gelingt, die erforderlichen Stimmen für einen Platz auf der Oppositionsbank zu erreichen.

Aber nicht jede Unterlegenheit muß sich als Ohnmacht und Wut auswirken. Erst dort, wo der Mächtige den Unterlegenen gegen dessen Willen manipuliert, wird Macht böse und erzeugt Ohnmacht und Wut.

Eine besondere Spielart der Macht ist die Institution. In ihr soll etwas gemacht, erhalten, gefördert oder verwaltet werden. In jeder Institution gibt es darum notwendigerweise eine gewisse Hierarchie. Je größer die Einrichtung ist, desto unpersönlicher können die Beziehungen der Mitglieder untereinander sein.

Die Institution hat Posten, Ämter, Funktionen, die jeweils mit besonderen Befugnissen ausgestattet sind. Je höher der Platz und je größer die Institution, desto größer auch die Vollmacht des Platzhalters.

Der einzelne erlebt sich einer Institution gegenüber oft als klein und ohnmächtig. Behörden, Konzerne, Staatsapparate lassen schnell Macht und Ohnmachtsgefühle entstehen.

Vielleicht kennt jemand die Situation aus seinem Vereinsleben, daß er es nach einer Vorstandswahl plötzlich nicht mehr mit seinem Freund zu tun hatte, sondern mit dem „Vorsitzenden". Unter Umständen hat dieser „Amtsinhaber" sogar persönlich eine andere Meinung, als er sie „von Amts wegen" sagen darf. Vorstände, Gremien, Ausschüsse und sogar Kollegien können zu einem unpersönlichen Machtinstrument werden. Der Mensch ist dann Diener des Apparates — ein Staatsdiener, ein Minister, ein Verwaltungsbeamter, ein Offizier, ein Funktionär. Er hat jetzt Machtbefugnisse. Er dient der Staatsmacht—Polizeimacht—Wehrmacht. Wer keiner Institution angehört, ist zunächst ohne Macht.

Die Beziehung zwischen Macht—Ohnmacht—Wut läßt sich an einem einfachen Modellbild darstellen.

Macht wird bewußt oder unbewußt von dem, der sie nicht besitzt, als Druck erlebt und erzeugt Ohnmacht. Die natürliche Reaktion auf das Erleben der Ohnmacht ist Wut. Echte Wut will die Situation verändern und richtet sich wieder gegen den, der die Macht ausübt.

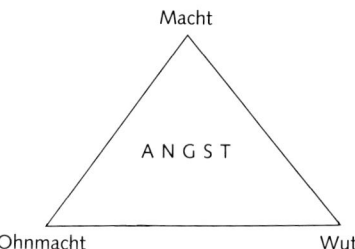

Der Motor, der die Dynamik in diesem Machtdreieck in Bewegung hält, ist die Angst. Auch der Mächtige hat Angst — die Angst, seine Position zu verlieren.

Unsere Sprache verrät sehr viel von den Mechanismen des Umgangs mit Macht. Eine Planstelle in der Institution wird nicht durch einen lebendigen Menschen „erfüllt, belebt" oder „gestaltet", sondern „besetzt". Der Sitz zeigt die Größe der Position an. Es gibt Sitze im Parlament, Ministersessel und schließlich sogar Throne, wenn auch deren Bedeutung meist nur noch repräsentativer Art ist. Wir haben — je nach Würde und Macht — bestimmte Sitzordnungen. Selbst in der Industrie ist die Position eines Angestellten an der Größe seines Schreibtischs und des dazugehörigen Sessels abzulesen. Das alles ist ebenso notwendig wie gefährlich — doch unsere Welt ist bis heute nicht anders zu regieren. Der Verzicht auf alle Institutionen würde ein lebensgefährliches Chaos auslösen. Andererseits nimmt das Potential an ohnmächtiger Wut in unserer Gesellschaft zu, was ebenso lebensgefährlich ist und uns nötigt, nach Lösungen des Problems der unpersönlichen Macht zu suchen.

An dieser Stelle beschäftigen wir uns weniger mit politischen Problemen als mit den ganz persönlichen, inneren Auseinandersetzungen mit Macht, Ohnmacht und Wut.

Ohnmachtsgefühle entstehen bereits in frühester Kindheit. Ein Säugling ist unfähig, sich selbst zu helfen. Er ist total auf andere angewiesen. Er kann noch nicht einmal sagen, was er braucht, wo es ihm weh tut, wie einsam er sich fühlt usw. Es dauert lange, bis wir die Entwicklung zu einem selbständigen — eigenmächtigen — Menschen durchgestanden haben und kein äußerer Anlaß mehr besteht, uns abhängig oder ohnmächtig zu fühlen. Wir bleiben aber lebenslang anfällig für diese Unterlegenheitsgefühle und versuchen deshalb auch in allen Beziehungen immer wieder zu entdecken, ob wir oben oder unten sind, ob wir etwas machen können oder ein anderer etwas mit uns macht. Wie oft wir solche Gefühlsprobleme haben, zeigt sich an der Häufigkeit der Wutgefühle. Manchmal erscheinen sie als Ärger, Eifersucht oder Gekränktsein oder als Gefühl der Entwürdigung und des Nichtbeachtetwerdens.

Wahrscheinlich gibt es nur sehr wenige Menschen, die nicht unter solchen Zwängen leben – die nicht Machteinflüssen ausgesetzt sind oder ihre Macht andere spüren lassen. Da wir alle mehr oder weniger dieses Problem der Macht/Ohnmacht/Wut-Struktur schicksalhaft im eigenen Leben erfahren, sind wir auch alle in unseren Gefühlen davon betroffen. Wir leben im Spannungsfeld der Angst.

Dadurch geraten unsere Gefühle oft außer Kontrolle und erzeugen Störungen und Krankheiten. Im gesellschaftlichen Bereich führt das zu Aufständen und Revolten.

Subjektive Erfahrungen mit Ohnmachtsgefühlen zeigen sich in typischen Störungen, die sich am Bild des „Macht-Dreiecks" aufzeigen lassen.

Das Macht-Dreieck

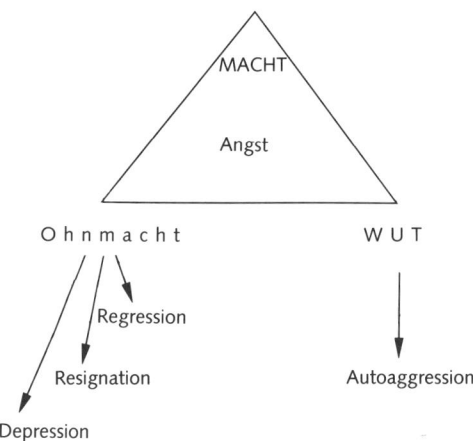

Fluchtwege aus der Macht

Der Zustand der Ohnmacht ist nicht lange zu ertragen. Nicht jeder entwickelt aber aus den Ohnmachtsgefühlen heraus eine ohnmächtige Wut. Es gibt drei andere Möglichkeiten, sich der Ohnmacht zu entziehen und aus der Machtdynamik auszusteigen: die Depression, die Resignation und die Regression.

Depression

Wer die Ohnmachtsgefühle nicht mehr erträgt und vom Gefühl der Hilflosigkeit und Ausweglosigkeit übermannt wird, kann in eine Depression verfallen. Damit entzieht er sich unbewußt dem Machtkampf. Er ist für keinen „Machthaber" mehr erreichbar. Depression ist eine Art fixierten Ohnmachtsgefühls.

Der Depressive verweigert sich seiner Lebenssituation und entzieht sich damit der Auseinandersetzung: zum Beispiel die Frau, die sich den Ansprüchen ihres Mannes und der Familie nicht mehr gewachsen fühlt, oder der Mann, der immer deutlicher spürt, daß er das Rennen um die höhere Position nicht mehr gewinnen kann.

Ein weiterer Grund zur Flucht in die Depression kann in einer vermeintlich unheilbaren Kränkung oder in der Verzweiflung über unlösbare Konflikte liegen.

Resignation

Auch der Resignierende verweigert sich. Er tut es aber bewußt und muß deshalb nicht krank werden. Er hat sich mit der Unlösbarkeit der Situation abgefunden und sieht keinen Sinn mehr in weiteren Auseinandersetzungen. Er überläßt die Macht und auch die Wut anderen. Er will nichts mehr verändern, weil er nicht mehr an eine machbare Veränderung glaubt. Man kann auch aus der Resignation eine Philosophie machen und diese als Lebensweisheit und Erfahrung ausgeben. Wer resigniert, steigt auch aus dem Machtkampf aus und zieht sich auf seine „Privatinsel" zurück.

Regression

Die dritte Haltung, die aus der Ohnmachtserfahrung entstehen kann, ist die Regression. Der Rückzug aus dem Kampf um die Macht geschieht hier durch Anerkennung der Verhältnisse und der eigenen Ohnmächtigkeit. Regression ist Rückzug in eine frühere Entwicklungsstufe, meist in eine Phase der Kindheit. Die Verantwortung wird abgegeben. Pflichterfüllung, Gehorsam und ein infantiles Vertrauen treten an ihre Stelle. Statt Auseinandersetzung geschieht Anpassung.

Bei vielen ist die Regression nur partiell. Im Bereich ihrer „Mächtigkeit" — vielleicht im Beruf, in der Politik oder im Verein — erscheinen diese Menschen erwachsen und verantwortungsbewußt. In ihrem Ohnmachtsbereich — vielleicht in der Ehe, in der Familie oder in anderen persönlichen Beziehungen — sind sie unreif, brav, zuverlässig und zufrieden. Ist die Politik oder ist der Beruf ihr Ohnmachtsbereich, dann stabilisieren sie durch ihre Regression das bestehende System. Der Regredierende ist sich seines Rückzugs nicht immer bewußt. Vielleicht fühlt er sich sogar wohl. Warum soll er kämpfen oder etwas verändern? Es geht doch gut so, wie es ist!

Gelingt es jedoch, aus dem Ohnmachtsgefühl heraus statt auszuweichen eine „ohnmächtige Wut" zu entwickeln, das heißt das aggressive Potential zuzulassen, geht der Ohnmächtig-Wütende auf den Mächtigen los. Er versucht, die Machtverhältnisse zu ändern.

Wird dabei die Kraft der Aggression gesteuert und nicht nur blindlings „Dampf abgelassen", kann eine Veränderung in Gang kommen. Ist die Wut nur explosiv, wirkt sie zerstörerisch. Aber ganz gleich, ob der bisherige Machthaber gestärkt aus dem Kampf hervorgeht oder der Aggressor an die Macht kommt, das Macht-Dreieck bleibt in jedem Fall erhalten.

Veränderungen, die durch Wut und Aggression entstehen, bringen meist keine dauerhafte Lösung. Ich bin meine Wut zwar losgeworden, aber mein Partner muß jetzt zusehen, wie er damit fertig wird. Nur selten gelingt es, die Aggression so zu äußern, daß der andere nicht verletzt wird und nicht wieder zurückschlägt. Die alte Methode „Auge um Auge, Zahn um Zahn" funktioniert nicht. Eine Kränkung kann nicht durch eine andere geheilt werden.

Wie schwierig ein solcher Aggressionsaustausch ist, weiß jeder, der in einer Dauerbeziehung lebt. Das Ideal „Streiten verbindet" führt selten zu einer idealen Lösung.

Wird die Wut aber verdrängt und nicht konstruktiv eingesetzt, verwandelt sie sich in Autoaggression − in eine nach innen, gegen die eigene Person gerichtete Zerstörungsenergie.

Autoaggression

Wahrscheinlich werden viele medizinisch noch nicht erfolgreich zu behandelnde Erkrankungen durch die selbstzerstörerischen Kräfte der Autoaggression verursacht oder zumindest chronifiziert. Die geschluckte Wut greift den Magen oder andere Verdauungsorgane an; die verdrängte Wut tobt sich im Kopf als Migräne aus. Die gestörten Gefühle, die inneren Verletzungen, die ohnmächtige Wut benutzen unseren Körper, um zu Wort zu kommen. Die „Körpersprache" verrät, welche Machtkämpfe sich im Inneren einer Person abspielen, wenn sie nach außen kein Ventil finden.

Die gewalttätigste Form der Autoaggression ist der Selbstmord. Wer Suicid begeht, tötet nicht nur sich selbst, sondern mit sich auch den übermächtigen Machthaber, den er nicht stürzen konnte. Weil er von ihm nicht freikommt, ist die Selbsttötung für ihn der einzige Ausweg, ihn endgültig loszuwerden.

Im Grunde sind auch alle Formen der Sucht eine Art Selbstbestrafung. Weil ich nicht das sein kann, was ich sein möchte oder was meinem inneren Ideal entspricht, muß ich mich selbst zerstören. In vielen Fällen läßt sich die verdrängte Wut und Enttäuschung am eigenen Ideal kaum mehr erkennen, weil Scham und Ohnmacht die Stelle der Wut eingenommen haben. Nicht mehr das Ideal übt jetzt die Macht aus, sondern das Suchtmittel.

Wenn ich den Ausdruck Macht in diesem Zusammenhang immer als negativ beschreibe, so halte ich das deshalb für berechtigt, weil ich neben den Begriff der Macht einen positiven Begriff setzen möchte: die Stärke.

Macht − einseitig, als eine Funktion der Angst verstanden − ist destruktiv und krankmachend. Stärke dagegen ist eine positive Kraft, die nicht durch Angst bestimmt wird, sondern durch Mut.

Die Starken und die Schwachen

Stärke ist im Gegensatz zur Macht eine Kraft, die im persönlichen und im gesellschaftlichen Leben konstruktiv wirkt.

In jeder Gemeinschaft gibt es Stärkere und Schwächere. Auch dadurch entsteht eine Art Hierarchie, ein Oben und ein Unten. Im Unterschied zur Machtstruktur, die aus Angst geboren ist, hat Stärke nichts mit Unterdrückung zu tun.

Der Mächtige braucht Schwache, um sich stark zu fühlen. Der Starke aber ist stark in sich und braucht keinen Schwächeren, um seine Stärke zu empfinden.

Stärke ist eine innere Substanz − ein Sein. Macht ist eine äußere Position − ein Haben.

Die Position, die ich habe, kann mir weggenommen werden. Das, was ich habe, ist bedroht durch die „Habenichtse". Darum darf der Mächtige keine Schwäche zeigen und sich keine Blöße geben. Der Starke kann seine Schwäche zugeben. Seine Kraft zeigt sich nicht in der Unterdrückung Schwächerer, sondern im Mut, auch seine Grenzen zu sehen und zuzugeben. Wer stark *ist*, braucht keine Macht zu *haben*.

Stärke kann sich in körperlicher Kraft, in Fähigkeiten und Fertigkeiten wie auch in geistiger Begabung zeigen.

Wo ein Starker ist, wird es unausweichlich auch Schwächere geben, die weniger können und sich vielleicht auch unterlegen fühlen.

Was unterscheidet dann aber dieses Unterlegenheitsgefühl vom Ohnmachtsgefühl, den Unterlegenen vom Ohnmächtigen?

Der Starke ist, nach unserer Definition, nicht von der Angst bestimmt. Er kann seine Schwäche zugeben und wirkt deshalb auch nicht angstmachend. Sein Mut, sich zu seinen Stärken und Schwächen zu bekennen, ist für den Schwächeren ermutigend. Angst löst Angst aus! Mut macht Mut!

Wer eine Machtposition besitzt, muß nicht unbedingt stark sein, denn die Macht liegt in seiner Position begründet. Die Macht „kraft Amtes" steht ständig unter dem Erwartungsdruck anderer, etwas zu machen. Sie muß sich beweisen, um das Amt zu rechtfertigen.

Weil das Amt sich manchmal für die Person, die es ausfüllen soll, als eine Nummer zu groß zeigt, ist es oft mit Angstgefühlen gekoppelt.

Da ist zum Beispiel der Chef, der sich eigentlich nicht kompetent fühlt. Er unterdrückt dieses Gefühl der Inkompetenz durch eine scheinbare Sicherheit. Innerlich wird er jedoch immer empfindlicher und nervöser aus der ständigen Angst heraus, seine Schwächen könnten entdeckt werden.

Da ist die Ehefrau, die sich in ihrer Weiblichkeit nicht sicher fühlt und deshalb mit Eifersucht beobachtet, wie sich ihr Partner anderen Frauen gegenüber verhält. Sie hat zwar die Position einer Ehegattin, fühlt sich aber unbewußt immer bedroht.

Wir können dieses Verhalten auch bei manchen Lehrern beobachten, die sich ihren Schülern gegenüber besonders autoritär aufführen und auf jede Disziplinlosigkeit nervös und hart reagieren.

Macht und Angst begegnen uns alltäglich – zum Beispiel bei einem Schalterbeamten, der uns demonstrativ langsam abfertigt, oder bei einem Polizisten, der den Verkehrssünder von oben herab behandelt.

Der Starke dagegen tut das, was seiner Kraft entspricht, und nicht das, was man von ihm erwartet. Er ist stark, auch wenn er nichts macht. Er zeigt seine Stärke, indem er seine Schwächen zugibt.

Im Unterschied zur Macht offenbart Stärke auch ihre Schwachseite und das Angewiesensein auf Unterstützung und Ergänzung. Der Mächtige wird bestenfalls bewundert, häufiger allerdings gefürchtet und am wenigsten geliebt. Er ist innerlich und oft auch äußerlich einsam.

Der Starke sucht Gemeinschaft, da er sie nicht fürchten muß. Er weiß, daß er andere braucht, und kann es zugeben.

Am deutlichsten wird der Unterschied von Stärke und Macht im Umgang mit Kritik. Der Starke ist für Kritik dankbar, auch wenn er sie nicht immer als angenehm empfindet. Er kann Fehler zugeben und Korrekturen annehmen. Sein Verhalten bewirkt Vertrauen. In seiner Nähe fühlt man sich ermutigt und herausgefordert, sich selbst einzubringen und eigene Stärken zu entwickeln.

Das Stärke-Dreieck

Der innere Motor in der Beziehung zwischen Starken und Schwachen ist Mut, im Unterschied zur Angst beim „Macht-Dreieck" (S. 10). Das wachsende Grundgefühl in einer solchen Gemeinschaft ist nicht mehr Wut, sondern Vertrauen.

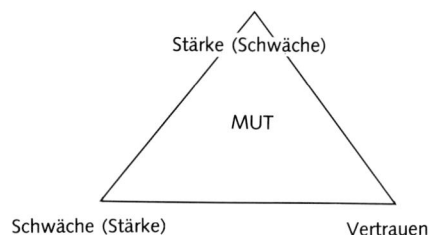

Wer unter Ohnmacht und Wut leidet, wird sich nach einem solchen Vertrauensverhältnis sehnen und fragen, wie die Dynamik der Angst im „Macht-Dreieck" verlassen werden kann und der Zugang zu einer Beziehung der Stärke und des Mutes zu finden ist.
  Wie kann das „Macht-Dreieck" in ein „Stärke-Dreieck" verwandelt werden?

Mut als neue Gesinnung

Um aus der Angst herauszutreten, ist Mut nötig. Der erste Schritt besteht darin, seine Angst zuzugeben. Wenn ein Machthaber es fertigbringt, zu sagen: „Ich habe Angst", zeigt er in Wahrheit Stärke. Wenn ein Ohnmächtiger zugibt, daß er sich ohnmächtig fühlt, zeigt er Vertrauen. Wenn einer, der wütend ist, zugibt, daß er verletzt ist, zeigt er seine Schwäche und beweist damit Mut. Offenheit ist der erste mutige Schritt ins Vertrauen.

Der Mut zur Offenheit ist ein Test für die Ernsthaftigkeit des Bemühens, aus den alten Verhaltens- und Beziehungsmustern herauszukommen.

Die Aggressionen einfach herauszulassen, bringt noch keine Lösung. Die Angst regiert dann immer noch in unseren Beziehungskisten. Wut ist noch keine Offenheit. Sie verdeckt eher die wirklichen Probleme.

Echte Stärke zeigt sich an ihrer Wirkung. Wo einer zu sich selbst steht — sowohl zu seinen Schwächen als auch zu seinen Stärken —, macht er sich zwar angreifbar und verletzbar, seine Wirkung ist aber entängstigend. Sie ist wie eine ansteckende Ermutigung, durch die echte, lebendige Beziehungen entstehen. Wer sich nur als schwach darstellt, täuscht andere ebenso wie der, der nur seine starken Seiten hervorkehrt. Beide Seiten zu zeigen, beweist Mut, weil das der Wirklichkeit entspricht. Tatsächlich gibt es niemanden, der nicht auch etwas zu geben hat. In einer Gemeinschaft, die von einer Atmosphäre des Vertrauens und der Offenheit geprägt ist, werden auch unentdeckte Begabungen geweckt und gefördert. Dadurch wächst die Fähigkeit zur gesunden Selbsteinschätzung.

Der Prozeß der „Erwachsenenbildung", der Reifung zur Persönlichkeit, hängt vom Mut ab, sich selbst in seinen Licht- und Schattenseiten zu erkennen und zu sich selbst zu stehen.

Mut ist immer dort erforderlich, wo Angst besteht. Wer seine Angst nicht kennt, kann auch keinen Mut entwickeln. Ein Kind, das einfach über die Straße rennt, zeigt damit keinen Mut, sondern es ist noch nicht fähig, die Gefahren einzuschätzen.

Erst wenn ich das Risiko kenne, das ich eingehe, die Angst spüre und trotzdem das Notwendige tue, beweise ich Mut. Mut schämt sich nicht der Angst, läßt sich aber auch nicht von ihr bestimmen.

Diese Haltung dem Leben gegenüber ist uns nicht in die Wiege gelegt worden. Von Natur aus sind wir feige und ängstlich. Je reifer ein Mensch wird, desto deutlicher wird er auch seine Ängste spüren und zugeben können. Reife entfaltet sich dort am stärksten, wo jemand trotz seiner Ängste mutig das Lebensnotwendige wagt, wo er sich nicht hinter seinen Schwächen versteckt, sondern seine Möglichkeiten nutzt und seine Begabungen entfaltet.

Ohnmachtsgefühle und Wut sind keine gute Startposition für Konfliktlösungen. Sie sind jedoch ein notwendiges Signal dafür, daß in unserem Leben etwas verändert werden muß.

Der Schritt über die Schwelle

Perspektiven eines neuen Menschenbildes

Die Entstehung der Wut hat ihre Wurzeln im Erleben sozialer Ohnmacht in den ersten Lebensjahren. Ich bin klein und hilfsbedürftig, die anderen sind groß und können alles — vor allem können sie alles mit mir machen! Ich bin ihnen ausgeliefert, ich bin ohnmächtig.

Habe ich mir dann im Lauf der Zeit einen Raum der Selbständigkeit erobert, wache ich argwöhnisch und sensibel über mein Territorium, meinen Schutzraum, meinen Machtbereich.

Diese Auseinandersetzungen um den besseren Platz, die im Spielzimmer beginnen, werden mit viel Energie und großem Aufwand lebenslang weitergespielt. Wenn Völker miteinander dieses Spiel treiben, nennen wir das Politik. Nehmen die Auseinandersetzungen massive und gewalttätige Formen an, beginnt der Krieg.

Aggressionen sind Kriege im Kleinformat. Sie haben den gleichen Ausgangspunkt — nämlich die Angst vor der Bedrohung und Benachteiligung durch andere, die letztlich eine Angst ums Leben ist. Kein Wunder, wenn wir Mittel und Wege suchen, aus diesem Druck herauszukommen — sei es durch Flucht, Anpassung oder Angriff.

Jeder hat sein eigenes Arsenal an Waffen, mit denen er um sein Leben kämpft, wenn er sich bedroht fühlt. Die Wut spielt in diesen Prozessen eine große Rolle.

Eine gute Erziehung, und vor allem eine gute Therapie, wird darauf ausgerichtet sein, den Innendruck, der durch unterdrückte Gefühle verursacht ist, entsprechend nach außen abzuleiten. Wir lernen, uns durchzusetzen, unseren Lebensraum zu behaupten und den Angreifer zurückzuweisen.

Wenn wir unsere Wut nicht wahrnehmen und freisetzen, werden wir krank, denn die Seele braucht Entlastung von gestautem Innendruck.

Das alles ist in den letzten Jahrzehnten besonders bewußtgemacht und betont worden. Das Zusammenleben wurde durch diese Erkenntnisse zwar nicht leichter, aber doch offener und freier. Die Opposition hat ihren Platz in der demokratischen Gesellschaft gefunden; die früher unterdrückten Arbeitnehmer haben ihre Gewerkschaft, die

Schüler ihre Mitverwaltung und Elternbeiräte; der Kranke hat sein gesichertes Recht auf Behandlung; die Frauen sind nicht mehr ohne Stimmrecht und können sich von ihren diktatorischen Partnern scheiden lassen. Eigentlich müßte es doch wunderbar zugehen in einer Gesellschaft, die so viele Kanäle anbietet, unterdrückte Gefühle loszuwerden, und die jedem seinen individuellen Raum und sein Lebensrecht zukommen läßt.

Trotz allen Fortschritts im gesellschaftlichen Zusammenleben ist die Zahl der „Gefühlskranken" jedoch nicht kleiner geworden, sondern sie wächst beängstigend. Wir leben heute gefühlsbewußter und sensibler für unsere Bedürfnisse. Wir haben uns dadurch aber auch eine Menge Nachteile eingehandelt.

Wut und Aggression sind notwendige Lebensäußerungen – aber sind sie tatsächlich „notwendend"?

Man darf heute weinen, schreien und wütend werden. Schimpfwörter sind in der Öffentlichkeit und selbst in „guten" Familien „in". Im Parlament werden aggressionsgeladene Rededuelle ausgetragen, und die ganze Nation kann dieses „Schauspiel" am Radio oder Fernseher miterleben. So hilfreich das im Augenblick für den Aggressiven sein mag – für die Aggressionen ist damit noch keine befriedigende Lösung gefunden. Die Gefühle werden durch solche „Entladungen" lediglich der anderen Seite zugeschoben und müssen nun dort bewältigt werden.

Gibt es eine konstruktivere Art, mit diesen Energien umzugehen, als sie einfach – wie bei einem Überdruckventil – abzulassen?

Der Umgang der Völker miteinander ist vorsichtiger geworden. Muß nicht auch im privaten Bereich ein neues „Muster" für das Zusammenleben gefunden werden?

Diese Frage entscheidet sich maßgeblich am Umgang mit unseren aggressiven Gefühlen.

Wir brauchen ein neues Menschenbild

Seit Beginn des Humanismus hat sich die Erforschung der Natur und ihrer Gesetze durch die Humanwissenschaften als großer Fortschritt erwiesen. Wir sind dabei, auch die Natur unseres Menschseins zu ergründen. Das Menschenbild orientierte sich an den Einsichten der

Evolution. Indem wir die Bausteine unseres Lebens entdeckten, entdeckten wir uns selbst.

Heute wird deutlich, daß dies allein nicht genügt. So entscheidend wichtig es ist, zu erkennen, woher wir kommen und wer wir sind – die Frage wird immer dringlicher: Wer sollen, wollen und können wir sein? Wie muß der Mensch aussehen, der den Herausforderungen der Zukunft entsprechen kann?

Wenn es überhaupt noch eine Zukunft geben soll, dann können wir diese nicht mit den Mitteln und Methoden der Vergangenheit erreichen. Wir brauchen für unser Denken und unser Verhalten ein neues Paradigma – ein neues Menschenbild.

Der neue Mensch ist nicht nur das Produkt seiner biologischen Herkunft und seiner Geschichte, sondern er ist herausgefordert, Geschichte zu machen!

Die Erfahrungen und Philosophien der Vergangenheit reichen nicht mehr aus. Wir brauchen Visionen und Phantasien, die über das bisher Erlebte hinausreichen. Das neue Denken ist ein Denken von der Zukunft her und kann nur durch göttliche Inspiration geschehen. Das Leben, das allein noch Zukunft hat, ist ein Leben aus dem Geist.

Immer wieder hat es Menschen gegeben, die aus dieser ewigen Quelle lebten. Sie gaben der Welt neue Impulse und eröffneten modellhaft neue Dimensionen des Denkens und Verhaltens. Für mich findet dieser Geist, der eine neue Art Leben in diese Welt bringt, in der Person des Jesus von Nazareth seinen klarsten Ausdruck. Es erscheint mir lebenswichtig, sein Leben und Verhalten unter dem Aspekt eines neuen Menschenbildes zu studieren.

Vielleicht muß dieser Jesus für viele Christen erst von seinen traditionellen frommen und die Kirchengeschichte prägenden Gewändern befreit und aus den Formeln und Bildern dogmatischer Verhüllungen herausgelöst werden, um ihn wiederzuerkennen. Jesus sprach von einem neuen Leben, das „von oben" – anders ausgedrückt: „von vorne" – kommt, von dem, was zukünftig ist. Er sprach von der neuen Zeit, vom neuen Menschen und auch von den Geburtswehen einer neuen Welt.

Christliche Theologie hat das Neue weitgehend ins Jenseits – in eine andere Welt – verlagert und dem Diesseits dabei wenig Chancen gelassen.

Für mich hat diese zukünftige Welt und der neue Mensch schon keimhaft mit Pfingsten, der Ausgießung des Geistes, begonnen.

Wut und Mut beim neuen Menschen

Jesus, die Inkarnation des neuen Menschen, hat sicher nicht weniger als wir unter den Machtstrukturen zu leiden gehabt. Auch er fühlte sich bestimmt wütend und ohnmächtig! Bibelkennern wird wahrscheinlich sofort die Geschichte von der Austreibung der Kaufleute aus dem Tempel (Mt 21,12—16 par.) einfallen, wo Jesus ja — Gott sei Dank! — auch einmal aus der Haut gefahren ist und seine Wut aus sich herausgelassen hat! Wie dieses Beispiel auch immer zu verstehen ist oder zu interpretieren sein mag — wichtiger sind die Beispiele und Aussagen, die uns nicht nur bestätigen und entschuldigen, sondern die darüber hinaus eine neue Perspektive für eine neue Lebensart eröffnen. Ob Jesus immer alles richtig gemacht hat oder nicht, ist für mich eine akademische, keine praktische Frage. Zu suchen sind bei ihm Modelle neuen Verhaltens, die zukunftsweisend sind.

Jesus hat sich nicht in das Dreieck von Macht—Ohnmacht—Wut einspannen lassen. Schon am Anfang seiner Laufbahn — in der Vorbereitungszeit und beim Reifetest in der Wüste — hat er das Angebot, Weltherrscher zu werden, abgelehnt. Er verzichtete damit auf die Demonstration der Macht über Menschen. Er befreite sie vielmehr aus den Machteinflüssen persönlichkeitsfremder Kräfte: Kranke und Besessene aus ihrer Lebensbedrohung — Dirnen und Zöllner aus ihrer sozialen Ächtung — Frauen aus der untergeordneten Rolle. Auch denen, die nicht mehr bei ihm bleiben wollten, hat er ohne Vorwurf die Freiheit zugestanden, sich von ihm zu trennen.

Er hat die Chancen seiner Laufbahn, ein Mächtiger zu werden, nicht genutzt. Selbst als es um sein Leben ging, verzichtete er auf Macht — und damit auf die Möglichkeit der Befreiung durch überirdische Mächte (12 Legionen Engel).

Jesus empfiehlt als Ausdruck einer neuen Einstellung zum Leben, nicht zurückzuschlagen, sondern statt dessen auch noch die andere Wange hinzuhalten. Beim Streit um einen Rock empfiehlt er, dem anderen nicht nur den Rock, sondern auch noch den Mantel zu geben (und damit den Prozeßgegner nicht nur zufriedenzustellen, sondern ihn darüber hinaus für sich zu gewinnen!).

War Jesus wirklichkeitsfremd? Oder lebte er schon im Blick auf eine neue Wirklichkeit, die noch in der Zukunft liegt?

Er erwartete von seinen Leuten keine moralischen Klimmzüge, sondern rechnete auch für sie mit einer neuen, inneren Kraft, aus der heraus er selbst lebte! An keiner Stelle macht er den Eindruck eines Moralisten, der ethische Bestleistungen fordert. Er lebte einfach die Art, von der er sprach, aus einem sicheren, gefestigten Selbstwertgefühl. Der wesentliche Unterschied zu uns lag in seinem starken Selbstwertgefühl. Auch sein Ich-Bewußtsein war deutlich ausgeprägt. Wie oft sagte er: „Ich bin ..." und „Ich aber sage euch ..."!

Er wußte sich als Mensch Gottes frei von den Machtstrukturen seiner Umwelt. Weder die Macht mütterlicher Fürsorge noch die Versuchung, König oder Führer eines Volksaufstandes zu werden, konnten seine Entscheidungen bestimmen. Er kannte zwar die Versuchung zur Macht, hatte ihr jedoch ein starkes Selbstbewußtsein entgegenzusetzen. Er lebte im Kraftfeld Gottes, das stärker und vor allem anders ist als alle menschlichen, politischen und gesellschaftlichen Mächte. Er wußte sich zu Wichtigerem berufen als zum Wettlauf von Erfolg und Karriere, Rückschlägen und Enttäuschungen. Selbst Verrat und Todesdrohung konnten ihn nicht umstimmen und von seiner Berufung abbringen.

Das Geheimnis seiner Ich-Stärke lag wahrscheinlich im Wissen und Erleben, umfassend von Gott geliebt zu sein. Aus der Erfahrung dieser Liebe heraus konnte er sich auch ohne Verlustangst den Ansprüchen seiner Nächsten und Liebsten verweigern.

Er war nicht der Übermensch im Sinne Nietzsches, ebensowenig paßte er in das Bild des griechischen Heros. Er war auch kein vom Himmel herabgestiegener Gott, sondern der mit Geist erfüllte Mensch. Seine Orientierung lag in dem, was kommt, und nicht in dem, was war. Deshalb konnte er auch nicht in irgendein schon vorhandenes Schema passen. Er war der neue Mensch.

Der konstruktive Umgang mit Aggressionen

Unsere Aggressionen sind Symptome für Ohnmachtsgefühle und Kennzeichen für ein gestörtes Wertbewußtsein und der Lebensangst.
Die Befreiung von diesem inneren Druck ist lebensnotwendig. Wie diese Befreiung geschieht, ist nicht entscheidend. Sie wird aber immer im Vorläufigen steckenbleiben, wenn nicht eine neue Dimension dazukommt.
Jesus weist auf den Geist hin, der nicht nur ein neues Bewußtsein, sondern auch ein neues Wertbewußtsein schafft. Derselbe Geist ermutigt uns, aus Abhängigkeiten innerer und äußerer Art auszusteigen. Der neue Mensch bezieht sein Wertgefühl nicht in erster Linie aus seinem sozialen Umfeld, nicht aus Anerkennung und Bessersein im Vergleich mit Schlechteren, sondern aus dem Wissen um seinen göttlichen Ursprung. Er gewinnt seine Bedeutung aus demselben Bewußtsein wie Jesus: ein Geliebter Gottes zu sein.
Die Wirkungen des Geistes geschehen nicht automatisch, sondern gleichsam unterwegs; sie sind der Weg. Das Bild vom Weg steht für den Wandlungsprozeß. Weg heißt: weg-gehen vom Bisherigen und Orientierung nach vorn. Ich verlasse das Alte – die Fixierung auf meine Minderwertigkeitsgefühle und Kränkungen –, überholte Wertvorstellungen und Geltungsbedürfnisse. „Ich vergesse, was hinter mir ist, strecke mich aber nach dem aus, was vorne ist" (Phil 3,13).
Manche haben schon ihre alten Lebensmuster verlassen und Neues kennengelernt, aber sie werden immer wieder von ihren Erinnerungen eingeholt. Sie können erlittenes Unrecht nicht vergessen und sind an traumatische Erlebnisse wie angebunden. Befreiung gibt es nur, wenn die Faszination des Neuen stärker ist als das Zurückliegende.
Wut und Aggressionen können uns so lange beherrschen, bis das alte Wertbewußtsein durch ein neues ersetzt ist.
Der Weg der Wandlung bis in unser Wertgefühl hinein beginnt mit einem neuen Bewußtsein. Es ist das Wissen, durch den Geist Gottes ein „neuer Mensch" werden zu können. Ich lerne unterwegs, mich selbst ernst zu nehmen und Verhaltensweisen einzuüben, die dem neuen Menschen entsprechen. Unser Wertgefühl ist ein guter Gradmesser dafür, wie die Entwicklung vorankommt. Die klassischen Beispiele aus der Bergpredigt führen uns an eine sensationelle nicht-

aggresssive Art des Umgangs miteinander heran. Wenn sie allerdings nicht aus einem neuen Bewußtsein heraus befolgt werden, machen sie uns lächerlich oder bewirken sogar eine Verschlimmerung der Situation.

Beispiel 1: „Wenn dir einer auf die rechte Wange schlägt, halte auch die linke hin!" (Mt 5,39).

Ohne ein neues Wertbewußtsein wird der Geohrfeigte immer der Gekränkte, der Leidende oder derjenige sein, der zurückschlägt. Schlägt er nicht zurück, dann wahrscheinlich aus Schwäche oder Selbstbeherrschung.

Als „neuer Mensch" erlebt er diese Beleidigung wohl ebenso schmerzhaft – sie kann ihm aber nicht seinen Wert nehmen. Äußerlich betrachtet ist der Geschlagene zwar in der Position des Schwachen – der eigentlich Schwächere ist jedoch der Schläger. Obwohl dieser nach außen hin stark erscheint, handelt er aus innerer Schwäche. Jemanden schlagen ist nicht gerade eine starke Leistung! Zurückschlagen ist ebenso eine Schwäche, ist eine aggressive Reaktion auf derselben Ebene. Die andere Wange hinhalten ist ein Zeichen von Stärke; denn wer die andere Wange hinhält, gibt damit seine Schwäche zu und macht sich verwundbar. Um sich so zeigen zu können, muß man stark sein.

Beispiel 2: Dasselbe gilt auch für die Feindesliebe (Mt 5,44). Als Forderung wäre sie unmenschlich. Aus einer neuen Sicht heraus ist sie menschliche Stärke in Vollkommenheit. Sie ist göttlich!

„Deshalb sollt ihr vollkommen sein, wie euer himmlischer Vater vollkommen ist! (Mt 5,48).

Wer sein Wertbewußtsein von Gott bezieht, weil er sich von ihm geliebt und sich ihm verbunden fühlt, kann dazu fähig werden.

Die höchste Tugend, die aus diesem neuen Wertbewußtsein wächst, ist die Vergebung.

Normalerweise verstehen wir Vergebung als Beendigung einer Spannung durch Nachgeben. Die Schuld wird nicht mehr angerechnet. Die zerbrochene Beziehung wird geflickt. Damit ist noch nichts Neues entstanden, der alte Zustand ist nur wiederhergestellt.

Neues, selbstbewußtes Vergeben hat darüber hinaus mit Geben zu tun. Es entsteht eine neue Beziehung, weil ich dem anderen nicht nur seine Schuld erlasse, sondern ihm etwas von mir schenke: meine Aufmerksamkeit, mein Bemühen, ihn zu verstehen, mein Wohlwollen.

Wer so vergeben kann, ist immer der Überlegene. Bei aller Benachteiligung, die er vielleicht dadurch erfährt, ist er im Grunde selbst der Beschenkte. Er hat seine Aggressionen nicht verdrängt, sondern positiv umgewandelt.

Die neue Wirklichkeit

Die epochalen Veränderungen in dieser Welt gehen nie von den Realisten aus. Sie können immer nur das denken, was war und was machbar ist. Sie kommen nicht über ihren Erfahrungshorizont hinaus. Sie rechnen nur mit dem, was bekannt und berechenbar ist. Liebe und bleibender Friede sind in ihren Augen utopisch; und doch tragen alle Menschen eine tiefe Sehnsucht danach in sich.

Realistisch sind dagegen Angst, Wut, Ohnmacht, Neid und verletzte Gefühle. Sie verhindern die Erfüllung dieser Wünsche und Hoffnungen.

Der neue Mensch, eine neue Gemeinschaft und eine neue Welt sind nur möglich, wenn es gelingt, die Macht der destruktiven Gefühle zu überwinden und sie zu erlösen.

Die Wut — unser Thema — ist ein Beispiel für destruktive Emotionen.

Zur Überwindung belasteter und selbstzerstörerischer Gefühle sind neue Erfahrungen nötig:
  ein neues Wertbewußtsein,
  ein neues Selbstkonzept,
  eine heilende und befreiende Gemeinschaft.

Ein *neuer Selbstwert* kann nicht im Vergleich mit anderen gewonnen werden. Ich bin nicht gut, weil ich besser bin als andere, und ich bin nicht darum wertvoll und wichtig, weil ich mehr leiste als andere. Ich bin nicht nur geliebt, weil andere mich brauchen. Ich fühle mich in meiner Liebe nicht nur sicher, wenn ich — wenigstens für einen Menschen — „ein und alles" sein kann, sondern ich bin liebenswert, weil ich bin.

Das neue, gesunde Selbstwertbewußtsein macht mich unabhängig vom Vergleich mit meiner Umwelt. Es wurzelt in mir selbst. Es gründet auf dem Wissen um meine Einmaligkeit und Einzigartigkeit. Weil ich ein Original bin, habe ich eine unauswechselbare Bedeutung. Unsere Zeit hat Bewertungsmuster, die sich an den Kategorien von Haben und Leistung, Brauchbarkeit und Nützlichkeit orientieren. Die neue Wertung liegt nicht in dem, was ich habe und tue, sondern in dem, was ich bin.

Mein Selbstkonzept besteht nicht aus ständigen Forderungen und Überforderungen: Ich muß mich beliebt machen! Ich muß viel leisten! Ich darf mir nichts zuschulden kommen lassen! Ich soll möglichst perfekt sein!

Das *neue Selbstkonzept* heißt: Ich darf sein, der ich bin, und werden, der ich sein kann!

Nicht Anpassung, Nützlichkeit oder Brauchbarkeit bestimmen dann mein Leben, sondern die Entdeckung und Entfaltung meiner Gaben und Möglichkeiten, die ich in meiner Einmaligkeit in mir trage.

Mein Wert liegt darin, daß ich bin, der ich bin!

Wie kann dieses neue Wertbewußtsein und Selbstkonzept entstehen und entwickelt werden?

Nach seinem Aufbruch aus Elternhaus und Beruf hatte Jesus in seiner Taufe ein grundlegendes Erlebnis. Eine Stimme sagte ihm: „Du bist mein lieber Sohn, du gefällst mir!" (Mk 1,11 par.). Diese Stimme wurde ihm zur Bestimmung, zur Berufung. Sie bildete die Grundlage seiner Gottesbeziehung. Vor allem Tun und Wirken stand bei ihm die totale Liebeserklärung Gottes. Eine solche Liebe ohne Vorbedingung war für ihn Freiraum und Motiv für alles spätere Reden, Leben und Handeln. Diese alle bisherigen Vorstellungen sprengende Erfahrung testete und verarbeitete er 40 Tage lang in der Einsamkeit der Wüste.

Seine spätere Aussage: „Viele sind berufen, aber nur wenige sind auserwählt" (Mt 22,14), hat wahrscheinlich mit dieser Anfangserfahrung zu tun. Er blieb nicht bei der Berufung stehen, sondern wurde sich in der Einsamkeit über die Konsequenzen klar. Berufen sind alle; wer die Konsequenzen daraus zieht, ist auserwählt. Wir verwenden die Worte „berufen" und „auserwählt" vielleicht mit allzuviel Respekt. Wir meinen, so etwas sei nicht für normale Leute gedacht, sondern eher für Propheten und Heilige. Viele ahnen, daß auch ihnen die Liebeserklärung Gottes gilt, aber sie reagieren nicht darauf. Dadurch bringen sie sich um ihre Auserwählung. Sie nehmen sich selbst in ihrer Einmaligkeit nicht ernst. Unsere Berufung besteht darin, sich selbst ernst zu nehmen und nicht mehr, wie üblich, von außen gelebt zu werden. Vielleicht beginnt dieses Ernstnehmen damit, daß ich mich darüber empöre, was ich alles mit mir habe machen lassen und was ich alles mitgemacht habe!

Bei den meisten kommt es nicht zum zweiten Schritt. Sie ziehen aus ihrer Berufung nicht die Konsequenzen und nehmen damit die Wahl nicht an. Sie verharren lieber in ihrem alten Selbstkonzept der Angepaßtheit und Unschlüssigkeit und entschuldigen sich mit Rücksichtnahme und Verantwortung, die sie anderen schuldig zu sein meinen.

Nach seiner Berufung und Auserwählung beginnt Jesus, eine *neue Gemeinschaft* aufzubauen. Er sucht sich Freunde, die mit ihm gehen, mit ihm leben. Es sind Leute seiner Wahl, keine schon bestehende Gruppe. Mit ihnen teilt er seine Erfahrung, sein Wissen und seine Erkenntnis. Ihnen öffnet er sein Herz. Zu jedem einzelnen hat er eine besondere, einmalige Beziehung. Die neue Gemeinschaft ist eine notwendige Voraussetzung für die neue Lebensart. Sie entspricht weder den üblichen Vorstellungen von Familie noch den gesellschaftlichen Bedingungen, die unser berufliches und soziales Leben bestimmen. Sie ist erfahrungsgemäß auch nicht identisch mit bereits bestehenden Gruppierungen.

Grundvoraussetzung für eine geisterfüllte Gemeinschaft ist die freie Wahl. Jesus sagt zu der Schar, die um ihn ist: „Nicht ihr habt mich erwählt, sondern ich habe euch erwählt" (Joh 15,16) — und man könnte hinzufügen: „und ihr habt meine Wahl angenommen." Die neue Gemeinschaft ist eine Wahlgemeinschaft und keine durch biologische oder soziologische Vorgaben entstandene Gruppe. Sie ist — um ein neutestamentliches Bild zu gebrauchen — eine Weggenossenschaft mit Menschen, die „des Weges sind". Sie kann nicht zur festen Einrichtung oder zur Institution werden. Der einzelne bleibt immer wichtiger als die Ordnungen und Verordnungen der Gruppe.

Der Verbleib in dieser Gemeinschaft ist vom persönlichen Weg abhängig. Keine Gruppe kann meinen ganzen Lebensweg begleiten. Es werden sich immer wieder neue lebendige Gemeinschaften bilden, die der nächsten Wegstrecke entsprechen. Eine solche flexible Lebendigkeit muß jeden starren Apparat konfus machen und Gesetzestreue in Panik versetzen. So ist es verständlich, daß man schon immer solche Freien und freien Gemeinschaften verfolgt und sie auszurotten versucht hat.

Ein Leben mit den Qualitäten eines neuen Selbstbewußtseins und einer neuen Gemeinschaft erfordert *Mut.* Es bietet für unsere Welt eine Möglichkeit, zu überleben. Es ist „Salz der Erde" und „Licht der Welt". Ein Dasein, das nur in den üblichen Kategorien der Leistungsgesellschaft, der öffentlichen Anerkennung und offiziellen Ehrungen gelebt wird, geht am eigentlichen Lebenssinn vorbei. Gefragt ist ein Leben aus dem Sein, nicht aus dem Machen und Tun!

Ein neuer Lebensstil

Im Bereich der Macht und des Machbaren ist der Glaube fehl am Platz. Wo der Erfolg garantiert ist, wo man ganz sicher sein kann, wo menschliches Versagen ausgeschlossen ist, braucht man keinen Glauben. Wo Mut als Leichtsinn oder Verantwortungslosigkeit deklariert wird, ist der Glaube nur eine letzte Rückversicherung dafür, daß am Ende auch noch Gott auf unserer Seite steht und unsere Richtigkeiten bestätigt. Dieser Glaube ist bestenfalls eine christliche Tünche über einem bürgerlichen Dasein. Er hat nichts mehr mit dem mutigen und unbequemen Jesus von Nazareth zu tun, der ohne Netz und doppelten Boden sein Leben wagte und andere in das Wagnis seines Lebens mit hineinnahm. Er kannte die Kraft des Glaubens und die Unberechenbarkeit der geistigen Welt. Er wagte immer wieder das Vertrauen, und auch im scheinbaren Scheitern vertraute er auf den Gott seines Glaubens. Er starb weder als Held noch verließ er seine Laufbahn als gefeierter Weltmeister. Er hinterließ keine Erfolgsrezepte für einen sicheren Aufstieg, für eine Karriere mit Applaus.

Diese Art des Lebens fordert den Mut heraus, das Unberechenbare zu wagen und Veränderungen zu erwarten. Der Glaube an Gott verspricht keinen sicheren Hafen – er entspricht eher einer kühnen Seefahrt.

Bei aller Kühnheit des Glaubens wird die Angst in unserem Leben bleiben und damit auch die von ihr verursachten Aggressionen. Es hat keinen Zweck, uns über diese Tatsache hinwegzutäuschen. Auch Jesus hat seine Jünger darüber nicht im unklaren gelassen. Er sagt ihnen: „In der Welt habt ihr Angst; aber seid getrost, ich habe die Welt überwunden" (Joh 16,33). Dieses „seid getrost" heißt im ursprünglichen Sinn: „faßt Mut!" Es ist eine Mutsache, sich gegen die Angst zu entscheiden. Täglich gibt es Situationen, in denen diese Entscheidung von uns getroffen werden kann. Die gewohnten Angstreaktionen können gestoppt werden.

Normalerweise reagiere ich auf einen Vorwurf spontan mit Abwehr und Rechtfertigung. Es ist eine Angstreaktion. Ungewohnt, aber mutig wäre es, den Vorwurf ruhig bis zu Ende anzuhören und darüber nachzudenken, was der andere damit meint. Spontane Selbstverteidigung ist meist von der Angst diktiert. Die Kritik an mich heranzulassen und sie in Ruhe zu prüfen, erfordert Mut.

Die Wandlungen im Umgang mit der Wut sind keine Frucht heroischer Augenblicke, sondern das Resultat kleiner und kleinster Schritte.

Manchmal wundern wir uns, wenn es bei scheinbar kleinen Anlässen zu großen Wutausbrüchen kommt. Solche aggressiven Reaktionen deuten meist darauf hin, daß hier die Spitze eines Eisbergs berührt worden ist. Darunter sitzen oft ganz massive Kränkungen, die bei dieser Gelegenheit auftauchen. So reagiert vielleicht eine Ehefrau überaus heftig auf eine Unaufmerksamkeit ihres Mannes, der selber wiederum darüber beleidigt ist, wie man aus einer Mücke so einen Elefanten machen kann. Diese Szene kann sich leicht zu einem ernsten Konflikt entwickeln, wenn es nicht gelingt, die versteckten Ängste und Bedürfnisse aufzudecken.

Unter jeder Aggression liegt in einer tieferen Schicht ein ungestilltes Bedürfnis. Die permanente Enttäuschung schafft eine dauernde Aggressionsbereitschaft.

Unter dem ungestillten Bedürfnis ist in einer noch tieferen Schicht die eigentliche Ursache verborgen − nämlich eine Angst.

Wenn wir genügend Mut besitzen und nicht durch eigene Betroffenheit unangemessen reagieren, können wir unseren Widersacher ruhig fragen, welches unerfüllte Bedürfnis hinter seiner Wut steckt und ob ich ihm vielleicht einen Wunsch erfüllen kann.

Wer seine eigenen Ängste kennt und in der Lage ist, sie zuzugeben, gewinnt dadurch eine gute Basis für den Umgang mit seinen Aggressionen.

In der Regel kennen wir nur zwei Wege, mit unseren verletzten Gefühlen und unserer Wut umzugehen.

Wir können sie verdrängen, sitzen dabei aber wie auf einem Pulverfaß, das jederzeit explodieren kann.

Oder wir lassen die Gefühle aus uns heraus und schlagen um uns mit der Möglichkeit, dabei einen anderen zu verletzen. Die Verletzungen können auch durch Schuldzuweisungen entstehen.

Ein dritter Weg ist der Weg nach innen. Er führt zur Entlarvung und Entmachtung der Angst. Angst zu erkennen und anzuerkennen, ist die notwendige Voraussetzung zur Bewältigung und Veränderung destruktiver Energien in meinem Gefühl.

Training

Von Paavo Nurmi, dem berühmten finnischen Weltrekordläufer, wird erzählt, daß er seine sportliche Höchstleistung erreichte, indem er allein gegen die Stoppuhr trainierte. Stundenlang lief er einsam seine Runden und kontrollierte und korrigierte sein Tempo nach der Uhr.

Es gibt sicher nur wenige „Nurmis", die ein Training – auf welchem Gebiet auch immer – ganz allein schaffen. Das ist auch nicht nötig.

Für mich ist der Kontakt mit Menschen, die auf der gleichen Bahn üben, eine große Ermunterung. Das ist mir besonders wichtig bei meinem Training zur Entwicklung der Persönlichkeit. Mein Erfolg stärkt andere, meine Pannen trösten sie. Die Einzelkämpfer haben es nicht nur unnötig schwer, sie sind auch für andere wenig hilfreich.

Die Gemeinschaft der Lernenden ist ein Vermächtnis Jesu. Er sammelt nicht eine Schar von Könnern und Experten um sich, die alle anderen belehren und bekehren, sondern eine Gruppe von Lernwilligen, die sich gegenseitig stärken.

Dieses gemeinsame Üben und der Erfahrungsaustausch sind besonders wertvoll, wenn es darum geht, mit den eigenen Gefühlstumulten zurechtzukommen. Ohne das „Feedback" anderer ist es schwer, die eigene Wirkung richtig einzuschätzen und positive Veränderungen wahrzunehmen. Selbst christliche Gruppen könnten sehr attraktiv werden, wenn sie solche Trainingsprogramme zur Arbeit am eigenen Charakter anbieten würden. Auch für den Umgang mit den eigenen Gefühlen wären sie ein hilfreiches Angebot.

Schwächen, Fehler, Pannen, Rückfälle und Versagen müßten in solchen Arbeitsgruppen erlaubt sein und nicht als peinliche Zwischenfälle angesehen werden, sondern als Chancen, daraus zu lernen.

Wertschätzung und Ermutigung

Du bist ein Schatz! In dir liegen unendliche, einmalige Werte. Das Leben ist für dich. Die Kräfte deiner Seele sind Energien, die das Leben reich machen können. Unser Gott ist kein Riesencomputer, der alles und alle registriert und auf DIN-Format normiert. Originalität und Einzigartigkeit ist seine Absicht mit jedem Menschen – so hat er es jedenfalls an seinem Sohn – Jesus – deutlich gemacht.

Mit dieser Botschaft vertraut zu werden, sie anzunehmen und sie wahr sein zu lassen, ist eine wichtige Voraussetzung für eine positive Veränderung in mir.

Nur wer sich wertschätzt und lernt, entsprechend mit sich umzugehen, wird auch anderen seine Wertschätzung vermitteln können.

Sich selbst zu lieben und dann seinen Nächsten, ist dabei die gesunde Reihenfolge.

Auf dem Übungsfeld des Umgangs mit destruktiven Gefühlen hängt letztlich alles davon ab, ob ich lerne, liebevoll und achtungsvoll zu mir zu sein.

Wer betet oder meditiert, kann üben, sich Gott als seinen Liebhaber vorzustellen, der alles in seinem Leben so eingerichtet hat, daß sich daraus Gutes entwickeln kann. Ohne eine persönliche Beziehung mit dem Urgrund des Lebens — der Liebe — ist es schwer, liebevoll zu sein.

Veränderungen fallen aber nicht vom Himmel. Sie wachsen tief in uns — verwandeln uns im innersten Kern durch das Bewußtsein der Wertschätzung.

Gefördert wird dieser innere Wandlungsprozeß durch ein entsprechendes bewußtes Verhalten anderen gegenüber. Wenn ich mich hoch einschätze, werde ich auch andere achtungsvoll behandeln.

Wie in einem Zweitakt bewegt sich die Entwicklung zur Reife. Mit mir selbst und mit meinen Gefühlen freundschaftlich umzugehen, ist das eine; die Gefühle des anderen ebenso freundschaftlich zu behandeln, ist das zweite.

Der Geist Gottes ist der Motor in dieser Bewegung. Er schafft einerseits in mir das neue Bewußtsein meines Wertes und ist gleichzeitig auch der Vermittler in unseren zwischenmenschlichen Beziehungen. Er bewirkt zunehmend die Souveränität für meinen Umgang mit mir selbst und gleichzeitig eine ermutigende Art im Kontakt mit anderen. Er ist die Atmosphäre der Liebe bei allen dynamischen Entwicklungsvorgängen.

Wilhard Becker

Geboren 1927 in Frankfurt/M. Nach 25 Jahren Tätigkeit als Theologe nimmt er seine ursprüngliche Intention, dem Menschen auch therapeutisch zu helfen, wieder auf.
Heil und Heilung — Christsein und ganz Menschsein gehören für ihn untrennbar zusammen. Z.Zt. in eigener Praxis für Beratung und Therapie.
Schulungsarbeit für Führungskräfte in der Industrie mit der Thematik »Persönlichkeitsbildung«. Wohnhaft in 7109 Schöntal 3, Obere Sonnenhalde 20.

Machine Intelligence and Pattern Recognition

Volume 5

Series Editors

L. N. KANAL

and

A. ROSENFELD

University of Maryland
College Park
Maryland
U.S.A.

NORTH-HOLLAND
AMSTERDAM · NEW YORK · OXFORD · TOKYO

UNCERTAINTY IN ARTIFICIAL INTELLIGENCE 2

Uncertainty in Artificial Intelligence 2

Edited by

John F. LEMMER
*Knowledge Systems Concepts
Rome
New York
U.S.A.*

and

Laveen N. KANAL
*University of Maryland
College Park
Maryland
U.S.A.*

1988

NORTH-HOLLAND
AMSTERDAM · NEW YORK · OXFORD · TOKYO

© ELSEVIER SCIENCE PUBLISHERS B.V., 1988

All rights reserved. No part of this publication may be reproduced stored in a retrieval system, or transmitted, in any form or by any means, electronic, mechanical photocopying, recording or otherwise, without the prior permission of the copyright owner.

ISBN: 0 444 70396 9

Publishers:
ELSEVIER SCIENCE PUBLISHERS B.V.
P.O. Box 1991
1000 BZ Amsterdam
The Netherlands

Sole distributors for the U.S.A. and Canada:
ELSEVIER SCIENCE PUBLISHING COMPANY, INC.
52 Vanderbilt Avenue
New York, N.Y. 10017
U.S.A.

```
                         LIBRARY OF CONGRESS
              Library of Congress Cataloging-in-Publication Data


Uncertainty in artificial intelligence 2 / edited by John F. Lemmer
  and Laveen N. Kanal.
        p.    cm. -- (Machine intelligence and pattern recognition ; v.
  5)
    Bibliography: p.
    ISBN 0-444-70396-9
    1. Artificial intelligence.  2. Uncertainty (Information theory)
  I. Lemmer, John F.   II. Kanal, Laveen N.   III. Title: Uncertainty in
  artificial intelligence two.   IV. Series.
  Q335.U532 1988
  006.3--dc19                                                    88-415
                                                                    CIP
```

PRINTED IN THE NETHERLANDS

PREFACE

The favorable reception accorded to our first volume on Uncertainty in Artificial Intelligence (Kanal &Lemmer, 1986; see e.g. review on IEEE Trans. on SMC, March—April 1987) has encouraged us to put together this second volume. The major portion of this second volume consists of expanded versions of papers originally presented at the Workshop on Uncertainty in Artificial Intelligence which was held August 8—10, 1986 at the University of Pennsylvania in Philadelphia. In addition, this volume contains a number of new papers.

At the time of final preparation the authors knew which other papers would appear, so there is considerable cross referencing among the papers. Because there is by no means a consensus of opinions within this volume, the cross referencing is particularly interesting.

We have placed the papers in four major sections: analysis, tools, theory, and applications. The analysis section contains papers which substantiate, dispute, or compare the attributes of various approaches to uncertainty. The papers in this first section raise many issues important for critical reading of the remaining sections. The tools section contains papers which provide sufficient information for one to implement uncertainty calculations, or aspects of uncertainty, without requiring deep understanding of the underlying theory. Papers in the theory section explicate various approaches to uncertainty without necessarily addressing how the approaches can be implemented. Finally, the applications section describes the difficulties involved in, and results produced by, incorporating uncertainty into implemented systems.

A number of interesting ideas emerge from the papers in this volume, and some are briefly mentioned here. Heckerman and Horvitz describe some newly discovered work showing that first order predicate calculus combined with some simple (and innocuous?) requirements for continuity imply the axioms of probability. They argue that this frees probability theory from its ties to repeatable events. Hummel and Landy show how Dempster—Shafer theory can be fully interpreted in the context of traditional probability theory. Three papers attempt to forge a link between probabilistic and non-numeric uncertainty approaches and thereby develop a basis for providing explanations for inferred probabilities: Norton attempts to directly explain inference results in terms of correlations; Su-Shing Chen attempts to bring probabilistic logic into the framework of probability theory; Hawthorne describes a theory that unifies into a single coherent system a symbolic approach to non-monotonic entailment and a quantitative (Bayesian) approach. Dalkey disproves by counter-example, an often cited property of distributions formed by product extension.

It is clear from the papers that there continues to be no consensus concerning the "best" approach to uncertainty for AI systems. Moreover, there is no agreement on how to measure "best". Further it is likely that best will always depend on the particular use to be made of uncertainty. Because in many experiments all approaches seem to imply essentially the same actions, the idea that the choice of any particular approach is not important was discussed at some length during the workshop without reaching a consensus.

We would stress that any choice of approach to uncertainty must be based on factors in addition to the merits of the uncertainty representation and calculus. These additional factors include the difficulty of acquiring the original uncertainty estimates (knowledge engineering), the computational complexity of inference, the semantics which guide the acquisition of the original estimates and guide the interpretation of computed results, and how the chosen representation is used in decision making.

We hope, that like volume 1, this volume will also stimulate further communication among researchers interested in handling uncertainty in AI systems. We thank all our colleagues who helped in organizing the workshop, and all the authors, reviewers, and the folks at North-Holland for their excellent collaboration in helping to produce the earlier volume and this volume on Uncertainty in Artificial Intelligence.

Laveen N. Kanal	John F. Lemmer
College Park, MD	Rome, NY

CONTRIBUTORS

Shoshana Abel *Mountain View, CA 94043*
Lee A. Appelbaum *Advanced Decision Systems, Mountain View, CA 94040*
Jonathan Baron *University of Pennsylvania, Philadelphia, PA 19104 and Medical College of Pennsylvania, Philadelphia, PA 19129*
Steven W. Barth *PAR Government Systems Corporation, New Hartford, NY 13413*
Lashon B. Booker *AI Center, Naval Research Laboratory, Washington, DC 20375*
Roger A. Browse *Queens University at Kingston, Ontario, Canada K7L 3N7*
Peter Cheeseman *NASA Ames Research Center, Moffett Field, CA 94035*
Kaihu Chen *University of Illinois at Urbana-Champaign, IL 61801*
Su-Shing Chen *University of North Carolina, NC 28223*
John R. Clarke *University of Pennsylvania, Philadelphia, PA 19104 and Medical College of Pennsylvania, Philadelphia, PA 19129*
A. Julian Craddock *Queens University at Kingston, Ontario, Canada K7L 3N7*
N.C. Dalkey *University of California, Los Angeles, CA 90024*
Hugh F. Durrant-Whyte *University of Pennsylvania, Philadelphia, PA 19104*
Brian Falkenhainer *University of Illinois, Urbana, IL 61801*
B.R. Fox *McDonnell Douglas Research Laboratories, St. Louis, MO 63166*
Sally A. Goldman *Massachusetts Institute of Technology, Cambridge, MA 02139*
Benjamin N. Grosof *Stanford University, Stanford, CA 94305*
Greg Hager *University of Pennsylvania, Philadelphia, PA 19104*
James Hawthorne *Honeywell Systems and Research Center, Minneapolis, MN 55418*

David Heckerman *Stanford University, Stanford, CA 94305*
Steven J. Henkind *Courant Institute of Mathematical Sciences, NYU, NY 10012 and Mount Sinai School of Medicine, New York, NY 10029*
Max Henrion *Carnegie-Mellon University, Pittsburgh, PA 15213*
Peter D. Holden *McDonnell Douglas Corporation, St. Louis, MO 63166*
Naveen Hota *JAYCOR, Vienna, VA 22180*
Eric Horvitz *Stanford University, Stanford, CA 94305*
Robert Hummel *Courant Institute of Mathematical Sciences, NYU, NY 10012*
Karl G. Kempf *FMC Corporation, Santa Clara, CA 95052*
Henry E. Kyburg *University of Rochester, Rochester, NY 14627*
Michael Landy *Courant Institute of Mathematical Sciences, NYU, NY 10012*
Todd S. Levitt *Advanced Decisions Systems. Mountain View, CA 94040*
Ze-Nian Li *University of Wisconsin, Milwaukee, WI 53211*
Ronald P. Loui *University of Rochester, Rochester, NY 14627*
Mary McLeish *University of Guelph, Guelph, Ontario, Canada N1G 2W1*
Khaled Mellouli *University of Kansas, Lawrence, KS 66045*
Steven W. Norton *PAR Government Systems Corporation, New Hartford, NY 13413*
Judea Pearl *University of California, Los Angeles, CA 90024*
Bruce M. Perrin *McDonnell Douglas Corporation, St. Louis, MO 63166*
Ronald L. Rivest *Massachusetts Institute of Technology, Cambridge, MA 02139*
Ross D. Shachter *Stanford University, Stanford, CA 94305*
Glenn Shafer *University of Kansas, Lawrence, KS 66045*
Prakash P. Shenoy *University of Kansas, Lawrence, KS 66045*
Shimon Shocken *New York University, NY 10003*
Stanley M. Schwartz *University of Pennsylvania, Philadelphia, PA 19104 and Medical College of Pennsylvania, Philadelphia, PA 19129*
Matthew Self *University of California, Berkeley, CA 94720*
Randall Smith *General Motors Research Laboratories, Warren, MI 48090*
Richard M. Tong *Advanced Decision Systems, Mountain View, CA 94040*
Leonard Uhr *University of Wisconsin, Madison, WI 53706*
Silvio Ursic *Ursic Computing, Madison, WI 53714*
David S. Vaughan *McDonnell Douglas Corporation, St. Louis, MO 63166*
Michael P. Wellman *MIT Laboratory for Computer Science, Cambridge, MA 02139*
Ben P. Wise *Thayer School, Dartmouth, NH 03755*
Robert M. Yadrick *McDonnell Douglas Corporation, St. Louis, MO 63166*
Ronald R. Yager *Iona College, New Rochelle, NY 10801*

CONTENTS

Preface   v

Contributors   vii

I. ANALYSIS

Models vs. Inductive Inference for Dealing with
   Probabilistic Knowledge
N.C. Dalkey   3

An Axiomatic Framework for Belief Updates
D.E. Heckerman   11

The Myth of Modularity in Rule-Based Systems for
   Reasoning with Uncertainty
D.E. Heckerman and E.J. Horvitz   23

Imprecise Meanings as a Cause of Uncertainty in Medical
   Knowledge-Based Systems
S.J. Henkind   35

Evidence as Opinions of Experts
R. Hummel and M. Landy   43

Probabilistic Logic: Some Comments and Possible Use for
   Nonmonotonic Reasoning
M. McLeish   55

Experiments with Interval-Valued Uncertainty
R.M. Tong and L.A. Appelbaum   63

Evaluation of Uncertain Inference Models I: PROSPECTOR
R.M. Yadrick, B.M. Perrin, D.S. Vaughan, P.D. Holden, and
K.G. Kempf   77

Experimentally Comparing Uncertain Inference Systems to
    Probability
B.P. Wise   89

II. TOOLS

Knowledge Engineering within a Generalized Bayesian
    Framework
S.W. Barth and S.W. Norton   103

Learning to Predict: An Inductive Approach
K. Chen   115

Towards a General-Purpose Belief Maintenance System
B. Falkenhainer   125

A Non-Iterative Maximum Entropy Algorithm
S.A. Goldman and R.L. Rivest   133

Propagating Uncertainty in Bayesian Networks by
    Probabilistic Logic Sampling
M. Henrion   149

An Explanation Mechanism for Bayesian Inferencing
    Systems
S.W. Norton   165

On the Rational Scope of Probabilistic Rule-Based
    Inference Systems
S. Schocken   175

DAVID: Influence Diagram Processing System for the
    Macintosh
R.D. Shachter   191

Qualitative Probabilistic Networks for Planning under
    Uncertainty
M.P. Wellman   197

On Implementing Usual Values
R.R. Yager 209

III. THEORY

Some Extensions of Probabilistic Logic
S.-S. Chen 221

Belief as Summarization and Meta-Support
A.J. Craddock and R.A. Browse 229

Non-Monotonicity in Probabilistic Reasoning
B.N. Grosof 237

A Semantic Approach to Non-Monotonic Entailments
J. Hawthorne 251

Knowledge
H.E. Kyburg, Jr. 263

Computing Reference Classes
R.P. Loui 273

Distributed Revision of Belief Commitment in Composite
  Explanations
J. Pearl 291

A Backwards View for Asssessment
R.D. Shachter and D. Heckerman 317

Propagation of Belief Functions: A Distributed Approach
P.P. Shenoy, G. Shafer, and K. Mellouli 325

Generalizing Fuzzy Logic Probabilistic Inferences
S. Ursic 337

IV. APPLICATIONS

The Sum-and-Lattice-Points Method Based on an
  Evidential-Reasoning System Applied to the
  Real-Time Vehicle Guidance Problem
S. Abel 365

Probabilistic Reasoning about Ship Images
L.B. Booker and N. Hota 371

Information and Multi-Sensor Coordination
G. Hager and H.F. Durrant-Whyte 381

Planning, Scheduling, and Uncertainty in the Sequence of Future Events
B.R. Fox and K.G. Kempf 395

Evidential Reasoning in a Computer Vision System
Z.-N. Li and L. Uhr 403

Bayesian Inference for Radar Imagery Based Surveillance
T.S. Levitt 413

A Causal Bayesian Model for the Diagnosis of Appendicitis
S.M. Schwartz, J. Baron, and J.R. Clarke 423

Estimating Uncertain Spatial Relationships in Robotics
R. Smith, M. Self, and P. Cheeseman 435

I

ANALYSIS

MODELS VS. INDUCTIVE INFERENCE FOR DEALING WITH
PROBABILISTIC KNOWLEDGE

N. C. DALKEY*

1. Introduction

Two different approaches to dealing with probabilistic knowledge are examined -- models and inductive inference. Examples of the first are: influence diagrams [1], Bayesian networks [2], log-linear models [3, 4]. Examples of the second are: games-against nature [5, 6], varieties of maximum-entropy methods [7, 8, 9], and the author's min-score induction [10].

In the modeling approach, the basic issue is manageability, with respect to data elicitation and computation. Thus, it is assumed that the pertinent set of users in some sense knows the relevant probabilities, and the problem is to format that knowledge in a way that is convenient to input and store and that allows computation of the answers to current questions in an expeditious fashion.

The basic issue for the inductive approach appears at first sight to be very different. In this approach it is presumed that the relevant probabilities are only partially known, and the problem is to extend that incomplete information in a reasonable way to answer current questions. Clearly, this approach requires that some form of induction be invoked. Of course, manageability is an important additional concern.

Despite their seeming differences, the two approaches have a fair amount in common, especially with respect to the structural framework they employ. Roughly speaking, this framework involves identifying clusters of variables which strongly interact, establishing marginal probability distributions on the clusters, and extending the subdistributions to a more complete distribution, usually via a product formalism. The product extension is justified on the modeling approach in terms of assumed conditional independence; in the inductive approach the product form arises from an inductive rule.

2. Structures on Event Spaces

An event space is a set $X = X_1, \cdots, X_n$ of descriptors which is presumed to cover the subject matter of interest. For example, in a medical context, the X_i's could be disease states, symptoms, test results, outcomes of treatment, and the like. Each descriptor X_i involves a set of states x_{ij}, which is a partition (exclusive and exhaustive division) of the "universe" of potential cases. The vector $x = (x_1, \cdots, x_n)$ is a joint state for a specific case. It is presumed that there is a joint probability distribution $P(X)$ on the set of joint states, so that

---

* Department of Computer Science, University of California, Los Angeles, CA. 90024. This work was supported in part by National Science Foundation Grant IST 84-05161.

$$\sum_X P(x) = 1$$

$$\sum_j P(x_{ij}) = 1$$

We define two types of components. An absolute component Y is a subset of descriptors. A conditional component $(Z \mid W)$ is an ordered pair of absolute components. A probability $P(Y)$ on an absolute component is a joint distribution on the states y for descriptors in Y; $P(Y)$ is a subdistribution (or marginal) of $P(X)$. Let $-Y$ denote the complement of Y (all descriptors in X not in Y). Thus

$$P(Y) = \sum_{-Y} P(X) \qquad (1)$$

A probability $P(Z \mid W)$ is a conditional probability distribution on the states z given the states w. Thus

$$P(Z \mid W) = \frac{\sum_{-Z.W} P(X)}{\sum_{-W} P(X)} \qquad (1a)$$

(The period in $-Z.W$ denotes the logical product "and".)

A set of components $C = Y_1, \cdots, Y_k$ is called a structure. The corresponding probability distributions on members of C, $PC = P(Y_1), \cdots, P(Y_k)$, is called a probability system (or system for short.) In this notation, Y may be either absolute or conditional.

A system PC is called consistent if there is a probability distribution $P(X)$ that fulfills (1) or (1a) for all components Y in PC. In general, if PC is consistent, there will be a set $K(PC)$ of distributions compatible with PC.

In the model approach, it is assumed that a system PC represents the clustering of descriptors with respect to dependence; i.e., within a component Y, the descriptors have "strong" probabilistic interactions, whereas if X_i and X_j do not occur together in any component, then they are conditionally independent. Specifically,

$$P(X_i.X_j \mid -X_i.X_j) = P(X_i \mid -X_i.X_j) P(X_j \mid -X_i.X_j) \qquad (2)$$

In the inductive approach, the system PC represents what is known concerning $P(X)$. If X_i and X_j do not occur in a common component, then nothing is known about their probabilistic relationship.

A structure C by itself exhibits many of the general properties of the available knowledge. Thus, it is possible to determine that one structure is uniformly more informative than another, or to specify which structures have a product extension, without reference to the probabilities PC [11]. As the developers of influence diagrams and Bayesian networks have noted, this feature allows a significant amount of preliminary analysis to be carried out before numbers are introduced.

3. Webs

Structures have an internal organization; e.g., components may overlap. There are a number of different ways to represent this organization. A common representation is as a graph, where the components are the nodes and one component is connected by an arc to another if they overlap. A more convenient representation for the purposes of this paper is what I call a web. Let $[C]$ designate the set of all descriptors which belong to some member of C. An absolute component Y is terminal if Y consists of two subcomponents Z and W, $Z.[C - (Y)] = 0$, $W \subset [C - (Y)]$. Thus, W "connects" Z to the remainder of C. (W may be vacuous, in which case Z is unconnected to the remainder of C.) A conditional component $Y = (Z \mid W)$ is terminal if the preceeding conditions hold for Z and W. (W cannot be vacuous for a conditional component.)

A web is a structure which fulfills the recursion:

1. Any absolute component is a web.
2. If Y is a terminal component, and $C - \{Y\}$ is a web, then C is a web.

From the definition, a web contains at least one absolute component. A web can be "unpacked" to generate a linear order on the components by starting with any terminal component Y, labeling it 1, choosing any terminal component in $C - \{Y\}$, labeling it 2, and so on. A web is called conditional if all absolute components are distinct, i.e., do not overlap.

A web is somewhat more general than influence diagrams or Bayesian networks. These can be characterized as conditional webs where for any conditional component $Y = (Z \mid W)$, Z consists of a single descriptor.

Conditional webs are significant for modeling probabilistic knowledge as a result of two basic properties:

a. The product $P^{\bullet}(X) = \prod_C \mid P(Y)$ is a joint probability distribution on X.
b. $P^{\bullet}(X)$ is an extension of PC; i.e., it fulfills (1) or (1a) for all Y in C.

Proofs for these assertions are readily constructed by induction on the number of components in a web.

What these two properties entail, in effect, is that if you can represent your knowledge concerning a distribution $P(X)$ by the sub-distributions PC for a web C plus assuming conditional independence for descriptors not in common components, then the product $P^{\bullet}(X)$ "automatically" expresses that knowledge.

From the modeling point of view, then, a web is a relatively manageable representation of probabilistic knowledge. All that need be input are the subdistributions PC. The product is quite convenient for computations; e.g., the manipulations feasible for influence diagrams are directly extendable to webs.

4. Induction and maximum-entropy

Turning to the inductive approach, in an earlier publication I demonstrated that for a subspecies of web, namely a forest, the product extension is the maximum entropy extension of PC [11]. A forest is a web in which all terminal components $Y = (Z:W)$ fulfill the additional restriction that W is contained some component Y' in $C - \{Y\}$. (In a general web, W need only be contained in the set of all descriptors "covered" by $C - \{Y\}$.) In the graphical representation mentioned earlier where arcs are defined by overlap of components, a forest is a graph with no loops. A forest corresponds to Goodman's decomposable model [3].

Maximum entropy is an instance of min-score inference which has the dual properties: (a) guaranteed expectation -- in the case of maximum entropy, the conclusion is always at least as informative as it claims to be -- and (b) positive value of information -- a conclusion based on additional knowledge will be at least as informative as a conclusion without that knowledge [10]. Thus, if all you know is a set of subdistributions PC, and PC is a forest, then the product extension is a supportable estimate of the total distribution.

One of the motivations for studying webs was the expectation that the product extension would also turn out to be the maximum entropy extension for a general web. The expectation was based on a purported result of P.M. Lewis frequently cited in the literature to the effect that for a structure with a product extension, the product is the maximum entropy extension [12]. Unfortunately, the Lewis "result" happens to be incorrect.

An elementary counter-example is furnished by the simplest of all possible webs that is not a forest, namely the structure $C = \{X_1, X_2, (X_3 | X_1 . X_2)\}$. Set $P(X_1) = P(X_2) = .5$ and define $P(X_3 | X_1 . X_2)$ by Table I, where "1" means occurrence in the list of cases.

Table I

X_1	X_2	$P(X_3 | X_1 . X_2)$
1	1	1
1	0	.5
0	1	.5
0	0	0

The product distribution $P^{\bullet}(X)$ is displayed in Table II, along with another distribution $P^{\circ}(X)$. $P^{\circ}(X)$ is an extension of PC -- which can easily be verified by summation -- and is also clearly a higher entropy distribution.

The entropy of $P^{\bullet}(X) = -\sum_X P(x) \log P(x) = 1.7329$, whereas the entropy of $P^{\circ}(X) = 1.7918$. The numerical difference in entropy is small, but the difference between .25 and 1/6 for $P(1, 1, 1)$, e.g., may not seem trivial.

The elementary structure C of the example is actually a substructure of any web that is not a forest. Hence a similar counter-example can be constructed for any such web. The example is also a counter to the Lewis "result".

Table II

X_1	X_2	X_3	$P^{\bullet}(X)$	$P^{\circ}(X)$
1	1	1	.25	1/6
1	1	0	0	0
1	0	1	.125	1/6
1	0	0	.125	1/6
0	1	1	.125	1/6
0	1	0	.125	1/6
0	0	1	0	0
0	0	0	.25	1/6

The upshot of this inquiry, then, is that a forest is the most general structure for which the product extension is always the maximum entropy extension.

5. Discussion

At first glance, the fact that the product extension of a web is not in general maximum entropy may appear benign. From the standpoint of the model approach, the basic properties of a web -- the product is a probability and an extension of PC -- make webs a highly convenient representation of probabilistic knowledge. All that is lost is a desirable, but by no means essential, fallback. In the case of a forest, for example, if the assumption of conditional independence for separated descriptors is shaky, then it can still be contended that the product is a reasonable estimate of the joint distribution, given PC. It would be a valuable safety feature if the same could be claimed for a web.

From the standpoint of the inductive approach, it is perhaps unfortunate that the product extension of a web is not maximum entropy. However, the maximum entropy extension can be sought by other means [13]. What is lost is the convenience of the product form. For the complex systems of many descriptors common in expert systems, maximum entropy formalisms are likely to be cumbersome.

On a somewhat deeper level, however, the result is thought-provoking. Independence is a common "simplifying" assumption in expert systems [14]. The maximum entropy property, where germaine, is a good justification of the "assumption" even when there is no evidence either for or against independence. However, as the example shows, maximum entropy does not imply independence, not even conditional independence, if the structure is not a forest. In the example, $P^{\circ}(x_1|x_3) = P^{\circ}(x_2|x_3) = 2/3$; but $P^{\circ}(x_1.x_2|x_3) = 1/3$, rather than 4/9 as required by conditional independence.

One route that can be taken is to "prune" the structure to a forest. Lemmer [15] has adopted this suggestion, following a program proposed by Lewis [12], Chow and Liu [16], and others. The advantages of this approach are clear: substantive inputs can be restricted to the subdistributions in PC for the forest, the product extension is automatically consistent with the inputs, and, as I mentioned above, the fact that the product extension is maximum entropy carries strong guarantees.

A basic element missing from this program is a measure of the information that is lost by the pruning process. Concomitantly, there is no systematic procedure for determining the most informative forest contained in the knowledge available to the analyst. Given a general probability system PC, if PC is consistent, the amount of information in PC can be defined as

$$\max_{P \in K(PC)} \text{Entropy}(P).$$

At present, there is no way to determine this quantity directly from PC -- or, for that matter, determining whether PC is consistent. These issues appear to be one area of potentially fruitful research.

References

1. Howard, R. A. and J. E. Matheson, "Influence Diagrams," in R. A. Howard and J. E. Matheson, *The Principles and Applications of Decision Analysis,* Vol. II, Strategic Decisions Group, Menlo Park, 1981.

2. Pearl, J., "Bayesian Networks: A Model of Self-Activated Memory for Evidential Reasoning," UCLA Computer Science Department *Technical Report* 850021 (R-43); in *Proceedings, Cognitive Science Society,* UC Irvine, August 15-17, 1985, pp. 329-334.

3. Goodman, L. A., "The Multivariate Analysis of Qualitative Data: Interaction among Multiple Classifications," *J. Amer. Statist. Assoc.,* 65, 1970, pp. 226-256.

4. Lauritzen, S. L., *Lectures on Contingency Tables,* Aalberg University Press, 1982.

5. Wald, A., *Statistical Decision Functions,* John Wiley and Sons, New York, 1950.

6. Blackwell, D. and M. A. Girshick, *Theory of Games and Statistical Decisions,* John Wiley and Sons, New York, 1954.

7. Kullback, S., *Information Theory and Statistics,* Wiley, New York, 1959.

8. Jaynes, E. T., "Prior Probabilities," *IEEE Transactions on Systems Science and Cybernetics, SSC-4,* 1968, pp. 227-241.

9. Shore, J. E. and R. W. Johnson, "Axiomatic Derivation of the Principle of Maximum Entropy and the Principle of Minimum Cross-Entropy," *IEEE Transactions on Information Theory,* Vol. IT-26, January, 1980, pp. 26-37.

10. Dalkey, N. C., "Inductive Inference and the Maximum Entropy Principle," in C. Ray Smith and W. T. Grandy Jr. (eds.) *Maximum-Entropy and Bayesian Methods in Inverse Problems,* D. Reidel, 1985.

11. Dalkey, N. C., "Min-Score Inference on Probability Systems," UCLA-ENG-CSL-8112, June, 1981.

12. Lewis, P. M., "Approximating Probability Distributions to Reduce Storage Requirements," *Information and Control, 2,* 1959, pp. 214-225.

13. Cheeseman, P., "A Method of Computing Generalized Bayesian Probability Values for Expert Systems," *Proceedings of the 1983 International Joint Conference on Artificial Intelligence.*

14. Duda, R., P. Hart, K. Konolige, and R. Reboh, "A Computer Based Consultant for Mineral Exploration," SRI Project 6415 Final Report, SRI International, Sept., 1979.

15. Lemmer, J., "Generalized Bayesian Updating of Incompletely Specified Distributions," in *Large Scale Systems, 5,* Elsevier, North-Holland, 1983, pp. 51-68.

16. Chow, C. K. and C. N. Liu, "Approximating Discrete Probabilities with Dependence Trees," *IEEE Transactions on Information Theory,* May 1968, pp. 462-467.

AN AXIOMATIC FRAMEWORK FOR BELIEF UPDATES

David E. Heckerman

Medical Computer Science Group, Knowledge Systems Laboratory
Medical School Office Building, Room 215, Stanford, California 94305

In the 1940's, a physicist named Cox provided the first formal justification for the axioms of probability based on the subjective or Bayesian interpretation. He showed that if a measure of belief satisfies several fundamental properties, then the measure must be some monotonic transformation of a probability. In this paper, measures of *change* in belief or *belief updates* are examined. In the spirit of Cox, properties for a measure of change in belief are enumerated. It is shown that if a measure satisfies these properties, it must satisfy other restrictive conditions. For example, it is shown that belief updates in a probabilistic context must be equal to some monotonic transformation of a likelihood ratio. It is hoped that this formal explication of the belief update paradigm will facilitate critical discussion and useful extensions of the approach.

1. INTRODUCTION

As researchers in artificial intelligence have begun to tackle real-world domains such as medical diagnosis, mineral exploration, and financial planning, there has been increasing interest in the development and refinement of methods for reasoning with uncertainty. Much of the work in this area has been focused on methods for the representation and manipulation of measures of *absolute* belief, quantities which reflect the absolute degree to which propositions are believed. There has also been much interest in methodologies which focus on measures of *change* in belief or *belief updates*[1], quantities which reflect the degree to which beliefs in propositions change when evidence about them becomes known. Such methodologies include the MYCIN certainty factor model [1], the PROSPECTOR scoring scheme [2], and the application of Dempster's Rule to the combination of "weights of evidence" [3].

In this paper, a formal explication of the belief update paradigm is given. The presentation is modeled after the work of a physicist named R.T. Cox. In 1946, Cox [4] enumerated a small set of intuitive properties for a measure of *absolute* belief and proved that *any* measure that satisfies these properties must be some monotonic transformation of a probability. In the same spirit, a set of properties or axioms that are intended to capture the notion of a belief update are enumerated. It is then shown that these properties place strong restrictions on measures of change in belief. For example, it is shown that the only measures which satisfy the properties in a probabilistic context are monotonic transformations of the likelihood ratio $\lambda(H,E,e) = p(E|H,e)/p(E|\neg H,e)$, where H is a hypothesis, E is a piece of evidence relevant to the hypothesis, and e is background information.

It should be emphasized that the goal of this axiomization is not to prove that belief updates can only take the form described above. Rather, it is hoped that a formal explication of the update paradigm will stimulate constructive research in this area. For example, the axioms presented here can serve as a tool for the identification and communication of dissatisfaction with the update approach. Given the properties for a belief update, a researcher may be able to pinpoint the source of his dissatisfaction and criticize one or more of the properties directly. In addition, a precise characterization of the update paradigm can be useful in promoting consistent use of the approach. This is important as methodologies which manipulate measures of change in belief have been used inconsistently in the past [5]. Finally, it is hoped that the identification of assumptions underlying the paradigm will allow implementors to better judge the appropriateness of the method for application in a given domain.

Although there has been much discussion concerning the foundations of methodologies which focus on measures of absolute belief [4, 6, 7], there have been few efforts directed at measures of change in belief. Notable exceptions are the works of Popper [8] and Good [9]. Popper proposed a set of properties or axioms that reflect his notion of belief update which he called *corroboration* and Good showed that the likelihood ratio $\lambda(H,E,e)$ satisfies these properties [9]. Unfortunately, Popper's desiderata are somewhat non-intuitive and restricted to a probabilistic context. The axiomization here is offered as an alternative.

2. SCOPE OF THE AXIOMIZATION

The process of reasoning under uncertainty can be decomposed into three components: problem formulation, belief assignment, and belief entailment. *Problem formulation* refers to the process of enumerating the propositions or events of interest as well as the possible outcomes of each proposition. *Belief assignment* refers to the process of constructing and measuring beliefs about propositions of interest. Finally, *belief entailment* refers to the process of deriving beliefs from beliefs assessed in the second phase.

It must be emphasized that most methods for reasoning with uncertainty, including those in which belief updates are central, focus primarily on the third component described above.[2] Indeed, it could be argued that a significant portion of the controversy over the adequacy of various methods for reasoning with uncertainty has stemmed from a lack of appreciation of this fact.[3] The axiomization of the belief update paradigm presented here similarly restricts its focus to the process of belief entailment.

3. FUNDAMENTAL PROPERTIES FOR A MEASURE OF ABSOLUTE BELIEF

Before presenting the axiomization for belief updates, it is useful to consider the properties Cox enumerated for a measure of absolute belief. This discussion will help motivate the characterization of measures of change in belief as it is similar in spirit. In addition, several of the properties for a measure of absolute belief will be needed for the explication of the belief update paradigm.

The first property proposed by Cox concerns the nature of propositions to which beliefs can be assigned. He asserted that propositions must be defined precisely enough so that it would be possible to determine whether a proposition is indeed true or false. That is, a proposition should be defined clearly enough that an all-knowing *clairvoyant* could determine its truth or falsehood. This requirement will be called the *clarity* property.[4]

A second property asserted by Cox is that it is possible to assign a degree of belief to any proposition which is precisely defined. This property will be termed the *completeness* property.

Cox also asserted that a measure of belief can vary continuously between values of absolute truth and falsehood and that the continuum of belief can be represented by a single real number. For definiteness, it will be assumed that larger numbers correspond to larger degrees of belief. The use of a single real number to represent continuous measures of belief will be called the *scalar continuity* property.

Another fundamental assumption made by Cox is that the degree of belief for a proposition will depend on the current state of information of the individual assessing the belief. To emphasize this, the term P|e, read "P given e," will be used to denote the degree of belief in proposition P for some individual with information e. This assumption will be termed the *context dependency* property.

Now consider two propositions P_1 and P_2 and two contexts e_1 and e_2. Cox asserted that if P_1 and P_2 are logically equivalent and if e_1 and e_2 are logically equivalent, then $P_1|e_1 = P_2|e_2$. In particular, if P_1 is true only when P_2 is true and vice versa, an individual should believe each proposition with equal conviction. Thus, for example, it must be that XY|e = YX|e where XY denotes the proposition "X AND Y." This axiom will be called the *consistency* property.

Another property asserted by Cox is that the belief in the conjunction PQ should be related to the belief in P alone and to the belief in Q given that P is true. Formally, Cox proposed that there exists some function F such that

$$PQ|e = F(P|e, Q|Pe). \qquad (1)$$

The function is asserted to be continuous in both arguments and monotonically increasing[5] in each argument when the other is held constant. This property captures the notion that individuals commonly assign belief to events conditioned on the truth of another. This property will be termed the *hypothetical conditioning* property.

Finally, Cox asserted that the belief in ¬P (not P) should be related to the belief in P. Formally, he asserted that there should be some function G such that

$$\neg P|E = G(P|e). \qquad (2)$$

The only restrictions placed on G are that it be continuous and monotonically decreasing. This assumption will be called the *complementarity* property.

After enumerating these properties, Cox proved that *any* measure which satisfies them must also satisfy the relations:

$$0 \leq H(P|e) \leq 1 \qquad (3)$$

$$H(TRUE|e) = 1 \qquad (4)$$

$$H(PQ|e) = H(P|e) \cdot H(Q|Pe) \quad \text{(product rule)} \qquad (5)$$

$$H(P|e) + H(\neg P|e) = 1. \quad \text{(sum rule)} \qquad (6)$$

where H is a monotonically increasing function. However, (3) - (6) implies that H(P|e) is a probability. That is, (3) - (6) correspond to the axioms of probability theory. Therefore, Cox demonstrated that if one accepts the above properties, one must accept that probability is the only admissible measure of absolute belief.

Cox's proof is simple and elegant. The reader is urged to consult the original work to gain a better appreciation of the argument. The work also contains an interesting discussion by Cox arguing for each of the properties he describes.

In the sections to follow, an argument analogous to Cox's for belief updates is presented. As mentioned above, there will be little effort made to justify the properties enumerated. Instead, it is hoped that this exposition will foster constructive discussion about the usefulness of the update paradigm.

4. FUNDAMENTAL PROPERTIES FOR A MEASURE OF CHANGE IN BELIEF

Suppose an individual with background information e has a belief in some hypothesis H for which a piece of evidence E becomes known. The basic assumption of the update paradigm is that a belief update, denoted U(H,E,e), in conjunction with the *prior* belief, H|e, is sufficient for determining the *posterior* belief H|Ee. More formally, it is assumed that there exists some function f such that

$$H|Ee = f(U(H,E,e), H|e). \qquad (7)$$

In the paradigm, the quantities U(H,E,e), H|e, and H|Ee are all single real numbers.[6] In addition, it is required that the function f be continuous in both arguments and that f be monotonically increasing in each argument when the other is held constant.

Equation (7) is the definition of a belief update. Note that only the context dependency property and the scalar continuity property for a measure of absolute belief have been assumed in this definition.

It is useful to view the function f in (7) as an *updating procedure* which operates on a prior belief and returns a posterior belief. The procedure, in turn, is parameterized by the single quantity U(H,E,e), a function of the hypothesis being updated, the evidence producing the update, and the background information in which the update takes place. This is depicted in the upper diagram of Figure 1.

For comparison, the Bayesian conditioning scheme is represented schematically in the lower diagram of the same figure. Corresponding to the updating procedure in the belief update paradigm is the axiomatic engine of probability theory. The axiomatic engine, in turn, is "parameterized" by the full joint distribution. Inputs to the Bayesian updating procedure include the propositions of interest and outputs consist of beliefs relating to these propositions.

An important difference between the two approaches is illustrated in the figure. In the Bayesian theory, the process of updating is implicit; it is a matter of course that the belief in a given proposition changes when the conditioning propositions are modified (recall Cox's context dependency property). In contrast, the process of updating is made explicit in the update paradigm. As a consequence, the Bayesian scheme can treat hypothesis and evidence symmetrically while the update approach cannot. For example, the calculation of p(E|He) in the Bayesian approach is no different in principle then the calculation of p(H|Ee). In the update approach, however, the roles of evidence and hypothesis would have to be exchanged in order to implement the calculation of p(E|He).

In addition to the definition above, there are two fundamental properties that are ascribed to belief updates. The first property is analogous to the consistency property for absolute beliefs. It is assumed that if the arguments of a belief update are logically equivalent, then the belief updates must have the same value. That is, if $H_1 \equiv H_2$, $E_1 \equiv E_2$, and $e_1 \equiv e_2$, then $U(H_1,E_1,e_1) = U(H_2,E_2,e_2)$. This will be called the *consistency* property for belief updates. Note that this property follows from the consistency property for absolute beliefs and the fact that the function f in (7) is invertable.

The second property concerns the combination of belief updates. Consider the situation corresponding to the upper path in Figure 2. The prior belief in hypothesis H, H|e, is updated by evidence E_1 in the context e. Then, the posterior belief, $H|E_1e$, is updated with a second piece of evidence E_2. Note the third argument of the second belief update, $U(H,E_2,E_1e)$, contains E_1 as part of the context. The result is the belief in H given both E_1 and E_2, $H|E_1E_2e$. Alternatively, the belief in H could be updated with both pieces of evidence simultaneously as depicted in the bottom path in Figure 2. In the belief update paradigm, it is asserted that the two separate updates, $U(H,E_1,e)$ and $U(H,E_2,E_1e)$, can be combined directly to give $U(H,E_1E_2,e)$. Formally, it is assumed that there exists some function g such that

An Axiomatic Framework for Belief Updates

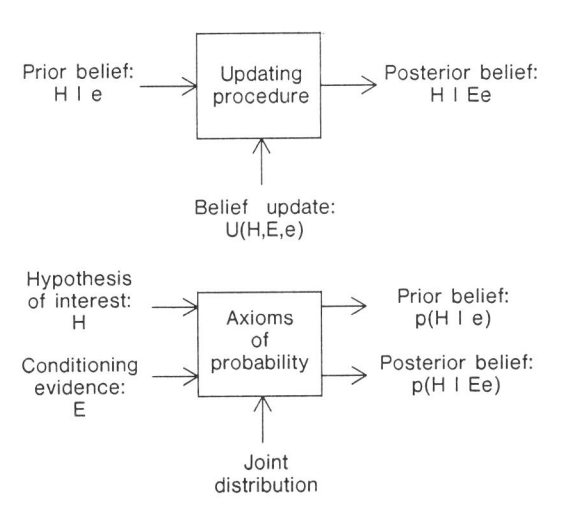

Figure 1: The belief update paradigm vs. Bayesian updating

$$U(H, E_1 E_2, e) = g(U(H, E_1, e), U(H, E_2, E_1 e)). \tag{8}$$

The only constraints on g is that it be continuous in both arguments and monotonically increasing in each argument when the other is held constant. This will be called the *combination* property for belief updates. Note that this property is independent of the properties for a belief update discussed previously.

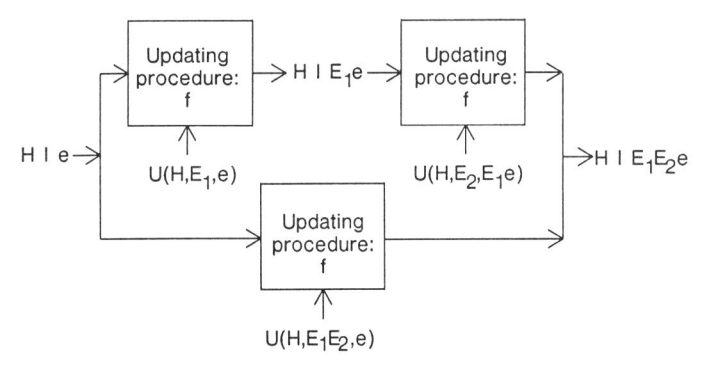

Figure 2: The combination of belief updates

5. A CONSEQUENCE OF THE AXIOMS

Although the properties above seem fairly general, they greatly restrict the quantities that may serve as belief updates. In particular, it is shown in this section that any measure which satisfies the definition of belief updates and the two properties above must also satisfy the relation:

$$h(U(H,E,e)) = i(H|Ee) - i(H|e) \tag{9}$$

where h and i are monotonic functions. In words, a belief update U(H,E,e) is simply the arithmetic difference of a posterior and prior belief, up to an arbitrary monotonic transformation. Of course, any quantity which satisfies (9) must also satisfy (7) and (8). Indeed, (9) is directly suggested by the term "update." However, in this section it is shown that (9) is a *necessary* condition for an update, a stronger result. Equation (9) will be called the *difference* property for belief updates.

Consider three items of evidence E_1, E_2, and E_3 for hypothesis H. Applying the combination property, (8), to (E_1E_2) and E_3 and then to E_1 and E_2 gives:

$U(H,(E_1E_2)E_3,e)$

$= g(U(H,E_1E_2,e), U(H,E_3,E_1E_2e))$

$= g(g(U(H,E_1,e), U(H,E_2,E_1e)), U(H,E_3,E_1E_2e))$.

Equation (8) can also be used to first expand E_1 and (E_2E_3) and then E_2 and E_3 giving:

$U(H,E_1(E_2E_3),e)$

$= g(U(H,E_1,e), U(H,E_2E_3,E_1e))$

$= g(U(H,E_1,e), g(U(H,E_2,E_1e), U(H,E_3,E_1E_2e)))$.

However, $(E_1E_2)E_3$ and $E_1(E_2E_3)$ are logically equivalent and therefore, by the consistency property, these two expressions must be equal. That is,

$$g(g(x,y), z) = g(x, g(y,z)) \tag{10}$$

where $x = U(H,E_1,e)$, $y = U(H,E_2,E_1e)$, and $z = U(H,E_3,E_1E_2e)$. Equation (10) is called a *functional equation*. Using group theory, Aczel has shown that the most general solution to this equation is

$h(g(x,y)) = h(x) + h(y)$

where h is some continuous, monotonic function [10]. Therefore, it follows from the combination property, (8), that

$$h(U(H,E_1E_2,e)) \tag{11}$$

$= h(U(H,E_1,e)) + h(U(H,E_2,E_1e))$.

Note the power of Aczel's result. It says that any continuous, monotonic function of two arguments that satisfies an associativity relation must necessarily be additive in some transformed space.

Now consider the definition of belief updates, (7). Given that the composition of two monotonic functions is another monotonic function, (7) can be rewritten as

$$H|Ee = f(h(U(H,E,e)), H|e). \tag{12}$$

Note that the function f in (12) is not equal to the function f in (7). The same symbol is used to avoid the proliferation of unnecessary terms.

Given this new version of the definition, consider again the situation in Figure 2. The upper path in the figure corresponds to the expansion:

$H|E_2(E_1e)$

$\quad = f(h(U(H,E_2,E_1e)), H|E_1e)$

$\quad = f(h(U(H,E_2,E_1e)), f(h(U(H,E_1,e)), H|e))$

while the lower path corresponds to the expansion:

$H|(E_1E_2)e$

$\quad = f(h(U(H,E_1E_2,e), H|e))$

$\quad = f(h(U(H,E_1,e)) + h(U(H,E_2,E_1e)), H|e)$

In the first expansion, (12) is applied to each item of evidence separately. In the second, (12) is applied to the combined evidence E_1 and E_2 and then (11) is used to expand the update. By the consistency property, these two expansions must be equal. Therefore,

$f(x + y, z) = f(x, f(y, z))$

where $x = h(U(H,E_2,E_1e))$, $y = h(U(H,E_1,e))$, and $z = H|e$. This is another functional equation. The most general solution is

$i(f(x,y)) = x + i(y)$

where i is another continuous, monotonic function [10]. Therefore, it can concluded from (7) that

$i(H|Ee) = h(U(H,E,e)) + i(H|e)$

which establishes the desired result.

6. PROBABILISTIC BELIEF UPDATES

In the remainder of the paper, measures of change in belief will be considered in a probabilistic context. That is, the implications of the axioms of belief updates will be explored under the assumption that each of Cox's properties are valid.

Before discussing the general case, however, it is useful to examine a particular probabilistic update. Consider the following version of Bayes' theorem for updating the probability of a hypothesis H given evidence E and the current state of information e:

$$p(H|Ee) = \frac{p(E|He)p(H|e)}{p(E|e)} . \tag{13}$$

Note that this relationship follows directly from (5). The corresponding formula for the negation of the hypothesis, $\neg H$, is

$$p(\neg H|Ee) = \frac{p(E|\neg He)p(\neg H|e)}{p(E|e)} . \tag{14}$$

Dividing (13) by (14) gives:

$$\frac{p(H|Ee)}{p(\neg H|Ee)} = \frac{p(E|He)}{p(E|\neg He)} \frac{p(H|e)}{p(\neg H|e)} . \tag{15}$$

Now the odds of some event X, denoted $O(X)$, is just

$$O(X) = p(X)/p(\neg X) = p(X)/(1 - p(X))$$

so that (15) can be written as

$$O(H|Ee) = \frac{p(E|He)}{p(E|\neg He)} O(H|E). \tag{16}$$

The ratio in (16) is called a *likelihood ratio* and is written $\lambda(H,E,e)$. With this notation, (16) becomes

$$O(H|Ee) = \lambda(H,E,e) \, O(H|e). \tag{17}$$

Equation (17) is called the *odds-likelihood* form of Bayes' theorem. Notice that $\lambda(H,E,e)$ and the prior odds are sufficient to determine the posterior odds. Moreover, since the odds of any event is a monotonic function of the probability of the event, it follows from (17) that the likelihood ratio $\lambda(H,E,e)$ satisfies the definition of a belief update (7).

It is also straightforward to show that $\lambda(H,E,e)$ satisfies the combination property for updates, (8). Consider two items of evidence E_1 and E_2. The likelihood ratio for the combined evidence E_1 and E_2 is

$$\lambda(H,E_1E_2,e) = \frac{p(E_1E_2|He)}{p(E_1E_2|\neg He)}.$$

Using the product rule (5), both the numerator and denominator in the above expression can be expanded giving:

$$\frac{p(E_1E_2|He)}{p(E_1E_2|\neg He)} = \frac{p(E_1|He)}{p(E_1|\neg He)} \frac{p(E_2|HE_1e)}{p(E_2|\neg HE_1e)}$$

From the definition of λ it follows that

$$\lambda(H,E_1E_2,e) = \lambda(H,E_1,e) \, \lambda(H,E_2,E_1e). \tag{18}$$

Thus, the likelihood ratio $\lambda(H,E,e)$ satisfies the combination property, (8), where the function g is simple multiplication. Moreover, since the consistency property for updates is trivially satisfied in a probabilistic context, it follows that the likelihood ratio λ is a legitimate belief update.

The quantity λ has several interesting properties. For example, λ satisfies the difference property, as it must given the previous discussion. In particular, taking the logarithm of (17) and subtracting gives

$$\log[\lambda(H,E,e)] = \log[O(H|Ee)] - \log[O(H|e)].$$

Another interesting property arises from assumptions of probabilistic independence. Suppose knowing E_1 does not influence one's belief in E_2 if it is known that either H or $\neg$H is true. That is,

$$p(E_2|HE_1e) = p(E_2|He) \quad \text{and} \tag{19}$$

$$p(E_2|\neg HE_1e) = p(E_2|\neg He).$$

Of course, this relationship is conditioned on the current state of information e. When (19) holds, it is said that E_2 is *conditionally independent* of E_1 given H and $\neg$H. With this assumption, it immediately follows from the definition of $\lambda(H,E,e)$ that

$$\lambda(H,E_2,E_1e) = \lambda(H,E_2,e). \tag{20}$$

That is, the belief update for E_2 given E_1 does not depend on E_1. More generally,

$$U(H,E_2,E_1e) = U(H,E_2,e). \tag{21}$$

Equation (21) will be called the *modularity* property for belief updates. This term is used because the above property closely resembles the informal notion of modularity associated with rule based systems [11].

Notice that the conditional independence assumption, (19), and the modularity property, (21), are both assumptions of independence but relate to different ways of thinking about the association between evidence and hypothesis. In asserting (19), one imagines that a *hypothesis* is either true or false with certainty and then contemplates the relationship between two pieces of evidence for the hypothesis. In asserting (21), one imagines that a *piece of evidence* is certain and then considers how this affects the updating of the hypothesis by a second piece of evidence. From above, it is clear that these two independence conditions are closely related in a probabilistic context. In particular, when the identification $U(H,E,e) = \lambda(H,E,e)$ is made, it follows that

$$p(E_2|HE_1e) = p(E_2|He) \quad \text{and}$$
$$p(E_2|\neg HE_1e) = p(E_2|\neg He)$$
$$\Rightarrow U(H,E_2,E_1e) = U(H,E_2,e). \tag{22}$$

This will be referred to as the *independence correspondence* for probabilistic belief updates.

In the remainder of this section, a general result concerning the independence correspondence will be derived. In particular, it will be shown that *any* probabilistic belief update satisfying the independence correspondence must be some monotonic transformation of λ.

To begin, consider the difference property in a probabilistic context[7]:

$$h(U(H,E,e)) = i(p(H|Ee)) - i(p(H|e)). \tag{23}$$

Because i is monotonic, (23) can be rewritten as

$$h(U(H,E,e))$$
$$= \log[j(p(H|Ee)/1-p(H|Ee))]$$
$$- \log[j(p(H|e)/1-p(H|e))]$$
$$= \log[j(O(H|Ee))/j(O(H|e))] \tag{24}$$

where j is another continuous, monotonic function. Now when the conditional independence assumption, (19), is valid, it follows from Bayes' theorem that

$$\frac{O(H|E_2E_1e)}{O(H|E_1e)} = \frac{O(H|E_2e)}{O(H|e)}.$$

In addition, it follows from (24) and the modularity property that

$$j(O(H|E_2E_1e))/j(O(H|E_1e))$$
$$= j(O(H|E_2e))/j(O(H|e)).$$

Therefore, the independence correspondence implies

$$w/x = y/z \Rightarrow j(w)/j(x) = j(y)/j(z)$$

where $w = O(H|E_1E_2e)$, $x = O(H|E_1e)$, $y = O(H|E_2e)$, and $z = O(H|e)$. The most general solution is [10]:

$$j(x) = \alpha \ x^A$$

where A and α are constants. This means that

$$i(x) = A \cdot \log[x/1-x]$$

and so

$$h(U(H,E,e)) = A \cdot \log \frac{O(H|Ee)}{O(H|e)} = A \cdot \log[\lambda(H,E,e)]$$

or

$$U(H,E,e) = h^{-1}\{A \cdot \log[\lambda(H,E,e)]\}$$

which establishes the desired result.

Thus, the likelihood ratio λ is a general belief update in the probabilistic context. The quantity λ and monotonic transformations of it are the only measures which satisfy the axioms of belief updates in addition to the correspondence between probabilistic conditional independence and modularity.

7. CONCLUSIONS

In this paper, a formal characterization of the belief update paradigm has been presented and several consequences of the characterization have been demonstrated. It is hoped that this explication will foster critical discussion and useful extensions of the approach.

ACKNOWLEDGEMENTS

I wish to thank Eric Horvitz for help with the development of this paper. I thank Eric Horvitz, Judea Pearl, and Peter Cheeseman for insightful discussions concerning belief updates. Support for this work was provided by the Josiah Macy, Jr. Foundation, the Henry J. Kaiser Family Foundation, and the Ford Aerospace Corporation. Computing facilities were provided by the SUMEX-AIM resource under NIH grant RR-00785.

NOTES

[1] The terms "weight of evidence" [12] "measure of confirmation" [13, 1, 3] and "measure of corroboration" [8] have also been ascribed to this quantity.

[2] An exception is the formalization of belief *measurement* in the Bayesian theory [14, 6]. However, the theory does not attempt to formalize the process of belief *construction*.

[3] The components of reasoning under uncertainty and the limited scope of most methods for reasoning under uncertainty are discussed in more detail in [15].

[4] The terminology for fundamental properties of belief is introduced in [15].

[5] Actually, the function need only be strictly monotonic in the interior of its domain. For example, when P is false, PQ will also be false no matter what the value of Q|Pe. Therefore, F is not increasing in its second argument when P|e takes on the extreme value corresponding to "FALSE." This caveat applies to all functions of two arguments mentioned in this paper that are required to be monotonic.

[6] Many researchers argue that a precise value cannot be assigned to a degree of belief [16, 17, 3] and such arguments can be extended to measures of change in belief. Indeed, it seems unreasonable to assess a belief update with precision exceeding a few significant figures. This paper, however, focuses strictly on methodologies for the entailment of single-valued belief updates. It is believed that the study of idealized point updates provides a strong foundation for methodologies which address the representation of imprecise belief updates. Evidence for this comes from the observation that analyses of idealized (point) absolute beliefs lie at the heart of techniques for the representation of imprecise beliefs including sensitivity analysis [18], probability bounds [16], and second-order theory [19]. In fact, it is likely that these techniques can be extended to measures of change in belief.

[7] The function i should be renamed since, by Cox's result, H|e and p(H|e) are related by a monotonic transformation. As before, the same name will be retained to avoid the proliferation of notation.

REFERENCES

[1] Shortliffe, E. H. and Buchanan, B. G., A model of inexact reasoning in medicine, *Mathematical Biosciences*, 23 (1975), pp. 351-379.

[2] Duda, R., Hart, P., and Nilsson, N., Subjective Bayesian Methods for Rule-based Inference Systems, *In* "Proceedings 1976 National Computer Conference", Vol. 45, AFIPS, 1976, pp. 1075-1082.

[3] Shafer, G., "A Mathematical Theory of Evidence", Princeton University Press, 1976.

[4] Cox, R., Probability, frequency and reasonable expectation, *American Journal of Physics*, 14 (1), January-February (1946), pp. 1-13.

[5] Horvitz, E. J., and Heckerman, D. E., The Inconsistent Use of Measures of Certainty in Artificial Intelligence Research, in "Uncertainty in Artificial Intelligence", (Kanal, L. and Lemmer, J., eds.), North Holland, 1986.

[6] de Finetti, B., "Theory of Probability", Wiley, New York, 1970.

[7] Gaines, B.R., Fuzzy and probability uncertainty logics, *Information and Control*, 38 (1978), pp. 154-169.

[8] Popper, K.R., Corroboration, the weight of evidence, in "The Logic of Scientific Discovery", Scientific Editions, New York, 1959, pp. 387-419.

[9] Good, I.J., Weight of evidence, corroboration, explanatory power, information and the utility of experiments, *J. R. Statist. Soc. B*, (22), (1960), pp. 319-331.

[10] Aczel, J., "Lectures on Functional Equations and Their Applications", Academic Press, New York, 1966.

[11] Heckerman, D.E., Probabilistic Interpretations for MYCIN's Certainty Factors, in "Uncertainty in Artificial Intelligence", (Kanal, L. and Lemmer, J., eds.), North Holland, 1986.
[12] Peirce, C.S., The probability of induction, in "The World of Mathematics, V.2", Simon and Shuster, 1956, pp. 1341-1354.
[13] Carnap, R., "Logical Foundations of Probability: Second Edition", Chicago University Press, 1962.
[14] Savage, L. J., "The Foundations of Statistics", Dover, New York, 1972.
[15] Horvitz, E. J., Heckerman, D. E., Langlotz, C. P., A framework for comparing alternative formalisms for plausible reasoning, *In* "Proceedings of the AAAI", Morgan Kaufman, AAAI, Philadelphia, August 1986, Knowledge Systems Lab Technical Report KSL-86-25, Stanford University
[16] Good, I.J., Subjective probability as the measure of a non-mearureable set, in "Logic, Methodology, and Philosophy of Science: Proceedings of the 1960 International Congress", Stanford University Press, 1962, pp. 319-329, Also in *Good Thinking: The Foundations of Probability and Its Applications*, I.J. Good, University of Minnesota Press, 1983
[17] Winkler, R.L., The consensus of subjective probability distributions, *Management Science*, 15 (2), October (1968), .
[18] Howard, R. A., Matheson, J. E., Influence Diagrams, in "Readings on the Principles and Applications of Decision Analysis", (Howard, R. A., Matheson, J. E., eds.), Strategic Decisions Group, Menlo Park, CA, 1981, pp. 721-762, ch. 37.
[19] Winkler, R., Scoring rules and the evaluation of probability assessors, *J. Amer. Statist. Ass.*, (64), (1969), pp. 1073-1078.

THE MYTH OF MODULARITY IN RULE-BASED SYSTEMS FOR REASONING WITH UNCERTAINTY

David E. Heckerman and Eric J. Horvitz

Medical Computer Science Group, Knowledge Systems Laboratory
Medical School Office Building, Room 215, Stanford, California 94305

In this paper, we examine the concept of *modularity*, an often cited advantage of the ruled-based representation methodology. We argue that the notion of modularity consists of two distinct concepts which we call *syntactic* modularity and *semantic* modularity. We argue that when reasoning under certainty, it is reasonable to regard the rule-based approach as both syntactically and semantically modular. However, we argue that in the case of plausible reasoning, rules are syntactically modular but are rarely semantically modular. To illustrate this point, we examine a particular approach for managing uncertainty in rule-based systems called the MYCIN certainty factor model. We formally define the concept of semantic modularity with respect to the certainty factor model and discuss logical consequences of the definition. We show that the assumption of semantic modularity imposes strong restrictions on rules in a knowledge base. We argue that such restrictions are rarely valid in practical applications. Finally, we suggest how the concept of semantic modularity can be relaxed in a manner that makes it appropriate for plausible reasoning.

1. INTRODUCTION

Researchers in the artificial intelligence community have concentrated their efforts on deductive problem solving methods. In doing so, they have developed numerous approaches for representing and manipulating propositions. One methodology that has been used frequently to build expert systems is the *rule-based* representation framework. In rule-based systems, knowledge is represented as rules of the form "IF A THEN B" where A and B are logical propositions.

An often cited advantage of the rule-based approach is that rules can be added or deleted from a knowledge base without the need to modify other rules [1]. This property is called *modularity*. To our knowledge the concept of modularity has never been formally defined. Nevertheless, modularity has been informally described in some detail. For example, the following two paragraphs are taken from a discussion of modularity by Davis [1]:

> We can regard the *modularity* of a program as the degree of separation of its functional units into isolatable pieces. A program is *highly modular* if any functional unit can be changed (added, deleted, or replaced) with no unanticipated change to other functional units. Thus program modularity is inversely related to the strength of coupling between its functional units.
>
> The modularity of programs written as pure production systems arises from the important fact that the next rule to be invoked is determined solely by the contents of the data base, and no rule is ever called directly. Thus the addition (or deletion) of a rule does not require the modification of any other rule to provide for or delete a call to it. We might demonstrate this by repeatedly removing rules from a PS [production system]: many systems will continue to display some sort of "reasonable" behavior. By contrast, adding a procedure to an ALGOL-like program requires modification of other parts of the code to insure that the procedure is

invoked, while removing an arbitrary procedure from such a program will generally cripple it.

In the above quotation and in other discussions of modularity, it seems that two different notions of modularity are defined without apparent distinction. One notion is that rules can be added or deleted from a knowledge base without altering the *truth* or *validity* of other rules in the system. The other notion is that rules can be added or deleted from a knowledge base without modifying the *syntax* of other rules; the inference process can continue in spite of such additions or deletions. We will call the former notion *semantic modularity* and the latter *syntactic modularity*.

By design, rules are syntactically modular. Furthermore, the validity of a rule in a deductive system does not depend on other rules in the system's knowledge base. For example, if a knowledge base contains the rule

    IF: A and B are parallel lines
    THEN: A and B do not intersect

then the addition or deletion of other rules will not affect the truth value of this rule. Once this fact is asserted, it cannot be falsified by additional facts. Of course, a rule might be added that contradicts rules already in the knowledge base. However, aside from this special case, categorical rules are semantically modular. Indeed, the syntactically modular rule-based representation scheme may have emerged from the recognition that logical rules are modular in the semantic sense.

As investigators have begun to tackle real-world problems such as mineral exploration, medical diagnosis, and financial management, methods for reasoning under uncertainty or *plausible reasoning* have received increasing attention. Popular AI approaches that have been developed for managing uncertainty include extensions of the production rule methodology. In these methodologies, a number is attached to each rule which represents the degree of association, in some sense, between the antecedent and the consequent of the rule.

In such approaches, the notions of syntactic and semantic modularity have been carried over from deductive systems. That is, the properties of both syntactic and semantic modularity have been ascribed to rules in plausible reasoning systems. It seems appropriate to attribute the property of syntactic modularity to rules in plausible reasoning systems. Just as in deductive systems, non-categorical rules can be added and deleted without the need to modify the syntax of other rules. However, in this paper, we argue that it is inappropriate to carry over the notion of semantic modularity from deductive systems and apply it to systems which must manage uncertainty. We shall see that fundamental differences between logical and plausible reasoning result in the breakdown of the assumption of semantic modularity in rule-based systems which reason under uncertainty.

To demonstrate that it is inappropriate to ascribe the property of semantic modularity to rules in plausible reasoning systems, we will examine a particular rule-based method for reasoning under uncertainty, the MYCIN certainty factor (CF) model [2]. We will first present a formal definition of semantic modularity with respect to the CF model. We will then illustrate several implications of semantic modularity and argue that these implications cannot be justified in most practical applications. Also in this paper, we will discuss a methodology for relaxing the assumption of semantic modularity to accommodate plausible reasoning.

We should emphasize that we are not the first to notice problems with the assumption of modularity in rule-based systems which reason under uncertainty. For example, in the closing remarks of their book on rule-based expert systems [3], Buchanan and Shortliffe state that many of MYCIN's rules do not have the property that we have termed semantic modularity. However to our knowledge, there have been no efforts to formally define the concept of semantic modularity nor have there been efforts to contrast the concepts of syntactic and semantic modularity in detail.

2. OVERVIEW OF THE MYCIN CERTAINTY FACTOR MODEL

In this section, we will describe the aspects of the MYCIN CF model that are essential for understanding the consequences of modularity in rule-based systems which manage uncertainty. As mentioned above, the model is an adjunct to the rule-based representation framework. A *certainty factor* is attached to each rule that represents the *change in belief* in consequent of the rule given the antecedent. Certainty factors range between -1 and 1. Positive numbers correspond to an *increase* in belief in a hypothesis while negative quantities correspond to a *decrease* in belief.[1] It is important to note that certainty factors do not correspond to measures of *absolute* belief. This distinction, with respect to certainty factors as well as other measures of uncertainty, has not been emphasized in the artificial intelligence literature [4].

The following notation will be used to represent a rule in the CF model:

$$E \xrightarrow{CF(H,E)} H$$

where H is a hypothesis, E is evidence relating to the hypothesis, and CF(H,E) is the certainty factor attached to the rule. In MYCIN, multiple pieces of evidence may bear on the same hypothesis. In addition, a hypothesis may serve as evidence for yet another hypothesis. The result is a network of rules such as the one shown in Figure 1. This structure is often called an *inference net* [5].

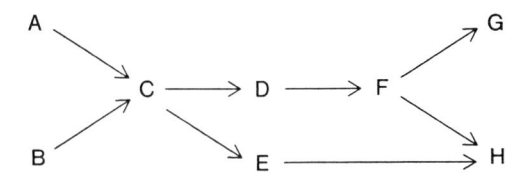

Figure 1: An inference net

The certainty factor model includes a prescription for propagating uncertainty through an inference net. For example, the CF model can be used to compute the change in belief in hypotheses G and H when A and B are true (see Figure 1). Details of the propagation scheme are described in [2] and [3].

3. DEFINITION OF SEMANTIC MODULARITY

In this section, we construct a formal definition of semantic modularity in the context of the MYCIN certainty factor model. To motivate the definition, consider the following classic example from probability theory. Suppose an individual is given one of the following two urns:

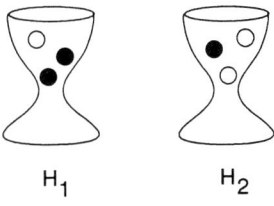

H_1 H_2

The first urn contains 1 white ball and 2 black balls while the second urn contains 2 white balls and 1 black ball. He is not allowed to look inside the urn, but is allowed to draw balls from the urn, one at a time, *without* replacement. Let H_1 be the hypothesis that the individual is holding the first urn and H_2 be the hypothesis that he is holding the second urn.

Suppose a black ball and then a second black ball are drawn from the urn. Upon drawing the second black ball, the individual's belief in H_1 increases to certainty. In contrast, suppose the result of the first draw is a white ball. In this case, the draw of the second black ball raises his belief in H_1 somewhat but does not confirm the hypothesis. Therefore, the effect of the second draw on his belief about the identity of the urn is strongly dependent on the result of the first draw.

This example illustrates that changes in belief may depend on information available at the time evidence becomes known. Therefore, a certainty factor which represents the change in belief in a hypothesis H given evidence E should be written as a function of three arguments, CF(H,E,e), where e denotes information that is known at the time of the update. The notion of semantic modularity, however, requires that the certainty factor for the rule "IF E THEN H" *not* depend on whether other rules which bear on H have fired. Therefore, we take as the formal definition of semantic modularity:

$$CF(H,E,e) = CF(H,E,\emptyset) \tag{1}$$

for all H and E in the network and for any evidence e that might be known at the time E updates H.[2] Since certainty factors in the CF model are functions of only two arguments, the model implicitly assumes (1).

4. CONSEQUENCES OF MODULARITY

Although little can be deduced from the modularity property alone, the creators of the CF model, in order to justify its use, outlined a set of properties or *desiderata* that should be satisfied by a propagation scheme. For example, one desideratum requires that the order in which evidence is considered should not affect the result of propagation. These desiderata provide tools that can be used to deduce the consequences of modularity.

In fact, we note that the desiderata alone lead to a significant consequence. It can be shown that *any* quantity which satisfies the desiderata *must* be a monotonic transformation of the likelihood ratio $\lambda(H,E,e) = p(E|H \wedge e)/p(E|\sim H \wedge e)$, where $p(E|H \wedge e)$ is the *probability* of evidence E given hypothesis H in the context of information e and $p(E|\sim H \wedge e)$ is the probability of evidence E given hypothesis H is false. That is, $CF(H,E,e) = F(\lambda(H,E,e))$ for some monotonic increasing function F. For example, the mapping

$$CF(H,E,e) = \begin{cases} (\lambda(H,E,e)-1)/\lambda(H,E,e) & \lambda \geq 1 \\ \lambda(H,E,e)-1 & \lambda < 1 \end{cases} \tag{2}$$

can be shown to be consistent with one of the central methods of propagation used in the CF model [6].

We will not present a formal proof of (2) nor proofs of the consequences of semantic modularity in this paper. Instead, we will state several consequences of modularity and provide examples that attempt to convey an intuitive understanding of the proofs. We refer those interested in the details of the correspondence to discussions in [6].

Conditional independence

The first consequence we discuss concerns a common situation where several pieces of evidence bear on a single hypothesis. This is shown below:

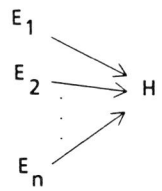

$$\begin{array}{c} E_1 \\ E_2 \\ \vdots \\ E_n \end{array} \longrightarrow H$$

Let ξ_H denote the set $\{E_1, E_2, \ldots E_n\}$.[3] Consider a single item of evidence E_i in ξ_H and let e be any subset of ξ_H which does not include E_i. In this situation, it can be proved that the modularity property (1) holds if and only if

$p(E_i|H \wedge e) = p(E_i|H)$ and   (3)

$p(E_i|\sim H \wedge e) = p(E_i|\sim H)$.

Equation (3) says that the belief in E_i does not depend on the knowledge that e is true when H is definitely true or definitely false. When (3) holds, it is said that evidence is *conditionally independent* given H and its negation.

Let us consider this correspondence between conditional independence and the modularity property in the context of the urn problem above. In the example, it is a simple matter to see why the modularity property is violated; draws are done *without* replacement, making evidence conditionally *dependent*. For example,

    p(2nd draw black | H₂∧1st draw black) = 0

and

    p(2nd draw black | H₂∧1st draw white) = 1/2.

Clearly, condition (3) is not satisfied in the example; this is consistent with our previous observation that modularity does not hold.

The urn problem can be modified such that the modularity property is satisfied. If draws are done *with* replacement, the conditional independence condition (3) is satisfied. In particular, for any e:

    p(W|H₁∧e) = p(W|H₁) = 1/3

    p(W|~H₁∧e) = p(W|H₂∧e) = p(W|H₂) = 2/3

where W denotes the draw of a white ball and e denotes draws made prior to W. Since (3) is satisfied, the modularity property holds and we can compute $CF(H_1,W)$, a function of only two arguments, using relation (2):

    λ(H₁,W) = (1/3)/(2/3) = .5

    CF(H₁,W) = .5 - 1 = -.5.

Other certainty factors relevant to the problem can be calculated in a similar fashion.

Unfortunately, semantic modularity only holds in extremely simple situations like the one above. Any small increase in the complexity of the problem will result in the loss of modularity. For example, suppose an individual is given one of *three* urns:

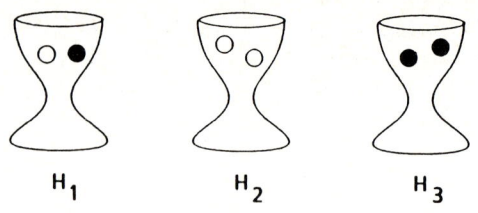

$$H_1 \qquad H_2 \qquad H_3$$

Making draws *with* replacement, evidence is conditionally independent given each of the hypotheses H_1, H_2, and H_3. However, evidence is no longer conditionally independent given the *negation* of any hypothesis. For example, if each hypothesis is equally likely before any draws, the initial probability of drawing a black ball given $\sim H_1$ is

$$
\begin{aligned}
p(B|\sim H_1) &\\
&= p(B \wedge \sim H_1) \,/\, p(\sim H_1) \\
&= [p(B \wedge H_2) + p(B \wedge H_3)] \,/\, p(\sim H_1) \\
&= [p(B|H_2)p(H_2) + p(B|H_3)p(H_3)] \,/\, p(\sim H_1) \\
&= [(0)(1/3) + (1)(1/3)] \,/\, (2/3) \\
&= 1/2
\end{aligned}
$$

However, if a white ball is drawn, H_3 is ruled out and the probability of drawing a black ball changes to

$$p(B|\sim H_1 \wedge W) = p(B|H_2) = 0.$$

Given the correspondence between the conditional independence assumption (3) and the modularity property (1) cited above, it follows that the rules describing this situation cannot be semantically modular. Indeed, using (2) we find that

$$\lambda(H_1, B, \emptyset) = 1 \quad \Longrightarrow \quad CF(H_1, B, \emptyset) = 0$$
$$\lambda(H_1, B, W) = \infty \quad \Longrightarrow \quad CF(H_1, B, W) = 1$$

and therefore

$$CF(H_1, B, \emptyset) \neq CF(H_1, B, W).$$

Intuitively, if a black ball is drawn first, one's belief in H_1 does not change significantly. However, if a black ball is drawn following the draw of a white ball, H_3 is ruled out and H_1 is confirmed. Thus, the certainty factor for H_1 depends on other pieces of evidence (other rules in the inference net). Consequently, the rules representing this knowledge are not modular.

The lack of modularity can be traced directly to the fact that there are more than two mutually exclusive and exhaustive events. In such cases, $\sim H_i$ is a "mixture" of hypotheses and thus evidence will not be conditionally independent given $\sim H_i$ even when evidence is conditionally independent given each H_i. Since the conditional independence assumption (3) is not satisfied, the modularity property cannot hold. This result can be rigorously derived. It can be shown that whenever a set of mutually exclusive and exhaustive hypotheses contains more than two elements, the conditional independence assumption (3), and hence the modularity assumption, is incompatible with multiple updating [7].

A restriction on the topology of inference nets

Another restrictive consequence of semantic modularity is that evidence *cannot*, in most circumstances, be propagated in a consistent manner through networks in which a single piece of evidence bears on more than one hypothesis[4] as shown below:

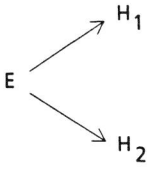

$$E \longrightarrow H_1$$
$$E \longrightarrow H_2$$

Notice the asymmetry between the case of *convergent* links discussed above and this case of *divergent* links. In the former case, the propagation of uncertainty is possible provided conditional independence is assumed. In the latter case, propagation in a manner consistent with the modularity property is essentially impossible.

To illustrate the difficulty associated with divergent links, consider the following story due to Kim and Pearl [8]:

> Mr. Holmes received a telephone call from his neighbor notifying him that she heard a burglar alarm sound from the direction of his home. As he was preparing to rush home, Mr. Holmes recalled that last time the alarm had been triggered by an earthquake. On his way driving home, he heard a radio newscast reporting an earthquake 200 miles away.

An inference net corresponding to this story is shown in Figure 2.

Phone call ⟶ Alarm ⟶ Burglary
                  ↘ Earthquake
Radio announcement ↗

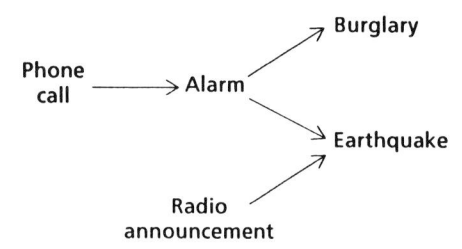

Figure 2: An inference net for Mr. Holmes' situation

A problem arises in trying to assign certainty factors to the rules which have "Alarm" as the antecedent. Since Mr. Holmes heard the radio announcement, the alarm sound tends to support the *earthquake* hypothesis. However, had Mr. Holmes not heard the radio announcement, the alarm sound would lend more support to the *burglary* hypothesis. Thus, the rules above are not modular since their impact depends on the belief about another proposition in the network.

There is an intuitive explanation for this lack of modularity. *A priori*, the earthquake hypothesis and burglary hypothesis are independent. However, knowledge of the alarm status induces a dependency between these hypotheses. In particular, once Mr. Holmes knows the alarm has sounded, evidence *for* one hypothesis is indirect evidence *against* the other. This dependency couples the rules in such a way that modularity is lost.

In this scenario, the loss of modularity is consistent with the general result cited above. Because the network contains divergent links ("IF Alarm THEN Burglary" and "IF Alarm THEN Earthquake"), updating is only possible if the semantic modularity property, (1), does not hold.

5. THE MYTH OF MODULARITY

Extremely few expert system domains satisfy the severely restrictive consequences of semantic modularity described in the previous section. Indeed, it is difficult to imagine a domain in which all sets of mutually exclusive and exhaustive hypotheses contain only two elements and in which divergent links do not occur. It follows, therefore, that semantic modularity rarely exists in rule-based systems which use the CF model to manage uncertainty. Earlier, however, we argued that rules in deductive systems (CF's = ± 1) are semantically modular.

The distinction between logical and uncertain rules is suggested by a fundamental difference between deductive and plausible reasoning alluded to earlier. Suppose a hypothesis is believed with certainty. In this case, no additional information can refute its truth. In particular, if a knowledge base contains the rule "IF E THEN H" (CF = 1), and if E is categorically established, then H is also established beyond any doubt. The addition of other rules to the knowledge base or the establishment of other rule antecedents cannot affect this conclusion. However, if a hypothesis is uncertain, the degree to which it is believed is sensitive to new information. If a knowledge base contains the rule "IF E THEN H" (CF $\neq$ ± 1), then additional information such as new evidence for H can affect the certainty factor for this rule.

In general, the strength of association between antecedent and consequent in a non-categorical rule will change when other rules are added to or deleted from a knowledge base. This suggests that semantic modularity (in a more general sense) will rarely hold in any rule-based system which must manage uncertainty. Thus, it appears that rules representing uncertain relationships will maintain syntactic modularity but *not* semantic modularity. The notion that syntactic and semantic modularity go hand in hand in uncertain reasoning as they do in logical reasoning is a myth.

6. A WEAKER NOTION OF MODULARITY

Since the assumption of semantic modularity places severe constraints on the relationships among propositions in a knowledge base, it seems useful to modify the ruled-based representation scheme to accommodate a weaker form of semantic modularity that is appropriate for plausible reasoning. In this section, we examine a methodology for representing and propagating uncertainty called *influence diagrams* [9] and show that this approach suggests a weaker form of modularity suited to plausible reasoning.[5]

We first informally describe the influence diagram methodology. In doing so, we show how this approach is used to represent the example problems discussed above. We next contrast the influence diagram methodology with the inference net approach. Finally, we develop the weaker notion of semantic modularity suggested by the approach.

An influence diagram is a two-level structure. The upper level of an influence diagram consists of a graph that represents the propositions relevant to a problem as well as relationships among them. Nodes (circles) are used to represent propositions and directed arcs are used to represent dependencies among the propositions. The bottom level represents all possible values or outcomes for each proposition together with a *probability distribution* for each proposition. The arcs in the upper level represent the notion of probabilistic conditioning or *influence*. In particular, an arc from proposition A to proposition B means that the probability distribution for B can be influenced by the values of A. If there is no arc from A to B, the probability distribution for B is independent of the values of A. Thus, the influence diagram representation is useful for representing assumptions of conditional independence. Notice that an arc from A to B may be interpreted as either a *causal* influence or an *associational* influence; no distinction is made between these two concepts in an influence diagram.

To illustrate these concepts, consider once again the three urn problem. An influence diagram

Level 1:

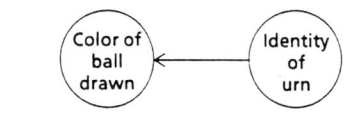

```
    Color of          Identity
     ball    ←─────      of
    drawn                urn
```

Level 2:

Node: Color of ball drawn			Node: Identity of urn	
Identity of urn	Values	p(Color|Identity)	Values	p(Identity)
H_1	White Black	1/2 1/2	H_1	1/3
H_2	White Black	1 0	H_2	1/3
H_3	White Black	0 1	H_3	1/3

Figure 3: An influence diagram for the three urn problem

for this problem is shown in Figure 3. The two nodes labeled "Identity of urn" and "Color of ball drawn" in the upper level of the diagram represent the propositions relevant to the problem. The tables in the lower level list the possible values for each proposition. The arc between the two nodes in the upper level means that the probability distribution for "Color of ball drawn" depends on the value of "Identity of urn." Consequently, the probability distribution for "Color of ball drawn" given in the second level of the diagram is conditioned on each of the three possible values of "Identity of urn": H_1, H_2, and H_3. Note that since there are no arcs into the "Identity of urn" node an unconditional or *marginal* distribution for this proposition is given. Also note that the same urn problem can be represented by an influence diagram with the arc reversed. In this case, a marginal probability distribution would be assigned to "Color of ball drawn" and a conditional probability distribution would be assigned to "Identity of urn."

We see that there are several significant differences between influence diagrams and inference nets. The first difference is that an influence diagram is a two-level structure while the inference net contains only one level. Another difference is that propositions in an influence diagram can take on any number (possibly infinite) of mutually exclusive and exhaustive values. In an inference net, propositions typically can only take on the values "true" and "false." Another distinction is that influence diagrams represent uncertain relationships among propositions using the concept of *probabilistic dependency* while inference nets represent uncertain relationships using the concept of *belief update*.

The story of Mr. Holmes illustrates another difference between influence diagrams and inference nets. The top level of an influence diagram for Mr. Holmes' situation is shown in Figure 4. Notice that many of the nodes in the graph are not directly connected by arcs. As mentioned earlier, the missing arcs are interpreted as statements of conditional independence. For example, the lack of a direct arc between "Burglary" and "Phone call" indicates "Burglary" influences "Phone call" only through its influence on "Alarm." In other words, "Burglary" and "Phone call" are conditionally independent given "Alarm." This would not be true if, for example, Mr. Holmes believed his neighbor might be the thief. We see from this example that influence diagrams provide a flexible means by which experts can assert assumptions of conditional independence that coincide with their beliefs. That is, assumptions of conditional independence are *imposed by the expert*. In contrast, assumptions of independence are *imposed by the methodology* in semantically modular inference nets.

Due to differences between inference nets and influence diagrams, problems that *cannot* be

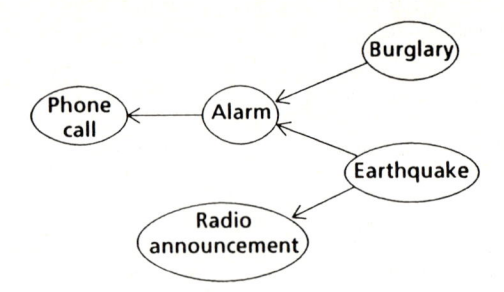

Figure 4: An influence diagram for Mr. Holmes' situation

represented in the former approach can be represented in the latter. For example, the three urn problem could not be represented using an inference net because there were three mutually exclusive and exhaustive hypotheses. However, representing more than two mutually exclusive and exhaustive hypotheses is straightforward in influence diagrams. The problem of Mr. Holmes could not be represented using an inference net because of strong dependencies among "Alarm," "Burglary," and "Earthquake." In an influence diagram, however, these dependencies are naturally represented by the two arcs entering the "Alarm" node. In particular, since there are arcs from both the burglary and earthquake propositions to the alarm proposition, the second level of the influence diagram will contain the probability distribution for "Alarm" as a function all the possible values of both of these propositions. That is, the following probabilities will be included in the lower level of the influence diagram:

p(Alarm|Burglary∧Earthquake)

p(~Alarm|Burglary∧Earthquake)

p(Alarm|Burglary∧~Earthquake)

p(~Alarm|Burglary∧~Earthquake)

p(Alarm|~Burglary∧Earthquake)

p(~Alarm|~Burglary∧Earthquake)

p(Alarm|~Burglary∧~Earthquake)

p(~Alarm|~Burglary∧~Earthquake)

The interaction between the burglary and earthquake hypotheses is completely captured by this probability distribution.[6] In general, it can be shown if an inference problem can be solved in a decision-theoretic framework then it can be represented with an influence diagram [10]. As we have seen, the same cannot be said for inference nets.

Now we are ready to consider a weaker notion of semantic modularity associated with the influence diagram representation. Imagine that a proposition is added to an influence diagram. When this occurs, the expert must first reassess the dependency structure of the diagram. For example, the new node may be influenced by other nodes, may itself influence other nodes, or may introduce conditional independencies or conditional dependencies among nodes currently in the network. Then, *the expert must reassess the probability distribution for each node which had its incoming arcs modified.* However, given the definition of an arc in an influence diagram, there is no need to modify the probability distributions for the nodes in the network whose incoming arcs were not modified. Similarly, if a proposition is deleted from an influence diagram, the expert must first reassess dependencies in the network and then modify only the probability distributions for those nodes which had their incoming arcs modified. The ability to add and delete propositions from an influence diagram without the need to reassign distributions for all nodes in the diagram is the weaker form of semantic modularity we have sought.

To illustrate the concept of weak semantic modularity, consider the following modification to Mr. Holmes' dilemma:

> Shortly after hearing the radio announcement, Mr. Holmes realizes that it is April first. He then recalls the April fools prank he perpetrated on his neighbor the previous year and reconsiders the nature of the phone call.

Given this new information, an "April fools" node should be added to the influence diagram as well as a conditioning arc from the new node to "Phone call." Furthermore, it appears that "April fools" directly influences only "Phone call" and that no other arcs need be added. Therefore, given the weaker form of semantic modularity we have outlined, only the probability distribution for "Phone call" need be reassessed; all other distributions remain intact. Note that the syntax of influence diagrams exactly parallels the weaker notion of semantic modularity we have defined. Thus, the influence diagram methodology is a framework in which notions of semantic and syntactic modularity can be united in the context of plausible reasoning.

7. SUMMARY

In this paper, we analyzed the concept of modularity in detail. We argued that this notion consists of two distinct concepts which we have called syntactic modularity and semantic modularity. We demonstrated that when reasoning under certainty, it is reasonable to regard the rule-based approach as semantically modular but when reasoning under uncertainty, semantic modularity rarely holds. To illustrate this point, we examined the concept of semantic modularity in the context of the MYCIN certainty factor model and demonstrated that the assumption of semantic modularity entails both a strong conditional independence assumption and a strong restriction on the topology of the network. We argued that such restrictions can rarely be met in practical applications and that consequently, semantic modularity does not hold in such situations. In addition, we discussed the implications of the semantic modularity assumption on knowledge engineering. Finally, we described influence diagrams as a representation approach which accommodates a weaker form of semantic modularity appropriate for plausible reasoning.

ACKNOWLEDGEMENTS

We wish to thank Judea Pearl and Peter Hart for several insightful discussions concerning divergence. We also thank Jack Breese, Curt Langlotz, Ted Shortliffe, and Larry Fagan for useful comments. Support for this work was provided by the Josiah Macy, Jr. Foundation, the Henry J. Kaiser Family Foundation, and the Ford Aerospace Corporation. Computing facilities were provided by the SUMEX-AIM resource under NIH grant RR-00785.

NOTES

[1] In another paper in this volume [11], the concept of a measure of change in belief or *belief update* is discussed in general terms.

[2] Technically, this assertion only holds for evidence e such that E does not lie on a directed path from e to H in the inference net. The certainty factor model explicitly handles the case where E lies on a directed path from e to H (see [6]).

[3] It is assumed that the pieces of evidence are logically distinct.

[4]Consistent propagation is possible if no other rules bear on H_1 or H_2.

[5]We note that the *Bayesian networks* of Pearl [12] and the *causal networks* of Cooper [13] are closely related to influence diagrams. In fact, all three approaches suggest the same form of semantic modularity.

[6]This example reveals a potential disadvantage of the influence diagram approach. In general, the number of probability assessments required for a single node is exponential in the number links converging on the node. However, Kim and Pearl [8] have developed a method whereby the probability distribution for a node can be calculated from "lower-order" probabilities in many situations. For example, their method can be used to calculate p(~Alarm|Burglary∧Earthquake) from p(~Alarm|Burglary) and p(~Alarm|Earthquake).

REFERENCES

[1] Davis, R. and King, J.J., The Origin of Rule-Based Systems in AI, in "Rule-Based Expert Systems", (Buchanan, B.G. and Shortliffe, E.H., eds.), Addison-Wesley, Menlo Park, 1984, ch. 2.

[2] Shortliffe, E. H. and Buchanan, B. G., A model of inexact reasoning in medicine, *Mathematical Biosciences*, 23 (1975), pp. 351-379.

[3] Buchanan, B. G., and Shortliffe, E. H., eds., "Rule-Based Expert Systems: The MYCIN Experiments of the Stanford Heuristic Programming Project", Addison-Wesley, Reading, Mass., 1984.

[4] Horvitz, E. J., and Heckerman, D. E., The Inconsistent Use of Measures of Certainty in Artificial Intelligence Research, in "Uncertainty in Artificial Intelligence", (Kanal, L. and Lemmer, J., eds.), North Holland, 1986.

[5] Duda, R., Hart, P., and Nilsson, N., Subjective Bayesian Methods for Rule-based Inference Systems, *In* "Proceedings 1976 National Computer Conference", Vol. 45, AFIPS, 1976, pp. 1075-1082.

[6] Heckerman, D.E., Probabilistic Interpretations for MYCIN's Certainty Factors, in "Uncertainty in Artificial Intelligence", (Kanal, L. and Lemmer, J., eds.), North Holland, 1986.

[7] Johnson, R., Independence and Bayesian updating methods, in "Uncertainty in Artificial Intelligence", (Kanal, L. and Lemmer, J., eds.), North Holland, 1986.

[8] Kim, J.H., and Pearl, J., A computational model for causal and diagnostic reasoning in inference engines, *In* "Proceedings 8th international joint conference on artificial intelligence", Karlsruhe, West Germany, IJCAI, 1983, pp. 190-193.

[9] Howard, R. A., Matheson, J. E., Influence Diagrams, in "Readings on the Principles and Applications of Decision Analysis", (Howard, R. A., Matheson, J. E., eds.), Strategic Decisions Group, Menlo Park, CA, 1981, pp. 721-762, ch. 37.

[10] Shachter, R., "Evaluating Influence Diagrams", To be published in *Operations Research*

[11] Heckerman, D.E., An Axiomatic Framework for Belief Updates, in "Uncertainty in Artificial Intelligence", (Lemmer, J. and Kanal, L., eds.), North Holland, 1987.

[12] Pearl, J., Fusion, propagation, and structuring in belief networks, *Artificial Intelligence*, 29 (3), September (1986), pp. 241-288.

[13] Cooper, G. F., "NESTOR: A Computer-based Medical Diagnostic Aid that Integrates Causal and Probabilistic Knowledge," PhD dissertation, Computer Science Department, Stanford University, November 1984, Rep. No. STAN-CS-84-48. Also numbered HPP-84-48.

IMPRECISE MEANINGS AS A CAUSE OF UNCERTAINTY IN MEDICAL KNOWLEDGE-BASED SYSTEMS

STEVEN J. HENKIND

New York University, Courant Institute of Mathematical Sciences, Department of Computer Science, 251 Mercer Street, New York, N.Y. 10012
and
Mount Sinai School of Medicine, Department of Cardiology, One Gustave L. Levy Place, New York, N.Y. 10029

There has been a considerable amount of work on uncertainty in knowledge-based systems. This work has generally been concerned with uncertainty arising from the strength of inferences and the weight of evidence. In this paper, we discuss another type of uncertainty: that which is due to imprecision in the underlying primitives used to represent the knowledge of the system. In particular, a given word may denote many similar but not identical entities. Such words are said to be *lexically imprecise*.

Lexical imprecision has caused widespread problems in many areas. Unless this phenomenon is recognized and appropriately handled, it can degrade the performance of knowledge-based systems. In particular, it can lead to difficulties with the user interface, and with the inferencing processes of these systems. Some techniques are suggested for coping with this phenomenon.

1. INTRODUCTION: LEXICAL IMPRECISION

Specialized fields of knowledge can be viewed as having their own languages. These languages, which are subsets of natural language, are known as *sublanguages* [1]. Typically, sublanguages have a specialized vocabulary: for example, the vocabulary of medicine as found in a medical dictionary, or the vocabulary of law as found in a legal dictionary.

Since sublanguages are generally used in complex situations where there are difficult problems to be solved, and critical decisions to be made, it is desirable that the underlying vocabularies be well defined. In particular, the words need to have precise meanings. Clearly, if a given word does not have a precise meaning, then a sentence containing that word may be imprecise as well. If the sentence is intended to convey information relevant to the solution of a problem, then the imprecision can lead to an incorrect solution.

Unfortunately, the vocabularies underlying most sublanguages are much less well defined than is commonly believed. For example, a word may be used to denote many similar, but not identical phenomena: In a recent review of the medical literature [2] we found more than a dozen definitions for the important clinical phenomenon *pulsus paradoxus*. All the definitions were intended to define the same phenomenon. Yet they differed enough that two physicians, given the same patient, could reach opposite conclusions as to the presence or absence of a paradoxical pulse. We will say that words which have several similar, but not identical, meanings are *lexically imprecise*.

The lexical imprecision to be found in medical terminology is not limited to certain exceptional words, but is, in fact, extremely common. For example, given that a patient has produced only 300 ml of urine during the past day, nearly every physician would state that the patient has oliguria (low urine output). But, if the the physicians were also told that the patient weighs 80 pounds, has received no fluids in the past 24 hours, and has been exercising heavily, then some would say that the patient is not oliguric, while others would continue to state that the patient has oliguria, albeit "to be expected under the circumstances." *Oliguria* is a term that is well-known to all physicians, but it is apparent that the use of the word is highly dependent upon who is using the word, under what circumstance, and so forth. A similar analysis can be performed for many other clinical entities, e.g., hypertension, etc.

It should be noted that we are not concerned here with words that are used to denote inherently imprecise entities. For example, the word *lethargic* must be somewhat imprecise because lethargy is very subjective in nature. However, we are extremely concerned with words that are used to denote ostensibly objective entities. The word *oliguria* can cause problems because although it is not well defined, nearly all physicians believe that it is. The word *lethargy*, on the other hand, is much less likely to cause difficulty because physicians recognize that it is subjective.

Lexical imprecision is more than just a theoretical curiousity: it has, in fact, caused widespread difficulties in medicine. For example, "There are varying schools of thought among specialists in interpreting petit mal seizures. Some assign the designation *petit mal* to 3 percent of all forms of epilepsy; others classify 80 percent of seizures under this rubric .... In three recent papers, the results reported by the authors on a newly introduced anti-epileptic drug for the treatment of petit mal were respectively that it was highly effective, moderately effective, and ineffective. How much of this discrepancy is to be attributed to the drug or conditions of the trials, and how much to the different conditions regarded by the experiments as being petit mal?" [3].

Lexical imprecision has also caused difficulties in other areas. For example, imprecision in word meanings is known to decrease the effectiveness of computerized information retrieval systems.

2. EFFECTS ON KNOWLEDGE-BASED SYSTEMS

One of the fundamental choices to be made in the construction of a knowledge-based system is the selection of an appropriate knowledge representation. Although rule-based representations are currently the most common choice, there are many other options, e.g., frames, semantic nets, scripts, etc.

At some point, however, all knowledge representations require a choice of semantic primitives. These primitives are the fundamental objects which a system will manipulate. In a knowledge-based system designed to perform medical diagnosis, for example, the semantic primitives would be various signs, symptoms, lab values, and diagnoses. Note that the semantic primitives are generally either lexical items (words), or numbers.

Consider a system which, when given some collection of signs and symptoms, deduces the patient's disease state. Call the set of all signs and symptoms, S, the set of all subsets of S (power set of S), $P(S)$, and the set of all diseases, D. Then diagnosis can be viewed as a map from $P(S)$ to D; i.e., $P(S) \rightarrow D$. For the sake of argument, it is assumed here that each patient has one and only one disease. Furthermore, it is assumed that the diagnostic map is provided by a single domain expert.

Suppose, now, that a user makes a certain set of observations O about a patient. In order to use the diagnostic system, the user will need to express these observations in terms of the semantic primitives of the system. In other words, O must be mapped by the user into $P(S)$. Therefore, the computer-assisted diagnostic process is actually $O \rightarrow P(S) \rightarrow D$.

Unfortunately, due to lexical imprecision, two individuals may map the same observations differently. This can, in turn, lead to a different set of deductions by the system. For example, suppose that an expert creates the following system:

IF pulsus-paradoxus
    THEN tamponade-likely
    ELSE tamponade-not-likely

Also, suppose that user U1 defines pulsus paradoxus as "an inspiratory decline in systolic arterial pressure of 10 mm Hg or more," and user U2 defines it as "a decline of 13 or more." If a patient has an inspiratory decline of 12, then U1 would map his observation into the semantic primitive pulsus-paradoxus, but U2 would not. Therefore, the system would provide U1 with the conclusion that tamponade is likely, but would provide U2 with the opposite conclusion.

Certainly, both conclusions cannot be correct. The difference in conclusions is due to the fact that the map $O \rightarrow P(S)$ is not uniquely specified. In particular, this map varies from individual to individual, depending on the definitions that each person happens to use. It is worth noting that the developers of the INTERNIST system [4] have, in fact, documented difficulties with the interface to their system due to variability in word meanings.

If a system is constructed by two or more domain experts, then lexical imprecision can lead to less than optimal performance of the diagnostic map $P(S) \rightarrow D$. Suppose, for example, that expert E1 provides the rule "IF A THEN B," and expert E2 provides the rule "IF B THEN C." Given A, the system will deduce C. But this may be incorrect if E1 and E2 have different definitions for the semantic primitive B. Of course, if a given expert is able to provide correct solutions to problems, then his knowledge must be, in some sense, internally consistent. The problem here, is that the components of his knowledge may be inconsistent with the components of another expert.

3. LEXICAL IMPRECISION IS NOT LEXICAL AMBIGUITY

Many words have several distinct meanings. For example, the word *beat* can be used as a verb to denote the act of physically abusing someone, as a verb to denote the act of sailing a boat close to the wind, as a noun to denote a policeman's patrol area, and so forth. This phenomenon of multiple distinct meanings is referred to as *lexical ambiguity*. Note that lexical ambiguity is not the same thing as lexical imprecision. A useful analogy is the following: If you open a dictionary and choose a word, it will have several distinct definitions. This is lexical ambiguity. If you open two dictionaries and choose the same word you will find sets of very similar, but not identical definitions. This is lexical imprecision.

Lexical ambiguity can lead to difficulties in the processing of natural language by computer. From a syntactic standpoint, the possibility that a given word may have multiple meanings makes it necessary to select the correct part-of-speech for the word. For example, in parsing the sentence "He is on his beat," it must be determined that *beat* is being used as a noun, and not as a verb. Since the meanings of a lexically imprecise word are all the same part-of-speech, lexical imprecision does not lead to problems in parsing.

Lexical ambiguity can also lead to difficulties in semantic analysis. Semantic analysis requires that the correct word-sense of an item be selected. For example, in analyzing the sentence fragment "Beat until you see the buoy," it must be determined that *beat* refers to the action of sailing close to the wind, and not to the infliction of physical violence. The dictionary of a typical natural language processing system may contain multiple definitions for a given word, but these definitions are invariably distinct. Hence, lexical imprecision has not posed many problems for semantic analysis.

It is at the level of pragmatics that lexical imprecision will cause the most difficulty for systems that use natural language. While subtle distinctions in meaning are of little consequence in the syntactic and semantic decomposition of sentences, these same distinctions can have profound consequences on a system that attempts to use those sentences.

There is much discussion in the literature of techniques for handling lexical ambiguity. Birnbaum [5] provides a detailed review and analysis. On the other hand, there seems to be little, if any, discussion of methods for coping with lexical imprecision. The following section describes some possible techniques.

4. COPING WITH LEXICAL IMPRECISION

The ideal solution to the problem of lexical imprecision would be to eliminate it entirely. This would require that a precise set of definitions be established in each specialized field of knowledge—presumably by a committee of experts. Furthermore, every individual in that field would need to agree upon and use those definitions. There has been, in fact, a great deal of effort in this direction, but with only mixed results. A notable success is the science of chemistry: once a molecule's structure has been determined, that substance has a name assigned to it that conveys the same meaning to every chemist. In the field of medicine, such efforts have been much less successful. For example, the American College of Cardiology, and the American Heart Association have published what they feel to be a standard definition for pulsus paradoxus [6], yet this definition was not to be found in any of the more than sixty papers in the literature that we surveyed [2].

Although efforts to standardize terminology are extremely important, it will never be possible to completely eliminate lexical imprecision. As a field of knowledge expands, new discoveries are made, new measurement techniques devised, and entities are viewed at finer levels of granularity. This in turn renders some previously precise words less precise. For example, to characterize a patient as being "hypertensive" was actually quite precise a hundred years ago; but in modern medicine, such a characterization is far from adequate. Lexical imprecision is, and will remain, a ubiquitous phenomenon, and high performance knowledge-based systems will need to handle it in a reasonable fashion.

As was discussed previously, lexical imprecision can lead to difficulties both at the interface to a knowledge-based system, i.e., $O \rightarrow P(S)$, and within the system, i.e., $P(S) \rightarrow D$. There are several ways to lessen the impact at the interface level. One way is to eliminate that level as much as possible. In particular, the more observations that a system can make directly (rather than through a human intermediary), the less the damage that will be done due to individual differences in the mapping $O \rightarrow P(S)$. In some situations a system should be able to gather most of its input directly: for instance, monitoring a chemical plant. In many other situations, however, a human intermediary is essential. For example, computer vision and robotics notwithstanding, no machine is yet capable of performing a complete physical examination of a patient.

Problems at the interface level can also be decreased by insisting on quantification. For example, the question "Does the patient have oliguria?" is highly susceptible to individual differences in the mapping $O \rightarrow P(S)$, but a request for the volume of urine output is much less problematical [7]. Unfortunately, not all phenomena can be quantified—e.g., petit mal. Even for those phenomena which can be quantified, there are still potential difficulties to be aware of. For example, the normal ranges of various biomedical tests, e.g., enzyme assays, are not standardized, but actually vary from laboratory to laboratory.

Another consideration is that it must be certain that all observers are in fact measuring the same phenomenon (e.g., is pulsus paradoxus the inspiratory decrease in pulse pressure, or the inspiratory decrease in systolic pressure?). This could be encouraged as follows: when the system requests the value of an entity, it also provides a definition. For example, "Please input the measured value of pulsus paradoxus (inspiratory decline in systolic arterial pressure)." Of course, these definitions would need to be built into the system.

The incorporation of definitions into a system is also a potential solution to problems in the construction of the diagnostic map $P(S) \rightarrow D$. In particular, each expert could be encouraged to record his definitions for the semantic primitives with which he is working. Thus, if expert E1 produces the rule "IF A THEN B," he would be expected to provide definitions for the primitives A and B. Before expert E2 entered the rule "IF B THEN C," he would be expected to check the definition of B, and so forth.

Unfortunately, it may be unreasonable to expect that definitions be provided for all the primitives of a large system. The demands in terms of increased development time and overhead could be enormous; nor is it clear how such definitions could be incorporated into existing systems. Furthermore, since the definitions of primitives are themselves composed from other primitives, it is impossible to enforce the complete consistency of the definitions within a system. It should be noted that there are currently a few knowledge-based systems which have (limited) facilities for the incorporation of definitions; e.g., MYCIN [8] and AI/RHEUM [9].

Fuzzy set theory [10] has some applicability as a tool to handle lexical imprecision. Many words are lexically imprecise because they are based upon cutoffs. For example, the lexical imprecision of *pulsus paradoxus* stems largely from the fact that different experts use different cutoffs, e.g., 10, 13, etc. These cutoffs in turn lead to discontinuous behavior, e.g., pulsus paradoxus is considered to be present given a cutoff of 10, but is considered to be absent given a cutoff of 13. By modeling pulsus paradoxus as a fuzzy concept, the damaging effects of lexical imprecision could be greatly reduced because the presence or absence of pulsus would no longer be treated in a discontinuous fashion.

Note, however, that fuzzy techniques are not a solution for all cases of lexical imprecision. For example, fuzzy techniques could not reconcile the imprecision due to one observer measuring the decrease in pulse pressure, and another another observer measuring the decrease in systolic pressure.

5. SUMMARY

Uncertainty is a major source of difficulty in the construction and use of knowledge-based systems. One type of uncertainty arises from the strength of the implication operator in inferences such as "IF A THEN B"; e.g., if A then there is a 40% chance of B. Another type of uncertainty arises from the weight of evidence: e.g., there is a 70% chance that the patient has A. In this paper, we have discussed another type of uncertainty – that which is due to imprecision in the underlying primitives: e.g., two experts have a different conception of A. Lexical imprecision has been described by other researchers [8,11] but it has received much less attention than other types of uncertainty.

Lexical imprecision can degrade the performance of knowledge-based systems. Effects can surface at both the user interface and inferencing levels.

Among the techniques to handle lexical imprecision are the direct acquisition of input data, quantification, the inclusion of definitions, and fuzzy set methods. Currently we are examining ways of incorporating these techniques into medical knowledge-based systems.

ACKNOWLEDGMENTS

I would like to thank Ronald Yager, Malcolm Harrison, Ernie Davis, Barbara de Vries, and Naomi Sager for their many helpful comments and suggestions.

REFERENCES

[1] Kittredege R, Lehrberger J, eds. Sublanguage: studies of language in restricted semantic domains New York: Walter de Gruyter, 1982.
[2] Henkind S, Benis A, Teichholz L. The paradox of pulsus paradoxus. Submitted for publication:1987.
[3] Kennedy J, Kossman C. Nomenclatures in medicine. Bulletin of the Medical Library Association 1973;61:238-52.
[4] Pople HE. Freeing the language of discourse for medical consultation systems. Proc fifth national AMSI congress 1986:272-3.
[5] Birnbaum L. Lexical ambiguity as a touchstone for theories of language analysis. Proceedings ninth IJCAI 1985:815-20.
[6] American College of Cardiology and American Heart Association. Glossary of cardiologic terms related to physical diagnosis: part IV. Arterial Pulses. American Journal of Cardiology 1971;27:708-9.
[7] Henkind SJ, Benis AM, Teichholz LE. Quantification as a means to increase the utility of nomenclature-classification systems. Proceedings of the fifth world congress on medical informatics 1986:858-61.
[8] Buchanan BG, Shortliffe EH, eds. Rule-based expert systems: the MYCIN experiments of the Stanford heuristic programming project. Reading: Addison-Wesley, 1984:210.
[9] Lindberg DAB, Kingsland III LC, Grant KD, Sharp GC. The AI/RHEUM knowledge-based consultant system in rheumatology (abstract). Proceedings of the fifth world congress on medical informatics 1986:1144.
[10] Zadeh L. Fuzzy Sets. Information and Control 1965;8:338-53.
[11] Bonissone PP, Tong RM. Editorial: Reasoning with uncertainty in expert systems. Int J Man-Machine studies 1985;22:241-50.

Evidence as Opinions of Experts

Robert Hummel
Michael Landy

Courant Institute of Mathematical Sciences
New York University

Abstract

We describe a viewpoint on the Dempster/Shafer "Theory of Evidence", and provide an interpretation which regards the combination formulas as statistics of the opinions of "experts". This is done by introducing spaces with binary operations that are simpler to interpret or simpler to implement than the standard combination formula, and showing that these spaces can be mapped homomorphically onto the Dempster/Shafer theory of evidence space. The experts in the space of "opinions of experts" combine information in a Bayesian fashion. We present alternative spaces for the combination of evidence suggested by this viewpoint.

1. Introduction

Many problems in artificial intelligence call for assessments of degrees of belief in propositions based on evidence gathered from disparate sources. It is often claimed that probabilistic analysis of propositions is at variance with intuitive notions of belief [1-3]. Various methods have been introduced to reconcile the discrepancies, but no single technique has settled the issue on both theoretical and pragmatic grounds.

One method for attempting to modify probabilistic analysis of propositions is the Dempster/Shafer "Theory of Evidence." This theory is derived from notions of upper and lower probabilities, as developed by Dempster in [4]. The idea that intervals instead of probability values can be used to model degrees of belief had been suggested and investigated by earlier researchers [2,5-7], but Dempster's work defines the upper and lower points of the intervals in terms of statistics on set-valued functions defined over a measure space. The result is a collection of intervals defined for subsets of a fixed labeling set, and a combination formula for combining collections of intervals.

Dempster explained in greater detail how these notions could be used to assess beliefs on propositions in [8]. The topic was taken up by Shafer [9,10], and led to publication of a monograph on the "Theory of Evidence," [11]. All of these works after [8] emphasize the values assigned to subsets of propositions (the "beliefs"), and the combination formulas, and de-emphasize the connection to the statistical foundations based on the set-valued functions on a measure space. This paper will return to the original formulation by Dempster in [8] to relate the statistical foundations of the Dempster/Shafer theory of evidence to notions of beliefs on propositions.

This paper has three main points. First, we show that the combination rule for the Dempster/Shafer theory of evidence may be simplified by omitting the normalization term. We next point out that the individual pairs of experts involved in the combination formula can be regarded as performing Bayesian updating. Finally, we present extensions to the theory, based on allowing experts to express probabilistic opinions and assuming that the logarithms of experts' opinions over the set of labels are multi-normally distributed.

2. The Rule of Combination and Normalization

The purpose of this section is to show how one can dispense with the normalization term in the Dempster rule of combination.

The set of possible outcomes, or labelings, will be denoted in this paper by Λ. This set is the "frame of discernment", and in other works has been denoted, variously, by Ω, Θ, or S. For convenience, we will assume that Λ is a finite set with n elements, although the framework could easily be extended to continuous label sets. More importantly, we will assume that Λ represents a set of states that are mutually exclusive and exhaustive.

An element (or state of belief) in the theory of evidence is represented by a probability distribution over the power set of Λ, $\mathbf{P}(\Lambda)$. That is, a state m is

$$m : \mathbf{P}(\Lambda) \to [0,1], \quad \sum_{A \subseteq \Lambda} m(A) = 1. \qquad (1a)$$

There is an additional proviso that is typically applied, namely that every state m satisfies

$$m(\emptyset) = 0. \qquad (1b)$$

Section 3.2 introduces a plausible interpretation for the quantities comprising a state.

A state is updated by combination with new evidence, or information, which is presented in the form of another state. Thus given a current state m_1, and another state m_2, a combination of the two states is defined to yield a state $m_1 \oplus m_2$ which for $A \neq \emptyset$ is given by

$$(m_1 \oplus m_2)(A) = \frac{\sum_{B \cap C = A} m_1(B) m_2(C)}{1 - \sum_{B \cap C = \emptyset} m_1(B) m_2(C)} \qquad (2a)$$

and is zero for $A = \emptyset$. This is the so called "Dempster Rule of Combination."

The problem with this definition is that the denominator in (2a) might be zero, so that $(m_1 \oplus m_2)(A)$ is undefined. That is, there exist pairs m_1 and m_2 such that the combination of m_1 and m_2 is not defined. This, of course, is not a very satisfactory situation for a binary operation on a space. The solution which is frequently taken is to avoid combining such elements. An alternative is to add an additional element m_0 to the space:

$$m_0(A) = 0 \text{ for } A \neq \emptyset, \quad m_0(\emptyset) = 1.$$

Note that this additional element does not satisfy the condition $m(\emptyset) = 0$. Then define, as a special case,

$$m_1 \oplus m_2 = m_0 \text{ if}$$
$$\sum_{B \cap C = \emptyset} m_1(B) m_2(C) = 1. \qquad (2b)$$

The binary operation is then defined for all pairs m_1, m_2. The special element m_0 is an absorbent state, in the sense that $m_0 \oplus m = m \oplus m_0 = m_0$ for all states m.

Definition 1: We define $(\mathcal{M}, \oplus)$, the *space of belief states*, by $\mathcal{M} = \{m$ satisfying (1a) and (1b)$\} \cup \{m_0\}$, and define $\oplus$ by (2a) when the denominator in (2a) is nonzero, and by (2b) otherwise. ∎

The set $\mathcal{M}$, together with the combination operation $\oplus$, constitutes a *monoid*, since the binary operation is closed and associative, and there is an identity element. In fact, the binary operation is commutative, so we can say that the space is an abelian monoid.

Still, because of the normalization and the special case in the definition of $\oplus$, the monoid $\mathcal{M}$ is both ugly and cumbersome. It makes better sense to dispense with the normalization. We have

Definition 2: We define $(\mathcal{M}', \oplus')$, the *space of unnormalized belief states*, by $\mathcal{M}' = \{m$ satisfying (1a) $\}$ without the additional proviso, and set

$$(m_1 \oplus' m_2)(A) = \sum_{B \cap C = A} m_1(B) \cdot m_2(C) \tag{3}$$

for all $A \subseteq \Lambda$ and for all pairs $m_1, m_2 \in \mathcal{M}'$. ∎

One can verify that $m_1 \oplus' m_2 \in \mathcal{M}'$, and that $\oplus'$ is associative and commutative, and that there is an identity element. Thus $\mathcal{M}'$ is also an abelian monoid. Clearly, $\mathcal{M}'$ is a more attractive monoid than $\mathcal{M}$.

We define a transformation $\mathbf{V}$ mapping $\mathcal{M}'$ to $\mathcal{M}$ by the formulas

$$(\mathbf{V}m)(A) = \frac{m(A)}{1 - m(\varnothing)}, \quad (\mathbf{V}m)(\varnothing) = 0 \tag{4}$$

if $m(\varnothing) \neq 1$, and $\mathbf{V}m = m_0$ otherwise.

A computation shows that $\mathbf{V}$ preserves the binary operation; i.e.,

$$\mathbf{V}(m_1 \oplus' m_2) = \mathbf{V}(m_1) \oplus \mathbf{V}(m_2).$$

Thus $\mathbf{V}$ is a *homomorphism*. Further, $\mathbf{V}$ is *onto*, since for $m \in \mathcal{M}$, the same m is in $\mathcal{M}'$, and $\mathbf{V}m = m$. The algebraic terminology is that $\mathbf{V}$ is an *epimorphism* of monoids, a fact which we record in

Lemma 1: $\mathbf{V}$ maps homomorphically from $(\mathcal{M}', \oplus')$ onto $(\mathcal{M}, \oplus)$. ∎

A "representation" is a term that refers to a map that is an epimorphism of structures. Intuitively, such a map is important because it allows us to consider combination in the space formed by the range of the map as combinations of preimage elements. Lemma 1 will eventually form a small part of a representation to be defined in the next section.

In the case in point, we see that combination can be done without a normalization factor. If it is required to combine elements in $\mathcal{M}$, one can perform the combinations in $\mathcal{M}'$, and project to $\mathcal{M}$ by $\mathbf{V}$ after all of the combinations are completed. In terms of the Dempster/Shafer theory of evidence, this result says that the normalization in the combination formula is essentially irrelevant, and that combining can be handled by Equation (3) in place of Equation (2a).

3. Spaces of Opinions of Experts

In this section, we introduce two new spaces, based on the opinions of sample spaces of experts, and discuss the evaluation of statistics of experts' opinions. Finally, we interpret the combination rules in these spaces as being a form of Bayesian updating. In the following section we will show that these spaces also map homomorphically onto the space of belief states. Thus our intent is to show that the Dempster/Shafer space of belief states can be interpreted as the statistics of experts updating their opinions in a Bayesian fashion. The reason why the formulas don't look like Bayesian updating is that instead of having a single expert, there are collections of experts, updating in pairs. Thus instead of keeping track of the opinion of a single expert receiving evidence from different sources, we will see that the space of beliefs can be viewed as the statistics of collections of experts, combining their opinions in a Bayesian fashion, where each collection of experts represents an independent source of information. We begin by giving a formal introduction to the spaces of expert and their methods of combination.

3.1. Opinions of Experts

We consider a set $\mathcal{E}$ of "experts", together with a map μ giving a weight or strength for each expert. It is convenient to think of $\mathcal{E}$ as a large but finite set, although the essential restriction is that $\mathcal{E}$ should be a measure space. Each expert $\omega \in \mathcal{E}$ maintains a list of possible labels: Dempster uses the notation $\Gamma(\omega)$ for this subset; i.e., $\Gamma(\omega) \subseteq \Lambda$. Here we will assume that each expert ω has more than just a subset of possibilities $\Gamma(\omega)$, but also a *probabilistic opinion* p_ω defined on Λ, such that $p_\omega(\lambda)$ is a probability distribution over $\lambda \in \Lambda$. The value $p_\omega(\lambda)$ represents expert ω's assessment of the probability of occurrence of the label λ. Except in the case that ω has no opinion (see below), we necessarily have

$$\sum_{\lambda \in \Lambda} p_\omega(\lambda) = 1.$$

If an expert ω believes that a label λ is possible, i.e., $\lambda \in \Gamma(\omega)$, then the associated probability estimate $p_\omega(\lambda)$ will be nonzero. Conversely, if ω thinks that λ is impossible ($\lambda \notin \Gamma(\omega)$), then $p_\omega(\lambda) = 0$. We also include the possibility that expert ω has no opinion which is indicated by the special element $p_\omega \equiv 0$. This state is included in order to ensure that the binary operation, to be defined later, is closed. We denote the collection of probabilistic opinions $\{p_\omega \mid \omega \in \mathcal{E}\}$ by P.

It will turn out that the central point in the theory of evidence is that the $p_\omega(\lambda)$ data is used only in terms of test for zero. Specifically, we set

$$x_\omega(\lambda) = \begin{cases} 1 & \text{if } p_\omega(\lambda) > 0 \\ 0 & \text{if } p_\omega(\lambda) = 0. \end{cases} \quad (5)$$

Note that x_ω is the characteristic function of the set $\Gamma(\omega)$ over Λ, i.e., $x_\omega(\lambda) = 1$ iff $\lambda \in \Gamma(\omega)$. The collection of all x_ω's will be denoted by X, and will be called the *boolean opinions* of the experts $\mathcal{E}$.

If we regard the space of experts $\mathcal{E}$ as a sample space, then each $x_\omega(\lambda)$ can be regarded as a sample of a random (boolean) variable $x(\lambda)$. In a similar way, the $p_\omega(\lambda)$'s are also samples of random variables $p(\lambda)$. In the next section, we will define the state of the system will be defined by statistics on the set of random variables $\{x(\lambda)\}_{\lambda \in \Lambda}$. These statistics are measured over the space of experts. If all experts have the same opinion, then the state should describe that set of possibilities, and the fact that there is a unanimity of opinion. If there is a divergence of opinions, the state should record the fact. The essential idea here is that we measure uncertainty in a probabilistic or boolean opinion by sampling a variety of opinions among a collection of experts, and observe the spread in those opinions.

A key aspect to the spaces of opinions of experts is that collections of experts are combined by taking product sets of experts. That is, suppose $\mathcal{E}_1$ is one set of experts with their opinions, and $\mathcal{E}_2$ is another set of experts with their opinions. The combination element will have as its set of experts the product set $\mathcal{E}_1 \times \mathcal{E}_2$. It might seem more desirable to make use of the disjoint union of $\mathcal{E}_1$ and $\mathcal{E}_2$, but then the connection with the Dempster/Shafer combination formula would not hold. The statistics of the combination element will depend on the statistics of the constituent elements because combination is defined by taking a product set of experts.

Pairs of experts combine their opinions in an essentially Bayesian fashion. Under fairly standard independence assumptions, two experts should update their probabilistic assignment for a given label by taking the product of their individual probabilities, and dividing by a prior probability. The resulting values have to be normalized so that they remain probabilities. In terms of the boolean opinions, Bayesian updating with the same independence assumption asserts that two experts agree that a label is possible only if both experts believe the label to be possible.

We are now ready to introduce the spaces which we will term "opinions of experts." The central point is that the set of labels Λ is fixed, but that the set of experts $\mathcal{E}$ can be different for distinct elements in these spaces.

Definition 3: The *space of boolean opinions of experts*, $(\mathcal{N}', \odot)$, is defined by:

$$\mathcal{N}' = \{(\mathcal{E}, \mu, X) \mid \#\mathcal{E} < \infty, \mu \text{ is a measure on } \mathcal{E},$$

$$X = \{x_\omega\}_{\omega \in \mathcal{E}}, \, x_\omega : \Lambda \to \{0,1\} \, \forall \, \omega\}.$$

If $(\mathcal{E}_1, \mu_1, X_1)$ and $(\mathcal{E}_2, \mu_2, X_2)$ are elements in $\mathcal{N}'$, define their product

$$(\mathcal{E}, \mu, X) = (\mathcal{E}_1, \mu_1, X_1) \odot (\mathcal{E}_2, \mu_2, X_2)$$

by

$$\mathcal{E} = \mathcal{E}_1 \times \mathcal{E}_2 = \{(\omega_1, \omega_2) \mid \omega_1 \in \mathcal{E}_1, \omega_2 \in \mathcal{E}_2\}$$

$$\mu(\{(\omega_1, \omega_2)\}) = \mu_1(\{\omega_1\}) \cdot \mu_2(\{\omega_2\}),$$

and

$$X = \{x_{(\omega_1, \omega_2)}\}_{(\omega_1, \omega_2) \in \mathcal{E}},$$

$$x_{(\omega_1, \omega_2)}(\lambda) = x^{(1)}_{\omega_1}(\lambda) \cdot x^{(2)}_{\omega_2}(\lambda),$$

where $X_i = \{x^{(i)}_{\omega_i} \mid \omega_i \in \mathcal{E}_i\}$, for $i = 1, 2$. ∎

Definition 4: Let $K = \{\kappa_\lambda\}$ be a set of positive constants indexed over the label set Λ. The *space of probabilistic opinions of experts* $(\mathcal{N}, K, \otimes)$ is defined similarly, except that $\mathcal{N}$ consists of triples $(\mathcal{E}, \mu, P)$, where P contains probabilistic opinions (as introduced earlier), and that combination of those probabilistic opinions is defined by

$$p_{(\omega_1, \omega_2)}(\lambda) = \frac{p^{(1)}_{\omega_1}(\lambda) p^{(2)}_{\omega_2}(\lambda) [\kappa_\lambda]^{-1}}{\sum_{\lambda'} p^{(1)}_{\omega_1}(\lambda') p^{(2)}_{\omega_2}(\lambda') [\kappa_{\lambda'}]^{-1}},$$

providing the denominator is nonzero, and

$$p_{(\omega_1, \omega_2)} \equiv 0$$

otherwise. ∎

To interpret this combining operation, consider two sets of experts $\mathcal{E}_1$ and $\mathcal{E}_2$, with each set of experts expressing opinions in the form of P_1 and P_2. We form a new set of experts, which is simply the set of all committees of two, consisting of one expert from $\mathcal{E}_1$, and another from $\mathcal{E}_2$. In each of the committees, the members confer to determine a consensus opinion. In the probabilistic case, one can interpret the formulas as Bayesian combination (where κ_λ is the prior probability Prob(λ) on λ). In the boolean case, the consensus is simply the intersection of the composing opinions (see Figure 1).

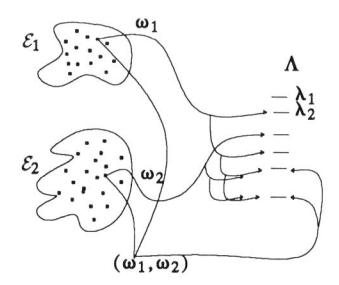

Figure 1. A depiction of the combination of two boolean opinions of two experts, yielding a consensus opinion by the element in the product set of experts formed by the committee of two.

3.2. Statistics of Experts

It will turn out that the Dempster/Shafer theory of evidence can be viewed as a mechanism for tracking statistics in the space of opinions of experts. We accordingly now define what is meant by the statistics of an element $(\mathcal{E}, \mu, X) \in \mathcal{N}'$.

Statistics will be computed by summing the weights of experts in subsets of $\mathcal{E}$. If the experts have equal weights, this is equivalent to counting the number of experts. In general, we will sum the weights of experts in a subset $\mathcal{F} \subseteq \mathcal{E}$, and denote the result by $\mu(\mathcal{F})$. Thus μ is in fact a measure on $\mathcal{E}$, although it is completely determined by the weights of the individual experts $\mu(\{\omega\})$ for $\omega \in \mathcal{E}$. (We are assuming that $\mathcal{E}$ is finite.)

For a given subset $A \subseteq \Lambda$, the characteristic function χ_A is defined by

$$\chi_A(\lambda) = \begin{cases} 0 & \text{if } \lambda \notin A \\ 1 & \text{if } \lambda \in A. \end{cases}$$

Equality of two functions defined on Λ means, of course, that the two functions agree for all $\lambda \in \Lambda$.

Given a space of experts $\mathcal{E}$ and the boolean opinions X, we define

$$\tilde{m}(A) = \frac{\mu\{\omega \in \mathcal{E} \mid x_\omega = \chi_A\}}{\mu\{\mathcal{E}\}} \tag{5}$$

for every subset $A \subseteq \Lambda$. It is possible to view the values as probabilities on the random variables $\{x(\lambda)\}$. We endow the elements of $\mathcal{E}$ with the prior probabilities $\mu(\{\omega\})/\mu(\mathcal{E})$, and say that the probability of an event involving a combination of the random variables $x(\lambda)$'s over the sample space $\mathcal{E}$ is the probability that the event is true for a particular sample, where the sample is chosen at random from $\mathcal{E}$ with the sampling distribution given by the prior probabilities. This is equivalent to saying

$$\underset{\mathcal{E}}{\text{Prob}}(\text{Event}) = \frac{\mu(\{\omega \in \mathcal{E} \mid \text{Event is true for } \omega\})}{\mu\{\mathcal{E}\}}.$$

With this convention, we see that

$$\tilde{m}(A) = \underset{\mathcal{E}}{\text{Prob}}(x(\lambda) = \chi_A(\lambda) \text{ for all } \lambda).$$

In fact, all of the priors and joint statistics of the $x(\lambda)$'s are determined by the full collection of $\tilde{m}(A)$ values. For example,

$$\text{Prob}(x(\lambda_0) = 1) = \sum_{\{A \mid \lambda_0 \in A\}} \tilde{m}(A)$$

and

$$\text{Prob}(x(\lambda_0) = 1 \text{ and } x(\lambda_1) = 1) = \sum_{\{A \mid \lambda_0, \lambda_1 \in A\}} \tilde{m}(A).$$

Further, the full set of values $\tilde{m}(A)$ for $A \subseteq \Lambda$ defines an element $\tilde{m} \in \mathcal{M}'$. To see this, it suffices to check that $\sum \tilde{m}(A) = 1$, which amounts to observing that for every ω, $x_\omega = \chi_A$ for some $A \subseteq \Lambda$.

Many of the quantities in the theory of evidence can be interpreted in terms of simple conditional probabilities on the $x(\lambda)$'s. For example, the belief on a set A,

$$\text{Bel}(A) = \sum_{B \subseteq A} m(B)$$

is simply the joint probability that $x(\lambda) = 0$ for $\lambda \notin A$ conditioned on the assumption that $x(\lambda) \neq 0$ for some $\lambda \in \Lambda$. In a similar way, plausibility values

$$\text{Pl}(A) = \sum_{B \cap A \neq \emptyset} m(B) = 1 - \text{Bel}(\bar{A})$$

can be interpreted as disjunctive probabilities, and the commonality values

$$Q(A) = \sum_{A \subseteq B} m(B)$$

are a kind of joint probability.

To recapitulate, we have defined a mapping from P values to X values, and then transformations from X to $\bar{m}$ and m values. The resulting element m, which contains statistics on the X variables, is an element in the space of belief states $\mathcal{M}$ of the of the Dempster/Shafer theory of evidence (Section 2).

4. Equivalence with the Dempster/Shafer Rule of Combination

At this point, we have four spaces with binary operations, namely $(\mathcal{N}, \otimes)$, $(\mathcal{N}', \odot)$, $(\mathcal{M}', \oplus')$, and $(\mathcal{M}, \oplus)$. We will now show that these four spaces are closely related. It is not hard to show that the binary operation is, in all four cases, commutative and associative, and that each space has an identity element, so that these spaces are abelian monoids. We also have

Definition 5: The map $T : \mathcal{N} \rightarrow \mathcal{N}'$, with $(\mathcal{E}, \mu, X) = T(\mathcal{E}, \mu, P)$, is given by equation (4), i.e., $x_\omega(\lambda) = 1$ iff $p_\omega(\lambda) > 0$, and $x_\omega(\lambda) = 0$ otherwise. ∎

There is another mapping U, given by

Definition 6: The map $U : \mathcal{N}' \rightarrow \mathcal{M}'$ with $\bar{m} = U(\mathcal{E}, \mu, X)$ given by equation (5), i.e., $\bar{m}(A) = \mu(\{\omega \in \mathcal{E} | x_\omega = \chi_A\}) / \mu(\{\mathcal{E}\})$. ∎

We claim that T and U preserve the binary operations. More formally, we show that T and U are homomorphisms of monoids. However, proofs are omitted here; we refer the interested reader to the larger report [12].

Lemma 2: T is a homomorphism of $\mathcal{N}$ onto $\mathcal{N}'$.

Lemma 3: U is a homomorphism of $\mathcal{N}'$ onto $\mathcal{M}'$.

Recall from Section 2 that the map $V: \mathcal{M}' \rightarrow \mathcal{M}$ is also a homomorphism. So we can compose the homomorphisms $T: \mathcal{N} \rightarrow \mathcal{N}'$ with $U: \mathcal{N}' \rightarrow \mathcal{M}'$ with $V: \mathcal{M}' \rightarrow \mathcal{M}$ to obtain the following obvious theorem.

Theorem: The map $V \circ U \circ T: \mathcal{N} \rightarrow \mathcal{M}$ is a homomorphism of monoids mapping onto the space of belief states $(\mathcal{M}, \oplus)$. ∎

This theorem provides the justification for the viewpoint that the theory of evidence space $\mathcal{M}$ represents the space $\mathcal{N}$ via the representation $V \circ U \circ T$.

The significance of this result is that we can regard combinations of elements in the theory of evidence as combinations of elements in the space of opinions of experts. For if $m_1, \cdots, m_k$ are elements in $\mathcal{M}$ that are to be combined under $\oplus$, we can find respective preimages in $\mathcal{N}$ under the map $V \circ U \circ T$, and then combine those elements using the operation $\otimes$ in the space of opinions of experts $\mathcal{N}$. After all combinations in $\mathcal{N}$ are completed, we project back to $\mathcal{M}$ by $V \circ U \circ T$; the result will be the same as if we had combined the elements in $\mathcal{M}$. The advantage to this procedure is that combinations in $\mathcal{N}$ are conceptually simpler: there are no funny normalizations, and we can regard the combination as Bayesian updatings on the product space of experts.

5. An Alternative Method for Combining Evidence

With the viewpoint that the theory of evidence is really simply statistics of opinions of experts, we can make certain remarks on the limitations of the theory.

(1) There is no use of probabilities or degrees of confidence. Although the belief values seem to give weighted results, at the base of the theory, experts only say whether a condition is possible or not. In particular, the theory makes no distinc-

tion between an expert's opinion that a label is likely or that it is remotely possible.

(2) Pairs of experts combine opinions in a Bayesian fashion with independence assumptions of the sources of evidence. In particular, dependencies in the sources of information are not taken into account.

(3) Combinations take place over the product space of experts. It might be more reasonable to have a single set of experts modifying their opinions as new information comes in, instead of forming the set of all committees of mixed pairs.

Both the second and third limitations come about due to the desire to have a combination formula which factors through to the statistics of the experts and is application-independent. The need for the second limitation, the independence assumption on the sources of evidence, is well-known (see, e.g., [13]). Without incorporating much more complicated models of judgements under multiple sources of knowledge, we can hardly expect anything better.

The first objection, however, suggests an alternate formulation which makes use of the probabilistic assessments of the experts. Basically, the idea is to keep track of the density distributions of the opinions in probability space. Of course, complete representation of the distribution would amount to recording the full set of opinions p_ω for all ω. Instead, it is more reasonable to approximate the distribution by some parameterization, and update the distribution parameters by combination formulas.

We present a formulation based on normal distributions of logarithms of updating coefficients. Other formulations are possible. In marked contrast to the Dempster/Shafer formulation, we assume that all opinions of all experts are nonzero for every label. That is, instead of converting opinions into boolean statements by test for zero, we will assume that all the values are nonzero, and model the distribution of their strengths.

In a manner similar to [14], set

$$L(\lambda|s_i) = \log\left[\frac{\text{Prob}(\lambda|s_i)}{\text{Prob}(\lambda)}\right],$$

where $\text{Prob}(\lambda|s_i)$ is a probability of label λ being the correct labeling, among labeling situations, conditioned on some information s_i shared by the collection of experts $\mathcal{E}_i$. (Note, incidentally, that the $L(\lambda|s_i)$ values are not the so-called "log-likelihood ratios"; in particular, they can be both positive and negative). Using some fairly standard assumptions in Bayesian updating, (see [14]), we obtain

$$\log[\text{Prob}(\lambda|s_1,\cdots,s_k)] \approx c + \log[\text{Prob}(\lambda)] + \sum_{i=1}^{k} L(\lambda|s_i),$$

where c is a constant independent of λ (but not of $s_1,\cdots,s_k$).

The consequence of this formula is that if certain independence assumptions hold, and if $\text{Prob}(\lambda)$ and $L(\lambda|s_i)$ are known for all λ and i, then the approximate values $\text{Prob}(\lambda|s_1,\cdots,s_k)$ can be determined.

Accordingly, we introduce a space which we term "logarithmic opinions of experts." For convenience, we will assume that experts have equal weights. An element in this space will consist of a set of experts $\mathcal{E}_i$, and a collection of opinions $Y_i = \{y_\omega^{(i)}\}_{\omega \in \mathcal{E}_i}$. Each $y_\omega^{(i)}$ is a map, and the component $y_\omega^{(i)}(\lambda)$ represents expert ω's estimate of $L(\lambda|s_i)$:

$$y_\omega^{(i)}: \Lambda \to \mathbb{R}, \quad y_\omega^{(i)}(\lambda) \approx L(\lambda|s_i).$$

Note that the experts in $\mathcal{E}_i$ all have knowledge of the information s_i, and that the estimated logarithmic coefficients $L(\lambda|s_i)$ can be positive or negative. In fact, since the experts do not necessarily have precise knowledge of the value of $\text{Prob}(\lambda)$, but instead provide estimates of log's of ratios, the estimates can lie in an unbounded range.

Combination in the space of logarithmic opinions of experts is defined much the same as our earlier combination formulas, except that now consensus opinions are derived by adding component opinions. Specifically, the combination of $(\mathcal{E}_1, Y_1)$ and $(\mathcal{E}_2, Y_2)$ is $(\mathcal{E}_1 \times \mathcal{E}_2, Y)$, where

$$Y = \{y_{(\omega_1, \omega_2)}\}_{(\omega_1, \omega_2) \in \mathcal{E}},$$

and

$$y_{(\omega_1, \omega_2)}(\lambda) = y^{(1)}_{\omega_1}(\lambda) + y^{(2)}_{\omega_2}(\lambda).$$

Next, in analogy with our map to a statistical space (Section 3.2), we can define a space that might be termed the "parameterized statistics of logarithmic opinions of experts." Elements in this space will consist of pairs $(\bar{u}, C)$, where $\bar{u}$ will be a mean vector in $\mathbb{R}^n$ and C is a symmetric n by n covariance matrix. To project from the space of logarithmic opinions to the space of parameterized statistics, define u_i to be the average value of $y_\omega(\lambda_i)$ over $\omega \in \mathcal{E}$, where $\Lambda = \{\lambda_1, \cdots, \lambda_n\}$ is a fixed ordering of the elements in the label set. Then the vector $\bar{u}$ is defined by $\bar{u} = (u_1, \cdots, u_n)$. Likewise, define c_{ij} as the average value of $(y_\omega(\lambda_i) - u_i) \cdot (y_\omega(\lambda_j) - u_j)$ over $\omega \in \mathcal{E}$, and set C equal to the matrix whose i,j-th component is given by c_{ij}.

Combinations in the space of statistics must be defined in such a way that the map from the collections of opinions to the mean and covariances forms a homomorphism. We are led, after some calculation, to the definition:

$$(\bar{u}^{(1)}, C^{(1)}) \oplus (\bar{u}^{(2)}, C^{(2)}) = (\bar{u}^{(1)} + \bar{u}^{(2)}, C^{(1)} + C^{(2)}).$$

That is, since the components are added on the product space of experts, the means and covariances separately add. An extension to the case where $\mathcal{E}_1$ and $\mathcal{E}_2$ have nonequal total weights is straight-forward.

To interpret a state $(\bar{u}, C)$ in the space of parameterized statistics, we must remember the origin of the logarithmic-opinion values. Specifically, after k updating iterations combining information s_1 through s_k, the updated vector $\bar{y} = (y_1, \cdots, y_n) \in \mathbb{R}^n$ is an estimate of the sum of the logarithmic coefficients,

$$y_j \approx \sum_{i=1}^{k} L(\lambda | s_j).$$

The *a posteriori* probability of a label λ_j is high if the corresponding coefficient $y_j + \log[\text{Prob}(\lambda_j)]$ is large in comparison to the other components $y_j + \log[\text{Prob}(\lambda_j)]$.

Since the state $(\bar{u}, C)$ represents a multinormal distribution in the log-updating space, we can transform this distribution to a density function for *a posteriori* probabilities. The vector $\bar{u}$ represents the center of the distribution (before bias by the priors). The spread of the distribution is given by the covariance matrix, which can be thought of as defining an ellipsoid in $\mathbb{R}^n$ centered at $\bar{u}$. The exact equation of the ellipse can be written implicitly as:

$$(\bar{y} - \bar{u})^T C^{-1} (\bar{y} - \bar{u}) = 1.$$

This ellipse describes a "one sigma" variation in the distribution, representing a region of uncertainty of the logarithmic opinions; the distribution to two standard deviations lies in a similar but enlarged ellipse. The eigenvalues of C give the squared lengths of the semi-major axes of the ellipse, and are accordingly proportional to degrees of confidence in the corresponding directions. Bias by the prior probabilities simply adds a fixed vector, with components $\log[\text{Prob}(\lambda_j)]$, to the ellipse, thereby translating the distribution. We seek an axis j such that the components y_j of the vectors $\bar{y}$ lying in the translated ellipse are relatively much larger than other components of vectors in the ellipse. In this case, the preponderant evidence is for label λ_j.

Clearly, the combination formula is extremely simple. Its greatest advantage over the Dempster/Shafer theory of evidence is that only $O(n^2)$ values are required to describe a state, as opposed to the 2^n values used for a mass distribution in $\mathcal{M}$. The simplicity and reduction in numbers of parameters has been purchased at the expense of an assumption about the kinds of distributions that can be expected. However, the same assumption allows us to track probabilistic opinions (or actually, the logarithms), instead of converting all opinions into boolean statements about possibilities.

6. Conclusions

We have shown how the theory of evidence may be viewed as a representation of a space of opinions of experts, where opinions are combined in a Bayesian fashion over the product space of experts. By "representation", we mean something very specific — namely, that there is a homomorphism mapping from the space of opinions of experts onto the Dempster/Shafer theory of evidence space. This map fails to be an isomorphism (which would imply equivalence of the spaces) only insofar as it is many-to-one. In this way the state in the theory of evidence represents a corresponding collection of elements.

Furthermore, combination in the space of opinions of experts, as defined in Section 3, leads to combination in the theory of evidence space. This allows us to implement combination in a somewhat simpler manner, since the formulas for combination without the normalization are simpler than the more standard formulas, and also permits us to view combination in the theory of evidence space as the tracking of statistics of opinions of experts as they combine information in a pairwise Bayesian fashion over the product space of experts.

From this viewpoint, we can see how the Dempster/Shafer theory of evidence accomplishes its goals, and what independence assumptions are needed. Degrees of support for a proposition, belief, and plausibilities, are all measured in terms of joints and disjunctive probabilities over a set of experts who are naming possible labels given current information. The problem of ambiguous knowledge versus uncertain knowledge, which is frequently described in terms of "withholding belief," can be viewed as two different distributions of opinions. In particular, ambiguous knowledge can be seen as observing high densities of opinions on particular disjoint subsets, whereas uncertain knowledge corresponds to unanimity of opinions, where the agreed upon opinion gives many possibilities. Finally, instead of performing Bayesian updating, a *set* of values are updated in a Bayesian fashion over the product space, which results in non-Bayesian formulas over the space of labels.

In meeting each of these goals, the theory of evidence invokes compromises that we might wish to change. For example, in order to track statistics, it is necessary to model the distribution of opinions. If these opinions are probabilistic assignments over the set of labels, then the distribution function will be too complicated to retain precisely. The Dempster/Shafer theory of evidence solves this problem by simplifying the opinions to boolean decisions, so that each expert's opinion lies in a space having 2^n elements. In this way, the full set of statistics can be specified using 2^n values. We have suggested an alternate method, which retains the probability values in the opinions without converting them into boolean decisions, and requires only $O(n^2)$ values to model the distribution, but fails to retain full information about the distribution. Instead, our method attempts to approximate the distribution of opinions with a Gaussian function.

Acknowledgements

This research was supported by Office of Naval Research Grant N00014-85-K-0077 and NSF Grant DCR-8403300. This is a conference report version of a longer paper, which appears as NYU Robotics Research Report Number 57 and can be obtained from the author at 251 Mercer Street, New York, New York, 10012, or by a request sent to "hummel@nyu.arpa". Many useful suggestions were given by Tod Levitt. We appreciate also the helpful comments given by George Reynolds, Deborah Strahman, and Jean-Claude Falmagne.

References

[1] J. C. Falmagne, "A random utility model for a belief function," *Synthese* **57**, pp. 35-48 (1983).

[2] B.O. Koopman, "The axioms and algebra of intuitive probability," *Ann. Math.* **41**, pp. 269-292 (1940). See also "The bases of probability", *Bulletin of the American Math. Society* 46, 1940, p. 763-774.

[3] Henry E. Kyburg, Jr., "Bayesian and non-bayesian evidential updating," University of Rochester Dept. of Computer Science Tech. Rep. 139 (July, 1985).

[4] A. P. Dempster, "Upper and lower probabilities induced by a multivalued mapping," *Annals of Mathematical Statistics* **38**, pp. 325-339 (1967).

[5] Peter C. Fishburn, *Decision and Value Theory*, Wiley, New York (1964).

[6] I. J. Good, "The measure of a non-measurable set," pp. 319-329 in *Logic, Methodology, and Philosophy of Science*, ed. E. Nagel, P. Suppes, and A. Tarski, Stanford University Press (1962).

[7] C. A. B. Smith, "Personal probability and statistical analysis," *J. Royal Statistical Society, Series A* **128**, pp. 469-499 (1965). With discussion. See also "Personal probability and statistical analysis", *J. Royal Statistical Society, Series B* 23, p. 1-25.

[8] A. P. Dempster, "A generalization of Bayesian inference," *Journal of the Royal Statistical Society, Series B* **30**, pp. 205-247 (1968).

[9] G. Shafer, "Allocations of Probability," Ph.D. dissertation, Princeton University (1973). Available from University Microfilms, Ann Arbor, Michigan.

[10] G. Shafer, "A theory of statistical evidence," in *Foundations and Philosophy of Statistical Theories in the Physical Sciences, Vol II*, ed. W.L. Harper and C.A. Hooker, Reidel (1975).

[11] G. Shafer, *A mathematical theory of evidence*, Princeton University Press, Princeton, N.J. (1976).

[12] Robert A. Hummel and Michael S. Landy, *A viewpoint on the theory of evidence*, Submitted. November, 1985.

[13] G. Shafer, "Constructive probability," *Synthese* **48**, pp. 1-60 (1981).

[14] Eugene Charniak, "The Bayesian basis of common sense medical diagnosis," *Proceedings of the AAAI*, pp. 70-73 (1983).

PROBABILISTIC LOGIC: SOME COMMENTS AND POSSIBLE USE FOR NONMONOTONIC REASONING

Dr. Mary McLeish

Department of Computer Science/Statistics, University of Guelph, Guelph, Ontario, Canada, N1G 2W1

Abstract

This paper considers recent work by Nils Nilsson on probabilistic logic and presents a way to extend it to represent default reasoning (and subsequent nonmonotonicity). This is done in the context of facts and rules which could be uncertain. Entailment results are presented and their meaning and usefulness discussed.

Introduction

Default and nonmonotonic reasoning have been discussed by many researchers [c.f. 8, 13]. Default logic has been considered as a reasoning mechanism for diagnostic systems by R. Reiter [14] and D. Poole [11, 12]. These systems do not employ any mechanism for dealing with uncertainty in facts or rules. More traditional diagnostic systems employ Bayesian statistical techniques [e.g. 9] or other quasi-probabilistic methods [2, 5, 16, 17]. However, the problem of dealing with uncertainty in the presence of nonmonotonicity or when default rules are used, has been little investigated. Recent work by Grosof [7] explores this situation and makes several suggestions of possible avenues for a solution.

This paper considers the entailment scheme used by Nils J. Nilsson in [10] for probabilistic logic. Nilsson states that 'probabilistic entailment' is actually monotonic and that the introduction of new facts can only reduce the region of consistent valuations. However, this work explores the effect of adding inconsistent valuation vectors to represent a nonmonotonic world and carries out entailment under these conditions. The implications of the results are discussed and a belief revision scheme is proposed. Some comments concerning computational problems are made in the final section. (An earlier version of some of these ideas appears in [6]).

Probabilistic Logic

Nilsson [10] has presented a semantical generalization of ordinary logic in which the truth values of sentences are probability values between 0 and 1. A review of the notaton used follows:

Let S represent a finite sequence L of sentences arranged in arbitrary order, e.g. $S = \{S_1, S_2 \cdots S_L\}$.

$$V = \begin{Bmatrix} v_1 \\ \cdot \\ \cdot \\ \cdot \\ v_L \end{Bmatrix} \text{ is a valuation vector for } S, \text{ where}$$

$$\begin{aligned} v_i &= 1 \quad \text{if } S_i \text{ has value true} \\ &= 0 \quad \text{otherwise.} \end{aligned}$$

V is consistent if it corresponds to a consistent valuation of the sentences of S. ν is the set of all consistent valuation vectors for S and let $K = |\nu|$ (cardinality). (Note $K \leq 2^L$). Each consistent V corresponds to an equivalence class of "possible worlds" in which the sentences in S are true or false according to the components of V.

Let M (sentence matrix) be the $L \times M$ matrix whose columns are the vectors in ν. Its rows will be denoted by S. If P is the i'th unit column vector, $MP_i = V_i$, where V_i is the ith vector of ν.

Example: Let $S = (A, A \supset B, B)$ $\nu = \left\{ \begin{pmatrix} 1 \\ 1 \\ 1 \end{pmatrix} \begin{pmatrix} 1 \\ 0 \\ 0 \end{pmatrix} \begin{pmatrix} 0 \\ 1 \\ 1 \end{pmatrix} \begin{pmatrix} 0 \\ 1 \\ 0 \end{pmatrix} \right\}$

and $M = \begin{Bmatrix} 1 & 1 & 0 & 0 \\ 1 & 0 & 1 & 1 \\ 1 & 0 & 1 & 0 \end{Bmatrix}$

However, if each of the sentences' truth values are uncertain in some sense, a probability distribution over classes of possible worlds is introduced. $P = \begin{Bmatrix} P_1 \\ \cdot \\ \cdot \\ \cdot \\ P_k \end{Bmatrix}$ with $0 \leq P_i \leq 1$ and $\sum_i P_i = 1$.

Here the i'th component of P represents the probability that 'our' world, is a member of the i'th class of worlds. Now a consistent probabilistic valuation vector V over the sentences in S is computed from the equation $V = MP$. The components of V are the probabilities of the S_i being true (or the probablity that 'our' world is a member of one of those classes of possible worlds in which sentence S_i is true).

Returning to example 1, we find that even if consistent valuations are known for the sentences A and $A \supset B$, the probability of B is not necessarily uniquely defined. One can determine the bounds $p(A \supset B) + p(A) - 1 \leq p(B) \leq p(A \supset B)$, which provide some restrictions. However, often a more precise value for $p(B)$ needs to be predicted. Thus methods for handling probabilistic entailment are needed.

The method will be illustrated using example 1.

Step 1: If s is the sentence we wish to add to S, append s to S and construct the set of all consistent true - false valuations

$$\text{Construct } M \text{ from } \nu'$$

e.g.

$$\begin{Bmatrix} 1 & 1 & 0 & 0 \\ 1 & 0 & 1 & 1 \\ 1 & 0 & 1 & 0 \end{Bmatrix}$$

in example 1

Step 2: Construct M' from M by deleting the last row of M.

Step 3: Make the first row of M' all 1's and the first entry of V also 1. (This ensures that $\sum p_i = 1$).

$$M' = \begin{Bmatrix} 1 & 1 & 1 & 1 \\ 1 & 1 & 0 & 0 \\ 1 & 0 & 1 & 1 \end{Bmatrix} \text{ for example 1.}$$

The entailment then consists of finding solutions to the matrix equation $M'P = V$. An 'acceptable' solution can then be used to solve the equation $p(s) = s.P$.

Methods for obtaining a Solution:

(i) Projection Method: Let s^* be the projection of s onto the subspace defined by the row vectors of M'. Then $s^* = \sum c_i s_i$ for some c_i and $p(s^*) = s^*.P = \sum c_i v_i$. Applied to example 1, with $s = (1\ 0\ 1\ 0)$, $s^* = (1,0,1/2,1/2)$ then $p(s^*) = p/2 + q - 1/2$, where $V = \begin{Bmatrix} 1 \\ p \\ q \end{Bmatrix}$. This is halfway between the earlier established bounds.

(ii) Method of Maximum Entropy:

This approach is borrowed from P. Cheeseman [3] and assumes minimum extra information. The entropy function becomes $H = -P.\log P + 1_1 (v_1 - S_1.P) + 1_2 (v_2 - S_2.P) + \cdots 1_L (v_L - S_L.P)$, where the 1_i are Lagrange multpliers. Following Cheeseman, the solution for maximum entropy becomes

$$P_i = e^{-1}.e^{-(1_1 S_{1i})}.......e^{-(1_L S_{Li})}$$

If one employs this method, at least for example 1, the solution for

$$P = \begin{Bmatrix} p+q-1 \\ 1-q \\ (1-p)/2 \\ (1-p)/2 \end{Bmatrix}, \text{ when } V = \begin{Bmatrix} 1 \\ p \\ q \end{Bmatrix} \text{ and thus } p(B) = p/2 + q - 1/2. \text{ (This is the same as}$$

that obtained by the projection method, although this fact does not hold in general.)

Nonmonotonic Reasoning:

Default reasoning is concerned with situations in which a certain assumption has been made, possibly due to the lack of information or in the face of no contradictory evidence. For example, one might assume that all birds fly [c.f. 11, 12] and that if Tweety is a bird, then the assumption is used to deduce that Tweety flies. However, if Tweety is a penguin, the reasoning strategy would produce a wrong result and possibly contradict a fact that might also be in the system (i.e. penguins don't fly) - hence the nonmonotonicity. Ways to handle this problem and still maintain many useful features of having defaults available when developing theories etc. have been studied in [11, 12, 13, 14].

In the schemes just referenced, the defaults are usually assumed to be true. When contradictory facts or rules are encountered, one is simply prohibited from using these in conjunction with the defaults to produce new conclusions. (That is, one is not allowed to find logical consequences involving them). All facts and rules are considered to be known with complete certainty.

Nonmonotonic probabilistic reasoning is concerned with the problem of defaults and subsequent nonmonotonicity in the presence of uncertain facts and rules. So, if example 1 is used with A being "Tweety is a bird", B being Tweety flies, then there could be a probability value of less than one assigned to $A \supset B$ (or indeed A, if the facts are also uncertain). Then, using logical entailment or some other probabilistic scheme, $p(B)$ may be found. If a new fact is entered saying B is false, this is not then inconsistent if $p(B)<1$. If the new fact is itself uncertain, so that a fact say $p'(B)<1$, is known which could have a different value from that derived by entailment, then a decision must be made about how to interpret the result. This could be difficult if there is reason to give some credibility to both $p(B)$ (derived) and $p'(B)$ (new fact).

The statement is made in [4] by P. Cheeseman that 'these logics' (referring to nonmonotonic and default reasoning) $\cdots$ "often attempt to force into a logical mode a type of reasoning that is not logical in nature" and that they are "mainly concerned with belief revision when new (logically contradictory) evidence is found".

In Nilsson's system, if the probability values assigned to the valuation vector V lie outside the region of consistent probability values, it will never be possible to solve the equation $MP = V$ for P. As pointed out in [10], the fact that M is a linear transformation forces MP to lie in the consistent region in V space. The entailment used will also never produce an inconsistent final valuation vector after applying any of the entailment schemes. As implied by Cheeseman's comments, nonmonotonic reasoning is really illogical or inconsistent in some sense. This section explores the possibility of adding inconsistencies to the 'world' through the matrix M itself, which then can produce valuation vectors outside the consistent region. This is applied initially to example 1.

An Inconsistent System

Suppose we agree that the world could in fact be illogical, at least in a certain sense. Going back to example 1, 2^L should be 8, and in fact 4 inconsistent vectors V have been dropped from ν. Motivated by the example of Tweety is a bird etc., consider what happens when the inconsistent vector $\begin{Bmatrix} 1 \\ 1 \\ 0 \end{Bmatrix}$ is added to ν.

Then M becomes $\begin{pmatrix} 1 & 1 & 0 & 0 & 1 \\ 1 & 0 & 1 & 1 & 1 \\ 1 & 0 & 1 & 0 & 0 \end{pmatrix}$. If now we seek bounds on $p(B)$, one obtains $0 \leq p(B) \leq p(A \supset B)$.

Consider the problem of entailment in the inconsistent system. M' becomes $\begin{pmatrix} 1 & 1 & 1 & 1 & 1 \\ 1 & 1 & 0 & 0 & 1 \\ 1 & 0 & 1 & 1 & 1 \end{pmatrix}$ and using the projection method, we find that $B^* = (1/2 \ 0 \ 1/2 \ 1/2 \ 1/2)$ and $p(B^*) = q/2$. (We note that this is mid-way between the bounds in the inconsistent case.) (A discussion of the significance and usefulness of this result will follow later.)

Consider now the maximum entropy approach (ii). To simplify, let $a_1 = e^{-1}e^{-1_1}$, $a_j = e^{-1j}$, $j = 2 \cdots L$ (as in [10]). Then $p_1 = a_1 a_2 a_3$, $p_2 = a_1 a_3$, $p_3 = a_1 a_3$, $p_4 = a_1 a_3$, $p_5 = a_1 a_2$. From $MP = V$ one obtains the equations:

$$2a_1 a_2 a_3 + a_1 a_2 + 2a_1 a_3 = 1$$

$$2a_1 a_2 a_3 + a_1 a_2 = p$$

$$2a_1 a_2 a_3 + 2a_1 a_3 = q$$

The solution for p is

$$\begin{bmatrix} \frac{p+q-1}{2} \\ 1-q \\ \frac{1-p}{2} \\ \frac{p+q-1}{2} \end{bmatrix}$$

$B = (10100)$ and $B.P = q/2$ (as for the projection method.)

Discussion of the Entailment Results

Relative Size and Range Restrictions:

If we compare the result to $p/2 + q - \frac{1}{2}$ we see that $q/2$ is smaller than this value if and only if $p+q \geq 1$. This condition on p and q is in fact necessary if the consistent or inconsistent systems are going to have valid solutions for P, as the expression $p+q-1$ appears in both for p_1 and $0 \leq p_1 \leq 1$ by definition. This would seem reasonable, as any chance of an inconsistency should decrease the probability of B.

Significance for Default Reasoning:

Consider the situation in which A is true (Tweety really is a bird) and you have no real evidence to decide $A \supset B$ is not true and would have difficulty trying to assign a precise probability value of less than 1 to this statement. However, you believe nonmonotonicity might occur. Using the nonmonotonic model would predict $p(B) = \frac{1}{2}$, whereas the monotonic model would give $p(B) = 1$. If there were later factual evidence that B was false, this would not be inconsistent with the prediction of the nonmonotonic model, but would be for the monotonic one. Thus, in situations where there is a suspicion that the default is not always true, but where one has no known probability value to assign to $p(A \supset B)$, it would seem more reasonable to use the nonmonotonic model to predict a value for $p(B)$.

Another situation to consider is one in which later evidence suggests $p(B)$ is .8. B. Grosof in [7] would allow the later evidence to override the entailment value and completely replace it. However, this later evidence (e) could really be a conditional value, $p(B/e) = .8$. There could even be uncertainty in the evidence, e.

A possible interpretation of this would be to consider the increase in belief due to this new piece of evidence. Following [2], we would look at expression as is used in the calculation of MB: (i.e.) $\frac{.8-q/2}{1-q/2}$. If $q = 1$, this becomes .6. Thus a certainty factor of .6 could be assigned to B. (Here the entailment value is really used as a Prior probability value for B). If the monotonic model were used, the CF would become $-.2$ from $MD = \frac{.8-1}{-1}$, because the new evidence would decrease the belief in B. The value .6 would seem to better represent the situation.

Bounding the Probability of an Inconsistency:

Another approach might be to add an additional constraint (constraints) when using the maximum entropy model. In the example under investigation, p_5 might be bounded by some value. To show the effect of this, suppose we add the constraint that $p_5 = .1$, for example, and introduce an additional Lagrange multiplier λ. We will have $(.1-p_5)$ added to our entropy expression. In the differentiation process this contributes only to one term,

$$a_4 = e^{-\lambda} \text{ and } p_5 = a_1 a_2 a_3 a_4$$

The equations in the a_i's change becoming

$$a_1 a_2 a_3 + a_1 a_2 + 2 a_1 a_3 + a_1 a_2 a_3 a_4 = 1$$

$$a_1 a_2 a_3 + a_1 a_2 + a_1 a_2 a_3 a_4 = p$$

$$a_1 a_2 a_3 + 2 a_1 a_3 + a_1 a_2 a_3 a_4 = q$$

$$a_1 a_2 a_3 a_4 = .1$$

The solution for P is given by:

$$\begin{bmatrix} p+q-1.1 \\ 1-q \\ (1-p)/2 \\ (1-p)/2 \\ .1 \end{bmatrix}$$

Now $p(B) = p/2 + q - .6$

Using this value allows for a situation where p and q are both taken to be 1 but there is a chance the world is not a 'logical' one and $p(B)$ becomes .9. Thus, if it turns out B is false, this will not be contradictory.

Some Computational Observations

(i) Concerning the calculations involved using the maximum entropy model, it may not be necessary to solve for the a_i, as Cheeseman does in his general model in [3] and Nilsson in [10]. When Cheeseman's method is applied to probabilistic logic, the equations that arise could as easily be thought of as equations in the p_i, by noting that the maximum entropy rule causes certain p_i to be related (e.g.) in the consistent version of example 1, Nilsson's equations in terms of the p_i become:

$$p_1 + p_2 + 2p_3 = 1$$
$$p_1 + p_2 = p$$
$$p_1 + 2p_3 = q \text{ and } p_3 = p_4.$$

These equations are easily solved for the p_i. A similar situation arises for the inconsistent case and other examples.

(ii) Consider the set of sentences: $\{A, B, A \cap B, (A \cap B) \supset C, C\}$. Suppose one wishes to predict $p(C)$ and $V = \begin{Bmatrix} 1 \\ p \\ q \\ r \\ s \end{Bmatrix}$.

Using the method of entailment $p(C)$ becomes $s + \frac{r}{2} - \frac{1}{2}$. Thus, although the system cannot be split quite as suggested in part 5 of [10], one can find the result of entailment for $\{A, B, A \cap B\}$, namely pq, and then find $p(C) = s + \frac{pq}{2} - \frac{1}{2}$. This would suggest that even more simplifications can occur for large sentence matrices than suggested in [10].

Conclusions

The approach to default and subsequent nonmonotonic reasoning taken in this paper admits to the inherently 'illogical' nature of this type of reasoning. It uses a model of the world in which logical inconsistencies can occur and make predictions in this setting. The results seem particularly applicable when a default is assumed true (in the absence of other information) and yet a logical result of this default does not always follow.

Further work need to be done to consider more complicated entailments and situations involving nonmonotonicity. The problem of how to handle new probabilistic information (probabilistic belief revision) in this context also needs to be more fully investigated.

References:

[1] Bundy, A. "Incidence Calculus: A Mechanism for Probabilistic Reasoning", Workshop on Uncertainty and Probability in A.I. Proceedings, 1985, pp.177-84.

[2] Buchanan, B.G., Shortliffe, E.H., "Rule-Based Expert Systems", Addison-Wesley, (May 1985).

[3] Cheeseman, P., "A Method of Computing Generalized Bayesian Probability Values for Expert Systems", Proc. Eighth International Joint Conference on Artificial Intelligence, Karlsruhe, (1983) pp. 198-292.

[4] Cheeseman, P., "In Defense of Probability", Proc. Ninth International Joint Conference on Artificial Intelligence, Los Angeles, (1985), pp. 1002-1009.

[5] Dempster, A.P., "A Generalization of Bayesian Inference", Journal of the Royal Statistical Society, Series B, Vol. 30, (1968) pp. 205-247.

[6] McLeish, M. "Dealing with Uncertainty in Nonmonotonic Reasoning", 1986 Proceedings of the Conference on Intelligent Systems and Machines, April (1986), Oakland University, Michigan, pp. 1-5.

[7] Grosof, B.N. "Non-monotonicity in Probabilistic Reasoning", Uncertainty in A.I. Workshop Proceedings, Philadelphia,(1986),pp. 91-98.

[8] Hanks, S. and McDermott, D. "Default Reasoning, Nonmonotonic Logics and the Frame Problem", AAAI Proceedings(1986), pp.328-333.

[9] Duda, R.O., Hart, P.E., Nilsson, N.J., "Subjective Bayesian Methods for Rule-Based Inference Systems", Proc. (1976) National Computer Conference, AFIPS, Vol. 45, pp. 1075-1082.

[10] Nilsson, N., "Probabilistic Logic", SRI Technical Report #321 (1984) and Artificial Intelligence, Vol. 28, Feb. (1986), pp. 71-87.

[11] Poole, D.L., "On the Comparison of Theories: Preferring the Most Specific Explanation", Proc. Ninth International Joint Conference on Artificial Intelligence, Los Angeles, (1985), pp. 144-147.

[12] Poole, D.L., "A Logical System for Default Reasoning", Proc. AAAI Workshop on Nonmonotonic Reasoning, New York (1984), pp. 373-384.

[13] Reiter, R., "A Logic for Default Reasoning", Artificial Intelligence (13), (1980), pp. 81-132.

[14] Reiter, R., "A Theory of Diagnosis from First Principles", University of Toronto Report, 1985. To appear in the Journal of A.I.

[15] Shafer, G.A., "Mathematical Theory of Evidence", Princeton University Press, Princeton, N.J., (1979).

[16] Zadeh, L.A., "Fuzzy Logic and Approximate Reasoning", Synthese 30: (1975), pp. 407-428.

EXPERIMENTS WITH INTERVAL-VALUED UNCERTAINTY

Richard M. Tong, Lee A. Appelbaum

Advanced Decision Systems,
201 San Antonio Circle, Suite 286, Mountain View, CA 94040, USA.

In this paper we describe the results of some recent experiments with interval representations of uncertainty. We have focussed on two basic models, one based on probability and one based on many-valued logic, and performed a series of tests to determine the resulting performance of a rule-based system for full-text information retrieval. Our results suggest that in this domain interval representations add little to our ability to capture the inherent uncertainty in the evidential reasoning process. We conjecture that concern over our ability to represent the semantics of the problem, and hence its principal reasoning structures, should dominate our concern over choices between competing formal models of uncertainty.

1. INTRODUCTION

The purpose of this paper is to report on the most recent developments in our ongoing investigation of the representation and manipulation of uncertainty in automated reasoning systems. In our earlier studies (Tong and Shapiro, 1985) we described a series of experiments with RUBRIC (Tong et al., 1985), a system for full-text document retrieval, that generated some interesting insights into the effects of choosing among a class of scalar valued uncertainty calculi. In order to extend these results we have begun a new series of experiments with a larger class of representations and calculi, and to help perform these experiments we have developed a general purpose inference engine.

Accordingly, the first three sections of the paper review the formal model of information retrieval that RUBRIC assumes, describe the extended models of uncertainty that the new engine supports, and describe the design and implementation of the engine. Then the fourth section reports on our experiments with a number of interval representations, and the final section summarizes our results.

2. THE INFORMATION RETRIEVAL MODEL

To set the context for our work, we suppose that there is a database of documents, denoted by S, in which the user is potentially interested. In response to a query, Q, the retrieval system returns a set of retrieved documents, denoted R, that are purported to be *relevant* to that particular query. In general, this set R will only be an approximation to the actual set of relevant documents, denoted R^*, contained in the database. The IR problem is thus one of developing a retrieval system that makes $R=R^*$ for all queries. Since this cannot be achieved in practice, we must design systems that maximize the intersection of R and R^* (i.e., maximizing *recall*) while minimizing $R-R^*$ (i.e., maximizing *precision*). In RUBRIC the ability to express retrieval requests in terms of hierarchical collections of rules with attached uncertainty weights results in both higher precision and higher recall than found in more conventional systems.

In developing our formal model we start from the view that the primary function of a retrieval system is to select a sub-set of the documents in the database as defined by their *relevance* to the user's query. To understand this, we must distinguish between the subject matter of a document and the utility of the document to the user. So for example, a retrieved document might be about the topic of the user's query, but it might not be useful because the user has seen it before, or because it is a summary of a longer document. Thus relevance includes a notion of usefulness for the task at hand. We have no way of describing this idea of a user goal in the current version of RUBRIC, so we approximate by asserting that a document is relevant if its subject matter is the same as the subject of the user's query.

Our notion of relevance is further modified by the recognition that in most cases the decision as to whether or not a document is about the topic of a query is inherently vague. That is, a document can be about a topic to a certain degree; ranging from not about a topic at all, to definitely about a topic. Notice too, that a document can be about many topics, so in RUBRIC we do not ask the question "What is the document about?" but rather we ask "Is the document about topic X?" RUBRIC's task is thus to decide to what degree the document under consideration is about the topic of the query.

So suppose that the user has a finite set of retrieval concepts, C, of interest:

$$C \triangleq \{c_1, c_2, \cdots, c_M\}$$

and that the database, S, contains a finite number of documents:

$$S \triangleq \{s_1, s_2, \cdots, s_N\}$$

then we assume that there is an underlying relevance relation, R, from C to S such that $R(m,n)$ is the true relevance of document s_n to concept c_m. Notice that the range of this relation is left unspecified since we are concerned with a number of possible representations for the degrees of uncertainty. Thus a row-tuple of R, denoted $R^*(c)$, is the "uncertain" subset of documents that are relevant to concept c.

A dual notion which arises is that which we call *typicality*. It refers to the fact that a document is an exemplar, to varying degrees, of documents that are about a particular retrieval concept. Since this notion of typicality also admits of degrees, we can define a typicality relation, T from C to S such that $T(m,n)$ is the typicality of document s_n for concept c_m. A row-tuple of T, denoted $T^*(c)$, can then be viewed as defining the subset of typical documents for that concept.

Now if we insist that R and T are in fact one and the same, we see that a rule-based query in RUBRIC can be thought of in two distinct, but related, ways. In the first interpretation, the rules used by RUBRIC constitute an algorithm for determining the degree of membership of a document in the set of relevant documents. That is, they define a network of relevance relationships for deciding how knowledge about the presence of a low-level concepts indicates the presence of a higher-level concept. In the second interpretation, the rules used by RUBRIC act as a definition of what constitutes a typical document. That is, they suggest what low-level concepts should appear if the goal is to find documents that are about a higher-level concept.

3. MODELS OF UNCERTAINTY

Since a major goal of the RUBRIC system is to provide a test-bed for the exploration of issues in evidential reasoning, we provide a number of uncertainty representations that can be selected by the users of RUBRIC. In the first class of models, uncertainty is represented as a real number in the interval [0,1] and the calculi are based on infinitely-valued logic. In the second class of models, sub-intervals of the [0,1] interval are used to represent uncertainty and the calculi are based on both probabilistic and logical assumptions. In the third class, uncertainty is represented by a linguistic variable whose domain is the unit interval and is manipulated using fuzzy logic. We consider each of these briefly:

3.1. Scalar Representations

In our first class of models we assert that relevance can be quantified as a real number in the interval [0,1]. Since there is an obvious fuzzy set theoretic interpretation of these values, we draw upon work on many-valued logics (Rescher, 1969), and on the use of triangular-norms as models of fuzzy set intersection (e.g., Dubois and Prade, 1982), to help us construct a calculus of scalar relevance values.

We allow three distinct pairs of definitions for conjunction (the *and* connective), and disjunction (the *or* connective). Negation is defined by $v\,[not\,A\,] = 1 - v\,[A\,]$.

In two-valued logic the *modus ponens* syllogism allows B to be inferred from A and $A =>B$. In an infinitely-valued logic, we need to extend this idea so that the relevance of B, denoted $v\,[B\,]$, can be computed from any given $v\,[A\,]$ and $v\,[A =>B\,]$, where "$=>$" is some infinitely-valued implication. Functions that allow us to compute $v\,[B\,]$ are called detachment operators (and are denoted *). It is usual to define them so that for a given definition of $=>$, $v\,[A\,] * v\,[A =>B\,]$ is a lower bound on the value of $v\,[B\,]$. We allow four distinct definitions corresponding to four distinct infinitely-valued implication operators.

3.2. Interval Representations

Our second class of models assumes that uncertainty can be represented by a sub-interval of the unit interval. That is rather than specify our uncertainty by means of single number we allow it to be expressed by means of a pair of numbers that correspond to the lower and upper values of the interval. So we have an interval such as $[\alpha, \beta]$ in which $\alpha, \beta \leq 1.0$ and $\alpha \leq \beta$. The primitive semantics of these intervals are that [0,0] corresponds to absolutely false (not relevant), [1,1] corresponds to absolutely certain (fully relevant), and [0,1] corresponds to completely unknown. Other sub-intervals reflect greater or lesser certainty, with the width of the interval (i.e. $\beta - \alpha$) representing additional information about the confidence we have in these certainty measures.

The advantage of such a representation is that it allows us to capture finer shades of meaning with respect to the uncertainty associated with propositions. The recent interest in AI in such interval-valued models largely derives from Shafer's influential book (1976) as well as more recent work that attempts to make Shafer's theory practically useful (see for example Gordon and Shortliffe, 1985). However, there are a number of competing models which although using an interval representation start from very different perspectives.

RUBRIC-III provides specific support for four distinct interval models, although it is trivial to add additional models as required. Specifically, we include:

[1] an interval-valued calculus based on Appelbaum and Ruspini (1985). This is an interval-valued probability calculus which makes minimal assumptions about the relationships between the events being modelled.

[2] a calculus based on the work of Baldwin (1986). This is also an extension of classical probability but with additional assumptions about the relationship between α and β. In this model α corresponds to the "support" for the base proposition, and β is equal to complement with respect to one of the support for the negation of the base proposition. In this respect it is similar to Shafer's model, but it differs in other particulars.

[3] a calculus derived from application of Zadeh's *extension principle* (1973) to the scalar calculi described in section 3.1. This is thus a logical view with minimal assumptions about the the relationships between α and β.

[4] a calculus derived from a combined application of *modus ponens* and *modus tollens* as discussed by Martin-Clouaire and Prade (1985). This is also a generalization of the calculi described in section 3.1 but with additional assumptions about the logical relationships between the relevant propositions.

3.3. Linguistic Representations

The third class of models assumes that uncertainty is primarily linguistic and that it can be operationalized by means of Zadeh's concept of a linguistic variable (Zadeh, 1975) together with a corresponding fuzzy logic. So in this model, uncertainty values are expressed by terms such as "very certain," "more or less false" and "not false but not certain."

RUBRIC-III supports this form of representation by providing the user with the ability to define and calibrate primary linguistic terms from which more complex terms can be generated automatically. The underlying computations are performed using extensions of the logical calculi defined for intervals in section 3.2 so that they can be applied to the fuzzy set definitions of the uncertainty terms.

4. THE INFERENCE ENGINE

The RUBRIC inference engine is designed for maximum flexibility. The emphasis has been placed on allowing for multiple uncertainty representations without having to modify any system code. The engine is thus a very useful research tool, although precisely because of its flexibility it is limited in its execution speed and space efficiency. It is an outgrowth of the earlier work by Appelbaum (Appelbaum and Ruspini, 1985), and makes use of a proprietary object-oriented programming environment developed at ADS (Cation, 1986).

The inference engine operates in two passes. First, a backward inference graph is explicitly created with the goal concept (from the user query) represented by the root node. Second, the inference graph is evaluated by assessing the relevance of the terminal nodes and then propagating and combining relevance values back up the graph to the root. The default operation mode generates the complete backward graph based on the rules, thus one graph may be used to test the relevancy of a collection of documents to a single concept without re-accessing the rule-base.

The implementation of the inference engine is based on the object-oriented programming paradigm. Each node of the inference graph is an object with associated handlers (methods) for expansion and evaluation. Rules are also objects, as are the collections of relevance representations, relevance calculi and the inference-graph itself. The backward and forward evaluation processes are carried out as a series of message passing between the different components mentioned above.

Since each node is an independent object with its own expansion and evaluation handlers, assigning different uncertainty functions is a very straight-forward procedure. Each node contains the name of the function to apply (in the LISP sense) to evaluate the relevance of the node given the relevance of its children. There is no restriction on the number of functions which may be employed; each node may use its own function. In practice, however, each node will point to a set of functions which are logically bound together. For example in a fuzzy set interpretation, min, max, and times would be three LISP functions for conjunction, disjunction, and detachment.

Three important "high level" considerations are addressed by this new engine: two control features and an explanation capability. One control feature is the creation of one node for each concept and terminal (a clause which contains only strings to be searched for in the documents) independently of how many times the concept or terminal may appear in the rules. It is from this feature that we produce a graph rather than a tree. It is still necessary, however, to keep track of all the references to the item. This is done through the arcs which link the concept or terminal nodes to their predecessors.

The second control feature is the actual control over graph traversal. Since the complete graph is generated before any evaluation, it is not possible to generate the minimal tree for a given application. However, it is a simple matter to order the rule nodes so that EVIDENCE rules are evaluated before IMPLIES rules and simpler IMPLIES before more complex ones. (EVIDENCE and IMPLIES rules are two of the several rule types available in RUBRIC.) This can be done in the expansion handlers. There is also the possibility of limiting the branches traversed below any node representing a complex clause. For example, in a node representing a conjunction, it may be possible to ascertain that the final result will be 0 (or below some predefined threshold given in the rule base) before all clauses have been evaluated. In this case it is not necessary to proceed any further with that node. There are similar tests for disjunctions and evidence combinations. Of course, these tests are all heavily dependent on the uncertainty calculus employed and thus require the user to supply all the tests (in LISP) before graph expansion.

Finally, a significant degree of explanation is possible through careful use of the action slot of rules. For example, it is possible to write out any string or variable binding to any node of the graph during graph evaluation. This could be simply printing the relevance value of the concept or generate a lengthy description of the environment at the time of evaluation. By traversing the graph upwards (i.e., towards the root) it is possible to reconstruct the reasoning employed in assigning any particular relevance value.

5. EXPERIMENTS

As in our earlier series of experiments, we have worked with a small collection of Reuters Newswire documents and a collection of rules that define the topic of terrorism. Figures 1 and 2 show a typical document from the collection and some example rules that might be used to define terrorism. The rules are, of course, greatly simplified; we include them here for illustration.

Although in our experiments we have explored a number of interval representations, our presentation will concentrate on two basic models; one derived from probability theory and one derived from many-valued logics. Before we describe these in detail, it is necessary to introduce some standard notation that we will use. A basic rule will be denoted $a \rightarrow z$ where a is an expression in the RUBRIC language and z is a retrieval concept, the conjunction of two expressions will be denoted $a \wedge b$, disjunction will be denoted $a \vee b$, and negation will be denoted $\neg a$. Then the value of an expression will be denoted $v(p)$, with the upper value written $\overline{v}(p)$ and the lower value written $\underline{v}(p)$.

The interval probability model is taken from Appelbaum and Ruspini (1985) and uses the following definitions for the basic logical combination operations:

$\underline{v}(a \wedge b) = \max(0, \underline{v}(a) + \underline{v}(b) - 1)$
$\overline{v}(a \wedge b) = \min(\overline{v}(a), \overline{v}(b))$

$\underline{v}(a \vee b) = \max(\underline{v}(a), \underline{v}(b))$
$\overline{v}(a \vee b) = \min(1, \overline{v}(a) + \overline{v}(b))$

$\underline{v}(\neg a) = 1 - \overline{v}(a)$
$\overline{v}(\neg a) = 1 - \underline{v}(a)$

which are, of course, straightforward extensions of the usual probabilistic definitions. The definition for inference, on the other hand, ensures that a conclusion is assigned the smallest possible interval, thus:

Guatemala City, Dec 28, Reuter -- A city mayor was shot dead and the bodies of seven people kidnapped on Christmas Eve were found yesterday dumped on a dusty road on the outskirts of the capital, Guatemalan police said today.

A spokesman said Gonzalo Quinonez Paredes, Mayor of Ciudad Vieja, adjoining the capital, was shot by three unidentified gunmen when he opened the door to his house in response to their knock. The kidnapped victims were residents of Ciudad Vieja, the spokesman added.

According to Church and human rights officials in Guatemala, about 3,500 people have been killed this year in political violence.

Figure 1 Reuters Document

$$\textbf{actor \& event} \longrightarrow \textbf{terrorism} \quad [0.8, 0.9]$$
$$\text{``TERRORIST''} \longrightarrow \textbf{actor} \quad [0.6, 0.9]$$
$$\text{``GUERILLA''} \mid \text{``GUERRILLA''} \longrightarrow \textbf{actor} \quad [0.0, 0.3]$$
$$\text{``PLO''} \longrightarrow \textbf{actor} \quad [0.7, 0.8]$$
$$\text{``IRA''} \longrightarrow \textbf{actor} \quad [0.7, 0.8]$$
$$\text{NEAR (``CAR'', ``BOMB'')} \longrightarrow \textbf{event} \quad [0.8, 0.8]$$
$$\text{PARAGRAPH (\textbf{device}, \textbf{explosion})} \longrightarrow \textbf{event} \quad [0.9, 0.9]$$
$$\text{``BOMB''} \longrightarrow \textbf{device} \quad [0.5, 0.8]$$
$$\text{``CHARGE''} \longrightarrow \textbf{device} \quad [0.2, 0.4]$$
$$\text{``MOLOTOV COCKTAIL''} \longrightarrow \textbf{device} \quad [0.8, 0.8]$$
$$\text{``BLAST''} \longrightarrow \textbf{explosion} \quad [0.2, 0.7]$$
$$\text{``EXPLOSION''} \longrightarrow \textbf{explosion} \quad [0.8, 1.0]$$

Figure 2 Terrorism Rules

$$\underline{v}(z) = \underline{v}(a \to z)\cdot\overline{v}(a) + \underline{v}(\neg a \to z)\cdot(1-\overline{v}(a)) \quad \text{if } \underline{v}(a \to z) \leq \underline{v}(\neg a \to z)$$
$$\underline{v}(z) = \underline{v}(a \to z)\cdot\underline{v}(a) + \underline{v}(\neg a \to z)\cdot(1-\underline{v}(a)) \quad \text{otherwise}$$

$$\overline{v}(z) = \overline{v}(a \to z)\cdot\underline{v}(a) + \overline{v}(\neg a \to z)\cdot(1-\underline{v}(a)) \quad \text{if } \overline{v}(a \to z) \leq \overline{v}(\neg a \to z)$$
$$\overline{v}(z) = \overline{v}(a \to z)\cdot\overline{v}(a) + \overline{v}(\neg a \to z)\cdot(1-\overline{v}(a)) \quad \text{otherwise}$$

Notice that this inference model requires us to supply additional information about the relationship between the antecedent a and the consequent z. That is, we need to specify the relevance value for $\neg a \to z$. We shall refer to this form of the rule in the remainder of the paper as the "negative rule," and its associated value will be referred to as the "negative value" or "negative weight." The semantics for this negative weight are clear; it expresses the degree to which we are willing to assert that a document is relevant to topic z when we are told that it does not mention topic a.

The interval logic model is based on results appearing in Martin-Clouaire and Prade (1985) and takes the following form:

$$\underline{v}(a \wedge b) = \underline{v}(a) \otimes \underline{v}(b)$$
$$\overline{v}(a \wedge b) = \overline{v}(a) \otimes \overline{v}(b)$$

$$\underline{v}(a \vee b) = \underline{v}(a) \oplus \underline{v}(b)$$
$$\overline{v}(a \vee b) = \overline{v}(a) \oplus \overline{v}(b)$$

$$\underline{v}(\neg a) = 1 - \overline{v}(a)$$
$$\overline{v}(\neg a) = 1 - \underline{v}(a)$$

with inference being defined as:

$$\underline{v}(z) = \underline{v}(a \to z) \otimes \underline{v}(a)$$
$$\overline{v}(z) = \overline{v}(\neg a \to z)) \oplus \overline{v}(a)$$

where $\otimes$ and $\oplus$ are triangular-norms and triangular-conorms respectively (see, for example, Dubois and Prade, 1982). Two interesting pairs are:

$$a \otimes b \triangleq a \cdot b \qquad a \oplus b \triangleq a + b - a \cdot b$$
$$a \otimes b \triangleq \min(a,b) \qquad a \oplus b \triangleq \max(a,b)$$

and we will make use of these in our experiments.

The main feature that distinguishes this logic model from the probabilistic one is the structure of the inference definitions. Notice that the lower value of the consequent, $\underline{v}(z)$, depends only on the lower values of the rule and the antecedent. Similarly, notice that the upper value, $\overline{v}(z)$, depends only on the upper values of the negative rule and the antecedent. This has some significant consequences as we shall see in the following sections.

5.1. Experiment One

Our first experiment explores the impact of adding intervals to our model of terrorism. That is we simply replace all the single-valued uncertainties in our original rule set (see Tong and Shapiro, 1985) with an interval having the same upper and lower values. So if the original rule has an uncertainty value of 0.7, then the revised form of the rule will have an uncertainty interval of [0.7,0.7].

To deal with the negative rules, we assume for this test that we we have no knowledge of the impact of lack of evidence. That being the case, we set the interval associated with the negative rule to [0,1]. Obviously this is the most conservative statement we can make about the absence of evidence. So rules now have the form:

$$\underline{v}(a \to z) = \overline{v}(a \to z) = \alpha$$
$$\underline{v}(\neg a \to z) = 0 \quad \overline{v}(\neg a \to z) = 1$$

where α denotes some real value in the interval [0,1].

With these assumptions, the inferential part of our probability model becomes:

$$\underline{v}(z) = \alpha \cdot \underline{v}(a)$$
$$\overline{v}(z) = 1 - \underline{v}(a) \cdot (1-\alpha)$$

Similarly, the inferential part of our logic model becomes:

$$\underline{v}(z) = \alpha \cdot \underline{v}(a)$$
$$\overline{v}(z) = 1$$

when the t-norm is *product*, and:

$$\underline{v}(z) = \min(\alpha, \underline{v}(a))$$
$$\overline{v}(z) = 1$$

when the t-norm is *min*.

These equations have some interesting features. In particular, we note that the logic models have upper bounds that are 1.0 whatever the values of the the antecedent and the rule. Even in the probability model, we see that if $\underline{v}(a) = 0$, a situation that will happen often (e.g., if the antecedent is "false"), then the upper value of the consequent will be one.

With these three calculi installed in the engine, we can perform a retrieval against the test collection using our revised definition of terrorism. Since there are three distinct calculi, we get three distinct sets of retrieval intervals. These are shown in Figure 3, where we have displayed

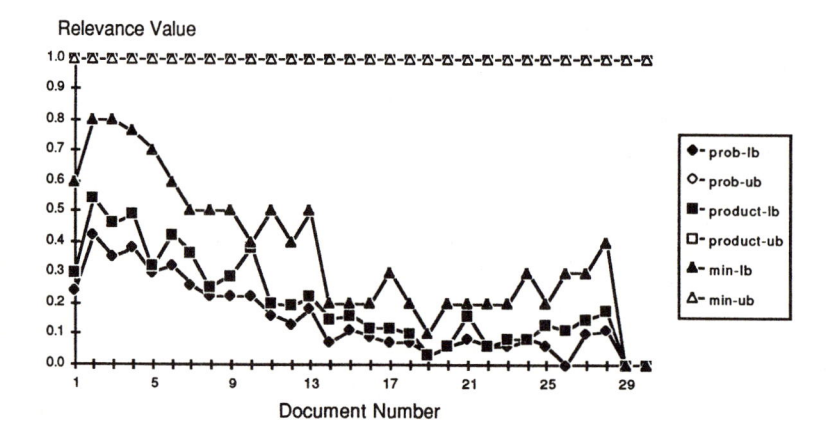

Figure 3 Results for Experiment One

both the lower relevance values (solid points on the curves) and the upper relevance values (open points) for each document in the collection (30 documents in all). Documents 1 through 13 are known to be relevant to the concept of terrorism; documents 14 through 30 are known to be not relevant. Thus, if we look only at the lower values we see that all three calculi give good absolute retrieval performance. More interesting of course is the behavior of the upper values. As we predicted, these are 1.0 for all documents for all calculi.

We conclude that in situations where no information is available about the negative weights, using an interval uncertainty representation is counter-productive. Extra knowledge engineering and computational effort is needed to input and manipulate the intervals, but they add almost nothing to our understanding about the conclusions reached. Not quite nothing, however, since we see that the values we get using a single-valued are actually the lower values of intervals of the form $[\alpha, 1]$.

5.2. Experiment Two

We could argue that the behavior of the upper values in the first experiment is due to the weak assumptions made about the negative weights. So in our second experiment we assume that a lack of evidence allows us to definitely conclude that a concept is absent. In this case we can set the negative weights to [0,0], clearly a very strong assumption. Rules now have the form:

$$\underline{v}(a \to z) = \overline{v}(a \to z) = \alpha$$
$$\underline{v}(\neg a \to z) = \overline{v}(\neg a \to z) = 0$$

So the probability model becomes:

$$\underline{v}(z) = \alpha \cdot \underline{v}(a)$$
$$\overline{v}(z) = \alpha \cdot \overline{v}(a)$$

and for the logic model becomes:

$$\underline{v}(z) = \alpha \cdot \underline{v}(a)$$
$$\overline{v}(z) = \overline{v}(a)$$

when the t-norm is *product*, and becomes:

$$\underline{v}(z) = \min(\alpha, \underline{v}(a))$$
$$\overline{v}(z) = \overline{v}(a)$$

when the t-norm is *min*.

Now we see that the upper values can be less than 1.0, although if we have a situation where $\overline{v}(a)$ is 1.0 (e.g., if the antecedent if "true") then the logic models will still give upper values that are 1.0. Notice that the lower values are unchanged from the first experiment.

Performing the same experimental procedure results in the retrieval values shown in Figure 4. Again as predicted, the upper values for the logic models are usually 1.0; the exceptions being documents 29 and 30, which on inspection reveal that they contain absolutely no evidence for any of the concepts involved in our definition of terrorism.

The probability model, on the other hand, gives upper values that are significantly different from 1.0. The reason becomes obvious if we consider the equation for the upper value. This is $\overline{v}(z) = \alpha \cdot \overline{v}(a)$, which implies that even if the upper value of the antecedent is 1.0 the upper value of the consequent will only be α. Since our definition for terrorism does not contain any rules for which $\alpha = 1.0$ we get the results as shown.

5.3. Experiment Three

Our first two experiments have explored extremes in terms of the assumptions about negative weights, so in the third we explore an intermediate set of assumptions. To do this we computed

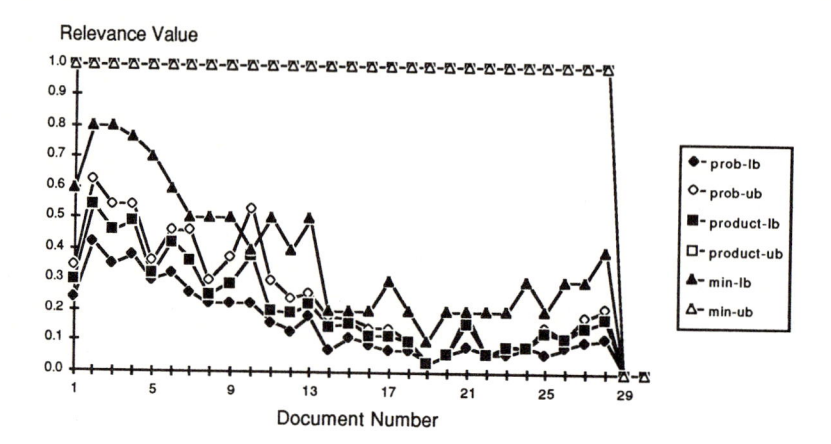

Figure 4 Results for Experiment Two

some statistics for the negative values to be attached to the EVIDENCE rules in the definition for terrorism. Our procedure involved reading all the documents in the collection, recording the presence and absence of the concept and the corresponding presence and absence of the evidential expressions. So for example, for a rule such as:

"TERRORIST" → **actor**

we computed the ratio of the number of documents in which the keyword "TERRORIST" did not appear but which were indeed about an **actor**, to the number of documents that did not contain the keyword. This value, denoted β, is then used to assign the interval value $[\beta, \beta]$ to the negative rule. The IMPLIES rules in our definition for terrorism receive a negative weight of $[0,0]$ as in experiment two. Thus rules now have the following form:

$$\underline{v}(a \to z) = \overline{v}(a \to z) = \alpha$$
$$\underline{v}(\neg a \to z) = \overline{v}(\neg a \to z) = \beta \quad \text{(E-rules)}$$
$$\underline{v}(\neg a \to z) = \overline{v}(\neg a \to z) = 0 \quad \text{(I-rules)}$$

In which case the probability model for EVIDENCE rules becomes:

$$\underline{v}(z) = \alpha \cdot \overline{v}(a) + \beta \cdot (1 - \overline{v}(a))$$
$$\overline{v}(z) = \alpha \cdot \underline{v}(a) + \beta \cdot (1 - \underline{v}(a))$$

if $\alpha \leq \beta$, and becomes:

$$\underline{v}(z) = \alpha \cdot \underline{v}(a) + \beta \cdot (1-\underline{v}(a))$$
$$\overline{v}(z) = \alpha \cdot \overline{v}(a) + \beta \cdot (1-\overline{v}(a))$$

otherwise.

Similarly for the logic model we get EVIDENCE rules of the form:

$$\underline{v}(z) = \alpha \cdot \underline{v}(a)$$
$$\overline{v}(z) = \overline{v}(a) + \beta \cdot (1-\overline{v}(a))$$

when the t-norm is *product*, and:

$$\underline{v}(z) = \min(\alpha, \underline{v}(a))$$
$$\overline{v}(z) = \max(\beta, \overline{v}(a))$$

when the t-norm is *min*.

Notice that although we have taken an intermediate position the effect on the logical models is such that if the upper value of the antecedent is 1.0, then the upper value of the consequent will also be 1.0. The lower values in the logic model remain unchanged. The probability model does undergo some modification though. Specifically, the negative value β influences both the lower and upper values of the consequent. Of the the two cases, the first (i.e., $\alpha \leq \beta$) is somewhat counter-intuitive in that it suggests that the lack of evidence is more indicative of the consequent than is the presence. Given the way in which rules are typically constructed, this condition would probably be translated into a positive rule in which the original antecedent is negated; the negative and positive weights would thus be interchanged. Consequently, it is the second condition (i.e., $\alpha > \beta$) that normally applies.

The results of applying these assumptions are shown in Figure 5. Notice that the sole effect on the logical models is to modify the upper values for documents 29 and 30. Since we know from the second experiment that there is no evidence at all for terrorism in these documents, the upper values represent some combination of the negative weights attached to all the EVIDENCE rules.

The probabilistic model shows marked changes to both the upper and lower values. In particular, the values are increased and there is less discrimination between values for relevant documents and values for non relevant ones. This is to be expected, since the effect of adding the negative weights is to increase relevance values in exactly those cases where there is a lack of evidence (i.e., in documents which not relevant).

6. DISCUSSION

We can draw a number of interesting conclusions from these experiments. First of all, we see that the addition of an interval representation apparently makes little difference to the overall behavior of our system. The fact that upper bounds tend to their maximum value means that we get little new information about the nature of our uncertainties, and the fact that the lower bounds behave (at least for the logic models) as if we were using a single-valued representation means that system performance is essentially unchanged.

When we look for explanations for this somewhat unexpected experimental outcome we uncover two primary reasons and a number of secondary ones. The leading technical cause is the fact that the detachment operators are such that as soon as the upper bound of the antecedent to a rule is 1.0, then the upper bound of the consequent will also be 1.0 (and of course will remain 1.0). Exacerbating this functional behavior is the fact that rules in RUBRIC tend to be "disjunctive" both in the sense that antecedent expressions are often disjunctions of clauses and in the sense that combination of evidence from different rules is performed using a operator that has disjunctive properties. This is then compounded by the fact that the "direct evidence" with which RUBRIC works is precise and error free. Thus once a text string has been detected, all subsequent deductions based on it will have have an upper bound of 1.0.

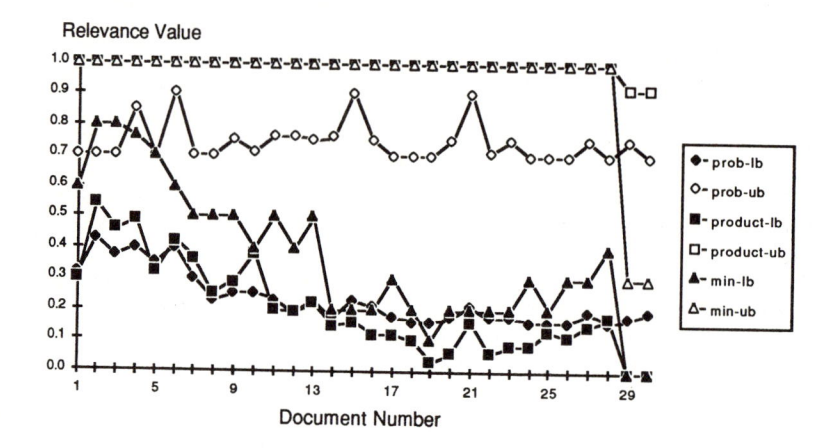

Figure 5 Results for Experiment Three

More importantly though, we must recognize that the reasoning performed in RUBRIC rests on two critical premises. The first is that it is not possible to make assertions about the negation of retrieval concepts (i.e., we have no rules of the form $a \rightarrow \neg z$), and the second is that a document can be about multiple topics (i.e., we are not attempting to select amongst competing hypotheses). Together these imply that we need not concern ourselves with contrary evidence, and so it should not be surprising that the use of an interval calculus produces upper bounds that contain little or no information. Clearly, the problem does no require that there be mechanisms for reducing the upper relevance values. We conclude that the evidential structure in RUBRIC is such that we can only really make statements about the lower bounds of relevance. That being the case, rule weights (i.e., $\underline{v}(a \rightarrow z)$) are the answer to the question:

> Given that you are interested in retrieving documents about topic z, what is the smallest degree of relevance you would be willing to assign to a document knowing only that it discussed topic a?

The variations produced by the choice of a specific calculus are then seen as a somewhat secondary issue to be resolved by thinking about the dependencies between the various evidence sub-structures. So we imagine that in developing knowledge structures for RUBRIC, the user has the opportunity to mark certain combinations of evidence as "independent," or "subsets," or whatever is appropriate, and can then select a calculus that models this properly. If nothing is known, then a calculus which makes the least assumptions (and is therefore the most conservative) should be chosen.

Our results can also be seen as further evidence for our conjecture that the problem of evidential reasoning is one which is to be resolved at the semantic level rather than at the syntactic one. We believe that in any given problem it is imperative that we develop an understanding of the major evidential structures and reasoning patterns before we attempt any formal modelling of the uncertainty. In AI systems we believe that this means that the quality of the reasoning will often be dominated by a proper structuring of the knowledge and reasoning, rather than by questions about the formal properties of the uncertainty calculus. That is not to say that we should ignore the question of uncertainty representation and manipulation, but that there may be higher-level questions that have more overall significance.

Although we do not have space to describe it here, our most recent work with RUBRIC is an attempt to separate the semantics from the syntax (Tong and Appelbaum, 1987). In this study we have shown that once the structure is properly described, some of the evidential reasoning questions become trivial. To be sure, there are still some interesting low-level questions, but we see them as relatively minor in the larger context of the problem that RUBRIC is trying to address.

REFERENCES

Appelbaum, L., E.H. Ruspini (1985). ARIES: A Tool for Inference Under Conditions of Imprecision and Uncertainty. *Proc. SPIE Vol. 548 Applications of Artificial Intelligence II*, Arlington, Va.

Baldwin J. (1986). Support Logic Programming. In A.I. Jones et al. (eds), *Fuzzy Sets Theory and Applications*, D. Reidel Publishing Co., Dordrecht.

Cation, M.K. (1986). SOPE: A Systems Oriented Programming Environment. *AI 1986, Artificial Intelligence and Advanced Computer Conference and Exhibition*, Long Beach, Ca.

Dubois, D., H. Prade (1982). A Class of Fuzzy Measures Based on Triangular Norms. *Int. J. General Systems*, 8:43-61.

Gordon, J., E.H. Shortliffe (1985). A Method for Managing Evidential Reasoning in a Hierarchical Hypothesis Space. *Artificial Intelligence*, 26:323-357.

Martin-Clouaire R., H. Prade (1985). On the Problems of Representation and Propagation of Uncertainty in Expert Systems. *Int. J. Man-Machine Studies*, 22(3):251-264.

Rescher, N. (1969). *Many Valued Logic*, McGraw-Hill, New York.

Shafer, G. (1976). *A Mathematical Theory of Evidence*, Princeton Univ. Press, Princeton NJ.

Tong, R.M., V.N. Askman, J.F. Cunningham, C.J. Tollander (1985). RUBRIC: An Environment for Full Text Information Retrieval. *Proc. 8th ACM-SIGIR Int. Conf. on R&D in Information Retrieval*, Montreal.

Tong, R.M., D.G. Shapiro (1985). Experimental Investigations of Uncertainty in a Rule-Based System for Information Retrieval. *Int. J. Man-Machine Studies*, 52:265-282.

Tong, R.M., L.A. Appelbaum (1987). Conceptual Information Retrieval using RUBRIC. *Proc. 10th ACM-SIGIR Int. Conf. on R&D in Information Retrieval*, New Orleans.

Zadeh, L.A. (1973). Outline of a New Approach to the Analysis of Complex Systems and Decision Processes. *IEEE Trans. Systems, Man and Cybernetics*, SMC-3:28-44.

Zadeh, L.A. (1975). The Concept of a Linguistic Variable and its Application to Approximate Reasoning (Part 1). *Information Science*, 8:301-357.

EVALUATION OF UNCERTAIN INFERENCE MODELS I: PROSPECTOR*

Robert M. Yadrick
Bruce M. Perrin
David S. Vaughan

McDonnell Douglas Astronautics Company
P.O. Box 516, St. Louis, MO 63166

Peter D. Holden
Karl G. Kempf**

McDonnell Douglas Research Laboratories
P.O. Box 516, St. Louis, MO 63166

This paper examines the accuracy of the PROSPECTOR model for uncertain reasoning. PROSPECTOR's solutions for a large number of computer-generated inference networks were compared to those obtained from probability theory and minimum cross-entropy calculations. PROSPECTOR's answers were generally accurate for a restricted subset of problems that are consistent with its assumptions. However, even within this subset, we identified conditions under which PROSPECTOR's performance deteriorates.

1. INTRODUCTION

Researchers in artificial intelligence (AI) have proposed or implemented several approaches to uncertain reasoning for knowledge-based systems, including the models inherent in MYCIN [1], PROSPECTOR [2], EMYCIN [3], and AL/X [4]; adaptations of fuzzy set theory [5], Dempster-Shafer belief functions [6], and set-covering theory [7]; as well as INFERNO [8] and endorsement theory [9]. Unfortunately, there is no consensus on which approach is best (or even suitable) for any particular application. One reason for this may be that empirical evidence concerning their accuracy has only recently begun to appear [10, 11].

In disciplines other than AI, there is a long history of systematic efforts to validate descriptive and inferential statistics. One important approach uses artificial or simulated data in which known parameters are varied in systematic ways so that correct outcomes can be calculated [e.g., 12]. Evaluation studies of this sort yield valuable insights into the relative strengths and weaknesses of the statistics under study. The uncertainty indices of knowledge-based systems are analogous to inferential statistics -- they reflect in some manner that the state of a condition is probabilistic. The adequacy of such indices can be assessed

---

* This research was conducted under the McDonnell Douglas Independent Research and Development program.

** Presently at FMC Corp., Central Engineering Lab, AI Group, 1185 Coleman Ave., Santa Clara, CA 95052.

by studying their response to changes in simulated data.

This paper is the first in a series that will examine uncertainty models by adopting a comparable rationale and using methods similar to those found in statistical evaluation studies. Our analyses are based upon the study of a large number of very simple inference networks that consist of two pieces of evidence and one conclusion. Such networks constitute one of the basic building blocks of larger networks, but are small enough to allow for explication of the sources of error. Inference in these networks requires both propagation and combining functions. Error is therefore symptomatic of problems that can accrue when many pieces of evidence bear on a conclusion or effects are propagated through several links in an inference chain. We will discuss the issues involved in extending our analyses to larger networks later in this paper.

We focus on the fundamental accuracy of the PROSPECTOR model, relative to the solutions provided by probability theory and under conditions in which we feel this comparison is valid and appropriate. By basing PROSPECTOR indices on known probability values, we eliminated a major source of error in an actual application -- human estimation of probabilities. We then compared PROSPECTOR's solutions to those produced by a probability-based inference procedure [13]. Moreover, by examining a large number of networks, we are conceptually evaluating PROSPECTOR's ability to deal with a wide range of problems that excercise a wide range of PROSPECTOR's parameter values, i.e., the reliability of a PROSPECTOR-based system in operational use.

2. OVERVIEW OF THE PROSPECTOR MODEL

A brief explanation of PROSPECTOR's model is in order before our methods and results are discussed. We will consider only the essential aspects of PROSPECTOR that deal with issues of combining evidence and propagating the effects of new evidence throughout the network. A number of features that are not directly related to evidence propagation or combination but that may nonetheless affect accuracy (e.g., calculations performed upon user responses to system inquiries), are not addressed here. Additionally, only the formulas used to handle uncertain evidence will be presented; the equations for certain evidence are simplifications of these formulas.

The basic formula PROSPECTOR uses to compute the conditional probability of a conclusion given new evidence is as follows:

$$P'(C|E) = \begin{cases} P(C|\overline{E}) + \dfrac{P(C) - P(C|\overline{E})}{P(E)} \times P'(E) & \text{FOR } 0 \leq P'(E) < P(E) \\[2ex] P(C) + \dfrac{P(C|E) - P(C)}{1 - P(E)} \times [P'(E) - P(E)] & \text{FOR } P(E) \leq P'(E) \leq 1 \end{cases}$$

In this equation, $P'(C|E)$ is the conditional probability of the conclusion that is inferred given new information; $P(C|E)$ is the original conditional probability of the conclusion, given that the evidence is certainly true; $P(C|\overline{E})$ is the original conditional probability of the conclusion, given that the evidence is certainly false; $P(C)$ is the base rate (prior probability) of the conclusion; $P(E)$ is the base rate of the evidence; and $P'(E)$ is the new probability (calculated from a user response to a request for diagnostic information) of the evidence. While this formula is written in terms of evidence bearing on a conclusion, the conclusion or the evidence could just as easily be an intermediate hypothesis in an inference chain. The equation essentially defines P'(C|E) as a piecewise linear function anchored at 0, P(E), and 1. Intermediate values are interpolated.

The new overall probability for evidence P'(E) is calculated in one of three ways when more than one piece of evidence bears on the conclusion. How it is calculated depends on the hypothesized relationship between the pieces of evidence and the conclusion. First, if the conclusion follows only if all pieces of evidence are believed true to some degree, then a conjunctive ("AND") rule is applied. In this case, P'(E) = MIN [(P'(Ei)], where the Ei are the various pieces of evidence. Second, if the conclusion follows if any of the pieces of evidence are true, a disjunctive ("OR") rule is applied and P'(E) = MAX [P'(Ei)]. In either case, P'(E) is used in the basic equation to estimate P'(C|E).

The third rule for determining the new evidence probability is to assume that each piece of evidence has an independent effect upon the conclusion. In this case, PROSPECTOR uses each P'(Ei) separately, yielding a set of P'(C|Ei). These conditional probabilities are then converted to odds according to the formula:

$$O'(C|Ei) = P'(C|Ei) / [1 - P'(C|Ei)].$$

These odds are converted to "effective likelihood ratios" by this formula:

$$L'i = O'(C|Ei) / O(C),$$

where O(C) is the odds of the conclusion. Next, the individual effective likelihood ratios are combined using this heuristic equation:

$$O'(C|E) = (\Pi L'i) O(C).$$

Finally, this odds is converted to a probability by the formula:

$$P'(C|E) = O'(C|E) / [1 + O'(C|E)],$$

yielding PROSPECTOR's estimate of the conditional probability of the conclusion given two or more pieces of independent evidence.

3. METHOD

An inference network can be represented as a multi-dimensional contingency table [14] which has a dimension for each piece of evidence and each conclusion. Each cell in the table contains the joint probability for the associated states of pieces of evidence and conclusions.

In real-world applications, it may be difficult and sometimes impossible to obtain satisfactory estimates of these cell entries. This was one of the motivations for the development of pseudo-Bayesian models like PROSPECTOR and MYCIN. (Several researchers have since developed methods for overcoming these problems in most cases, e.g., [15], [16].)

For theoretical studies, however, there is no difficulty in generating simulated data for such tables. If these tables are taken as representing actual situations, one may focus directly on the question of how well a particular inference model can approximate answers which are correct according to some standard. Tables that exhibit a variety of potentially interesting properties can be produced. For example, the degree of association (i.e., conditional dependence) between pieces of evidence and conclusions can be examined systematically.

Figure 1 shows a contingency table which represents a two-evidence, one conclusion network. We implemented a problem generator to produce sets of small networks in contingency table form. The process for producing contingency tables was necessarily somewhat different for tables representing associated and independent evidence nodes.

For associated evidence nodes, the base rate for each piece of evidence and the conclusion was set randomly to a number between zero and one. Then each cell entry was likewise set randomly between zero and one. The

EVIDENCE 1	EVIDENCE 2	CONCLUSION TRUE	CONCLUSION FALSE	MARGINALS
FALSE	FALSE	$P(\bar{E}_1 \& \bar{E}_2 \& C)$	$P(\bar{E}_1 \& \bar{E}_2 \& \bar{C})$	$P(\bar{E}_1 \& \bar{E}_2)$
FALSE	TRUE	$P(\bar{E}_1 \& E_2 \& C)$	$P(\bar{E}_1 \& E_2 \& \bar{C})$	$P(\bar{E}_1 \& E_2)$
TRUE	FALSE	$P(E_1 \& \bar{E}_2 \& C)$	$P(E_1 \& \bar{E}_2 \& \bar{C})$	$P(E_1 \& \bar{E}_2)$
TRUE	TRUE	$P(E_1 \& E_2 \& C)$	$P(E_1 \& E_2 \& \bar{C})$	$P(E_1 \& E_2)$

FIGURE 1
Contingency Table for a 3-Node Network

table was rescaled by an algorithm called iterative proportional fitting [14]. The base rates and associations in the resulting tables were both randomly assigned and independent of each other. This assured that any error effects resulting from one factor (e.g., conclusion base rate) could not be attributed to any other table characteristic. It also assured that a full range of base rates and associations would be sampled.

For independent evidence nodes, the table marginals equal the product of the base rates (i.e., the joint probability is the product of the simple probabilities.). The first step was to compute marginals from the base rates, and then to randomly apportion each marginal between the two corresponding table cells. For example, the $P(\bar{E}1 \& \bar{E}2)$ marginal in Figure 1 was apportioned between the two first-row cells. The resulting table exhibited both statistical independence between peices of evidence and random associations between each piece of evidence and the conclusion. We generated four hundred independent and four hundred associated networks using these procedures.

Initial analysis showed that many networks contained counterintuitive relationships, e.g., indicating support of the conclusion if one piece of evidence was true but negating the conclusion if both were true. We also found that PROSPECTOR's error for such networks often exceeded .50. PROSPECTOR apparently does not model these situations adequately (Shortliffe and Buchanan [1] noted explicitly that MYCIN was not capable of modeling such phenomena). To provide a conservative test, these problems must be considered outside of PROSPECTOR's domain. Therefore, we required that the networks exhibit one of the following patterns of conditional probabilities:

$$P(C|\bar{E1} \& \bar{E2}) \geq P(C|\bar{E1} \& E2), \ P(C|E1 \& \bar{E2}) \geq P(C|E1 \& E2) \quad [1]$$

or

$$P(C|\bar{E1} \& \bar{E2}) \leq P(C|\bar{E1} \& E2), \ P(C|E1 \& \bar{E2}) \leq P(C|E1 \& E2) \quad [2]$$

These restrictions left 66 independent and 73 associated networks. Each remaining network was solved for a set of "new evidence probabilities." PROSPECTOR updates evidence probabilities when users respond to system inquiries, or, indirectly, as a result of propagation. For present purposes, we simply assigned new probabilities to each evidence node. These nodes independently assumed values of 0.0, 0.2, 0.5, 0.8, and 1.0, in turn, to simulate the wide range of probabilities that could arise as a result of user responses. Thus each network was solved for 25 sets of new evidence probabilities. Our analysis is based upon a total of 3,475 test cases.

Each test case was solved twice: once by a program that implemented the PROSPECTOR model described in section 2 (and gave answers for each of the three rule sets), and once by an inference procedure we developed for this comparison. The details of this inference engine are discussed elsewhere [13]. Briefly, the joint probabilities in the original table are updated in a manner which preserves the original table's pattern of associations. As it turns out, this procedure is a special case of maximum entropy/minimum cross-entropy updating [17]. The resulting table entries are the statistically correct answers, according to probability theory and extensions provided by the principles of entropy theory [18].

4. RESULTS

The stated intention of PROSPECTOR's designers was that answers be reasonably close approximations to those that would result from a rigorous probability analysis, if one could be performed. Consequently, we have focused on measuring the average PROSPECTOR error for each network over the set of new evidence updates. We defined error as the absolute difference between each correct answer and the corresponding PROSPECTOR estimate. Finally, we also examined the maximum error, i.e., the greatest error resulting from a single new evidence probability update.

A case study will illustrate these points. Suppose that a network is generated for which the base rate of the conclusion and the base rates of each piece of evidence are all equal, say $P(C) = P(E1) = P(E2) = 0.50$. Further, the network was produced by the procedure that yields independent evidence. Also, the truth of either piece of evidence alone tends neither to strongly support nor negate the conclusion. Finally, the conclusion is rather strongly suggested if both pieces of evidence are true. All this is so if, say, $P(C|\overline{E1}\ \&\ \overline{E2}) = .10$; $P(C|\overline{E1}\ \&\ E2) = P(C|E1\ \&\ \overline{E2}) = .50$; and $P(C|E1\ \&\ E2) = .90$. Figure 2 shows the contingency table representation of this problem (Part A) and plots PROSPECTOR's error (correct - PROSPECTOR) across the range of new E1 and E2 probabilities (Part B).

This particular example is rather unrealistic (e.g., all base rates of 0.50), but does illustrate a few pertinent points. First, the average signed error over all new probability values is zero, showing that averaging over signed errors can be particularly misleading. Second, the average absolute difference (unsigned error) is approximately .0098. This can be considered the expected error for this network if all new evidence probabilities (i.e., user responses) are thought to be equally likely over the life of the system. The actual error PROSPECTOR would exhibit in operational use, of course, depends on how the new evidence probabilities are distributed. Finally, the maximum error for this network is about .055. Because this table and the error plot are symmetrical, the maximum error occurs twice. This will not generally be the case. For this example, however, the maximum error occurs when the user responds that both pieces of evidence are either definitely true or definitely false.

4.1. PROSPECTOR Rule Sets

The overwhelming majority of our sample problems were solved most accurately by PROSPECTOR's independence rule. The actual independence (or lack of it) inherent in the data does little to determine which rule set works best in terms of reducing overall error. As Table 1 shows, 61 of 66 independent evidence examples and 58 of 73 associated evidence examples were solved best using independence rules. The errors shown are the averages, over all problems, of the two error measures discussed above.

	CONCLUSION		
	FALSE	TRUE	
E1 FALSE, E2 FALSE	.225	.025	
E1 FALSE, E2 TRUE	.125	.125	PART A
E1 TRUE, E2 FALSE	.125	.125	
E1 TRUE, E2 TRUE	.025	.225	

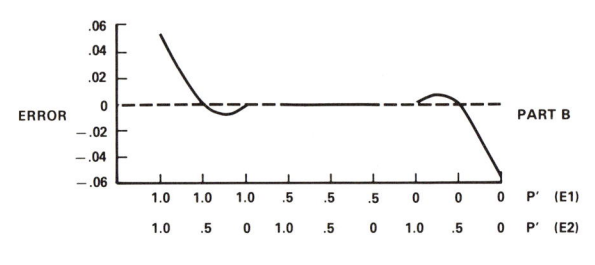

FIGURE 2
PROSPECTOR Case Study 1

TABLE 1. MOST ACCURATE PROSPECTOR RULE
SET FOR INDEPENDENT AND ASSOCIATED EVIDENCE

Relation of Evidence	Rule Set Type			Overall Average Error	Overall Maximum Error
	Conjunctive	Disjunctive	Independent		
Independent	5	0	61	.014	.055
Associated	9	6	58	.022	.083

Average absolute error is low. It is particularly low when the evidence is independent, rather than associated. In any event, PROSPECTOR's estimates are quite accurate most of the time. However, maximum error averages are considerably higher. This suggests that some user responses result in relatively inaccurate solutions, a point that will be examined in greater detail later in this paper. For the present, we turn to a discussion of what factors result in each of PROSPECTOR's rule sets being relatively accurate or inaccurate.

4.2 Error in Conjunctive and Disjunctive Rule Sets

The adequacy of PROSPECTOR's conjunctive rule was found to rest heavily upon the degree to which:

$$P(C|\overline{E1}\ \&\ \overline{E2}) \approx P(C|\overline{E1}\ \&\ E2) \approx P(C|E1\ \&\ \overline{E2}).$$

This is so because PROSPECTOR approximates each of these separate conditional probabilities by a single formula:

$$\frac{P(\overline{E1}\ \&\ \overline{E2}\ \&\ C) + P(\overline{E1}\ \&\ E2\ \&\ C) + P(E1\ \&\ \overline{E2}\ \&\ C)}{1 - [P(E1) * P(E2)]}.$$

The disjunctive rule set generally requires networks for which:

$$P(C|\overline{E1}\ \&\ E2) \approx P(C|E1\ \&\ \overline{E2}) \approx P(C|E1\ \&\ E2).$$

PROSPECTOR approximates each of these conditional probabilities by the formula:

$$\frac{P(\overline{E1}\ \&\ E2\ \&\ C) + P(E1\ \&\ \overline{E2}\ \&\ C) + P(E1\ \&\ E2\ \&\ C)}{1 - [P(\overline{E1}) * P(\overline{E2})]}.$$

By examining our data, we found that the respective conditional probabilities for a given problem must conform closely to these ideals. Even relatively small variations from equality between these conditional probabilities result in the independence rule set being more accurate than either the conjunctive or disjunctive rule sets.

The size of conjunctive or disjunctive error depends in large measure upon two factors, each of which interacts with the other to mitigate or increase the impact of the other. The first factor is the degree to which the actual conditional probabilities given above are approximated by the corresponding PROSPECTOR formulas. This condition will be met only when the conditional probabilities are equal and the evidence is independent.

The second factor is the difference between the fourth conditional probability and the average of the other three. For example, with a disjunctive rule set the difference between $P(C|\overline{E1}\ \&\ \overline{E2})$ and the average of $P(C|\overline{E1}\ \&\ E2)$, $P(C|E1\ \&\ \overline{E2})$, and $P(C|E1\ \&\ E2)$ is critical. Larger inaccuracies result as this difference becomes larger, unless the first condition is fully satisfied.

4.3 Independence Rule Sets

It is considerably more difficult to identify the sources of error for networks solved by the independence rule set. It is possible, however, to write an equation for error in such cases. We will use a simplified notation here, since the expressions become very long otherwise. Let:

Pi = joint probabilities, e.g., $P1 = P(\overline{E1}\ \&\ \overline{E2}\ \&\ \overline{C})$, as shown in Figure 1
Bi = evidence base rates, e.g., $B1 = P(E1)$
$\overline{Bi} = 1 - Bi$
Ci = new evidence probabilities, e.g., $C1 = P'(E1)$
$\overline{Ci} = 1 - Ci$

Even with this notation, PROSPECTOR's independence rule solution for our

3-node networks is long, and is given in Figure 3. The correct answer is

[(P2 / $\overline{B1}$ * $\overline{B2}$) * $\overline{C1}$ * $\overline{C2}$] + [(P4 / B1 * $\overline{B2}$) * C1 * $\overline{C2}$]
+ [(P6 / $\overline{B1}$ * B2) * $\overline{C1}$ * C2] + [(P8 / B1 * B2) * C1 * C2],

if the evidence is independent. Note that the independence rule set often

$$P(C) = \{[(P2+P4)(B1\ \overline{C1}) + (P6+P8)(\overline{B1}\ C1)] \times [(P2+P6)(B2\ \overline{C2}) + (P4+P8)(\overline{B2}\ C2)] \times \overline{B3}\}$$

$$+ \left(\{[(P2+P4)(B1\ \overline{C1}) + (P6+P8)(\overline{B1}\ C1)] \times [(P2+P6)(B2\ \overline{C2}) + (P4+P8)(\overline{B2}\ C2)] \times \overline{B3}\}\right.$$

$$+ \{[(B1\ \overline{B1}) - (P2+P4)(B1\ \overline{C1}) - (P6+P8)(\overline{B1}\ C1)]$$

$$\left. \times [(B2\ \overline{B2}) - (P2+P6)(B2\ \overline{C2}) - (P4+P8)(\overline{B2}\ C2)] \times B3\}\right)$$

FIGURE 3
PROSPECTOR Independence Rule Solution

provided the best solution even when evidence was not independent (Table 1). This formula, however, cannot be used to compute the correct answer for associated evidence cases because joint probabilities cannot be obtained by multiplying simple probabilities. Unfortunately, it is not easy to look at the formula and quickly estimate which network configurations will produce sizeable error and which will not.

It is possible to identify a single factor which relates strongly to independence rule set error. PROSPECTOR's estimates are increasingly inaccurate as the association between evidence and conclusion becomes stronger. PROSPECTOR is most accurate in trivial cases in which uncertain inference is unnecessary. Stated another way, error is smallest when the conditional probability of the conclusion is approximately the same whether the evidence is true or not. This relationship is shown in Figure 4, which plots a function we fit to our error data.

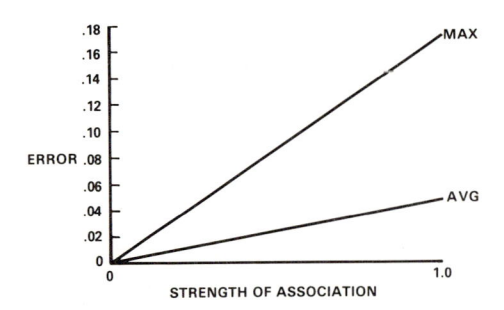

FIGURE 4
Error as a Function of Associative Strength

The function shows the relationship between a simple measure of the strength of the evidence-conclusion association (ABS [$P(C|\overline{E1}\ \&\ \overline{E2})$ - $P(C|E1\ \&\ E2)$]) and error. Thus, the function averages across a wide range of values for the base rates, new evidence probabilities, and conditional probabilities.

To illustrate the significance of the function in Figure 4, we developed a fairly realistic case study. Suppose that a three-node network must

represent the situation in which all evidence and conclusion base rates
are low. Further, the conclusion is likely true if either piece of
evidence is true and very likely true if both pieces of evidence are
true. To make the calculations simpler, the two pieces of evidence are
independent of each other.

For example, let P(E1) = .01, P(E2) = .02, P(C) = .05, P(C|E1) = .60,
P(C|E2) = .70, and P(C|E1 & E2) = .95. Figure 5 shows the only
contingency table that represents this situation exactly.

	CONCLUSION	
	FALSE	TRUE
E1 FALSE, E2 FALSE	.94001	.03019
E1 FALSE, E2 TRUE	.00599	.01381
E1 TRUE, E2 FALSE	.00399	.00581
E1 TRUE, E2 TRUE	.00001	.00019

FIGURE 5
Case Study 2 -- Contingency Table

Rather than summarizing unsigned error in this situation, we present
Figure 6, which plots PROSPECTOR's error across the range of new evidence
probabilities P'(E1) and P'(E2). It is apparent that PROSPECTOR's answers
for a considerable range of new probabilities are very inaccurate. Again,

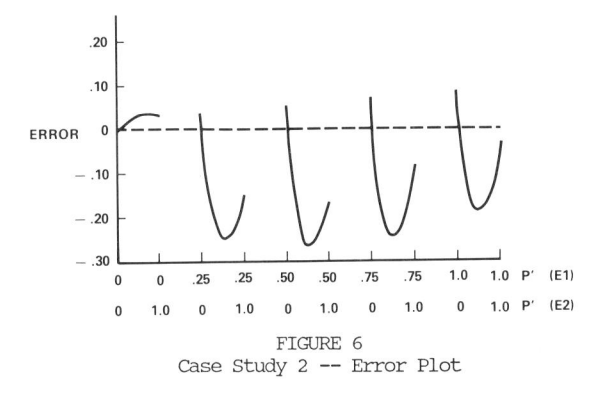

FIGURE 6
Case Study 2 -- Error Plot

some of this error results from complex interactions between conditional
probabilities, base rates, new probabilities, etc. But an important
determinant of the actual size of these errors is simply the large
difference between $P(C|\overline{E1} \& \overline{E2})$ and $P(C|E1 \& E2)$, a rough measure of the
association between the evidence and the conclusion.

5. DISCUSSION AND CONCLUSIONS

An apparently reasonable extension to this study would be to examine
PROSPECTOR's accuracy with networks involving several pieces of evidence,
intermediate nodes, and conclusions. However, the issues involved in such
extensions are deceptive in their apparent simplicity. The important
matter for bigger networks is simply the final amount of error, which
reflects the degree to which errors are compounded or canceled as effects
are propagated through the network.

It is hard to predict in advance just what insights might result from this effort. It may be difficult to discover general principles, and findings would be of little interest if causes of error can be determined only on a case-by-case basis. Additionally, we could deliberately configure networks to yield large or small amounts of error. This would not be very informative for anyone interested in a specific application. Another matter concerns just how to represent particular networks so as to constitute a rigorous yet fair test for PROSPECTOR. A given contingency table can be interpreted using various combinations of PROSPECTOR conjunctive, disjunctive, and independence rules. The number of possible combinations could quickly become unmanageable as the size of the network increases.

An additional extension to this study would be to examine the issue of system tuning. It is often argued that by working with an expert, the parameters and rule sets of a model such as PROSPECTOR's can be adjusted to improve system accuracy. Our findings suggest that it would be difficult to find a single rule set and set of parameters that would adequately handle different sets of new evidence probabilities. In practice, this means that a system developed using, for example, cases in which a piece of evidence is predominantly true would work poorly on cases in which that evidence is false. If cases with both positive and negative evidence were used in system development, it could be impossible to identify a single rule set that would work consistently. In this instance, performance over a broad range of problems would almost certainly deteriorate with any effort to adjust some of the parameters. We plan future research to examine these issues.

In fairness, PROSPECTOR is satisfactorily accurate in many instances within its problem domain (i.e., consistent with the restrictions given by inequalities 1 and 2 above). Even so, the networks that are least-well represented by PROSPECTOR are those in which evidence strongly influences the probablility of the conclusion. It seems reasonable that these will be the cases of critical interest in implementing a PROSPECTOR-based system. Furthermore, for any given network, new evidence probabilities can either compound or mitigate this problem. This means that accuracy in practice may be undeterminable if the system builder does not roughly know the distribution of expected user responses.

REFERENCES

[1] Shortliffe, E.H. and Buchanan, B.G. A model of inexact reasoning in medicine. Mathematical Biosciences, 23, 351-379, 1975.

[2] Duda, R.O., Hart, P.E., Nilsson, N.J., Reboh, R., Slocum, J., and Sutherland, G.L. Development of a computer-based consultant for mineral exploration. Annual Report, Projects 5821 and 6415, SRI International, Oct. 1977.

[3] Van Melle, W. A domain-independent system that aids in constructing knowledge-based consultation programs. Computer Science Department, Stanford University, Report STAN-CS-80-820, 1980.

[4] Reiter, J. AL/X: An expert system using plausible inference. Oxford: Intelligent Terminals, Ltd., 1980.

[5] Zadeh, L.A. The role of fuzzy logic in the management of uncertainty in expert systems. Electronics Research Laboratory Memorandum UCB/ERL M83/41, University of California, Berkeley, 1983.

[6] Shafer, G. Probability judgment in artificial intelligence. In: Kanal, L.N. and Lemmer, J.F. (Eds.), Uncertainty in Artificial Intelligence. Amsterdam: North-Holland, 1986.

[7] Nau, D.S., Reggia, J.A., and Wang, Y.W. Knowledge-based problem solving without production rules. Procedural Trends and Applications, IEEE Computer Society, 105-108, 1983.

[8] Quinlan, J.R. INFERNO: A cautious approach to uncertain inference. The Computer Journal, 26(3), 255-267, 1983.

[9] Cohen, P.R. Heuristic reasoning about uncertainty: an artificial intelligence approach. Boston: Pitman Publishing Company, 1985.

[10] Wise, B.P. and Henrion, M. A framework for comparing uncertain inference systems to probability. In: Kanal, L.N. and Lemmer, J.F. (Eds.), Uncertainty in Artificial Intelligence. Amsterdam: North-Holland, 1986.

[11] Wise, B.P. Experimentally comparing uncertain inference systems to probability, this volume.

[12] Games, P.A. and Howell, J.F. Pairwise multiple comparison procedures with unequal N's and/or variances: A Monte Carlo study. Journal of Educational Statistics, 1976, 1, 113-125.

[13] Vaughan, D.S., Perrin, B.M., Yadrick, R.M., Holden, P.D., and Kempf, K.G. An odds ratio based inference engine. In: Kanal, L.N. and Lemmer, J.F. (Eds.) Uncertainty in Artificial Intelligence. Amsterdam: North-Holland, 1986.

[14] Bishop, Y.M.M., Fienberg, S.E., and Holland, P.W. Discrete multivariate analysis, theory and practice. Cambridge, MA: The MIT Press, 1975.

[15] Cheeseman, P. A method of computing generalized Bayesian probability values for expert systems. Proceedings of the Eighth International Joint Conference on Artificial Intelligence, Karlsruhe, W. Germany, 1983.

[16] Pearl, J. How to do with probabilities what people say you can't. Proceedings of the IEEE Second Conference on Artificial Intelligence Applications, Miami, 1985.

[17] Wise, B.P. Experimental comparison of uncertain inference systems. Unpublished Ph.D. Dissertation, Carnegie-Mellon University, 1986.

[18] Shore, J.E. and Johnson, R.W. Axiomatic derivation of the principle of maximum entropy and the principle of minimum cross-entropy. IEEE Transactions on Information Theory, Vol. IT-26, 26-37, 1980.

Experimentally Comparing Uncertain Inference Systems to Probability

Ben P. Wise
Thayer School, Dartmouth
Hanover, NH 03755

1. Abstract

This paper examines the biases and performance of several uncertain inference systems: Mycin, a variant of Mycin, and a simplified version of probability using conditional independence assumptions. We present axiomatic arguments for using Minimum Cross Entropy inference as the best way to do uncertain inference. For Mycin and its variant, we found special situations where its performance was very good, but also situations where performance was worse than random guessing, or where data was interpreted as having the opposite of its true import. We have found that all three of these systems usually gave accurate results, and that the conditional independence assumptions gave the most robust results. We illustrate how the importance of biases may be quantitatively assessed and ranked. Considerations of robustness might be a critical factor is selecting UIS's for a given application.

2. Introduction

Uncertainty is a pervasive feature of the domains in which expert systems are supposed to function. There are several mechanisms for handling uncertainty, of which the oldest and most widely used is probability theory. It is also the only one which is derived from a formal description of rational behavior [5]. There are many axiomatic arguments that no other system can do better than probability theory in terms of *results* [1]. For use in pattern-directed inference systems, or rule-based inference engines, artificial intelligence researchers have favored others (such as fuzzy set theory, Dempster-Shafer theory, or the algorithms used in the Prospector or Mycin expert systems), largely for reasons of simplicity, speed, low data requirements, and explainability. We will present techniques with which to measure how well these alternatives approximate the results of probability theory, to assess how well they perform by those measures, and to find out what underlying features of a problem cause strong or weak performance. The object of such assessment is to provide an "off-line standard" against which other, simpler and faster, systems may be calibrated.

Because the amount of data required to fully specify a probability distribution is enormous for problems of practical size, some technique must be used to estimate a distribution when only partial information is given. Moreover, there is no formally correct, Bayesian way to handle the type of uncertain information which expert systems must use. We give intuitive and axiomatic arguments that fitting maximum entropy priors and using minimum cross entropy updating are the most appropriate, or the most nearly Bayesian, ways to meet both requirements. More extensive discussion may be found in [7].

We have concentrated on an analysis of the system used in MYCIN [4], largely because it is familiar to many researchers, but also because varients are being widely disseminated by various corporations. Its operations have been analyzed to elucidate both which basic problem-features affect, or bias, the answers, and the directions of the biases. Series of experiments have been done on test cases to find out how these biases affect the performance of the uncertain inference systems. We present and discuss both the motivation and design of our analysis techniques, and the specific structures which were found to have strong effects on bias and on performance.

3. Outline of Our Method

The basic goal of our work is to suggest what conditions produce significant differences in the outputs of uncertain inference systems (UIS's). The emphasis is on comparing the outputs, not the simplicity, explicability, or ease of construction of the UIS itself. We will present the method by giving the rationale for each part of the experimental procedure, as given in figure 1. The bottom is where the ME/MXE inference is performed, while the inference of the UIS being explored is done in the top row.

Conversions: To answer questions about differences in performance, a common interpretation of the inputs and results is required to make them commensurable. Presumably, the ultimate purpose of any expert system is to lead to better decisions - either directly by the system or indirectly by the human user. If two different representations of uncertainty lead to making the same decision, then they are operationally equivalent. According to Bayesian Decision theory, decisions can reveal probabilistic beliefs about the outcomes on which the decisions are based. Even if the decision-maker does not think in probabilistic terms, if he chooses coherently he will act as though he did. In principle, if a non-probabilistic approach to uncertainty provides an integrated theory of how to make both inferences and decisions based on its representations of uncertainty, then this would imply an operational equivalence between uncertain beliefs expressed in the probabilistic and non-probabilistic forms, where they produced the same decision. This would allow direct comparison of the representations. Notably, however, the non-probabilistic approaches do not provide agreed upon decision strategies, and so this is unfortunately impossible.

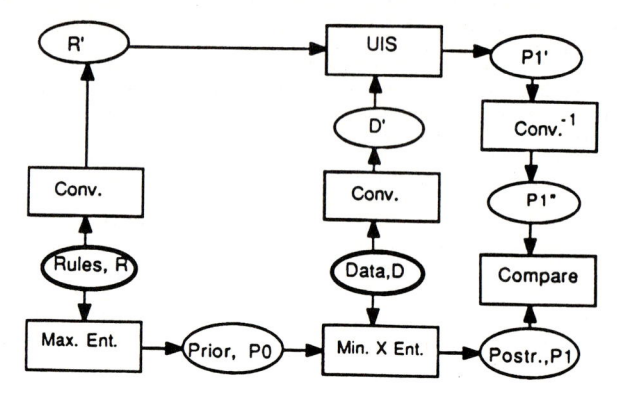

Figure 1: Basic Experiment Design for Comparisons

Nevertheless, there are obvious, simple ways to make transformations from to probability for at least some UIS's. For MYC, the conversions are taken from the verbal and equational definitions of Certainty Factors [4]: $CF = 1$ means true, so $\text{Pr}_0(x) = 1$; $CF = 0$ means no evidence, so we stay at the prior probability, $\text{Pr}_1(x) = \text{Pr}_0(x)$; and $CF = -1$ means definitely false, so $\text{Pr}_1(x) = -1$. Values between these three points are found by piecewise linear interpolation. As these definitions were provided by the system's designers, we regard them as being quite accurate statements of the originally intended interpretation; we will demonstrate that some alternative interpretations suggested for CF's do not change our essential conclusions. One simplified version of probability consists of always assuming that antecedents are conditionally independent, given their common conclusion; we will denote this version as CI. For this system, the correspondance is direct. Using these conversions, we can state some inference rules and data in terms of probabilities, convert them into an alternative representation, and remain confident that the two still represented the same knowledge. At the end of an experiment, we can then invert the conversion to change the UIS's conclusions to probabilities, for direct comparison.

UIS Inference: The rule-strengths and data obtained by the above conversions are fed into the UIS currently being tested, and propagated up a rule-tree according to the particular UIS's rules for "and", "or", "not", and implication ("&", "v", "¬", and "*modus ponens*"respectively) evaluating the reliability of evidence, or combining the results of different rules with the same consequent. The "&", "v", "¬", and "*modus ponens*"operations for MYC are given in equations 1 to 4. The "&" and "v" operations are assumed; the "¬" operation is easily derivable from the probabilistic definition of a CF .

$$CF(A_1 \ \& \ A_2) = \min[CF(A_1), \ CF(A_2)] \qquad (1)$$

$$CF(A_1 \ \text{or} \ A_2) = \max[CF(A_1), \ CF(A_2)] \qquad (2)$$

$$CF(\neg A) = -CF(A) \qquad (3)$$

$$CF_1(C) = CF(C|A)CF_1(A), \ \text{if} \ CF_1(A) \geq 0$$
$$= 0, \text{otherwise} \qquad (4)$$

One should note that this last rule for "*modus ponens*" contradicts what Bayesian theory requires. That is, if A's being true increase $\text{Pr}_1(C)$ above its prior value, then A's being false must lower $\text{Pr}_1(C)$ below its prior value. But in MYC, A's being false causes C to stay at its prior probability. We can define a new UIS which is identical to MYC in every way, except that it also repsonds to negative CF's for A. Because we call it Two-Sided Mycin, we will refer to it as TSM.

The definition of a MYC rule-strength is quite similar to that for the CF of a proposition, except that we look at the change in the conclusion's probability, given the antecedent, relative to its prior probabilitiy. That is, we compare $\text{Pr}_0(C|A)$ and $\text{Pr}_0(C)$. The idea here is that the CF's on the input evidence represent the change in belief which is attributable to some external evidence available only to the expert, while the rule CF's represent the change in belief in C which is attributable changed belief in A, when C and A are both represented in the expert system.

When two rules refer to the same consequent, C, we use rule the rule in equation 5 for combining their results. The result of rule R_1 is denoted by x, and the result of rule R_2 by y, and the resulting CF in C by $x \oplus y$. Surprisingly, this rather complicated rule is commutative and associative, so it can be applied to an arbitrary number of rules, in arbitrary order.

$$\begin{aligned} x \oplus y &= x + y - xy, \quad \text{if } x \geq 0, y \geq 0 \\ &= x + y + xy, \quad \text{if } x \leq 0, y \leq 0 \\ &= \frac{x+y}{1 - \min(|x|,|y|)}, \quad \text{if mixed signs} \end{aligned} \qquad (5)$$

We will very briefly discuss another UIS, called CI, which is a simplified version of probability which represents all its rules as having their antecedents conditionally independent, given the consequent. Propositions A_1 and A_2 are conditionally independent, given C, if equation 6 holds.

$$p(A_1 \ \& \ A_2|C) = p(A_1|C)p(A_2|C) \qquad (6)$$

Intuitively, this states that the factors which affect A_1 and A_2 are unrelated, once we have compensated for all those which affect their relationship to C. Of course, it is not always possible for A_1 and A_2 to be related only through that one C, particularly if they themselves share a common antecedent, but the approximate formula can be used nonetheless. To do "modus ponens", we use equation 7, which states that the updated odds-ratio for C is determined from its old odds-ratio, and the product of a series of factors, one for each antecedent. This equation also assumes that A_1 and A_2 are conditionally independent given $\neg C$ and uses the abbreviations $\text{Pr}_0(C) = c$, $\text{Pr}_1(C|A_1 \& A_2) = \text{Pr}_1(C)$, $\text{Pr}_0(A_1|C) = p_{1c}$, $\text{Pr}_0(A_1|\neg C) = p_{1n}$, $\text{Pr}_0(A_2|C) = p_{2c}$, and $\text{Pr}_0(A_2|\neg C) = p_{2n}$.

$$\frac{\text{Pr}_1(C)}{1 - \text{Pr}_1(C)} = \left(\frac{p_{1c}}{p_{1n}}\right)\left(\frac{p_{2c}}{p_{2n}}\right)\left(\frac{c}{1-c}\right) \qquad (7)$$

An approximate interpolation formula is used when the A_i are between 0 and 1, as in equation 8, using the abbreviations $\text{Pr}_1(A_1) = a$, $\text{Pr}_1(A_2) = b$, $\text{Pr}_2(A_1) = A$, $\text{Pr}_2(A_2) = B$, and $\text{Pr}_1(C) = \text{Pr}_1(C|a\&b)$. In PROSPECTOR, a multi-stage procedure is used; the closed-form of its result is in equation 8.

$$\frac{\text{Pr}_1(C)}{\text{Pr}_1(\neg C)} = \left(\frac{p_{1c}(1-A)a + (1-p_{1c})A(1-a)}{p_{1n}(1-A)a + (1-p_{1n})A(1-a)}\right)\left(\frac{p_{12}(1-B)b + (1-p_{2c})B(1-b)}{p_{2n}(1-B)b + (1-p_{2n})B(1-b)}\right)\left(\frac{\text{Pr}_0(C)}{\text{Pr}_0(\neg C)}\right) \qquad (8)$$

In [3], Heckerman argues for an interpretation of CF's which causes MYCIN's $\oplus$ operator to be equivalent to the assumption of conditional independence, when the posterior probabilities of A_0 and A_1 are each either 0 or 1. It is not clear what interpolation formula is implied, as his re-formulation is quite difficult to invert. As will be discussed later, the significant problems with MYCIN are in the "&", "v", and "modus ponens" operations, not $\oplus$. We have duplicated all the following analysis under Heckerman's new interpretation, with no significant change in the results.

ME/MXE Inference: The ME/MXE inference is a simple generalization of Bayesian conditioning. There are no special rules for "&" , "v" , "modus ponens" , evaluating the reliability of evidence, or combining the results of different rules with the same consequent. The first two "operations" are done simply be reading the appropriate numbers off the posterior. The last three "operations" happen automatically when we update.

Before proceeding farther, we must define a particular rule for uncertain inference which will appear several times throughout this paper - Jeffrey's Rule. Where x is some arbitrary event, and y_i are an exhaustive and exclusive set of alternatives, equation 9. must hold for any distribution. In words, it says that our prior probability of any event x must be a combination of our probabilities for x given other events, y_i, weighted by our prior probabilities for those events.

$$\Pr_0(x) = \sum_{i=1}^{n} \Pr_0(x|y_i) \Pr_0(y_i) \qquad (9)$$

One may extend equation 9 from a consistency requirement to an updating rule by forming equation 10, which is the usual definition of Jeffrey's Rule.

$$\Pr_1(x) = \sum_{i=1}^{n} \Pr_0(x|y_i) \Pr_1(y_i) \qquad (10)$$

Equation 10 has several notable characteristics. The rule always results in another coherent probability distribution. If x is quite likely given a particular y_i, then raising the probability of that y_i will raise the probability of x, so it exhibits an intuitively pleasing sensitivity. The new probabilities may be specified only over an exhaustive and exclusive set of events. The requirement of exhaustiveness is not really a problem - if new probabilities are given over a non-exhaustive set of events, one need only specify that the remaining probability fall over the remaining events, and so obtain an exhaustive set of events. One should especially note the corrollary that $\Pr_1(x \& y_i) = \Pr_0(x \& y_i)(\Pr_1(y_i)/\Pr_0(y_i))$ because we will later show how it describes Mycin's updating rule.

As discussed in [2], Jeffrey's Rule is a special case of many other generalized updating methods. In particular, it is a special case of the iterative proportional fitting procedure (IPFP), which is in turn a special case of minimum cross entropy (MXE) updating, as proved in [7]. The IPFP is an extension to the case where $y_i \cap y_j$ is non-empty, simply by using Jeffrey's Rule for each y_i in turn, over and over, until the result no longer changes significantly. The IPFP is the only form of MXE which we will need in this paper. However, we will briefly review the general justification of MXE.

Surprisingly, the maximum entropy estimation of priors and the minimum cross entropy updating method are completely defined by several weak properties, as proven by Shore and Johnson [6] They proved that any method for forming or updating a prior which possessed these properties would give the same answer as maximum entropy or minimum cross entropy, respectively. Thus, ME/MXE analysis has been singled out as not just one more heuristic among many, but as the only one which has these four simple consistency properties. One should note especially that it has been singled out whether it is considered as a "stand alone" method or as a computationally feasible *approximation* to Bayesian analysis. It is quite important to note that this proof does not specify that only an answer generate by the general MXE algorithms will satisfy these four properties. It states only that the *result* should be the same.

The four properties are defined so as to make the answer invariant when we re-phrase the input data in ways which are by definition equivalent. First, the method should give a single, unique answer for the distribution. Second, the answer should be invariant under 1-to-1 coordinate transformations of the data or the prior distribution. Third, the answer should be invariant under different ways of specifying the probabilities of events which are independent. That is, we should be able to give marginal distributions over y and over x, specifying that they are independent, or to give the resulting joint distribution, and still get the same answer. This basically means that the inference system must understand what the word "independent" means. Lastly, the answer should be invariant under different ways of specifying the probabilities of sets of events which are independent. Many more arguments for and against ME/MXE, as well as many comparisons to standard Bayesian analysis, can be found in [7].

Comparisons: Given the conclusions of MXE and the conclusions (converted back to probabilities) of a UIS, we can then do several comparisons. Some are useful in elucidating when biases will be apparent and how large they will be, others are useful in estimating how significant those biases may be to the user.

We can measure one form of bias by seeing if the UIS has shifted the probabilities by the same additive amount, or by the same multiplicative factor. We will denote the prior probability by p_0, the UIS estimate by $p_{U,1}$, and the MXE estimate by $p_{M,1}$. That is, we can look compare the UIS-shift, $\Delta_U = p_{U,1} - p_0$ to the MXE-shift, $\Delta_M = p_{M,1} - p_0$. We can run a whole series of tests, for different data, and do a regression of the UIS-shift against the MXE-shift, to see if there is consistent over- or under-response to the data, and if there is a constant bias in one direction, independent of the data.

We can also do comparisons of performance by evaluating how close the UIS's estimate is to the MXE answer. Because different p_i allow different margins for error, we compare the actual error to a perfect match, random guessing, or the worst possible match. This can be done either for the absolute error ($|\epsilon|$) or the squared error (ϵ^2); we will use squared error. For MYC and TSM, with random guessing of CF's over the interval [+1,-1], the average of the expected error in an estimate of $p_{M,1}$ is given in equation 11. The p_0 term is present because the value guessed for CF can only be converted to a p_1-estimate by using p_0. We may use the squared error to define a normalized performance measure, ζ which is 1 if there is zero error, 0 if the squared error is $\mu(\epsilon^2)$, and -1 if the squared error is the largest possible, with linear interpolation between.

$$\mu(\epsilon^2) = \frac{2p_0^2 - 6p_{M,1}p_0 + 6p_{M,1}^2 + 1 + p_0 - 3p_{M,1}}{6} \qquad (11)$$

4. Outline of Biases in MYC and TSM

In this section, our main concern will be to assess the biases which Mycin (MYC) displays. Again, we should emphasize that the main concern is not to criticize a particular (old) scheme of inference, but to illustrate the general style of analysis on a familiar example. We will also briefly discuss the modified version, TSM. As discussed earlier, the standard of comparison will be ME/MXE analysis. Our general conclusions will be that each UIS is sometimes accurate, but sometimes quite inaccurate. The factors underlying those differences are described and discussed.

The rules for MYC contain implicit assumptions; a fact which Shortliffe and Buchanan very briefly discuss at two places in [4]. The "&" and "v" rules for MYC operate on confidence factors which denote not belief but *changes* in belief. Thus, we need to do some algebra in order to state what the assumptions are, but the end result is that the "&" and "v" operations are equivalent to Jeffrey's Rule, but using only one piece of the given data. Suppose that $CF(A_1) \leq 0$ and $CF(A_1) \leq CF(A_2)$, then equation 12 holds. Given the definition of a MYC CF as a re-scaling, we can restate 12 as 13, and follow the algebra to the last line, which as one can see is exactly the answer which MXE gives if we use only $\Pr_1(A_1)$ and ignore evidence about A_2.

$$CF(A_1 \& A_2) = CF(A_1) \tag{12}$$

$$\frac{\Pr_1(A_1 \& A_2) - \Pr_0(A_1 \& A_2)}{\Pr_0(A_1 \& A_2)} = \frac{\Pr_1(A_1) - \Pr_0(A_1)}{\Pr_0(A_1)} \tag{13}$$

$$\Pr_1(A_1 \& A_2) = \Pr_0(A_1 \& A_2)\frac{\Pr_1(A_1)}{\Pr_0(A_1)} \tag{14}$$

A similar derivation gives equation 15, when $0 \leq CF(A_1) \leq CF(A_2)$. For this equation, the odds-ratio answer is identical only under the additional assumption that A_1 is a proper sub-set of A_2 (or, equivalently, that A_2 logically implies A_1). Also, equation 15 is exactly the MXE result if $\Pr_1(A_2)$ is 1.0, implying that MYC will often over-estimate the probability of a conjunction when both CF's increase. Note however, that this extra assumption is invoked only some of the time, and depends not on prior probabilities but on how much they are changed and in which direction.

$$\Pr_1(\neg(A_1 \& A_2)) = \Pr_0(\neg(A_1 \& A_2))\frac{\Pr_1(\neg A_1)}{\Pr_0(\neg A_1)} \tag{15}$$

For the "v" operation, we may also do similar algebra. For the case that $CF(A_1) \geq 0$ and $CF(A_1) \geq CF(A_2)$, we get equation 16, which is exactly the MXE answer, if we ignore evidence about A_2. For the case that $0 \geq CF(A_1) \geq CF(A_2)$, we get equation 17, which is the MXE answer if we ignore evidence about A_2 and assume that A_2 is a proper subset A_1. Again, this additional assumption is only invoked sometimes.

$$\Pr_1(\neg(A_1 \vee A_2)) = \Pr_0(\neg(A_1 \vee A_2))\frac{\Pr_1(\neg A_1)}{\Pr_0(\neg A_1)} \tag{16}$$

$$\Pr_1(A_1 \vee A_2) = \Pr_0(A_1 \vee A_2)\frac{\Pr_1(A_1)}{\Pr_0(A_1)} \tag{17}$$

The fact that MYC updates with only one piece of data while systematicly ignoring the rest has certain implications. For example, one would expect MYC to under-estimate the impact of new data. In fact, if one takes the original graphical data presented in [4], which plots the MYC estimate versus the correct probability, and does a linear regression, one finds that MYC's response is only about 51% of the correct amount (which explains 74% of the variance). When there are N pieces of input data, MYC's "&" and "v" operators will ignore $N-1$ of them. This can cause extreme errors. For example, let us say $\Pr_0(A_1)$ is quite near 1.0, and $\Pr_0(A_i)$ is near 0.0 for $2 \leq i \leq N$; the prior probability of their conjunction will generally be nearly zero. If $CF(A_1) = 0$, and $CF(A_i) = 1$ for all other i, then MYC will estimate the CF of their conjunction as 0.0, and hence estimate the posterior probability of the conjunction to remain at nearly zero, even though it has actually risen to be quite near 1.0. In fact, it is exactly $\Pr_0(A_1)$. Also, in the face of contradictory data, MYC will not balance one against the other, but simply update with one or the other. Updating with one will have an impact in the right direction; updating with the other will have an impact in the wrong direction.

We compared the "&" rule for MYC and TSM, on two input items, to the results of "&" in minimum cross entropy updates. Surprisingly, we found that the following results were true whether the propositions were positively correlated, negatively correlated, or independent: if both input CF's are negative, MYC understates the impact of the data, and if either one or both of the input CF's are positive, MYC overstates the impact of the data. The analysis was done as follows. We assumed a prior distribution in which the prior probabilities of A_1 and A_2 are both one half, and a prior probability of $A_1 \& A_2$ is one ninth. The results for this particular distribution are given in figure 4.1; results for other distributions with negative correlation were qualitatively similar.

$CF(A_1)$	$CF(A_2)$	$CF_{myc}(A_1\&A_2)$	$CF_{mxe}(A_1\&A_2)$
+.8	+.8	+.8	+.776
−.8	+.8	−.8	.501
−.8	−.8	−.8	−.991

Figure 4.1: Negative Correlation Comparison of "and" rule.

If we set their CF's to +0.8 and +0.8, this gives posterior probabilities of 0.9 to A_1 and 0.9 to A_2. If we do an MXE update with those new probabilities, we find a posterior probability for $(A_1 \& A_2)$ of 0.801, which given the prior of one ninth, corresponds to a CF of +0.776 for the conjunction. MYC's value of +0.8 CF for the conjunction corresponds to a posterior probability of 0.822. In this case, MYC has overstated the impact by only 3.08%, which may be negligible.

If we set their CF's to +0.8 and -0.8, this gives posterior probabilities of 0.9 to A_1 and 0.1 to A_2. If we do an MXE update with those new probabilities, we find a posterior probability for $(A_1 \& A_2)$ of 0.05543, corresponding to a CF of -.501. The -0.8 CF for the conjunction corresponds to a posterior probability of 0.022. In this case, MYC has overstated the impact by 59.6%, which may be significant.

If we set their CF's to -0.8 and -0.8, this gives posterior probabilities of 0.1 to A_1 and 0.1 to A_2. If we do an MXE update with those new probabilities, we find a posterior probability for $(A_1 \& A_2)$ of 0.001, or a CF of -.991. The -0.8 CF for the conjunction corresponds to a posterior probability of 0.022. In this case, MYC has understated the impact.

These results are simply explained if one bears in mind that MYC updates using Jeffrey's Rule, but ignores all save one piece of data. In the case of CF's with opposite signs, the impact of the data is over-stated because only the disconfirming evidence is used. The confirming evidence, which should have lessened the impact, is totally ignored. When both have negative signs, the impact is under-stated, because MYC ignores the fact that it has multiple pieces of disconfirming evidence, and acts as if it only had one. When both are positive, MYC also assumes that one, say A_1, is a logical consequence of the other, A_2, as shown by equation 15. If that "assumed rule" were true, then A_2 itself would actually be additional evidence for A_1. Of course, this is not true in our case, and so MYC overstates the impact, because it thinks it has received more information than it really has. Equivalently, MYC treats A_2 as having probability 1.0, and hence it overstates the probability of $(A_1 \& A_2)$.

This line of reasoning implies that the higher the positive correlation between A_1 and A_2, the less significant will be the underestimation when both CF's are negative. Similarly, we would expect the overestimation to be more significant when both CF's are positive and there is positive correlation, because then the two CF's are more redundant, and hence less informative. Both hypotheses are confirmed by the experiments on a distribution in which A_1 and A_2 are positively correlated (i.e. $\text{Pr}_0(A_1) = \text{Pr}_0(A_2) = .5$ and $\text{Pr}_0(A_1 \& A_2) = .3889$) with the results in figure 4.2.

$CF(A_1)$	$CF(A_2)$	$CF_{myc}(A_1\&A_2)$	$CF_{mxe}(A_1\&A_2)$
+.8	+.8	+.8	+.746
−.8	+.8	−.8	−.746
−.8	−.8	−.8	−.885

Figure 4.1: Positive Correlation Comparison of "and" rule.

We may similarly compare MYC's "v" rule to the MXE results. Again, and for similar reasons, MYC understates the impact of the data whenever both CF's are positive, but the underestimation decreases when A_1 and A_2 increase in correlation. For "v", MYC always overestimates the impact of data whenever there are CF's of mixed sign, because the disconfirming evidence is ignored. Whenever both CF's are negative, it makes the same assumption as before that one antecedent is a logical consequence of the other, and hence behaves as if there were an additional rule, which exaggerates the impact.

The MYC rule, $\oplus$, for combining the results of multiple rules which bear on one consequent is rather complex. Because it is quadratic in the input CF's, which are non-linearly related to the probabilities, inverting and solving in the fashion of equations 12 through 17 generally yields equations which have no clear intuitive interpretation. Hence, we choose numerical analysis. We compared it to the ordinary "v" rule of MYC and the "v" results of MXE, for the previous two prior distributions over A_1 and A_2, as well as one in which they were independent. In figure 4.3, the prior distribution is flat over all possible combinations of A_1 and A_2, which makes them independent with probability 0.5 each. The table displays the CF's for A_1

and A_2 at the far left. The CF's yielded by using the MYC "v" and $\oplus$ rule are in the middle. On the far right is the CF obtained for $(A_1$ or $A_2)$ if one converts the two input CF's to posterior probabilities, does the MXE update, reads the probability of the disjunction off the posterior, and converts that back to a CF (using the prior probability of the disjunction).

$CF(A_1)$	$CF(A_2)$	$CF_{myc\ or}$	$CF_\oplus$	CF_{mxe-or}
$+.8$	$+.8$	$+.8$	$+.96$	$+.9600$
$+.8$	$-.8$	$-.8$	0.00	$+.6400$
$+.4$	$+.4$	$+.4$	$+.64$	$+.6400$
$-.8$	$-.8$	$-.8$	$-.96$	$-.7467$

Figure 4.3: Independence Comparison of "or" rules.

Whenever the CF's are of equal magnitude but opposite signs, the "v" result overestimates the MXE result, both of them are positive, and the $\oplus$ result predicts no change at all. Whenever both CF's are positive the $\oplus$ result is exactly the MXE result, and "v" underestimates the impact of the data. But when both are negative, the $\oplus$ and "v" results both overestimate the impact of the data, which is a puzzling asymmetry. We will now argue that the $\oplus$ rule is equivalent to assuming independence when both CF's are positive, and that there is a strong negative correlation when both CF's are negative.

Let us suppose that $CF(A) > 0$ and $CF(B) > 0$. Recalling the definitions of positive CF's and of $\oplus$, we get equation 18, which after a little algebra gives equation 19. For brevity, we have designated $Pr_0(A)$ by A_0, $Pr_1(A)$ by A_1, and so on. This equation states that the CF for A or B, assuming that they are independent, is the $\oplus$ combination of their individual CF's. Surprisingly, equation 19 is an identity, true for any choice of $A_0, A_1, B_0,$ and B_1 with $A_0 \neq 1$ and $B_0 \neq 1$. Hence, it is also true for any choice which satisfies $0 \leq A_0 < A_1 \leq 1$ and $0 \leq B_0 < B_1 \leq 1$. One should note that the assumption of independence was something which MYC was explicitly designed to avoid. Instead, it seems merely to have been obscured by MYC's notation, taking a very simple probabilistic model and casting it in opaque terminology. This result illustrates the point that without careful analysis, it is not clear what a heuristic UIS really does, whether it avoids what it should not be doing, or whether it does what it was designed to do.

$$CF(A \oplus B) = CF(A) + CF(B) - CF(A)CF(B) \tag{18}$$

$$\frac{(A_1 + B_1 - A_1 B_1) - (A_0 + B_0 - A_0 B_0)}{1 - (A_0 + B_0 - A_0 B_0)} = \frac{A_1 - A_0}{1 - A_0} + \frac{B_1 - B_0}{1 - B_0} - \frac{(A_1 - A_0)(B_1 - B_0)}{(1 - A_0)(1 - B_0)} \tag{19}$$

If we take the same approach when both CF's are negative, we get equation 21 But this equation can not be satisfied if $0 < A_1 < A_0$ and $0 < B_1 < B_0$, because the left side will always be larger than the right.

$$CF(A \oplus B) = CF(A) + CF(B) + CF(A)CF(B) \tag{20}$$

$$\frac{1}{A_1} + \frac{1}{B_1} = \frac{1}{A_0} + \frac{1}{B_0} \tag{21}$$

Hence, for negative CF's, $\oplus$ does not model independence. In fact, if one combines the "v" results from the distributions with negative, zero, and positive correlation which we mentioned earlier, one can see from the following table that $\oplus$ corresponds to assuming a very strong negative correlation - more than is possible for any distribution. This is particularly significant because the commonly accepted assumption of conditional independence always produces non-negative correlation.

$CF(A)$	$CF(B)$	$\oplus$	MXE_{minus}	MXE_{indep}	MXE_{plus}
$-.8$	$-.8$	$-.96$	$-.776$	$-.747$	$-.746$

Most authors regard it as quite desirable that an inference system obey DeMorgan's Laws, which are that $\neg(A \vee B) = (\neg A) \& (\neg B)$ and $\neg(A \& B) = (\neg A) \vee (\neg B)$ At first glance, it seems that MYC's "&" , "v" , $\oplus$, and "$\neg$" rules obey them. However, the CF's refer to *change* in belief, not to belief itself. Hence, it is not clear from their definitions alone whether MYC will actually obey DeMorgan's Laws in terms of belief. But the evidence above clearly shows that the $\oplus$ and "v" operations, *when combined* with the non-linear definition of CF's, generally violate DeMorgan's Laws. This is because MYC assumes independence when CF(A) and CF(B) are both positive, but if we reverse the signs of the CF's by talking about $CF(\neg A)$ and $CF(\neg B)$, then it assumes a strong negative correlation. Hence, the results in the first case will directly contradict those from the second.

Clearly, we have not really changed the content of the data-base, just re-named the propositions within it. Thus, because the operations are sensitive to the *signs* of the CF's, MYC will make completely different implicit assumptions, and get very different answers, purely because the propositions have been re-named. One will recall that invariance under 1-to-1 one transformations was one of the desirable, defining characteristics of MXE updating. Not only does the MYC result depend on trivial restatements of the prior, but also it makes different, contradictory, assumptions about the prior depending on which update is performed.

The results of the various detailed comparisons may be integrated and summarized as follows. Shortliffe and Buchanan's original MYC data shows an overall tendency to under-estimate the impact of new data by about 49%. Our more detailed analysis shows that the "&" , "v" , and "*modus ponens*" rules systematically ignore data and hence typically underestimate the aggregate impact. Only the operation for combining the results of several rules consistently produces over-estimations of the impact, and it may have a significant bias toward negative CF's. Hence, we may conjecture that in the complete rule-system which Shortliffe and Buchanan tested, the under-estimation effect of the first three operations dominated the over-estimation effect of the last one. This suggests that efforts to improve the MYC system are better directed at the way it does "&" , "v" , and "*modus ponens*" than at the way it combines the results of separate rules, via $\oplus$. Even though the latter issue may have more intellectual appeal than the first three, it seems to have less practical importance.

5. Experiments on Performance

While we have clarified some biases in MYC and TSM, we have not yet addressed the problem of how important those biases really are. To answer this question, we examined their ζ-performance over a broad range of differently structured sample rule-sets, and multiple trials of each rule-set. Space limitations preclude complete discussion of the data, but the general method is more important. It is important to note that our tests do cover a broad range of basic structures. This type of broad coverage and comparison of results has been lacking in the few previous studies which examined UIS's performance.

For each rule-set, a collection of input data were evaluated, and each UIS assigned its average performance - the average value of ζ - over that set of cases. This was done by cycling each input node through a range of four probabilities. Thus, if there were n input leaves, there would be 4^n cases tried, one for each possible combination of the inputs. The four values were always close to 0.05, 0.35, 0.65, 0.95. They were actually chosen to be random within .01 of those values; for example, $(0.053, 0.349, 0.643, 0.945)$ would be a possible set of values. They were generated afresh for each of the 4^n trials. This sampling method was chosen for two reasons. First, it spanned the space of input possibilities, and thus approximated an even distribution over the space of possible input probabilities. Second, it enabled rule-sets with different numbers of input nodes to have their performance compared, as only the averages were compared. Thus, the numbers derived are an estimate of average performance, which is distinct from the biases, which were explored earlier. The small examples came in eight sets, totaling 36 small examples. Each example was run for between 16 and 256 individual trials, for each of six different UIS's. We will present some data on MYC's and TSM's performance over the first six sets. In each set, one or several factors were changed in systematic way to see the effect of different structures.

Depth: The first two examples (dpth-2 and dpth-1) tested effects of depth. This was done by setting up a tree two rules deep and solving for the ME solution, giving the prior for dpth-2. The resulting probabilities for the intermediate nodes, B_1 and B_2, were then included as constraints on a rule-set which was just the top of the first set, giving the prior for dpth-1. Separate series of experiments were then run on each, giving average ζ performance over the top node, A.

Rule Strength and Bushiness: The second four examples were each just one rule. They tested of varying bushiness and of varying lower rule strength. The first case, bsh2-upr, just has the upper ruler strength for A given the conjunction of B_1 and B_2. We add a lower rule strength in bsh2-u&l, a third antecedent, B_3, in case bsh3-upr, and both the lower rule strength and third antecedent in case bsh3-u&l. Thus, the four cases form a two by two matrix of options.

Shared antecedents: The third set of six examples tested some simple correlations. Cases 2cnc-2rls-neg and 2cnc-2rls-pos had two consequents, A_1 and A_2, each referred to by its own rule. A_1 depended on B_1 and B_2, while A_2 depended on B_2 and B_3, so the rules shared an antecedent. In case 2cnc-2rls-pos, this antecedent was shared directly, creating positive correlation between A_1 and A_2. In 2cnc-2rls-neg, the antecedent has its negation used in the second rule, creating a negative correlation between A_1 and A_2. In cases 1cnc-2rls-neg and 1cnc-2rls-pos, use the same two rules to make conclusions about one shared consequent, A. Similarly to the first two cases, the two rules in 1cnc-2rls-pos share the same antecedent, and so the satisfaction of their compound antecedent terms is positively correlated, while in case 1cnc-2rls-neg, the negation is shared, and so the satisfaction is negatively correlated. Cases 1cnc-2lyrs-neg and 1cnc-2lyrs-pos are just like 2cnc-2rls-neg and 2cnc-2rls-pos, respectively, except that another rule has been added, so that the final conclusion is separated by one more layer of rules from the source of correlation.

One should note that 1cnc-2rls-neg, 1cnc-2rls-pos, 1cnc-2lyrs-neg, and 1cnc-2lyrs-pos all contain undirected cycles, and hence cannot be perfectly modeled by the CI system's assumptions.

Shared Conclusions: The fourth set of two examples (cnd-ind-2 and cnd-ind-3) test the effect of varying bushiness in cases where several rules bear on one consequent. As derived in an appendix to [7], in the ME prior conditional independence holds exactly for such cases.

Rule Strength, Bushiness, and Correlated Inputs: The fifth set of examples (bsh2-upr-pos bsh2-upr-neg bsh2-u&l-pos bsh2-u&l-neg bsh3-upr-pos bsh3-upr-neg bsh3-u&l-pos bsh3-u&l-neg) test the effects of varying bushiness, lower rule strength, and correlation of inputs. They reproduce the two-by-two experimental design of the second set of of examples, but add the extra factor of explicitly introducing either the minimum or maximum possible correlation of the antecedents, giving a two-by-two-by-two design.

Extreme Correlations of Inputs: The sixth set of four examples test the effects of varying correlation of consequents and of rules. In cases 2cnc-min-shr-ruls-pos 2cnc-max-shr-ruls-pos, the rules share an antecedent, and so instances of their being satisfied are positively correlated; in cases 2cnc-min-shr-ruls-neg 2cnc-max-shr-ruls-neg, negatively. In cases 2cnc-min-shr-ruls-pos and 2cnc-min-shr-ruls-neg, the consequents have the minimum possible overlap; in cases 2cnc-max-shr-ruls-pos and 2cnc-max-shr-ruls-neg, the maximum possible. Hence, we again have a two-by-two design.

6. Best and Worst Results for MYC and TSM

The best and worst performances for MYC are listed in table 6.1; some relevant sensitivities are pictured in figure 6.2.

ζ	Casename	Casenumber
0.998	1cnc − 2lyrs − neg	3.5
0.996	bsh2 − upr − neg	5.1
0.994	bsh3 − upr − neg	5.2
0.799	cnd − ind − 3	4.2
0.788	bsh3 − u&l − pos	5.8
0.735	bsh2 − u&l − pos	5.7
0.517	cnd − ind − 2	4.1

Figure 6.1: Best and Worst MYCIN Results

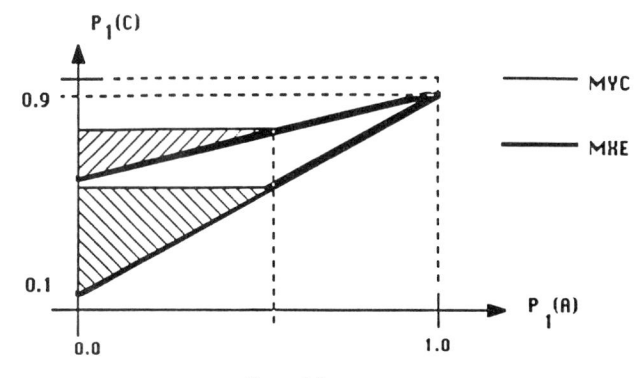

Figure 6.2

We can see that sensitivity to rule-strength should outweigh the sensitivity to antecedent correlations. The higher the upper rule strength, the better MYC should do The performance on cases where the lower rule strength was explicitly forced down (e.g. 5.8 and 5.7) confirms this. Similarly, bsh2-upr-neg and bsh3-upr-neg have no lower rule strength specified, which lets them drift higher, and MYC does quite well.

ζ	Casename	Casenumber
0.997	$cnd - ind - 2$	4.1
0.983	$2cnc - min - shr - ruls - neg$	6.2
0.981	$2cnc - min - shr - ruls - pos$	6.1
0.981	$bsh2 - u\&l$	2.2
0.972	$bsh3 - u\&l$	2.4
0.230	$bsh2 - upr - pos$	5.5
0.138	$bsh3 - upr$	2.3
0.128	$bsh3 - upr - neg$	5.2
0.011	$bsh3 - upr - pos$	5.6

Figure 6.3: Best and Worst Results for TSM

The TSM system does read the rule-strengths off the prior, hence the only effects on accuracy are those which pertain to the correlations of inputs. Note that most of the best cases were with only two antecedents rather than with three (as is typical of the worst cases). Recalling that TSM ignores all but one of the input items, this accords well with our expectation that it would do worse when ignoring 2/3 of the data than when only ignoring 1/2 of it.

Another way of looking at these results is suggested by the fact that TSM's worst four cases were all among MYC's best cases. Moreover, TSM's average performances on its four best and four worst cases are lower than the corresponding averages for MYC. This is because MYC essentially has "canceling errors". The problem appears when we get a mixture of confirming and disconfirming evidence. Because it responds to only one piece of data and ignores cancellation, TSM tends to over-react in one direction or the other when mixed data is present. However, MYC stays put at the prior value. In many cases, it is better to not react at all than to over-react in the wrong direction. This is an example of how fixing only one error (no sensitivity to disconfirming data), but not the other (using only one piece of data in Jeffrey's Rule) can actually worsen performance.

The following table lists the worst ζ-performance for each of the UIS's discussed here, and gives some information about robustness. Explaining the differing degrees of robustness provides a useful, extremely brief, summary of the relevant interactions and biases for each UIS.

CI	MYC	TSM
+.643	+.517	+.011

Figure 6.4: Worst performance for each UIS

Referring to the table, one can see that the UIS with the best worst-ζ was CI, suggesting that it is the most robust of those tested here. We hypothesize that this is simply because CI uses more parameters than do the other UIS's, and hence it has more degrees of freedom to "bend to fit the data" even in cases where its assumptions are unmet. For example, it can model antecedants' as having negative, zero, or positive correlation. In spite of having only one operation different, TSM performed worse than did MYC, reflecting the fact that it only corrects one of two canceling errors. In fact, of the six UIS's tested, these three were the best; the others all had average performance which was worse than random guessing (i.e. $\zeta < 0$) on at least cases.

7. Summary

Our theoretical predictions of bias are born out by numerical analysis performance. Thus, we have gained some insight into what the relative strengths of the effects are - suggesting that past efforts to improve and update MYCIN have concentrated on correcting relatively minor effects, while leaving the major ones unaddressed. Also, we have seen how some deleterious, or meritorious, conditions arise for subtle reasons, hence we have more clues to check for while trying to estimate how well a UIS will do in a given application. For Mycin and its variant, we found special situations where its performance was very good, but also situations where performance was worse than random guessing, or where data was interpreted as having the opposite of its true import. We have uncovered independence assumptions in MYC, inspite of the fact that eliminating such assumptions was one of the designers' goals. We have found that all three of these systems usually gave accurate results, and that the conditional independence assumptions gave the most robust results. Considerations of robustness might be a critical factor is selecting UIS's for a given application.

8. References

1. DeFinetti, B. *Theory of Probability*, Wiley, New York (1974)
2. Diaconis, P., Zabell, S. L. "Updating Subjective Probability", *Journal of the American Statistical Association*, December 1982.

3. Heckerman, D "Probabilistic Interpretations for MYCIN's Certainty Factors", *Uncertainty in Artificial Intelligence*, edited by Kanal and Lemmer.
4. Shortliffe, E. H., *Computer-Based Medical Consultations: MYCIN*, American Elsevier (1976)
5. Savage, L. J. *The Foundations of Statistics* John Wlley & Sons, New York (1954)
6. Shore, J. E., Johnson, R. W., "Am Axiomatic Derivation of the Maximum Entropy Principle" *IEEE Transactions on Information Theory*, January 1980.
7. Ben P. Wise, *An Experimental Comparison of Uncertain Inference Systems*. PhD Thesis, Carnegie-Mellon University (1986).

II

TOOLS

KNOWLEDGE ENGINEERING WITHIN A GENERALIZED BAYESIAN FRAMEWORK

Stephen W. Barth and Steven W. Norton*

PAR Government Systems Corporation
220 Seneca Turnpike
New Hartford, NY 13413

During the ongoing debate over the representation of uncertainty in Artificial Intelligence, Cheeseman, Lemmer, Pearl, and others have argued that probability theory, and in particular the Bayesian theory, should be used as the basis for the inference mechansims of Expert Systems dealing with uncertainty. In order to pursue the issue in a practical setting, sophisticated tools for knowledge engineering are needed that allow flexible and understandable interaction with the underlying knowledge representation schemes. This paper describes a Generalized Bayesian framework for building expert systems which function in uncertain domains, using algorithms proposed by Lemmer. It is neither rule-based nor frame-based, and requires a new system of knowledge engineering tools. The framework we describe provides a knowledge-based system architecture with an inference engine, explanation capability, and a unique aid for building consistent knowledge bases.

1. INTRODUCTION

Recent arguments have been made for the use of Bayesian inferencing techniques for expert systems dealing with uncertainty [1] [2] [3] [4]. Some expert system (ES) applications involving reasoning under uncertainty may best be handled by mechanisms that are as purely Bayesian as possible. This paper describes a Generalized Bayesian framework for constructing expert systems using networks of probability distributions, based on Lemmer's approach to Generalized Bayesian Inference (GBI) [5] [6] [7].

The knowledge representation scheme for our GBI framework consists of a network of intersecting sets of events, and their associated probability distributions. The GBI Framework contains the key ingredients of a classic knowledge-based system architecture: an inference engine with an explanation capability, and a tool for creating, editing, and maintaining consistency in the knowledge base. These individual components, however, are very different from those of rule-based probabilistic systems such as PROSPECTOR [8]. The purpose of this paper is to describe the GBI framework for building expert systems, its tools for estimating consistent prior probability distributions (the CMD Estimation Aid), and its facilities supporting the utilization and incremental development of knowledge bases, the

---

* Steven W. Norton is now employed at Siemens RTL, 105 College Rd. East, Princeton, NJ 08540

Updating Mechanism and Explanation Facility. The description of the Explanation Facility will be ommitted here, since it is described in detail in [9] in this volume.

The system described in this paper was developed for application to a problem of real-time discrimination of object types from sensor information. The original approach to this problem involved using a Markov model with a sequence of discriminant tests to classify objects. This approach had several difficulties. Order dependancies among the tests made it hard to tune the system for accurate classifications. Heuristic estimates of probabilities incorporated into state transition matrices caused instabilities in the decision process. In general, the original approach lacked a framework for understanding the results from system test and evaluation and using those results for improving system performance. A knowledge-based approach to the problem was taken to alleviate these problems. The Generalized Bayesian Framework was developed to provide the tool for knowledge-based handling of the rich environment of probabilistic information available for the problem.

Unfortunately the details of the problem domain are classified. Therefore, in this paper, we will illustrate knowledge representation in the system with a small knowledge base for predicting the weather in Upstate New York; in particular, providing expert estimates of the probability of precipitation. This toy problem example has a similar diagnostic character to the real problem: the goal is to infer the correct identification or prediction from observed characteristics or measurable quantities. The advice provided by the system, or an expert, for both problem domains, always takes the form of a probabilistic recommendation, because of the uncertainty of the data and its interpretation.

2. KNOWLEDGE ENGINEERING WITHIN THE GENERALIZED BAYESIAN FRAMEWORK

GBI is a tool for building expert systems to solve Bayesian hierarchical inferencing problems. The initial phases of knowledge engineering for an expert system using this framework proceed as in any other hierarchical inferencing problem [10]. Together with one or more domain experts, the knowledge engineer considers the expert thought process used in solving the problem at hand. A series of stages is sketched out which takes observable evidence, relates it to intermediate hypotheses, and uses these intermediate hypotheses to determine the validity of one or more goal variables. The problem variables (evidence, hypothesis, and goal variables) represent assertions of interest. Sets of these variables form the nodes in the network structure of a GBI knowledge base.

In a typical rule-based expert system framework, the knowledge engineer, in cooperation with one or more domain experts, specifies the relationships between the problem variables using rules. In GBI, the knowledge engineer groups together those variables for which some probabilistic constraints (correlation information) are known. These structures are called Local Event Groups by Konolige in an appendix to [8]. A LEG Network (LEG Net) is a collection of LEGs, some of which share common variables. The LEG Net structure arises naturally from the hierarchical problem organization.

The aim of our sample knowledge base is to combine information from many sources to match the weather predicting capability of local experts in Upstate New York. An initial LEG Net for this knowledge base is shown in Figure 1. Each LEG is indicated by a round edged box labeled with a name in bold type.The names of the variables

Knowledge Engineering within a Generalized Bayesian Framework 105

Kind-of-Precip
- Snow-Tomorrow, Rain-Tomorrow, No-Precip-Tomorrow
- Rain-Temp, Others-Precip, Change-to-Clear
- Snow-Temp, Folk-Precip

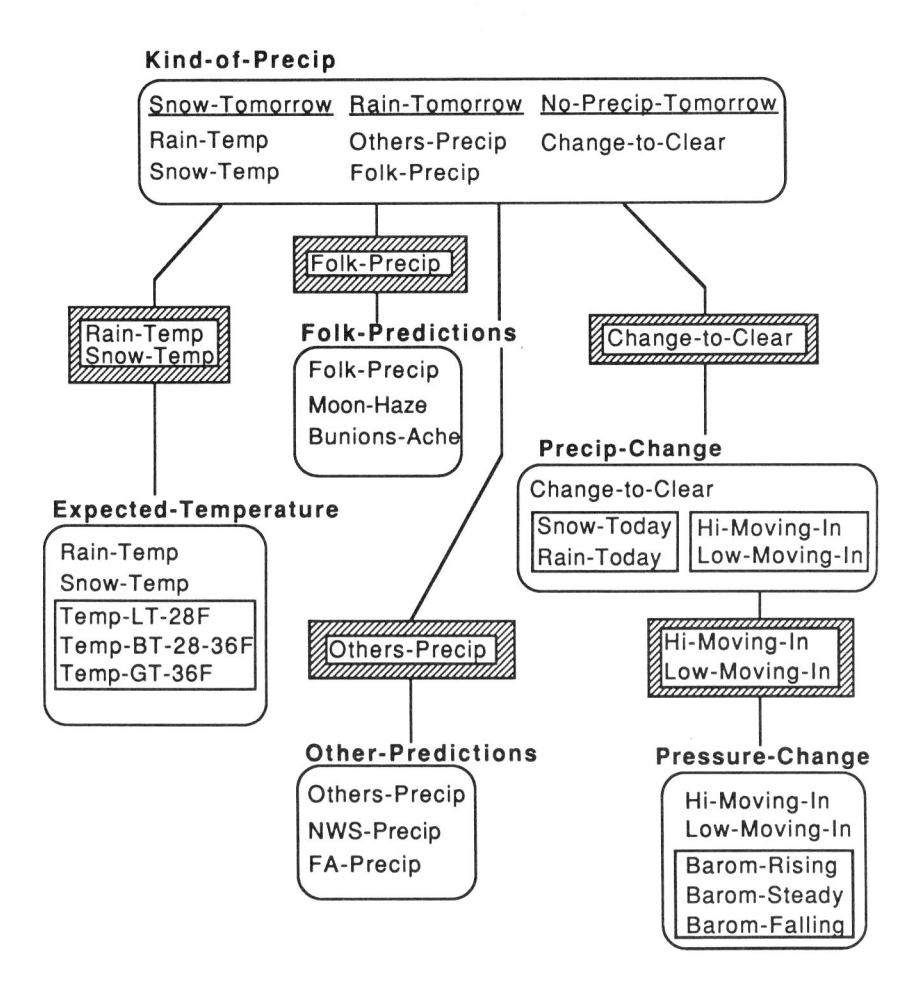

Folk-Predictions
- Folk-Precip
- Moon-Haze
- Bunions-Ache

Expected-Temperature
- Rain-Temp
- Snow-Temp
- Temp-LT-28F
- Temp-BT-28-36F
- Temp-GT-36F

Other-Predictions
- Others-Precip
- NWS-Precip
- FA-Precip

Precip-Change
- Change-to-Clear
- Snow-Today, Hi-Moving-In
- Rain-Today, Low-Moving-In

Pressure-Change
- Hi-Moving-In
- Low-Moving-In
- Barom-Rising
- Barom-Steady
- Barom-Falling

Figure 1. LEG Net for Precipitation Prediction

in the LEG are listed inside the box. Square shaded boxes show the variables in LEG intersections, and are attached to lines connecting the intersecting LEGs.

In our example the goal variables are Snow-Tomorrow, Rain-Tomorrow, and No-Precip-Tomorrow, in the Kind-of-Precip LEG, representing the events or assertions "it will rain tomorrow," "it will snow tomorrow," and "there will be no precipitation tomorrow." The advice to the user will be whatever values are attained by their posterior probabilities. The hypothesis variables Folk-Precip and Others-Precip represent the assertions that folk signs and other agencies should be considered in predicting precipitation for tomorrow. Examples of evidence variables are Moon-Haze and Bunions-Ache in the Folk-Precip LEG. Bunions-Ache will be true if Grandma has complained about her feet lately, and Moon-Haze will be true if haze appears around the moon. Other evidence variables in the example are mutually exclusive. In Figure 1 mutually exclusive events are shown boxed within their LEG. The evidence variables in this example represent events that either occur or do not occur and hence have a posterior probability of either 0.0 or 1.0. Such variables are called Binary Evidence Variables or BEVs.

If all the problem variables were grouped together, we could, in principle, establish a single underlying probability distribution. In practice that is quite infeasible since the storage requirements for probability distributions are exponential (2^n) in terms of the number of variables covered. Even for the simple weather example of Figure 1, over 8 million probabilities may be required for the underlying distribution.

Lemmer's GBI approach avoids this problem by using only Component Marginal Distributions (CMDs) for each LEG [6]. Each LEG in a LEG Net is associated with a CMD which covers just those variables in the LEG. Taken together, the CMDs for a LEG Net are an approximation to the underlying distribution. It is an approximation in the sense that no n-variate constraints are specified. If the largest LEG contains only $\underline{m}$ variables then the LEG Net can contain no constraints of order greater than $\underline{m}$. This approximation is reasonable since by breaking up the event space into LEGs we are specifying which constraints are important, and which are not. The size requirement for the network is the total of the sizes of the CMDs. The CMDs which are to be specified for the network in Figure 1 will have a total of 368 elements versus more than 8 million in the underlying distribution.

The Lemmer approach requires $2^m - 1$ constraints to fully specify an m-variate CMD. However, it allows the system to make use of information about mutually exclusive or implied events which may cause many of the constraints to be set to zero. The CMD Estimation Aid exploits this capability, so that in practice the knowledge engineer has many fewer probabilities to determine or estimate than the product of the number of LEGs and ($2^m - 1$). The number of constraints to be specified can be reduced still further by accepting minimum information default values for the higher order constraints, which are automatically generated. The examples in the next section illustrate these features of the system.

2.1. Specifying LEGs and CMDs

The CMD Estimation Aid of the GBI framework provides an interactive, menu-driven interface for defining events, LEGs, LEG Nets, and estimating CMDs. LEG intersections, through which probability is propagated, are managed automatically. In the following paragraphs we describe knowledge engineering within the GBI framework by walking through the features of the CMD Estimation Aid and illustrating the thought processes used during estimation in terms of the example in Figure 1.

One body of evidence weighed by our local expert is that of precipitation predictions from other sources. Our example considers two: the probability of precipitation predicted by the National Weather Service, NWS-Precip, and that predicted by the Farmers Almanac, FA-Precip. The heuristic that our local expert uses is that when either one of these sources predicts precipitation it increases the chances of rain or snow tomorrow. The hypothesis variable Others-Precip is introduced to indicate the probability of precipitation predicted from either of these two sources, and we form the LEG Other-Predictions to handle it and the two evidence variables. The constraints on the distribution for Other-Predictions are that if either or both of the variables NWS-Precip and FA-Precip are certain, then Others-Precip is certain. In addition, let us say we know, from statistical information, that the National Weather Service predicts precipitation 55% of the time, that the Farmers Almanac predicts precipitation 45% of the time, and that the two sources agree on the prediction 35% of the time.

Using the CMD Estimation aid requires the knowledge engineer to specify the constraints on a LEG in a canonical order, to support efficiency in the algorithm for constructing the distribution; however, the knowledge engineer has the freedom to select the style of constraints by choosing the order of variables for consideration and the form of the constraint that is most easily understood or calculated, either a joint or conditional probability. (The details of the CMD estimation algorithms are described in [5] and [11].) In the LEG Other-Predictions we chose the constraints with a diagnostic "style" in mind; since we wanted to specify the conditional probabilities of the hypothesis variable given the evidence variables as symptoms. To accomplish this we proceed by specifying the marginal probabilities for FA-Precip and NWS-Precip first, 0.45 and 0.55, respectively. The system prompts next for either the conditional of FA-Precip given NWS-Precip, or the marginal joint probability of FA-Precip and NWS-Precip. The latter we know to be 0.35. Now, we must specify the marginal probability for the hypothesis variable Others-Precip. A simple calculation with a Venn diagram shows that it must be 0.65. From here on out the system prompts us for constraints of either Others-Precip conditioned on the evidence variables, or the related joint probabilities. The former is easiest to specify, since P(Others-Precip | FA-Precip), P(Others -Precip| NWS-Precip), and P(Others-Precip | FA-Precip, NWS-Precip) are all 1.0. Figure 2 shows the constraints in the canonical order and the resulting distribution for the Other-Predictions LEG. The bit patterns in the left column under CMD indicate the joint events in the distribution and the right column holds their probabilities.

```
       Bit 0    F    FA-Precip
       Bit 1    N    NWS-Precip
       Bit 2    P    Others-Precip

       Constraints                CMD
                             000    0.35
       Pr(F)        0.45    001    0.00
       Pr(N)        0.55    010    0.00
       Pr(N&F)      0.35    011    0.00
       Pr(P)        0.65    100    0.00
       Pr(P|F)      1.00    101    0.10
       Pr(P|N)      1.00    110    0.20
       Pr(P|N&F)    1.00    111    0.35
```

Figure 2. Constraint Set for Other-Predicitons

As another example, consider the LEG Folk-Predictions. Here, the knowledge engineer wants to weigh together the results from two evidence variables, Bunions-Ache, and Moon-Haze. The former we estimate to occur about 45% of the time, the latter about 65%, and that both events happen together about 30% of the time. The hypothesis variable Folk-Precip represents the belief we have that the folk signs indicate rain, which we estimate at 0.55; i.e. they are slightly predisposed to predict rain. If there's haze around the moon, however, we're 60% sure that a folksy prediction is being made. If Grandma is complaining about her feet, we're 85% sure. And if both of these events occur then it's 99% certain that folk signs are telling us that precipitation will occur. The constraints just described are summarized in Figure 3. The effect of knowing that the folk signs indicate rain on our actual prediction is

Bit 0 M	Moon-Haze	
Bit 1 G	Bunions-Ache	
Bit 2 P	Folk-Precip	

Constraints			CMD
		000	0.1255
Pr(M)	0.65	001	0.2570
Pr(G)	0.45	010	0.0645
Pr(G&M)	0.30	011	0.0030
Pr(P)	0.55	100	0.0745
Pr(P|M)	0.60	101	0.0930
Pr(P|G)	0.85	110	0.0855
Pr(P|G&M)	0.99	111	0.2970

Figure 3. Constraint Set for Folk-Predictions

taken account of in the constraints on the goal leg between Folk-Precip and the other variables.

2.2 Expediting CMD Estimation

The examples above show how a simple probabilistic OR relationship and weighing of beliefs can be specified using the CMD Estimation Aid. Generally, however, the knowledge engineer needs to make use of shortcut facilities that the CMD estimation aid provides. These are: allowing minimum information values as defaults for constraint probabilities, and taking advantage of "forbidden" and "cutoff" relationships among events. Whenever the CMD Estimation Aid prompts the user to specify a constraint it offers a range of values possible for the constraint that is consistent with the previously specified constraints. Within this range the value offered as a default for the constraint is the probability that satisfies a minimum information condition on the distribution under construction [11]. In the example above the default value for the constraint P(FA-Precip & NWS-Precip) was 0.2475, which represents independence of the two variables. For small LEGs of only three or four variables, or larger ones that are highly constrained by cutoff or forbidden relationships, such default values are not so important except as a convenient function of the user interface. In other cases the ability to take default values for constraints that are needed to determine the distribution, but for which values are not known or cannot be estimated easily, is a critical feature. For example in the goal LEG Kind-Of-Precip, the user may not feel comfortable estimating constraints on more than four variables, such as P(Rain-Temp, Snow-Temp, Others-Precip, Folk-Precip), or any conditional form of these four variables, though it is not desirable to decompose Kind-Of-Precip into smaller LEGs. The mechanism for default values allows the user to ignore constraints above a certain order, or specify only those for which some justification is available, taking defaults for the rest.

The CMD Estimation Aid also allows the user to specify "forbidden" and "cutoff" relationships between variables that automatically limit the number of constraints required to specify the distribution. Forbidden relationships indicate that the occurrence of two variables in a joint event is impossible, as is the case for mutually exclusive events. In the LEG Expected-Temperature the three evidence variables Temp-LT-28F, Temp-BT-28-36F, and Temp-GT-36F are mutually exclusive (and collectively exhaustive) and so are given the forbidden relationship. As a result, the knowledge engineer needs to specify only 12 constraints on joint events, instead of 26, and, if defaults are taken for constraints on more than two variables, then only six constraint probabilities need to be specified.

Cutoff relationships between variables indicate that one variable cannot occur in a joint event unless another does, in an implication relation. For example, in the Other-Predictions LEG, we might have specified that NWS-Precip only occurs if FA-Precip occurs. This means that joint events in which NWS-Precip occurs, but FA-Precip does not occur, have probability 0.0. Thus the number of constraints required to specify the distribution is reduced.

The knowledge engineer can make use of all of these mechanisms to reflect the expertise being modeled, and to reduce the amount of information needed to define the knowledge base. As might be expected, our experience has been that cutoff and forbidden relationships nearly always exist among evidence variables but are harder to find in LEGs where hypothesis variables have been introduced to represent a concept or summarize an effect. In either case, but especially the latter, the default values mechanism makes it easy to specify what low order constraints are known for a distribution, while letting the system make reasonable assumptions for the higher order constraints that the expert or knowledge engineer may be unable to specify.

3. GENERALIZED BAYESIAN INFERENCE

Once prior CMDs for each LEG have been estimated by the knowledge engineer using the CMD Estimation Aid, posterior CMDs are calculated by the GBI Updating mechanism as evidence is gathered; i.e. as the posterior probabilities of the evidence variables are determined from observable data. Summing out the marginal probability of a LEG variable from a posterior CMD provides the advice about the occurrence of the event represented by that variable, based on the evidence gathered so far. As more evidence is gathered, a new posterior CMD may be calculated for a LEG, and new marginal probabilities determined for the LEG variables. When the posterior probabilities for all evidence variables have been determined the marginal probabilities of the goal variables represent the final advice of the system.

The GBI Updating rule has been formally described in [6] and [7]. Inferences are propagated through the CMDs over LEG intersections. If $\underline{A}$ and $\underline{B}$ are two intersecting LEGs, the formula for updating the CMD of $\underline{A}$ after a new posterior CMD for $\underline{B}$ has been determined is:

$$\Pr'(A,a) = \Pr(A,a) * \frac{\sum_{\substack{b \subseteq B \\ a \cap I = b \cap I}} \Pr'(B,b)}{\sum_{\substack{b \subseteq B \\ a \cap I = b \cap I}} \Pr(B,b)} \quad \text{where } I = A \cap B$$

where a is a subset of the variables in A, and P(A,a) represents the prior probability for the joint event in which the variables of a occur and the other variables of A do not. (As a ranges over the subsets of A, P(A,a) ranges over the prior probabilities of the joint events in A's CMD). Similarly, P'(A,a) represents the posterior probability of the joint event in which the variables of a occur and the other variables of A do not.

It is important to realize that P(A,a) represents probabilities in the most recent posterior that was determined for A. Initially P(A,a) has the value that was assigned during the knowledge engineering phase with the CMD Estimation Aid, but as evidence is collected and udating proceeds, several new CMDs may be calculated for A. Each time a new CMD needs to be calculated the P(A,a) values in the formula are the ones from the last update to the CMD, not the *a priori* distrbution.

Viewed as a sequential process, the updating formula means that for each joint event e in A (P(e) = P(A,a) for some a) we

1. Determine the joint event i in the LEG intersection of A and B which is a component of e.
2. Sum out from the previous CMD of B to obtain the prior probability of i. This is the denominator of the fraction given in the formula.
3. Sum out from the new CMD of B to obtain the new posterior marginal probability of i. This is the numerator of the fraction in the formula.
4. Multiply P(e) by the quotient of the values obtained in 2 and 3 above to obtain its posterior P'(e).

As an example of the Updating mechanism consider an update of the CMD of the goal LEG Kind-of-Precip from the evidence LEG Folk-Predictions in Figure 1. Figure 4 shows the transformations of the CMDs for part of the Kind-of-Precip LEG, and the entire Folk-Predictions and Other-Precip- Predictions LEGs, for the situation in which the events Bunions-Ache, NWS-Precip, and FA-Precip occur.

After it is determined (through querying the user or accessing a data base) that the event Bunions-Ache occurs and that Moon-Haze does not occur, the posterior distribution of Folk-Predictions is calculated by applying the GBI Updating rule with the marginal distribution of the two evidence events as the updating distribution. In this instance, the GBI Updating rule is equivalent to Bayes' Rule applied to the CMD of Folk-Predictions, since the conditioning events are certain [6]. In the next step, the new CMD for the intersection of Folk-Predictions and Kind-of-Precip is calculated by summing out over the CMD of Folk-Predictions. Now, the CMD of Kind-of-Precip is calculated using the GBI Updating rule. For example, the prior probability of the joint event that Snow-Tomorrow, Folk-Precip, Others-Precip, and Snow-Temp occurred, but No-Precip-Tomorrow, Rain-Tomorrow, and Rain-Temp did not occur, in the Kind-of-Precip LEG, is multiplied by the quotient of the posterior and prior probabilities for the event Folk-Precip in the LEG intersection. (0.160 = 0.154 * 0.570 / 0.550). Next the CMD of Other-Predictions is updated using the CMD for

Knowledge Engineering within a Generalized Bayesian Framework

Kind-Of-Precip

No-Precip-Tomorrow	Rain-Tomorrow	Snow-Tomorrow	Folk-Precip	Others-Precip	Rain-Temp	Snow-Temp	Prior	0	1
0	0	1	0	1	1	0	0.001	0.001	0.002
0	0	1	1	1	0	1	0.154	0.160	0.245
0	1	0	1	1	0	0	0.008	0.009	0.013
0	1	0	1	1	1	0	0.059	0.062	0.094
1	0	0	0	1	0	1	0.071	0.068	0.105
1	0	0	1	0	0	1	0.036	0.037	0.0

Folk-Precip

	Prior	0	1
0	0.450	0.430	0.366
1	0.550	0.550	0.634

Σ

Snow-Tomorrow

	Prior	0	1
0	0.400	0.596	0.572
1	0.600	0.404	0.428

Others-Precip

	Prior	0	1
0	0.350	0.347	0.0
1	0.650	0.653	1.000

Folk-Predictions

Folk-Precip	Bunions-Ache	Moon-Haze	Prior	0	1
0	0	0	0.126	0.0	0.0
0	0	1	0.257	0.0	0.0
0	1	0	0.065	0.430	0.366
0	1	1	0.003	0.0	0.0
1	0	0	0.075	0.0	0.0
1	0	1	0.093	0.0	0.0
1	1	0	0.086	0.570	0.634
1	1	1	0.297	0.0	0.0

Other-Predictions

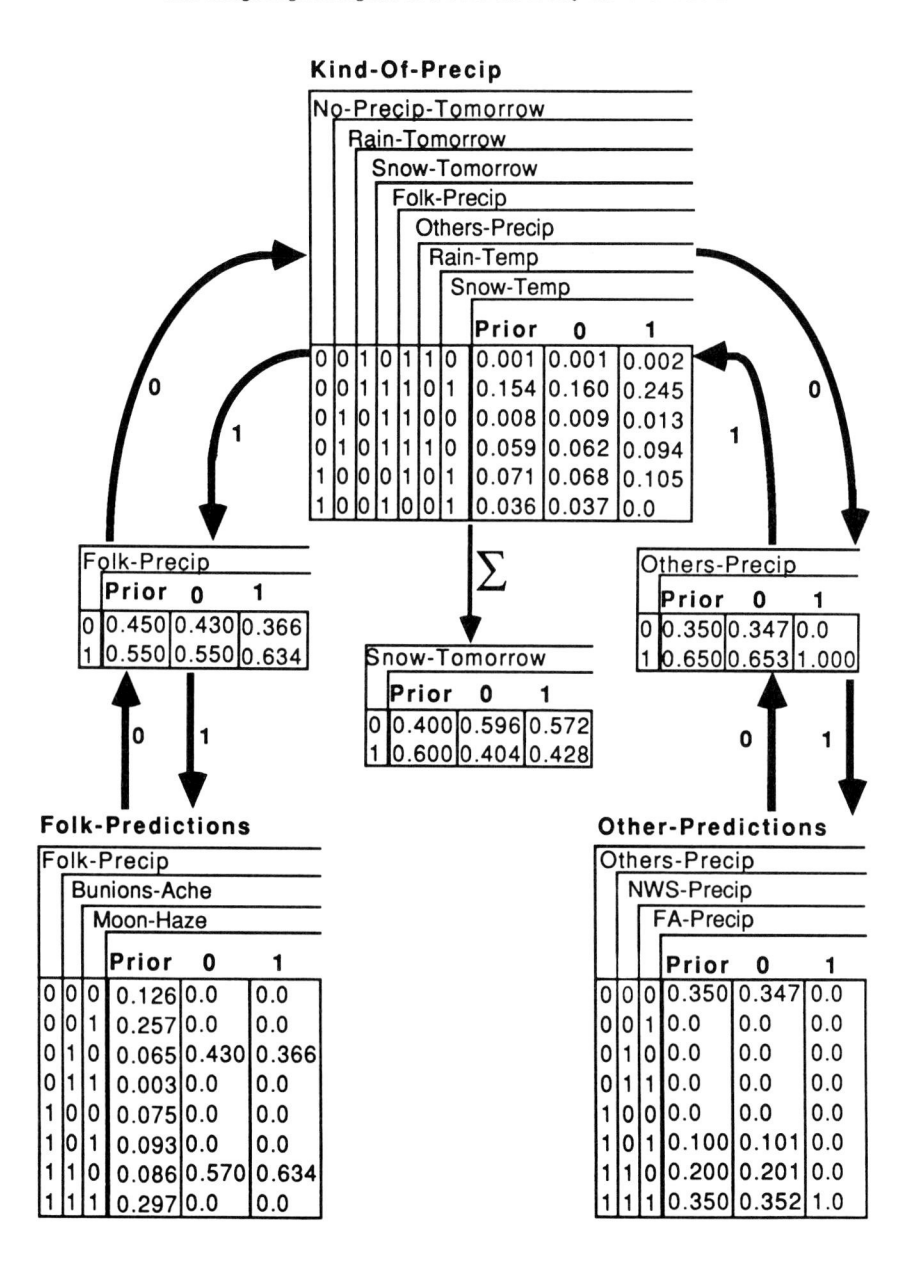

Others-Precip	NWS-Precip	FA-Precip	Prior	0	1
0	0	0	0.350	0.347	0.0
0	0	1	0.0	0.0	0.0
0	1	0	0.0	0.0	0.0
0	1	1	0.0	0.0	0.0
1	0	0	0.0	0.0	0.0
1	0	1	0.100	0.101	0.0
1	1	0	0.200	0.201	0.0
1	1	1	0.350	0.352	1.0

Figure 4. Example of the GBI Updating Mechanism

the LEG intersection between Kind- of-Precip and Others-Predictions. The posterior CMD for the LEG intersection is calculated by summing out from the new posterior CMD for Kind-of-Precip to obtain the probabilities of Others-Precip and not Others-Precip. The GBI Updating rule is then used to calculate the new posterior CMD for the Other-Predictions LEG. Posterior CMDs for the other LEGs would also be calculated from the effects of the update to Folk-Predictions so that consistent CMDs are maintained throughout the network after the completion of each update.

The fact that propagation of probability occurs throughout the LEG Net is an important difference between the the GBI Updating rule and the mechanisms used in systems like MYCIN [12] and PROSPECTOR. In PROSPECTOR for example, probability is only propagated from evidence to goal variables, and the prior probabilities for unexamined evidence remain unmodified. In the GBI mechanism consistent probability distributions are maintained: summing out the marginal probability for a variable in a LEG intersection from either CMD that it belongs to yields the same value. A practical advantage of the GBI mechanism is that it allows the system to look for the evidence that is next most or least likely to occur, determined from the marginal probabilities of evidence variables summed out from their most recent posterior CMD. Whether such evidence does or does not in fact occur in a given situation can be used to control the inference mechanism; e.g. by computing expected costs and benefits of evidence tests.

4. GENERALIZED BAYESIAN EXPLANATION

As with any Expert System knowledge representation scheme, the GBI representation offers a means of explaining inferences which provides a knowledge engineer with the information needed to tune the knowledge base. A trace of the inference mechanism is available during a consultation session, when only partial results are available, or after the system has exhausted all evidence, as a post-mortem explanation. The GBI Explanation Mechanism is described in "An Explanation Mechanism for Bayesian Inferencing Systems" [9] appearing elsewhere in these proceedings.

5. FUTURE WORK

Although our GBI framework has been successfully applied to a real problem other than the example discussed here, much work remains to develop an industrial strength Expert System building tool. The issues we are currently concerned with are:

1. Mining CMDs for richer explanations of Updating Mechanism results. Much more useful information on expected and unexpected relationships between variables can be presented to the knowledge engineer to aid in tuning the knowledge base. Multi-variate relationships and the effects of initial prior constraints can be easily obtained. A better man-machine interface can be developed with graphics for use of the system in consultation mode.

2. Allowing distributions over evidence variables as inputs during Updating. Uncertain marginal probabilities for evidence variables, or, in cases where all possible data has been collected, for joint evidence events, define posterior CMDs for evidence LEGs other than those currently allowed in which some joint event must have unit probability.

3. Exploiting parallelism. The GBI framework has proven quite efficient for the relatively small problems to which it has been applied. However, the GBI Updating rule has characteristics which would allow fast implementations for larger knowledge bases.

4. Providing more CMD Estimation Aid facilities. Ways of easily backtracking through the canonical constraints and and other estimation shortcuts can be provided. A graphic presentation of the low order constraints, and a separate explanation mechanism for the CMD estimation process are also desirable.

6. SUMMARY

Our GBI framework provides a knowledge-based system architecture for a Generalized Bayesian knowledge representation and inferencing technique. The CMD Estimation Aid provides the needed knowledge engineering tool for estimating distributions of prior probabilities over sets of events. The Updating Mechanism provides an inference engine for using the knowledge base to obtain advice in the form of marginal probabilities associated with goal variables. An explanation facility provides feedback to allow the knowledge engineer to refine the knowledge base.

Although the current system is in the embryonic stage, it has been successfully applied to develop a prototype knowledge base for discriminating types of objects from real time sensor data. With further development we feel that the GBI framework will allow knowledge engineers and application users to take advantage of the richness of the Bayesian representation for uncertain reasoning.

REFERENCES

[1] Charniak, "The Bayesian Basis of Common Sense Medical Diagnosis", Proceedings of the National Conference on Artificial Intelligence 1983, (AAAI-83). pp 70-73.

[2] Cheeseman, "In Defense of Probability," Proceedings of the Ninth International Conference on Artificial Intelligence, August 1985.

[3] Pearl, "Reverend Bayes on Inference Engines: A Distributed Hierarchical Approach," Proceedings of the National Conference on Artificial Intelligence, 1982, (AAAI-82). pp 133-136.

4] Yeh, "PLY: A System of Plausibility Inference with a Probabilistic Basis," Master's Thesis, Massachusetts Institute of Technology, June 1983.

[5] Lemmer, "Algorithms for Incompletely Specified Distributions in a Generalized Graph Model for Medical Diagnosis", PhD Thesis, Dept. of Computer Science, University of Maryland, 1976.

[6] Lemmer, "Generalized Bayesian Updating of Incompletely Specified Distributions," Large Scale Systems 5, Elsevier Science Publishers, 1983.

[7] Lemmer and Barth, "Efficient Minimum Information Updating for Bayesian Inferencing in Expert Systems," Proceedings of the National Conference on Artificial Intelligence 1982, (AAAI-82). pp 424-427.

[8] Duda, Hart, Konolige, and Reboh, "A Computer Based Consultant for Mineral Exploration", Appendix D, Final Report for SRI Project 6415, Menlo Park, CA, SRI International, 1979.

[9] Norton, "An Explanation Mechanism for Bayesian Inferencing Systems," in this volume.

[10] Hayes-Roth, Waterman, and Lenat (ed.), Building Expert Systems, Addison-Wesley Publishing Co., 1983.

[11] Lemmer and Norton, "Eliciting Probabilities," submitted for publication in 1986, copies available from the author upon request.

[12] Buchanan, and Shortliffe, Rule-Based Expert Systems, Addison-Wesley Publishing Co., 1984.

LEARNING TO PREDICT: AN INDUCTIVE APPROACH

Kaihu Chen

Artificial Intelligence Laboratory
Department of Computer Science
University of Illinois at Urbana-Champaign[*]

The ability to predict the future in a given domain can be acquired by discovering empirically from experience certain temporal patterns that tend to repeat unerringly. Previous works in time series analysis allow one to make *quantitative predictions* on the likely values of certain linear variables. Since certain types of knowledge are better expressed in symbolic forms, making *qualitative predictions* based on symbolic representations require a different approach. A domain independent methodology called TIM (Time-based Inductive Machine) for discovering potentially uncertain temporal patterns from real time observations using the technique of inductive inference is described here.

1. INTRODUCTION

An important class of human concepts involves the notion of time, and based on which the notion of causality. Causal knowledge allows one to predict consequences from causes, and diagnose problems from symptoms. Although the notion of time is indispensable in many domains, many previous AI systems conveniently simplify their temporal representations to disallow important temporal concepts that are prevalent in real world problem, such as time intervals, transient states, and monotonously changing states. A domain independent methodology called TIM (*Time-based Inductive Machine*) is described here, for learning incrementally from examples those concepts that are described as temporal processes occurring in real time. An example of such a temporal process is the history of a patient that suffered from a particular disease. The history may contain time-related information such as the time and durations of treatments, and the time and duration of the measurements of vital signs.

The problem of discovering temporal patterns from observations can be viewed as a problem in concept acquisition [Michalski, 1983], where the event to be predicted can be viewed as a class designator, and the "causes" to be discovered as the hypotheses for the class. Under this construct, the "causes" of the event to be predicted can be discovered by the application of generalization and specialization operators to partial hypotheses in an orderly way. Several important issues that decides the viability of the methodology in real world applications are addressed here:

- *Incremental learning.* The introduction of temporal information into the representation language greatly increases the complexity of the problem. It is hardly affordable if a inductive program has to learn the concept from scratch whenever a new set of data become available.

- *Learning uncertain concepts.* Real world concepts tend to be uncertain for many reasons. The uncertainty can be caused by erroneous data, missing information, or simply because the concepts are *fuzzy* in nature (e.g. there is no clear cut boundary between the concept *tall* and the concept *short*). Since perfect hypotheses may not exist or are too costly to find, the utility of an inductive program in real world domains thus is partially decided by the program's capacity to discover less than perfect hypotheses.

---

[*] This work was supported in part by the National Science Foundation under grant DCR-84-06801, the Office of Naval Research under grant N00014-82-K-0186, and the Defense Advanced Research Project Agency under grant N00014-K-85-0878.

An alternative approach to deciphering the temporal patterns hidden in raw data is typified by the time series analysis [Box & Jenkins, 1976]. The inductive approach differs from time series analysis in several important ways:
- Temporal patterns (or causal relationships) are derived through the technique of symbolic inductive generalization instead of numerical methods.
- Relations between variables are characterized in terms of symbolic relations instead of bindings in the form of equations.
- A temporal process is described as objects, attributes of objects, relations between objects, and the change or sustenance of attributes/relations of objects in time.
- Time is viewed as a variable with complex structures rather then just a real variable. For example, the absolute time point at 3 p.m., February 3, 1987, may have addition properties such as "daytime", "Tuesday", etc.
- The program uses a set of background knowledge that contains constructive induction rules that generate new attributes not present in the initial data. Background knowledge may also include models of the world, which may aid the inductive algorithm in generating plausible hypotheses.

In the context of *concept acquisition*, as defined in [Michalski, 1983], an example (or observation) of a *concept* is described as an implicative rule

$$d(A) \rightarrow K(A) \qquad (1)$$

which states that "an object A that is described as $d(A)$, is known to belong to class $K(A)$". In light of this definition, *concept acquisition* can be defined as the problem of generating generalized concept descriptions from examples (and possibly also counter examples) of the concept. That is, given a set of observational statements F_i of class K, where each F_i is of the form shown in (1), discovers a hypothesis (or rule) H of the form:

$$\forall x, D(x) \rightarrow K(x)$$

such that for all observed examples F_i of class K,

$$H \rhd F_i$$

where $\rhd$ means *more general than* (and $\lhd$ means *more special than*). Since the inductive assertion H represents a hypothesized description about the class K, it is also sometimes called a *hypothesis*. H is considered to be *more general than* F_i if H either tautologically implies F_i, or H weakly implies F_i with a given set of background knowledge. For example, it can be asserted that

$$\{A \ \& \ B \rightarrow K\} \ \lhd \ \{A \rightarrow K\}$$

because $A \rightarrow K$ tautologically implies $A \ \& \ B \rightarrow K$; it can also be asserted that

$$\{A > 5 \rightarrow K\} \ \rhd \ \{A = 8 \rightarrow K\}$$

because $A > 5 \rightarrow K$ implies $A = 8 \rightarrow K$, provided that the axioms concerning integer numbers (assuming that A is an integer) are given.

Constructing inductive assertions from observational statements involves the transformation of the observational statement (training instances) using a set of refinement operators. A refinement operator is either a specialization operator or a generalization operator. When applied to an inductive assertion or observational statment, a generalization/specialization operator transforms it into a more general/special statement. That is, given generalization/specialization operators G/S and a rule R, the transformed rule $G(R)$ or $S(R)$ has the following relations with R:

$$G(R) \rhd R$$
$$S(R) \lhd R$$

A rule R_1 is said to *cover* another rule R_2 if R_1 is more general than R_2.

1.1. The Acquisition of Temporal Concepts

The observation of a temporal process, called an *episode*, is a collection (conjunction) of temporal expressions (called *events*) that represents a chronological record of a collection of objects. An event can be expressed using realization operator R for *temporal realization*. The expression $R_t(P)$ indicates the assertion P is realized (i.e. has boolean value *true*) at time t [Rescher and Urquhart, 1971]. The classification of an episode is based on the occurrence of a particular event, called *classifying event*. A training instance to the inductive engine is given as an episode and its corresponding classification in the following form:

$$R_{t_1}(event_1) \ \& \ R_{t_2}(event_2) \ \& \ ..R_{t_n}(event_n) \rightarrow R_{t_k}(K)$$

which states that an episode, described as a collection of events $event_i$, each occurring at t_i, is observed to have led to the occurrence of the classifying event K at a later time t_k.

Given training episodes, the goal of TIM is to discover a generalized temporal description that will predict the occurrence of K with a certain precision. The hypothesis to be found can be formally expressed as follows:

$$\forall t_1, t_2, \cdots H \rightarrow R_{f(t_1, t_2, \ldots)}(K) \qquad (2)$$

where H is a generalized description of the training episodes, t_i are temporal variables appeared in H, and $f(t_1, t_2, ...)$ indicates the temporal relations between the classifying event K and the generalized events in H. In other words, if H is satisfied by certain observation, then it is expected that K will realize at the time as indicated by the temporal relation f.

Given any set of refinement operators that generates reasonably expressive hypotheses, the number of possible hypotheses is likely to be astronomical. Although a given representation language may permit various forms of hypotheses, only a small subset of them are likely to be useful. It is assumed here that given a set of episodes $\{E_i\}$ of class K, the goal of the inductive engine is to find a generalization of $\{E_i\}$, G_E, such that G_E is temporally related to K. In other words, a temporal variable that appeared in G_E must be directly or indirectly related to the temporal variables in the classifier K. Restricting rules to the form given in (2) allows the inductive engine to concentrate only on rules that may represent causality or temporal patterns.

Assumption of causality: TIM assumes that there exist certain temporal relations between the events in a given episode E, and the classifying event of E.

This assumption greatly reduces the size of the search space while permitting useful rules that describe likely causal relations or temporal patterns to be discovered.

Discovering the plausible causes of a given event K involves two parts: hypothesizing an event (or a set of events) that may be the cause, and hypothesizing the temporal relations between these events and K. For example, given two observed events $R_{T_1}(P)$ and $R_{T_2}(K)$, if we are to hypothesize that P is the cause of K, then the observed events can be turned into the following rule:

$$\forall t, R_t(P) \rightarrow R_{t+T_2-T_1}(K)$$

which states that "whenever P is observed, then K will realize in T_2-T_1 time units". In general, the goal of the inductive engine is to find a rule of the form as given in (1) that will explain all (or most) of the observed events. This is called a *causal template*. Subsequent refinements of a rule are achieved by either refining the antecedent of the rule, as well as by refining the function f that represents the temporal relations between causes and effects. The causal template given here serves two important functions: it excludes complex temporal patterns (that cannot be represented with the template given above) from consideration by TIM, thus reduce the problem to a manageable magnitude; it also represents a useful class of knowledge that is abundant in human concepts, thus the automation in the acquisition of such knowledge can be beneficial.

Although theoretically f can be arbitrary function, it is obviously unrealistic to expect a program to be able discover arbitrary f with limited computing resources. A simplifying assumption is thus made to limit f to certain simple types.

> *Assumption*: TIM assumes that the function f, which expresses the temporal relations between causes and effects, is limited to simple symbolic or arithmetic relations.

Here the relationships permitted between two temporal variables are limited to the following:

> t_1 REL t_2, where REL is one of $\{=, \neq, >, <, \leq, \geq\}$; or
> $t_1 = t_2$ A−REL $linear-range$, where A−REL is one of $\{+, -\}$.

The following are examples of temporal patterns that TIM cannot/can find.

> *Example 1*: TIM cannot discover rules of the form $\forall t, \{R_t(P) \rightarrow R_{2 \cdot t}(K)\}$ because the antecedent of the rule and the classifying event K is not related in the form of simple symbolic or arithmetic relations as given above.

> *Example 2*: the following is an example of the type of temporal pattern that can be discovered by TIM:
>
> $$\forall t, \{R_t(P) \rightarrow R_{t+3..5}(K)\}$$
>
> which indicates that whenever P is observed, K will be observed in three to five time units.

With the causality template given above, the problem of discovering temporal patterns from observations can be viewed as a problem in concept acquisition, where generalized form are generated for the training episodes, as well as for the function f that relates temporally the generalized descriptions with the classifying events.

2. BASIC INDUCTIVE COMPONENTS FOR INCREMENTAL LEARNING

An approach to incremental inductive learning to use a set of refinement operators to repair the partial hypotheses, until satisfactory ones are found. The simplest rule refinement criteria can be given as follows:

> Generalize whenever a hypothesis is over-specialized (e.g. the hypothesis does not cover certain *positive* examples), and specializes whenever a hypothesis is over-generalized (e.g. the hypothesis covers *negative* examples) [Mitchell, 1977].

the criteria represent general principles that need to be further refined in order to achieve practical efficiency in complex domains. As the complexity of the domain increases, the need for spending computing resources sparingly also intensifies. An approach to efficient inductive learning is through the technique of incremental learning. A inductive system is said to learn incrementally if given a set of new training examples, the system generate hypotheses by modifying the existing hypotheses. A simple algorithm for incremental learning is given as follows:

(1) Input a new training instance T.

(2) Decide which rules $\{R_i\}$ in the rulebase are affected by T, and have the greatest prospect of being further improved (*rule invocation*).
(3) From $\{R_i\}$ generates through refinement operators a new set of refined rules $\{R'_i\}$ (*rule generation*). Put $\{R'_i\}$ into the rulebase.
(4) Decide if the rules in $\{R'_i\}$ satisfy the predefined criteria (*rule evaluation*). If the answer is yes, then exit; else go to (1).

Note that three basic components for incremental learning are identified in the algorithm for making the following decisions:

(1) How to decide if a rule satisfies predefined criteria. This is called the problem of *rule evaluation*. Such criteria may include the predictive power of a rule, the total number of times a rule has been confirmed or disproved (confidence level), the syntactical complexity of the rule, and many others that jointly evaluate the desirability of a rule.

(2) How to select from the rulebase those partial rules (hypotheses) that have the highest promise of being improved by the current training instance. This is called the problem of *rule invocation*. Here we assume that the number of rules in the rulebase is so great that exhaustive rule invocation is impractical. The issue here is to maximize the efficiency of the system by investing computing resources only on those partial hypotheses that are more likely to be improved further.

(3) How to repair the invoked rules in a most efficient way. This is the problem of *rule generation*. Here we assume that the number of allowable refinements is so great that exhaustive rule refinement is impractical.

2.1. Refinement Operators

Refinement operators can be divided into two categories: atemporal refinement operators and temporal refinement operators. Static refinement operators are defined on the atemporal language representations. Many atemporal refinement operators, such as "closing an interval", "dropping conjunctive terms", "turning constants into variables", etc., are described in [Michalski, 1983].

Temporal refinement operators are used to derive temporal relationships not explicitly specified in the given data. Temporal generalization from a pair of conjointed events e_1 and e_2 can be derived by turning the temporal marks into variables, then adding (by conjunction) the relationships between these temporal variables to the expression. For example, given two events e_1 and e_2, each described as d_i occurring between the time interval from t_{s_i} to t_{f_i}, $i = 1$ or 2, the following temporal attributes can be generated:

$$T_1 = t_{s_2} - t_{s_1}$$
$$T_2 = t_{s_2} - t_{f_1}$$
$$T_3 = t_{f_2} - t_{s_1}$$
$$T_4 = t_{f_2} - t_{f_1}$$
$$T_5 = t_{f_1} - t_{s_1}$$
$$T_6 = t_{f_2} - t_{s_2}$$

The temporal attributes T_1 to T_4 manifest the temporal relationship between d_1 and d_2, while T_5 and T_6 represent the *duration* of d_1 and d_2 respectively. This way, a total of six simple generalizations can be produced. Arbitrary combination of these six generalizations also constitute a generalization of the original expression.

Temporal marks, like atemporal structured attributes, can have its own value hierarchy. A set of refinement operators based on this value hierarchy can be created. For example, the temporal mark *12:00 pm* can be generalized to *daytime*, and *January 10* can be generalized to *winter*.

Another temporal generalization operator, works by hypothesizing temporal invariance. That is, if it is observed that P is true at two time points t_1 and t_2, then it can be hypothesized that P remains unchanged throughout the time interval between t_1 and t_2. Similarly, monotonous changes of a linear attribute of a certain object during a time interval can be hypothesized even if only finite number of observations are available. For example, if it is known that John's body temperature at t_2 has increased compared to John's body temperature at an earlier time t_1, than it can be assumed that John's temperature has been *increasing monotonously* throughout the time interval between t_1 and t_2.

The set of the refinement operators used by an inductive engine plays an important role in deciding the computation complexity of the system, as well as the type of expressions that the system is capable of generating. Allowing the system to generate arbitrary hypotheses that are permitted by the representation incurs severe penalties in both computing time and memory space requirement. A compromise can be reached either by limiting the type and number of refinement operators to be used, or by constraining the applications of refinement operators. The refinement operators also provide an implicit control over the ways a hypothesis may change. Instead of allowing hypotheses to be generalized/specialized in all conceivable ways, a well-controlled path of refinements can be defined by restricting the type and usage of refinement operators.

2.2. Rule Evaluation

The purpose of rule evaluation is to provide a measurement of the desirability of the rules in the rulebase, so that "good" rules can be reported to the user of the inductive system. The desirability of a given rule can be decided by a set of criteria that evaluate the *merits* of the rule. Two types of merit-measuring criteria that are used by TIM are distinguished here: **efficacy criteria**, and **efficiency criteria**. Efficacy criteria measure the confidence level and the performance of a rule, disregarding other properties of a rule. The confidence level of a rule is proportional to the total number of training instances covered by the rule, while the performance of a rule is in general related to the percentage of positive/negative instances covered by the rule.

The efficiency criteria measure desired properties such as the syntactical complexity of a rule, which are indications of the computing resources required in storing and evaluating the rule. The efficiency criteria dictate that all else being equal, the one rule that is more efficient is also preferred over that ones that are less efficient.

2.3. Rule Invocation

The number of partial hypotheses contained in the rulebase in a complex domain (e.g. domain described with large number of attributes, relations, objects, etc.) can be tremendous. To ensure that the system will achieve maximal net improvement with the given computing resource, it is necessary to identify those hypotheses that are likely to improve more than the others. Two issues are involved here: the definition of the "desirability" of a hypothesis, which has been described earlier; and the problem of identifying those hypotheses that have more potential of being improved. The prospect of improvement of a rule can be identified in two ways: using the measurement of *expected maximum entropy variation* (EMEV) to decide how much improvement a rule may achieve by tallying new evidences; and using the *uniformness* measurement to decide if a rule is over-generalized or over-specialized and consequently adopt appropriate measures to remedy the situation. These are described in details below.

2.3.1. Entropy-Based Rule Invocation

The purpose of rule refinement is to generate rules that satisfy predefined criteria, such as the simplicity or the generality of the rules. One criterion for measuring the performance of a rule can be defined in terms of its *entropy*. The entropy of a rule R is given by the following formula:

$$entropy(R) = -q^+ \log q^+ - q^- \log q^-$$

where q^+/q^- are the percentage of positive/negative instances covered by R respectively. A *consistent* classification rule covers either all positive or all negative instances, thus has zero entropy; otherwise it has non-zero entropy. Entropy thus can be viewed as a partial measurement of the desirability of a rule, where rules of low entropy are preferred. The *expected improvement* of a rule can be defined as the expected maximal variation in its entropy as a new training instance is registered. Rule invocation based on the EMEV (Expected Maximal Entropy Variation) value of the rules has many interesting properties. For example, consider the following rules:

$$R_1 \equiv H_1 \rightarrow Class_k : 1000:10$$
$$R_2 \equiv H_2 \rightarrow Class_k : 100:1$$
$$R_3 \equiv H_3 \rightarrow Class_k : 50:50$$
$$R_4 \equiv H_4 \rightarrow Class_k : 1:1$$

where $R_i \equiv H_i \rightarrow Class_j : P:N$ means that the rule R_i, described as H_i implies $Class_j$, covers P positive training instances, and N negative training instances. Intuitive judgement of the above rules in terms of the prospect for further improvement in entropy shows that R_1 is the least interesting of the four, since it is a rule well-established with 1010 evidences, and the prospect of seeing further improvements is slim. R_3 is also uninteresting since it covers equally large number of positive and negative instances. R_2 and R_4 are much more interesting because new evidence may cause large reductions in their entropy (large amount of information gain), thus worth spending more effort for further refinements. The EMEV for the four rules are respectively:

$$EMEV(R_1) = 0.0045$$
$$EMEV(R_2) = 0.041$$
$$EMEV(R_3) = 0.0055$$
$$EMEV(R_4) = 0.057$$

which correspond closely to our intuitive notion of the prospect of improvement of a rule. The *interestingness of a training instance* e to a rule R can be defined as the entropy change of R caused by e. This measurement provides a way to pinpoint:

- training instances that can be important new evidences in forming new hypotheses (which cause high EMEV).
- spurious training instances that can be *noise*, which cause high EMEV in rules with *high confidence* (which cover many training instances) in a not-too-noisy domain. These events should be either verified or deleted from the training set.
- commonplace training instances (which cause low EMEV) that are forgettable by the system.

Entropy reduction can be viewed as a form of information gain. Rule invocation based on EMEV thus maximizes the prospect of gaining information through refinement. Using EMEV as guidance, each unit of computing resource is likely to achieve greater reduction in the overall entropy of the system, thus improves the overall efficiency.

2.3.2. Uniformness-Based Rule Invocation

In light of entropy, many inductive algorithms [Michalski, 1978; Quinlan, 1983; Mitchell, 1977; Rendell, 1985] can be viewed as algorithms that generate entropy plateaus in the description space. Programs such as ID3 [Quinlan, 1983] and PLS/1 [Rendell, 1985] explicitly use entropy or entropy-like measurements to find maximum entropy gradients in order to divide the space into regions that are relatively flat in entropy. The Aq algorithm [Michalski, 1978] generates zero entropy regions by maximally extending from a zero entropy point (a positive instance). In ID3 or version space [Mitchell, 1977] the need for further specialization is detected by the mere fact that the given rule has non-zero entropy, while in PLS/1 it is detected by a gradient exceeding certain threshold. To counteract the complexity of the temporal domain, we propose a strategy of *lazy evaluation* as an efficient way of detecting the non-uniformness in the entropy distribution of a given rule. A rule R is considered *non-uniform* (in entropy) if there exist in the rulebase a specialization of R, R_s, such that the difference in entropy between R and R_s exceeds certain threshold. A rule is considered to be uniform until proven otherwise by one of its specializations. By evaluating the entropy relationships between related rules in the rulebase, it is possible to prognosticate the internal entropy structure of a rule, hence deciding the proper refinements that should take place.

There are many ways one can read from the uniformness of a rule in order to derive more information:

- A non-uniform rule may indicate over-generalization. In this case further specialization is required.

- A non-uniform rule may indicate that the concept to be learned is intrinsically probabilistic. In this case, further specialization is fruitless. Probabilistic concepts (assuming uniform probability distributions) can be identified as uniform rules with non-zero entropies.
- The non-uniformness can be the result of spurious data, or noise. Such data should be verified, deleted, or the concept can be treated as probabilistic.
- The non-uniformness may be the result of the intrinsically fuzzy boundaries in the concepts to be learned, as is the case in many human concepts. In this case, a region that is relatively flat in entropy can be used to approximate the intended concept.

Rule refinement based on the uniformness measurement will eventually yield rules that are entropy plateaus. Perfectly consistent zero entropy rules can be generated if they do exist, otherwise variable precision rules still can be discovered.

2.4. Rule Generation

Rule generation can be achieved by either generating totally new rules by applying refinement operators to the old rules, or repairing incrementally the existing rules.

Some rules of thumb for rule refinement are listed below:

(1) If the number of training instances that cause non-uniformness are few, then these instances can be registered as *exceptions* to the rule.

(2) If the number of training instances that cause non-uniformness are moderate, then generate a local generalization of these instances and registered them as *exceptions* to the rule.

(3) If no rule repairing seems to work, then generate a completely new rule. This is detailed in the following section.

Since rule repairing by registering exceptions does not requirement reevaluation of the repaired rules, it is a very efficient form of rule refinement and is preferred whenever possible.

2.4.1. Dependency Directed Rule Generation

The dependencies between rules (of the same class/action) are marked by the generalization relationship between them. By examining the uniformness and performance of a rule, and the generalization relationship between rules, it is possible to derive powerful domain independent heuristics that suggest the proper refinements that should take place. Given two rules R and R_G such a that R_G is a generalization of R, derivable by applying the generalization operator G to R:

- an over-generalization is indicated if the difference between the entropy of R_G and R is greater than certain threshold. If R is uniform, then a generalization operator G_s that is more specific than G can be used to generate an intermediately general rule $G_s(R)$. This amounts to extending the coverage of a known entropy plateau until an "entropy cliff" is reached. The *extend-against* operation in the Aq algorithm can be used here as an efficient way of reaching the entropy cliff.

- an over-specialization is indicated if the entropy of R_G is the same as R, and both R and R_G are uniform. In this case certain static criteria can be used to select the one rule that achieves higher score.

Another type of dependency comes in the form of associations through temporal/spatial proximity. Two rules R_1 and R_2 can be refined to a common specialization R_S (where R_S is more specialized than both R_1 and R_2), if they are temporal/spatially associated. Temporal association is marked by the facts that the two rules in question tend to be invoked at the same time (or nearly the same time). Spatial association is marked by the fact that the rules tend to be invoked by the same object (or same set of objects).

2.4.2. Knowledge Space Decomposition

Another technique to reduce of the complexity of the inductive process is to divide the description space into hierarchies in a fashion similar to those used in INDUCE [Larson, 1977]. In the INDUCE method, the description space is divided into a structure-only space and an attribute-only space. The structure space is searched first to find relationships that characterize the given training instance, then the attribute–only space is searched to fill out the detail generalization. The complexity is thus reduced as a result of reduced search space and simplified graph matching. In the temporal domain, this idea can be extended further by dividing the structure–only space into a atemporal–relation space and a temporal–relation space. The searching precedence can then be arranged in the order of temporal–relation space first, atemporal–relation space second, and attribute–only space last. Such searching precedence is by no means foolproof, thus should be treated as a form of inductive bias that is subject to change from domain to domain.

3. CONCLUSIONS

The application of inductive inference to realtime domain have been hampered by many problems. Notably the presence of uncertainty, the lack of expressive power in the representation languages, the lack of strong heuristics, and the batch nature of many previous systems. As the complexity of the problem domain increases, the capability to learn incrementally becomes increasingly important. The method presented here is an attempt to address these problems and lay a framework for future researches in the inductive acquisition of knowledge in temporal domains.

ACKNOWLEDGEMENTS

The author is grateful to R. S. Michalski and R. E. Stepp III for their comments and suggestions.

REFERENCES

[Box and Jenkins, 1982]
Box, G. E. P., and Jenkins, G. M., "Time–Series Analysis: Forecasting and Control," Revised Edition, Holden–Day, San Francisco, 1976.

[Larson, 1977]
Larson, J. B., "Inductive Inference in the Variable–Valued Predicate Logic System VL_{21}: Methodology and Computer Implementation," Ph.D. Thesis, Report No. 869, Department of Computer Science, University of Illinois, Urbana, Illinois, May 1977.

[Michalski and Larson, 1978]
Michalski, R. S., and Larson J., "Selection of the Most Representative Training Examples and Incremental Generation of VL1 Hypotheses: the Underlying Methodology and the Description of Programs ESEL and AQ11," report No. 867, Department of Computer Science, University of Illinois at Urbana–Champaign, Urbana, Illinois, May, 1978.

[Michalski, 1983]
Michalski, R. S., "A Theory and Methodology of Inductive Learning," In: *Machine Learning, An Artificial Intelligence Approach*, R. S. Michalski, J. G. Carbonell and T. M. Mitchell (eds), Tioga Publishing Company, Palo Alto, CA, 1983, pp. 461–481.

[Mitchell, 1977]
Mitchell, T. M., "Version Space: A candidate Elimination Approach to Rule Learning," IJCAI 5, pp. 305–310, 1977

[Quinlan, 1983]
Quinlan, J. R., "Learning Efficient Classification Procedures and their Application to Chess End Games," in *Machine Learning, An Artificial Intelligence Approach*, R. S. Michalski, J. G. Carbonell and T. M. Mitchell, eds. Tioga, Palo Alto, CA, 1983, pp. 461–481.

[Rendell, 1985]
Rendell, L. A., "Substantial Construction Induction Using Layered Information Compression: Tractable Feature Formation in Search," Proceedings of *Ninth International Joint conference on Artificial Intelligence*, 1985, pp. 650–658.

[Rescher and Urquhart, 1971]
Rescher, N., and Urquhart, A., "Temporal Logic," Springer–Verlag New York–Wien, 1971.

TOWARDS A GENERAL-PURPOSE BELIEF MAINTENANCE SYSTEM

Brian Falkenhainer

Qualitative Reasoning Group
Department of Computer Science
University of Illinois
1304 W. Springfield Avenue, Urbana, Illinois, 61801

1. INTRODUCTION

There currently exists a gap between the theories proposed by the probability and uncertainty community and the needs of Artificial Intelligence research. These theories primarily address the needs of expert systems, using knowledge structures which must be pre-compiled and remain static in structure during runtime. Many AI systems require the ability to dynamically add and remove parts of the current knowledge structure (e.g., in order to examine what the world would be like for different causal theories). This requires more flexibility than existing uncertainty systems display. In addition, many AI researchers are only interested in using "probabilities" as a means of obtaining an ordering, rather than attempting to derive an accurate probabilistic account of a situation. This indicates the need for systems which stress ease of use and don't require extensive probability information when one cannot (or doesn't wish to) provide such information. This paper attempts to help reconcile the gap between approaches to uncertainty and the needs of many AI systems by examining the control issues which arise, independent of a particular uncertainty calculus, when one tries to satisfy these needs.

Truth Maintenance Systems have been used extensively in problem solving tasks to help organize a set of facts and detect inconsistencies in the believed state of the world. These systems maintain a set of true/false propositions and their associated dependencies. However, situations often arise in which we are unsure of certain facts or in which the conclusions we can draw from available information are somewhat uncertain. The non-monotonic TMS [2] was an attempt at reasoning when all the facts are not known, but it fails to take into account degrees of belief and how available evidence can combine to strengthen a particular belief.

This paper addresses the problem of probabilistic reasoning as it applies to Truth Maintenance Systems. It describes a *Belief Maintenance System* that manages a current set of beliefs in much the same way that a TMS manages a set of true/false propositions. If the system knows that belief in $fact_1$ is dependent in some way upon belief in $fact_2$, then it automatically modifies its belief in $fact_1$ when new information causes a change in belief of $fact_2$. It models the behavior of a TMS, replacing its 3-valued logic (true, false, unknown) with an infinite-valued logic, in such a way as to reduce to a standard TMS if all statements are given in absolute true/false terms. Belief Maintenance Systems can, therefore, be thought of as a generalization of Truth Maintenance Systems, whose possible reasoning tasks are a superset of those for a TMS.

2. DESIGN

The design of the belief maintenance system is based on current TMS technology, specifically a monotonic version of Doyle's justification-based TMS [2]. As in the TMS, a network is constructed which consists of nodes representing facts and justification links between nodes representing antecedent support of a set of nodes for some consequent node. The BMS differs in that nodes take on a *measure of belief* rather than true or false and justification links become *support links* in that they provide partial evidence in favor of a node.

The basic design consists of three parts: (1) the conceptual control structure, (2) the user hooks to the knowledge base, and (3) the uncertainty calculus. A simple parser is used to translate user assertions (e.g. `(implies (and a b) c)`) into control primitives. This enables the basic design to be semi-independent of the belief system used. All that is required of the belief formalism is that it is invertible. Specifically, if A provides support for B and our belief in A changes, we must be able to remove the effects the previous belief in A had on our belief in B.

2.1. An Overview of Dempster-Shafer Theory

The particular belief system used here is based on the Dempster-Shafer theory of evidence [12]. Shafer's representation expresses the belief in some proposition A by the interval [s(A), p(A)], where s(A) represents the current amount of support for A and p(A) is the plausibility of A. It is often best to think of p(A) in terms of the lack of evidence against A, for $p(A) = 1 - s(\neg A)$. To simplify calculations, the BMS represents Shafer intervals by the pair $(s(A)\ s(\neg A))$ rather than the interval [s(A) p(A)] (as in [6]).

Dempster's rule provides a means for combining probabilities based upon different sources of information. His language of belief functions defines a *frame of discernment*, Θ, as the exhaustive set of possibilities or values in some domain. For example, if the domain represents the values achieved from rolling a die, Θ is the set of 6 propositions of the form "the die rolled a j." If m_1 and m_2 are two basic probability functions over the same space Θ, each representing a different knowledge source, then Dempster's *orthogonal sum* defines a new combined probability function m which is stated as $m = m_1 \oplus m_2$.

Since the primary concern here is the use of uncertainty in a deductive reasoning system, we are interested in the case where Θ contains only two values, A and $\neg A$. For this case, the basic probability function has only three values, m(A), m($\neg$A), and m(Θ). This allows the derivation of a simplified version of Dempster's formula [11,6]:

$$(a\ b) \oplus (c\ d) = \left[1 - \frac{\bar{a}\bar{c}}{1 - (ad + bc)} \quad 1 - \frac{\bar{b}\bar{d}}{1 - (ad + bc)} \right]$$

where $\bar{a}$ means $(1 - a)$. We may also formulate an inverse function for subtracting evidence [6].

The decision to choose Dempster-Shafer Theory over some other system of beliefs was purely pragmatic. Dempster-Shafer has been shown to be invertible, it distinguishes between absolutely unknown (no evidence) and uncertain, and it is simple to use. However, the design of the BMS is not based on a particular uncertainty calculus and there should be little difficulty (as far as the BMS itself is concerned) in adapting it to use some other belief system.

2.2. A Logic of Beliefs

The conventional meaning of two-valued logic must be redefined in terms of evidence so that the system can interpret and maintain its set of beliefs based on the user-supplied axioms.

NOT: Because Dempster-Shafer theory allows us to express belief for and against in a single probability interval, (not A) and A can simply be stored under the same proposition, A.

AND: There are a number of approaches to the meaning of AND. The interpretation used here corresponds to that of Garvey et al [5]. The -2 term represents (1 - cardinality(conjuncts)):

$$A_{(s_A\ s_{\neg A})} \wedge B_{(s_B\ s_{\neg B})} \wedge C_{(s_C\ s_{\neg C})} \rightarrow (A\ \&\ B\ \&\ C)_{(\max(0, s_A + s_B + s_C - 2),\ \max(s_{\neg A},\ s_{\neg B},\ s_{\neg C}))}$$

OR: The belief in OR is the maximum of the individual beliefs [5]:

$$A_{(s_A\ s_{\neg A})} \wedge B_{(s_B\ s_{\neg B})} \rightarrow (A \vee B)_{(\max(s_A,\ s_B),\ \max(0,\ s_{\neg A} + s_{\neg B} - 1))}$$

IMPLIES: There are two theories in the literature for the interpretation of IMPLIES using Dempster-Shafer. Dubois and Prade [3], suggest that, for A→B, we take into account the value of Bel(B→A). Because the BMS should be simple to use and because Bel(B→A) can be difficult to obtain, the use of IMPLIES will be the same as given in [3,6]:

$$A_{(s_A\ s_{\neg A})} \wedge (A \rightarrow B)_{(s_i\ s_{\neg i})} \rightarrow B_{(s_A s_i\ s_A s_{\neg i})}$$

For example, if full belief in A implies $B_{0.8}$, then a half belief in A should imply $B_{0.4}$.

With these operators defined, the system can parse all user assertions and construct the necessary support links with the appropriate belief functions attached to them.

2.3. Support Links

A support link consists of a list of antecedent nodes, a consequent node, its current positive and negative support for its consequent, and a function for recalculating its support based on the current belief of the antecedents (when the support is provided by the user, forming a *premise link*, no such function exists). Figure 1 shows a sample support link network. The system recognizes two types of support links – *hard links* and *invertible links*.

2.3.1. Hard Support Links

A hard support link is one which provides an absolute statement of its consequent's belief. For example, statements of the form
$$(\text{implies x (and y z)})$$
are translated into
$$(\text{implies x y}) \quad \text{and} \quad (\text{implies x z})$$
As a result, nodes are never allowed to give support directly to an "and" node and the only support entering an "and" node must come from the individual conjuncts. A support link for an "and" node is therefore given the status hard link and the value of the consequent node equals the link's support. In Figure 1, if the belief in A changes, a new value is calculated for the conjunctive link using its attached formula for AND, and the node for (AND A B) is set to the new value.

2.3.2. Invertible Support Links

Links representing implication or user support act as only one source of evidence for their consequent node. Such links are designated invertible since a change in their support means that their old support must be subtracted (using the inverted form of Dempster's rule) before the new value is added. In Figure 1, if the belief in D changes, then the current support provided by D's link into C is subtracted, the link support is recalculated, and the new support is added to C.

2.4. Control

The basic control structure of the BMS is similar to that of a TMS. When the belief in a node is modified, the affects of this new belief are propagated throughout the system. This is done by following the node's outgoing links and performing the appropriate operations for modifying hard and invertible links' support. Propagation of evidence may be defined so as to terminate early [7]. If the system sees that the change it has just made to a node's belief state is sufficiently small, there is no need for it to propagate this change to every node dependent upon it. A threshold value, *propagation–delta*, is defined so that, when the change to a node's positive and negative beliefs are less than the threshold, the system will not continue to propagate changes past this node. The default threshold is 10^{-3}.

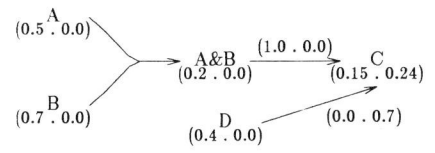

Figure 1. A sample BMS network.

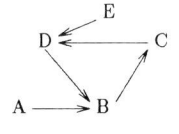

Figure 2. Circular support structure.

In a TMS architecture, only one justification is needed to establish truth. Any independent justifications are extraneous. Using a probabilistic architecture, each source of support adds to the node's overall belief. All incoming supports must be combined (using Dempster's rule) to form the overall belief for the node. If one tries to combine two contradicting, absolute beliefs, (1 0) $\oplus$ (0 1), the system would simply detect the attempt and signal a contradiction as a TMS would. Thresholds could also be used so that if a strongly positive belief is to be combined with a strongly negative belief, the system could signal a contradiction. Caution should be used for this case, however, because non-monotonic inferences should not be interpreted as contradictions.

2.4.1. New Control Issues

Circular support structures (e.g., Figure 2) cause a number of problems for belief maintenance. Because of these problems, the current implementation requires that no such structures exist. There are a variety of problems which the structure in Figure 2 can cause:

(1) *Interpretation of circular evidence.* When A is partially believed and the status of E is unknown, what can be said about the support which D provides to B? All of the evidence D is supplying to B originally came from B in the first place. Because all links entering B will combine according to Dempster's rule to form a single belief, B may be believed more strongly than A simply because B supplies evidence in favor of D through C. This does not seem intuitively correct.

(2) *Problems with possible cures.* There are several potential solutions to this problem. First, D could be allowed to provide support for B. This situation is undefined under normal probability theory. Second, the chain can be stopped at D by not allowing any node to provide support to one of its supporters (by transitivity). This introduces a new problem. What should happen when E is providing independent support for D? Forcing the system to only propagate those supports for D which are independent of B would require a much more sophisticated control structure.

(3) *Retraction or modification of support.* Modifying support links becomes much more difficult if circular support structures are allowed to exist. Any time the support A provides for B changes, the old support A provided must be retracted. This means removing all support from A, propagating the change in B, adding in the new support from A, and propagating the new belief in B. This will cause the belief in C to be propagated four times (twice when B changes the first time and twice when B changes the second time), the belief in D to be propagated 8 times, etc. In addition, retracting the support A provides for B means that we must retract all support for B (to remove the effects D has on B), propagate the new lack of belief in B, and then recalculate a new belief for B based on the new value for A and the current values of its other support links. Doing this every time the belief for any node changes makes such a system untenable. When we assume there is no circular support in the network, modifying belief in A simply involves subtracting its old support for B, adding in its new support for B, and then propagating the new belief in B.

The use of beliefs also causes problems for systems that explicitly calculate transitivity relations. Suppose we were to assert A → C based on A → B and B → C. This would cause belief in C to increase, even though we were simply making existing information explicit.

2.5. User Support

The system has been designed so that it will appear to operate in exactly the same manner as the standard justification-based TMS. Thus, it is able to handle assertions using the connectives AND, OR, NOT, and IMPLIES. If a contradiction occurs, the system will notify the user and seek to resolve the contradiction. In addition, the BMS supports operations corresponding to its belief-oriented knowledge. For example, since truth is measured here in terms of belief, the truth status query language can be extended. Truth is redefined in terms of a threshold, so that a belief over a certain threshold is considered to be true:

$$\text{true?} \quad = \text{belief+(node)} > \text{*belief-threshold*}$$

In addition, functions such as `absolutely-true?` support queries which require a strict true, false, or unknown distinction, enabling the system to accurately emulate a traditional TMS.

2.5.1. Frames of Discernment

In addition to the default usage of the simplified version of Dempster's rule, where each node is treated as a frame of discernment, Θ, containing $\{A, \neg A\}$, the user may define a specific frame of discernment by the function call:

$$(\text{frame-of-discernment } node_1\ node_2\ \ldots\ node_n)$$

This establishes a frame-of-discernment stating that the given nodes represent an exhaustive set of possibilities or values in some domain. Evidence in favor of one node acts to discredit belief in the other members of the set. Evidence may be provided to support any of the nodes from outside the set, but no support link is allowed to change once it has a non-zero value. This is due to the (current) uninvertibility of the general form of Dempster's rule. When new evidence is provided for one of the nodes in the set, the belief in all the nodes is recalculated according to Dempster's orthogonal sum so that the sum of the beliefs for the nodes in the set is less-than or equal-to one. The affect of these changes are then propagated to the rest of the system.

2.6. Rule Engine

Because the BMS does not allow variables in the knowledge base, pattern-directed rules are required to provide demons that trigger on certain events [9]. For example, the rule

```
(rule ((:INTERN (dog ?x)))
   (assert (implies (dog ?x) (mammal ?x))))
```

causes the implication `(implies (dog fido) (mammal fido))` to be asserted when `(dog fido)` first appears in the knowledge base (whether it is believed or not).

The rule

```
(rule ((:BELIEF+ (foo ?x) 0.8 :test (numberp ?x))
       (:BELIEF- (bar ?y) 0.9))
  (print "Support for Foo is now > 0.8")
  (print "Support against Bar is now > 0.9"))
```

fires when the belief in some `(foo ?x)`, where `?x` is a number, exceeds 0.8 and the belief in some `(not (bar ?y))` exceeds 0.9. There are three types of rule triggers. The `:INTERN` trigger causes the rule to fire each time a new fact is added to the knowledge base which matches the given pattern. The `BELIEF+` trigger causes the rule to fire each time the support in favor of an instance of its pattern first exceeds the specified value. A `BELIEF-` rule fires when the support against its pattern exceeds the specified value.

3. EXAMPLES

There are a number of possible uses for a belief maintenance system. It enables us to perform normal TMS, three-valued, deductive logic operations if all statements are given in absolute true/false terms. In addition, the BMS is able to reason with probabilistic or uncertain information. It is able to state the current partial belief in a particular item and the sources of this belief. Such a system is also able to handle non-monotonic reasoning much more elegantly than a two or three valued logic is able to [6,8]. Consider the classic non-monotonic problem about birds "in general" being able to fly. If one were to replace a rule about birds using Doyle's [2] consistency operator with a probabilistic one stating that roughly 90 to 95% of all birds fly

$$(\text{bird ?x}) \;\rightarrow\; (\text{fly ?x})_{(0.90\ 0.05)}$$

the desired non-monotonic behavior comes automatically from negative rules such as

$$(\text{ostrich ?x}) \;\rightarrow\; (\text{fly ?x})_{(0\ 1)}$$

No modifications of the control structure are needed to perform non-monotonic reasoning.

3.1. Rule-Based Pattern Matching

The belief maintenance system has been used to implement a rule-based, probabilistic pattern matching algorithm which is able to form the type of matching typical in analogies in a manner consistent with Gentner's Structure-Mapping Theory of analogy [5,4]. For example, suppose we tried to match

(a)
```
(AND (CAUSE (GREATER (PRESSURE beaker) (PRESSURE vial))
           (FLOW beaker vial water pipe))
     (GREATER (DIAMETER beaker) (DIAMETER vial)))
```

with

(b)
```
(AND (GREATER (TEMPERATURE coffee) (TEMPERATURE ice-cube))
     (FLOW coffee ice-cube heat bar))
```

A standard unifier would not be able to form the correspondences necessary for those two forms to match. First, the forms are different in their overall structure. Second, the arguments of similar substructures differ, as in (FLOW beaker vial water pipe) and (FLOW coffee ice-cube heat bar). The rule-based pattern matcher, however, is able to find all consistent matches between form (a) and form (b). These matches correspond to the possible interpretations of the potential analogy between (a) and (b). They are

(1)
```
(GREATER (PRESSURE beaker) (PRESSURE vial))
    ↔   (GREATER (TEMPERATURE coffee) (TEMPERATURE ice-cube))
(FLOW beaker vial water pipe) ↔ (FLOW coffee ice-cube heat bar)
```

(2)
```
(GREATER (DIAMETER beaker) (DIAMETER vial))
    ↔   (GREATER (TEMPERATURE coffee) (TEMPERATURE ice-cube))
```

The pattern matcher works by first asserting a *match hypothesis* for each potential predicate or object pairing between (a) and (b) with a belief of zero. For example, we could cause all predicates having the same name to pair up and all functional predicates (e.g. PRESSURE) to pair up if their parent predicates pair up (e.g. GREATER). The likelyhood of each match hypothesis is then found by running *match hypothesis evidence rules*. For example, the rule

```
(assert same-functor)    { provide a name for the source of the rule's support }
(rule ((:intern (MH ?i1 ?i2) :test (and (fact? ?i1) (fact? ?i2)
                                        (equal-functors ?i1 ?i2))))
      (assert (implies same-functor (MH ?i1 ?i2) (0.5 . 0.0))))
```

states "If two items are facts and their functors are the same, then supply 0.5 evidence in favor of their match." After running these rules, the BMS would have the beliefs shown in Table 1.

The pattern matcher then constructs all consistent sets of matches to form *global matches* such that no item in a global match is paired up with more than one other item. (1) and (2) are examples of such global matches. Once the global matches are formed, the pattern matcher must

Table 1. BMS State After Running Match Hypothesis Evidence Rules.

Match Hypothesis	Evidence	Match Hypothesis	Evidence
(MH GREATER$_{Pressure}$ GREATER$_{Temperature}$)	0.650	(MH FLOW$_{water}$ FLOW$_{heat}$)	0.790
(MH GREATER$_{Diameter}$ GREATER$_{Temperature}$)	0.650	(MH beaker coffee)	0.932
(MH PRESSURE$_{beaker}$ TEMPERATURE$_{coffee}$)	0.712	(MH vial ice-cube)	0.932
(MH PRESSURE$_{vial}$ TEMPERATURE$_{ice-cube}$)	0.712	(MH water heat)	0.632
(MH DIAMETER$_{beaker}$ TEMPERATURE$_{coffee}$)	0.712	(MH pipe bar)	0.632
(MH DIAMETER$_{vial}$ TEMPERATURE$_{ice-cube}$)	0.712		

select the "best" match. To do this, a frame of discernment consisting of the set of global matches is created and global match evidence rules are used to provide support for a global match based on various syntactic aspects such as overall size or "match quality". For example, we could have match hypotheses provide support in favor of the global matches they are members of. Thus, the pattern matcher would choose global match (1) because the match hypotheses provide the most support for this interpretation. This is a sparse description of the system discussed in [4].

4. CONCLUSIONS

The design of a *belief maintenance system* has been presented and some of its possible uses described. This system differs from other probabilistic reasoning systems in that it allows dynamic modification of the structure of the knowledge base and maintains a current belief for every known fact. Previous systems have used static (compiled) networks [1,10] which cannot be dynamically modified or simple forward chaining techniques which don't provide a complete set of reason-maintenance facilities [1,6,7,8].

There are still a number of unsolved problems. First, the interpretation and efficient implementation of circular support structures needs to be examined further. Second, operations such as generating explicit transitivity relations cause new problems for belief based reasoning systems. What is important to note is that the basic design is independent of the belief system used. For any given uncertainty calculus which is invertible, the assertion parser can be modified to construct the appropriate network.

ACKNOWLEDGEMENTS

Thanks to Peter Haddawy, Boi Faltings, Larry Rendell, Ken Forbus, and Barry Smith for helpful discussions and proofreading skills. The BMS was modeled after a simple justification-based TMS written by Ken Forbus. This research is supported by the Office of Naval Research, Contract No. N00014-85-K-0559.

REFERENCES

[1] Buchanan,B.G., E.H.Shortliffe, *Rule-Based Expert Systems: the MYCIN Experiments of the Stanford Heuristic Programming Project*, Addison-Wesley, Reading, MA., 1984.

[2] Doyle,J., "A Truth Maintenance System," *Artificial Intelligence* **12**, 1979.

[3] Dubois,D., Prade,H., "Combination and Propagation of Uncertainty with Belief Functions," *Proceedings of the 9th International Joint Conference on Artificial Intelligence*, 1985.

[4] Falkenhainer,B., K.Forbus, D.Gentner, "The Structure-Mapping Engine," *Proceedings of the Fifth National Conference on Artificial Intelligence*, August, 1986.

[5] Gentner,D., "Structure-Mapping: A Theoretical Framework for Analogy," *Cognitive Science*, **7**(2), 1983.

[6] Ginsberg,M.L., "Non-Monotonic Reasoning Using Dempster's Rule," *Proceedings of the Fifth National Conference on Artificial Intelligence*, August, 1984.

[7] Ginsberg,M.L., "Implementing Probabilistic Reasoning," *Workshop on Uncertainty and Probability in Artificial Intelligence*, August, 1985a.

[8] Ginsberg,M.L., "Does Probability Have a Place in Non-monotonic Reasoning," *Proceedings of the 9th International Joint Conference on Artificial Intelligence*, 1985b.

[9] McAllester,D.A., "Reasoning Utility Package User's Manual," MIT AI Memo 667, April, 1980.

[10] Pearl,J., "Fusion, Propagation, and Structuring in Belief Networks," *Artificial Intelligence* **29**(3), September, 1986.

[11] Prade,H., "A Synthetic View of Approximate Reasoning Techniques," *Proceedings of the 8th International Joint Conference on Artificial Intelligence*, 1983.

[12] Shafer,G., *A Mathematical Theory of Evidence*, Princeton University Press, Princeton, New Jersey, 1976.

A NON-ITERATIVE MAXIMUM ENTROPY ALGORITHM

Sally A. Goldman and Ronald L. Rivest

Laboratory for Computer Science
Massachusetts Institute of Technology
Cambridge, Massachusetts 02139

We present a new algorithm for computing the maximum entropy probability distribution satisfying a set of constraints. Unlike previous approaches, our method is integrated with the planning of data collection and tabulation. We show how *adding constraints* and performing the associated additional tabulations can substantially speed up computation by replacing the usual iterative techniques with a non-iterative computation. We note, however, that the constraints added may contain significantly more variables than any of the original constraints so there may not be enough data to collect meaningful statistics. These extra constraints are shown to correspond to the intermediate tables in Cheeseman's method. Furthermore, we prove that acyclic hypergraphs and decomposable models are equivalent, and discuss the similarities and differences between our algorithm and Spiegelhalter's algorithm. Finally, we compare our work to Kim and Pearl's work on singly-connected networks.

1 Introduction

Many applications require reasoning with incomplete information. For example, one may wish to develop expert systems that can answer questions based on an incomplete model of the world. Having an incomplete model means that some questions may have more than one answer consistent with the model. How can a system choose reasonable answers to these questions?

Many solutions to this problem have been proposed. While probability theory is the most widely used formalism for representing uncertainty, ad-hoc approximations to probability have been used in practice. The problem with pure probabilistic approaches is that their computational complexity seems prohibitive. One way to reduce the complexity of this problem is to make the strong assumption of conditional independence. However, this assumption is typically not valid and generates inaccurate results. A probabilistic method which shows promise for solving some of the problems with uncertain reasoning is the maximum entropy approach.

This research was supported in part by NSF Grant DCR-8006938. Sally Goldman received support from an Office of Naval Research Fellowship.

A preliminary version of this paper was presented at the 6th Annual Workshop on Maximum Entropy and Bayesian Methods in Applied Statistics; Seattle, Washington, August 1986.

This paper discusses efficient techniques, based on the principle of maximum entropy, for answering questions when given an incomplete model. The organization is as follows. Section 2 contains a formal definition of the inference problem. In sections 3 and 4, we introduce the maximum entropy principle, and review iterative methods for calculating the maximum entropy distribution. Section 5 contains a discussion of some non-iterative techniques which use a conditional independence assumption rather than maximum entropy to obtain a unique probability distribution. In sections 6 and 7, we examine Malvestuto's work on acyclic hypergraphs, and present a new technique which makes maximum entropy computations non-iterative by adding constraints. Section 8 discusses Spiegelhalter's non-iterative algorithm for estimating a probability distribution. In section 9, we present some interesting comparisons between our technique and those of Cheeseman, Spiegelhalter, and Kim and Pearl. We conclude with some open problems.

2 Formal Problem Definition

In this section, we formally define the inference problem which this paper addresses. We begin by defining some notation. Let $V = \{A, B, C, \ldots\}$ be a finite set of binary-valued variables, or attributes. (The generalization to finite-valued variables is straightforward.) Consider the event space Ω_V defined to be the set of all mappings from V to $\{0,1\}$. We call such mappings *assignments* since they assign a value to each variable in V. It is easy to see that $|\Omega_V| = 2^{|V|}$. If $E \subseteq V$, we have Ω_V is isomorphic to $\Omega_E \times \Omega_{V-E}$; we identify assignments in Ω_E with subsets of Ω_V in the natural manner.

We are interested in probability distributions defined on Ω_V. We use the following convention throughout this paper. If $E \subseteq V$, we write $P(E)$ to denote the probability of an element of $\Omega_E \subseteq \Omega_V$. In other words, we specify only the variables involved in the assignments and not their values. For example,

$$P(V) = P(A)P(B)P(C)\cdots \qquad (1)$$

represents $2^{|V|}$ equations, stating that the variables are independent. (We do not assume equation (1).) By convention, all assignments in an equation must be consistent. We also write $P(A)$ instead of $P(\{A\})$, $P(AB)$ instead of $P(\{AB\})$, and so on.

We use a similar convention for summations: $\sum_E$ stands for a summation over all assignments in Ω_E, when $E \subseteq V$. Using these conventions, we see that $Y \subseteq E \subseteq V$ implies that

$$P(Y) = \sum_{E-Y} P(E) \qquad (2)$$

For example, if $E = \{ABCD\}$ and $Y = \{AB\}$ then $P(Y) = \sum_{CD} P(E)$.

For conditional probabilities we use similar notation. For $Y \subseteq E \subseteq V$ the probability of E given Y is written as $P(E|Y)$ and defined to be

$$P(E|Y) = P(E-Y|Y) = \frac{P(E \wedge Y)}{P(Y)}. \qquad (3)$$

We say that X and Y are *conditionally independent* given S if

$$P(X \wedge Y|S) = P(X|S)P(Y|S) \qquad (4)$$

where $X, Y, S \subseteq V$.

A Non-Iterative Maximum Entropy Algorithm

We are interested in probability distributions on Ω_V satisfying a set of constraints. We assume that the constraints are supplied in the form of *joint marginal probabilities*. Let $E_1, \ldots, E_m$ be distinct but not necessarily disjoint subsets of V. Let us suppose that for each i we are given the $2^{|E_i|}$ constraint values $\{P(E_i)\}$. Furthermore, we assume that these values are *consistent*. By consistent we mean that there exists at least one probability distribution on Ω_V which satisfies the constraints. Note that equation (2) states that a constraint on the values $P(Y)$ is implied by a constraint on the values $P(E)$ when $Y \subseteq E$. A common way of ensuring that the constraints are consistent is to derive the constraints by computing the observed marginal probabilities from a common set of data [1].

Many techniques require that constraints are given in the form of *conditional probabilities*. Here, each element of $E_1, \ldots, E_m$ has a distinguished subset e_i, and the input is the $2^{|E_i|}$ constraint values $\{P(E_i - e_i | e_i)\}$ for each i. This approach is frequently used when obtaining information form experts because it is often easier for experts to give information in terms of conditional probabilities. In general, we find that joint marginal distributions are easier to handle. Since we plan to obtain the constraint values from raw data, we are free to use joint marginal distributions. By doing so, we avoid both the possibility of inconsistent data, and the difficulty in transforming conditional distributions to joint marginal distributions.

In general, there may be many probability distributions satisfying the constraints. There are two problems which must be addressed. First, assuming that there are many probability distributions satisfying the constraints, which one should be chosen? And second, how can one *efficiently* calculate the desired distribution? Most of our attention shall be given to the second of these two problems, but we briefly address the first in the following section.

3 The Maximum Entropy Principle

In this section, we formally define the maximum entropy principle. When faced with an underconstrained problem, a reasonable way to get a unique answer is to apply the principle of maximum entropy. The entropy function, H, is defined as follows:

$$H(P) = -\sum_V P(V) \log(P(V)). \qquad (5)$$

The maximum entropy probability distribution, P^*, is the unique distribution which maximizes H while satisfying the supplied constraints. Informally, the maximum entropy principle says that when one makes inferences based on incomplete information, one should draw them from the probability distribution that has the maximum uncertainty permitted by the data. That is, the maximum entropy distribution is the unique distribution which is maximally noncommittal with regard to missing information. Motivation for this choice are discussed by Jaynes [18,19]. Arguments formally justifying the choice of the maximum entropy distribution are provided by Rissanen, Shore and Johnson, and Tikochinsky, Tishby and Levine [20,28,31,35].

Given that the distribution of choice is the one with maximum entropy, an efficient algorithm for calculating the maximum entropy distribution is desired. The remaining sections of this paper will address this goal.

One problem that is immediately apparent is that space required to store a probability distribution is exponential in $|V|$. An advantage of the maximum entropy distribution,

---
[1] Using "experts" to provide subjective probability estimates is a well-known way of deriving a set of *inconsistent* constraints [36].

P^*, is that it has a simple representation. For each ω in Ω_{E_i}, there is a non-negative real parameter $\alpha_{E_i}(\omega)$ (i.e., one parameter set per constraint set and $2^{|E_i|}$ parameters in the parameter set for E_i), that determine P^* as follows. Let us write $\alpha_i(\omega)$ instead of $\alpha_{E_i}(\omega)$ for brevity, and omit the argument ω when it can be deduced from context. Now we may simply write

$$P^*(V) = \alpha_1 \alpha_2 \ldots \alpha_m. \qquad (6)$$

Each element of Ω_V is assigned a probability which is the product of the appropriate α's where each α determines its argument from the assignment to V. This is known as a *log-linear* representation. For example, suppose we have the variables A, B, C and constraint sets $E_1 = \{AB\}$ and $E_2 = \{BC\}$. Then we will have the parameter sets α_{AB} and α_{BC}, where the corresponding parameters are $\alpha_{AB}(00), \ldots, \alpha_{AB}(11)$ and $\alpha_{BC}(00), \ldots, \alpha_{BC}(11)$. The maximum entropy distribution is given by the log–linear model

$$P^*(V) = \alpha_{AB} \alpha_{BC}.$$

If $P_{ABC}(010)$ (i.e., the probability that $A = 0$, $B = 1$, and $C = 0$) is desired, it can be calculated by

$$P^*(010) = \alpha_{AB}(01) \alpha_{BC}(10).$$

Thus, the maximum entropy distribution can be represented in a linear amount of space in the number of constraints.

4 Iterative Maximum Entropy Methods

Most existing methods for calculating the maximum entropy distribution are iterative. They typically begin with a representation of the uniform distribution and converge towards a representation of the maximum entropy distribution. Each step adjusts the representation so that a given constraint is satisfied. To enforce a constraint $P(E_i)$, all of the elementary probabilities $P(V)$ relevant to that constraint are multiplied by a common factor. Because constraints are dependent, adjusting the representation to satisfy one constraint may cause a previously satisfied constraint to no longer hold. Thus, one must iterate repeatedly through the constraints until the desired accuracy is reached. (We note that the implicit constraint — that the probabilities sum to one — must usually be explicitly considered.) Examples of this type of algorithm are discussed in [5,6,13,17,21,23].

Representing the probability distribution explicitly as a table of $2^{|V|}$ values is usually impractical. For this problem, it is most convenient to store only $\alpha_1, \alpha_2, \ldots \alpha_m$; this is a representation as compact as the input data, which represents the current probability distribution implicitly via equation (6). To represent the uniform distribution, every α is set to 1, except for the α corresponding to the requirement that entries of the probability distribution must sum to 1 — which is set to $2^{-|V|}$. To determine if a constraint is satisfied, one must sum the appropriate elements of the probability distribution; any particular element can be computed using equation (6). If the constraint is not satisfied, the relevant α is multiplied by the ratio of the desired sum to the computed sum. Thus, in originally calculating the α's and later in evaluating queries it is necessary to evaluate a sum of terms, where each term is a product of α's. This sum is difficult to compute since it may involve an exponential number of terms.

Cheeseman [6] proposes a clever technique for rewriting such sums to evaluate them more efficiently. For example

$$\alpha \sum_{A\ldots F} \alpha_{AB} \, \alpha_{ACD} \, \alpha_{DE} \, \alpha_{AEF}$$

is rewritten as follows. First, $\sum_{A...F}$ is broken into six sums, each over one variable. Arbitrarily choosing the variable ordering $CDFEAB$, we obtain

$$\alpha \sum_B \sum_A \sum_E \sum_F \sum_D \sum_C \alpha_{AB} \alpha_{ACD} \alpha_{DE} \alpha_{AEF}.$$

Now each α is moved left as far as possible (it stops when reaching a sum over a variable on which it depends). The above sum then becomes

$$\alpha \sum_B \sum_A \alpha_{AB} \sum_E \sum_F \alpha_{AEF} \sum_D \alpha_{DE} \sum_C \alpha_{ACD}.$$

The sums are evaluated from right to left. The result of each sum is an *intermediate table* containing the value of the sum evaluated so far as a function of variables further to the left which have been referenced. The variable ordering must be chosen carefully in order to take full advantage of this technique. A poor choice of variable ordering can yield a sum which is not much better than explicitly considering all $2^{|V|}$ terms; a good choice may dramatically reduce the work required. While picking a good variable ordering is important, the success of this technique depends greatly on the interconnectedness of the constraints. If the constraints are highly connected, no ordering can significantly reduce the complexity of evaluating the summation.

Some alternative approaches to the standard iterative schemes have been proposed. One of the more interesting proposals is due to Geman [14,24]. Instead of considering one constraint at a time, this algorithm uses stochastic relaxation to simultaneously adjust the probability distribution to meet all of the constraints. In particular, a convex function, whose minimum gives the maximum entropy distribution, is calculated. Then a technique to approximate the gradient and a gradient descent algorithm are used to find this minimum.

An approach which comes immediately from the Lagrange multiplier technique is discussed by Agmon, Alhassid, and Levine [1,2]. First they calculate the "potential function" $F(\lambda^t)$. They show that F is strictly convex, and has a unique global minimum for λ^t which solves $\nabla F(\lambda^t) = 0$. Finally, they use the modified Newton-Raphson procedure to find the global minimum.

Unlike most approaches which are based on the Lagrange multiplier technique, Csiszár [9] uses I-divergence geometry to prove that a generalized version of the standard iterative technique converges. His proof is more general than those which are derived from the Lagrange multiplier technique.

5 Non–Iterative Techniques

The iterative techniques of the previous section are applicable in most situations, but computationally they are rather inefficient. We want a model that is powerful enough to handle real-world situations, yet simple enough for the maximum entropy distribution to be calculated efficiently. In this section, we discuss some non–iterative approaches which use conditional independence instead of the principle of maximum entropy to obtain a unique result.

Chow and Liu [8] consider the class of product approximations in which only second-order distributions are used. If there is a product approximation such that for some ordering of the variables $x_1 \ldots x_n$, each x_i depends on at most one variable from the set $\{x_1, \ldots x_{i-1}\}$, then this approximation forms a *dependence tree*. They discuss how to build the best dependence tree when supplied with the complete probability distribution. They also present a method to construct an optimal dependence tree from samples.

Similar to their work is the work of Kim and Pearl [22]. They construct a *Bayesian network* where the nodes represent variables and directed links represent direct dependencies; all direct influences on a node come from its parents. We will use the following notation for stating their formula: S_x is the set of the *immediate* predecessors (parents) of node x in the network, T_x is the set of *all* predecessors of node x in the network, and $\mathcal{R}$ is the set of roots (sources). All conditional probabilities of the form $P(x|S_x)$ for all $x \notin \mathcal{R}$ and $P(x)$ for all $x \in \mathcal{R}$, along with the independence assumptions that $P(x|S_x) = P(x|T_x)$ suffice to define the following unique probability distribution:

$$P^*(V) = \left(\prod_{x \in \mathcal{R}} P(x)\right) \left(\prod_{x \notin \mathcal{R}} P(x|S_x)\right). \tag{7}$$

They define a network to be *singly-connected* if there is at most one *undirected* path between any pair of nodes. One of the most interesting results of this work is that the propagation of new evidence through a singly-connected network can be accomplished by a network of parallel processors in time proportional to the longest path in the network. Pearl [27] addresses the problem of propagating new evidence through *multiply-connected* networks.

Dalkey [10] has shown that if a Bayesian network is a tree (i.e. all nodes have at most one parent), equation (7) gives the maximum entropy distribution. So for a Bayesian network which is a tree, a non-iterative technique exists for calculating the maximum entropy distribution when the input is all conditional probabilities of the form $P(x|S_x)$ for all $x \notin \mathcal{R}$ and $P(x)$ for all $x \in \mathcal{R}$.

6 Acyclic Hypergraphs

Even with Cheeseman's summation technique, the general iterative algorithm discussed in section 4 still has a very high (exponential) computational cost since many iterations through the constraints are required before the distribution converges. The non-iterative techniques discussed in the previous section are efficient, but they assume conditional independence which is rarely present. What we want is an non-iterative maximum entropy algorithm. If we are willing to put restrictions on the supplied constraints, this goal can be achieved.

Malvestuto [25] introduced a way to model constraints which are joint probability distributions as a hypergraph and presented a non-iterative maximum entropy algorithm for hypergraphs which are acyclic. In this section we introduce his work. We begin by describing how to model a set of variables and associated constraints as a hypergraph. It is interesting to note that the work on acyclic hypergraphs first appeared in the database literature [3,4,26,34]. The variables in our problem replace the attributes of the database, and the constraint sets replace the relations. If the database schema is acyclic, many problems can be simplified.

A hypergraph is like an ordinary undirected graph, except that each edge may be an arbitrary subset of the vertices, instead of just a subset of size two. We define the hypergraph $H = (\mathcal{V}, \mathcal{E})$ to contain a vertex for each variable, and a hyperedge for each constraint. For example the hyperedge $\{ABC\}$ corresponds to the constraint set $E_i = \{A, B, C\}$. We say that hyperedge X *subsumes* hyperedge Y if $Y \subseteq X$. It is important to observe that the constraints on a sub-hypergraph induced by restricting attention to a subset of the vertices can be inferred from the original hypergraph constraints using equation (2).

We define the graph $C(H)$ of a hypergraph H to be the graph whose vertices are those of H and whose edges are the vertex pairs $\{v, w\}$ such that v and w are in a common hyperedge of H. A hypergraph H is *conformal* if every clique of $C(H)$ is contained in a hyperedge of H. A graph, H, is *chordal* if for every cycle of length greater than three, there is an edge of H joining two non-consecutive vertices A hypergraph H is *acyclic* if H is conformal and $C(H)$ is chordal.

An equivalent definition is that a hypergraph is acyclic if repeatedly applying the following reduction steps results in the empty hypergraph (containing no hyperedges and no vertices):

1. Delete any vertices which belong to only one hyperedge.

2. Delete any hyperedges which are subsumed by another hyperedge.

Graham's algorithm is the procedure of applying reduction steps 1 and 2 until either the empty set is reached, or neither can be applied [16].

Before proceeding, we shall define some notation regarding the above reduction procedure. Let $\mathcal{E}^{(0)} = \{E_1^{(0)}, \ldots, E_m^{(0)}\}$, where $E_i^{(0)}$ is the ith hyperedge of H. Let $Y_i^{(k)}$ be the set of variables which appear in at least one hyperedge other than $E_i^{(k)}$. Finally let $\mathcal{E}^{(i+1)}$ be the result of applying reduction step (1) and then (2) to $\mathcal{E}^{(i)}$. If H is acyclic then there exists an l such that $\mathcal{E}^{(l+1)} = \emptyset$.

For acyclic hypergraphs, Malvestuto [25] gave the following formula for the maximum entropy distribution, $P^*(V)$:

$$P^*(V) = \left(\prod_{k=0}^{l-1} \frac{\prod_i P\left(E_i^{(k)}\right)}{\prod_i P\left(Y_i^{(k)}\right)} \right) \left(\prod_i P\left(E_i^{(l)}\right) \right) \quad (8)$$

Note that no α's are needed; the formula depends only on joint marginal distributions of the constraints. This formula is an immediate extension of the following theorem due to Malvestuto [25].

Theorem 1 *Given the constraints* $\{E_1, \ldots, E_m\}$, *the maximum entropy distribution is given by the following.*

$$P^*(V) = \frac{P(E_1) \cdots P(E_m)}{P(Y_1) \cdots P(Y_m)} P^*(Y)$$

where Y_i is the set of variables which appear in at least one hyperedge other than E_i and $P^*(Y)$ is the maximum entropy distribution for the constraints $\{Y_1, \ldots, Y_m\}$.

Proof: From the marginal constraints we have the following

$$P(E_i) = \sum_{V-E_i} \alpha_1 \cdots \alpha_m$$
$$= \alpha_i \sum_{V-E_i} \prod_{j \neq i} \alpha_j \quad (9)$$

Similarly we have,

$$P(Y_i) = \sum_{Z_i} \sum_{V-E_i} \alpha_1 \cdots \alpha_m$$
$$= \left(\sum_{Z_i} \alpha_i \right) \left(\sum_{V-E_i} \prod_{j \neq i} \alpha_j \right) \quad (10)$$

Let $\beta_i = \sum_{Z_i} \alpha_i$. Combining equations (9) and (10) from above gives:

$$\alpha_i = \frac{P(E_i)}{P(Y_i)} \beta_i \qquad (11)$$

Now writing $P^*(V)$ in its product form we get

$$\begin{aligned} P^*(V) &= \alpha_1 \cdots \alpha_m \\ &= \frac{P(E_1) \cdots P(E_m)}{P(Y_1) \cdots P(Y_m)} \beta_1 \cdots \beta_m \end{aligned} \qquad (12)$$

We want to show that $\psi(Y) = \beta_1 \cdots \beta_m$ is $P^*(Y)$, the maximum entropy distribution for the constraints $P(Y_i)$. To do this, it is suffices to prove that the marginal constraints hold.

$$\begin{aligned} P^*(E_i) &= \sum_{V-E_i} \left(\prod_j \frac{P(E_j)}{P(Y_j)} \right) \psi(Y) \\ &= \sum_{V-E_i} \psi(Y) \frac{P(E_i)}{P(Y_i)} \prod_{j \neq i} \frac{P(E_j)}{P(Y_j)} \\ &= \frac{P(E_i)}{P(Y_i)} \sum_{Y-Y_i} \left(\psi(Y) \prod_{j \neq i} \frac{1}{P(Y_j)} \sum_{Z-Z_i} \left(\prod_{j \neq i} P(E_j) \right) \right) \end{aligned} \qquad (13)$$

where $Z = Z_1 \cup \cdots \cup Z_m$, so that $V = Y \cup Z$. Now, since the Z_j's are disjoint,

$$\begin{aligned} \sum_{Z-Z_i} \prod_{j \neq i} P(E_j) &= \prod_{j \neq i} \sum_{Z-Z_i} P(E_j) \\ &= \prod_{j \neq i} \sum_{Z_j} P(E_j) \\ &= \prod_{j \neq i} P(Y_j) \end{aligned} \qquad (14)$$

Substituting equation (14) into equation (13) gives:

$$P^*(E_i) = \frac{P(E_i)}{P(Y_i)} \sum_{Y-Y_i} \psi(Y)$$

However since $P^*(E_i) = P(E_i)$ we get $P(Y_i) = \sum_{Y-Y_i} \psi(Y)$, so $\psi(Y)$ satisfies the constraints $P(Y_i)$. ∎

7 A New Maximum Entropy Method

While Malvestuto's work provides a non-iterative maximum entropy algorithm for acyclic hypergraphs, in practice, this technique is not very useful since typically constraint sets do not form acyclic hypergraphs. While one could make a hypergraph acyclic by removing some hyperedges, this approach would lead to inaccurate results. In this section, we propose a new maximum entropy algorithm which is based on the observation that a hypergraph can be made acyclic by *adding* hyperedges. In other words, maximum entropy computations can actually be simplified by adding constraints. The main advantage of our procedure is that it avoids the iteration previously required by providing a non-iterative formula for the desired answer. The major disadvantage is that the method cannot ordinarily be applied if the data is already tabulated and the constraints already derived; the method requires that one "plan ahead" and tabulate additional constraints when processing the data.

We begin by describing our algorithm. Equation (8) allows one to avoid iteration when calculating the maximum entropy distribution for schemas having acyclic hypergraphs. What should one do for *cyclic* hypergraphs? Our method is based on the observation that *a hypergraph can always be made acyclic by adding hyperedges.* (This is trivial to prove, since at worst a hypergraph can be made acyclic by adding the hyperedge containing all vertices.) For example, the hypergraph:

$$(\mathcal{V}, \mathcal{E}) = (\{ABCDEF\}, \{\{AB\}, \{ACD\}, \{DE\}, \{AEF\}\})$$

becomes acyclic when the hyperedge $\{ADE\}$ is added (see figures 1 and 2).

Thus, by adding additional constraints (edges) the maximum entropy calculation can be

$$\{\underline{AB}, \underline{ACD}, \underline{DE}, \underline{AEF}\}$$
$$\Downarrow$$
$$\{\underline{AD}, \underline{DE}, \underline{AE}\}$$

Figure 1: The hypergraph consisting of the hyperedges $\{AB\},\{ACD\},\{DE\}$, and $\{AEF\}$ is cyclic as shown be the reduction above. (Elements of Y_i are underlined.)

$$\{\underline{AB}, \underline{ACD}, \underline{ADE}, \underline{AEF}\}$$
$$\Downarrow$$
$$\{ADE\}$$
$$\Downarrow$$
$$\emptyset$$

Figure 2: The hypergraph consisting of the hyperedges $\{AB\}$, $\{ACD\}$, $\{ADE\}$, and $\{AEF\}$ is acyclic as shown be the reduction above. (Elements of Y_i are underlined.)

simplified so that no iteration is required. Here is a summary of how our method works:

1. We begin with a set of variables (attributes) and constraint sets deemed to be of interest. (Cheeseman [7] discusses a learning program which uses the raw data to find a set of significant constraints. Edwards and Kreiner [12] also discuss how to choose a good set of constraints.) Here a "constraint set" is a set of variables; the intent is that during data-gathering there will be one joint marginal distribution table created for each constraint set, and the observed events will be tabulated once in each table according to the values of the attributes in the constraint set. For example, if $\{A, B, C\}$ is a constraint set of three binary–valued attributes, then there will be a table of size 8 used to categorize the data with respect to these three attributes. This results in 8 constraints on the maximum-entropy distribution desired, one for each of the eight observed probabilities $P(ABC)$.

2. Construct the corresponding hypergraph $H = (\mathcal{V}, \mathcal{E})$, where there is one vertex for each variable and one hyperedge corresponding to each constraint group.

3. Perform Graham's algorithm on H, and let H' denote the resulting hypergraph. If H' is the empty hypergraph, then H is acyclic, and the following step is skipped.

4. Find a set $\mathcal{X}$ of *additional* hyperedges (constraint groups) which can be added to H' to make it acyclic. Note that any original edges subsumed by edges in $\mathcal{X}$ are eliminated. These additional hyperedges should be chosen to minimize the space required to store the joint marginal distributions.

5. Collect data for the expanded set $\mathcal{E} \cup \mathcal{X}$ of constraints [2].

6. Apply equation (8) to calculate individual elements of the maximum entropy distribution.

With the exception of step 4, we have completely described how to perform each of the steps. We now discuss how to find a good set of hyperedges to add which makes a hypergraph acyclic. Finding the optimal set of hyperedges to add is extremely similar to the minimum fill-in problem which has been proven to be NP-complete [37], and thus we conjecture that our problem is also NP-complete. See Rose, Tarjan, and Lueker [29,30] for a discussion of the fill-in problem. There are many heuristics which have been studied for the minimum fill-in problem. We plan on using one of these heuristics, the minimum-degree heuristic, to find a good set of hyperedges to add. Here is our proposal for performing step 4 of our algorithm. We define the *degree* of a vertex v to be the number of vertices in a common hyperedge with v. We begin by calculating the degree of each vertex in H'. Let v be the vertex with the smallest degree (break ties at random). Add to $\mathcal{X}$ the hyperedge e which contains v and any vertices in a common hyperedge with v. Next, modify H' by adding e to it and performing Graham's algorithm. If H' is now the empty hypergraph then we are done, otherwise return to the step of calculating the degree of each vertex. The reason for choosing this algorithm, is that it usually keeps the hyperedges in $\mathcal{X}$ as small as possible.

We will now demonstrate our algorithm on the example of figure 3. First we must perform Graham's algorithm on H. The result is shown below, where elements of Y_i are underlined.

$$\{\underline{AB}, \underline{AC}, \underline{BC}E, \underline{BD}F, \underline{CD}\}$$
$$\Downarrow$$
$$\{\underline{AB}, \underline{AC}, \underline{BC}, \underline{BD}, \underline{CD}\}$$

So after performing step 3 of our algorithm we have the hypergraph H' shown in figure 4. Now we must find the set $\mathcal{X}$ of hyperedges to make H' acyclic. We start by calculating the degree of the vertices in H'. We find that A and D both have a degree of two, and B and C both have a degree of three. Since A (we could have picked D) has the smallest degree we let $\mathcal{X} = \{\{ABC\}\}$. After adding $\{ABC\}$ to H' and performing Graham's algorithm, we find that $H' = (\{BCD\}, \{\{BC\}, \{BD\}, \{CD\}\})$. Since H' is a complete graph the only way to make it acyclic is to add a hyperedge which contains all vertices of H'. Thus, $\mathcal{X} = \{\{ABC\}, \{BCD\}\}$. Finally after adding the hyperedges in $\mathcal{X}$ to those in H and removing any hyperedges subsumed by another, we obtain the acyclic hypergraph

---

[2] Our method is unusual in that it extends the set of tables (constraints) used to tabulate the data. To fill in the entries of a new table, the raw data must still be available in step (5). So, steps 1-4 may be considered to be "planning" steps.

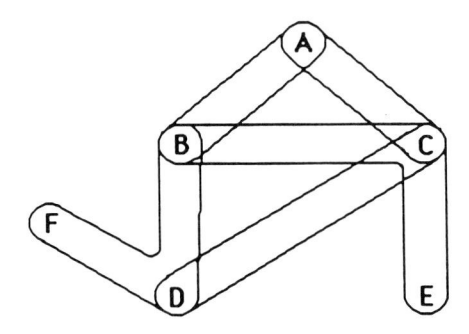

Figure 3: The original hypergraph $H = (\{ABCDEF\}, \{\{AB\}, \{AC\}, \{BCE\}, \{BDF\}, \{CD\}\})$.

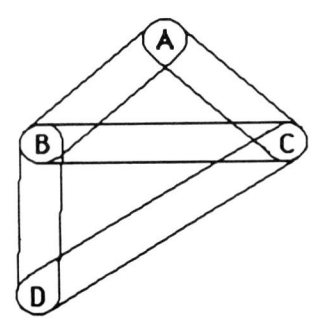

Figure 4: The hypergraph $H' = (\{ABCD\}, \{\{AB\}, \{AC\}, \{BC\}, \{BD\}, \{CD\}\})$ is obtained by performing Graham's algorithm on H.

$(\{ABCDEF\}, \{\{ABC\}, \{BCD\}, \{BCE\}, \{BDF\}\})$. So the set of constraints for which the data must be collected is $E_1 = \{ABC\}$, $E_2 = \{BCD\}$, $E_3 = \{BCE\}$, $E_4 = \{BDF\}$. Now in order to apply equation (8) we must perform Graham's algorithm on this new set of constraints.

$$\{A\underline{BC}, \underline{BCD}, \underline{BC}E, \underline{BD}F\}$$
$$\Downarrow$$
$$\{BCD\}$$
$$\Downarrow$$
$$\emptyset$$

Now applying equation (8) we get the the maximum entropy distribution is as follows:

$$\begin{aligned} P^*(V) &= \frac{P(ABC)}{P(BC)} \frac{P(BCE)}{P(BC)} \frac{P(BDF)}{P(BD)} P(BCD) \\ &= \frac{P(ABC)P(BCE)P(BDF)P(BCD)}{P(BC)P(BC)P(BD)} \end{aligned} \quad (15)$$

Finally, we consider possible inefficiencies of our method. First, it may be necessary to add "large" hyperedges containing many vertices in order to make the hypergraph acyclic. For example, to make the complete undirected graph (containing all hyperedges of size two) acyclic, one must add the "maximum" hyperedge containing all vertices. Since the size of the table corresponding to a hyperedge is an exponential function of the size of the hyperedge, adding large hyperedges creates a problem. Furthermore, the table corresponding to the maximum hyperedge is itself the probability distribution that we are estimating, so the above situation is clearly undesirable. This kind of behavior depends on the structure of the hypergraph; hypergraphs which are "highly connected" will tend to require the addition of large hyperedges. However, when the graph is highly connected other techniques seem to "blow up" as well.

Finally, because of our method's unique approach, we have a unique concern. Recall that since the data is tabulated *after* adding the additional constraints; steps 1-4 of our algorithm must be performed while the source of the constraints (i.e., the raw data) is still available. If the added hyperedges are too large, there may not be enough data to calculate meaningful statistics. Tabulating 100,000 data points in a table of size approximately 1,000 will give reasonable estimates, while tabulating them in a table of size approximately 1,000,000 will not.

8 Spiegelhalter's Algorithm

In this section, we briefly describe a method independently introduced by Spiegelhalter [32,33] for calculating the maximum entropy distribution. His work is based on *decomposable models* as discussed by Darroch, Lauritzen and Speed [11]. Spiegelhalter takes advantage of the fact that the maximum entropy probability distribution for decomposable models may be expressed as a simple function of the joint probabilities of the constraints from the model and their intersections.

A major difference between his work and our work is that he assumes that the data is given as *conditional* probability distributions rather that joint marginal distributions. From these conditional probabilities he finds a set of joint marginal distributions which form a decomposable model. To obtain the needed data, he used equation (7) to calculate the joint probability distributions. Since equation (7) only gives the maximum entropy distributions for networks which are singly-connected, in general Spiegelhalter's technique does not produce the maximum entropy distributions.

9 Comparisons

In this section we compare our technique for estimating the probability distribution to Cheeseman's algorithm, Spiegelhalter's algorithm, and Kim and Pearl's algorithm. In this paper we will just state the results which we have obtained. For a more complete discussion and proofs of the stated results see Goldman [15].

We begin by comparing our algorithm to Cheeseman's algorithm. We have proven that for a given problem, the hyperedges (tables) added by our technique are like the intermediate tables used by Cheeseman's summation technique. The only difference between these tables is that for Cheeseman's technique they are half the size, since they are summed over one of the variables in the table.

In terms of time complexity, Cheeseman's method specifies an iterative approximation of the αs, whereas our method requires no such iteration. So, if Cheeseman's method requires 10 iterations on the average, our method should yield an average speed-up of a factor of 10. In terms of space complexity, both methods use approximately the same amount of space. However, our method adds what might be called "permanent" edges, since they correspond to tabulations of the raw data. Note, however, that new edges may subsume and eliminate original edges, so the space required by our method may not be quite as great as it first appears. In Cheeseman's method the tables exist only temporarily during the course of the computation, and not all such tables may be needed at the same time. And finally, in terms of the "precomputation" needed, both methods need to compute a vertex ordering to use. We observe that a good summation ordering is a good ordering for eliminating vertices. So the problem of choosing the hyperedges to make a graph acyclic is essentially equivalent to the problem of choosing an optimal summation ordering. Therefore, we conclude that our algorithm will be generally more efficient than Cheeseman's algorithm, where both are applicable.

Next we compare our algorithm to Spiegelhalter's algorithm. We have shown that a graphical model is decomposable if and only if the corresponding hypergraph is acyclic. We also have proven that if the decomposable model obtained by Spiegelhalter's technique is the same as the acyclic hypergraph obtained after step 4 of our technique, then these techniques produce the same formula for the estimated probability distribution.

We now consider the additional data required by our technique and the additional data required by Spiegelhalter's technique. As we have mentioned, adding hyperedges to the original hypergraph corresponds to requiring joint marginal probability distributions which were not included in the original data. Now let's look at the data requirements for Spiegelhalter's algorithm. In order to get a decomposable model, Spiegelhalter must add edges to the original directed graph. In doing so, he may form cliques in the corresponding undirected graph which are larger than any of the original maximal cliques. These large cliques correspond to joint marginal probability distributions which are not contained in the original data. Finally, let's compare how we propose getting the additional data to how Spiegelhalter proposes doing so. We propose that this additional data is collected with the original data by having the first four steps of our algorithm be "planning" steps. On the other hand, Spiegelhalter's technique assumes conditional independence to get the additional data from the given constraints.

Finally, we will compare our technique to Kim and Pearl's technique which uses conditional independence instead of maximum entropy to obtain a unique distribution. We show that acyclic hypergraphs generalize singly-connected networks. We know that in the case where the Bayesian network is a tree, equation (7) gives the maximum entropy distribution, and when the network is not a tree, equation (7) does not give the maximum entropy distribution. However, if the independence constraints assumed by Kim and Pearl are supplied as additional constraints to a maximum entropy algorithm, then the two techniques give equivalent results. This is because the conditional independence constraints uniquely define a probability distribution. So, in some sense one could argue that a maximum entropy algorithm is more general that the one used by Kim and Pearl.

10 Conclusions and Open Problems

We have presented an efficient algorithm for calculating the maximum entropy distribution for a given set of attributes and constraints. Using a hypergraph to model the attributes and constraints, we have shown the benefits of making the corresponding hypergraph *acyclic*. We also have shown how to make a hypergraph acyclic by adding hyperedges (constraints). Finally, we have compared this new technique to Cheeseman's technique, Spiegelhalter's technique and Kim and Pearl's technique.

An open problem is to determine whether or not the problem of choosing the best set of hyperedges which will make a hypergraph acyclic is an NP-complete problem. We conjecture that this is the case, but have not yet been able to exhibit a proof. We would like either to find an NP-completeness proof, or to find a polynomial time algorithm to solve the problem.

Another direction of future research is to determine how well our new algorithm works on real-life problems. We intend to try our technique on some realistic examples. Our goal is to determine if the size of the hyperedges will remain within reasonable limits for realistic examples. We expect that in practice our new method will give substantial improvements in running time. Since our method adds tables which may be larger than the original ones, it may be interesting to explore how these larger tables impact data accuracy.

Another interesting problem is to find a condition which ensures the existence of a non-iterative algorithm for approximating the maximum entropy distribution when the input can consist of joint marginal probability distributions, conditional probability distributions, and some clearly defined independence constraints.

References

[1] Agmon, N., Y. Alhassid, R.D. Levine, "An Algorithm for Determining the Lagrange Parameters in the Maximal Entropy Formalism," In Levine and Tribune, editors, *The Maximum Entropy Formalism*, M.I.T. Press, (1979).

[2] Agmon, N., Y. Alhassid, R.D. Levine, "An Algorithm for Finding the Distribution of Maximal Entropy," *Journal of Computational Physics* 30,2 (February 1979), 250-259.

[3] Berri, C., R. Fagin, D. Maier, A. Mendelzon, J.D. Ullman and M. Yannakakis, "Properties of Acyclic Database Schemas," in *Proc. 13th Annual ACM STOC* (1981), 355-362.

[4] Berri, C., R. Fagin, D. Maier and M. Yannakakis, "On the Desirability of Acyclic Database Schemas," *J. ACM*, **30**,3 (1983), 355-362.

[5] Brown, D.T., "A Note on Approximations to Discrete Probability Distributions," *Information and Control*, **2** (1959), 386-392.

[6] Cheeseman, P.C., "A Method For Computing Generalized Bayesian Probability Values For Expert Systems," in *Proc. Eighth International Conference on Artificial Intelligence* (August 1983), 198-202.

[7] Cheeseman, P.C., "Learning of Expert Systems From Data," in *Proc. IEEE Workshop on Principles of Knowledge Based Systems* (1984), 115-122.

[8] Chow, C.K. and C.N. Liu, "Approximating Discrete Probability Distributions With Dependence Trees," *IEEE Trans. on Info. Theory*, **IT-14**,3 (May 1968), 462-467.

[9] Csiszár, I., "I-Divergence geometry of probability distributions and minimization problems," *Annals of Probability*, **3**,1 (1975), 146-158.

[10] Dalkey, N.C., "Min-Score Inference on Probability Systems," *University Of California, Los Angeles Dept. of Computer Science Technical Report UCLA-ENG-CSL-8112*, (June 1981).

[11] Darroch, J.N., S.L. Lauritzen, and T.P. Speed, "Markov Fields and Log-Linear Models for Contingency Tables," *Annals of Statistics*, **8** (1980), 522-539.

[12] Edwards, D., and S. Kreiner, "Analysis of Contingency Tables by Graphical Models," *Biometrika* **70**,3 (1983), 553-565.

[13] Fienberg, S.E., "An Iterative Procedure For Estimation In Contingency Tables," *The Annals of Mathematical Statistics*, **41**,3 (1970), 907-917.

[14] Geman, S., "Stochastic Relaxation Methods For Image Restoration and Expert Systems," In Cooper, D.B., R.L. Launer, and E. McClure, editors, *Automated Image Analysis: Theory and Experiments*, New York: Academic Press, (to appear).

[15] Goldman, S.A., "Efficient Methods for Calculating Maximum Entropy Distributions," S.M. thesis, Massachusetts Institute of Technology, Department of Electrical Engineering and Computer Science, (May 1987).

[16] Graham, M.H., "On the Universal Relation," *University of Toronto Technical Report* (1979).

[17] Ireland, C.T., and S. Kullback, "Contingency tables with given marginals," *Biometrika* **55**,1 (1968), 179-188.

[18] Jaynes, E.T., "Where Do We Stand On Maximum Entropy," In Levine and Tribune, editors, *The Maximum Entropy Formalism*, M.I.T. Press, (1979).

[19] Jaynes, E.T., "On the Rationale of Maximum-Entropy Methods," *Proceedings of the IEEE*, **70**,9 (September 1982), 939-952.

[20] Johnson, R.W., and J.E. Shore, "Comments and corrections to 'Axiomatic derivation of the principle of maximum entropy and the principle of minimum cross-entropy'," *IEEE Trans. Inform. Theory* **IT-29**, 6 (Nov. 1983), 942-943.

[21] Ku, H.H. and S. Kullback, "Approximating Discrete Probability Distributions," *IEEE Trans. on Info. Theory*, **IT-15**,4 (July 1969), 444-447.

[22] Kim, J.H. and J. Pearl, "A Computational Model for Causal and Diagnostic Reasoning in Inference Systems," *Proc. Eighth International Conference on Artificial Intelligence* (August 1983), 190-193.

[23] Lewis, P.M., "Approximating Probability Distributions to Reduce Storage Requirements," *Information and Control*, **2** (1959), 214–225.

[24] Lippman, A.F., "A Maximum Entropy Method for Expert System Construction," Ph.D. thesis, Brown University, Division of Applied Mathematics, (May 1986).

[25] Malvestuto, F.M., "Decomposing Complex Contingency Tables to Reduce Storage Requirements," *Proceedings of 3rd International Workshop on Statistical and Scientific Database Management* (July 1986), 66–71.

[26] Malvestuto, F.M., "Modeling Large Bases of Categorical Data with Acyclic Schemes," *Proceedings of the International Conference on Database Theory* (September 1986).

[27] Pearl, J., "Fusion, Propagation and Structuring in Bayesian Networks," *University Of California, Los Angeles Dept. of Computer Science Technical Report CSD-850022 R-42*, (April 1985).

[28] Rissanen, J., "A Universal Prior for Integers and Estimation by Minimum Description Length," *The Annals of Statistics*, **11**,2 (1983), 416–431.

[29] Rose, D.J. and R.E. Tarjan, "Algorithmic Aspects of Vertex Elimination in Directed Graphs," *SIAM Journal Applied Math*, **24** (1978), 176–197.

[30] Rose, D.J., R.E. Tarjan, and G.S. Lueker, "Algorithmic Aspects of Vertex Elimination on Graphs," *SIAM Journal Comput.*, **5**,2 (June 1976), 266–283.

[31] Shore, J.E., and R.W. Johnson, "Axiomatic Derivation of the Principle of Maximum Entropy and the Principle of Minimum Cross-Entropy," *IEEE Trans. Inform. Theory*, **IT-26**,1 (Jan. 1980), 26–37.

[32] Spiegelhalter, D.J., "Probabilistic Reasoning in Predictive Expert Systems," in *Uncertainty in Artificial Intelligence*, (eds. Kanal, L.N. and Lemmer, J.) North Holland Amsterdam, 47–68.

[33] Spiegelhalter, D.J., "Coherent Evidence Propagation in Expert Systems," to appear in the *The Statistician*.

[34] Tarjan, R.E. and M. Yannakakis, "Simple Linear-Time Algorithms to Test Chordality of Graphs, Test Acyclicity of Hypergraphs, and Selectively Reduce Acyclic Hypergraphs," *SIAM J. Comp.*, **13**,3 (August 1984), 566–579.

[35] Tikochinsky, Y., N.Z. Tishby, and R.D. Levine, "Consistent Inference of Probabilities for Reproducible Experiments," *Physical Rev. Letters* **52**, 16 (16 April 1984), 1357–1360.

[36] Tversky, A. and Kahneman, D., "Judgment Under Uncertainty: Heuristics and Biases," *Science*, **185**, (September 1974), 1124–1131.

[37] Yannakakis, M., "Computing the Minimum Fill-in is NP-Complete," *SIAM Journal Alg. Disc. Meth.*, **2**,1 (March 1981), 77–79.

Propagating Uncertainty in Bayesian Networks by Probabilistic Logic Sampling

Max HENRION[*]

Carnegie Mellon University, Department of Engineering and Public Policy, and Department of Social and Decision Sciences, Pittsburgh, Pa 15213, USA.

Bayesian belief networks and influence diagrams are attractive approaches for representing uncertain expert knowledge in coherent probabilistic form. But current algorithms for propagating updates are either restricted to singly connected networks (Chow trees), as the scheme of Pearl and Kim, or they are liable to exponential complexity when dealing with multiply connected networks. Probabilistic logic sampling is a new scheme employing stochastic simulation which can make probabilistic inferences in large, multiply connected networks, with an arbitrary degree of precision controlled by the sample size. A prototype implementation, named Pulse, is illustrated, which provides efficient methods to estimate conditional probabilities, perform systematic sensitivity analysis, and compute evidence weights to explain inferences.

1. Introduction

Several recent papers have advocated the use of Bayesian or personalist probability as the best approach for representing uncertainty in rule-based expert systems, arguing that earlier criticisms of probability as inappropriate or impractical have been misplaced [12, 2, 15, 7]. Among the suggested advantages of probability are that it has a clear theoretical basis combined with a theory of rational decision-making, an operational definition, a language for expressing uncertain dependence, and an ability to integrate diagnostic and predictive reasoning. The most promising current candidates for a coherent probabilistic representation appears to be the *Bayesian belief network* or *causal network* [13] and the closely related *influence diagram* [9, 14]. The influence diagram generalizes the Bayesian network by including decision variables in addition to uncertain chance variables.

An ingenious and computationally efficient algorithm is available for propagating updates through a Bayesian network, provided it is singly connected [10]. However, existing algorithms to deal with multiply connected networks are liable to exponential complexity when there are many intersecting cycles. This paper introduces *probabilistic logic sampling*, a scheme designed to make inferences efficiently in multiply connected Bayesian networks. Before describing the technique, I shall first review the basic notions of Bayesian networks, introducing a simple example, and examine the treatment of dependent evidence in uncertain inference systems.

---

[*]This work was supported in part by the National Science Foundation under grant IST-8603493.

2. Bayesian Belief Networks

Each node in a Bayesian network represents a variable, which in general may be uncertain. It may have many possible values, but for simplicity of exposition I shall restrict the discussion to logical variables or propositions, with just two possible values, true and false. The links between variables are directed, and they represent predictive influences on each variable of its immediate predecessors (its *parents*). A Bayesian network must have no *directed* cycles (i.e. no variables that are their own descendants), but it may be multiply connected (i.e. with more than one directed path from a variable to one of its descendants).

The network provides a clear graphical form to express qualitative judgments about the probabilistic dependencies and conditional independences among the variables. Specifically, each variable is independent of its indirect ancestors conditional on its parents, i.e. immediate predecessors; and sibling variables (i.e. with one or more common parents) are independent conditional on their parents. The usefulness of the Bayesian network, and indeed the usefulness of any inference network or rule-based representation of knowledge, rests on the assumption that knowledge is decomposable and can be adequately represented by a sparse graph, in which each variable is directly influenced by only a few other variables.

We shall illustrate this scheme with a simple example, borrowed from [3] via [16]:

> "Metastatic cancer is a possible cause of a brain tumor, and is also an explanation for increased total serum calcium. In turn either of these could explain a patient falling into a coma. Severe headache is also possibly associated with a brain tumor."

This information about qualitative dependences is represented by the Bayesian network in Figure 2-1. Note that it is multiply connected, having a single cycle, A,B,C,D.

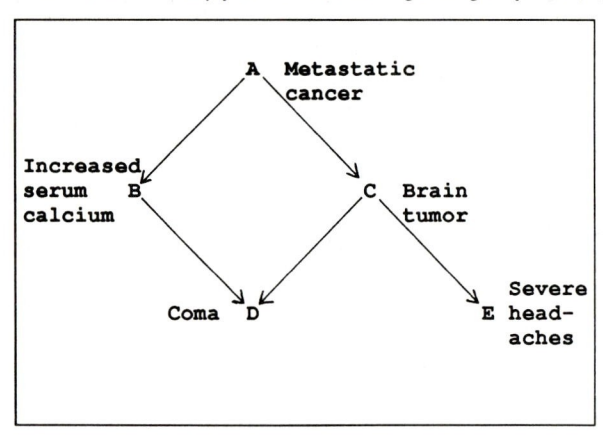

Figure 2-1: An example Bayesian belief network

In this example we will assume for simplicity that all five variables are logical propositions denoting the presence or absence of each disease or symptom. Uppercase letters, such as A, will be used to represent random logical variables, which can take values *true* or *false*, represented by the corresponding lowercase letters, a and $\bar{a}$.

In a Bayesian network, each influence is quantified as the probability distribution of each child conditional on its parents. For example, the influence of A on B is quantified by the conditional probability distribution, $p(B|A)$. This requires specification of two independent parameters, $p(b|a)$ and $p(b|\bar{a})$. The influence of variables B and C on their common child, D, is expressed by the conditional distribution, $p(D|B,C)$. This requires specification of four independent parameters, e.g. $p(d|b,c), p(d|b,\bar{c}), p(d|\bar{b},c), p(d|\bar{b},\bar{c})$. To complete the specification, we also need a prior probability distribution for the "top level" source nodes, in this case variable $p(A)$.

For any Bayesian network, the priors assessed for the source nodes together with the conditionals for all the other nodes are guaranteed to specify a joint probability distribution over all the variables, which is both *coherent*, i.e. not overdetermined, and *complete*, i.e. not underdetermined. It is this feature that underlies much of the appeal of the approach for eliciting uncertain expert knowledge.

Formal statistical theory says nothing about which direction the arrows should go, as long as the network has no directed cycles. However, where a causal relation is believed to exist, it is usually much easier to assess the conditional probabilities as p(effect|cause) than as p(cause|effect). Consequently it is more convenient to initially structure the network with the arrows from cause to effect. Moreover knowledge about causal relations can be very helpful in judging dependence and independence relationships between variables [4]. Pearl conjectures that the psychological usefulness of the notion of causality is closely tied to its heuristic role in structuring probabilistic relationships [13].

In a medical example, the top or *source* nodes, with indegree 0, may represent disease hypotheses, such as variable A, metastatic cancer, in this case, or factors or conditions that might influence disease probabilities, such as age or exposure to carcinogenic chemicals. The bottom or *sink* nodes, with outdegree 0, represent manifestations or symptoms of their parent hypotheses (such as variables, D, coma, and E, severe headaches). *Predictive* or *causal* inference involves reasoning from evidence about source nodes down through the network in the direction of the arcs to the sink nodes, e.g. to infer the probability that particular symptoms will be observed if a disease or conditioning factor is known to be present. *Diagnostic* inference involves reasoning in the reverse direction, from observations of manifestations to infer probabilities of possible causes, e.g. from observations of symptoms to diseases. A coherent probabilistic inference scheme can support both predictive and diagnostic inference and combinations of the two, according what evidence is available and what hypotheses are of interest. This is a major advantage of such schemes over the better known incoherent schemes, such as Mycin or Prospector, which are incapable of supporting this kind of mixed inference in a flexible and general manner [7].

The following probability distributions completely specify the example network. They are taken from [16]:

$p(a) = .20$

$p(b|a) = .80$ $p(c|a) = .20$
$p(b|\bar{a}) = .20$ $p(c|\bar{a}) = .05$

$p(d|b,c) = .80$
$p(d|\bar{b},c) = .80$
$p(d|b,\bar{c}) = .80$ $p(e|c) = .80$
$p(d|\bar{b},\bar{c}) = .05$ $p(e|\bar{c}) = .60$

These probabilities may be estimated from empirical data, if available, but more often will be derived from expert opinion, perhaps a medical specialist in this case. Note that the knowledge engineer may not necessarily ask for the conditional probabilities precisely in this form. Conditionals may be specified as likelihood ratios or log-likelihood ratios. In general, an influence with n parents requires 2^n parameters, but simpler forms of influence, such as "noisy And gates" and "noisy Or gates", may often be sufficient, requiring many fewer parameters [13]. Some influences may be essentially deterministic. In many cases the sensitivities to the precise numerical values may be small, and verbal expression of the strength of evidential relationships may be sufficient. There is still considerable scope for research on finding the most convenient and reliable methods for eliciting knowledge about probabilistic relationships. But for the purposes of this paper, we shall assume that, however the influences were elicited, the results have been converted into the form of conditional distributions as used above.

In principle, it is simple to compute the joint distribution over all variables in a network as the product of all the specified prior and the conditional distributions. In the example, this would be:

$$p(A,B,C,D,E) = p(A) \times p(B|A) \times p(C|A) \times p(D|B,C) \times p(E|C)$$

From this it is straightforward to calculate the marginal probability for any proposition, or its conditional probability given observations of the truth or falsity of any set of observables. For example, using the notation,

$$\sum_X p(X,y) = p(x,y) + p(\bar{x},y),$$

we can compute the probability of a, given the patient is not in a coma, $\bar{d}$, but has severe headaches, e:

$$p(a|\bar{d},e) = \frac{p(a,\bar{d},e)}{p(\bar{d},e)} = \frac{\sum_{B,C} p(a,B,C,\bar{d},e)}{\sum_{A,B,C} p(A,B,C,\bar{d},e)} = 0.097$$

The problem with this approach is that the number of parameters in the joint distribution over n propositions is 2^n, and so explicit representation is intractable for networks of reasonable size, having hundreds or thousands of variables. As mentioned, Pearl and Kim have devised an ingenious and highly efficient algorithm for propagating evidence through a Bayesian network, using predictive and/or diagnostic inference, provided the network is singly connected, i.e. a *Chow tree*, [10, 13]. This Pearl-Kim algorithm is linear in the size of the network, and requires only local computations at each variable, exchanging information only with its neighbours. It could therefore be implemented very efficiently by a network of parallel processors.

3. Dependent evidence and multiply connected networks

The Pearl-Kim algorithm relies on the assumption that evidence from different neighbours (parents or children) of a variable is independent, which would be violated in a multiply connected network, such as our example. Indeed most schemes proposed for use in expert systems have problems with treating dependence between convergent lines of evidence. Any scheme for combining two or more sources of uncertain evidence, whether diagnostic or predictive, needs to know about the dependence between the sources, or at least has to make some assumptions about it. Proponents of some non-probabilistic approaches, notably Fuzzy Set theory and the Emycin scheme, have argued that by avoiding the use of probabilities, they can avoid having to make any such assumptions. But in fact such approaches can still be compared with probabilistic schemes, and it turns out that they are equivalent to probabilistic schemes with particular assumptions [18, 6, 7]. For example, the Fuzzy Set combination rules for conjunction and disjunction are equivalent to assuming "maximum correlation" between the operands, i.e. that the less likely one *implies* the more likely one. The Emycin algorithm for combining evidence from multiple rules turns out to be equivalent to assuming marginal independence for confirming evidence [17]. Most deliberately probabilistic schemes, including Prospector and the Pearl-Kim scheme for Bayesian Networks, assume conditional independence when combining rules with diagnostic evidence.

In the real world, evidence from different sources is often dependent. If an inference network has multiple paths from one node to another, then the convergent lines of evidence bearing on the second node will be inherently dependent in general. This ought to affect how the evidence from the two paths is combined, but it cannot in schemes in which the dependence is not represented. Unfortunately, any local propagation scheme that represents the uncertainty associated with a proposition by only one or two numbers, as do the numerical schemes used in the standard expert systems and the Pearl-Kim scheme is unable to represent the richness of multiple dependencies. Hence it is inherently incapable of taking dependence properly into account in its combining rules, other than by some arbitrary assumption of independence or total dependence. On the other hand a scheme that attempts to represent explicitly the dependence between all propositions in the domain (as does a naive "complete" probabilistic scheme), or even just between all propositions which are direct or indirect antecedents, seems doomed to exponential complexity.

Pearl [13] discusses four possible approaches for dealing with multiply connected networks (with undirected cycles). One method is to group interconnected variables within a cycle into *cliques* or *local event groups (LEGs)*, and thus convert a cyclic graph of simple variables into a tree of compound variables. Spiegelhalter describes a similar method derived from the statistical theory of *graphical models* in contingency tables [16]. This is similar in effect to collapsing the n binary nodes in a cycle into a single compound node or *clique* with 2^n states. It works well if the cycles are few, but runs into problems with networks with cycles that are themselves in cycles. Shachter has described and implemented an approach to evaluation of influence diagrams, which can deal with networks of modest size containing cycles, but this also appears to become impractical for large networks with many cycles [14]. Another approach is *stochastic relaxation*, but Pearl suggests this is liable to take a very long time to reach convergence. A third method is *conditioning*, which involves cutting open the cycles by instantiating key variables within them, and combining the results from different instantiations. Again this is liable to exponential complexity with multiple loops [13]. The fourth approach suggested by Pearl, is to introduce auxiliary variables, which can sometimes allow conversion of a multiply connected network to a tree. He suggests that this mirrors the conceptual development of causal models in humans, and is how we construct cognitively manageable representations for dealing with an uncertain World. While each of these approaches may be useful in some situations, none of them appears to be computationally tractable in general for large and complex, multiply connected networks.

4. Probabilistic Logic sampling

Probabilistic Logic sampling employs a stochastic simulation approach to provide a way out of this apparent impasse between oversimplifying by ignoring dependences between lines of evidence on one hand, and risking exponential complexity on the other. In this approach a probabilistic Bayesian network is represented by a finite sample of deterministic *scenarios* or *possible worlds* generated at random from the probabilistic model. It is similar in spirit to the independently developed *Incidence Calculus*, which has been used for estimating the probabilities of arbitrary boolean expressions with dependent terms [1]. Bundy points out the advantages of this approach in dealing with probabilistic dependence. Logic sampling generalizes this approach to represent conditional relationships and so perform inference in Bayesian networks. The idea of representing a probabilistic inference as a generalization of logical inference in a set of deterministic possible worlds is related to Nilsson's Probabilistic Logic [11]. However, here we solve the combinatorial problem of considering all possible worlds by contenting ourselves with merely a random sample of them. While a finite sample will not produce exact estimates of the required probabilities, we can obtain an arbitrary degree of accuracy by choice of the appropriate sample size. Moreover we can easily estimate the precision with standard statistics.

Suppose we represent a Bayesian network by a sample of m deterministic *scenarios*, $s=1,2,...m$. Suppose $L_s(x)$ is the truth of event x in scenario s. Then uncertainty about x can be represented by a *Logic sample*, that is the vector of truth values for the sample of scenarios:

$$L(x) \equiv [L_1(x), L_2(x), ... L_m(x)].$$

If we are given the prior probability $p(x)$, we can use a random number generator to produce a logic sample for x. If we use *equiprobable sampling* then each $L_s(x)$ is set true with the specified probability, otherwise false.

Conversely, given a logic sample, $L(x)$, we can estimate the probability of x as the *truth fraction* of the logic sample, i.e. the proportion of scenarios in which x is true:

$$p(x) \approx T[L(x)] \equiv \sum_{s=1}^{m} L_s(x)/m$$

For each conditional probability distribution given, e.g. $p(X|Y)$, we can generate a logic sample for each of its independent parameters using the corresponding probabilities, e.g. $p(x|y)$, $p(x|\bar{y})$. We denote these *conditional logic samples* as $L(x|y)$, $L(x|\bar{y})$. Each can be viewed as a vector of implication rules from the parent(s) to child. For a given scenario s, the values of the two conditional logic samples specify the state of x for any state of its parent, y:

$$L_s(x|y) \equiv (L_s(y) => L_s(x))$$
$$L_s(x|\bar{y}) \equiv (L_s(\bar{y}) => L_s(x))$$

Figure 4-1 shows the example Bayesian network with each influence expressed as a conditional probability distribution in tabular form. Figure 4-2 shows a particular deterministic scenario from the sample with each of the corresponding influences is expressed as a truth table.

Figure 4-3 presents the first few scenarios from a sample. Each horizontal vector of truth values represents a logic sample for the specified variable or conditional relation. Each

Figure 4-1

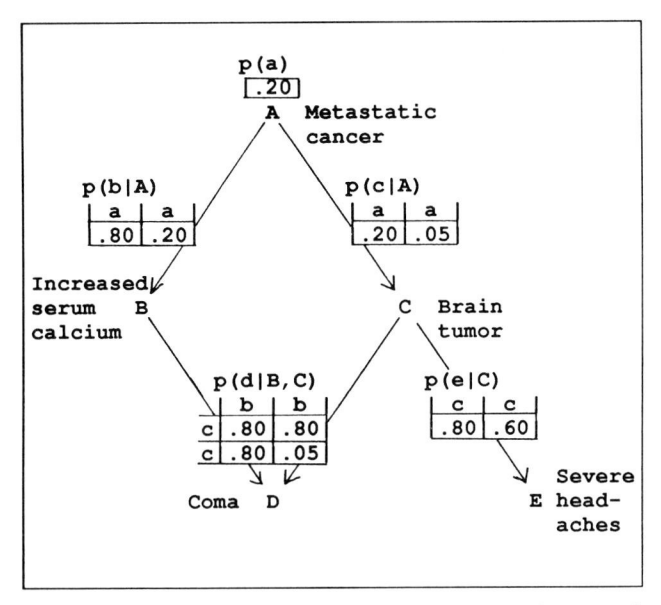

```
                      p(a)
                      .20
                    A  Metastatic
                       cancer
      p(b|A)                  p(c|A)
      | a  | ā  |             | a  | ā  |
      |.80 |.20 |             |.20 |.05 |
Increased ↙                        ↘
serum    B                          C  Brain
calcium                                tumor
              p(d|B,C)          p(e|C)
              |   | b  | b̄  |   | c  | c̄  |
              | c |.80 |.80 |   |.80 |.60 |
              | c̄ |.80 |.05 |
                  ↓   ↙              ↓    Severe
              Coma  D                E    head-
                                          aches
```

Figure 4-1: Bayesian network with probabilities for the example

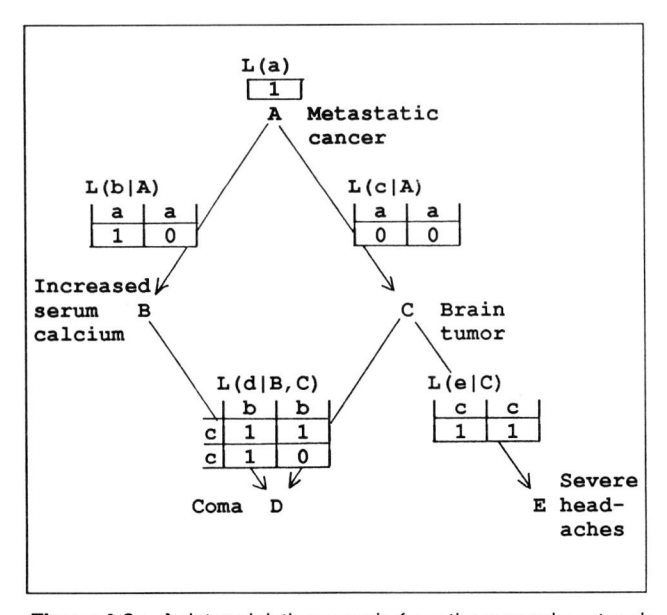

Figure 4-2

```
                      L(a)
                       1
                    A  Metastatic
                       cancer
      L(b|A)                  L(c|A)
      | a  | ā  |             | a  | ā  |
      | 1  | 0  |             | 0  | 0  |
Increased ↙                        ↘
serum    B                          C  Brain
calcium                                tumor
              L(d|B,C)          L(e|C)
              |   | b  | b̄  |   | c  | c̄  |
              | c | 1  | 1  |   | 1  | 1  |
              | c̄ | 1  | 0  |
                  ↓   ↙              ↓    Severe
              Coma  D                E    head-
                                          aches
```

Figure 4-2: A deterministic scenario from the example network

of the columns of truth values represents one of the m scenarios. The first column of probabilities are those given for the Bayesian network and used to generate the logic samples to their left.

Logic sample	Given Probs	Scenario # 1 2 3 4 ...m	Estimated probs
L(a)	.20	[1 0 0 0 ...]	
L(b|a)	.80	[1 0 1 1 ...]	
L(b|a)	.20	[0 1 0 1 ...]	
L(b)		[1 1 0 1 ...]	0.32
L(c|a)	.20	[0 1 0 0 ...]	
L(c|a)	.05	[0 0 1 0 ...]	
L(c)		[0 0 1 0 ...]	0.08
L(d|b,c)	.80	[1 0 1 1 ...]	
L(d|b,c)	.80	[0 1 1 1 ...]	
L(d|b,c)	.80	[1 1 1 0 ...]	
L(d|b,c)	.05	[0 0 0 1 ...]	
L(d)		[1 1 1 0 ...]	0.34
L(e|c)	.80	[0 1 0 0 ...]	
L(e|c)	.60	[0 0 1 0 ...]	
L(e)		[0 0 1 0 ...]	0.63
L(a&e)		[0 0 0 0 ...]	0.13

Figure 4-3: Logic sampling example

It is straightforward to compute the truth of each variable given the state of its parents and the deterministic influence of its parents. For example, for scenario s, we obtain the truth of b given its parent a, thus:

$$L_s(b) = L_s(b|a)\&L_s(a) \vee L_s(b|\overline{a})\&L_s(\overline{a}). \tag{1}$$

In this way we can work down from the source node(s) to their successive descendants, using simple logical operations to compute the truth for each variable:

$$L_s(c) = L_s(c|a)\&L_s(a) \vee L_s(c|\overline{a})\&L_s(\overline{a})$$

$$L_s(d) = [L_s(d|b,c)\&L_s(c) \vee L_s(d|b,\overline{c})\&L_s(\overline{c})]\&L_s(b) \vee$$
$$[L_s(d|\overline{b},c)\&L_s(c) \vee L_s(d|\overline{b},\overline{c})\&L_s(\overline{c})]\&L_s(\overline{b})$$

$$L_s(e) = L_s(e|c)\&L_s(c) \vee L_s(e|\overline{c})\&L_s(\overline{c})$$

Note that identity (1) is the deterministic counterpart of the probabilistic chain rule:

$$p(b) = p(b|a) \times p(a) + p(b|\overline{a}) \times [1-p(a)]$$

The problem with performing simple probabilistic chaining in this example is that to compute $p(d)$ we would need the joint distribution over its parents $p(B\&C)$, but probabilistic chaining would only give us the marginals, $p(B)$ and $p(C)$, and assuming independence would be incorrect in general. But in a deterministic case, the individual truth values determine the joint truth value, e.g.:

$L_s(b\&c) = L_s(b)\&L_s(c)$.

While a single scenario says little about the probabilities, a sample of several scenarios can be used to estimate them. The marginal probability for each variable x, is estimated as the truth fraction of its Logic sample, $T[L(x)]$. In Figure 4-3, the second column of probabilities are those estimated from the logic samples to their right. Similarly, we can estimate the joint probability of any set of variables, or indeed the probability of any Boolean combination of variables from the truth fraction of that Boolean combination of their Logic Samples. Hence, for example:

$p(\overline{d}\&e) \approx T[L(\overline{d}\&e)]$,

$p(a\&\overline{d}\&e) \approx T[L(a\&\overline{d}\&e)]$.

Any conditional probability can be computed directly from its definition, as the ratio of the joint probability to the probability of the conditioning event, each of which may be estimated from their Logic samples. For example, the posterior probability of a given the patient is not in a coma, $\overline{d}$, but has severe headaches, e, may be estimated as the ratio of the truth fractions of the corresponding Logic samples, which we just computed:

$$p(a|\overline{d},e) = \frac{p(a,\overline{d},e)}{p(\overline{d},e)} \approx \frac{T[L(a\&\overline{d}\&e)]}{T[L(\overline{d}\&e)]} = 0.11$$

In summary, probabilistic logic sampling proceeds as follows, assuming we start with a Bayesian network with priors specified for all source variables and conditional distributions for all others:

1. Use a random number generator to produce a sample truth value for each source variable, and a sample implication rule for each parameter of each conditional distribution, using the corresponding probabilities.

2. Proceed down through the network following the arrows from the source nodes, using the simple logical operations to obtain the truth of each variable from its parents and the implication rules.

3. Repeat steps 2 and 3 m times to obtain a logic sample for each variable.

4. Estimate the prior marginal probability of any simple or compound event by the truth fraction of its logic sample, i.e. the fraction of scenarios in which they are true.

5. Estimate the posterior probability for any event conditional on any set of observed variables as the fraction of sample scenarios in which the event occurs out of those scenarios in which the condition occurs.

5. Pulse: An Implementation

Pulse (Propagation of Uncertainty by Logic Sampling) is a program that implements this scheme in the Demos language [8]. The following are some of the basic functions Pulse provides for defining and analyzing Bayesian networks:

Bern(*p*) Generates a logic sample (Bernoulli sample) of truth values each with probability, *p*, of being true.

Influence1(*x, pax, panx*)
Generates a logic sample for a variable *a* influenced by a single parent *x*, with conditional probabilities, $pax = p(a|x)$, $panx = p(a|\bar{x})$.

Influence2(*x, y, pxy, pnxy, pxny, pnxny*)
Generates a logic sample for a variable *a* influenced by two parents *x* and *y*, and specified conditional probabilities, $pxy = p(a|x,y)$, $pnxy = p(a|\bar{x},y)$, $pxny = p(a|x,\bar{y})$, $pnxny = p(a|\bar{x},\bar{y})$.

Influence3(*x, y, z, pxyz, ...*)
Generates a logic sample for a variable with three parents, *x*, *y*, and *z*, and the required nine conditional probabilities, defined similarly.

Pr(*x*) Estimates the probability of *x* as the truth fraction of its logic sample.

Cpr(*x, y*) Estimates the conditional probability of *x* given *y*.

The coma example is completely represented by the following Pulse expressions:
```
A:=Bern(.20)
B:=Influence1(A, .80, .20)
C:=Influence1(A, .20, .05)
D:=Influence2(B, C, .80, .80, .80, .05)
E:=Influence1(C, .80, .60)
```

The following table compares the prior probabilities for each variable estimated by Pulse using a sample size, m=200, with the exact probabilities:

	A	B	C	D	E
Pulse	[.20	.32	.08	.34	.63]
Exact	[.20	.32	.08	.32	.62]
S.d.	[.02	.03	.02	.03	.03]

S.d. denotes an estimate of the standard deviation of the results from Pulse, expressing the expected accuracy. (Calculation of this is explained below.) The following table gives the posterior probabilities, conditional on severe headaches, E, being observed, as estimated by Pulse and the exact answers.

	A	B	C	D
Pulse	[.21	.34	.11	.38]
Exact	[.21	.33	.10	.33]
S.d.	[.03	.04	.02	.04]

Again, the agreement seems good, but we will return to the question of precision below.

6. Explanation and sensitivity analysis

With this logic sampling scheme it is computationally cheap to estimate the probability of any event conditional on any simple or compound event which has significant probability. Once prior logic samples have been computed for the network, it is an order *m* operation, independent of network size. This is useful for estimating posterior probabilities given specific observations, for estimating the relative importance of individual observations for hypotheses of interest, and for examining the sensitivity of conclusions to initial probability assessments.

For uncertain inference systems, and "expert systems" in general, to be acceptable to users, it is essential to be able to explain how conclusions were obtained and what they depend on. Some have suggested that probabilistic inference is inherently hard to explain, being "alien" to human reasoning. We certainly have some way to go in understanding just how we reason intuitively under uncertainty, but in any case there exist convenient ways to explain probabilistic inference comprehensibly. Many statisticians have suggested the use of Evidence Weights as a simple-to-understand method of comparing the relative importance of different sources of evidence, for and against a probabilistic conclusion [15]. The Evidence Weight of any evidence y for a hypothesis x is defined as the log likelihood of y with respect to x, times a factor of 100 for convenience:

$$EW(x,y) \equiv 100 \times \ln(\frac{p(y|x)}{p(y|\bar{x})})$$

The variable y may be diagnostic evidence for x, a causal influence, or indeed any other variable in the network. Supporting evidence has positive weight and evidence against has negative weight: If the sources of evidence are independent conditional on X, the Evidence Weights may simply be added and subtracted from the prior log-odds in a kind of "ledger book" format. If Evidence Weights for two sources are superadditive, i.e.

$$EW(x, y \wedge z) > EW(x,y) + EW(x,z),$$

or conversely, subadditive, this may be useful information about whether one source strengthens or weakens the impact of the other.

Evidence Weights are straightforward to compute using logic samples, provided the prior probability $p(x)$ is not too near 0 or 1. This table illustrates the Evidence Weights of e and d, separately and combined on each of their predecessors, as computed by Pulse;

	A	B	C
EW(x,E)	[8	7	29]
EW(x,D)	[96	208	93]
EW(x,D&E)	[101	185	101]

A second important practical issue is uncertainty or vagueness about probability assessments. This is leading to increasing interest in assessing and propagating ranges of probabilities to represent "second order uncertainty". Where there is uncertainty about the probability, which there usually is, it is desirable to examine the sensitivity on the probability of key conclusions (e.g. disease hypotheses). The sensitivity of a computed probability $p(y)$ to an input probability $p(x)$, may be computed as:

$$\frac{dp(y)}{dp(x)} = p(y|x) - p(y|\bar{x})$$

7. Precision and Computational effort

The values of each generated logic sample are independent, and so all scenarios are independent. Hence the values of each computed logic sample, $L(x)$, are independent, and the number of true values is a random sample from a Binomial distribution with mean $mp(x)$, and size, m. The standard deviation of the truth fraction $T[L(x)]$ as an estimate of $p(x)$, may be estimated as $\sqrt{p(x)[1-p(x)]/(m-1)}$. The sample size for estimating a conditional probability $p(x|y)$ is equal to the number of points for which y is true. Thus the truth fraction $T[L(x|y)]$ is an estimate of $p(x|y)$ with standard deviation approximately

$$\sqrt{p(x|y)p(\bar{x}|y)/[mp(y)-1]}.$$

Using the truth fractions to estimate each of the probabilities in these expressions, we can easily estimate the accuracy of each of our probability estimates.

In the description of logic sampling, each scenario is generated separately, but in fact it is likely to be easier to generate and evaluate many scenarios in parallel to obtain logic samples for all variables. Obviously, logic samples can be efficiently represented as bitstrings. All operations to compute logic samples for derived variables and compound events then involve simple Boolean operations on these bitstrings.

To compute the marginal logic samples for all variables requires a single pass through the network from the source variables downward. With a bitstring representation the effort to compute the priors with a sample size of a few hundred should be comparable with a single pass for a numerical scheme for representing uncertainty using a few numbers per variable. However there is an important difference: When new evidence is observed in numerical schemes, such as Mycin or the Pearl-Kim algorithm, the impact is propagated through all or part of the network, depending on the control strategy and use of thresholds. In the logic sampling scheme, once the priors have been propagated down through the network, the effect of any observation or combination of observations from a particular case on any variable can be computed directly from the logic samples representing the observed variables and the impacted variable, without need for any additional propagation through the network. The same is true for computing conditional probabilities to obtain Evidence Weights and or to conduct sensitivity analyses. In each case, the incremental computational cost is independent of the size of the network or the path length between the observed variable(s) and the variable of interest. The information about the relationships between variables is, in effect, already inherent in the logic samples. Thus it can be computationally cheap to do very thorough, systematic sensitivity analysis to explore the robustness of the conclusions, and to suggest what additional information would be most valuable to the conclusions of interest.

For any given m the computational complexity of this scheme is linear in the size of the network, the number of nodes and arcs. But the uncertainty in estimates of conditional probabilities, $p(x|y)$, varies inversely with the probability of the observed event $p(y)$. Essentially scenarios incompatible with the observations are ignored. Thus if individual observed values are improbable, or if there are many observed variables in unlikely combinations, the uncertainty of the estimate may be large. If the observed variables are nearly independent, simply increasing the sample size m may not be a very effective solution, since the standard deviation is inversely proportional to $\sqrt{m}$, but proportional to $2^{L/2}$ where L is the number of observed variables. In other words, the complexity is potentially exponential.

However, two mitigating points should be noted: First, it is much more important to be linear in the size of the network, which may be measured in the thousands, than in the number of observed variables, which may be typically from a few to a few dozen. Secondly, the observations of interest will generally *not* be independent. Observations which are manifestations of a common cause (e.g. symptoms of a disease), will of course be highly correlated. Thus the probability of their co-occurence will be vastly greater than the independence assumption would predict. While unusual combinations of observations may occur, by definition they will be rare.

8. Improvements to efficiency

There are several possible approaches to improve the efficiency of this approach:

Latin Hypercube Sampling: This is a stratified sampling technique, in which logic samples are generated so that the fraction true is the same as the specified probability p, (or as close as possible to it if $m \times p$ is not an integer), instead of each sample value being generated independently with the specified probability. This is currently implemented in Pulse, and it provides modest increases in precision for a given m.

Weighted sampling: Instead of generating all values of a logic sample with equal probability, outcomes of low probability, but great interest are generated more often, but with a compensating lower weight. For example, serious but rare diseases would be contained in more scenarios. Thus, instead of the scenarios being equiprobable, they each have a probability proportional to the product of the weights of values from all the logic samples for all the input probabilities. The function for computing the truth fraction of a logic sample must take into account these weights to compensate, so it will produce unbiased estimates. One approach is for all logic samples to be generated with equal numbers of true and false values, i.e. with actual probability 0.5, and with weights $p(x)$ for the true values and $1-p(x)$ for the false values. This could substantially increase accuracy relative to equiprobable sampling.

Ignoring irrelevant data: Some observed variables will have little or no impact on variables of interest. If there is little correlation between the observed variable and variable of interest, then you can simply ignore the observation when computing a posterior. You can test the statistical significance of the correlation with a Chi-square test. In deciding which observations can safely be ignored, care must be taken to examine interactions between observations, since two observations taken together may have a strong effect, where each alone has little. Judicious examination of the network links can help in identifying possible interactions, without exhaustive testing of all possible combinations of observations.

9. Final remarks

One feature of logic sampling that may be appealing to some AI researchers, is the way it develops probabilistic reasoning as a direct extension of categorical logical inference, and thus can build on existing theory and methods. For example, it appears to have some interesting relationships with assumption-based reasoning [5]. Another possible attraction is the way in which reasoning under uncertainty is performed by construction of alternative deterministic scenarios, which some psychologists have suggested as typical of human reasoning under uncertainty. It explicitly represents probabilities as "frequencies" in a sample of truth values, which may be easier to understand for those more comfortable with the frequentist interpretation of probability. However it is in no way based on such an interpretation, and the input probabilities may very well be subjective probabilities judged by experts.

Logic sampling shows considerable potential as a coherent probabilistic scheme that can combine dependent evidence correctly, and still be computationally tractable. Unlike other proposed schemes, the computational effort and correctness of results are unaffected by the size and complexity of cycles within the Bayesian network. It also supports simple, yet powerful ways of explaining probabilistic inference and conducting sensitivity analysis. The precision of the output probabilities can be estimated statistically, and may be controlled directly by the sample size. Further work is required to show how to deal effectively with multiple, low probability observations, but at least one approach appears promising.

Acknowledgments

I am grateful to Judea Pearl for helpful suggestions.

References

1. Bundy, A. Incidence Calculus: A mechanism for probabilistic reasoning. Proceedings of Workshop on Uncertainty and Probability in AI, AAAI, Los Angeles, August, 1985.

2. Cheeseman, P. In Defense of Probability. Proceedings of 9th International Joint Conference on AI, Los Angeles, Ca, 1985, pp. 1002-9.

3. Cooper, C.F. NESTOR: A computer-based medical diagnostic that integrates causal and probabilistic knowledge. Report HPP-84-48, Stanford University, 1984.

4. Cooper. G.F. "A diagnostic method that uses causal knowledge and linear programming in the application of Bayes' formula". *Computer Methods and Programs in Biomedicine*, 22 (1986), 223-237.

5. de Kleer, J. "An Assumption-Based Truth Maintenance System". *Artificial Intelligence 28*, 2 (1986), 127-162.

6. Heckerman, D. Probabilistic Interpretations for Mycin's Certainty Factors. Workshop on Uncertainty and Probability in AI, 1985.

7. Henrion, M. Uncertainty in Artificial Intelligence: Is probability epistemologically and heuristically adequate? In J. Mumpower, Ed., *Expert Systems and Expert Judgment*, NATO ISI Series: Springer-Verlag, (in press) 1987.

8. Henrion, M. & M.G. Morgan. "A Computer Aid for Risk and other Policy Analysis". *Risk Analysis 5*, 3 (1985).

9. Howard, R.A. & J. E. Matheson. Influence Diagrams. The Principles and Applications of Decision Analysis: Vol II, 1984.

10. Kim, J. & Pearl, J. A Computational Model for Combined Causal and Diagnostic Reasoning in Inference Systems. Proceedings of IJCAI-83, 1983, pp. 190-193.

11. Nilsson, N.J. "Probabilistic Logic". *Artificial Intelligence*, 28 (1986), 71-87.

12. Pearl, J. How to do with probabilities what people say you can't. Tech. Rept. CSD-850031, Cognitive Systems Laboratory, Computer Science Department, University of California, Los Angeles, CA, 1985.

13. Pearl, J. "Fusion, Propagation, and Structuring in Belief Networks". *Artificial Intelligence 29*, 3 (September 1986), 241-288.

14. Shachter, R.D. "Evaluating Influence Diagrams". *Operations Research (in press)* (1987).

15. Spiegelhalter, D. J. A statistical view of uncertainty in expert systems. In *AI and Statistics*, Addison-Wesley: Reading, MA, 1986, pp. 17-48.

16. Spiegelhalter, D.J. Probabilistic Reasoning in Predictive Expert Systems. Uncertainty in Artifical Intelligence, 1986, pp. 47-67.

17. Wise, B.P. *An experimental comparison of Uncertain Inference Systems.* Ph.D. Th., Carnegie Mellon University, The Robotics Institute and Department of Engineering and Public Policy, 1986.

18. Wise, B.P. & Henrion, M. A Framework for Comparing Uncertain Inference Systems to Probability. In *Uncertainty in Artificial Intelligence*, North-Holland: Amsterdam, 1986, pp. 69-84.

AN EXPLANATION MECHANISM FOR BAYESIAN INFERENCING SYSTEMS

Steven W. Norton

PAR Government Systems Corporation
New Hartford, NY 13413 *

Explanation facilities are a particularly important feature of expert system frameworks. It is an area in which traditional rule-based expert system frameworks have had mixed results. While explanations about control are well handled, facilities are needed for generating better explanations concerning knowledge base content. This paper approaches the explanation problem by examining the effect an event has on a variable of interest within a symmetric Bayesian inferencing system. We argue that any effect measure operating in this context must satisfy certain properties. Such a measure is proposed. It forms the basis for an explanation facility which allows the user of the Generalized Bayesian Inferencing System to question the meaning of the knowledge base. That facility is described in detail.

1. INTRODUCTION

The area of Expert Systems (ES) is currently one of considerable interest. Much of this interest arises because ES technology is returning real benefits to ES users [1]. It is fair to say, however, that ES technology has not yet fully matured. A complete, fully functional ES framework must provide a range of features. One of these is an explanation capability. Explanation is particularly important since in most critical applications the human user bears the ultimate responsibility for action. In medicine, for example, the human practitioner utilizing an ES as a consultant requires an explanation of the machine inferencing process whenever its recommendation is not precisely as expected. There are many other critical areas in which expert systems will be called upon to explain themselves (nuclear, military, etc.).

The explanation facilities of current ES frameworks are chiefly directed at control mechanisms [2,3]. However, we often desire explanations of the contents of the knowledge base itself. A summary of how particular values in the knowledge base were computed may be insufficient. The uncertainty representations and inferencing mechanisms of various rule based expert systems have impeded the development of robust explanation capabilites through ill-defined actions and inconsistent semantics.

---

* Now employed by Siemens Research and Technology Laboratories, 105 College Road East, Princeton, NJ 08540.

This paper addresses both theoretical and practical issues related to explanation. In Bayesian inferencing systems, not only can explanations of control be generated, but also meaningful explanations of database content. We propose a measure of the effect that an event has on a variable of interest. That measure, summarizing correlation information, prior probabilities, and posterior probabilities, is at the core of the explanation facilities of the Generalized Bayesian Inferencing System (GBI). In the following sections we detail the most relevant features of GBI, of our effect measure, and of our explanation facility. Finally, we describe a number of enhancements possible within our implementation which would significantly enhance its explanation capabilities.

2. THE GENERALIZED BAYESIAN INFERENCING SYSTEM

The Generalized Bayesian Inferencing System is a framework for building expert systems, which supports inferencing under uncertainty according to the Bayesian hierarchical inferencing paradigm. It differs significantly from other systems reasoning under uncertainty (PROSPECTOR, MYCIN) in several respects, and the reader is referred to [4,5,6,7] for more detail. In this section, we highlight the features of GBI most relevant to the topic of explanation and provide an example to fuel further discussion.

GBI's knowledge base is a network of probability distributions over intersecting sets of events. Each event set is a Local Event Group (LEG [8]). It should be a set of importantly correlated variables. Since a LEG does not encompass all the problem variables, it has a marginal probability distribution called a Component Marginal Distribution (CMD [5]). A LEG Network (LEG Net) is made up of several LEGs, some of which share common variables. Two LEGs sharing common variables must be consistent, meaning that the computation of joint probabilities over those common variables yields identical results no matter which CMD is used.

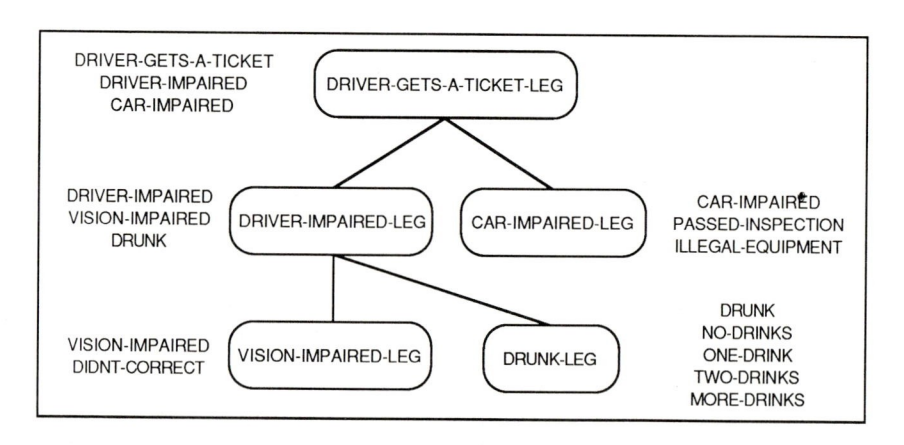

FIGURE 1: A SAMPLE LEG NETWORK

Figure 1 contains a simple example network for reasoning about whether or not the driver of an automobile receives a ticket at the scene of an accident. The events are listed beside each LEG. It's an obvious simplification since it doesn't consider any parameters of the accident itself. If the observation is made that TWO-DRINKS occured, the CMD associated with DRUNK-LEG is altered. Using the updating rule given in [4], the effect of the observation is propagated to the DRIVER-IMPAIRED-LEG through the action of the event DRUNK. If the CMD for the DRIVER-IMPAIRED-LEG is actually changed, then that effect will have to be propagated to the VISION-IMPAIRED-LEG and to the DRIVER-GETS-A-TICKET-LEG. If the CMD for DRIVER-GETS-A-TICKET-LEG changes, then the CAR-IMPAIRED-LEG will be updated as well.

3. EXPLANATION FACILITIES

At some point during a consultation session with GBI, the user will want an explanation of the expert system's behavior. In this paper, we address neither the natural language aspects of automatically generated explanations nor the explanation of control decisions. These topics have been covered elsewhere in the literature for other expert system frameworks. The same techniques may be used here. Instead we focus on explaining the contents of the LEG Net, and why changes occured in the LEG Net in order to highlight the possibilities for explanation in Bayesian expert systems.

The GBI framework was created out of a desire to incorporate correlations between variables directly into the knowledge base of an expert system. In fact, the correlations guide LEG Net construction and CMD specification [7]. Two events are correlated if information about one yields information about the other. For example, the probability of DRIVER-GETS-A-TICKET given CAR-IMPAIRED is greater than the probability of DRIVER-GETS-A-TICKET. Hence, those events are positively correlated. CAR-IMPAIRED and PASSED-INSPECTION are negatively correlated since the probability of CAR-IMPAIRED given PASSED-INSPECTION is less than the probability of CAR-IMPAIRED. This can serve as a basis for generating explanations. Why did an event become more likely? Either because a positively correlated event became more likely, or because a negatively correlated event became less likely.

We require a class of explanations for the GBI framework generated solely within a single LEG, after a single evidence update. We classify any explanation which makes explicit use of information about the exact sequence of evidence observations in order to trace back from a hypothesis to that particular evidence variable as an explanation of control information. While this type of explanation is important, we leave it out of the present discussion. This decision is not entirely arbitrary since all the available evidence could be gathered and its effects propogated in a single step using the GBI framework. In that case, there is no sequencing of evidence observations. Even in the event that evidence updates occur in sequence, there may be multiple paths through the LEG Net leading from the evidence to the hypothesis of interest. But most of all, there may be no direct relationship (in terms of correlations) within a given LEG between the variable which is changing (or any joint variable containing it) and the hypothesis of interest. Such examples are not hard to develop. Let a local explanation be any explanation for a change in a variable of interest which is expressed solely in terms of variables coexisting with it in a LEG.

Suppose that three updates altered the DRIVER-GETS-A-TICKET network, that the first was from CAR-IMPAIRED-LEG, the second from DRUNK-LEG, and the third from VISION-IMPAIRED-LEG. During the first update, PASSED-INSPECTION occurred, and ILLEGAL-EQUIPMENT did not. During the second update, NO-DRINKS occurred.

Focusing our attention after the second update and asking GBI for a local explanation of DRIVER-GETS-A-TICKET might yield the explanations given in Figure 2. The first one was generated with a level of detail appropriate for a typical user. In the second example the level of detail is more appropriate for a knowledge engineer.

The probability of DRIVER-GETS-A-TICKET decreased because the probability of DRIVER-IMPAIRED decreased after the update of DRUNK-LEG.

Events DRIVER-GETS-A-TICKET and DRIVER-IMPAIRED are positively correlated (P[DRIVER-GETS-A-TICKET | DRIVER-IMPAIRED] - P[DRIVER-GETS-A-TICKET] = 0.70). The probability of DRIVER-GETS-A-TICKET decreased (from 0.09 to 0.06) because the probability of DRIVER-IMPAIRED decreased (from 0.05 to 0.01) after the update of DRUNK-LEG.

FIGURE 2: LOCAL EXPLANATIONS

In order to generate this type of explanation, we are proposing a heuristic measure of the impact an event has had on a variable of interest within the same LEG. To quantify this effect (here the effect of evidence on a hypothesis variable), a three step calculation is performed. The first part is a measure of correlation equal to the difference between the probability of the hypothesis and the evidence, and the product of their marginal probabilities. The magnitude of the effect must increase with the amount of change in the probability of either event, and so the second and third parts of the calculation are the amounts by which the probabilities of the hypothesis and evidence change. We are left with a quantity which can always be maximized to achieve an appropriate result. Thus, if we are interested in the effect an evidence event E has had on a hypothesis variable H, we compute it as in Equation 1.

$$Ef(H,E) = [\ Pr(HE) - Pr(H)Pr(E))\ ]\ \times\ [\ Pr\ '(H) - Pr(H)\ ]\ \times\ [\ Pr\ '(E) - Pr(E)\ ] \qquad (1)$$

This measure, the Effect, is intuitively pleasing. Compare two different Effects, *Ef1* and *Ef2*, computed for a single hypothesis variable. They can be expressed as the products of correlations, changes in the evidence probabilities, and the change in the hypothesis probability. Let these be *Corr1*, *Delta1*, *Corr2*, *Delta2*, and *DeltaH* so that *Ef1* = *Corr1* x *DeltaH* x *Delta1* and *Ef2* = *Corr2* x *DeltaH* x *Delta2*. Assume that *DeltaH* is positive, indicating that the hypothesis variable became more likely. If the changes in the evidence probabilities are positive and equal, then the greater Effect will come from the variable with the larger correlation. If the changes in the evidence probabilities are negative and equal, then the greater Effect will come from the variable with the smaller correlation. And if the correlations are positive and equal, the greater Effect will come from the evidence variable which undergoes the greater positive change. The same analysis shows the measure is reasonable when the *DeltaH* term is negative.

There are two properties that an Effect measure should have, stemming from desirable properties of Bayesian systems. The first is symmetry: *Ef(H,E)* = *Ef(E,H)*. Symmetry is desirable because in a symmetric Bayesian system (such as GBI) initiating an update with a change in evidence has similar (if not identical) consequences to initiating an update with a change in the hypothesis. The other property is that $Ef(H, \text{not } E) = Ef(H,E)$. Since a Bayesian system requires that the probability of an event occurring and the probability of the same event not occurring sum to one (in the limit anyway), we cannot distinguish between the effect of those opposites except by introducing additional structure.

The measure in Equation 1 satisfies both of the above properties. It is the basis for the current GBI explanation capability. We have only implemented explanation for the univariate case, but have plans to extend it since the measure can clearly be applied to generation of multivariate explanations. For example, the joint event DRIVER–IMPAIRED & CAR–IMPAIRED may have a stronger effect on DRIVER–GETS–A–TICKET than either evidence variable alone. There may also be cases in which we want a change in a joint event to be explained.

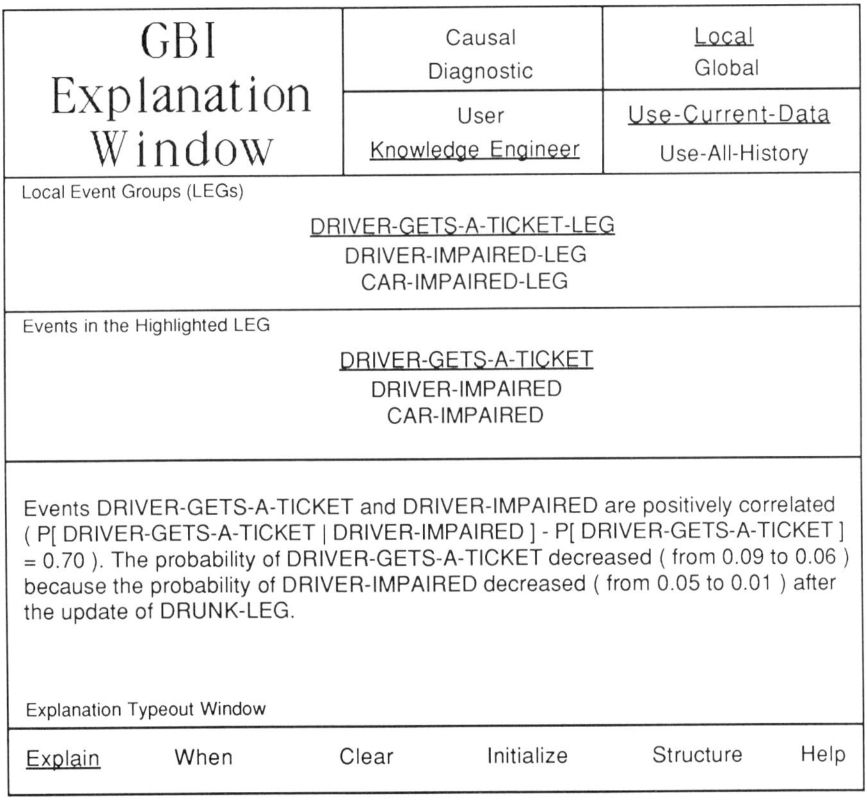

GBI Explanation Window	Causal	Local
	Diagnostic	Global
	User	Use-Current-Data
	Knowledge Engineer	Use-All-History
Local Event Groups (LEGs)		
	DRIVER-GETS-A-TICKET-LEG	
	DRIVER-IMPAIRED-LEG	
	CAR-IMPAIRED-LEG	
Events in the Highlighted LEG		
	DRIVER-GETS-A-TICKET	
	DRIVER-IMPAIRED	
	CAR-IMPAIRED	
Events DRIVER-GETS-A-TICKET and DRIVER-IMPAIRED are positively correlated (P[DRIVER-GETS-A-TICKET | DRIVER-IMPAIRED] - P[DRIVER-GETS-A-TICKET] = 0.70). The probability of DRIVER-GETS-A-TICKET decreased (from 0.09 to 0.06) because the probability of DRIVER-IMPAIRED decreased (from 0.05 to 0.01) after the update of DRUNK-LEG.		
Explanation Typeout Window		
Explain When Clear Initialize Structure Help		

FIGURE 3: THE GBI EXPLANATION FACILITY

An alternative measure of effect is the likelihood ratio used in Prospector [8]. We note, however, that it is a measure of potential effect rather than actual effect. As such, it is most useful (directly so) in controlling inference and subsequently explaining control decisions. If the likelihood ratio is substituted for the correlation measure in Equation 1, the measure fails because the likelihood ratio is non-negative. Using one minus the likelihood ratio also fails since the likelihood ratio ranges between zero and infinity. The result is to favor events positively correlated with the hypothesis over events negatively correlated with the hypothesis.

Kosy and Wise [9] make use of still another effect measure. Their measure differs from ours because there is no requirement in the domain of financial models corresponding to the symmetry requirement in the domain of LEGs. In order to express $Ef(H,E)$ and $Ef(E,H)$ in their terms, two different model functions are needed. One model sums over the evidence variables, and the other over the hypothesis variables. As a consequence, symmetry is not generally maintained.

Figure 3 portrays the GBI explanation facility in action. In the upper righthand corner are switches which control the explanation. Below the switches are the LEGs and Events menus, as well as the explanation typeout window and the explanation command menu. The LEGs menu allows the user to roam within the LEG Net. As he does so, the Events menu reflects the contents of the current LEG. In the figure, LOCAL and KNOWLEDGE ENGINEER switches are set to generate a detailed local explanation.

Since several updates occur during a typical session, the GBI explanation facility needs mechanisms to handle sequenced updates. While the fact that updates occur sequentially is used explicitly in the explanation computations, information about the particular evidence variables observed is not.° The WHEN option from the command menu allows the user to focus on a particular evidence update. In that context, the USE-CURRENT-DATA and USE-ALL-HISTORY switches determine the temporal extent of the explanation. If USE-CURRENT-DATA is selected, the current update alone is used to generate the explanation. On the other hand, if USE-ALL-HISTORY is selected GBI summarizes the effects of all the earlier updates on the variable of interest. Figure 4 illustrates local explanations using a series of several updates. Given identical switch settings, the current GBI explanation facility presents this same information although with somewhat less polished delivery.

The probability of DRIVER-GETS-A-TICKET increased because the probability of CAR-IMPAIRED increased after the update of the CAR-IMPAIRED-LEG, and because the probability of DRIVER-IMPAIRED increased after the update of the DRUNK-LEG.

DRIVER-GETS-A-TICKET is positively correlated with CAR-IMPAIRED (0.73) and with DRIVER-IMPAIRED (0.80). The probability of DRIVER-GETS-A-TICKET increased (from 0.05 to 0.35) because the probability of CAR-IMPAIRED increased (from 0.05 to 0.60) after the update of CAR-IMPAIRED-LEG, and because the probability of DRIVER-IMPAIRED increased (from 0.02 to 0.40) after the update of DRUNK-LEG.

FIGURE 4: HISTORICAL EXPLANATIONS

A limitation of this approach becomes apparent when, after the update of CAR–IMPAIRED–LEG, we ask for an explanation of CAR–IMPAIRED without moving to the CAR–IMPAIRED–LEG. Since the default mode of the GBI explanation facility is to look in the current LEG for an explanation, GBI may suggest that CAR–IMPAIRED became more likely because DRIVER–GETS–A–TICKET became more likely. If the evidence came from above rather than from below this would have been a pleasing explanation.

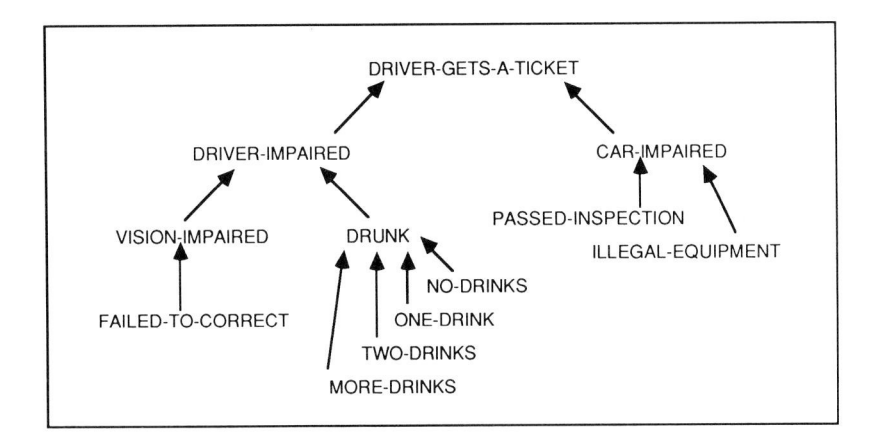

FIGURE 5: CAUSAL STRUCTURE

The probability of DRIVER–GETS–A–TICKET increased because the probability of DRIVER–IMPAIRED increased, because the probability of DRUNK increased, because MORE–DRINKS occurred after the update of DRUNK–LEG.

DRIVER–GETS–A–TICKET is positively correlated (0.73) with DRIVER–IMPAIRED, which is positively correlated (0.80) with DRUNK, which is positively correlated (0.85) with MORE–DRINKS. The probability of DRIVER–GETS–A–TICKET increased (from 0.05 to 0.80) because the probability of DRIVER–IMPAIRED increased (from 0.04 to 0.65), because the probability of DRUNK increased (from 0.01 to 0.25), because the probability of MORE–DRINKS increased (from 0.10 to 1.00) after the update of DRUNK–LEG.

FIGURE 6: GLOBAL EXPLANATIONS

In this particular case, we are seeking an explanation in terms of the causes of CAR–IMPAIRED. However, GBI itself has no real knowledge of causal structure. With the STRUCTURE option from the explanation command menu, the knowledge engineer is able to input structural information. Figure 5 shows the causal structure for our simple

LEG Net. The link from DRIVER-IMPAIRED to DRIVER-GETS-A-TICKET may be read as "DRIVER-IMPAIRED causes DRIVER-GETS-A-TICKET" or "DRIVER-GETS-A-TICKET is a symptom of DRIVER-IMPAIRED." Strict interpretation of these relationships, at least in the context of this example, may not be very productive. Instead we view these links as additional control information for the explanation process itself. When the CAUSAL switch is set, GBI will only generate explanations in terms of the designated causes of the hypothesis of interest. DIAGNOSTIC, on the other hand, leads to the generation of explanations in terms of the hypotheses symptoms. Very simply, if either switch is activated, an additional filter is applied to candidate explanations. If the filter is so restrictive that GBI cannot satisfy the request for explanation, it informs the user of the problem.

The next logical step, now that the causal structure has been introduced, is to attempt to generate global explanations. For GBI this means tracing along the causal links looking at the most significant effects at each stage. Consequently, when the GLOBAL setting is in effect, the GBI explanation facility requires that either CAUSAL or DIAGNOSTIC be set. Figure 6 illustrates the use of the GLOBAL and CAUSAL switches. GBI delivers similar explanations when the GLOBAL and DIAGNOSTIC switches are set.

4. CONCLUDING REMARKS

The explanation capability of the Generalized Bayesian Inferencing System can be extended in several interesting ways. Two compatible avenues are available for improving the presentation of explanations. The first is simply to add a better natural language capability to replace the tedious fill-in-the-blank style. Natural language could even be used effectively in querying the system. The advantage of GBI is that there is a meaningful semantic foundation for explanations. The "richness" of information in the CMDs can provide a solid basis for generating and quantifying linguistic statements of relationships between variables. A further enhancement might be the graphical display of the LEG Net and causal structures. Not only would this replace the menu driven interface with something more convenient, but a graphical display would make the explanations much easier to understand. It would also make it easier for the user to direct the system towards the desired explanation whenever it strays.

Candidate computational changes include the availability of multivariate queries and multivariate explanations. Multivariate events might be taken as indirect causes for a change in a hypothesis variable, although that view is not entirely applicable under GBI. It is easy to think of instances when a joint event exerts the strongest influence on a hypothesis of interest. Inside a complicated LEG, these events could be the equivalent of the global explanations. Our system should also be able to recognize and then handle special relationships between variables such as mutual exclusion and implication.

Finally, while this paper has left out the issue of explaining control information, knowledge of control must be available for explanation. It can be used as is, or it can augment the kinds of explanations described above. It would be helpful to tell the user not only which variable had the greatest direct effect upon the hypothesis of interest, but also through which variable that effect had propagated in the path from the evidence.

FOOTNOTES AND REFERENCES

° In the update to the LEG Net of Figure 1 due to CAR-IMPAIRED-LEG, two evidence variables are observed simultaneously. To GBI, there is no sequencing of ILLEGAL-EQUIPMENT and PASSED-INSPECTION. Therefore a typical explanation which traces from DRIVER-GETS-A-TICKET to these evidence variables could only report that one of them was the cause. A mechanism such as the one we propose offers a more satisfactory explanation in this case.

[1] Andriole, S.J., (ed.), Applications in Artificial Intelligence (Petrocelli Books, Princeton NJ, 1985).
[2] Buchanan, B.G., and Shortliffe, E.H., Rule-Based Expert Systems (Addison-Wesley, 1984).
[3] Neches, R., Swartout, W.R., and Moore, J., Explainable (and Maintainable) Expert Systems, in: Proceedings of the IJCAI-85 Conference (Morgan Kaufman, Los Altos CA, 1985).
[4] Barth, S.W., and Norton, S.W., Knowledge Engineering within a Generalized Bayesian Framework, this volume.
[5] Lemmer, J.F., Generalized Bayesian Updating of Incompletely Specified Distributions, Large Scale Systems 5, Elsevier Science Publishers, pp. 51-68, 1983.
[6] Lemmer, J.F., and Barth, S.W., Efficient Minimum Information Updating for Bayesian Inferencing in Expert Systems, in: Proceedings of the AAAI-82 Conference (Morgan Kaufmann, Los Altos CA, 1982).
[7] Lemmer, J.F., and Norton, S.W., Eliciting Probabilities, in print.
[8] Duda, R.O., Hart, P.E., Konolige, K., and Reboh, R., A Computer Based Consultant for Mineral Exploration, Appendix D, Final Report for SRI Project 6415, Menlo Park CA. SRI International, 1979.
[9] Kosy, D.W., and Wise, B.P., Self-Explanatory Financial Planning Models, in: Proceedings of the AAAI-84 Conference (Morgan Kaufmann, Los Altos CA, 1984).

ON THE RATIONAL SCOPE OF PROBABILISTIC RULE-BASED INFERENCE SYSTEMS

Shimon Schocken[*]

Information Systems Area
Graduate School of Business Administration
New York University

Belief updating schemes in artificial intelligence may be viewed as three dimensional languages, consisting of a *syntax* (e.g. probabilities or certainty factors), a *calculus* (e.g. Bayesian or CF combination rules), and a *semantics* (i.e. cognitive interpretations of competing formalisms). This paper studies the rational scope of those languages on the syntax and calculus grounds. In particular, the paper presents an endomorphism theorem which highlights the limitations imposed by the conditional independence assumptions implicit in the CF calculus. Implications of the theorem to the relationship between the CF and the Bayesian languages and the Dempster-Shafer theory of evidence are presented. The paper concludes with a discussion of some implications on rule-based knowledge engineering in uncertain domains.

1. INTRODUCTION

In order for a computer program to be a plausible model of a (more or less) rational process of human expertise, the program should be capable of representing beliefs in a language that is (more or less) calibrated with a well-specified normative criterion, e.g. the axioms of subjective probability [1], the theory of confirmation [2], formal logic, etc. According to Shafer and Tversky, the building blocks of a probabilistic language are syntax, calculus, and semantics [3]. The syntax is a set of numbers, commonly referred to as *degrees of belief* (e.g. standard probabilities or certainty factors), used to parameterize uncertain facts, inexact rules, and competing hypotheses. Typically, a set of atomic degrees of belief is elicited directly from a human expert, while compound degrees of belief are computed through a set of operators collectively known as a belief calculus. The semantics of the language can be viewed as a mapping from a real-life domain of expertise onto the belief language. This mapping provides a cognitive interpretation as well as descriptive face-validity to both the syntax and the calculus dimensions of the language.

Given the critical role that a belief language plays in determining both the low-level mechanics and the high-level ordinal ranking of the recommendations generated by an expert system, it is clear that the implicit rationality of the language is directly related

---

[*]This Research was carried out while the author was at the Decision Sciences Department, the Wharton School of the University of Pennsylvania. The author's current address is 624 Tisch Hall, Washington Square, New York, NY 10003.

to both the internal and external validities of computer-based expertise. By 'rationality' I refer here to the normative criteria of *consistency* and *completeness* [1] as well as to the psychometric criteria of *reliability* and *validity* [4]. It is argued that the performance of any expert, whether a human being or a computer program, should be evaluated and rated along those lines.

The two mainstream belief languages in rule-based inference systems are the normative *Bayesian* and the descriptive *certainty factors* (CF) languages, the latter being representative of a wide variety of ad-hoc calculi of uncertainty. It seems that the CF method is currently the most widely used belief language in applied expert systems, primarily due to the popularity of such CF-based shells as EMYCIN [5], M.1 [6], and Texas Instrument's Personal Consultant [7]. Bayesian inference has been traditionally much less popular, with the exception of some notable examples, e.g. PROSPECTOR [8], which uses a Bayesian syntax and an ad-hoc version of a Bayesian calculus. Recently, new techniques designed to cope with the computational complexity of a complete Bayesian design are emerging, giving rise to the concept of a *Bayesian inference net* [Pearl,9].

Notwithstanding the critical importance of exploring the practical scope of non-categorical rule-based inference systems, few studies have compared belief languages on rational as well as cognitive grounds. Furthermore, practitioners are often oblivious to the theoretical limitations inherent in the representation and synthesis of degrees of belief. This has led to a number of commonly held misconceptions regarding some properties of the CF and the Bayesian languages, such as the following two conjectures:

C1: Classical Bayesian methods are either too simplistic or too complex: in order for a Bayesian updating procedure to be computationally feasible, strict statistical independence must prevail. This requirement is rarely met in practice, where interaction effects among clues and hypotheses make the Bayesian solution unmanageable on combinatorial grounds. The CF calculus, on the other hand, does not make explicit assumptions of statistical independence; therefore, it can be used to model realistically complicated problems that defy a normative Bayesian interpretation.

C2: Both the Bayesian and the CF calculi are special cases of the general Dempster-Shafer theory of evidence [10]. Hence, they may be construed as two alternative and competing belief languages, each specialized to deal with a particular class of problems and probabilistic designs.

Toward the end of the paper a rather different interpretation of both C1 and C2 will be presented. The organization of the paper is as follows: Section 2 presents some necessary background and terminology. Section 3 provides a brief review of the CF language and its rational (Bayesian) interpretation. Section 4 presents three lemmas that are further integrated into an endomorphism theorem. This theorem shows that the CF language is a special case of the Bayesian language. Similar results have been proven in the past by Adams [11], Heckerman [12], and Grosof [13]. Section 5 presents some preliminary thoughts about the computational complexity of wholistic (not conditionally independent) inference problems. The paper concludes with some implications on knowledge engineering and future research directions.

2. BACKGROUND AND NOMENCLATURE

Consider an n-dimensional propositional space S defined over a certain domain of expertise, e.g. medical diagnosis. Each dimension of S is interpreted as an attribute of the domain, e.g. chest pain, headache, allergy, etc. An *inference problem* in S is a tuple $<h,e_1,...,e_m>$, $0 \leq m \leq n$, where the attribute h is interpreted as a prospective hypothesis and the attributes $e_1,...,e_m$ are interpreted as pieces of evidence relevant to h. Let $F:S \rightarrow [0,1]$ be a (possibly transcendental) joint distribution function defined over S. Although we don't have direct access to F, we assume that there exists a domain expert who is capable of making judgments that can be further interpreted as a subjective function BEL which approximates F. In particular, given an inference problem $<h,e_1,...,e_m>$, the *posterior belief* $BEL(h|e_1,...,e_m)$ reflects the expert's belief that h is true in light of the evidence $e_1,...,e_m$.

In order to avoid the apologetic debate of whether or not the function F exists, we note that F is presented here primarily for the sake of clear exposition. In fact, the relationship between BEL and F is at the center of an intensified philosophical debate that has been going strong for more than 300 years. In short, under a Bayesian interpretation (e.g. Ramsey), $BEL = P \equiv F$, where P is the standard Savage/de Finetti subjective probability function. Objectivists (like Popper) argue that F stands aloof from P (or, for that matter, from any personal BEL), and, hence, in general, $P \neq F$. Proponents of the logical school of probability model BEL through Carnap's "confirmation" function $C(\cdot)$ [2]. A similar approach is taken by the certainty factors formalism, which sets $BEL = CF$.

Finally, pragmatic Bayesians (like myself) feel that $BEL = P$ is our best shot at F, a shot whose accuracy is directly related to the operational characteristics of the elicitation procedure designed to construct P. Since P is subject to an internal axiomatic system, I term |BEL-P| an 'internal bias' and |BEL-F| an 'external bias.' Attempts to reduce those biases are termed 'debiasing' or 'corrective procedures' in the cognitive psychology literature [e.g. 14].

Let V be the subset of all "interesting" (i.e. non-arbitrary) inference problems $<h,e_1,...,e_m>$ defined over S. The following set of definitions partitions V into three classes of problems that vary in terms of their computational (and cognitive) complexity. This partitioning is a reflection of the fact that some problems that require expertise may be simple 'open and shut' cases, while other problems may be complicated and vague. In what follows, I wish to provide a more precise definition of this taxonomy of problems, based on the underlying complexity of their diagnostic structures.

<u>Diagnostic Structure</u>: the diagnostic structure of a problem $q = <h,e_1,...,e_m>$ is the conditional distribution $F(e_1,...,e_m|h)$.

Weakly Decomposable Problems: the set of weakly decomposable problems WD is defined as follows:

$$WD = \{q \mid q = \{h, e_1, ..., e_m\} \in V \text{ and } F(e_1, ..., e_m \mid h) = F(e_1 \mid h) \cdot ... \cdot F(e_m \mid h)\}$$

Decomposable Problems: the set of decomposable problems D is defined as follows:

$$D = \{q \mid q = \{h, e_1, ..., e_m\} \text{ is weakly decomposable and } F(e_1, ..., e_m) = F(e_1) \cdot ... \cdot F(e_m)\}$$

Wholistic Problems: a problem q is wholistic if $q \in V - WD$

Corollary: $D \subset WD \subset V \subset S$

Note that "decomposability" is a weaker notion of statistical independence. The latter requires that events be independent in all subsets, e.g. $P(abc) = P(a)P(b)P(c)$, $P(ab) = P(a)P(b)$, $P(ac) = P(a)P(c)$, and $P(bc) = P(b)P(c)$. Decomposability requires only the first constraint, i.e. $P(abc) = P(a)P(b)P(c)$.

3. THE CF LANGUAGE AND ITS RATIONAL INTERPRETATION

This section provides a brief account of the definition and interpretation of the certainty factors language, as stated by Shortliffe and Buchanan in [10]. Given a problem $q = <h, e_1, ..., e_m> \in V$, the CF syntax approximates the posterior belief associated with q through the difference between a measure of increased belief (MB) and a measure of increased disbelief (MD) in the hypothesis h in light of the clues $<e_1, ..., e_m>$:

$$-1 \leq CF(h \mid e_1, ..., e_m) = MB(h \mid e_1, ..., e_m) - MD(h \mid e_1, ..., e_m) \leq 1$$

The CF calculus is a set of operators designed to combine atomic CF's into compound CF's (e.g. compute BEL(h|a,b) from BEL(h|a) and BEL(h|b)). This paper focuses only on a subset of this calculus, denoted hereafter (M1-M2):

$$MB(h \mid a,b) = \begin{cases} 0 & \text{if } MD(h \mid a,b) = 1 \\ MB(h \mid a) + MB(h \mid b) \cdot (1 - MB(h \mid a)) & \text{otherwise} \end{cases} \quad (M1)$$

$$MD(h \mid a,b) = \begin{cases} 0 & \text{if } MB(h \mid a,b) = 1 \\ MD(h \mid a) + MD(h \mid b) \cdot (1 - MD(h \mid a)) & \text{otherwise} \end{cases} \quad (M2)$$

Note that (M1-M2) appears to convey a certain descriptive appeal: if you open the parentheses of (M1) for example, you obtain the sum of MB(h|a) and MB(h|b) minus their multiplicative interaction effect. The resulting combination rule is both commutative and associative, as one would expect.

Shortliffe and Buchanan have also suggested a syntactical mapping from Bayesian probabilities to certainty factors, defined as follows:

$$MB(h|a) = \begin{cases} 1 & \text{if } P(h)=1 \\ \frac{\max\{P(h|a),P(h)\}-P(h)}{1-P(h)} & \text{otherwise} \end{cases} \quad (R1)$$

$$MD(h|a) = \begin{cases} 1 & \text{if } P(h)=0 \\ \frac{\max\{P(h|a),P(h)\}-P(h)}{-P(h)} & \text{otherwise} \end{cases} \quad (R2)$$

I term the (R1-R2) mapping a *rational interpretation* for three reasons. First, the mapping is intended to convey a certain degree of descriptive face-validity to the CF syntax. For example, (R1) represents the measure of increased belief in h in light of the piece of evidence a as a normalized difference between the posterior $P(h|a)$ and the prior $P(h)$. Second, the mapping relates CF's to a subset of the real interval [0,1] which is consistent with the seven rational postulates of Savage and de Finetti (i.e. the axioms of subjective probability). Third, my notion of a rational interpretation is consistent with Shortliffe and Buchanan who suggest: *"Behavior is irrational if actions taken or decisions made contradict the result that would be obtained under a probabilistic analysis of the behavior"* [10, p. 251].

Note in passing that (M1-M2) is very different from (R1-R2). The former pair of combination rules is the nucleus of the CF calculus, designed to compute the compound strength of belief of two parallel pieces of evidence. The latter pair of definitions is a suggested ex-post Bayesian interpretation of certainty factors which is not necessarily unique.

4. THE CF LANGUAGE AS A SPECIAL CASE OF THE BAYESIAN LANGUAGE

<u>Lemma 1</u> If the MB combination rule (M1) is used to approximate the posterior belief associated with a problem $<h,e_1,...,e_m>$, then (M1) is mutually consistent with the rational MB interpretation (R1) if and only if $<\neg h,e_1,...,e_m>$ is decomposable.

<u>Lemma 2</u> If the MD combination rule (M2) is used to approximate the posterior belief associated with a problem $<h,e_1,...,e_m>$, then (M2) is mutually consistent with the rational MD interpretation (R2) if and only if $<h,e_1,...,e_m>$ is decomposable.

<u>Lemma 3</u> If the CF calculus (M1-M2) is used to approximate the posterior belief associated with a problem $<h,e_1,...,e_m>$, and if (M1-M2) is mutually and jointly consistent with the rational interpretation (R1-R2), then both $<h,e_1,...,e_m>$ and $<\neg h,e_1,...,e_m>$ are weakly decomposable.

<u>The Endomorphism Theorem</u> Let CF be the set of all problems that have an approximate posterior solution derived by the CF calculus (M1-M2). Let V be the set of all problems that have an approximate posterior solution derived by a Bayesian calculus. Let T be the rational interpretation (R1-R2). Under these conditions, T is an endomorphic transformation T:CF → WD ⊂ V, where WD is the subset of weakly decomposable problems in V.

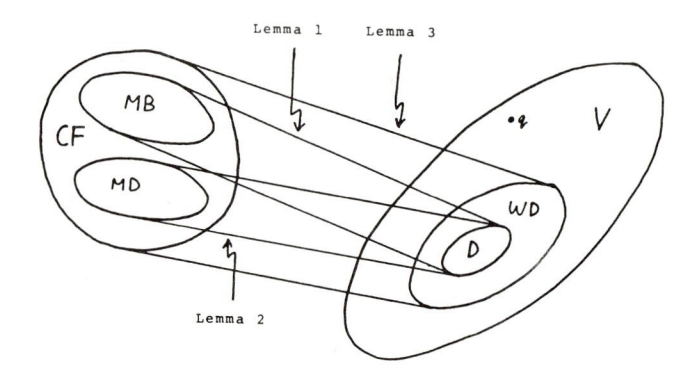

Figure 1

5. DISCUSSION

The endomorphism theorem says that the CF calculus (R1-R2) has a rational interpretation if and only if it is restricted to weakly decomposable problems. Under these conditions, the CF belief synthesis rule is equivalent to the likelihood ratio version of the Bayesian belief updating rule. As was mentioned at the beginning of the paper, the fact that the CF calculus makes implicit assumptions of conditional independence was proved elsewhere, e.g. by Adams [11], Heckerman [12], and Grosof [13]. The present theorem is useful in that it highlights the important implications of the CF/Bayesian relationship on the rational scope of CF-based inference systems.

In the pictorial illustration of the theorem, q is a wholistic problem that is outside the rational scope of the CF language (e.g. q = <h,a,b> has a "synergistic" diagnostic structure, i.e. $F(a,b|h) > F(a|h) \cdot F(b|h)$). At the same time, however, q does have a (complicated) Bayesian posterior belief, by virtue of its membership in V. This dichotomy means that one cannot trade rationality for efficiency, as is sometimes being done in AI. Furthermore, the likelihood that real-life problems exist in WD is very small, due to the underlying complexity of inference problems that require expertise [15].

The preceding paragraph implies that most CF-based expert systems (and, hence, most applied expert systems) are inconsistent with their rational interpretation (R1-R2). This finding is disturbing in view of the impressive decision-making performance of some CF-based systems [8]. There may be (at least) two potential explanations for the disparity between the narrow normative foundation and the de-facto face-validity of the CF language.

First, I argue that experienced knowledge engineers intuitively know that the endomorphism theorem is true, and, in fact, take advantage of it. In particular, designers of complicated expert systems often feel that the more granular the knowledge-base, the higher is the validity of the system [16]. This heuristic amounts to augmenting an evidence/hypotheses inference net with a multitude of sub hypotheses and intermediate states, designed to partition the knowledge-base and achieve a higher degree of granularity. This judicious decomposition is done in an attempt to explicitly account for interaction effects, and, thereby, induce more conditional independence on the evidence/hypotheses space, as was proposed by Charniak [15] and by Winter and Girse [17].

In the context of the present paper, we can describe this practice as follows: when a CF knowledge engineer faces a wholistic problem q which is outside the scope of a rational interpretation, he or she first modifies the diagnostic structure of the original problem, thus creating a transformation from q to q' $\in$ WD, which is a rational CF territory. If there exists a problem q' whose diagnostic structure is indeed a plausible (weak) decomposition of q, a CF-based system applied to q' is likely to provide a (close) rational belief representation to q as well.

The second explanation of the CF descriptive/normative contrast may be that the original rational interpretation of certainty factors (R1-R2) is subject to doubt. In other words, it seems that the CF language is indeed a novel formalism that deserves a serious look, especially on practical and descriptive grounds. Indeed, the fact that the CF language has been going strong for more than a decade in spite of its unrealistically narrow rational interpretation suggests that the model is basically powerful although its normative foundation is weak. Hence, future research is needed to explore new interpretations to the CF language that will be more plausible on rational, cognitive, and philosophical grounds. An Example of such an undertaking may be found in Heckerman's work [12] on alternative probabilistic interpretations of certainty factors.

5.1. Conjecture C1 Revisited

We now turn to the casual conjecture C1, which attributes the impracticality of the Bayesian language vis a vis the CF language to the fact that real life domains of expertise are not statistically independent. The reader has perhaps realized by now that this statement is based on a semantic rather than a substantive argument. In particular, note that the phenomenon of statistical independence is not directly expressible in the CF formalism. This is consistent with Shafer and Tversky, who observe that some mathematical properties are not translatable from one belief language to another [3]. However, the fact that a particular characteristic of the world cannot be described in a certain language does not necessarily imply that this characteristic in nonexistent.

The statistical independence phenomenon is an attribute of nature which stands aloof
from the CF/Bayesian debate. To clarify this distinction, we may use an analogy from
physics. The presence or absence of statistical independence is a unique property of a
domain of expertise just as the mass is a unique physical property of a brick.
Notwithstanding the mass uniqueness, the weight of the brick varies with different
scales (or on different planets). Thus an absolute unique property of nature may be
mapped onto different manifestations under different circumstances. Similarly, the
manifestation of the independence property may be explicit in some belief languages
and vague or even null in others. The crispness of this expression should be construed
as a property of the language, not a property of nature.

5.2. Conjecture C2 Revisited

The C2 conjecture suggests that both the CF and the Bayesian languages are special
cases of the Dempster-Shafer theory of evidence. Although this premise is indeed
correct, this truth is quite different from its popular interpretation. That the Bayesian
design is a special case of the Dempster-Shafer model is a trivial corollary that can be
found in [18]. Similarly, Gordon and Shortliffe gave a Shaferian belief interpretation to
the CF calculus. They then proceeded to conclude that *"The Dempster-Shafer
combination rule includes the Bayesian and the CF functions as special cases"*
[19, p.273].

In my view, the popular interpretation of this correct argument is depicted in Figure 2a:

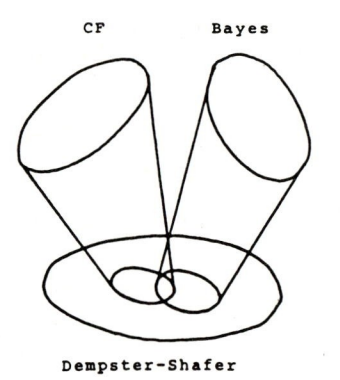

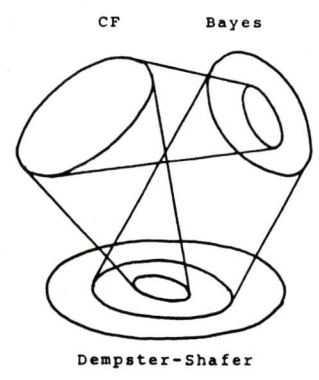

Figure 2a

Figure 2b

However, in light of the endomorphism theorem, a more accurate description of the
CF/Bayesian/Shafer relationships is as depicted in Figure 2b. The relationships
depicted in the latter figure are consistent with Grosof's analyses of the
CF/Bayesian/Shafer interplay [13]. Grosof has also provided the explicit
transformations under which the CF and the Bayesian languages are special cases of the
Dempster-Shafer language.

In short, the present discussion indicates that within the subset of weakly decomposable problems (WD), CF's are remarkably Bayesian after all. Outside the subset WD, the CF language may have a variety of free-form and appealing descriptive interpretations. At the same time, those ad-hoc interpretations will not be accountable or testable on rational (Bayesian) grounds. Of course, this restriction may be lifted if either (R1-R2) or (M1-M2) are modified or extended in order to cover a larger superset of WD.

6. IMPLICATIONS ON KNOWLEDGE ENGINEERING AND FUTURE RESEARCH

Several authors have stressed the fact that most real-life domains of expertise include problems that are *dependant, adjacent,* or *wholistic*. Clearly, all those definitions basically imply that the diagnostic structure of realistically complex problems is not weakly decomposable. This observation has far-reaching computational implications which may be summarized in the following proposition, which has not yet been proven:

Proposition: If a problem $<h,e_1,...,e_m>$ is wholistic, then the rule-based computation of the posterior belief $BEL(h|e_1,...,e_m)$ is *NP*-Complete.

Heuristic argument: This proposition is based on the intuition that an m-cities Travelling Salesman Problem (TSP) is reducible to the integer programming (IP) formulation of the rule-based comutation of $BEL(h|e_1,...,e_m)$, provided that such plausible formulation exists. The objective function of the IP model might be based on a logarithmic transformation of $BEL(h|e_1,...,e_m)$ which amounts to a linear combination of all the possible interaction effects within subsets of the $\{h,e_1,...,e_m\}$ space. Each individual interaction effect might be multiplied by an integer $0-1$ variable that determines whether or not the interaction obtains. Furthermore, it is felt that the typical TSP constraint designed to avoid a sub-tour among $k \leq m$ cities can be mapped onto the constraint that given that the underlying inference problem is wholistic, the computation of BEL cannot afford to disregard a dependency of degree k within the $\{h,e_1,...,e_k\}$ space. The objective here is to design these 2^m logical constraints in a way that will force the appropriate $0-1$ variables to be set to 0 or 1, thus determining whether or not the respective interaction effect should enter the computation of $BEL(h|e_1,...,e_m)$ in the objective function.

We now turn to the implications of the endomorphism theorem on knowledge engineering in light of the proposition just presented. In particular, we wish to focus on the key question that ought to be addressed, namely: how can a rule-based expert system compute the posterior belief associated with a wholistic problem. Basically, there seem to be three alternative options:

1. Apply a rule-based algorithm as though the problem in not wholistic:

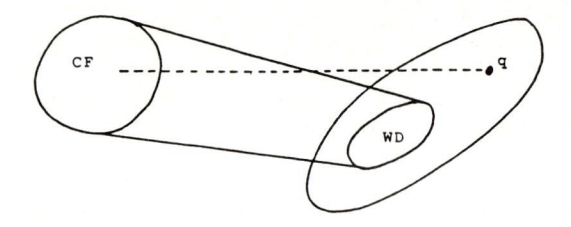

Figure 3a

2. Devise a new rule-based algorithm to wholistic problems:

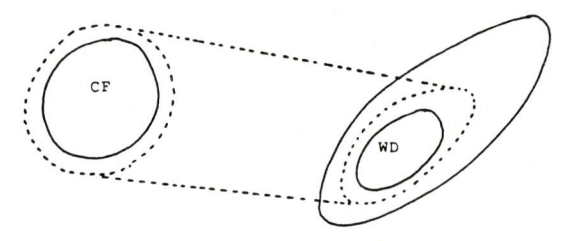

Figure 3b

3. Transform the wholistic problem q into a more complicated problem q' that nonetheless is (roughly) weakly decomposable. Then apply a rule-based algorithm to q':

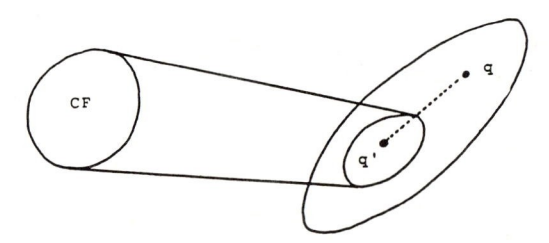

Figure 3c

Option 1, which basically amounts to fudging, is, in my opinion, the leading practice among practitioners who use rule-based expert system shells (this impression is not supported by any firm empirical evidence). Moreover, the endomorphism theorem shows that it doesn't really matter if you use a decomposable Bayesian or a CF approach; both fail to handle wholistic diagnostic structures, although the latter appears to be oblivious of this limitation.

Option 2 presents a very tough challenge. Basically, it requires the development of an optimal belief updating solution to wholistic problems which is also rule-based, or polynomial in the size of the problem, in some sense. In light of the proposition regarding the computational complexity of wholistic problems, such algorithm will imply that $P = NP$, amounting to the most staggering finding in complexity theory, and a very unlikely one. This leaves us with more realistic lines of attack which are suboptimal, but, nonetheless, feasible. Examples of such efforts are Lemmer's work on incompletely specified distributions [20] and Cheeseman's maximum entropy algorithm [21].

It seems that proponents of the classical rule-based approach to inference are left with the pragmatic option 3, which, in my view, has not received a sufficient amount of research. If we manage to construct a plausible decomposition q' of q, then we can safely apply a rule-based algorithm to q'. Moreover, the goodness of this solution will be a function of the structural proximity of q' to q, which might be estimated by the knowledge engineer. Decomposition might be carried out syntactically, as in Pearl's technique of structuring causal trees [9], or semantically, as in Charniak's notion of 'intermediate states' [15].

If we view the optimal solution of q as a complete combinatorial Bayesian design, and the rule-based solution of q' as a heuristic solution of q, we may bring upon some very strong findings from the probabilistic analysis of the TSP. For example, there is a greedy algorithm that solves the TSP in polynomial time, giving a solution that may not be optimum but is guaranteed to be no worse than twice the optimum path. Furthermore, if some very plausible assumptions are made regarding the layout of the cities (viz, the topology of the diagnostic structure of the problem), this error can become as small as 5% [22].

7. CONCLUSION

The approach taken in this paper was to explicitly define the class of inference problem that are solvable in the CF language in a way which is consistent with the theory of probability. The resulting endomorphism theorem is yet another way to show that the CF language makes strong independence assumptions. In the final analyses, it is obvious that conditional dependencies is a phenomenon that we cannot afford to ignore, regardless of the belief language that we choose to adopt. Moreover, it seems that the conditional independence assumption is structurally inherent in any rule-based algorithm, when applied to probabilistic domains. This is unfortunate, since the rule-based architecture is a well established inference technique with some very appealing characteristics. With that in mind, it is argued that future research should concentrate on manipulating the problem space, rather than the algorithm, in order to make it more amenable to a rule-based solution which will also be valid on probabilistic grounds.

8. Appendix: Proofs

For the sake of brevity, the following proofs are limited to inference problems with two pieces of evidence. Due to the commutative and associative nature of both Bayes rule and (M1-M2), these results can be easily extended to any finite number of pieces of evidence.

8.1. Proof of Lemma 2

Applying (M2) to an inference problem q={h,a,b} amounts to

$$MD(h|a,b) = MD(h|a) + MD(h|b) \cdot (1-MD(h|a)) \qquad \text{(M2)}$$

It is easy to show (from the (R2) interpretation of MD) that

$$MD(h|e) = 1 - \frac{P(e|h)}{P(e)} \qquad \text{(if } P(h), P(e) > 0\text{)}$$

Applying this to the r.h.s. of (M2) gives:

$$MD(h|a,b) = \left(1 - \frac{P(a|h)}{P(a)}\right) + \left(1 - \frac{P(b|h)}{P(b)}\right) \cdot \frac{P(a|h)}{P(a)} = 1 - \frac{\cancel{P(a|h)}}{\cancel{P(a)}} + \frac{\cancel{P(a|h)}}{\cancel{P(a)}} - \frac{P(a|h)}{P(a)} \cdot \frac{P(b|h)}{P(b)}$$

Hence, (M2) is equivalent to

$$MD(h|a,b) = 1 - \frac{P(a|h) \cdot P(b|h)}{P(a) \cdot P(b)} \qquad \text{(M2')}$$

Alternatively, the rational interpretation (R2) of MD(h|a,b) gives:

$$MD(h|a,b) = \frac{P(h|a,b) - P(h)}{-P(h)} \qquad \text{(R2')}$$

To prove the IF direction, we begin with a decomposable {h,a,b}:

$$P(a,b|h) = P(a|h) \cdot P(b|h) \qquad (1)$$

$$P(a,b) = P(a) \cdot P(b) \qquad (2)$$

Now, plugging (1) and (2) in the r.h.s. of (M2') and using Bayes Rule yields:

$$1 - \frac{P(a|h) \cdot P(b|h)}{P(a) \cdot P(b)} = 1 - \frac{P(a,b|h)}{P(a,b)} = 1 - \frac{P(h|a,b) \cdot P(a,b)}{P(h) \cdot P(a,b)} =$$

$$= \frac{P(h) - P(h|a,b)}{P(h)} = \frac{P(h|a,b) - P(h)}{-P(h)}$$

which is identical to (R2'). Alternatively, we could have applied Bayes rule to (R2'), plug (1)-(2) in the result, yielding an expression which is identical to (M2'). Since (M2') and (R2') are consistent with (M2) and (R2), respectively, we have proven that (M2) and (R2) are mutually consistent.

To prove the ONLY IF direction, we assume that (M2') and (R2') are mutually consistent, and equate them:

$$\frac{P(h|a,b) - P(h)}{-P(h)} = 1 - \frac{P(a|h) \cdot P(b|h)}{P(a) \cdot P(b)}$$

Which, after some algebraic manipulations, gives

$$P(h|a,b) = -\cancel{P(h)} + \frac{P(a|h) \cdot P(b|h) \cdot P(h)}{P(a) \cdot P(b)} + \cancel{P(h)} \qquad (3)$$

Now, if {h,a,b} is subject to probabilistic interpretation, then Bayes rule dictates that:

$$P(h|a,b) = \frac{P(a,b|h) \cdot P(h)}{P(a,b)} \qquad (4)$$

Equating (3) and (4) recovers the implicit assumptions:

$$P(a,b|h) = P(a|h) \cdot P(b|h)$$

$$P(ab) = P(a) \cdot P(b)$$

which imply that {h,a,b} is a decomposable problem.

8.2. Proof of Lemma 1

We begin by applying the fact $MB(h|a) = MD(\neg h|a)$ to (R1), obtaining:

$$MD(\neg h|a,b) = MD(\neg h,a) + MD(\neg h,b) \cdot (1 - MD(\neg h,a))$$

Applying Lemma 2 to this completes the proof.

8.3. Proof of Lemma 3

The proof follows from lemmas 1 and 2: The former says that (M1) is equivalent to the Bayesian computation of $P(\neg h|a,b)$ under the assumption that $\{\neg h,a,b\}$ is decomposable. The latter says that (M2) is equivalent to the Bayesian computation of $P(h|a,b)$ under the assumption that $\{h,a,b\}$ is decomposable. Taken together, these two belief updating operations are equivalent to the odds-ratio form of Bayes rule:

$$\frac{P(h|a,b)}{P(\neg h|a,b)} = \frac{P(a|h)}{P(a|\neg h)} \cdot \frac{P(b|h)}{P(b|\neg h)} \cdot \frac{P(h)}{P(\neg h)}$$

Which is based on the assumption that {h,a,b} and {¬ h,a,b} are weakly decomposable.

8.4. Proof of the Endomorphism Theorem:

Let the rational interpretation (R1-R2) be a transformation T, $T:CF \to V$. Let $WD \subseteq V$ be the subset of weakly decomposable problems in V. Since there exist many wholistic problems in V which are not weakly decomposable, we get $WD \subset V$. Let q be such a wholistic problem with $q \in V$ and $q \notin WD$. According to Lemma 3, $T(CF) = WD$. Hence, we have found a problem $q \in V$ which is outside the range of T. This implies that $T:CF \to V$ is an endomorphism.

REFERENCES

[1] Savage, L. J., The Foundations of Statistics, Wiley, 1954.

[2] Carnap, R., Logical Foundations of Probability, Chicago: University of Chicago Press, 1954.

[3] Shafer G., and Tversky, A., "Languages and Designs for Probability Judgment," Cognitive Science 9, 1985.

[4] Wallsten, T. A., and Budescu, D. V., "Encoding Subjective Probabilities: a Psychological and Psychometric Review," Management Science, Vol. 29, No. 2, Feb. 1983.

[5] Van Melle, W., Shortliffe, E. H., and Buchanan B. G., "EMYCIN - a Knowledge Engineer's Tool for constructing Rule-Based Expert Systems," in: Buchanan, B. G., and Shortliffe, E. H. (Eds.), Rule-Based Expert Systems, Addison-Wesley, 1984, pp. 302-313.

[6] Webster, R., "M.1 Makes a Direct Hit," PC Magazine, April 16, 1985, pp. 145-157.

[7] Personal Consultant Expert Systems Development Tools (User Guide), Texas Instruments, January, 1985.

[8] Duda, R. O., Hart, P. E, and Nilsson, N. J., "Subjective Bayesian Methods for Rule-Based Inference Systems," Proceedings of the 1976 National Computer Conference, AFIPS, Vol 45, 1976, pp. 1075-1082.

[9] Pearl, J., "Fusion, Propagation, and Structuring in Belief Networks," Artificial Intelligence, September, 1986.

[10] Shortliffe, E. H., and Buchanan, B. G., "A Model of Inexact Reasoning in Medicine," in: Buchanan, B. G., and Shortliffe, E. H. (Eds.), Rule-Based Expert Systems, Addison-Wesley, 1984, pp. 233-262.

[11] Adams, J. B., "Probabilistic Reasoning and Certainty Factors' in Rule-Based Expert Systems," in: Buchanan, B. G. and Shortliffe, E. H. (Eds.), Rule-Based Expert Systems, Addison-Wesley, 1984, pp. 263-271.

[12] Heckerman, D. E., "Probabilistic Interpretation for MYCIN's Certainty Factors," in Kanal, L., and Lemmer, J. F.(eds.), Uncertainty in Artificial Intelligence. North Holland, 1986.

[13] Grosof, B. N., "Evidential Confirmation as Transposed Probability," in Kanal, L., and Lemmer, J. F.(eds.), Uncertainty in Artificial Intelligence. North Holland, 1986.

[14] Fischhoff, B., "Debiasing," in: Kahneman, D., Slovic, P., and Tversky A. (Eds.), Judgment under Uncertainty, Heuristics and Biases, Cambridge University Press, 1982.

[15] Charniak, E., "The Bayesian Basis of Common Sense Medical Diagnosis," Proceedings of the National Conference in Artificial Intelligence, 1983, 3, pp. 70-73.

[16] Barr, A., and Feigenbaum, E. A. (Eds.), "The Handbook of Artificial Intelligence." Los Altos, CA: William Kaufmann, 1981, p 195.

[17] Winter, C. L., and Girse, R. D., "Evolution and Modification of Probability in Knowledge Bases," The 2nd Conference on Artificial Intelligence Applications, Miami Beach, Florida, 1985.

[18] Shafer, G., A Mathematical Theory of Evidence, Princeton University Press, 1976.

[19] Gordon, J., and Shortliffe, E. H., "The Dempster Shafer Theory of Evidence." in: Buchanan, B. G., and Shortliffe, E. H. (Eds.), Rule-Based Expert Systems, Addison-Wesley, 1984, pp. 272-294.

[20] Lemmer, J. "Generalized Bayesian Updating of Incompletely Specified Distributions," Large Scale Systems 5, Elsvier Science Publishers, 1983.

[21] Cheeseman, P., "A Method of Computing Generalized Bayesian Probability Values for Expert Systems," Proceedings of the 8th International Joint Conference on Artificial Intelligence, Vol. 1, Karlsruhe, West Germany, 1983.

[22] Papadimitriou, C. H., and Steiglitz, K., Combinatorial Optimization: Algorithms and Complexity, Prentice-hall, 1982, pp.406-429.

DAVID: Influence Diagram Processing System for the Macintosh

Ross D. Shachter*
Department of Engineering-Economic Systems
Stanford University
Stanford, CA 94305-4025

Influence diagrams are a directed graph representation for uncertainties as probabilities. The graph distinguishes between those variables which are under the control of a decision maker (decisions, shown as rectangles) and those which are not (chances, shown as ovals), as well as explicitly denoting a goal for solution (value, shown as a rounded rectangle). Figure 1 shows the influence diagram for the oil wildcatter problem from Raiffa [3], as it is represented in DAVID. The arcs in the diagram indicate the probabilistic dependence among random variables with respect to a particular factorization of the joint distribution, and also indicate the time at which information becomes available. (The informational arcs, into decisions, are indicated by dashed lines.)

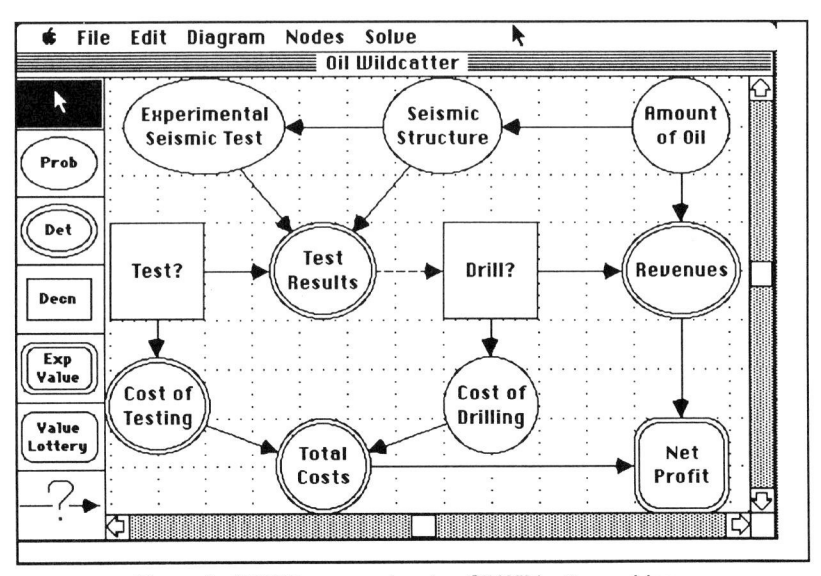

Figure 1. DAVID screen showing Oil Wildcatter problem.

---

*Currently visiting at the Center for Health Policy Research and Education, Duke University, PO Box GM, Durham, NC 27706.

Influence diagrams have been used for the last ten years as a model structuring and elicitation device in the practical field of decision analysis. They have been a powerful communication tool during the initial discussion about a problem, as well as when explaining results after analysis. Because the diagrams are hierarchical, with the numbers "hidden" within the nodes, attention is focused on the relationship among variables and the assumptions of timing and observability. (Figure 2 shows the "opened" node for seismic structure.) Traditionally, the actual analysis has been performed using other data structures, principally trees, and the problem has been converted from its assessed version to be analyzed.

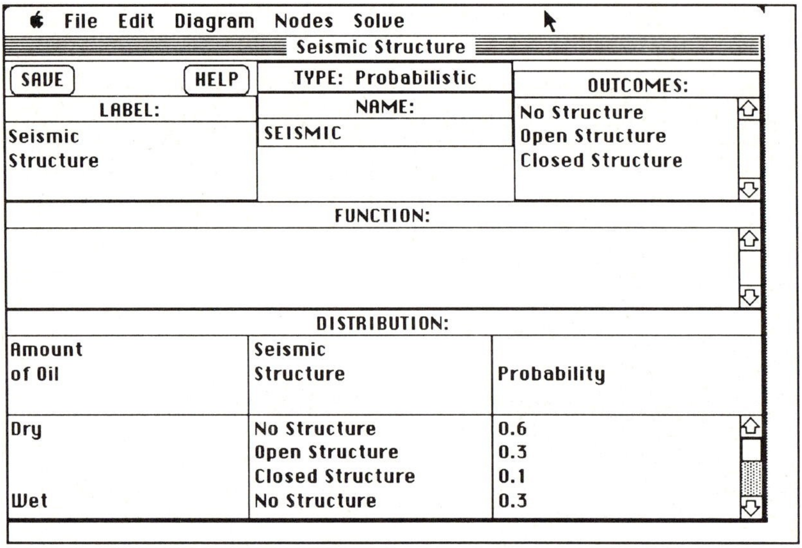

File Edit Diagram Nodes Solve			
	Seismic Structure		
SAVE HELP	TYPE: Probabilistic		OUTCOMES:
LABEL:	NAME:		No Structure
Seismic Structure	SEISMIC		Open Structure
			Closed Structure
	FUNCTION:		
	DISTRIBUTION:		
Amount of Oil	Seismic Structure	Probability	
Dry	No Structure	0.6	
	Open Structure	0.3	
	Closed Structure	0.1	
Wet	No Structure	0.3	

Figure 2. Open node screen for the Seismic Structure variable.

Within the last few years, a number of theoretical results allow for the analysis to be performed directly on the influence diagram, as assessed. In fact, for many problems, this representation offers computational advantages, since it explicitly captures conditional independence among variables. (For example, the experimental test results are conditionally independent of the amount of oil, given the seismic structure.) Another benefit is in the calculation of sensitivities, wherein we consider changes to the original problem structure. In particular, we can easily adjust the informational assumptions in a problem, to determine the relative value of observing variables at different times. (For example, we could see the value of knowing the amount of oil at the time of our drilling decision by adding an arc from amount of oil to drill.) In general, these techniques apply a sequence of transformations to different influence diagrams, to solve either probabilistic inference or decision analysis problems.

The latest version in the recent series of software efforts to manipulate influence diagrams is the DAVID program on the Macintosh. It is written in LISP (ExperCommonLisp) so it is fairly transportable and could be wrapped into a shell within an expert system. The focus, however, is on the use of graphical interaction in the construction, manipulation and analysis of influence diagram models. The system is a working demonstration of the ability of people to think about models within a probabilistic framework. Many of the criticisms of probabilistic models of uncertainty are overcome by an intelligent graphical interface that explicitly incorporates conditional independence. Figure 3 shows how the conditional distribution for seismic structure is entered into DAVID. By storing the model how it is initially formulated and allowing graphical modification, DAVID encourages analysts to reassess and experiment.

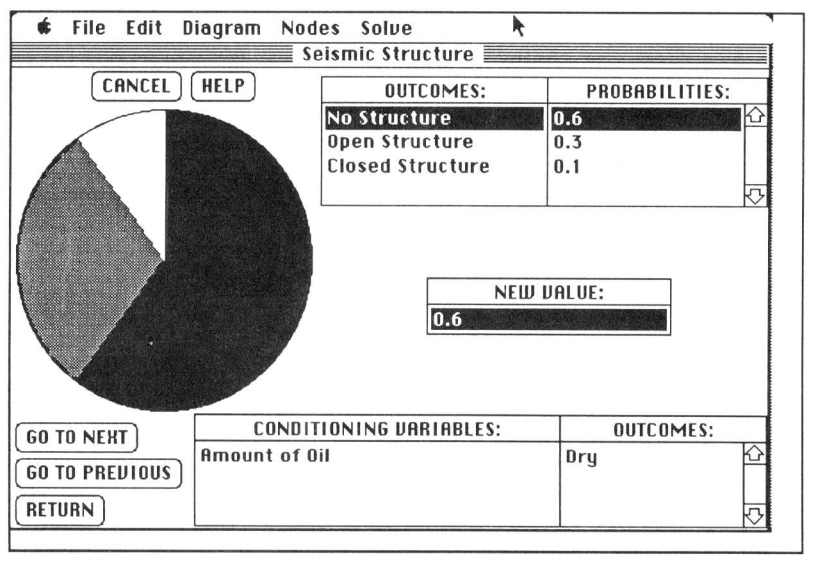

Figure 3. Entering the conditional probability distribution for Seismic Structure.

A problem is evaluated in DAVID by "reducing" nodes through a series of value-preserving transformations. Fundamentally, these operations are conditional expectation, maximization of expected utility and the application of Bayes' Theorem. In the influence diagram, these appear as the removal of a chance node, removal of a decision node, and the reversal of an arc between chance nodes, respectively (Howard and Matheson [1], Olmsted [2], and Shachter [4, 5]). Any completely specified influence diagram can be solved using these operations. At the end, the decision nodes are replaced by deterministic "policies," showing the optimal decisions given the information available at the time of the decision. If we look inside the value node after the problem is reduced, then we can see the optimal value of objective function.

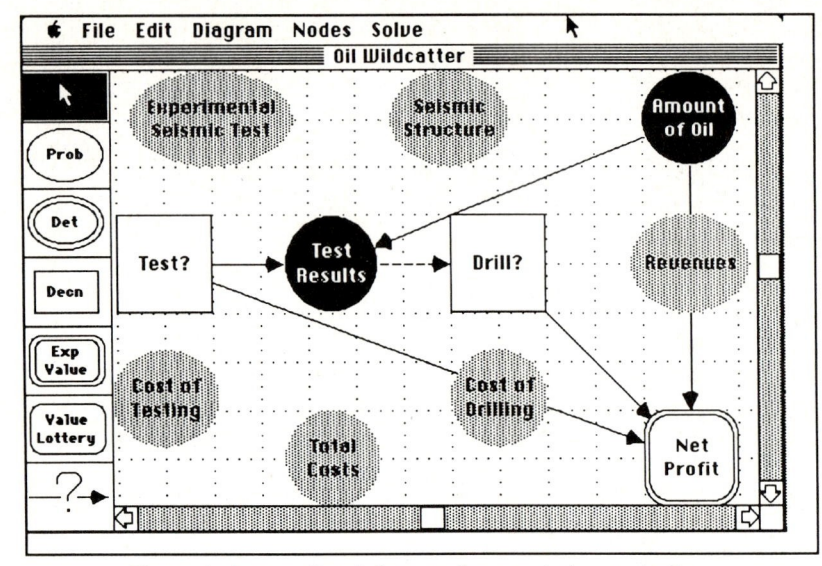

Figure 4. Intermediate influence diagram during evaluation.

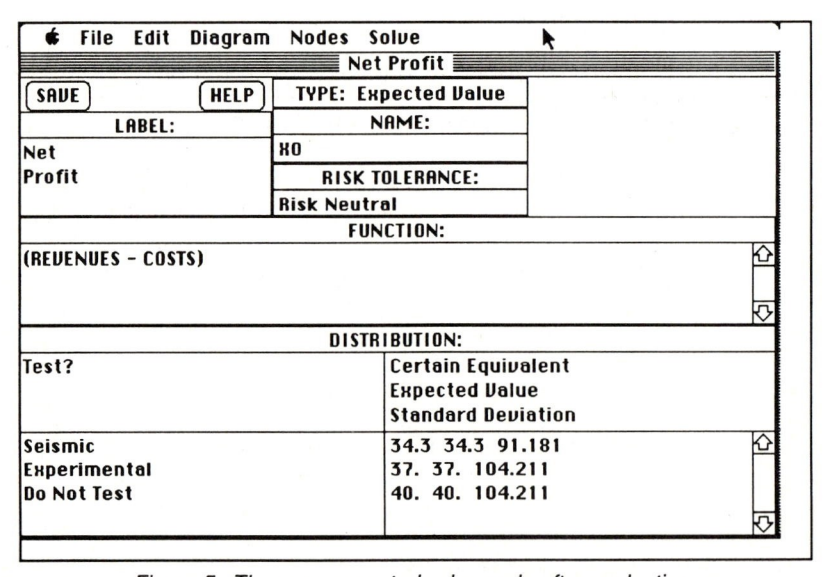

Figure 5. The open expected value node after evaluation.

Another benefit of the reduction process is that every intermediate product is a valid influence diagram, so one can think of the reduction process as "consolidating" the information in the model. (Figure 4 shows the diagram halfway through the evaluation.) DAVID takes advantage of this property to increase the power available to the user willing to think in terms of influence diagrams. For example, it is straightforward to obtain the value lottery for the optimal policy in the oil wildcatter problem.

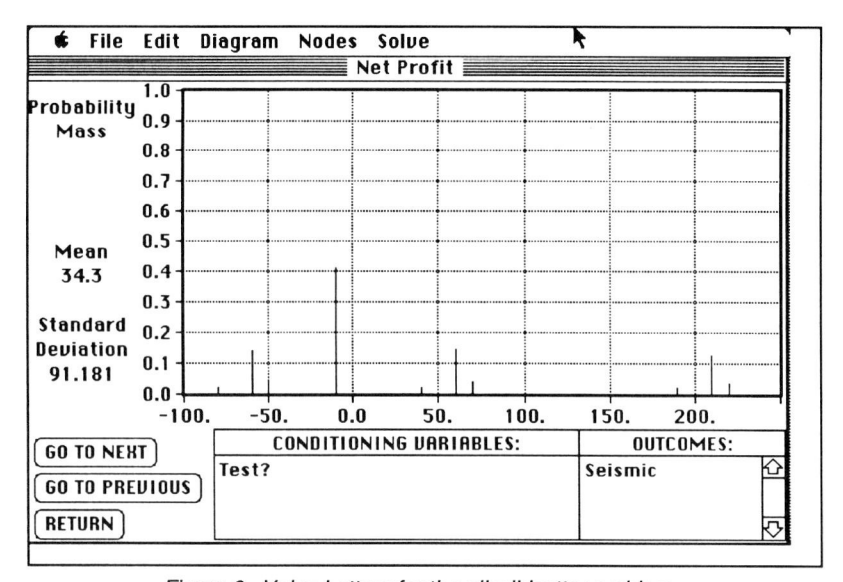

Figure 6. Value Lottery for the oil wildcatter problem.

One of the goals of the DAVID project is to develop an environment in which people can be comfortable thinking in probabilistic models. While DAVID is a prototype implementation of an influence diagram processor, the results have been most encouraging. Not only have students been able to quickly build and solve decision models with DAVID, but it has stimulated their interest and understanding of influence diagram and decision theory as well.

There are many features and conveniences built into DAVID program which there is insufficient space to illustrate here, including:
- Many of the Macintosh features are supported, such as cutting and pasting text, nodes, probability disributions and pictures of the influence diagram.
- Nodes and text are selected with the mouse (or other commands) for operations.
- There are many keystroke and mouse equivalents to provide multiple modes of data entry.
- Files are opened and saved with the standard minifinder.
- The influence diagram is a full 16 by 24 inches, and can be viewed at three

different magnifications. The "normal size" views shown in the article show one-sixteenth of the whole diagram, while a "show page" view reduces the entire diagram to the same window.

There are also many computational features. For example:
- The paradigm is able to exploit the principle of optimality and dynamic programming whenever possible (Tatman [6]).
- The system features automated sensitivity analysis for probabilistic and deterministic outcomes and risk tolerance.
- An optional smart display routine suppresses the display of conditional expressions which have probability zero.

There are many exciting possibilities using influence diagrams as a representation for communication among people and machines, and as a language for the development of expert systems. Because DAVID is written in LISP, there are a variety of expert system shells available from which it could be invoked.

REFERENCES

[1] Howard R. A., and Matheson, J. E., Influence Diagrams, in: Howard, R. A. and Matheson, J. E., (eds.), The Principles and Applications of Decision Analysis, Vol. II (Strategic Decisions Group, Menlo Park, CA, 1984) pp. 719-762.
[2] Olmsted, S. M., On Representing and Solving Decision Problems, Ph.D. Thesis, EES Department, Stanford University (1983).
[3] Raiffa, H. A., Decision Analysis (Addison-Wesley, Reading, MA, 1968).
[4] Shachter, R. D., Evaluating Influence Diagrams, to appear in Operations Research, (1986).
[5] Shachter, R. D., Probabilistic Inference and Influence Diagrams, EES Department, Stanford University (1986).
[6] Tatman, J. A.,Decision Processes in Influence Diagrams: Formulation and Analysis, Ph.D. Thesis, EES Department, Stanford University (1985).

Qualitative Probabilistic Networks for Planning Under Uncertainty

Michael P. Wellman*

MIT Laboratory for Computer Science
Cambridge, Massachusetts 02139

Bayesian networks provide a probabilistic semantics for qualitative assertions about likelihood. A qualitative reasoner based on an algebra over these assertions can derive further conclusions about the influence of actions. While the conclusions are much weaker than those computed from complete probability distributions, they are still valuable for suggesting potential actions, eliminating obviously inferior plans, identifying important tradeoffs, and explaining probabilistic models.

1 Introduction

In the traditional planning paradigm, the effects of actions are represented as logical functions of the state in which they are applied. In practice, the representation is restricted by difficulties of expression and deductive limits of the reasoner. When the planner's knowledge of the environment is uncertain, the representation problem is substantially more complicated. Because the result of an action is not uniquely determined by the model, it is necessary to enumerate the set of possible results that can obtain along with their respective likelihoods.

One class of representations is the *probabilistic model*. Probabilistic models have the virtue of completeness; the output is a complete probability distribution of outcomes for any plan of interest. Furthermore, the model has a decision-theoretic semantics that can be used to validate and interpret its component parts. However, opponents of this approach argue that this completeness and semantic adequacy is an illusion, since structurally correct and numerically precise probabilistic models cannot be constructed in practice. Alternative uncertainty calculi and various deterministic approaches to uncertainty have been proposed as competing methodologies.

The scheme described here attempts to answer some of the concerns of non-probabilists without abandoning probabilistic semantics. Essential characteristics of the influence of actions on the world can often be captured with qualitative assertions that are much easier to specify than complete probabilistic models. Conclusions derived from qualitative abstractions of probabilistic models can be justified by decision theory, with the added assurance that they are not an artifact of unreasonable precision in our specification of the model. Of course, such conclusions will be weaker than those drawn from completely

---

*This research was supported by National Institutes of Health Grant No. R01 LM04493 from the National Library of Medicine and National Institutes of Health Grant No. R24 RR01320 from the Division of Research Resources.

specified models, and are not sufficient in general to select a uniquely optimal plan. Nevertheless, qualitative models will often reduce the space of admissible plans, help to focus the search for good plans, identify central tradeoffs in the decision problem, and improve explanations provided to human users.

2 Probabilistic Networks

Two related graph-based formalisms that have been advocated for computer representation of probabilistic knowledge are Pearl's *Bayesian networks* [10] and the *influence diagrams* of Howard and Matheson [7]. Graph representations are computationally attractive and have conceptual advantages in their focus on dependencies among the probabilistic variables [11].

Bayesian networks and influence diagrams both encode probabilistic models as directed graphs, with the nodes representing uncertain variables and the links denoting probabilistic dependence. Within each node is a table recording the distribution of the node's values given each combination of values for its direct predecessor nodes. Distributions of nodes of interest under various scenarios or decisions may be computed through propagation or graph reduction techniques. Influence diagrams also include specially-designated decision nodes and informational links to indicate which chance variables are known at the time decisions are made. A single value node indicates the utility of outcomes represented in the network.

Because decision-making is the focus of work on qualitative probabilistic networks, I will discuss the methodology within the influence diagram paradigm. The presentation of manipulation techniques below closely parallels Shachter's description of the algorithm for evaluating numeric influence diagrams [13].

3 Qualitative Influences

3.1 Definitions

Qualitative probabilistic networks replace the conditional distribution table within each node with a specification of the *direction* of a predecessor's influence. Consider an influence diagram with binary chance nodes.[1] Lowercase letters are variables corresponding to each node, and uppercase letters are literals denoting the proposition's truth or falsity (for example, A and $\bar{A}$). Often the literal X serves as an abbreviation for the proposition $x = X$. We say that node a positively influences node b—denoted $S^+(a,b)$—if and only if

$$\forall x \ \Pr(B|Ax) \geq \Pr(B|\bar{A}x) \tag{1}$$

Equivalently,

$$\forall x \ \Pr(\bar{B}|Ax) \leq \Pr(\bar{B}|\bar{A}x) \tag{2}$$

Here, x ranges over the propositional formulas consistent with both A and $\bar{A}$. Negative and zero influences are defined analogously. An unknown dependence between a and b is written $S^?(a,b)$.

---

[1] The extension to multi-valued chance variables appears in a forthcoming paper [16].

It is also useful to provide a notation for conditional influence assertions. We can assert that a positively influences b given y:

$$S^+(a,b,y) \equiv \forall x \; \Pr(B|Ayx) \geq \Pr(B|\bar{A}yx) \tag{3}$$

Such an assertion says nothing about a's influence on b when y does not hold. Notice that unconditional influence is just a special case of conditional influence where $y = \text{true}$.

These influences can be depicted graphically by placing the appropriate direction notation on the links between nodes. Figure 1 displays a fragment of a qualitative probabilistic network consisting of one node influenced by several others. Conditional influences are indicated by writing the condition after the direction, separated by a vertical bar. A link may contain several influences, but the conditions for each must be mutually exclusive.

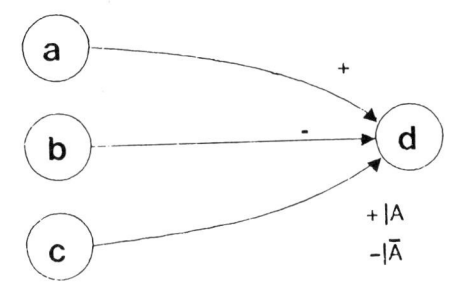

Figure 1: Graphical notation for qualitative influences.

Assertion of qualitative influences is far weaker than the conditional distribution table specified for complete influence diagrams. In general, the influences acting on a node induce a partial order on the conditional probabilities for the node's event given its predecessors. For example, in the diagram of Figure 1, the assertions imply $\Pr(D|ABC) \geq \Pr(D|\bar{A}BC)$. The partial order determined by the influences in this case is shown in Figure 2.

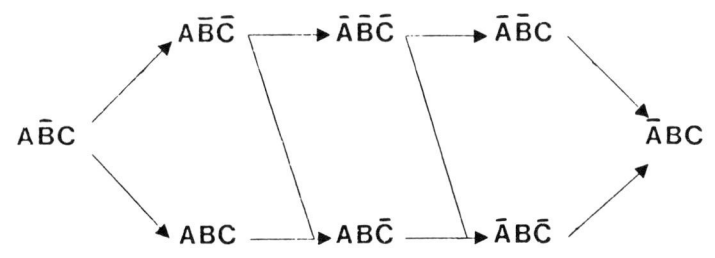

Figure 2: Partial order on the conditional probabilities for D given a, b, and c. An arrow from x to y indicates that $\Pr(D|x) \geq \Pr(D|y)$.

This partial order could be further constrained by assertions of pairwise influence. For example, we might assert that for any x, $\Pr(D|ABx) \geq \Pr(D|\bar{A}\bar{B}x)$. Joint influence assertions are not considered here, but the techniques can be extended to accommodate them.

Influences on the value node of an influence diagram are defined in a similar manner. The assertion $U^+(a, y)$ means that node a has a positive influence on the utility function u given y.

$$U^+(a, y) \equiv \forall x \; u(x, A, y) \geq u(x, \bar{A}, y) \qquad (4)$$

where x is an assignment of values to nodes other than a and those included in y.

3.2 Graph Manipulations

Like numeric influence diagrams, qualitative influence diagrams are "evaluated" by successive removal of nodes from the network. Any chance node with a single direct successor may be removed by "splicing" its direct predecessors to its successor, determining appropriate influences for the new links. These new influences can be computed from the influences on the old links according to a simple qualitative algebra. The operations for combining influences are similar to those for combining qualitative measures in other applications of qualitative reasoning in AI (see, for example, Kuipers [8] and the papers in Bobrow [1]).

Influence Chains

Consider the simple chain shown in Figure 3. If there are no other influences in the network on b or c, then it is clear that $S^+(a,b) \land S^+(b,c) \Rightarrow S^+(a,c)$.

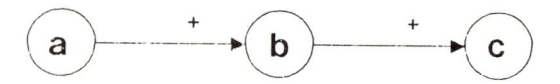

Figure 3: A simple influence chain.

To verify that this also holds if there are other influences on b and c (possibly including additional indirect paths from a to c), see Figure 4.

It is convenient to define an operator, $\otimes$, for combining chains of qualitative influences. The complete definition for $\otimes$ is provided in Table 1.

$\otimes$	+	−	0	?		$\oplus$	+	−	0	?
+	+	−	0	?		+	+	?	+	?
−	−	+	0	?		−	?	−	−	?
0	0	0	0	0		0	+	−	0	?
?	?	?	0	?		?	?	?	?	?

Table 1: The $\otimes$ operator for combining influence chains and the $\oplus$ operator for combining parallel influences. For example, $S^{+|x} \otimes S^{-|y} = S^{-|x \land y}$.

It is apparent from the table that $\otimes$ is just sign multiplication with conjunction of the conditioning propositions. Combination of influences is thus associative and commutative.

Let x_0 be any assignment of values to the other nodes in the network. We have

$$\begin{aligned} \Pr(C|Ax_0) &= \Pr(BC|Ax_0) + \Pr(\bar{B}C|Ax_0) \\ &= \Pr(C|ABx_0)\Pr(B|Ax_0) + \Pr(C|A\bar{B}x_0)\Pr(\bar{B}|Ax_0) \end{aligned} \quad (5)$$

Because a and c are conditionally independent given b and x,

$$\Pr(C|Ax_0) = \Pr(C|Bx_0)\Pr(B|Ax_0) + \Pr(C|\bar{B}x_0)\Pr(\bar{B}|Ax_0) \quad (6)$$

and using $\Pr(B|Ax) + \Pr(\bar{B}|Ax) = 1$,

$$\Pr(C|Ax_0) = \Pr(B|Ax_0)\left[\Pr(C|Bx_0) - \Pr(C|\bar{B}x_0)\right] + \Pr(C|\bar{B}x_0) \quad (7)$$

Similarly,

$$\Pr(C|\bar{A}x_0) = \Pr(B|\bar{A}x_0)\left[\Pr(C|Bx_0) - \Pr(C|\bar{B}x_0)\right] + \Pr(C|\bar{B}x_0) \quad (8)$$

Given the inequalities expressed by the influence assertions,

$$\forall x \; \Pr(C|Bx) \geq \Pr(C|\bar{B}x) \text{ and } \forall x \; \Pr(B|Ax) \geq \Pr(B|\bar{A}x) \quad (9)$$

it follows that $\Pr(C|Ax_0) \geq \Pr(C|\bar{A}x_0)$. Since x_0 was chosen arbitrarily, we have $S^+(a,c)$.

Figure 4: A demonstration that $S^+ \otimes S^+ = S^+$.

Influence Addition

The derivation above assumed that there were no direct links between a and c.[2] But even if there are such links, it still makes sense to say that a positively influences c *along this particular path*. After removing node b, however, we are left with two direct links from a to c. This situation is illustrated in Figure 5.

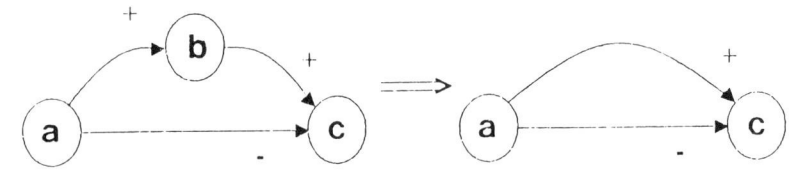

Figure 5: Removing node b leaves two paths from a to c.

Parallel influences can be combined in a way analogous to the serial influence chains described above. The influence addition operator, $\oplus$, is defined by the right-hand side of Table 1. Note that the situation of Figure 5 is ambiguous; we cannot determine the direction of the overall influence of a on c.

---
[2] If there were, then the conditional independence assumption necessary for going from equation (5) to equation (6) would not be valid.

Arc Reversal

In validating the algorithm for influence diagram evaluation, Shachter [13] shows that there is always a candidate node for removal, sometimes requiring arc reversals first. It is possible to reverse arcs in a qualitative network as well, with similar requirements for updating the predecessor relations for the nodes involved. The reversed influence has the same direction as the original one (by Bayes's rule), and each node adds the direct predecessors of the other to its own. New predecessor influences are computed from the old values according to the diagram of Figure 6.

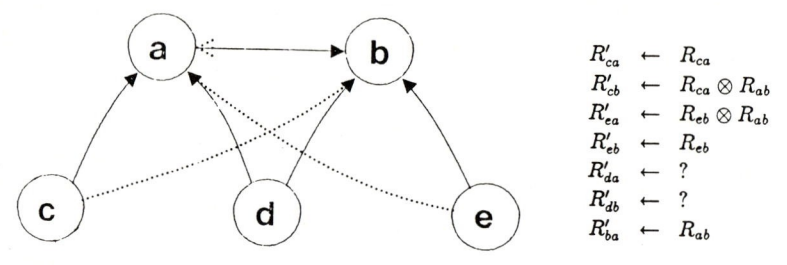

$$R'_{ca} \leftarrow R_{ca}$$
$$R'_{cb} \leftarrow R_{ca} \otimes R_{ab}$$
$$R'_{ea} \leftarrow R_{eb} \otimes R_{ab}$$
$$R'_{eb} \leftarrow R_{eb}$$
$$R'_{da} \leftarrow \; ?$$
$$R'_{db} \leftarrow \; ?$$
$$R'_{ba} \leftarrow R_{ab}$$

Figure 6: Reversal of the arc from a to b. The dotted lines indicate influences added as a result of the flip. R_{ij} and R'_{ij} denote the sign on the link from a to c before and after the reversal, respectively.

Decision Nodes

Decision nodes may be removed from the network if the optimal choice is apparent from the influences in the reduced diagram. For example, if the decision node is an unambiguous positive or negative influence on utility, then the choice is obvious. Given particular values for the informational predecessors, the decision can be determined if the conditional influence of the decision on utility given those values is unambiguous.

More generally, decision nodes cannot be easily removed. Such cases require more powerful analysis techniques, such as those illustrated in the next section.

4 An Example: The Generic Test/Treat Decision

Consider the following rather vague description of a medical decision problem:

> Patient P might have the undesirable disease D. Patients with D are sometimes "cured," which is preferred over uncured disease. A treatment exists that improves the likelihood that P will be cured, but unfortunately, this treatment may result in unpleasant side-effects. There is also a test for which a positive result is somewhat indicative of disease D. The test carries some risk of undesirable complications.

The information presented thus far is obviously insufficient for deciding the fate of poor patient P. Nevertheless, it conveys enough of the structure of the decision problem to construct the qualitative influence diagram depicted in Figure 7.

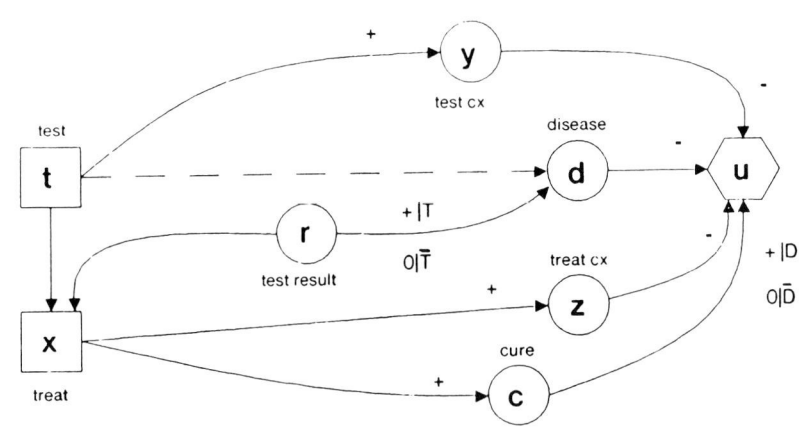

Figure 7: Qualitative influence diagram for the generic test/treat decision.

As the diagram indicates, utility (the hexagon node) is a function of the four variables c, d, y, and z. The result is conditionally independent of the decisions (square nodes) and the test result given those four values. Note that cure only influences utility in the presence of disease.

The influence of the test result on the likelihood of disease is similarly conditioned on whether or not the test was performed. Because of this conditioning, node d depends probabilistically on node t. But since this dependence is totally described by the condition on the r influence, we do not need a separate influence for t. The dependence is indicated on the diagram by a dashed line to avoid portraying a redundant influence in the network.

The first step in evaluating the diagram is to apply the graph manipulations described in section 3.2 to reduce the model as much as possible. In our example, removing nodes c, z, and y and reversing the influence between r and d leaves us with the diagram of Figure 8.

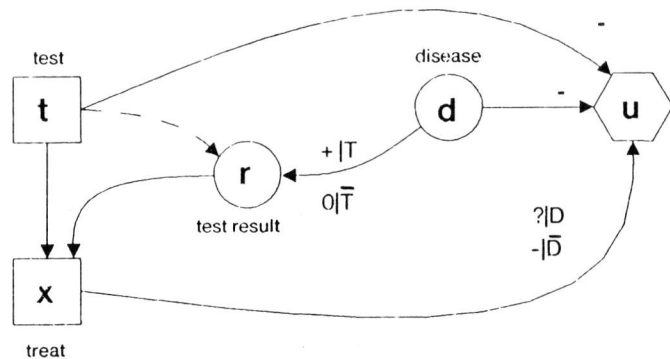

Figure 8: The reduced influence diagram.

4.1 Planning

Before proceeding further, let us consider our objectives in this decision problem. We are certainly not going to derive a unique decision from this information. Instead, an analysis of the model serves two main purposes: to separate the sensible plans from the senseless ones and to identify the indeterminacies of the model that are most important for resolving the decision at hand. The remainder of this discussion is devoted to the first purpose.

A naive planning program or influence diagram evaluator considers all syntactically valid plans. In a representation that consists of a collection of available actions, the set of syntactically valid plans is simply all possible sequences of actions. If there are uncertain variables that may become known along the way, then plans must include contingencies.

In the reduced diagram of Figure 8, the set of syntactically valid plans is defined by the combinations of t and x, with x expressed as policies given t and r. This makes for a total of eight distinct strategies. While many of these combinations are reasonable, others (more than half in this example) either violate common sense or are not coherent plans at all. For example, the combination of T with the treatment policy $x(r) = X$ seems like a ridiculous strategy, because we are performing the test but then treating the patient regardless of the result. The strategy of not doing the test but treating only if positive is also syntactically valid in this model, though it has no coherent meaning in the domain.

In the following section we will see that—at least in this example—the intuitively nonsensical plans correspond exactly to those not admissible under qualitative influences.

4.2 Determining Admissibility

A variety of techniques are available for computing admissibility within a qualitative probabilistic network. This section explores a few of these by examining their conclusions about the generic test/treat example.

Hypothetical Optimality

The "hypothetical optimality" technique explores the space of possible plans by postulating that the optimal strategy includes particular components. For example, we might start on the current problem by assuming that the best plan includes a test operation ($t = T$). Examining the diagram of Figure 8, we see that node t has two paths to the value node: an unambiguously negative path due to the effect of test complications, and an indeterminate path which includes the informational link from the test result to the treatment decision.

If testing is indeed optimal, then it must be the case that the indeterminate path actually has a positive influence on utility. Otherwise, performing the test would have an overall negative value. An informational path can only have positive value if a downstream decision depends on the value of a chance node. That is, the value of x that is preferred given R is not the preferred value given $\bar{R}$. Thus, one of the following two conditions must hold:

$$U^+(x, TR) \wedge U^-(x, T\bar{R}) \tag{10}$$

$$U^-(x, TR) \wedge U^+(x, T\bar{R}) \tag{11}$$

The second conjunct of condition (11) implies that negatives should be treated. But since $\Pr(D|R) \geq \Pr(D|\bar{R})$, this clause contradicts the first. Thus, given that testing is optimal, the strategy of treating only the positives is best.

Similar hypothetical reasoning can show, for example, that if treating negatives is optimal then it does not make sense to perform the test. Proofs of this type rule out all strategies in this example except

- no test, no treatment
- test, treat if positive
- no test, treat (empiric therapy)

Stochastic Dominance

Though the previous technique has substantial intuitive appeal, it is not clear that such nice admissibility results can always be derived via simple inspection. Therefore, we seek a more systematic approach that will eliminate as many nonsensical strategies as possible.

Figure 9 displays the partial order on utility induced by the influences in the reduced influence diagram. We can use this partial ordering to prove strategies inadmissible through a generalized form of *first-order stochastic dominance* [17]. Strategy A dominates strategy B in the first order if for every possible outcome, the likelihood of getting that outcome or a worse one is greater for B than for A. This can be generalized to partially ordered outcomes by requiring that the condition hold within directed paths in the order graph, being careful to avoid double-counting of outcomes.

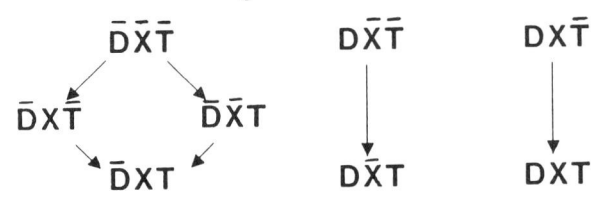

$$\bar{D}X\bar{T} \qquad D\bar{X}\bar{T} \qquad DX\bar{T}$$

$$\bar{D}X\bar{T} \qquad \bar{D}\bar{X}T$$

$$\bar{D}XT \qquad D\bar{X}T \qquad DXT$$

Figure 9: Partial order on outcome desirability determined from the diagram.

We can rule out a particular strategy by finding another feasible strategy that dominates it according to this criterion. To perform this comparison, we determine the outcomes of each strategy given the various possibilities for relevant chance nodes in the network. For example, Table 2 is a case analysis of the two syntactically valid strategies "no test, no treat" and "test, no treat."

The table records the outcome for each case, along with its probability (symbolic). Notice that the value of node r is irrelevant here, since there is no path to utility except through an informational link which is not being used. Looking at Table 2, it is easy to see that the first strategy dominates the second. For each case, the first strategy has an outcome that is preferred (based on the partial order) to the corresponding outcome in the second strategy, which occurs with equal probability. In this example, the two strategies are ranked by an application of Savage's "sure-thing principle" [12, page 21]. Note that this ranking does not depend at all on the prevalence of the disease.

By an almost identical argument, the strategy "test, treat" is dominated by the empiric therapy strategy.

Strategy	Case	Prob	Outcome
$t = \bar{T},\ x = \bar{X}$	D	$\Pr(D)$	$D\bar{X}\bar{T}$
	$\bar{D}$	$\Pr(\bar{D})$	$\bar{D}\bar{X}\bar{T}$
$t = T,\ x = \bar{X}$	D	$\Pr(D)$	$D\bar{X}T$
	$\bar{D}$	$\Pr(\bar{D})$	$\bar{D}\bar{X}T$

Table 2: Case analysis of two strategies.

Unfortunately, pairwise dominance testing is not sufficient to rule out all inadmissible strategies. In our example, the strategy "test, treat iff negative" is not dominated by any of the other strategies under consideration. While the strategy of treating only the positives may seem to make more sense, it is actually the inferior choice when, for example, the test is very insensitive and the treatment complications are relatively unlikely or benign.

To prove that treating the negatives is a suboptimal policy, it is necessary to show that there is always some strategy that is preferred, though the superior strategy may vary from case to case. In the scenario mentioned above where this policy is better than treating the positives, it is clear that there are other strategies that would be even better. Indeed, this is always the case in our example. For this kind of situation, dominance proofs take the form

$$S_1 \succeq S_2 \Longrightarrow S_3 \succeq S_1 \qquad (12)$$

When (12) holds, we say that S_1 is dominated with respect to S_2 and S_3.

Three-way (or k-way) dominance proofs are more cumbersome to construct, however. A related technique that might be computationally more direct is to demonstrate suboptimality by comparison with *mixed strategies* [5]. A mixed strategy is simply a probabilistic combination of feasible deterministic strategies. For our example, consider

Strategy 9: No test, treat if heads on an α coin flip.

It can be shown that strategy 9 with $\alpha = \Pr(\bar{R}|D)$ is guaranteed to dominate the treat on negative strategy, even though no nonrandom strategy was uniquely superior. Because mixed strategies are always suboptimal [12], our problematic strategy of treating only the negatives may be ruled inadmissible.

5 Conclusions

Within a probabilistic network formalism, we can provide a precise probabilistic semantics for qualitative influences among uncertain variables. A qualitative algebra for combining influences in the network can be used within an algorithm for isolating the influences of interest, such as the overall influence of decisions on expected utility.

Given a reduced influence diagram, several techniques are available for determining the admissible strategies among the syntactically valid plans. The source of indeterminacy in a failed dominance proof may be a reliable indicator of the importance of further information and assumptions to a problem solver capable of generating more detailed models.

The scheme presented here is intended to form only part of a comprehensive planning program. Although these kinds of qualitative influences are not sufficient to resolve true tradeoffs, the techniques described can be useful in planning under uncertainty for a variety of reasons.

First, the qualitative reasoner can work in tandem with a more traditional planner or decision algorithm, noticing the "obvious" conclusions before precise information is supplied. This argument suggests that a program that rules out "test but do not treat" based on a lower numeric expected utility is missing the point, because the conclusion does not depend on the absolute values of any quantities in the model. Recognition of the minimal assumptions necessary for a result provides for more coherent and compelling explanations than those generated under complete information.

Second, the mechanisms described here may be "scaled up" to handle more precise information when it is available, with decision-making power varying smoothly within the continuum of model specification. Expansion of indeterminacy with increased detail can be avoided somewhat by maintaining the more abstract influences while exploring the more detailed structure. Thus, this work is complementary with other recent AI work on reasoning with incomplete probabilistic information [3,6,9] as well as incomplete utility specification [15].

Finally, the formalism provides a means for exploring probabilistic interpretations of other schemes that use qualitative influence among uncertain variables. Work on "causal networks" (for example, CASNET [14]) and Cohen's endorsement approach [2] fall in this category.

Further development and integration will buttress these arguments. Current work includes application of these techniques to analyze and critique models generated by human decision analysts [4].

References

[1] Daniel G. Bobrow, editor. *Qualitative Reasoning about Physical Systems.* M. I. T. Press, 1985.

[2] Paul R. Cohen. *Heuristic Reasoning about Uncertainty: An Artificial Intelligence Approach.* Volume 2 of *Research Notes in Artificial Intelligence*, Pitman, 1985.

[3] Gregory Floyd Cooper. NESTOR: *A computer-based medical diagnostic aid that integrates causal and probabilistic knowledge.* PhD thesis, Stanford University, November 1984.

[4] Mark H. Eckman and Michael P. Wellman. Decision tree construction advisor: A knowledge based system for the automated critiquing of medical decision tree models. Abstract presented at the NLM Trainee Meeting, March 1986.

[5] Peter C. Fishburn. Analysis of decisions with incomplete knowledge of probabilities. *Operations Research*, 13:217–237, 1965.

[6] Benjamin N. Grosof. An inequality paradigm for probabilistic knowledge: The logic of conditional probability intervals. In Laveen N. Kanal and John F. Lemmer, editors, *Uncertainty in Artificial Intelligence*, North-Holland, 1986.

[7] Ronald A. Howard and James E. Matheson. Influence diagrams. In Ronald A. Howard and James E. Matheson, editors, *The Principles and Applications of Decision Analysis*, pages 719–762, Strategic Decisions Group, Menlo Park, CA, 1984.

[8] Benjamin Kuipers. Qualitative simulation. *Artificial Intelligence*, 29:289–338, 1986.

[9] Nils J. Nilsson. Probabilistic logic. *Artificial Intelligence*, 28:71–87, 1986.

[10] Judea Pearl. Fusion, propagation, and structuring in belief networks. *Artificial Intelligence*, 29:241–288, 1986.

[11] Judea Pearl. *Markov and Bayes networks: A comparison of two graphical representations of probabilistic knowledge*. Technical Report R-46, UCLA Computer Science Department, September 1986.

[12] Leonard J. Savage. *The Foundations of Statistics*. Dover Publications, New York, second edition, 1972.

[13] Ross D. Shachter. Evaluating influence diagrams. To appear in *Operations Research*.

[14] Sholom M. Weiss, Casimir A. Kulikowski, Saul Amarel, and Aaron Safir. A model-based method for computer-aided medical decision making. *Artificial Intelligence*, 11:145–172, 1978.

[15] Michael Paul Wellman. *Reasoning about preference models*. TR 340, Massachussetts Institute of Technology, Laboratory for Computer Science, 545 Technology Square, Cambridge, MA, 02139, May 1985.

[16] Michael P. Wellman. Probabilistic semantics for qualitative influences. Submitted for publication.

[17] G. A. Whitmore and M. C. Findlay, editors. *Stochastic Dominance: An Approach to Decision Making Under Risk*. D. C. Heath and Company, Lexington, MA, 1978.

ON IMPLEMENTING USUAL VALUES*

Ronald R. Yager

Machine Intelligence Institute
Iona College
New Rochelle, N.Y. 10801

In many cases commonsense knowledge consists of knowledge of what is usual. In this paper we develop a system for reasoning with usual information. This system is based upon the fact that these pieces of commonsense information involve both a probabilistic aspect and a granular aspect. We implement this system with the aid of possibility-probability granules.

1. INTRODUCTION

An ability to handle commonsense reasoning is a crucial need in the development of the artificial intelligence [1]. A number of variants of so-called non-monotonic logics have been introduced as aids in developing these commonsense reasoning mechanisms [2-4].
Recently L.A. Zadeh has suggested that a central role in a theory of commonsense must be played by a concept of "usuality". This concept reflects the fact that in many cases commonsense reasoning involves reasoning with usual values for variables. For example, the statement
"a cup of coffee costs fifty cents,"
is more precisely reflected by the statement
"a cup of coffee usually costs fifty cents."
In a number of recent presentations Zadeh [5-7] has suggested some properties which must be present in any theory of usuality. In this paper we introduce a formal mechanism for representing and manipulating usual values. This formalism allows for both logical and arithmetic manipulations of usual values. The formal structure used to represent these usual values are Possibility-Probability granules (Poss-Prob granules). These structures have been studied by Yager [8-10] and are based upon a combination of the linguistic variables introduced by L.A. Zadeh in his theory of approximate reasoning [11] and the evidential structures introduced by G. Shafer [12].
As we shall see, the idea of usuality implies some random or probabilistic phenomenon at play as well as some idea of granularity. The idea of granularity necessitates the use of set theoretic constructs in the form of possibility distributions which enable us to account for the fact that humans conceptualize

---

* This research was in part supported by grants from the NSF program in Information Science and the AFOSR.

in terms of gross concepts. The introduction of the
probabilistic aspect also provides a departure from the approach
taken by the non-monotonic logicians.
    We further note that these usual values play a central role
as default values in frames and other similar type structures
[13-15].
    Since much of the information in knowledge-based systems
involves the use of commonsense knowledge. This theory of
usuality will greatly impinge in this area.

2. ON POSSIBILITY-PROBABILITY GRANULES

    In preparation for presenting our representation scheme for
usual values we briefly review the idea of
possibility-probability granules. For more details on these
structures see [8-10].
    Assume V is a variable which takes its value in the set X.
Assume A is a fuzzy subset of X a <u>canonical statement</u> of
knowledge about V is of the form <u>V is A</u>. A canonical statement
is meant to be interpreted as a proposition indicating that the
value of V lies in the subset A. These type of statements
provide a restriction on the value of V. A canonical statement
provides a formal way of representing many natural language
statements. Consider the statement "Bill is young." This can be
represented as V is A where V would indicate the attribute Bill's
age and A would be the subset of ages constituting the user's
definition of young. Canonical statements of this type provide a
mechanism for associating values to attributes when there exists
some uncertainty as to the value of the attribute. In particular
a canonical statement associates a set of <u>possible</u> values, those
elements in the set A, with the variable V. We denote the type
of uncertainty associated with these statements as possibilistic
uncertainty.
    A more general data structure which subsumes these canonical
statements is what we shall call a Possibility-Probability
granule. Again assume V is a variable which takes its value in
the set X. Let A_k, $k = 1,2,\ldots\ldots n$, be a collection of fuzzy
subsets on X. Again in this framework <u>V is A_k</u> is a canonical
statement restricts the value of the variable V. However in this
more general setting of Poss-Prob granules we allow for some
probabilistic uncertainty as to which is the appropriate
canonical statement restricting the value of V. In particular we
associate with each statement <u>V is A_k</u> a probability p_k, which
indicates the probability that V is A_k is the appropriate
proposition expressing our knowledge about V. We note that their
exists no restriction on the relationship between the A_k's, other
than they be non-null fuzzy subsets of X, however the p_k's must
sum to one.
    Care should be taken to understand that p_k is not the
probability that the value of an experiment on X results in an
element in A_k but more in the following vain. There exists some
other space $Y = \{y_1, y_2, \ldots\ldots,y_n\}$ in which we perform a random
experiment in which p_k is the probability that y_k is the outcome.
If as a result of this experiment y_k occurs then we say that <u>V is
A_k</u> is the canonical statement restricting V.
    In [10] Yager has shown that the structure captured by these
Poss-Prob granules is similar to that of a Dempster-Shafer belief
structure in which the A_k's are the focal elements and the p_k's

are the weights. However, we note in this Poss-Prob framework the A_k's can be fuzzy subsets. Because of the similarity with the Dempster-Shafer belief structure we shall denote the knowledge that a variable's value is controlled by a Poss-Prob granule as

V is m,

where m is a basic probability assignment function (bpa) with focal elements $\{A_k\}$ and weights $m(A_k) = p_k$.

Two important concepts associated with Dempster-Shafer are the measures of plausibility and belief defined on subsets of X. Because of the allowance for fuzzy sets as focal elements we must provide more general definitions for these measures in the framework of Poss-Prob granules. For any subset B of X

$$Pl(B) = \sum_k (Poss[B/A_k] * m(a_k))$$

and $Bel(B) = \sum_k (Cert[B/A_k] * m(A_k))$,

where $Poss[B/A_k] = Max_x [B(x) \wedge A_k(x)]$ and $Cert[B/A_k] = 1-Poss[B^-/A_k]$. In the above $B(x)$ and $A_k(x)$ are membership grades of x in the respective sets and B^- is defined by $B^-(x) = 1-B(x)$.

In [10] Yager has shown that when the focal elements are restricted to be crisp subsets of X these definitions collapse to those of Shafer.

As is well established in the Dempster-Shafer setting these two measures provide bounds on the probabilities of events in the space X of outcomes for V. In particular, if we denote Prob(B) ti indicate the probability that the value for V lies in the set B then

$$Bel(B) \leq Prob(B) \leq Pl(B).$$

The use of Poss-Prob granules provides a very powerful mechanism for representing various different types of knowledge about the variable V in a unified structure. One particular type of knowledge we shall find useful in this paper is the case in which we know that Prob(B) is "at least α." Formally this can be stated as $\alpha \leq Prob(B) \leq 1$. Thus in this case we require that $Bel(B) = \alpha$ and $Pl(B) = 1$. It can easily be shown that the least restrictive Poss-Prob granule which can represent this information is a bpa m on X such that $m(B) = \alpha$ and $m(X) = 1-\alpha$.

3. ON USUAL VALUES AND THEIR REPRESENTATION

As we noted in a number of recent papers L.A. Zadeh has introduced the concept of usuality and discussed its central role in any theory of commonsense reasoning. In particular Zadeh argues that in many cases the types of knowledge which constitutes commonsense involves the knowledge about the _usual_ value of some variable. Furthermore we understand Zadeh to suggest that in many cases these usual values are vague and imprecise of the type best represented by a linguistic value and the associated ideas of a fuzzy subset and a possibility distribution. This imprecision is due to the granular nature of human conceptualization.

If V is a variable taking its value in the set X and A is a fuzzy subset of X representing the usual value of V, we could then say, "usually V is A" or equivalently U(V) is A, where U(V) denotes the usual value of V. Examples of the above of linguistic structure would be
"usually basketball players are tall,"
"usually birds fly"
"usually Mary comes home at about 8 o'clock.

In many instances of natural language discourse we suppress the word usually and simply say, for example, "birds fly" rather than "usually birds fly." If one doesn't recognize this shorthand many difficulties follow.

The statement "usually Mary comes home at 8 o'clock," as formalized by Usually V is A embodies a number of different forms of uncertainty. We see that the statement U(V) is A implies some probabilistic phenomenon in our knowledge about the variable V. We shall now provide a formal framework for representing this type of knowledge.

According to Zadeh the statement Usually V is A should be interpreted as indicating that the probability that the event A occurs as the value for the variable V is "at least α", where α is some number close to one. The usual the occurrence of A the closer α is to one.

As we have indicated in the previous section this type of information on the variable V can be represented as a Poss-Prob granule. In particular the knowledge that usually V is A can be represented as the Poss-Prob granule
$$V \text{ is } m,$$
where m is a bpa on X, the frame of V, such that $m(A) = \alpha$ and $m(X) = 1-\alpha$.

Thus we see that the effect of the statement usually V is A is to say that α portion of the time the value of V is determined by the proposition V is A and that for $1-\alpha$ of the time V is unknown.

The form V is m shall constitute a canonical type of representation for usual information. In the next section we shall provide for the translation of various linguistic structures involving usual values into these structures.

Before preceding we note that a non-probabilistic assertion such as "John is about 30 years old" can be written in this formation as V is m_1 where V is the attribute John's age and m_1 is a bpa such that $m_1(B) = 1$ where B is "about thirty."

4. TRANSLATION OF COMPOUND STATEMENTS

In this section we shall provide some procedures for translating compound linguistic statements involving usual values into formal structures in terms of Poss-Prob granules. Our purpose here is to put these complex linguistic statements into forms which enable us to use the sophisticated mechanisms available for combining these structures as necessary in the course of the reasoning process. The approach here is based upon a generalization of the approach used in Zadeh's theory of approximate reasoning [11].

We first start with the representation of linguistic structures in which propositions involving linguistic variables are qualified by the modifier "usually."

Assume V is a variable taking values in the set X. We recall a statement of the form V is A, where A is a fuzzy subset of X, is called a canonical proposition. As we discussed in the previous section the effect of the qualification of this proposition by usually to Usually (V is A) is to transform this statement into a Poss-Prob granule of the form V is m* where m* is a bpa on X such that $m(A) = \alpha$ and $m(X) = 1-\alpha$.

Assume V_1 and V_2 are two variables taking their values in the sets X and Y respectively. Consider the conditional

statement
"if V_1 is A then V_2 is B,"
where A and B are fuzzy subsets of X and Y respectively. From the theory of approximate reasoning, this conditional statement translates into compound canonical propositions (V_1, V_2) is H where H is a fuzzy subset of X × Y which can be defined by
$$H(x, y) = \text{Min} [1, 1-A(x) + B(y)].$$
Alternatively H can be defined as $H(x,y) = \text{Max} [1-A(x), B(y)]$. Now consider the qualified version of this statement "usually if V_1 is A then V_2 is B." This can be seen to be equivalent to usually (V_1, V_2) is H which can be represented as any usuality qualified canonical proposition as a Poss-Prob granule (V_1, V_2) is m where m is a bpa on X × Y such that m (H) = α and m (X × Y) = 1-α.

Consider now the statement usually (V_1 is A or V_2 is B). Since the statement V is A or V_2 is B translates into the compound canonical proposition (V_1, V_2) is H* where H is a fuzzy subset of X × Y such that $H^*(x, y) = \text{Max} [A(x), B(y)]$ then the statement usually (V_1 is A or V_2 is B) which is equivalent to usually (V_1, V_2) is H* translates into the Poss-Prob granule (V_1, V_2) is m* where m* is a bpa on X × Y such that m*(H*) = α and m*(X × Y) = 1-α.

Similarly usually (V_1 is A and V_2 is B) translates into (V_1, V_2) is m$^\perp$ where m$^\perp$ is a bpa on X × Y such that m$^\perp$(H$^\perp$) = α and m$^\perp$(X × Y) = 1-α where H$^\perp$ is a fuzzy subset of X such that $H^\perp(x, y) = \text{Min} [A(x), B(y)]$.

In the above we have essentially applied this new usuality qualification operation to statements which are canonical forms from the theory of approximate reasoning, ie. V is A or (V_1, V_2) is H. All the logical operations were performed on canonical statements before the usuality qualification transformed them into granules. In the next section we shall look at situations in which we combine under various logical operations structures which are of the form of Poss-Prob granules. This will enable us to translate compound statements in which the usuality qualification is more deeply embedded in the structure.

5. LOGICAL TRANSLATION RULES

Let $\perp$ be any operation definable in terms of operations on sets. Based upon the work of Yager [10] we can extend this operation to apply to Poss-Prob granules. Assume V_1 is m_1 and V_2 is m_2 are two Poss-Prob defined over the sets X and Y respectively, the rule developed by Yager states that (V_1 is m_1) $\perp$ (V_2 is m_2) translates into (V_1, V_2) is $m_1 \perp m_2$ where m = $m_1 \perp m_2$ is a bpa defined on X × Y such that for all the focal elements A_k of m_1 and B_j of m_2
$$m(A_k \perp B_j) = m_1(A_k) * m_2(B_j).$$
Equivalently we can define m such that for any A ⊆ X × Y
$$m(A) = \Sigma \ m_1(A_k) * m_2(B_j),$$
where the summation is taken over all A_k, B_j such that $A_k \perp B_j$=A. We note in the special case where $V_1 = V_2$ = V defined on X then (V is m_1) $\perp$ V is m_2 translates into V is m where m is a bpa on X defined as in the above. Dempster's rule is a special case when $\perp$ = $\cap$.

Let us use this rule to translate some linguistic statements which involve an embedded usuality qualification.

Consider the statement "if V_1 is A then usually V_2 is B." This statement can be seen to be of the form "if V_1 is m_1 then v_2 is m_2," where m_1 is a bpa on X such that m_1(A) = 1 and m_2 is a bpa on Y such that $m_2(B) = \alpha$ and $m_2(Y) = 1-\alpha$. Applying our translation rule to this situation we get, (V_1, V_2) is m where $m(A_k \perp B_j) = m_1(A_k) * m_2(B_j)$ and $A_k \perp B_j = G_{kj}$. G_{kj} is a fuzzy subset of $X \times Y$ such that $G_{kj}(x, y) = \text{Min } [1, 1-A_k(x) + B_j(y)]$.

In the case we are interested in with $A \perp B = D$ and $A \perp Y = X \times Y$ we get (V_1, V_2) is m^* where m^* is a bpa on $X \times Y$ such that $m^*(D) = \alpha$ and $m^*(X \times Y) = 1-\alpha$. We note in this case $D(x, y) = \text{Min } (1, 1-A(x) + B(y))$. Parenthetically we note that this is the same translation as the statement "usually if V_1 is A then V_2 is B."

Consider next the statement, "if usually V_1 is A then V_2 is B." This can be translated into "if V_1 is m_1 then V_2 is m_2" where m_1 is on X such that $m_1(A) = \alpha$ and $m_1(X) = 1-\alpha$. m_2 is on Y such that $m_2(B) = 1$. Using our translation rule we get (V_1,V_2) is m^*. m^* is a bpa on $X \times Y$ such that $m^*(D) = \alpha$ and $m^*(H) = 1-\alpha$ in which $D(x, y) = \text{Min } [1, 1-A(x) + B(y)]$ and $H(x, y) = B(y)$.

Next consider the statement "if usually V_1 is A then usually V_2 is B." This can be first translated as "if V_1 is m_1 then V_2 is m_2" where m_1 is a bpa on X such that $m_1(A) = \alpha$ and $m_1(X) = 1-\alpha$ and m_2 is a bpa on Y such that $m_2(B) = \alpha$ and $m_2(X) = 1-\alpha$. Using our logical translation rule this becomes (V_1, V_2) is m^*, where m^* is a bpa on $X \times Y$ such that $m^*(A \perp B) = \alpha^2$, $m^*(A \perp Y) = \alpha(1-\alpha)$, $m^*(X \perp B) = (1-\alpha)\alpha$ and $m^*(X \perp Y) = (1-\alpha)(1-\alpha)$. Since $A \perp B = D$, $A \perp Y = X \perp Y$ and $X \perp B = H$, then m^* can be seen to be $m^*(D) = \alpha^2$, $m^*(H) = (1-\alpha)\alpha$ and $m^*(X \times Y) = 1-\alpha$.

Consider next the proposition "usually V_1 is A and usually V_2 is B." Formally this becomes V_1 is m_1 and V_2 is m_2 where m_1 is a bpa on X such that $m_1(A) = \alpha$ and $m_1(X) = 1-\alpha$. m_2 is a bpa on Y where $m_2(B) = \alpha$ and $m_2(Y) = 1-\alpha$. This can be seen to be equivalent to (V_1, V_2) is m^* where m^* is on $X \times Y$ such that $m^*(D_1) = \alpha^2$, $m^*(D_2) = \alpha(1-\alpha)$, $m^*(D_3) = \alpha(1-\alpha)$ and $m^*(D_4) = (1-\alpha)^2$. In this structure $D_1(x,y) = \text{Min}(A(x), B(y))$, $D_2(x, y) = A(x)$, $D_3(x, y) = B(y)$ and $D_4(x, y) = 1$.

On the other hand "V_1 is m_1 or V_2 is m_2" becomes (V_1,V_2) is m^* where $m^*(D) = \alpha^2$ and $m^*(X \times Y) = 1-\alpha^2$ where $D(x, y) = \text{Max}[A(x), B(y)]$.

6. REASONING WITH USUAL VALUES

In this section we shall look at the structure of some examples of reasoning with usual values. Consider the following two propositions

P_1: Usually [if V_1 is A then V_2 is B]
P_2: V_1 is C.

In the above we are assuming that A and C are fuzzy subsets of X, the base set of V_1 and B is a fuzzy of Y, the base set of V_2. These two pieces of data can be written as Poss-Prob granules,

P_1: (V_1, V_2) is m_1 and P_2: (V_1) is m_2.

In the above m_1 is a bpa on $X \times Y$ such that $m_1(H) = \alpha$ and $m_1(X \times Y) = 1-\alpha$ where $H(x, y) = (1-A(x)) \vee B(y)$. m_2 is a bpa on X such that $m_2(C) = 1$. Taking the conjunction of these two pieces of data we get "(V_1, V_2) is m_3" where m_3 is a bpa on $X \times Y$ such that $m_3(E) = \alpha$ and $m_3(E_1) = 1-\alpha$ where

$E(x, y) = H(x, y) \wedge C(x) = ((1-A(x)) \vee B(y)) \wedge C(x)$

and $E_1(x, y) = C(x)$. Finally to get the inferred value of V_2, V_2 is m_4, we take the projection of m_3 on Y. Thus m_4 is a bpa on Y such that $m(F) = \alpha$ and $m(F_1) = 1-\alpha$, where $F_1 = \text{Proj}_Y E_1 \rightarrow F_1(y) = $

$\text{Max}_x \; E_1(x, y) = 1$, thus $F_1 = Y$. $F = \text{Proj}_Y E$. Thus
$F(y) = \text{Max}_x \; [(1-A(x)) \vee B(y)) \wedge C(x)]$.
Thus the inferred information about V_2 from P_1 and P_2 is that usually V_2 is F.

We note that in the special case when $A = C$ we get $F = \text{Max}_x \; [(A^-(x) \wedge A(x)) \vee (B(y) \wedge A(x))]$. Furthermore if A is crisp then $F = B$.

Consider next the situation in which both propositions involve usual values

$\qquad P_1$: Usually (if V is A then V_2 is B)
$\qquad P_2$: Usually (V is C).

In this case as in the previous case P_1: (V_1, V_2) is m_1 where m_1 is the bpa on $X \times Y$ such that $m_1(H) = \alpha$ and $m_1(X \times Y) = 1-\alpha$. However in this case
$\qquad P_2$: v is m_2^*
where m_2^* is a bpa on X such that $m_2^*(C) = \alpha$ and $m_2^*(X) = 1-\alpha$.
Taking the conjunction of these two pieces of data we get
$\qquad\qquad (V_1, V_2)$ is m_3^*
where $m_3^*(E) = \alpha^2$, $m_3^*(H) = \alpha(1-\alpha)$, $m_3^*(C \times Y) = \alpha(1-\alpha)$ and $m_3^*(X \times Y) = (1-\alpha)^2$.
Finally we can infer that
$\qquad\qquad V_2$ is m_4^*
where m_4^* is a bpa on Y and its focal elements are obtained as the projection onto Y of the focal elements of m_3^*. We note
$\quad \text{Proj}_Y [H] = \text{Proj}_Y [C \times Y] = \text{Proj}_Y [X \times Y] = Y$.
Since have already shown Proj $[E] = F$ we get
$\quad m_4^*(F) = \alpha^2$ and $m_4^*(Y) = 1-\alpha^2$.
Thus in this situation we have obtained (usually)^2 (V_2 is F).

Consider the two Poss-Prob granules V_2 is m_4 and V_2 is m_4^* where
$\qquad\qquad m_4(F) = \alpha \qquad\qquad m_4^*(F) = \alpha^2$
$\qquad\qquad m_4(Y) = 1-\alpha \qquad\quad m_4^*(Y) = 1-\alpha^2$
which were obtained as a result of the preceding reasoning processes. Let us look at the plausibility and certainty measures associated with some arbitrary subset A of Y under each of these granules. From our definitions
$\qquad\qquad Pl(A) = \alpha \; \text{Poss} \; [A/F] + (1-\alpha) \; \text{Poss} \; [A/Y]$
$\qquad\qquad Pl^*(A) = \alpha^2 \; \text{Poss} \; [A/F] + (1-\alpha^2) \; \text{Poss} \; [A/Y]$
Since Poss $[A/Y] \geq$ Poss $[A/F]$ and for any $\alpha \in [0,1]$, $\alpha \geq \alpha^2$ then it follows that $Pl^*(A) \geq Pl(A)$. Furthermore
$\qquad\qquad Bel(A) = \alpha \; \text{Cert} \; [A/F] + (1-\alpha) \; \text{Cert} \; [A/Y]$
$\qquad\qquad Bel^*(A) = \alpha^2 \; \text{Cert} \; [A/F] + (1-\alpha^2) \; \text{Cert} \; [A/Y]$.
Since Poss $[A^-/Y] \geq$ Poss $[A^-/F]$ it follows that Cert $[A/F] \geq$ Cert $[A/Y]$. Hence Bel$(A) \geq$ Bel$^*(A)$. Thus we see that the case of a usually qualified proposition provides tighter bounds on the probability of events then that of a usually squared qualified proposition.

6. ARITHMETIC OPERATIONS WITH USUAL OPERATIONS

In the preceding sections we have mainly concerned ourselves with the manipulation of usual values under logic operations. In many cases we may have to perform mathematical or arithmetic operations on these usual values. In this section we develop the calculus necessary to perform these operations. The ability to handle both logical and arithmetic manipulations provides this approach with a very sophisticated mechanism for building expert systems.

Assume V_1 and V_2 are two variables taking their values in the real line R. Let V_1 is m_1 and V_2 is m_2 be two Poss-Prob granules in which m_1 and m_2 are basic probability assignments on R. Let $\{A_k\}$ be the focal elements of m_1 and let $\{B_j\}$ be the focal elements of m_2. We note that both the A's and B's are fuzzy subsets of R. Let "$V = V_1 \perp V_2$" where $\perp$ is any arithmetic operation, (addition +, subtraction -, multiplication *, division /, or exponentiation). In [10] Yager has shown that in this situation "V is m" where m is a bpa on R such that for any $A \subseteq R$
$$m(A) = \Sigma\ m_1(A_i) * m_2(B_j),$$
where the summation is taken over all A_i and B_j such that $A_i \perp B_j = A$. In order to evaluate the above we must use fuzzy arithmetic [17]. In particular if E and F are two fuzzy numbers, fuzzy subsets of the real line, then $E \perp F = G$, where G is a fuzzy subset of R such that
$$G = \bigcup_{y,z \in R} \{E(y) \wedge F(z)/y \perp z\}.$$

Let us look at the situation for various forms of m_1 and m_2. Consider the case in which our knowledge is
P_1: Usually V_1 is A and P_2: V_2 is B
in which A and B are fuzzy subsets of R. First we see that these two pieces of data can be represented in terms of granules in the following way. P_1: V_1 is m_1 in which m_1 is a bpa on R defined by $m_1(A) = \alpha$ and $m_1(R) = 1-\alpha$. P_2: V_2 is m_2 where m_2 is also a bpa on R defined by $m_2(B) = 1$. If $V = V_1 \perp V_2$ then V is m where m is a bpa on R defined by $m(A \perp B) = \alpha$ and $m(R \perp B) = 1-\alpha$. Since for any mathematical operation, except division by $B = 0$, $R \perp B = R$ we get $m(A \perp B) = \alpha$ and $m(R) = 1-\alpha$, thus this translates to usually (V is $A \perp B$).

Consider next the situation in which both pieces of data involve usual values; P_1: usually V_1 is A and P_2: usually V_2 is B. In this case we get V_1 is m_1 and V_2 is m_2 where $m_1(A) = m_2(B) = \alpha$ and $m_1(R) = m_2(R) = 1-\alpha$. If $V = V_1 \perp V_2$ then V is m^* where $m^*(A \perp B) = \alpha^2$, $m^*(A \perp R) = \alpha\ (1-\alpha)$, $m^*(R \perp B) = (1-\alpha)\ \alpha$ and $m^*(R \perp R) = (1-\alpha)^2$. However again since $A \perp R = R \perp B = R \perp R = R$ we get $m^*(A \perp B) = \alpha^2$ and $m^*(R) = 1-\alpha^2$. Thus this translates into
(usually)^2 (V is $A \perp B$).

7. CONCLUSION

We have presented a calculus for reasoning with usual valued knowledge. This system can provide a mechanism for implementing expert systems with commonsense knowledge.

REFERENCES

[1] McCarthy, J., "Applications of circumspection to formalizing commonsense knowledge," Proc. of Non-Monotonic Reasoning Workshop, AAAI, 295-324, 1984.
[2] Reiter, R., "A logic for default reasoning," Artificial Intelligence 13, 81-132, 1980.
[3] McDermott, D.V., & Doyle, J., "Non-Monotonic logic," Artificial Intelligence 13, 41-72, 1980.
[4] McCarthy, J., "Circumspection-a form of non-monotonic reasoning," Artificial Intelligence 13, 27-39, 1980.

[5] Zadeh, L.A., "Fuzzy sets and commonsense reasoning," Institute of Cognitive Studies report 21, University of California, Berkeley, 1984.
[6] Zadeh, L.A., "Fuzzy sets as a basis for the management of uncertainty in expert systems," Fuzzy Sets and Systems 11, 199-227, 1983.
[7] Zadeh, L.A., "A computational theory of dispositions," in Proc. of 1984 Int. Conference on Computation Linguistics, Stanford, 312-318, 1984.
[8] Yager, R.R., "Reasoning with uncertainty for expert systems," Proc. 9th Int. Joint Conference on Artificial Intelligence, Los Angeles, 1295-1297, 1985.
[9] Yager, R.R., "Toward a general theory of reasoning with uncertainty Part I: Non-Specificity and Fuzziness," Int. J. of Intelligent Systems 1, 45-67, 1986.
[10] Yager, R.R., "Arithmetic and other operations on Dempster-Shafer structures," Int. J. of Man-Machine Studies (To Appear).
[11] Zadeh, L.A., "A theory of approximate reasoning," in Machine Intelligence Vol 9, Hayes, Michie & Kulich (eds.), Wiley, 1979.
[12] Shafer, G., "A Mathematical Theory of Evidence," Princeton University Press: Princeton, N.J., 1976.
[13] Minsky, M., "A framework for representing knowledge," in the Psychology of Computer Vision, Winston, P.(ed.), McGraw-Hill, New York, 1975.
[14] Bobrow, D.G., Kaplyn, R.M., Kay, M., Norman, D.A., Thompson, H., & Winograd, T.," GUS, a frame driven dialog system." Artificial Intelligence 8, 155-173, 1977.
[15] Yager, R.R., "Linguistic representation of default values in frames," IEEE Trans. on Systems, Man and Cybernetics 14, 630-633, 1984.
[16] Yager, R.R., "Toward a general theory of reasoning with uncertainty Part II: Probability," Int. of Man-Machine Studies (To Appear).
[17] Dubois, D. & Prade, H., Fuzzy Sets and Systems: Theory and Applications, Academic Press: New York, 1980.
[18] Zimmermann, H.J., Fuzzy Set Theory and Its Applications, Kluvier-Nijhoff Publishing: Hingham, Mass., 1985.

III

THEORY

SOME EXTENSIONS OF PROBABILISTIC LOGIC

Su-shing Chen

Department of Computer Science
University of North Carolina
Charlotte, NC 28223, U.S.A.

1. INTRODUCTION

In [12], Nilsson proposed the probabilistic logic in which the truth values of logical propositions are probability values between 0 and 1. It is applicable to any logical system for which the consistency of a finite set of propositions can be established. The probabilistic inference scheme reduces to the ordinary logical inference when the probabilities of all propositions are either 0 or 1. This logic has the same limitations of other probabilistic reasoning systems of the Bayesian approach. For common sense reasoning, consistency is not a very natural assumption. We have some well known examples: { Dick is a Quaker, Quakers are pacifists, Repulicans are not pacifists, Dick is a Republican } and { Tweety is a bird, birds can fly, Tweety is a penguin }.

In this paper, we shall propose some extensions of the probabilistic logic. In the second section, we shall consider the space of all interpretations, consistent or not. In terms of frames of discernment, the basic probability assignment (bpa) and belief function can be defined. Dempster's combination rule is applicable. This extension of probabilistic logic is called the evidential logic in [1]. For each proposition s, its belief function is represented by an interval [Spt(s), Pls(s)]. When all such intervals collapse to single points, the evidential logic reduces to probabilistic logic (in the generalized version of not necessarily consistent interpretations). Certainly, we get Nilsson's probabilistic logic by further restricting to consistent interpretations.

In the third section, we shall give a probabilistic interpretation of probabilistic logic in terms of multi-dimensional random variables. This interpretation brings the probabilistic logic into the framework of probability theory. Let us consider a finite set $S = \{s_1, s_2, ..., s_n\}$ of logical propositions. Each proposition may have true or false values; and may be considered as a random variable. We have a probability distribution for each proposition. The n-dimensional random variable $(s_1, ..., s_n)$ may take values in the space of all interpretations of 2^n binary vectors. We may compute absolute (marginal), conditional and joint probability distributions. It turns out that the permissible probabilistic interpretation vector of Nilsson [12] consists of the joint probabilities of S. Inconsistent interpretations will not appear, by setting their joint probabilities to be zeros. By summing appropriate joint probabilities, we get probabilities of individual propositions or subsets of propositions. Since the Bayes formula and other techniques are valid for n-dimensional random variables, the probabilistic logic is actually very close to the Bayesian inference schemes.

In the last section, we shall consider a relaxation scheme for probabilistic logic. In this system, not only new evidences will update the belief measures of a collection of propositions, but also constraint satisfaction among these propositions in the relational network will revise these measures. This mechanism is similar to human reasoning which is an evolutive process converging to the most satisfactory result. The main idea arises from the consistent labeling problem in computer vision. This method is originally applied to scene analysis of line drawings. Later, it is applied to matching, constraint satisfaction and multisensor fusion by several authors [8], [16] (and see references cited there). Recently, this method is used in knowledge aggregation by Landy and Hummel [9].

2. EVIDENTIAL LOGIC

We consider the set $S = \{s_1, ..., s_n\}$ of logical propositions. In [12], Nilsson introduced the concept of a binary semantic tree of S which represents 2^n possible interpretations. At each node, we branch left or right, indicating a proposition and its negation. Below the root, we branch on s_1, then on s_2, and so on. We may assign truth values to these branches according to propositions and their negations. Since we are dealing with evidential reasoning, logically inconsistent interpretations are kept.

Let Θ denote the set of 2^n interpretations. Each proposition s in S is either true or false in Θ, thus, is completely characterized by the associated subset A of Θ to s containing those interpretations where s is true. We shall say that s is suuported by A. A basic probability assignment (bpa) m is a generalization of a probability mass distribution and assigns a number in [0,1] to every subset B of Θ such that the numbers sum to 1.

$$m: \Theta \to [0,1], \quad \Sigma_B m(B) = 1.$$

If a proposition s is supported on a subset A of Θ, then for all B in A,

$$\text{Spt}(s) = \Sigma_B m(B), \quad \text{Pls}(s) = 1 - \text{Spt}(\neg s).$$

We have a linear system of equations of $\text{Spt}(s_i)$ and $\text{Pls}(s_i)$ for $i = 1,...,n$ which gives the collection $\{[\text{Spt}(s_i),\text{Pls}(s_i)]\}$ of evidential intervals. If the evidential interval of a proposition s collapses to a point, then we have the probability (or generalized truth value) of s in [12]. We may very well have a mixed situation which allows some intervals and some points for the set **S** of logical propositions.

There are various kinds of evidential reasoning schemes, Nilsson's probabilistic inference scheme [12] can be extended as follows:
1. Construct **S'** by appending a new proposition s to **S**.
2. Extend the binary semantic tree for **S'**.
3. Construct the space Θ'.
4. Find a bpa **m'** from the system of evidential intervals of **S**.
5. Calculate the evidential interval of s using **m'**.

The Dempster combination rule applies also. For two bpa $\mathbf{m}_1$ and $\mathbf{m}_2$, the combination $\mathbf{m}_1 + \mathbf{m}_2$ may be calculated over intersecting subsets of Θ.

3. SEMANTICS AS RANDOM VARIABLES

Given the set $\mathbf{S} = \{s_1,...,s_n\}$ of n logical propositions, the binary semantic tree gives 2^n possible assignments of truth values $\{0,1\}$ to **S**. For each s, there are two possible outcomes 0 and 1. A probability measure on the Borel field on $\{0,1\}$ gives a probability distribution **p** of the random variable s. The values of **p** at two outcomes 0 and 1 are nonnegative and they sum to be one.

Without much ambiguity, we shall use the same symbol **S** for the n-dimensional random variable $\mathbf{S} = (s_1,...,s_n)$. **S** may assume value in the set of interpretation vectors (n-dimensional binary vectors) v_j, $j = 1, ..., 2^n$ in [12]. The permissible probabilistic interpretation vector turns out to be the joint probability distributions $\mathbf{p}(v_j)$, $j = 1,...,2^n$. For inconsistent v_j, its joint probability $\mathbf{p}(v_j)$ is zero and does not contribute to the permissible probabilistic interpretation vector.

In [12], a consistent probabilistic valuation vector over **S** is computed by multiplying the sentence matrix **M** to a permissible probabilistic interpretation vector. The components of this valuation vector are the generalized truth values or probabilities of propositions s in $\mathbf{S}$. These components are the marginal (or absolute) probability distributions $p(s_i=1)$ for $i = 1,...,n$, because the marginal probability distribution of any component of a n-dimensional random variable is the sum of joint probabilities over the remaining components. For any m ($1 \le m \le n-1$), we denote by $\mathbf{S}_m$ a m-dimensional random variable whose components are chosen from $\mathbf{S}$ and denote by $\mathbf{S}_{n-m}$ the complementary (n-m)-dimensional random variable with respect to $\mathbf{S}$. Let $\mathbf{v}$ denote an arbitrary n-dimensional binary vector that $\mathbf{S}$ may take as value. Let $\mathbf{u}$ denote an arbitrary m-dimensional binary vector and $\mathbf{w}$ denote an arbitrary (n-m)-dimensional binary vector that $\mathbf{S}_m$ and $\mathbf{S}_{n-m}$ may take as values respectively. The marginal probability distribution

$$p(\mathbf{u}) = \Sigma_\mathbf{w} p(\mathbf{u},\mathbf{w})$$

can be computed easily according to the binary semantic network. Similarly, the conditional probability distribution

$$p(\mathbf{u}|\mathbf{w}) = p(\mathbf{v})/p(\mathbf{w}),$$

where $p(\mathbf{w})$ has to be positive, can also be computed easily. Thus, we may compute joint generalized truth value of any subset $\mathbf{S}_m$ of $\mathbf{S}$ and the conditional probability of $\mathbf{S}_m$ given the complement $\mathbf{S}_{n-m}$ from the joint probabilites of $\mathbf{S}$. This is an extension of [12] which deals with individual propositions. Moreover, we can derive the Bayes formulas easily for $\mathbf{S}_m$ and $\mathbf{S}_{n-m}$ as

$$p(\mathbf{u}) = \Sigma_\mathbf{w} p(\mathbf{u}|\mathbf{w}).p(\mathbf{w}), \quad p(\mathbf{w}|\mathbf{u}) = p(\mathbf{w}).p(\mathbf{u}|\mathbf{w})/p(\mathbf{u}).$$

We may also compute joint probabilities (or permissible probabilistic interpretation vector) from marginal and conditional probabilities, provided that they are known. Here, we have a slight variation of Nilsson's probabilistic inference scheme which is described as follows. We are given a set $\mathbf{S}$ of propositions with known joint probabilities from which all marginal and conditional probabilities of $\mathbf{S}$ may be computed. For a new proposition s, we like to know its marginal probability in terms of the joint probabilities of the set $\mathbf{S}'$, the union of $\mathbf{S}$ and $\{s\}$. Construct a binary semantic tree for $\mathbf{S}'$ by appending the tree for $\mathbf{S}$. We simply assign permissible conditional probabilities of s, given those of $\mathbf{S}$, to the appended binary semantic tree to obtain the joint probabilities of $\mathbf{S}'$. The marginal probability of s can be readily computed.

4. PROBABILISTIC LOGIC AS CONSISTENT LABELING

The labeling problem is to find a consistent labeling of all objects, given a set of objects $\{a_1,...,a_n\}$, a set of labels (meanings) $\{\lambda_1,...,\lambda_m\}$, a set of relations among objects, and a set of constraints. In the case of probabilistic logic, we have a set S of logical propositions which are to be labeled by only two labels $\{0,1\}$. Relations among propositions are whether they are involve in a deductive database or in inference rules. Constraints are the logical dependencies among them. Here, we are having the same problem as Bayesian networks of logical dependencies.

First of all, we extend the probabilistic logic to a probabilistic multi-valued logic. There is a set of logical truth values $\{\lambda_1,...,\lambda_m\}$, instead of $\{0,1\}$, that the set S of propositions may take. Now, we formulate probabilistic multi-valued logic in the framework of probabilistic consistent labeling. For each proposition s, the weight assigned to a label λ of s is the probabilty that λ is the correct label of s. For s_i, we have

$$0 \le p_i(\lambda_k) \le 1, \quad \Sigma_{k=1}^m p_i(\lambda_k) = 1.$$

The entropy of s_i, under a given probabilistic consistent labeling, is given by

$$H_i = -\Sigma_{k=1}^m p_i(\lambda_k) \log p_i(\lambda_k).$$

We are able to extend some of the entropy arguments in [12] to the current situation. We may also derive a probability modification algorithm to decrease the entropies of propositions in order to increase the certainties of the correct labeling of propositions in S.

The relaxation scheme is to start with an initial assignment of probabilities $\{p_i^{(0)}\}$ to the set S of propositions with respect to the label set; and to define a relaxation operator R that changes the k-th probabilities $\{p_i^{(k)}|i=1,...,n\}$ to (k+1)-th probabilities $\{p_i^{(k+1)}|i=1,...,n\}$ so that the limit of $\{p_i^{(k)}\}$ as k approaches to infinity is an unambiguous labeling under given compatibility constraints. Experiments have shown that after a reasonable steps definite results are obtained. This relaxation scheme is computationally intensive for logical propositions and is similar to the paper [15] of J. Pearl. Currently, we are working on implementing this relaxation scheme on a neural network processor [3]. Some of the computational difficulties will be eliminated by this distributed processor.

In [16], update equations are given by the following:

$$p_i^{(k+1)}(\lambda) = p_i^{(k)}(\lambda) + q_i^{(k)}(\lambda),$$

$$q_i^{(k)}(\lambda) = \Sigma_j \, d_{ij} \, \Sigma_{\lambda'} r_{ij}(\lambda,\lambda') p_j^{(k)}(\lambda'),$$

where j-indices are indices of source nodes leading to the node at the i-th index, d_{ij}'s are certain weighting factors, r_{ij}'s indicate compatibility measure of assignment of λ to the i-th node, given λ' to the j-th node. In our relaxation scheme, the Hepp learning mechanism is assumed on the links so that their weights w_{ij} may be modified in the process by factors $\Delta w_{ij}^{(k)}$. Our update equations are

$$p_i^{(k+1)}(\lambda) = \min[1, p_i^{(k)}(\lambda) + \max(0, q_i^{(k)}(\lambda))],$$

$$q_i^{(k)}(\lambda) = \Sigma_{\lambda',j}(w_{ij}(\lambda,\lambda') + \Delta w_{ij}(\lambda,\lambda')) p_j^{(k)}(\lambda'),$$

$$\Delta w_{ij}^{(k+1)}(\lambda,\lambda') = a_{ij} \Delta w_{ij}^{(k)}(\lambda,\lambda') + b_{ij} p_i^{(k+1)}(\lambda) p_j^{(k)}(\lambda').$$

The detail of this study will appear in [3].

REFERENCES

[1] Chen, S., Evidential logic and Dempster-Shafer theory, Proc. ACM SIGART International Symposium of Methodologies for Intelligent Systems, Knoxville, Tenn., Oct. 22-24, 1986, 201-206.
[2] Chen, S., Some extensions of probabilistic logic, Proc. AAAI Workshop on Uncertainty in Artificial Intelligence, Philadelphia, Penn., August 8-10, 1986, 43-48.
[3] Chen, S. and Cruz-Young, C. A., Evidential reasoning on parallel associative networks, in preparation.
[4] Cruz, C. A. and Myers, H. J., Associative Networks, IBM Palo Alto Scientific Center Report ZZ20-6459, October, 1982.
[5] Cruz, C. A. and Myers, H. J., Associative Networks II, IBM Palo Alto Scientific Center Report G320-3446, 1983.
[6] Dempster, A. P., A generalization of Bayesian inference, Journal of the Royal Statistical Society, Series B, 30 (1968), 205-247.
[7] Gordon, J. and Shortliffe, E. H., A method for managing evidential reasoning in a hierarchical hypothesis space, Artificial Intelligence, 26 (1985), 323-357.

[8] Hummel, R. A. and Zucker, S. W., On the foundations of relaxation labeling processes, IEEE Trans. PAMI, 5 (1983), 267-287.

[9] Landy, M. S. and Hummel, R. A., A brief survey of knowledge aggregation methods, New York University, Courant Institute Technical Note 177, September 1985.

[10] Lowrance, J. D. and Garvey, T. D., Evidential reasoning: An implementation for multisensor integration, SRI AI Center Tech. Note 307, December 1983.

[11] Lukasiewicz, J., Logical foundations of probability theory, Jan Lukasiewicz Selected Works, ed. by L. Berkowski, North-Holland, 1970, 16-43.

[12] Nilsson, N. J., Probabilistic logic, Artificial Intelligence, 28 (1986), 71-87.

[13] Pearl, J., On evidential reasoning in a hierarchy of hypotheses, Artificial Intelligence, 28 (1986), 9-15.

[14] Pearl, J., Fusion, propagation, and structuring in Bayesian networks, UCLA Technical Notes, April 1985.

[15] Pearl, J., Distributed revision of belief commitment in multi-hypotheses interpretations, Proc. AAAI Workshop on Uncertainty in Artificial Intelligence, Philadelphia Penn, August 8-10, 1986, 201-210.

[16] Rosenfeld, A., Hummel, R. A. and Zucker, S. W., Scence labeling by relaxation operations, IEEE Trans. Systems, Man and Cybernetics, 6 (1976), 420-433.

[17] Shafer, G. A., Mathematical Theory of Evidence, Princeton University Press, 1979.

Belief as Summarization and Meta-Support

A. Julian Craddock & Roger A. Browse†

Department of Computing and Information Science
Department of Psychology
Queen's University at Kingston
Ontario, Canada
K7L 3N7

A model of knowledge representation is described in which propositional facts and the relationships among them can be supported by other facts. The set of knowledge which can be supported is called the set of cognitive units, each having associated descriptions of their explicit and implicit support structures, summarizing belief and reliability of belief. This summary is precise enough to be useful in a computational model while remaining descriptive of the underlying symbolic support structure. When a fact supports another supportive relationship between facts we call this *meta-support*. This facilitates reasoning about both the propositional knowledge, and the support structures underlying it.

1. Introduction

The research described in this chapter pursues the problem of developing representational and inference mechanisms which are capable of dealing with incomplete and inaccurate knowledge about facts, and which can also be used to reason about the support structures which relate facts. The direction taken is based on the assumption that methods which deal effectively with uncertain knowledge and with supportive relationships must play an integral role in both models of human reasoning and flexible computational reasoning systems.

Network models of knowledge representation and belief maintenance typically distinguish between *factual knowledge* and *relational knowledge*. The factual knowledge, encoded as network nodes, represents propositions such as IT IS COLD INSIDE. Such propositions are labelled with parameters indicating probability [8, 12], possibility [18], plausibility [9, 4] or logical truth. In the simplest case, the existence of the proposition indicates a binary truth value. The relational knowledge, encoded as network connections, depicts relations and support among propositions, so for example, the proposition IT IS WINTER might support the proposition IT IS COLD OUTSIDE. In the most straightforward case, these relations may depict the origins of inferences in a belief maintenance system [6].

Recently, Cohen [3] has formulated a model of belief which does not rely on labels assigned to factual knowledge, but rather centralizes reasons for believing or disbelieving propositions (called *endorsements*) in order to establish a more clear indication of the

---

†This work was supported in part by Natural Sciences and Engineering Research Council of Canada, Grant A2427.

status of the proposition. Our approach is similar, but we accomplish the representation of endorsements in a network of support. An individual node in the network is surrounded by a localized structure indicating endorsements for and against the proposition.

Within the network, nodes are assigned numeric labels which summarize their underlying support structure. Such numeric labels must be simple and precise enough to enable effective inferential reasoning, and yet remain descriptive of the local network of support. Most formal reasoning systems represent belief as a single value, whether binary or continuous-valued [3, 7, 18]. Craddock and Browse [5] suggest that the compression of a node's label into a single value, whether binary or continuous-valued, is justified in many cases, but there are many instances for which this simple summary is inadequate. Consider the proposition, RICK LIKES MATH. The extent of belief in this proposition may be high whether it is quite reliable (Rick has taken, and enjoyed a wide variety of math courses) or quite unreliable (Rick has only taken a single math course). As soon as we attempt to summarize the underlying support structure a single value becomes clearly inadequate. We have proposed instead that two values, belief and reliability of belief more precisely summarize the support structure.

We have incorporated a further extension by recognizing that the extent of support that one proposition offers another is itself subject to positive and negative endorsements, and should be permitted the same representational capabilities as the propositions themselves. For example, the proposition WINDOW IS OPEN may support the proposition IT IS COLD INSIDE, but the extent of this support is itself supported by the proposition IT IS WINTER. We propose that we must be able to reason about support for support (called *meta-support*), and that by doing so, there is a resultant increase in the expressive power of the network model of knowledge representation and belief.

The direction we have taken in developing representational and inference mechanisms to describe reasoning under conditions of uncertainty is based on the belief that methods which model the way people think under uncertainty may be used in the construction of flexible and more understandable computational reasoning systems. The model developed here involves collecting reasons for believing or disbelieving propositional knowledge [3] and relational knowledge, and then summarizing these reasons by a measure of belief and reliability of belief. The belief and reliability values can be used: (1) to determine how supportive a body of evidence for a particular hypothesis is and (2) to reason with evidential relationships such as conflicts among decisions [4].

2. The Network Model

We shall now illustrate how the languages of set theory, (eg. [13]) and graph theory, (eg. [2]), can be used to build a framework of precise definitions for a network model of knowledge representation. We shall demonstrate in the course of this section how the model is extended to represent meta-support and continuous belief summarization.

First, let a set of propositions $P = \{n_1 \ldots n_m, T\}$ represent the set of factual knowledge, such as RICK LIKES MATH, where T, represents the source of the factual knowledge. T denotes the factual knowledge which is implicit in the knowledge model. We can then define $A = P \times P$ as the set of all possible relationships among elements of P.

P and A provide a framework for modelling behavior of many existing knowledge representations. Facts and relationships encountered in structures such as influence networks [10], and inference networks [7] can be depicted. Within this framework the propositions may be labelled with numeric or non-numeric quantifiers and qualifiers.

Similarly, the relationships in A can also be labelled, providing a model of inference or belief maintenance. However, the labels themselves are not subject to inference. As a result we can only reason about the factual knowledge P and not about the relationships which combine it to form more complex knowledge representations. We now introduce an extension to this framework called *meta-support* which will provide us with this facility.

Meta-support allows the model to reason about relationships by relating elements in P to facts in A. As a result, the set of knowledge which can be related to the set of facts P must be extended as the set C - known, for lack of a better word, as the set of cognitive units. C includes not only all the elements in P but also all the elements in A. Thus, C can be defined formally as the union of the arcs A, and the propositions P, $(A \cup P)$. The set of relationships A can then be extended using C to include the relationships between arcs and facts, as the set of supports S. S is formally defined as the set of relationships between elements in P and elements in C by $S = P \times C$.

Any support relationship s_{ij} in S is represented by the pair (p_i, c_j), where p_i is a particular member of P, and c_j is a particular member of C. If a particular p_i is the source of the knowledge model, T, then we say that s_{Tj} is equivalent to c_j. In a like fashion s_{iT} is equivalent to T. We shall use this shorthand notation throughout the remainder of the paper. If c_j in the pair, $s_{ij} = (p_i, c_j)$ is a member of P, p_j, then p_i is said to support p_j. If, on the other hand, c_j is a member of A, (p_j, p_k), then p_i is said to *meta-support* the relationship c_j between two facts p_j and p_k. In the former case a fact is supported and in the latter a relationship is meta-supported. Only elements of A are subject to meta-support. The meta-supports, $\{(p_i, c_j) \mid c_j \in A\}$, are not subject to reasoning within the current model.

The meta-support and support relationships for a cognitive unit form the support structure of that unit. Any cognitive unit c_i with an underlying support structure can be labelled with a summarization of the structure called the *Rationale*. The Rationale labels a unit with two parameters, the *rationale belief* and the *rationale reliability*. The belief, $b \in [-1, 1]$, is a measure of the completeness and the strength of the supports for a cognitive unit. As b is a continuous value from -1 to 1 we may view cognitive units as statements in fuzzy logic [18] in which a belief of -1 indicates unbelievability and a belief of +1 indicates believability. The reliability, $r \in [0, 1]$, is the reliability of the evidence which was used to calculate the belief. A value of 0 represents complete unreliability and a value of 1 represents complete reliability.

The meta-supports and those cognitive units with no explicit support structure, and indeed any cognitive unit, are labelled with an Intuition. Labelling a structure with the Intuition provides an *Intuitive belief*, b', and an *Intuitive reliability*, r'. These structures appear much the same as those produced by the Rationale except that they are never computed, but remain available to take part in the computation of other beliefs. Intuitive values correspond to the usual direct assignment of belief and reliability to a cognitive unit from which other beliefs and reliabilities are to be determined. The application of the *Intuition* to T, is such that $I(T) = (1, 1)$. The external or *source knowledge* is thus assumed to be completely believable and this belief is completely reliable.

To illustrate the distinction between the belief and reliability of the Intuition and Rationale, consider the simple cognitive unit composed of the single proposition I LIKE MATH. This may have, for example $b_i = 0.4$ indicating moderately strong support for liking mathematics. On the other hand, the reliability, r_i, of this value might be high or low, depending on the person's exposure to mathematics. It is thus important to note that the measure of proposition's reliability is not closely related to its belief. A statement can be highly believable but still be very unreliable. In a similar fashion, a statement can be unbelievable but its incredibility may be very reliable [5] though there are cases in which these two summary aspects of support may be combined to provide a more concise belief estimate.

The supportive relationship between any two cognitive units is represented as a link and the strength of the relationship is specified by labelling the arc with the Intuition or Rationale. For example, in figure 1: I LIKE PSYCHOLOGY may support I LIKE COMPUTING. An Intuition may be assigned to the cognitive unit representing this relationship describing the strength of the support. However, the measure of this support may be contingent on the believability of the cognitive unit COMPUTATION MAY MODEL COGNITION. If COMPUTATION MAY MODEL COGNITION is unbelievable then the support relationship between I LIKE PSYCHOLOGY and I LIKE COMPUTING will be unsupported and will subsequently be labelled as unbelievable by the Rationale. In summary the model of knowledge representation described in this paper consists of a set of supportable knowledge, C, and a set of supports and meta-supports, S. We shall now go on to consider the mechanisms which permit the dynamic evaluations and maintenance of support based on the assigned values.

3. Computing Belief and Reliability values

While any cognitive unit, c_j, may simply be assigned values of belief and reliability of belief through the use of I_j, we wish to develop ways of computing the values of Rationale, R_j, for a cognitive unit c_j on the basis of the available supports. The strength of support between two cognitive units must be computed with consideration of the Rationale, R_i, of the supporting cognitive unit c_i, and the Rationale, R_k, of the supporting relationship, c_k. For example, given the support relation represented by the cognitive unit c_k in figure 2, the net endorsement of the cognitive unit c_j, I LIKE COMPUTER SCIENCE, must be dependent on the extent of our Rationale in the support, R_k, as well as in the Rationale of the supporting cognitive unit I LIKE WRITING.

We must first be able to calculate the strength of the support relationship, c_k, which is equal to R_k, or I_k if the rationale has not been defined. We can define the Rationale R_j of a cognitive unit, c_j, supported by c_i with the relationship c_k, as

$$R_j = (1, 1) \quad \text{if } c_j = T$$
$$R_j = Z(\{R_i, R_k \mid c_i \text{ supports } c_j \text{ with } c_k\})$$

If a person enjoys writing (see Figure 2), ie. $b_i = 0.8$, and they believe that enjoying writing is non-supportive of liking computing, ie. $b_j < 0$, then a net negative belief for the cognitive unit, I LIKE COMPUTER SCIENCE, results. If, on the other hand, they believe that enjoying writing is supportive of enjoying computer science, ie. $b_j > 0$, a net positive endorsement would result. The summarization function, Z, will therefore take a set of pairs of Rationales, (R_i, R_k), and compute a new Rationale. We shall now describe how Z can calculate the belief and reliability of the new Rationale.

Given a supported cognitive unit c_j we can define a measure of the relative reliability of each of its supports, c_i in $\{c_1 \ldots c_n\}$, as:

$$w_{r_i} = \frac{r_i}{r^*}$$

where r^* is the maximum reliability of all of its supports. We can also define a measure of the *relative belief of support*, $w_{b_{ij}}$, and *relative reliability of support*, $w_{r_{ij}}$, for each cognitive unit, s_{ij}, representing a supportive relationship between an element c_i and an

Belief as Summarization and Meta-Support 233

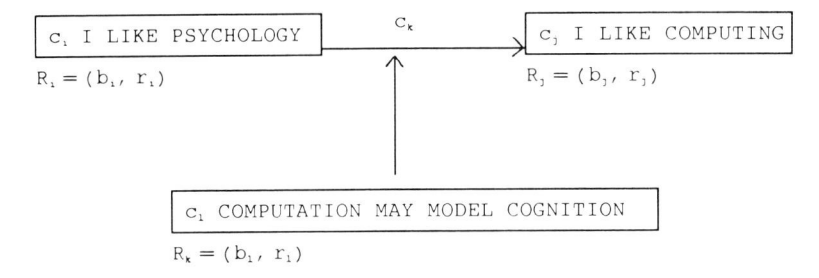

```
┌─────────────────────────┐        C_k         ┌─────────────────────────┐
│ c_i  I LIKE PSYCHOLOGY  │───────────────────▶│ c_j  I LIKE COMPUTING   │
└─────────────────────────┘          ▲         └─────────────────────────┘
 R_i = (b_i, r_i)                    │          R_j = (b_j, r_j)
                                     │
                    ┌────────────────┴──────────────────┐
                    │ c_l  COMPUTATION MAY MODEL COGNITION │
                    └───────────────────────────────────┘
                     R_k = (b_l, r_l)
```

Figure 1. : An example of an endorsement c_k which influences the strength of support, R_l, between two other nodes.

---

element c_j, where b_{ij} and r_{ij} represent the belief and reliability of the supportive relationship.

$$w_{r_{ij}} = \frac{r_{ij}}{r^*}$$

$$w_{b_{ij}} = \frac{b_{ij}}{\sum_i b_{ij}}$$

Thus b_j, the *Rationale belief* of c_j, then becomes a function of the beliefs of each support and their relative reliabilities, w_{r_i}, and the relative beliefs and reliabilities for the supportive relationships:

$$b_j = \sum_i w_{r_i} \, b_i \, w_{b_{ij}} \, w_{r_{ij}}$$

The Rationale belief is a weighted measure of the beliefs of its supports. As its supports, beliefs, and relative reliabilities increase the aggregate belief will also increase. The reliability of this new belief may then be calculated as a function of the *agreement* between the beliefs of the supporting items and the newly calculated belief, b_j. Thus, belief must be calculated before reliability. The individual's agreement values are once again weighted by the relative reliability of the source support. This effect may be modelled in formula such as:

$$r_j = 1 - [\sum_i |b_i - b_j| \, w_{r_i} \, w_{r_{ij}}]$$

to provide r_j, the *Rationale reliability* of c_j, a measure of agreement among supports.

```
┌─────────────────────┐                      ┌───────────────────────────┐
│ c_i  I LIKE WRITING │──R_k = (b_k, r_k)──▶│ c_j  I LIKE COMPUTER SCIENCE│
└─────────────────────┘                      └───────────────────────────┘
 R_i = (0.8, r_i)                             R_j = (b_j, r_j)
```

Figure 2. : An example of an endorsement which may have net positive or net negative support.

The formula for calculating belief and reliability provide a means of incorporating basic heuristics such as those described by Kahneman and Tversky [11] to evaluate supports and their underlying structure. The use of relative reliabilities and Rationales are a simple example of how we can allow a network model to utilize reasoning strategies which are satisfactory within constraints, but not necessarily optimal with respect to formal mathematical theory. Kahneman and Tversky [11] provide numerous examples in which subjects reach decisions which run counter to those reached by mathematical theories. It is important, therefore, that we be able to model not only the formal capabilities of mathematical reasoning but also the more human ones.

4. A Network of Cognitive Units

The model described so far is similar to many existing connectionist models, particularly the spreading activation models of Anderson [1], Rumelhart and McClelland [16], and McClelland and Rumelhart [14, 15]. The model which we have described can be used to represent the equivalent structures by restricting the set of cognitive units to those of solitary vertices and by labelling these units with the correct values. However, the model has several important differences which allow it to become a much more flexible form of knowledge representation.

- First, as discussed by Craddock & Browse [5] the uncertainty of a piece of information is represented numerically as the values of the Rationale, and non-numerically as the structure of supports.

- Second, once the supports have been collected, they are subject to reasoning and natural heuristics [4] to compute the belief and reliability values as depicted in section 3. In contrast most connectionist models ignore, or do not explicitly deal with the non-numeric representation of uncertainty, depending instead on numeric values which provide no evidence as to how they are calculated, what they represent, or how reliable they are [3]. Both non-numeric justifications and numeric summarizations are necessary to adequately describe knowledge.

- Third, is the ability to reason about the supportive relationships between facts, allows us to not only reason about an elements belief and reliability but also to reason about its underlying support structure. In this manner, we can represent such evidential relationships as disjunction, (that is, strong belief which may be propagated on the basis of only one of many supports [4]) without structures such as Rumelhart and Zipser's [17] "Inhibitory Clusters" which may incorrectly inhibit a nodes activation level instead of its support for another node.

- Finally, we can also represent *Contradictions* in supporting evidence. *Rationale contradictions* among endorsements are defined as follows: If c_i is compelling evidence against c_j but c_k is equally compelling evidence for c_j then the supports for c_j are inconsistent. In addition to a rationale contraction an *Intuition contradiction* can also be defined: If the intuitive belief, b'_i, of the Intuition is not equal to the rational belief, b_i, of the Rationale then the two beliefs are inconsistent. Intuitive contradictions are useful for recognizing changes in belief through a knowledge base when knowledge is added and removed and for controlling cycles which may force more global interpretations on input propositions. When cycles exist within a network $<C, S>$, belief and reliability values will only be calculated for nodes in a partial network $<C', S'>$, where $C' \subseteq C$, and $S' \subseteq S \cap (C \times C')$, where there exists a $c_i \in P - P'$ such that there is an elementary path from c_i to C' and $|I_i - R_i|$ is greater than some threshold T_i.

5. Conclusions

The model discussed in this paper describes the numeric parameters associated with a piece of knowledge, the cognitive unit, as the summarization of the explicit and implicit underlying support structures. Of major issue is the observation that a single numeric value is an inadequate representation of reasoning. Instead we propose that two values, belief and reliability, more adequately provide a summarization of, and a means of reasoning computationally with, the symbolic structures of support. In addition, the two numeric values can form both an *Intuition* and a *Rationale*. The Rationale provides a summary calculated form the explicit support structure while the Intuition is a summary of the implicit structure, that represented by the source T. The Rationale and the Intuition need not be identical for any cognitive unit and as a result can be used to diagnose evidential contradictions and to control the inference process.

Second, the model supports heuristics such as those proposed by Kahneman and Tversky [11]. The heuristics can be used not only to determine the relevance of information in an inference but also to summarize it in a manner supported by cognitive research.

Finally, a major issue is that both propositional and relational knowledge should be subject to inference. The inclusion of meta-support makes this possible. It is argued that meta-support both facilitates the control and representation of inference. Currently the model is restricted in two ways. First, the set of cognitive units is limited to propositions and arcs. Clearly C could be extended to include sub-graphs built form A and P, providing the model with the facility to reason with complex knowledge structures such as schema [15]. Second, only elements of C are subject to meta-support. The meta-supports themselves, $\{s_{ij} = (p_i, c_j) \mid c_j \in A\}$ are not. The effect of removing both these restrictions is currently being evaluated.

References

[1] Anderson, R, *The architecture of cognition.* Harvard University Press, 1982.
[2] Bondy, J. A., and Marty, *Graph Theory with Applications.* North-Holland Publishing Co., 1976.
[3] Cohen, R, "The use of heuristic knowledge in decision theory," Diss. Stanford University, 1983.
[4] Craddock, A. J., "Modelling uncertainty in a knowledge base," Computing and Information Sciences Technical Report, number 87-189, Queen's University at Kingston, 1987.
[5] Craddock, A. J., and Browse A. R, *Reasoning with uncertain knowledge.* Proceedings of the Workshop on Uncertainty and Probability in Artificial Intelligence. August 8-10, 1986. University of Pennsylvania: Philadelphia, Pennsylvania, 1986, pp.57-62.
[6] Doyle, J., "A model for deliberation, action and introspection." Diss. Massachusetts Institute of Technology, 1980.
[7] Duda, R., Hart, P., and Nilsson, N., *Subjective Bayesian Methods for Rule-based Inference Systems.* Proceedings 1976 National Computer Conference, AFIPS, 1976, pp.1075-1082.

[8] Edwards, W., "Conservatism in human information processing". *Judgment under uncertainty: Heuristics and Biases*, Cambridge University Press, 1982, pp.355-358.
[9] Fox, J., *Strong and weak methods: A logical view of uncertainty.* Proceedings of Uncertainty and Probability in Artificial Intelligence. UCLA: Los Angeles, California, 1985.
[10] Heckerman, D. E., and Horvitz, E. J., *The myth of modularity in Rule-based systems* Proceedings of the Workshop on Uncertainty and Probability in Artificial Intelligence. August 8-10, 1986. University of Pennsylvania: Philadelphia, Pennsylvania, 1986, pp. 115-121.
[11] Kahneman D., and Tversky A., *Judgment under uncertainty: Heuristics and Biases*. Cambridge University Press, 1982.
[12] Lee, W., *Decision theory and human behavior.* New York: Wiley, 1971.
[13] Matt, J. L., Kandel, A., and Baker, T. P., *Discrete Mathematics for Computer Scientists*. Reston Publishing Company, Inc., 1983.
[14] McClelland, J. L., and Rumelhart, D. E., "An interactive activation model of context effects in letter perception: Part 1. An account of basic findings," *Psychological Review*, 88 (1981) pp. 375-407.
[15] McClelland, J. L., and Rumelhart, D. E., *Parallel Distributed Processing: Psychological and Biological Models*. The MIT Press, 1986.
[16] Rumelhart, D. E., and McClelland, J. L., "An interactive activation model of context effects in letter perception: Part 2. The contextual enhancement effect and some tests and extensions of the model," *Psychological Review*, 89 (1982), pp. 60-94.
[17] Rumelhart, D. E. and Zipser D., "Feature Discovery by Competitive Learning," *Cognitive Science*, 9: 1985, pp. 75 - 112.
[18] Zadeh, L.A., "Commonsense knowledge representation based on Fuzzy Logic", *Computer*, Vol 16, 10 (1983), pp.61-66.

NON-MONOTONICITY IN PROBABILISTIC REASONING

Benjamin N. Grosof[*]

Computer Science Department, Stanford University
Stanford, California 94305-2140

We start by defining an approach to non-monotonic probabilistic reasoning in terms of non-monotonic categorical (true-false) reasoning. We identify a type of non-monotonic probabilistic reasoning, akin to default inheritance, that is commonly found in practice, especially in "evidential" and "Bayesian" reasoning. We formulate this in terms of the *Maximization of Conditional Independence (MCI)*, and identify a variety of applications for this sort of default. We propose a formalization using *Pointwise* Circumscription. We compare MCI to Maximum Entropy, another kind of non-monotonic principle, and conclude by raising a number of open questions.

1 Introduction

Probabilistic reasoning is often rather loosely referred to as being non-monotonic. But how can we make this notion of non-monotonicity precise? In particular, what sort of non-monotonicity characterizes probabilistic reasoning? We will be addressing both of these questions in this paper. Our approach is to use the same definition of non-monotonicity as for "categorical" reasoning, i.e. reasoning where each sentence may only take on a truth value of 0 or 1. This requires that we cast probabilistic reasoning in terms of categorical reasoning

2 Probabilistic Logic

A way to do so is provided by the approach of "Probabilistic Logic", as introduced in [17] and extended in [3].

Suppose we start with a (finite) set $\mathcal{A}$ of statements about the probabilities of some sentences S_i in a (categorical) logical language $\mathcal{L}_b$. The basic idea of Probabilistic Logic is to express the probabilistic statements $\mathcal{A}$ in a second logical language $\mathcal{L}_m$ which is classical and categorical, e.g. first-order. The formulas of $\mathcal{L}_b$ are *reified*: they become terms in $\mathcal{L}_m$. The connectives of $\mathcal{L}_b$ become functions in $\mathcal{L}_m$. The logical properties of $\mathcal{L}_b$ (e.g. its tautologies) are encoded as a set of axioms **LOG$_\mathbf{b}$** in $\mathcal{L}_m$. We can represent an assertion G in $\mathcal{L}_b$ by an axiom $P(G) = 1$ in $\mathcal{L}_m$ which says it holds with certainty.[1] For example we can write as an axiom in **LOG$_\mathbf{b}$**:

$$\forall XY. P((X \wedge (X \to Y)) \to Y)) = 1$$

There is a subtlety, however, that eases the job of writing **LOG$_\mathbf{b}$**. The only formulas of $\mathcal{L}_b$ that we need to describe in $\mathcal{L}_m$ are those formed (by application of logical connectives) from the members of the set $\mathcal{F}$ of interpretation classes of $\mathcal{S} = \{S_i\}$. Then we do not need to encode in **LOG$_\mathbf{b}$** all the tautologies of $\mathcal{L}_b$, only those of propositional logic involving propositions corresponding to the space $\mathcal{W} = 2^{\mathcal{F}}$. See [17] for details.

The definitional axioms of standard probability **AXPROB**, are also encoded in $\mathcal{L}_m$, e.g. [2] :

$$P(True) = 1$$

---

[*]This work was supported by the author's National Science Foundation Graduate Fellowship; by the author's Fannie and John Hertz Foundation Fellowship; and by the Defense Advanced Research Projects Agency, the Office of Naval Research, and Rockwell International under contracts N00039-83-C-0136, N00014-81-K-0004, and B6G3045.

$$\forall XY.\{P(\neg(X \wedge Y)) = 1\} \Rightarrow \{P(X \vee Y) = P(X) + P(Y)\}$$
$$\forall XY.\{P(Y) \neq 0\} \Rightarrow \{P(X|Y) = \{P(X \wedge Y)/P(Y)\}\}$$
$$\forall XY.\{P(X \equiv Y) = 1\} \Rightarrow \{P(X) = P(Y)\}$$

From these we can get the usual probabilistic identities, including Bayes' Theorem.

Thus by recourse to a meta-language, probabilistic knowledge and reasoning can be described in terms of categorical logic and reasoning.

We have assumed that $\mathcal{A}$ contains statements in which there is only one level of nesting of $\{$probability of $\ldots\}$ before reaching a proposition in a categorical language. However, one could apply our approach iteratively to express some sorts of "second-order" or "higher-order" probabilistic theories. Above, we assumed $\mathcal{L}_b$ was zero-th order in P. Then $\mathcal{L}_m$ was order 1 in $\overset{.}{P}$. However, more generally, we could let $\mathcal{L}_b$ be of order n in P, and then $\mathcal{L}_m$ would be of order $n+1$ in P.

In [3], we defined a family of probabilistic logics which in terms of the above are all order 1 in P. There and in [4], we discussed the relationship between Probabilistic Logic and "evidential" or "Bayesian" reasoning in AI. In particular we showed how to formulate in terms of Probabilistic Logic

- the PROSPECTOR system, which performs Bayesian updating of probabilities [2];
- the MYCIN system, which employs the avowedly "non-Bayesian" Certainty Factors formalism introduced in [22];
- and the also avowedly "non-Bayesian" Dempster-Shafer Belief Functions formalism [20].

We showed in [4] that the assumptions underlying the combination rules in Certainty Factors and Dempster-Shafer bear a strong relationship to the assumptions of conditional independence underlying the odds-likelihood Bayesian updating method employed in PROSPECTOR. In this paper, we extend our previous work on formulating "Bayesian" and "evidential" reasoning via Probabilistic Logic, in the direction of making more rigorous the formulation of Bayesian updating as *inference* in a logical *theory*.

3 Non-Monotonic Probabilistic Theories

Let $\mathbf{Th}(\mathcal{Q})$ denote the closure of $\mathcal{Q}$ under logical implication in $\mathcal{L}_m$. Furthermore, let

$$\mathbf{Th^a}(\mathcal{A}) \overset{\triangle}{=} \mathbf{Th}(\mathcal{A} \cup \mathbf{LOG_b} \cup \mathbf{AXPROB})$$

Then $\mathbf{Th^a}(\mathcal{A})$ is what [17,3] call "the" *probabilistic theory* which is *probabilistically entailed* by $\mathcal{A}$. There $\mathcal{L}_m$ was implicitly first-order logic.

We say $\mathcal{A}$ is of *Type-1-ci* form (terminology of [3]) iff it consists of axioms of the form $P(S_{i1}|S_{i2}) \geq q_i$, where q_i is a number in the real unit interval $[0,1]$. (Note that $P(X|Y) \leq r$ can be re-written equivalently as $P(\neg X|Y) \geq (1-r)$.) In such a case, $\mathbf{Th^a}(\mathcal{A})$ is equivalent to a *lower probability distribution* $\mathbf{P}^-(\mathcal{W}|\mathcal{W})$ giving lower (and upper) bounds on all the conditional probabilities defined on $\mathcal{W}$.

Definition 3.1: A set operator $\mathbf{T}$ is *monotonic* iff

$$\forall \mathbf{B}_1 \mathbf{B}_2.\{\mathbf{B}_1 \subseteq \mathbf{B}_2\} \Longrightarrow \{\mathbf{T}(\mathbf{B}_1) \subseteq \mathbf{T}(\mathbf{B}_2)\}$$

Definition 3.2: A set operator $\mathbf{T}$ is *non-monotonic* iff it is not monotonic, i.e. iff

$$\exists \mathbf{B}_1 \mathbf{B}_2.\{\mathbf{B}_1 \subseteq \mathbf{B}_2\} \wedge \{\mathbf{T}(\mathbf{B}_1) \not\subseteq \mathbf{T}(\mathbf{B}_2)\}$$

Probabilistic Logic allows us to consider $\mathcal{A}$ to be a set of statements in $\mathcal{L}_m$. Suppose we have some rule for generating the set of conclusions (in $\mathcal{L}_m$) that we draw from $\mathcal{A}$. We can then ask whether the set of conclusions grows monotonically as we add to $\mathcal{A}$. We call this conclusion-drawing set operation *theory-closure*. $\mathbf{Th^a}$ above is an example of a theory-closure operator. *Logical (non-)monotonicity* is (non-)monotonicity of theory-closure. If $\mathbf{T}$ is (non-)monotonic, we say that $\mathbf{T(B)}$ is a (non-)monotonic theory.

Definition 3.3: A sentence C in a non-monotonic theory $\mathbf{T(B_1)}$ is *defeasible* iff

$$\exists \mathbf{B_2}.\{\mathbf{B_1} \subset \mathbf{B_2}\} \wedge \{C \notin \mathbf{T(B_2)}\}$$

We also call a defeasible conclusion a *non-monotonic conclusion*. A monotonic conclusion is one which is not defeasible. Thus we can partition any theory $\mathbf{T(B)}$ into a monotonic part and a non-monotonic part. We will say that *reasoning* (inference) is monotonic or non-monotonic according to whether the conclusions drawn are monotonic or non-monotonic. We write $\models_\mathbf{T}$ for entailment of a monotonic conclusion, and $\approx_\mathbf{T}$ for entailment of a non-monotonic conlusion.

Definition 3.4: An *update* $\mathbf{\Delta}$ to $\mathbf{T(B)}$ is *non-monotonic* iff $\mathbf{T(B)} \not\subseteq \mathbf{T(B \cup \Delta)}$.

Note that when $\mathbf{T}(\mathcal{A})$ is of Type-1-ci form, logical monotonicity corresponds to the functional monotonicity of the equivalent $\mathbf{P}^-(\mathcal{W}|\mathcal{W})$. In other words, if when we add new probabilistic statments to $\mathcal{A}$, the lower bound of every probability does not decrease, then the update is monotonic. If this condition is violated, then the update is non-monotonic.

Probabilistic Logic as defined in [17,3] draws its notions of logical implication and entailment from classical categorical logic, in fact implicitly from first-order logic. It is thus monotonic, since first-order logic is.

However, just as classical logic can be extended to perform non-monotonic reasoning, so can Probabilistic Logic. Thus we can represent non-monotonic probabilistic reasoning via non-monotonic categorical reasoning in $\mathcal{L}_m$, i.e. via non-monotonic reasoning in Probabilistic Logic. To do so will require us to adopt theory-closure operators different from $\mathbf{Th^a}$, since $\mathbf{Th^a}$ is monotonic. However, we might want to include $\mathbf{Th^a}$ in the monotonic part of whatever non-monotonic $\mathcal{T}$ we employ. Later when we define a circumscriptive approach to one kind of non-monotonic probabilistic reasoning, we will do just that. We will call the monotonic sentences (e.g. $\mathbf{Th^a}(\mathcal{A})$) *hard* information (beliefs). Relatively speaking, the non-monotonic conclusions are *soft*, i.e. tentative. Hard beliefs are not retractible, while soft beliefs are. We might regard hard versus soft in terms of confidence; hard beliefs being ones about which we are absolutely confident.

Non-monotonic probabilistic reasoning requires us to employ principles for drawing conclusions which properly extend (i.e. go beyond) the axioms of classical probability. Thus each of the types of non-monotonic probabilistic reasoning discussed below takes the axioms of a classical probability as a constraining point of departure rather than as an equivalent model.

3.1 A Monotonic Example

As an example of monotonic probabilistic reasoning using $\mathbf{Th^a}$ as our theory-closure operator, consider the case of a rather rowdy fellow named Igor. Let *Fights* denote the proposition that Igor gets in a bar fight; let *Drunk* denote the proposition that Igor has more than three drinks. Suppose to begin with we are given (i.e. $\mathcal{A}_1$ consists of):

$$P(Fights|Drunk) = .6$$
$$P(Drunk) = .3$$

Then we can infer

$$\mathcal{A}_1 \models_{\mathbf{Th^a}} \{P(Fights) \geq .18\} \tag{1}$$

If we next learn (i.e. add to $\mathcal{A}_1$ to get $\mathcal{A}_2$)

$$P(Fights|\neg Drunk) = .2$$

then we can infer

$$\mathcal{A}_2 \models_{\mathbf{Th^a}} \{P(Fights) = .32\} \quad (2)$$

which is consistent with, but stronger than, (1). The conclusions (1) and (2) are forced or determined by the given information in a strong sense which depends only on the standard axioms and definitions of classical probability.

3.2 A Non-Monotonic Example

Next we investigate an example of what appears to be one important type of non-monotonic probabilistic reasoning. Consider the case of 1985 model-year cars made by Neptune Corporation. Let L denote the proposition that a car is so severely defective that it mechanically breaks down in its first 1000 miles. Let N denote the proposition that a car's maker is Neptune. To begin with we are given (i.e. $\mathcal{A}_1$ consists of)

$$P(L|N) = .1$$

(No wonder you have never heard of Neptune Corporation before.) Suppose we are now asked what is $P(L|(N \wedge T))$, where T means the car is a Triton model. $\mathbf{Th^a}(\mathcal{A}_1)$ tells us nothing about the value of $P(L|(N \wedge T))$: it could consistently be anything between 0 and 1.

However, a commonly-found pattern of probabilistic reasoning is to presume in this circumstance that

$$P(L|(N \wedge T)) = P(L|N)$$

A variety of rationales might be offered. One is that as long as we have no information to the contrary, the best estimate of the proportion of lemons in the class of Neptune Tritons is to use the information we are given about the proportion of lemons in the overall class of Neptunes. Another rationale is that since we have no evidence that the property of being a Triton model is indeed relevant to whether Neptunes are lemons, we will presume it is irrelevant.

In effect,

$$P(L|(N \wedge T)) = .1$$

is adopted as a *default*. We are using a non-monotonic theory-closure operator $\mathcal{T}$ to generate a non-monotonic conclusion:

$$\mathcal{A}_1 \mathrel{|\!\approx}_{\mathcal{T}} \{P(L|(N \wedge T)) = .1\} \quad (3)$$

Suppose next we learn (i.e. add to $\mathcal{A}_1$ to form $\mathcal{A}_2$)

$$P(L|(N \wedge T)) = .05 \quad (4)$$

i.e. we get definitive, hard information about the value of $P(L|(N \wedge T))$. (4) contradicts and overrides our previous non-monotonic conclusion (3): it is a non-monotonic update. If next we are asked what is $P(L|(N \wedge T \wedge W))$, where W means that the car is a station-wagon, our circumstance is similar to that above. Again, $\mathbf{Th^a}$ tells us nothing: only that $P(L|(N \wedge T \wedge W))$ may consistently take on any value between 0 and 1. Later, as we did in (4), we may get specific, hard information. In the meanwhile, we might apply the same sort of non-monotonic reasoning as we performed before to get (3). This time there is an added complexity, though. We have two different pieces of hard information bearing on the probability of L: both are conditioned on classes which are more general than $(N \wedge T \wedge W)$. Often a refinement to the above rationales is invoked: in cases of such competition, we choose to adopt the "most specific" information, i.e. the one which is conditional on the most specific class. So in the choice between

$$P(H|(N \wedge T \wedge W)) = P(H|N); \text{ and} \quad (5)$$
$$P(H|(N \wedge T \wedge W)) = P(H|(N \wedge T)) \quad (6)$$

we favor the latter. Thus we infer

$$\mathcal{A}_2 \approx_\mathcal{T} \{P(L|(N \wedge T \wedge W)) = .05\} \tag{7}$$

Similarly, if we are asked about the probability of L for progressively more specific classes (e.g. by adding blue, air-conditioned, etc. as further conditions), we might employ the same pattern of non-monotonic reasoning to conclude from $\mathcal{A}_2$ that:

$$P(L|(N \wedge T \wedge W \wedge Blue)) = .05,$$
$$P(L|(N \wedge T \wedge W \wedge Blue \wedge AirCond)) = .05, \ldots$$

4 Default Inheritance of Probabilities

Our non-monotonic example above illustrates what appears to be one commonly-found type of non-monotonic probabilistic reasoning. Now we will formulate the example more abstractly. Define

$$H \triangleq L$$
$$C_1 \triangleq N$$
$$C_2 \triangleq (N \wedge T)$$
$$S \triangleq (N \wedge T \wedge W)$$
$$q_1 \triangleq .1$$
$$q_2 \triangleq .05$$

$\mathcal{A}_2$ consisted exactly of:

$$P(H|C_1) = q_1$$
$$P(H|C_2) = q_2$$

while $\mathbf{LOG_b}$ contained:

$$P(C_2 \to C_1) = 1$$
$$P(S \to C_1) = 1$$
$$P(S \to C_2) = 1$$

In our example, we *inherited* a defeasible (default) value for the probability of H for the conditioning class S from the most specific conditioning class C_i for which we had a hard value for the probability of H.

> **The "Default Inheritance" Principle:** Let $P(H|S)$ denote the probability of some hypothesis H of interest, given the situation S at hand. Suppose our hard information $\mathcal{A}$ consists only of values for the probability of H, conditional on various propositions C_i which form a chain. Then in order to conclude a defeasible value for $P(H|S)$, we look for the most specific C_j such that $S \to C_j$, and make $P(H|S)$ equal to $P(H|C_j)$.

The structure of this sort of non-monotonic reasoning is analogous to that of default inheritance in categorical reasoning, e.g. in the classic example of whether birds and ostriches fly. In default inheritance, a particular class S inherits an attribute A from the most specific class C_j of a chain of S's super-classes $\{C_i\}$ for which information about A is available. In the categorical case of default inheritance, the attribute is inherited with certainty, e.g. *Flies* or else $\neg Flies$. We can represent this as inheriting either $P(A) = 0$ or else $P(A) = 1$[3]. The "default inheritance" type of non-monotonic reasoning with probabilities corresponds to inheriting the probability $P(A)$ of the attribute, which is not always 0 or 1. Thus it can be formalized as a generalization of the usual default inheritance. Alternatively, we can think of it as inheriting with certainty an attribute which is a probability, e.g. $P(H)$ above.

5 Specificity-Prioritized Maximization of Conditional Independence

We can formulate our non-monotonic example in terms of (non-monotonically inferred) conditional independence statements. Let $CIG(\{x,y\},z)^4$ mean that the propositions x and y are conditionally independent given the proposition z, i.e. that:

$$P((x \wedge y)|z) = P(x|z)P(y|z)$$

which is equivalent (when $P(y|z) \neq 0$) to:

$$P(x|(y \wedge z)) = P(x|z)$$

; and (when $P(x|z) \neq 0$) to:

$$P(y|(x \wedge z)) = P(y|z)$$

Since $P((S \to C_i)) = 1$ for $i = 1, 2$:

$$P(S \equiv (S \wedge C_i)) = 1$$

Thus (5) is equivalent to:

$$P(H|(S \wedge C_1)) = P(H|C_1); \text{i.e.,} \quad CIG(\{H,S\}, C_1).$$

Similarly, (6) is equivalent to:

$$P(H|(S \wedge C_2)) = P(H|C_2); \text{i.e.,} \quad CIG(\{H,S\}, C_2)$$

Note that after (4), because $P(H|C_2)$ differs from $P(H|C_1)$, $CIG(\{H,S\}, C_2)$ and $CIG(\{H,S\}, C_1)$ cannot hold simultaneously. In effect, we have a competition and conflict between the two. According to the "default inheritance" principle, we try to non-monotonically conclude at least one of the two, and $CIG(\{H,S\}, C_2)$ takes precedence when (as after (4), though not before (4)) there is conflict. Thus we can formulate the precedence of more specific information as a *priority* among default conditional independence statements.

We *propose* formulating the "default inheritance" principle as the *Specificity-Prioritized Maximization of Conditional Independence (SPMCI)*. That is, given some hard probabilistic axioms, we non-monotonically conclude conditional independence statements corresponding to inheritance chains. (If such conditional independence statements are inconsistent with the given hard axioms, then as usual with defaults we block them as conclusions.) In case of the sort of conflict above, we apply precedence based on specificity in the above sense.

An important (and open) question is which conditional independence statements to maximize. We may only want to apply the "default inheritance" principle to some hypotheses H^k and some chains C_i^l and situations S^m. If we are only interested in inheriting a default value the way we did above for the probability of a particular H conditional on a particular S, then it appears we need consider only CIG tuples $\langle \{u,v\}, w \rangle$ such that H or $\neg H$ is in $\{u,v\}$ and $P(S \to w) = 1$.

6 Non-Monotonicity in "Evidential" Reasoning

An important type of probabilistic reasoning in AI has been what we will call "evidential" reasoning, in which we are given hard information about $P(H|E_i)$ for each of several E_i's. Importantly, no E_i subsumes any other, though they may (and usually do) overlap. They do not form a chain. By making the assumptions of conditional independence of the E_i's given both H and given $\neg H$, one can then infer a value for

$$P(H|(E_1 \wedge \ldots \wedge E_n))$$

(E.g., see PROSPECTOR [2], as well as MYCIN and Dempster-Shafer [4].)

6.1 "Default Inheritance"

Typically, this value for $P(H|(E_1 \wedge \ldots \wedge E_n))$ is in effect combined (rather implicitly) with the "default inheritance" principle to yield non-monotonically a value for $P(H|S)$, when (S is the situation at hand and) we believe with certainty that:

$$S \rightarrow (E_1 \wedge \ldots \wedge E_n)$$

and when S implies no other E_j's for which $P(H|E_j)$ is available. This step corresponds to an application of SPMCI; more specific conjunctions of the E_i's take precedence.

6.2 "Soft-Coding" Assumptions

A problem with "evidential" reasoning schemes is that the conditional independence assumptions of the E_i's given H and given $\neg H$ are often too strong: there are so many such assumptions that they are inconsistent either with each other, or with given (hard) information about the probability of H given conjunctions of various E_i's. We observe that MCI can be used to make such assumptions by default. Past approaches have been to "hard-code" or "build" such assumptions into the probabilistic inference machinery in a way which is monotonic and thus frequently inconsistent. "Soft-coding" via defeasibility retains the advantages (conceptual simplicity, representational parsimony, and computational ease) afforded by making the assumptions, to the greatest extent possible without sacrificing consistency and expressiveness. We can regard this as maximizing, rather than inflexibly assuming, a sort of "modularity" or "locality".

Another issue in evidential reasoning is that often $P(E_i|S)$ is uncertain rather than certain. In such cases, commonly (e.g. in PROSPECTOR [8]) the assumption is made that for each of several EJ_k representing most specific conjunctive formulae in the E_i's and their negations:

$$P(H|(EJ_k \wedge S)) = P(H|EJ_k)$$

i.e. that:

$$CIG(\{H, S\}, EJ_k)$$

Of course this assumption may be inconsistent with other hard information. In particular, the presumption that it is consistent in practice seems to have been made by implicitly limiting what sorts of probabilistic information will be present, i.e. can be expressed, in the AI system making this assumption (e.g. in the PROSPECTOR project [9]). If we "soft-code" this assumption as a "default inheritance" step, then we can avoid the choice between expressive limitation and inconsistency.

7 Graphoids, Influence Diagrams, and Irrelevance

Recently both the AI and the Decision Analysis research communities have developed interest in the idea of reasoning about the structure of (conditional) dependencies and independencies among a complexly-related collection of probabilistic events, in a fashion abstracted from the details of the particular underlying probabilistic values It appears that especially for humans it is a natural and helpful way to factor probabilistic reasoning. This makes it important for explanation, justification, and validation of probabilistic reasoning, and suggests that there may be computational advantages as well.

One direction of this research is represented by *influence diagrams* [7]. Influence diagrams implicitly specify conditional independencies by omission of "links" representing conditional probability statements (constraints). This suggests the use of a *non-monotonic specification convention* for influence diagrams: a sort of "closed dependency" assumption analogous to the "closed world assumption" familiar in categorical reasoning.

A related direction of research is the alternative formulation of conditional independence provided by the abstraction of Graphoids [18][5]. A Graphoid is the theory of a trinary relation, $I(x, z, y)$, which we can take to denote $CIG(\{x,y\},z)$, but with the additional generality that x, y, and z denote (non-intersecting) *sets* of propositions. Informally,

$$I(\{a_1,\ldots,a_l\},\{c_1,\ldots,c_n\},\{b_1,\ldots,b_m\})$$

denotes

$$\bigwedge_{i_1,\ldots,i_l,j_1,\ldots,j_m,k_1,\ldots,k_n} I(\{\bigwedge_{q=1}^{l}\sigma_{i_q}a_q\},\{\bigwedge_{s=1}^{n}\sigma_{k_s}c_s\},\{\bigwedge_{r=1}^{l}\sigma_{j_r}b_r\})$$

(where the σ's are sign variables). That is, Graphoids can be expressed in terms of conditional independence statements.

As with influence diagrams, we can imagine employing non-monotonic reasoning about Graphoids, e.g. as a specification convention. MCI in terms of Graphoids is the maximization of the I relation. Thus given partial constraints on the relation I, we might non-monotonically conclude additional positive literals in I.

Another way to think about conditional (in)dependence is in terms of *(ir)relevance*. $CIG(\{x,y\},z)$ means that given z, learning y is irrelevant to our estimate of the probability of x; and vice versa, that given z, learning x is irrelevant to our estimate of the probability of y. MCI then corresponds to the non-monotonic *maximization of irrelevance*. This has a flavor of maximizing simplicity in the sense of Occam's Razor. The more that we can decide is irrelevant to some problem-solving task, the easier that task becomes; thus maximization of irrelevance holds out the ultimate promise of substantial computational advantages if that maximization itself is not too complex.

8 A Circumscriptive Formalization of (SP)MCI

We can try to formalize MCI in a variety of formalisms for non-monotonic categorical reasoning, e.g. Circumscription [14,15], Default Logic [19], or Non-Monotonic Modal Logic (a.k.a. Autoepistemic Logic) [16]. However, we also want to express the precedence of more specific information in the sense discussed earlier. For this purpose, a recently-developed version of Circumscription, called Pointwise Circumscription [12], is most apt. In it, we can conveniently express priorities among the various defaults corresponding to particular conditional independence statements.

We lack space to go into the details here of circumscription and its pointwise version. The following treatment is necessarily rather schematic.

Circumscription accomplishes non-monotonic reasoning from a base theory **B** by applying the (monotonic) theory-closure of classical *second*-order logic to **B** augmented by an additional second-order *circumscription axiom* which is formed from **B** according to a *circumscription policy* specifying the non-monotonic behavior. The circumscription axiom expresses the minimality of a predicate.

$$\mathbf{T}^{\mathbf{circ}}_{\mathbf{policy}}(\mathbf{B}) \triangleq \mathbf{Th_2}(\mathbf{B} \cup Circ(\mathbf{B};\mathbf{policy}))$$

We now sketch a *proposed* method to construct an appropriate **B** and **policy** to accomplish (SP)MCI. We are currently investigating [5] a number of unresolved outstanding technical issues involved in proving that the following indeed accomplishes its intended effect.

Let $\mathcal{B}_0$ (e.g. $\{\mathcal{A} \cup \mathbf{LOG_b} \cup \mathbf{AXPROB}\}$) be our "base" theory consisting of given, monotonic (hard), probabilistic axioms (both certain and uncertain), e.g. $P(C_2 \to C_1) = 1$; $P(H|C_1) = .15$; etc.. $\mathcal{B}_0$ is in a first-order logical language $\mathcal{L}_m$. For simplicity, let us assume here that P is the only function symbol, and CIG is the only predicate symbol, of $\mathcal{L}_m$ that appear in $\mathcal{B}_0$

We introduce an abnormality predicate AB characterized by the following axiom which we add to $\mathcal{B}_0$ to form $\mathcal{B}$. (By employing a slight variant of circumscription, which we dub "hyperscription", in which predicates are maximized rather than minimized, we can actually avoid the need to introduce an AB and the following axiom. We just maximize CIG directly. However the following formulation will be easier for most readers to follow.)

$$\neg AB(\{x,y\},z) \Rightarrow CIG(\{x,y\},z)$$

We then express MCI via a pointwise circumscription axiom (following the notation of [12]):

$$C_{AB}(B; AB/V_{AB}, P/V_P, CIG/V_{CIG})$$

This says that (the extension of) the predicate AB is minimized in the theory B, with the predicates AB and CIG and the function P being variable respectively when (the newly-introduced predicates) V_{AB}, V_{CIG}, and V_P hold. Intuitively, constraints on the variability of the predicates and functions represent constraints on the minimization. V_{CIG} and V_P we make be always true, so that there are no constraints on the minimization from those "directions".[6]

Two interesting sorts of questions about MCI are: which tuples $\langle\{x,y\},z\rangle$ to try to presume by default; and with what priorities. Pointwise circumscription gives us a way to specify these in some detail. We can express via V_{AB} both the delimitation of the scope of MCI, and the priorities among various conditional independence (CI) defaults.

$V_{AB}(\langle\{u,v\},w\rangle,\langle\{r,s\},t\rangle)$ means that when minimizing AB (i.e. maximizing CIG) at tuple $\langle\{u,v\},w\rangle$, the tuple $\langle\{r,s\},t\rangle$ is variable. To specify that we want MCI to apply to a particular tuple $\langle\{a,b\},c\rangle$, we include in B the axiom:

$$V_{AB}(\langle\{a,b\},c\rangle,\langle\{a,b\},c\rangle) \qquad (8)$$

If (8) is absent from $\mathbf{Th_2}(B)$, e.g. if its negation is present, then MCI will not apply to that tuple. To specify that the CI default on tuple $\langle\{a,b\},c\rangle$ has greater priority than the CI default on tuple $\langle\{d,e\},f\rangle$, we include in B the axiom:

$$V_{AB}(\langle\{a,b\},c\rangle,\langle\{d,e\},f\rangle)$$

Thus we can write a general *Specificity-Prioritization Axiom*:

$$\forall C_1, C_2.(P(C_2 \rightarrow C_1) = 1) \Rightarrow$$
$$(\forall x, y. V_{AB}(\langle\{x,y\},C_2\rangle,\langle\{x,y\},C_1\rangle))$$

We can imagine specifying other kinds of prioritizations among CI defaults as well. We may wish to infer some CI defaults before considering others. We can do so by making the former have higher priority, i.e. be relatively "harder" or more confident.

Thus in pointwise circumscription it appears we can[7] express Maximization of Conditional Independence with and without Specificity-Prioritization ((SP)MCI), restricted to arbitrary collections of tuples and with arbitrary additional priorities among the CI defaults.

(Note that above we are *not* circumscribing, i.e. minimizing truth values, in $\mathcal{L}_b$. That would be in the spirit of forcing selected probabilities to their lower bounds in $\mathbf{Th^a}(\mathcal{A})$.)

9 Maximum Entropy

So far we have discussed two major types of non-monotonic probabilistic reasoning: "default inheritance" (formulable as SPMCI) and default locality/irrelevance/$I_{Graphoid}$ (formulable as MCI). A third type of non-monotonic probabilistic reasoning is the use of the Maximum Entropy assumption, which has attracted considerable attention in the AI community (e.g. [10,8,1,17,3])

Maximum Entropy (ME) is a method of selecting a non-monotonic extension of given ("base") hard axioms B. The base axioms are treated as a set of constraints on the maximization of the entropy of the joint probability distribution $\mathbf{P}(\mathcal{F})$:

$$-\sum_{F_i \in \mathcal{F}} P(F_i) log(P(F_i))$$

ME always produces a unique, *complete* extension. By "complete", we mean that every $P(W_i|W_j)$ has a unique single real value in the ME extension: the lower conditional probability distribution on $\mathcal{W}$ is equal to the upper probability distribution.

Intuitively, ME tries to "flatten" the joint distribution $\mathbf{P}(\mathcal{F})$. In the extremal case, i.e. if the base theory is empty, then the result of ME is that each $P(F_i)$ is the same as every other. This is sometimes called the *uniform prior*, or *LaPlacian prior*, assumption.

ME often non-monotonically entails a large number of conditional independence statements. It has some elegant properties in this regard. A well-known result [11] is the Product Extension Theorem, which partially characterizes the sorts of conditional independence statements produced by ME, in terms of propositional subspaces.

A natural question is the relationship between ME and (SP)MCI.

Clearly they are not in general identical. Consider the case of an empty base theory. Here ME entails a uniform distribution, while (SP)MCI entails only conditional independence constraints which are satisfiable by non-uniform distributions. Also, in general (SP)MCI does not entail a unique, complete extension: e.g. it may result in bounds on, rather than point values for, some probabilities.

ME is a rather different flavor of non-monotonic principle than (SP)MCI. It is expressed in terms of numerical properties of probabilities rather than dependency properties. (Of course, there are important relationships between these two sorts of properties; and there exists a considerable body of work on high-level axiomatic characterizations of ME, e.g. [21].) One example of the difference in flavor is that ME often in effect gives "partial credit" for approximate conditional independence, whereas MCI is by definition "all or nothing".

An interesting open question we are investigating is how fully to characterize the sort of conditional independence statements produced by ME, including in relation to specificity-prioritization.

10 Discussion

Selective, prioritized MCI appears to represent several important kinds of non-monotonicity in probabilistic reasoning. SPMCI can express the commonly-found "default inheritance" principle. We can use MCI as a specification convention for Graphoids or influence diagrams. We can use MCI to maximize irrelevance in a particular sense. MCI also promises to provide a tool to specify the presumption of "locality" of updating in the sense of "evidential" reasoning. MCI overlaps substantially with Maximization of Entropy (ME). Compared to ME, it is a more precisely controllable assumption. It separates the assumption of maximizing conditional independence from the uniform prior assumption; ME conflates the two. SPMCI can yield a non-monotonic theory with bounds, not just point values, for probabilities. Moreover, we can specify in much greater detail the tuples to which to apply MCI and SP. Hopefully that this will carry over to more control and goal-directedness in computation as well. Current ME algorithms are global, numerical relaxation procedures which calculate the entire joint probability distribution. It is thus often impracticably costly to apply the ME assumption. An open challenge is to make any of these three types of non-monotonic probabilistic reasoning reasonably efficient. One important criterion we might want to impose is that the non-monotonic conclusions about CIG be *definite* in the sense of logic, i.e. that every non-monotonically entailed clause mentioning CIG be a positive unit clause.

As usual with non-monotonic reasoning, there are at least two sorts of intepretations or justifications for adopting a non-monotonic theory-closure principle. One is as a representational or specification convention. Another is as a conjectural decision rule. We have concentrated here rather more on the form than on the pragmatic substance of non-monotonicity in probabilistic reasoning. One interesting lead we are investigating is the basis in Bayesian statistical estimation and decision theory for what we have called the "default inheritance" principle.

11 Conclusion

Probabilistic Logic casts monotonic probabilistic reasoning in terms of monotonic categorical (i.e. true-false) reasoning with probabilistic statements. We extended this approach, and cast non-monotonic probabilistic reasoning in terms of non-monotonic categorical reasoning. We identified a type of non-monotonic probabilistic reasoning, akin to default inheritance in categorical reasoning, that is commonly found in practice, especially in "evidential" and "Bayesian" reasoning. We formulated this as a principle: *Specificity-Prioritized Maximization of Conditional Independence (SPMCI)*. We then identified another interesting type of non-monotonic probabilistic reasoning, akin to default irrelevancy, and showed that it can be formulated in similar terms: as Maximization of Conditional Independence (MCI). We suggested a formalization of (SP)MCI using *Pointwise* Circumscription, a recently developed variant of the circumscription formalism for non-monotonic (categorical) reasoning. We noted the Maximum Entropy assumption as a third type of non-monotonic probabilistic reasoning, and compared it to (SP)MCI.

A pay-off of our approach is that it makes it possible to apply to probabilistic and "evidential" reasoning the very substantial body of theoretical results and practical methods developed for non-monotonic (and monotonic) categorical reasoning. In particular:

- the semantics of agents' uncertain beliefs are clarified;
- reasoning procedures can be evaluated for soundness and completeness;
- existing methods for probabilistic and "evidential" reasoning can be generalized to incorporate more kinds of information, and more types of updating and inference.

In uncertain reasoning, especially "evidential" reasoning, an outstanding problem is how to employ assumptions, particularly of conditional independence, that are useful for drawing strong conclusions and doing efficient inference, without sacrificing consistency or expressive capability. Our approach shows how to express non-monotonic logical solutions to this challenge.

12 Directions for Future Research

The main intent of this paper is to help to define and provoke an area of investigation. We have offered more conjectures and suggestions than answers.

Several open questions were mentioned in passing. When, i.e. for which tuples, do we want to do MCI? Are there additional sorts of prioritizations besides SP which are desirable or useful? (Our preliminary investigations indicate that it is often undesirable to perform indiscriminate MCI, and that prioritization beyond specificity indeed often is desirable.) What are the statistical and decision-theoretic justifications for the default inheritance principle? When and to what extent does ME produce MCI? Insofar as ME produces MCI, is it compatible with SP? Are there ways to employ (SP)MCI in relatively efficiently in goal-directed computations, i.e. without computing the entire lower probability distribution non-monotonically entailed by SPMCI? Does our proposed circumscriptive formalization of (SP)MCI have its intended models?

We discussed a default inheritance principle in terms of inheriting point-valued probabilities in single chains of specificity. Our motivation was to start simple. More generally, *multiple* inheritance of *bounds* and *"higher-order"* (in P, e.g. probabilities of probabilities) information appears interesting. Loui [13] discusses some of these complexities.

Acknowledgements

Thanks to Peter Cheeseman, Michael Genesereth, David Heckerman, Eric Horvitz, Henry Kyburg, Vladimir Lifschitz, Ronald Loui, Nils Nilsson, Judea Pearl, Devika Subramanian, Michael Wellman and the participants of the Stanford Logic Group MUGS seminar, for valuable discussions and encouragement. I am grateful to Michael Wellman for pointing out an error in an earlier draft.

Notes

1. Instead, another way to use certain "background" axioms in $\mathcal{L}_b$ is to constrain the generation of the interpretation classes of $\mathcal{S} = \{S_i\}$ (see below).
2. cf. [6], modified so that the probability function is defined on propositions rather than sets
3. We have considered here only binary attributes, but the property of certainty holds for n-ary attributes as well.
4. $\{x, y\}$ is a set not a tuple, since $CIG(\{x,y\}, z)$ is symmetric in $x \leftrightarrow y$. It is also useful to define the case of mutual independence among a set of n propositions conditional on z, but we will not take the space here.
5. Below we follow their notation.
6. Technically, we accomplish this by including in $\mathcal{B}$ the two axioms:

$$\forall uvwxyz. V_{CIG}(\langle\{u,v\}, w\rangle, \langle\{x,y\}, z\rangle)$$

$$\forall uvwx. V_P(\langle\{u,v\}, w\rangle, x)$$

7. see the caveat above

References

[1] Cheeseman, Peter, "A Method of Computing Generalized Bayesian Probability Values for Expert Systems", *Proceedings of the Eighth IJCAI*, Aug. 1983.

[2] Duda, Richard O., Hart, Peter E., and Nilsson, Nils J., "Subjective Bayesian Methods for Rule-Based Inference Systems", in: Proceedings of the 1976 National Computer Conference, *AFIPS* Vol. 45, pp. 1075-1082, 1976.

[3] Grosof, Benjamin N., "An Inequality Paradigm for Probabilistic Knowledge", in: Kanal, L.N., & Lemmer, J.F., eds., *Uncertainty in Artificial Intelligence*, pp. 259-275. North-Holland, 1986.

[4] Grosof, Benjamin N., "Evidential Confirmation As Transformed Probability", in: Kanal, L.N., & Lemmer, J.F., eds., *Uncertainty in Artificial Intelligence*, pp. 153-166. North-Holland, 1986.

[5] Grosof, Benjamin N., *Non-Monotonic Theories: Structure, Inference, and Applications* (working title). Ph. D. thesis (in preparation), Stanford University, 1987.

[6] Hoel, Paul G., Port, Sidney C., and Stone, Charles J., Introduction to Probability Theory. Houghton Mifflin Co., 1971.

[7] Howard, Ron A., and Matheson, J. E., "Influence Diagrams", in: Howard, Ron A., and Matheson, J. E., (eds.) Readings on the Principles and Applications of Decision Analysis, chapter 37, pp. 721-762. Strategic Decisions Group, Menlo Park, CA., 1981.

[8] Konolige, Kurt, "An Information-Theoretic Approach to Subjective Bayesian Inference in Rule-Based Systems". SRI International Working Paper, Menlo Park, CA., Mar. 1982.

[9] Kurt Konolige, private communication, Apr. 1986

[10] Lemmer, John F. and Barth, S.W., "Efficient Minimum Information Updating for Bayesian Inferencing in Expert Systems", *Proceedings National Conference on Artificial Intelligence*, pp. 424-427, 1982.

[11] Lewis, P.M., "Approximating Probability Distributions to Reduce Storage Requirements", *Information and Control* Vol. 2, pp. 214-225, 1959.

[12] Lifschitz, Vladimir, "Pointwise Circumscription: Preliminary Report", in: *Proceedings of AAAI-86*, pp. 406-410, Aug. 1986.

[13] Loui, Ronald P., "Computing Reference Classes", in this volume.

[14] McCarthy, John, "Circumscription — A Form of Non-Monotonic Reasoning", *Artificial Intelligence* Vol. 13, Nos. 1-2, pp. 27-39, 1980.

[15] McCarthy, John, "Appplications of Circumscription to Formalizing Common-Sense Knowledge", *Artificial Intelligence* Vol. 28, No. 1, pp. 89-116, Feb. 1986.

[16] Moore, Robert C., "Semantical Considerations on Non-Monotonic Logic", *Artificial Intelligence* Vol. 25, No. 1, pp. 75-94, Jan. 1985.

[17] Nilsson, Nils J., "Probabilistic Logic", *Artificial Intelligence* Vol. 28, No. 1, pp. 71-88, Feb. 1986.

[18] Pearl, Judea, and Paz, Azaria, "GRAPHOIDS: A Graph-Based Logic for Reasoning About Relevance Relations". UCLA Technical Report R-53-L-I, April 1986.

[19] Reiter, Raymond, "A Logic for Default Reasoning", *Artificial Intelligence* Vol. 13, Nos. 1-2, pp. 81-132, 1980.

[20] Shafer, Glenn A., *A Mathematical Theory of Evidence*. Princeton University Press, Princeton, N.J., 1976.

[21] Shore, John E., and Johnson, Rodney W., "Axiomatic Derivation of the Principle of Maximum Entropy and the Principle of Minimum Cross-Entropy", *IEEE Transactions on Information Theory*, Vol. IT-26, No. 1, pp. 26-37, Jan. 1980.

[22] Shortliffe, Edward H., and Buchanan, Bruce G., "A Model of Inexact Reasoning in Medicine", *Mathematical Biosciences*, Vol. 23, pp. 351-379, 1975. Also available as Stanford University Knowledge Systems Laboratory Report HPP-75-1. Reprinted as chapter 11 in: *Rule-Based Expert Systems: The MYCIN Experiments of the Stanford Heuristic Programming Project* (Addison-Wesley, Reading, MA., 1984).

A SEMANTIC APPROACH TO NON-MONOTONIC ENTAILMENTS

James Hawthorne

Intelligent Systems Technology Section
Department of Man-Machine Sciences
Honeywell Systems and Research Center
Minneapolis, Minnesota 55418

Any inferential system in which the addition of new premises can lead to the retraction of previous conclusions is a non-monotonic logic. Classical conditional probability provides the oldest and most widely respected example of non-monotonic inference. This paper presents a semantic theory for a unified approach to qualitative and quantitative non-monotonic logic. The qualitative logic is unlike most other non-monotonic logics developed for AI systems. It is closely related to classical (i.e., Bayesian) probability theory. The semantic theory for qualitative non-monotonic entailments extends in a straightforward way to a semantic theory for quantitative partial entailment relations, and these relations turn out to be the classical probability functions.

1. OVERVIEW

Formal logics for AI systems are usually implemented as a controlled sequence of syntactic transformations on expressions in a formal language. The syntactic transformations are designed to compute some underlying notion. -- e.g., some notion of logical entailment, logical consistency, or justified degree of certainty. Ideally the underlying logical notion is made precise by a semantic theory. The semantic theory identifies certain primitive semantic concepts (e.g., truth or satisfaction), and defines more complex semantic concepts in terms of the primitives (e.g., consistency and logical entailment). It provides for the establishment of important semantic theorems (e.g., that some collection of syntactic transformations is truth preserving).

This ideal is well illustrated by automated systems for sentential logic. The underlying semantic theory takes the notion of a truth-value assignment to every sentence as primitive. Semantic rules govern how truth-values may be assigned to complex sentences in terms of the truth-values of constituents. Logical entailment is *defined*. A sentence A is a logical consequence of B just in case every possible truth-value assignment that makes B true also makes A true. Semantic theorems establish that certain syntactic transformations (e.g., resolution) suffice to deduce every logical entailment of any set of premises. Other semantic theorems establish that interesting weaker syntactic deduction systems (e.g., Horne-clause resolution) are incomplete. Some truth preserving inferences escape them. Semantic theorems characterize the usually more efficiently computable subset of logical entailments that weaker deduction systems compute.

Systems for predicate logic and some modal logics also fit the ideal of syntactic deduction systems motivated by precise formal semantic theories. But many of the logics for AI systems have no rigorous semantic theory. The syntactic transformations are motivated by rough intuitions, and are adjusted to particular applications in a pragmatic but ad hoc fashion. A semantic theory furnishes a deduction system with justified *principles of correct inference*. Applications of the system turn mainly on implementing techniques for using the *principles* to make desired inferences.

This paper will present a formal semantic theory for a class of qualitative non-monotonic entailment relations. It will describe several interesting properties of these entailment relations. Then it will show how to extend the semantics to represent a class of quantitative non-monotonic partial entailment (i.e., degree of entailment) relations. These relations turn out to be the classical (i.e., Bayesian) probability functions, but with a twist. The semantics permits non-monotonic, non-Bayesian jumps from one classical probability function to another when sentences considered previously to be "impossible" (i.e., they had probability zero) are accepted as new premises.

I won't discuss syntactic deduction methods for the semantic relationships described in this paper. Nor will I prove any of the semantic theorems that establish the characteristics of the entailment relations. These theorems are proven elsewhere [3]. The purpose of this paper is to introduce an approach to a non-monotonic logic that unifies a qualitative and a quantitative notion of non-monotonic entailment into a single coherent system.

The systems in this paper will be restricted to the language of sentential logic, but the semantic theories and theorems are easily extended to a language for first-order predicate logic. Hartry Field [2] first introduced a probabilistic semantics of this kind for first-order logic in 1977. That paper initiated several investigations into probabilistic semantics, including this one. For an excellent recent treatment see the papers of Bas van Fraassen [5] [6]. Other investigations are citied in its references.

The next section illustrates a typical truth-value semantics for sentential logic. This will be used in succeeding sections as a standard for comparison. Those sections will develop the semantic theory for non-monotonic entailments.

2. TRUTH

Let L be a formal language for sentential logic. L contains the following categories:

    sentential letters: $P_1, P_2, ...$
    logical symbols: &, -
    parentheses:), (

sentences: 1) sentential letters
2) if A is a sentence, $-A$ is a sentence
3) if A and B are sentences, then $(A\&B)$ is a sentence.

Let S be the set of all sentences of L. We use 'A', 'B', etc. as metalinguistic variables ranging over members of S.

The only logical symbols of L are '&' and '-'. Other standard symbols are considered abbreviations:

$(A \vee B)$ for $-(-A\&-B)$,
$(A \rightarrow B)$ for $-(A\&-B)$,
$(A \leftrightarrow B)$ for $(-(A\&-B)\&-(-A\&B))$.

A truth-value semantics for L specifies all possible ways the sentences of L can be simultaneously assigned truth-values -- i.e., be true or false. For sentential logic the concept of truth is the semantic primitive. Presumably the truth or falsehood of a sentence depends on the meanings of constituent terms and the actual state-of-the-world they refer to. In more complex logics (e.g., predicate logic, modal logic) the semantics may take meaning assignments and possible states-of-the-world as primitive, and define the notion of truth in terms of them. But for the purposes of sentential logic meaning and possible states add nothing essential beyond their contribution to truth. It suffices to formalize the semantics in terms of truth, and to leave meaning and world states as an informal account of how truth is determined.

A semantics for sentential logic may be specified in terms of truth-sets. Initially each subset of the set of all sentences S can be thought of as a possible truth set. Let T_a, T_b, etc. be subsets of S. If a sentence A is in T_a we say that T_a makes A true, abbreviated "$T_a(A)$". If A is not in T_a, then T_a makes A false, abbreviated "not $T_a(A)$". So each subset T_a of S can represent a possible truth-value assignment to all members of S. But not every T_a in S is a *permissible* truth-value assignment.

For T_a to be a truth-value assignment it must satisfy certain semantic rules that constrain the notion of truth:

for all A, B in S:
1) $T_a(-A)$ iff not $T_a(A)$,
2) $T_a((A\&B))$ iff $T_a(A)$ and $T_a(B)$,
("iff" abbreviates "if and only if").

Let *TVA* be the set of all T_a such that T_a is a subset of *S* that satisifies these semantic rules. *TVA* represents the set of all coherent truth-value assignments to *L*. Every possible meaning assignment to sentences of *L* together with a possible state-of-the-world corresponds to some member of *TVA*. And each member of *TVA* is a truth set for some possible meaning assignment and state-of-the-world. But the contributions of meaning and the world to truth need not be formalized in the semantics for sentential logic. The semantic rules don't require such distinctions, so they stay informally in the background.

The only notion of entailment usually associated with sentential logic is the notion of logical entailment. Logical entailment is the relation of truth preservation for all possible truth-value assignments:

> definition: $A=/B$ (read "*A* is logically entailed by *B*") iff
> for every T_a in *TVA*, if $T_a(B)$, then $T_a(A)$.

Logical entailment is both monotonic and transitive:

> Monotonicity $A=/B$ only if $A=/(B\&C)$;

> Transitivity $A=/B$ and $B=/C$ <u>only if</u> $A=/C$.

Monotonicity and transitivity are closely related in the non-monotonic entailments described in the next section.

3. ENTAILMENT

Truth-value semantics is inadequate as a basis for non-monotonic entailments because the concept of truth it explicates is monotonic to the core. Any truth-value assignment that makes *A* true will also make *(A&B)* true if *B* is true.

Non-monotonic logic presumes that there is more to the meaning of a sentence than the determination of truth-values at possible worlds. The meaning of a sentence (and, perhaps, the state-of-the-world) imbues a sentence with an inferential connection to other sentences. This connection is commonly expressed in one of the following ways:

1) If *B* were the case, then *A* would be.
2) *A* is true if *B* is, ceteris paribus.
3) *B* would make *A* nearly certain.

Each of these expressions indicates that A is entailed by B in some sense. And each expression tends to be non-monotonic. Replacing B by (B&C) can undermine the entailment. The standard example is:

1. "it flies" is entailed by "it's a bird";

2. "it flies" is not entailed by "it's a bird and it lives in the Antarctic";

3. "it doesn't fly" is not entailed by "it's a bird and it lives in the Antarctic";

4. "it flies" is entailed by "it's a bird and it lives in the Antarctic and it's a tern";

5. "it doesn't fly" is entailed by "it's a bird and it's a penguin";

6. "it's a bird" is entailed by "it's a penguin";

7. "it doesn't fly" is entailed by "it's a penguin".

The breakdown of monotonicity is illustrated by 1-5. Transitivity fails for this notion of entailment, as 1, 6, and 7 illustrate.

Truth-value semantics takes the notion of truth as primitive, and specifies truth preserving relationships. The semantics for non-monotonic entailments will take entailment as a primitive notion, and will specify entailment preserving relationships.

For language L let $S \times S$ be the set of all pairs of sentences, $<A,B>$. Each subset of $S \times S$ is a potential entailment relation among sentences. Let $=/_a$, $=/_b$, etc. represent subsets of $S \times S$. If an ordered pair of sentences $<A,B>$ is in $=/_a$ we say that A is entailed by B under entailment-value assignment $=/_a$, abbreviated "$A=/_a B$". If $<A,B>$ is not in $=/_a$ we say that A is not entailed by B in $=/_a$, abbreviated "not $A=/_a B$".

Not all subsets of $S \times S$ are permissible entailment relations. The class of entailment relations of interest should satisfy certain plausable semantic rules. For each $=/_a$ in $S \times S$, $=/_a$ is in *ERA* (the set of permissible entailment relation assignments) just in case it satisifies the following semantic rules:

1) for some A and B, not $A=/_a B$;
and for all A,B,C:
2) $A=/_a A$;
3) $A=/_a(B\&C)$ only if $A=/_a(C\&B)$;
4.1) $(A\&B)=/_a C$ only if $(B\&A)=/_a C$;

4.2) $-(A\&B)=/_a C$ only if $-(B\&A)=/_a C$;
5.1) $--A=/_a B$ only if $A=/_a B$;
5.2) $A=/_a B$ and $-A=/_a B$ <u>only if</u> $C=/_a B$;
6.1) $(A\&B)=/_a C$ <u>iff</u> $A=/_a(B\&C)$ and $B=/_a C$;
6.2) $-(A\&B)=/_a C$ <u>iff</u> $-A=/_a(B\&C)$ or $-B=/_a C$.

ERA characterizes a set of entailment relations. Each entailment relation assigns entailment to hold or not hold between each pair of sentences. Presumably the meanings of the sentences and the state-of-the-world contribute to the specification of an entailment relation. But for our purposes we can take the concept of an entailment relation as primitive. What is more important is that the semantic rules governing entailment relations are plausible restrictions on the intuitive notions of non-monotonic entailment we are after.

The semantic rules for *ERA* are plausible when $A=/_a B$ is read "among possible states (possible worlds) where B is true, A is almost always true". With this reading rules 1-5.2 are clearly plausible. Notice that an instance of 1 is "not $-B=/_a B$, for some B". The converse of 5.1 is provable as a semantic theorem. Rule 5.2 says that if B make both A and $-A$ nearly certain, then B makes every sentence nearly certain. In that case we shall say that B is inconsistent in entailment relation $=/_a$.

Rule 6.1 contains a weak form of transitivity. It only permits

$A=/_a(B\&C)$ and $B=/_a C$ <u>only if</u> $A=/_a C$.

Full transitivity would say that

$A=/_a B$ and $B=/_a C$ <u>only if</u> $A=/_a C$.

Full transitivity doesn't generally hold for members of *ERA*.

The weak transitivity fits the penguin case pretty well.

[it flies]$=/_a$ [it's a bird], and
[it's a bird]$=/_a$[it's a penguin],
but not [it flies]$=/_a$[it's a penguin],
because not [it flies]$=/_a$ ([it's a bird] & [it's a penguin]).

Rule 6.1 also permits the conjunction of entailed conjuncts. For every member $=/_a$ of *ERA*:

$A=/_a C$ and $B=/_a C$ <u>iff</u> $(A\&B)=/_a C$.

This can be proved as a semantic theorem.

Rule 6.2 contains a weak form of the deduction theorem. It implies

$(B \to A) = /_a C$ only if $A = /_a (B \& C)$ or $-B = /_a C$,

where the deduction theorem would have

$(B \to A) = /_a C$ only if $A = /_a (B \& C)$.

The strong form of the deduction theorem would threaten to force monotonicity. From $A = /_a C$ we can get $(B \to A) = /_a C$, which would lead to $A = /_a (B \& C)$ with the strong version. Reading "$= /_a$" as "is made nearly certain by", the weak version permits:

[it flies] $= /_a$ [it's a bird],
so ([it's a penguin] $\to$ [it flies]) $= /_a$ [it's a bird],
though not [it flies] $= /_a$ ([it's a bird] & [it's a penguin]),
because -[it's a penguin] $= /_a$ [it's a bird],
(i.e., given only that it's a bird, it almost certainly is not a penguin).

Notice that the semantics does not involve the notion of logical entailment in the truth-value sense. It is totally autonomous with respect to truth-value semantics. *ERA* semantics does not presuppose that logically equivalent sentences can be substituted in an *ERA* entailment to determine other entailments. Nor does it assume that members of *ERA* respect logical entailment. Rather, *ERA* permits an alternative definition of logical entailment.

We may define *ERA* logical entailment as entailment in every member of *ERA*:

definition: *A* is *ERA* logically entailed by *B* iff for every $= /_a$ in *ERA*, $A = /_a B$.

Semantic theorems about *ERA* show that the logical entailments in the classical *TVA* sense are just those entailments that hold in every member of *ERA*, the *ERA* logical entailments:

$A = /B$ iff for every $= /_a$ in *ERA*, $A = /_a B$.

So the members of *ERA* may be thought of as all possible ways of extending the classical logical entailment relation to permit additional non-monotonic entailments.

Other semantic theorems show that within each member of *ERA* one can substitute $= /_a$ -- equivalent sentences:

for all C, $A = /_a (B \& C)$ and $B = /_a (A \& C)$ only if for all D, $A = /_a D$ only if $B = /_a D$.

I.e., if A and B are monotonically equivalent in $=/_a$ (but not necessarily logically equivalent), then whatever entails A in $=/_a$ also entails B in $=/_a$. The substitution rules for the premise of a relation in *ERA* doesn't require monotonic equivalence:

$$A=/_a B \text{ and } B=/_a A \underline{\text{ only if }} \text{ for all } D, D=/_a A \text{ only if } D=/_a B.$$

When do montonicity and transitivity break down for an *ERA* entailment relation? Monotonicity only fails with the addition of a new premise that was previously considered almost certainly false:

$$A=/_a B \text{ and not } A=/_a(B\&C) \underline{\text{ only if }} -C=/_a B.$$

And for transitivity the following theorem holds:

$$A=/_a B \text{ and } B=/_a C \text{ and not } A=/_a C \underline{\text{ only if }} -C=/_a B.$$

Indeed, B monotonically entails A for a member $=/_a$ of *ERA* just in case whatever entails B also entails A in $=/_a$, i.e.:

$$\text{for every } C, A=/_a(B\&C) \underline{\text{ iff }} \text{ for every } D, B=/_a D \text{ only if } A=/_a D.$$

The syntactic structure of *ERA* entailment relations is quite different from that of other non-monotonic logics. Other systems state explicitly in a non-monotonic inference rule what condition will counter-act the inference. In *ERA* interference with transitivity and monotonicity are signaled by other entailments that hold between the sentences involved:

$$A=/_a B \text{ and not } A=/_a(B\&C) \text{ can only occur when } -C=/_a B.$$

The syntactic structure for *ERA* non-monotonic entailments resembles the non-monotonicity of conditional probabilities associated with probabilistic dependence and independence. The next section shows how closely entailments in *ERA* are related to classical probability functions.

4. PROBABILITY

The entailment semantics of the previous section extrapolates in a straightforward way to a semantics for partial (i.e., probabilistic) entailments. The class of probabilistic entailment relations turns out to be almost precisely the class of all classical (i.e., Bayesian) probability functions. They satisfy the standard axioms for probability theory -- up to a point.

A typical semantic approach to classical probability theory for a sentential language *defines* the set *PROB* of probability functions on L:

P_a is in *PROB* iff
1) P_a is a function from S into the real interval $[0,1]$;
2) $P_a(A)=1$ if A is a logical truth;
3) $P_a((A \vee B)) = P_a(A) + P_a(B)$ if $-(A \& B)$ is a logical truth.

Some versions have the additional rule that logically equivalent sentences have the same probability. But that rule can be derived from 1-3 above.

On this approach probability is sometimes taken to represent the degree of certainty that a sentence is true. An alternative interpretation takes expressions like $P_a(A)=r$ to say, roughly, that given the meaning of A (that P_a presupposes), A is true in $100 \times r$ percent of the possible states-of-affairs (possible worlds).

In *PROB* semantics conditional probability is a defined notion:

definition: $P_a(A/B) = P_a((A \& B)) \div P_a(B)$ if $P_a(B) \neq 0$, and is undefined if $P_a(B) = 0$.

Intuitively, $P_a(A/B)=r$ might be understood to say that A is true in $100 \times r$ percent of the states in which B is true.

PROB semantics relies on the concept of logical truth. It's semantic rules employ that concept. The concept of logical truth is borrowed from truth-value semantics -- i.e., truth in all members of *TVA*. Strictly speaking, the semantics employs two primitives, the concept of truth and the concept of probability.

The *ERA* semantics suggests a different approach to probabilistic semantics. For *ERA* we took certain subsets of $S \times S$ as relations which qualify as entailments. Each relation $=/_a$ maps each pair of sentences onto either "entailment holds" (i.e., the pair is in $=/_a$) or "entailment doesn't hold" (i.e., the pair is not in $=/_a$). Let R be the set of all mappings from $S \times S$ into the real interval from 0 to 1, inclusive. Each member of R is a set of triples of form $<A,B,r>$, where A and B are in S and r is in $[0,1]$. I will characterize a class of these functions in R that capture the notion "A is entailed by B to degree r". Members of R will be represented by symbols like $'/_a'$, and we write "$A_r/_a B$" for "$<A,B,r> \in /_a$". $/_a$ is a mapping, i.e., a function, so $<A,B,r> \in /_a$ and $<A,B,s> \in /_a$ only if $r=s$ (r and s reals in $[0,1]$). R contains all and only such functions. Every sentence is entailed by each sentence to some unique degree for each partial entailment function $/_a$ in R.

Define *PVA* as the set of all probabilistic entailment value assignments $/_a \in R$ that meet the following conditions:

1) for some $A,B \in S$, not $A_1/_a B$;
and for every $A,B,C \in S, r,s,q, \in [0,1]$:

2) $A_1/_aA$;
3) $A_r/_a(B\&C)$ only if $A_r/_a(C\&B)$;
4) $(A\&B)_r/_aC$ only if $(B\&A)_r/_aC$;
5) $A_r/_aB$ and $-A_s/_aB$ and $r+s\neq 1$ <u>only if</u> $C_1/_aB$;
6) $(A\&B)_r/_aC$ and $A_s/_a(B\&C)$ and $B_q/_aC$ <u>only if</u> $r=s\times q$.

Each rule is the obvious extension of a similarily numbered rule for *ERA*. Rule 5 is the natural extension of 5.2, and covers 5.1 Rules 4 and 6 extend 4.1 and 6.1. The connection between a sentence and its negation imposed by Rule 5 is sufficiently strong to cover the counterparts to 4.2 and 6.2.

Since $/_a$ is a function we can establish a notational convenience. We will rewrite $A_r/_aB$ as $P_a(A/B)=r$, and say $P_a \in PVA$ rather than $/_a \in PVA$. Rewriting 1 through 6 we have:

1) for some $A,B \in S$, $P_a(A/B) \neq 1$;
and for all $A,B,C \in S$:
2) $P_a(A/A)=1$;
3) $P_a(A/(B\&C))=P_a(A/(C\&B))$;
4) $P_a((A\&B)/C)=P_a((B\&A)/C)$;
5) $P_a(A/B)+P_a(-A/B)=1$ or $P_a(C/B)=1$;
6) $P_a((A\&B)/C)=P_a(A/(B\&C))\times P_a(B/C)$.

Notice that it is not *assumed* that the members of *PVA* are classical probability functions, nor that logical entailments have conditional entailments of *1*. *PVA* contains just those P_a that are functions from $S \times S$ into *[0,1]* satisfying conditions 1-6.

Presumably, sentences are true or false because of their meanings and the state-of-the-world. *TVA* doesn't make such distinctions because they contribute nothing essential to sentential logic. Only when the formal language is extended to intentional contexts (e.g., modal operators) need the semantics explicitly reflect the separate contributions to truth by meaning and the possible world or state-of-affairs that an interpretation takes the sentences to be about.

Similarily, the semantics for partial entailments given by *PVA* need not make explicit the separate contributions made by meaning and the nature of possible states. Presumably, $A_r/_aB$ holds under interpretation $/_a$ because $/_a$ represents both a way of associating meaning with *A* and *B*, and certain probabilistic relationships among the possible states-of-affairs that *A* and *B* are about. Roughly, $A_r/_aB$ says that *r* is the measure or frequency of *A* being true among possible states (possible worlds) where *B* is true. Parsing members of *PVA* into these components may play an essential role in a semantics for an intentional language. But, for our purposes it is only a useful heuristic for understanding what partial entailment represents. Understood in this way, the semantical rules are plausible principles for partial entailments.

Semantic Rules 1-4 seem totally uncontroversial. Rule 5 is plausible, too. Presumably each possible state makes either A true or $-A$ true. So their truth-frequencies should add to 1 among states where B is true. Rule 6 is also a plausible principle when read in terms of truth-frequencies among possible states. Of course any other interpretation of partial entailments (e.g., as conditional degrees of belief) is also captured by PVA provided it satisifies the semantic rules.

PVA semantics does not presuppose a notion of logical entailment. Like ERA, it permits an independent *definition* of logical entailment:

A is PVA logically entailed by B iff for all P_a in PVA, $P_a(A/B)=1$.

Then a semantic theorem establishes that the defined notion coincides with classical TVA logical entailment. Logical truth is just logical entailment by every sentence. So that notion, too, is definable in PVA semantics.

Relative to any given sentence C, for each P_a in PVA the function $P_a(\ /C)$ satisfies the classical probability rules of $PROB$. This is provable as a semantic theorem. Observe that Rule 6 for PVA requires that conditionalization relative to a sentence B fits the classical definition of conditional probability when $P_a(B/C) \neq 0$:

$P_a(A/(B\&C)) = P_a((A\&B)/C) + P_a(B/C)$ if $P_a(B/C) \neq 0$.

So $P_a(\ /C)$ behaves as classical probability unless conditionalized on a sentence B that is "nearly impossible", has measure 0, relative to C. But entailment to degree 0 need not make B absolutely impossible. Rule 6 permits $P_a(\ /(B\&C))$ to behave as a new classical probability function. It, too, behaves classically until some new condition D for which $P_a(D/(B\&C))=0$ is added. Then $P_a(\ /(D\&(B\&C)))$ behaves classically, and so on.

Bayes' theorem is a direct consequence of classical conditionalization:

$P_a(A/(B\&C)) = P_a(A/C) \times [P_a(B/(A\&C)) + P_a(B/C)]$ for $P_a(B/C) \neq 0$.

It states how adding a new premise B influences the degree to which A is entailed by C. Rule 6 requires members of PVA to transform in classical Bayesian fashion when $P_a(B/C) \neq 0$. When $P_a(B/C)=0$, Rule 6 permits $P_a(A/(B\&C))$ to take a non-Bayesian leap -- $P_a(\ /(B\&C))$ becomes a different classical probability function than $P_a(\ /C)$, and they are not related by a Bayesian transformation. In effect each member of PVA is a class of Bayesian probability functions with non-Bayesian jumps from one to another impelled by new conditions considered nearly impossible under previous conditions.

5. CONCLUSION

Probabilistic inference is itself non-monotonic, and some have suggested it subsumes the qualitative notion. Cheeseman [1] and Heurion [4] have argued extensively that classical probability theory is sufficient for all forms of reasoning under uncertainty. They argue that the numerous other theories for uncertain inference developed for AI applications suffer disorders ranging from being simply unnecessary (i.e., classical probability would do as well), to ad hoc and misleading, to unsound. While I largely share their views regarding quantitative alternatives to classical probability, I take a different view of qualitative non-monotonic inference.

The semantic theories described above show that classical probability theory is a simple quantitative extension of an underlying semantic theory of non-monotonic entailments. Entailments are not subsumable under the Bayesian conditionalization mechanism of classical probability. Rather, non-monotonic entailments can furnish non-Bayesian jumps from one classical probability function to another. The semantic theory suggests a general approach to uncertain inference that unifies qualitative and quantitative non-monotonic inference into a single coherent system.

ACKNOWLEDGEMENTS

The writing of this paper was partly supported by the Intelligent Systems Technology Section of the Man-Machine Sciences Group at Honeywell's Systems and Research Center. I especially want to thank my Section Chief, Jan Wald, for his interest and encouragement. He suggested a number of improvements. My colleague, Tim Colburn, contributed helpful discussions. My secretary, Rhona Driggs, deserves special thanks.

REFERENCES

[1] Cheeseman, P. In Defense of Probability. In *Proceedings of 9th International Joint Conference on AI*. Los Angeles, CA, 1985.

[2] Field, H. *"Logic, Meaning, and Conceptual Role"*, Journal of Philosophy, 74, pp. 374-409, 1977.

[3] Hawthorne, J. *A Formal Semantics for Statistical Entailments and Inductive Inference*. Ph.D Thesis, University of Minnesota (in progress).

[4] Henrion, M. *"Should we use Probability in Uncertain Inference Systems?"*, Eigth Annual Conference of the Cognitive Science Society, pp. 320-330, 1986.

[5] van Fraassen, B.C. *"Probabilistic Semantics Objectified: I. Postulates and Logic"*, Journal of Philosophical Logic, 10, pp.371-394, 1981.

[6] van Fraassen, B.C. *"Probabilistic Semantics Objectified: II. Implications in Probabilistic Model Sets"*, Journal of Philosophical Logic,10, pp. 495-510, 1981.

KNOWLEDGE

Henry E. Kyburg, Jr.

Departments of Philosophy and Computer Science
University of Rochester
Rochester, NY 14627*

1. BACKGROUND.

One purpose -- quite a few thinkers would say the main purpose -- of seeking knowledge about the world is to enhance our ability to make good decisions. An item of knowledge that can make no conceivable difference with regard to anything we might do would strike many as frivolous. Whether or not we want to be philosophical pragmatists in this strong sense with regard to everything we might want to enquire about, it seems a perfectly appropriate attitude to adopt toward artificial knowledge systems.

If is granted that we are ultimately concerned with decisions, then some constraints are imposed on our measures of uncertainty at the level of decision making. If our measure of uncertainty is real-valued, then it isn't hard to show that it must satisfy the classical probability axioms. For example, if an act has a real-valued utility $U(E)$ if the event E obtains, and the same real-valued utility if the denial of E obtains, so that $U(E) = U(\neg E)$, then the expected utility of that act must be $U(E)$, and that must be the same as the uncertainty-weighted average of the returns of the act, $p \cdot U(E) + q \cdot U(\neg E)$, where p and q represent the uncertainty of E and $\neg E$ respectively. But then we must have $p + q = 1$.

2. SUBJECTIVE MEASURES.

There are reasons for rejecting real-valued -- i.e., strictly probabilistic measures of uncertainty, though not all the reasons that have been adduced for doing so are cogent. One is that these probabilities seem to embody more knowledge than they should: for example, if your beliefs are probabilistic, and you assign a probability of

.01 to a drawn ball's being purple (on no evidence), and a probability of .02 to a second ball's being purpole on the evidence that the first one is, and regard pairs of balls as "exchangeable" then you should be 99% sure that in the infinitely long run no more than 11% of the balls will be purple. You know beyond a shadow of a doubt (with probability .99996) that no more than half will be purple. (In fact, we need much less than full exchangeability for this: all we need is that both individual events and pairs of events are treated independently of their place in the sequence -- [Kyburg, 1968]).

Peter Cheeseman [1985] has given a defense of classical probability, and perhaps would not find even such results as the foregoing distasteful. But it is hard to see how to defend the real-valued point of view from charges of subjectivity. Cheeseman refers to an "ideal" observer, but offers us no guidance in how to approach ideality, nor any characterization of how the ideal observer differs from the rest of us. It is therefore quite unclear what the ideal observer offers us, other than moral support: each of us is no doubt convinced that the ideal observer assigns probabilities much as he does himself. One man's subjective bias is another man's rational insight.

One defense against charges of subjectivity is to be found in the "convergence" theorems, of which the most famous is de Finetti's [de Finetti, 1937]. Roughly: if S is a sequence of trials, each resulting in success or failure, and you and I agree that the sequence is exchangeable, then no matter how divergent our initial views of the probability of success -- so long as they are not given by probabilities of 0 or 1 -- and no matter what degree of agreement we seek, there is a number n such that after observing n trials you and I will agree to that degree on the probability of success on the *next* trial.

Of course such a theorem has a less gratifying counterpart: given any degree of disagreement that we find abhorrent, and given any amount of evidence n, there exists a degree of initial disagreement such that even after n trials our degree of disagreement about the probability of succcess on the $n + 1$'st trial will be intolerable. And nothing precludes our disagreeing that much to start with.

It could be argued -- and has been -- that subjective probabilities don't vary so dreadfully much, and so in fact subjectivity is a mere hobgoblin. It may be philosophically troubling to those of that turn of mind, but is of little importance.

But I think it can be argued that a small difference in some subjective probabilities can lead to a very large difference in others. Furthermore, it is well known that we all fail to conform to the probability calculus in our degrees of belief. That just means that we have to make some adjustments. Since small differences can lead to large ones, though, the particular adjustments we make can create large disagreement about courses of action.

There are other ways of representing uncertainty than by real numbers between 0 and 1. If these uncertainties are to be used in making decisions, however, they must be compatible with classical point-valued probabilities. My preference is for intervals, because they can be based on objective knowledge of distributions, and because this compatibility is demonstrable. [Kyburg, 1974].

In what follows, I will sketch the properties of interval-valued epistemic probability, and exhibit a structure for knowledge representation that allows for both uncertain inference from evidence and uncertain knowledge as a basis for decision. Along the way I make some comparisons to other approaches.

3. PROBABILITY

Probability is a function from statements and sets of statements to closed subintervals of $[0, 1]$. The sets of statements represent hypothetical bodies of knowledge. The idea behind $\text{Prob}(S, K) = [p,q]$ is that someone whose body of knowledge is K should, ought to, have a 'degree' of belief in S characterized by the interval $[p,q]$. The cash value of having such a 'degree' of belief is that he should not sell a ticket that returns to the purchaser $ 1.00 for less than $100p$ cents, and he should not buy such a ticket for more than $100q$ cents. The relation in question is construed as a purely objective, logical, relation.

Every probability can be based on knowledge of statistical distributions or relative frequencies, since statements known to have the same truth value receive the same probability, and every such equivalence class of statements (we can show) contains some statements of the appropriate form. This statistical knowledge may be both uncertain and approximate (we may be practically sure that between 30% and 40% of the balls are black), but it is objective in the sense that any two people having the same evidence should have the same knowledge.

Classical point-valued probabilities constitute a special case, corresponding to the extreme hypothetical (and unrealistic) case in which K embodies exact statistical knowledge.

The connection between statements and frequencies is given by a set of formal procedures for finding the right reference class for a given statement. The reference set may well be multi-dimensional -- the set of urns, each paired with the set of draws made from it. It may be only "accidentally" related to the sentence for which we want a probability -- as when we assign a probability to the act of someone who makes a choice on the basis of a coin toss. What is the right reference class for a given statement S depends (formally and objectively) on what is in K, our body of knowledge. In some cases we can implement a procedure for finding the right reference class.

It is natural to suppose that statistical knowledge in K is represented by the attribution to each reference set of a convex set of distributions -- for example, we have every reason in the world to suppose that heads among sets of coin-tosses in general is nearly binomial, with a parameter close to a half. (We have no reason to suppose that the parameter has the real value 0.4999...). Or we may have good reason to believe that two quantities are uncorrelated in their joint distribution, though we know little about their individual distributions. Or we may be able to rule out certain classes of extreme distributions. We can know of a certain bent coin that heads will be binomially distributed in sequences of its tosses, with a parameter p at least equal to a half. In a wide range of cases of practical importance, what we can know of the set of distributions is that conditional independence obtains among certain variables. (Judea Pearl [1985] has made conditional independence the cornerstone of his constraint propagation approach to evidential updating; conditional independence, among other things, is what is required to warrant the use of Dempster's rule of combination. (See [Kyburg, forthcoming])

Henceforth, we assume convexity. Here are some immediate results [Kyburg, 1961, 1974]:

(1) If $\text{Prob}(S,K) = [p,q]$ then $\text{Prob}(\neg S,K) = [1-q,1-p]$.

(2) If $\neg(S \,\&\, T)$ is in K, and $\text{Prob}(S,K) = [p_1,q_1]$ and $\text{Prob}(T,K) = [p_2,q_2]$ and $\text{Prob}(S \vee T) = [p,q]$, then there are numbers in $[p_1,q_1]$ and $[p_2,q_2]$ whose sum is in $[p,q]$. To see that $[p,q]$ can be a proper subset of $[p_1+p_2, q_1+q_2]$, consider a die that you know to be biassed toward the one at the expense of the two, or toward the two at the expense of the one. Reasonable probability for the disjunction "one or two" would be very close to 1/3, even though the reasonable probabilities for "one" and "two" would be significantly spread above and below 1/6.

(3) We can show that: given any finite set of sentences SS, and a body of knowledge K, there exists a classical probability function B, satisfying the classical probability axioms, such that for every sentence S_i in SS, $B(S_i) \in \text{Prob}(S_i,K)$.

(4) Let KE be the body of knowledge obtained from K when evidence E is added to K. Let E be in the finite set of sentences SS. Then there may be no classical Bayesian probability function B satisfying both $B(S_i) \in \text{Prob}(Si,K)$ and $B(S_i/E) \in \text{Prob}(S_i,KE)$ for all S_i in SS. Classical conditionalization is not the only way of updating probabilities.

(5) The randomness relation is definable, and in fact for one kind of database, rules for picking the right reference class have been implemented [Loui, 1987].

4. UNCERTAIN KNOWLEDGE

One problem that subjectivistic Bayesian and other approaches to uncertainty have is that there is no formal way of representing the acquisition of knowledge. We can represent the having of knowledge (by the assignment of probability 1 to the item), but since there is no interesting way in which $P(S,E)$ can be 1 unless $P(S)$ is already 1, conditionalization doesn't get us knowledge. This has been noticed, of course; Cheeseman [1985, p. 1008] simply says, "A reasonable compromise is to treat propositions whose probability is close to 0 or 1 as if they are known with certainty..." But of course it is well known that this cannot be done generally: the conjunction of a number of certainties is a certainty, but the conjunction of a large enough number of certainties in Cheesman's sense is what he would have to consider an impossibility.

McCarthy and Hayes [1969] are seduced into following this primrose path, when they suggest (p. 489) "If $\theta_1, \theta_2, \ldots \theta_n \vdash \theta$ is a possible deduction, then probably(θ_1), probably(θ_2), ... ,probably(θ_n) $\vdash$ probably(θ) is also a possible deduction." This is clearly ruled out, on our scheme -- and even acceptable(θ_1), ... , acceptable(θ_n) $\vdash$ acceptable(θ) is ruled out as a consequence of the logical conditional. If we are to formalize uncertain inference at all and not merely the deductive propagation of probabilities, we must somehow accommodate sets of conflicting statements. Purely probabilistic rules of inference do this easily.

We can accommodate Cheeseman's intuition that we should accept what is "practically certain" by considering two sets of sentences in the representation of knowledge. One of them we will call the evidential corpus, and denote by K_e; the other we will call the practical corpus, and denote by K_p.

We will accept a sentence into K_p if and only if its lower probability relative to K_e is greater than p. The conjunction of two statements that appear in K_p will also appear in K_p only if the conjunction itself is probable enough relative to the evidential corpus K_e. Thus K_p will not be deductively closed. Of course if a conjunction appears in K_p, each conjunct will also appear in K_p, since we can show that the lower probability of a conjunct has to be at least as great as the lower probability of the conjunction. In fact, we can show that if a statement S appears in K_p, and S entails T, T must also appear there because it must have a lower probability greater than that of S. This reflects a natural feature of human inference: we must have reason, not only to accept each premise in a complex argument, but to accept the conjunction of the premises, in order to be confident of the conclusion.

In fact, the uncertain inference that generates K_p from K_e has a number of the desirable features of non-monotonic inference. Add "Tweety is a bird" to the evidential corpus K_e, and "Tweety is capable of flight" will appear in K_p exactly because practically all birds fly. In addition, add "Tweety is an ostrich" to K_e, and "Tweety is not capable of flight" will appear in K_p, since practically no ostriches can fly. In the former case, you should base your decisions on the assumption that Tweety can fly; in the latter, you no longer need worry about that merely logical possibility.

But to warrant the detachment that yields the addition of a sentence to our stock of practical certainties, we need more than a mere preponderance of evidence. We don't want to infer that two tosses of a coin will yield one head and one tail just because this is the most probable outcome. Similarly we don't want to infer that a die will not yield a six: we want to say that the probability of an outcome other than a six is about five sixths.

This is just to say that the level of practical certainty p is exactly what distinguishes (in a given context) sentences that we are willing to bet either for or against (at the right odds!) from sentences that we take for granted or whose denials we take for granted.

We have a picture that looks like this:

$$K_e$$

Uncertain Inference: $S \in K_p$ iff $\text{Prob}(S, K_e) > p$.

$$K_p$$

It is relative to K_p, the practical corpus, that we make our (practical) decisions. It is thus the (convex sets of) distributions -- including conditional distributions -- embodied in the practical corpus that we use in our decision theory.

But there are a lot of questions. What is the value of p that we are taking to characterize practical certainty? How do statements get in the evidential corpus K_e? What is the decision theory that goes with this kind of structure?

Let us first consider the value of p. Suppose the widest range of stakes we can come up with is 99:1. For example, Sam and Sally are going to bet on some event, each has $100, and neither has any change. Then a probability value falling outside the range of [0.01,0.99] would be useless as a betting guide. A probability less than .01 would (in this context) amount to a practical impossibility; one greater than .99 would amount to a practical certainty.

The range of stakes can determine the level of "practical certainty" p. What counts as practical certainty depends on context, but in an explicit way: it depends on what's at stake.

How do statements qualify as evidence in K_e? Not by being "certain." It can be argued that anything that was really incorrigible would have to be devoid of empirical content. (The worry about uncertain evidence is not misplaced; it is just misconstrued.) One typical form of evidence statment is this: "the length of x is $d \pm r$ meters." Whatever our readings may have been these statements are not "certain" -- they admit of error. This is so however large r is. The same is true of all ordinary observation statments.

So a statement gets into K_e by having a low probability of being in error: equally, by having a high probability (at least e, relative to yet another corpus -- say an observational one, or a phenomenological one) of being veridical. How high? In virtue of the fact that conjunctions of pairs of statements in K_e appear in K_p, it seems plausible to take $e = (p)^{1/2}$. For a number of technical reasons [Kyburg, 1984] it turns out to be best to construe the corpus containing the theory of error as metalinguistic.

This is as one might think: after all, the theory of error concerns the relation between readings -- e.g. numerals written in laboratory books -- and values: the real quantities characterizing things in the real world. For present purposes we need note only that this is not the beginning of an infinite regress. We can maintain objectivity; we can avoid "presuppositions" and other unjustified assumptions.

5. DECISION

It has been objected [Seidenfeld, 1979] that there is no decision theory that is tailored to Shafer's theory of evidential support. Indeed, it is pretty clear that using support functions alone to measure uncertainties as if they were probabilities would lead to conflict with the principle of maximizing expected utility (because they're not additive). On the other hand, since Shafer's system of support functions is a special case of the representation by convex sets of distributions, we can have very nearly a normal decision theory using Shafer's system. In computing the value of an act, we need to consider not only the support assigned to the various possible outcomes or states of affairs (corresponding to lower probabilities), but also the plausibilities -- corresponding to upper probabilities.)

This is true also, of course, for the more general convex set representation. We can construct an interval of expected utilty for each act. A natural reinterpretation of the principle of dominance would take an alternative a_1 to dominate an alternative a_2 whenever, for every distribution in the convex set of distributions that is regarded as possible, the expectation of a_1 is greater than that of a_2.

This eliminates some alternatives, but in general there will be a number of courses of action that are not eliminated. What we do here is another matter, one which is certainly worthy of further study. But it seems natural that minimax and minimax regret strategies are appropriate candidates for consideration under some conditions. There may well be other candidates, such as satisficing, that are appropriate under other conditions. And it may even be that the guidance proided by the motto:

Eliminate dominated alternatives! is as far as rationality alone takes us. Further pruning may depend on constraints that are local to the individual decision problems.

BIBLIOGRAPHY

Cheeseman, Peter [1985]: In Defense of Probability, IJCAI 1985, v. II, pp. 1002-1009.

de Finetti, Bruno [1937]: La Prevision: Ses Lois Logiques, Ses Sources Subjectives, Annales de l'Institute Henri Poincare 7, pp. 1-68.

Kyburg, Henry E., Jr. [1968]: Bets and Beliefs, American Philosophical Quarterly 5, pp. 54-63.

------------ [1961]: Probability and the Logic of Rational Belief, Wesleyan University Press, Middletown, Ct.

------------ [1974]: The Logical Foundations of Statistical Inference, Reidel, Dordrecht.

------------ [1984]: Theory and Measurement, Cambridge University Press, Cambridge.

------------ [1987]: Bayesian and Non-Bayesian Evidential Updating, AI Journal (forthcoming).

Loui, Ronald P. [1987]: Compputing Reference Classes, this volume.

McCarthy, John, and Hayes, Patrick [1969]: Some Philosophical Problems from the Standpoint of Artificial Intelligence, Machine Intelligence 4, pp. 463-502.

Pearl, Judea [1985]: Fusion, Propagation, and Structuring in Bayesian Networks, TR CSD-850022, UCLA, Los Angeles.

Seidenfeld, Teddy [1979]: Statistical Evidence and Belief Functions, PSA 1978, Asquith and Hacking (eds), Philosophy of Science Association, East Lansing.

Computing Reference Classes

Ronald P. Loui

Depts. of Computer Science and Philosophy
University of Rochester
Rochester, NY 14627

For any system with limited statistical knowledge, the combination of evidence and the interpretation of sampling information require the determination of the right reference class (or of an adequate one).

The present note (1) discusses the use of reference classes in evidential reasoning, and (2) discusses implementations of Kyburg's rules for reference classes. This paper contributes the first frank discussion of how much of Kyburg's system is needed to be powerful, how much can be computed effectively, and how much is philosophical fat.

1. Reference Classes.

AI discussions on probability have perenially revolved around two problems: what to do with conflicting evidence, and how to get by without a lot of statistical knowledge. Each of these problems can be addressed by an adequate theory of how reference classes are selected. This section introduces reference classes.

Hans Reichenbach left modern philosophers of probability with a single task: in order to determine an event's probability, determine the most specific class to which the event belongs, and about which adequate statistics are known [Rei49]. This class is the reference class; we refer to its statistics in order to determine the probability. Suppose I know about the next Mets game, "m", that it is one in which Dwight Gooden will pitch, "Dm", and one to be played at home, "Hm", and one in which Keith Hernandez will bat, "Km"; I want to know the probability that the game will be a Mets' victory, P("Vm"). I have statistics about (or have an expert's degree of belief in) the per cent of Mets home games that are Mets' victories,

%($\{x : Hx\}$, $\{x : Vx\}$), or just %(H, V),

and the per cent of Dwight Gooden home games that are Mets' victories,

%(H & D, V),

but no statistics (or beliefs) relating Keith Hernandez games to victories, whether at home or not, whether in conjunction with Dwight Gooden or not.

Some are willing to supply the missing numbers,

e.g. %(H & D & K, V),

by procedure or by fiat. But A.I. has left the age when inventing such numbers was condoned. Something must be done with the statistics that are legitimately known.

According to Reichenbach and his followers, if %(H & D, V) is known, then it gives the probability of the win. This is because "H & D" defines a more specific class than "H".

Statistics for the most specific class may not be available. Consider the most specific possible class: the singleton set. Suppose "m" is an "M" game, "Mm" is true, where "M" is the predicate that individuates "m": i.e., "games identical to m". "M" could be analyzed as:

"(λx)(Hx & Dx & $M_1 x$ & $M_2 x$ & . . .)"

Then "M" defines the most specific class to which m belongs, and is a singleton. But %(M, V) is surely not known, or else P("Vm") is a trivial query. We don't usually want the probability to come from statistics on V's among M's. Rules are needed to point out that only the "H & D" part of "M" is useful here. Systems of probability have been constructed on such rules.

Reichenbachian rules say what to do with evidence when it is conflicting or incomplete. When appropriate, the rules mandate combination of evidence via purely set-theoretic axioms. Set theory allows the construction of "%" statements from other "%" statements. At other times, the rules throw out information that is simply irrelevant. For example, the "M_1 & M_2 . . ." part of "M" is useless. Discarding irrelevant information is natural in evidential reasoning, though it is suppressed by the applied statistician in practice. Rules governing this practice need to be made explicit.

There is a way of making this point forceful to Bayesians. If

"Hm & Dm & Km"

is the total evidence, then P("Vm") is given by

P("Vm" | "Hm & Dm & Km").

Suppose, however, that this conditional is not known, and that what is known is just

P("Vm" | "Hm & Dm") and P("Vm" | "Hm").

Then some logical principles should determine that the total relevant, or total useful knowledge is "Hm & Dm". These logical principles should say what to do when there is some knowledge about P("Vm" | "Hm & Dm & Km") when it is only poor knowledge, such as belonging to the interval [.1, .9].

Even if the Bayesian knows these conditionals precisely, there is the matter of interpreting sampling information. Some Bayesians feel they should base their probability judgements not only on opinion, but on prior opinion modified by the experience of sampling. Sampling leads to k victories out of n Mets games, which leads to a posterior distribution on the probability of a victory. But which sampling? There are the samples of (a) Mets games played at home, (b) Mets games pitched by Dwight Gooden at home, and (c) Mets games in which Keith Hernandez went to bat. There may be no games in which Gooden pitched, Hernandez went to bat, and the Mets were at home. What if there was only one such game? There are no doubt differences in the amount of data in each sample; hence, different samples lead to posteriors based on different amounts of experience. If the Bayesian values experience, the choice matters.

Before asking in knee-jerk fashion what are to be the "weights for combination," some have asked what are the logical grounds for choosing among them. If the Mets are different from last year, last year's record doesn't matter. If they're on a winning streak, the relevant sample information should again be restricted. What would reflect this in the data? There may be Bayesian answers to such questions, but they are answers to the question of which reference class to use.

2. Kyburg's Strategy and Its Capabilities.

Henry Kyburg based his theory of probability on the determination of reference classes (so did John Pollock [7, 8]). Kyburg's definitions first appeared in 1961 as a solution to the problems that led Carnap to Bayesianism. So it cannot be classified under Peter Cheeseman's taxonomy [2] as "invented new formalism." [4] is the complete presentation. [5] is a more cogent formulation.

2.1. The Idea.

The system follows Reichenbach, except that it uses interval-valued statistics instead of real-valued statistics. Intervals are associated with classes; e.g., %(H, V) = [.3, .5].

A class is better than another if it is more specific, unless its interval is weaker. An interval is weaker than another if the first contains the second (it is stronger if the converse holds; see figure 1).

Consider what should happen if

%(H & D & K, V) is [.1, .6], and
%(H, V) is [.4, .8].

The former is better, because its class is more specific ("H & D & K" is a subset of "H") and its interval is not weaker. Meanwhile, if

%(H & D & K, V) is [0, 1], and
%(H, V) is [.3, .5],

the latter is better, due to the strength of its interval ([.3, .5] is contained in [0, 1]).

Nested intervals are supposed to signal agreement; non-nested intervals are supposed to signal disagreement, even if they overlap considerably.

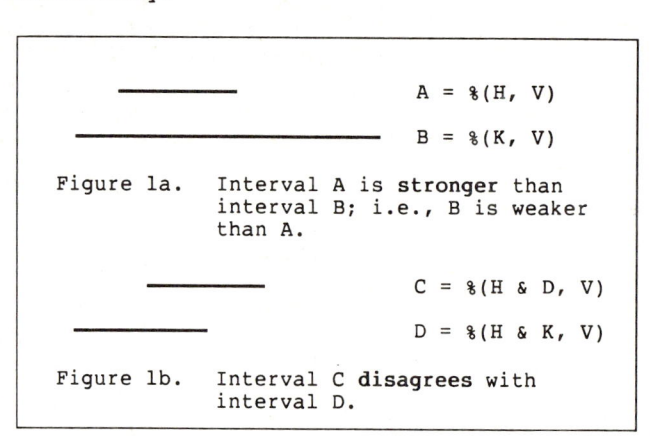

```
                ─────────────              A = %(H, V)
           ─────────────────────           B = %(K, V)

   Figure 1a.    Interval A is stronger than
                 interval B; i.e., B is weaker
                 than A.

                  ──────────               C = %(H & D, V)
       ──────────                          D = %(H & K, V)

   Figure 1b.    Interval C disagrees with
                 interval D.
```

Comparing

%(H, V) = [.4, .8], and
%(K, V) = [.3, .7],

neither is better. Between the classes H and K, neither is more specific. As for the intervals [.4, .8] and [.3, .7]; they are non-nested, so they disagree. Since neither class is useable, another class must be sought. Note that Kyburg doesn't just intersect or take unions of non-nested intervals in order to resolve their disagreement.

In order to determine the probability of t, a sentence in a formal language, relative to a base of knowledge,
   1. Find statements of the form: "t ≡ (x ∈ Z)";
      i.e., isolate the events relevant to determining the

probability in question;
e.g., "(I win bet b) ≡
(m ∈ the set of Mets victories)".

2. Now for each sentence "x ∈ Y",
   i.e., for each property Y of x,
   e.g., "m ∈ the set of home games: {x : Hx}"
   find the strongest statistical statement for property Z
   among class Y: "%(Y, Z) = [p, q]".
   These are the potentially useful statistics.
   Y's are "candidate" reference classes.

3. The 4-tuple < x, Y, Z, [p, q] > is an "inference structure for t."

4. Collect all such inference structures and call the set S.

5. Find IS*, the strongest member of S that "dominates" every member of S that disagrees with it (these are defined below).

6. If IS* is < x*, Y*, Z*, [p*, q*] >,
   then Prob(t) = [p*, q*].

Inference structures disagree when their intervals disagree (i.e., when their intervals don't nest). IS1 dominates IS2 when IS1 "reflects" IS2 and IS2 doesn't "reflect" IS1. IS1 can reflect IS2 in any of a number of ways. The most interesting way is for the class of one to be a subset of the class of the other. This is "subset reflection." If the statistics for Gooden games at home disagree with the statistics for games at home, then subset reflection will make the statistics for Gooden games at home preferred. Subset reflection takes the most specific class when there is disagreement.

2.2. The Achievement.

Here's the achievement. Distinguish probability assertion,

   Prob("x ∈ Z") = [p, q],

from statements about specific frequencies in classes,

   "%(Y, Z) = [p, q]".

Then provide rules for selecting among such frequency statements in order to determine probability. Whatever information had been used to determine or combine probabilities, whether subjective or objective, can now be used to determine or combine frequencies. But where there is conflict there is no special problem. If one source of conflict reflects the other, there is deference. If there is no reflection, appeal is made to a third source, usually one that permits only a weaker conclusion. Where there is lack of information, again there is no special problem. The strongest

	Relation between Classes		
	IS1's Class Subset of IS2's Class	IS1's Class Superset of IS2's Class	Neither
Relation between intervals			
IS1 Stronger than IS2	IS1	IS1	IS1
IS1 Weaker than IS2	IS2	IS2	IS2
IS1 in Disagreement with IS2	IS1	IS2	neither

Figure 2. Arbitration, assuming there are only two inference structures, IS1 and IS2. Table entries say to use IS1, to use IS2, or to use neither.

permissible conclusion is drawn relative to the accepted knowledge.

2.3. Specific Constructions.

If %(H, V) and %(K, V) are known, but not %(H & K, V), some bounds on the latter can be constructed with computational effort, if there is knowledge of %(H, K), %(K, H), and so forth. The problem in general is an extremization of a non-linear objective with linear constraints.

But even if %(H & K, V) can't be determined to an informative interval, there are other interesting things to construct.

When the knowledge base contains:

"%(H, V) = $[p_1, q_1]$" and
"%(K, V) = $[p_2, q_2]$".

it should also contain:

"x ∈ V ≡ <x, x> ∈ V x V";
"<x, x> ∈ H x K"; and
"%(H x K, V x V) = [$p_1 p_2$, $q_1 q_2$]",

i.e., the knowledge base contains an inference structure based on
H x K.   (ISX)

This product class always leads to an inference structure that is relevant, and it represents something like an independence assumption. The inference structure based on the product class reflects both the inference structure based on H and the inference structure based on K.

It will almost always be reflected, in turn, by the inference structure based on the class:

$$\{<x, y> : (x \in H) \text{ and } (y \in K) \text{ and } (x \in V \equiv y \in V)\} .$$ (ISXB)

The per cent of this class's members that are in V x V is the interval

$$[g(p_1, p_2), g(q_1, q_2)]; \text{ where}$$
$$g(x, y) = xy / (1 - x - y + 2xy),$$

which is easily calculated. Using this inference structure would also be like making a kind of independence assumption (in this system, a provably better one. (ISX) and (ISXB) inference structures will disagree, and since the latter reflects the former but not vice versa, the (ISXB) construction is the most interesting.

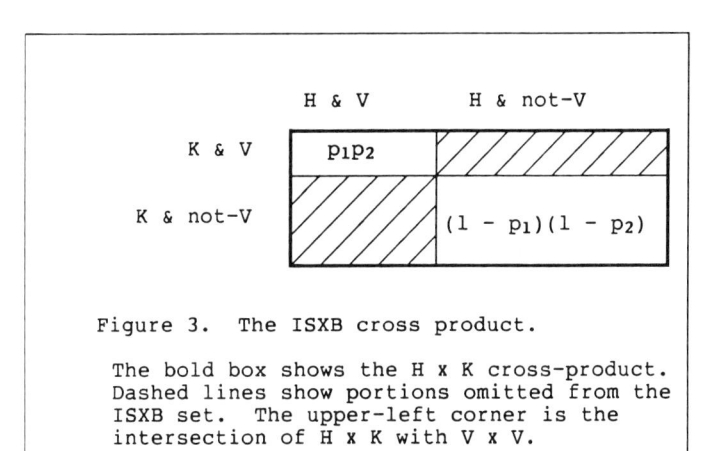

```
                    H & V           H & not-V
        K & V      ┌─────────┬─────────────┐
                   │  p₁p₂   │/////////////│
                   │         │/////////////│
        K & not-V  │/////////│             │
                   │/////////│ (1-p₁)(1-p₂)│
                   └─────────┴─────────────┘
```

Figure 3. The ISXB cross product.

The bold box shows the H x K cross-product. Dashed lines show portions omitted from the ISXB set. The upper-left corner is the intersection of H x K with V x V.

But it too can't be used unless it dominates all others with which it disagrees, including whatever is known about joint information; %(H & K, V), or equivalently, the per cent of (V x V)'s among

$$\{<x, y> : (x \in H \& K) \text{ and } (y \in H \& K) \text{ and } (x = y)\}$$

(we call the inference structure based on this latter percentage "statistically equivalent" to the inference structure based on

%(H & K, V); note that this 2-dimensional form of H & K is a subset of ISXB, but H & K is not).

In general, interference could come from any structure of the form

{<x, y> : (x ∈ H) and (y ∈ K) and
(x ∈ W ≡ y ∈ W) and other conditions}

where V is not a subset of W. For instance,

{<x, y> : (x ∈ H) and (y ∈ K)
and (x ∈ V & K ≡ y ∈ V & H)}

could interfere if its statistics were known to disagree.

We've identified only the inference structures based on (ISX) and on (ISXB) which reflect structures based on H and on K, which have statistics that are easily computable from %(H, V) and %(K, V). The one based on (ISXB) always dominates the one based on (ISX), so it is most interesting when there is conflict, and weak joint information.

What about Bayesian-like constructions? Suppose we don't know whether Dwight Gooden, Sid Fernandez, or Ron Darling will pitch, but we know the frequency with which each is picked to pitch,

%(DSR-selections, D) = $[d_3, d_4]$,
%(DSR-selections, S) = $[s_3, s_4]$,
%(DSR-selections, R) = $[r_3, r_4]$.

and we know their individual frequencies of victory:

%(D, V) = $[d_1, d_2]$,
%(S, V) = $[s_1, s_2]$,
%(R, V) = $[r_1, r_2]$.

From these statistics, we can compute bounds on

%({<x, y> : (y ∈ DSR-selections) and (x ∈ Games-of(y))},
V),

which is just what the Bayesian would have calculated. If all of the intervals are degenerate, i.e., are points, then this percentage is just the familiar weighted sum.

We also know the following facts, which allow us to use the Bayesian bounds in an inference structure:

(m ∈ V) ≡ (<m, p> ∈ V x DSR-selections),

<m, p> ∈ {<x, y> : (y ∈ DSR-selections) and
(x ∈ Games-of(y))}

We can potentially use the same weighted sum that the Bayesian is willing to use. Of course, we can't use these bounds unless the inference structure that uses them turns out to be IS*. It must, as always, reflect all other inference structures with which it disagrees.

3. Lessons from Implementation.

Figure 4 shows a trivial query, using part of the program.

```
-> (setq KBASE '(
    (% (Home Victory) (.6 .8))
    (% ((I D-Gooden Home) Victory) (.65 .95))
    (% ((I D-Gooden K-Hernandez Home) Victory) (.4 .99))
    (MEMBER m-game (I K-Hernandez D-Gooden Home))))
t
-> (prob 'm-game 'Victory)
    (I D-Gooden K-Hernandez Home) (I D-Gooden Home)
        (0 1) pass;
    (I D-Gooden K-Hernandez Home) Home
        (0 2) pass;
    (I D-Gooden Home) Home
        (1 2) pass;
    (I D-Gooden K-Hernandez Home) (I D-Gooden Home) Home
        (0 1 2) pass;

<       new candidate  Home (.60 .80)
failed > (I D-Gooden Home) (.65 .95)

<       new candidate (I D-Gooden Home) (.65 .95)
no dis > (I D-Gooden K-Hernandez Home) (.40 .99)
no dis > (I D-Gooden Home) (.65 .95)
reflect > Home (.60 .80)

        Prob (MEMBER m-game Victory) = (.65 .95)
        w.r.c. (I D-Gooden Home)
```

Figure 4. A short trace on simple data.

The lines preceding and including the word "pass" refer to (ISXB) combinations, which the reasoner chose not to add to KBASE. The candidate class "Home" failed because of an unreflected disagreement with the class "(I D-Gooden Home)", which is the intersection of D-Gooden games and Home games.

This latter class turns out to be the reference class, as its inference structure reflects the inference structure based on the candidate class "Home".

3.1. So Much Set Theoretic Computation.

> Lesson:
> The better you are with set theory, the better you'll be at computing reference classes.

Finding candidate reference classes and determining reflection are by far the major computations. Both are intensively set-theoretic.

3.1.a. Finding Classes.

Finding candidate classes starts with chaining on biconditionals. We implemented the biconditional chaining, but in practice, it's dispensable logical convenience. We want the probability of t. The equality/biconditionality reasoner leads to a set of pairs $<x_i, z_i>$, such that for each i,

(IFF t (MEMBER x_i z_i)) is true.

For each of these x_i, we have to find the sets to which it is known to belong. There is a choice (we implemented the latter, but now prefer the former):
 a) chain forward on those sets to which x_i is known to belong, and their supersets, y_j. Then either look for statistical statements

(% (y_j z_i) (p q)) , i.e., %(y_j z_i) = [p, q],

or construct them.
 b) chain backward to try to prove

(MEMBER x_i y_j)

for each y_j whose z_i statistics are known. This method requires that all inferred statistics be done by forward chaining. For classes y_k and y_l, each of which is found to contain x_i, try to discover reflection by attempting proofs of the form

(SUBSET y_k y_l).

3.1.b. Computing Reflection.

Then there is the matter of reflection. Determining reflection is either determining that one class is a subset of another, or chaining on statistically equivalent inference structures whose to find classes that do bear the subset relation. Again, the computation is intensively set-theoretic.

With educated algorithmic design, it's possible to avoid having to compute some reflection relations. Deciding disagreement of inference structures is a tremendously cheaper computation than trying to decide reflection. If IS1 and IS2 are inference structures, IS1 disagrees with IS2, and IS1 reflects IS2, then IS2 can't possibly be the reference class. So at the very least, consider the control structure in figure 5.

```
           S is the set of inference structures, obtained under (b).
           CHOICES ← S.
           CHOICES is a priority queue ordered by strength.
           Until CHOICES empties do {
              Select s* from CHOICES
              (s* is maximally strong among CHOICES).
              For every s ∈ S that disagrees with s* do {
                 If s* reflects s
                 then {
(i)                    CHOICES ← CHOICES - s;
(ii)                   if s reflects s* then exit with FAILURE.
                 }
                 else exit with FAILURE.
              } * repeat For *
              If not(FAILURE) then exit.
           } * repeat Until *

           If not(FAILURE) then take statistics from s*.

           Figure 5.  Control of search.
```

The deletions in (i) are the improvement over the naive algorithm. The line, (ii) can also be omitted for most purposes; reflection is anti-symmetric in consistent knowledge bases.

3.1.c. Reflection without Proofs.

We can now explain why (a) seems more attractive than (b). Even with the shortcuts for computing reflection, there are too many proofs attempted. Instead, chain forward through known inclusion relations using one's favorite set-theoretic axioms. For every set found, one has simultaneously determined a candidate class and identified which other classes it reflects, i.e., which sets are its supersets.

The relations between inference structures direct the search, rather than lead to more proofs.

3.2. Reducing the Language.

> Lesson:
> Set-theoretic language just gets in the way. The rules are too general: use the most basic of Kyburg's rules (those that I've outlined) and restrict the languages over which probability is computed.

The set-theory that is needed is significantly less elaborate than what Kyburg envisions, or what Brown [1] or Pastre [6] have provided for, in the past.

3.2.a. Restricting the Set-Forming Operations.

It is important to represent and manipulate sets like

$\{x : (x \in H)$ and $(y \in K)$ and $(x \in V \equiv y \in V)\}$.

But for all the effort required to implement this set-theoretic structure faithfully, it is quite inexpensive to supply the relevant information manually. In fact, rather than name the set with a complex expression that shows its structure, in practice we found it easier just to give it an atomic name and assert the relevant relations to other sets.

We found we could get along with a quite restricted language, where all sets are named by creative intersection. The details are not important. What is important is that the cross-product constructions from section 2.3, and the Bayesian constructions can be named with less set-theoretic machinery.

> EMORPH is the union of
> $\{<x, y> : x = y\}$, and
> $\{<x, y, z> : x = y = z\}$, etc.

(so it acts like it has polymorphic dimension on intersections; "E" for "equality").

> (BMORPH V) is also a union, of
> $\{<x, y> : x \in V \equiv y \in V\}$, and
> $\{<x, y, z> : x \in V \equiv y \in V \equiv z \in V\}$, etc.

("B" for "biconditional").
Now

> (INTERSECTION (X a b) EMORPH) names the set
> $\{<x, y> : (x \in a)$ and $(y \in b)$ and $(x = y)\}$,

And

(INTERSECTION (X a b) (BMORPH V)) names the set
$\{<x, y> : (x \in a) \text{ and } (y \in b) \text{ and } (x \in V \equiv y \in V)\}$.

With this kind of naming, all of the classes we've identified as important can be named and manipulated easily. A simple reasoner about inclusions, such as a type reasoner, will suffice if it can be made to handle multidimensional objects, intersections, and some sophisticated functions like those of functional programming languages.

We no longer need to provide for set abstractions that use arbitrary logical and mathematical syntax. For instance, we no longer need to worry about "and" and "iff" in our names of sets.

3.2.b. A Minimal Language.

An even starker language we've considered for applications uses no asserted subset relations. No two sets with atomic names are known to be subsets. One set is a subset of another just in case the name of the first set syntactically shows that it is the intersection of the second set with some additional sets. In this language, we represent only the classes, their intersections, and their "BMORPH" combinations: i.e., the (ISXB)-like products discussed in section 2.3.

Define the function EXTERN-PROD. Let

(EXTERN-PROD ((a b c d)) V),

or just

$[abcd]_V$,

be

$\{<x, y, z, t> : (x \in a) \text{ and } (y \in b) \text{ and } (z \in c) \text{ and } (t \in d) \text{ and } (x = y = z = t)\}$.

Also let

(EXTERN-PROD ((a b c) (d)) V),

or just

$[abc,d]_V$,

be

$\{<x, y, z, t> : (x = y = z) \text{ and } (z \in V \equiv t \in V) \text{ and } (z \in a \& b \& c) \text{ and } (t \in d)\}$.

We'll continue to use the notation that uses only brackets and commas, with V implicit. [abc,d] is the class that would be formed if one took the joint information about the class a & b & c, and did the (ISXB)-style product with the class d. Since this kind of product is commutative, and so is set-intersection, it doesn't matter if we write [abc,d] or [d,abc] or [d,bca], etc.

In this language, it's very easy to see which classes to appeal to when there is conflict, and what are the reflection relations among inference structures built on these classes. Suppose x ∈ [abcd]. For the probability of x in V, appeal first to

%([abcd] , V).

If there is knowledge about

%([abc] , V) and
%(d, V),

then compute

%([abc,d] , V).

Consider using it, if it is stronger than

%([abcd] , V).

If it is, then [abc,d] must also agree with all that are computable among:

[ab,cd], [abd,c], [ac,bd], [acd,b], [ad,bc],
[bcd,a], [bd,a,c],

and so forth. The only classes that [abc,d] is allowed to disagree with are those reflected classes such as

[ab,c,d] and [ab,c],

which can be determined by the following easy rule. Reflected classes are composed of constituents, such as "ab", and "c", and "d". For each constituent in the reflected class (e.g., "ab" in [ab,c,d]) there is some constituent of the reflecting class (e.g. "abc" in [abc,d]) that contains all of the first constituent's characters (here, characters correspond to names of sets).

The implementation based on this minimal language was pleasingly fast; computing reference classes bacame faster than estimating intervals from sampling information.

4. Concluding Discussion.

Kyburg's system does solve some perplexing questions inherent in evidential reasoning, including: 1) when does an independence assumption conflict with joint information; 2) which conclusion can be drawn, if any, when there is disagreeing evidence; and 3) how to choose between evidence that is strong but ill-founded, and evidence that is well-founded but weak.

The key elements are: 1) the use of intervals, so that probability assertions can vary in strength, and 2) the distinction between frequency and probability assertion, so that conflict among statistical information can be arbitrated outside of the probability calculus.

We implemented the system in some generality, and found that the difficulties were in deciding how much set-theoretic language and how much set-theoretic inference to use.

In order to simplify, we studied exactly which inference structures would be useful, of the many that satisfy the definitions. In particular, we know that when there is conflict between two classes, e.g., %(H, V) and %(K, V), one should appeal to %(H & K, V) if it is precise, or else to %([H, K] , V), if it is agreeable with what is in fact known about %(H & K, V).

We have thus demonstrated the ideas, both in a rich theorem-proving-like inference engine, and also in a fast, effective engine capable of processing a lot of data quickly. A satisfactory general inference engine could be based on a multidimensional type reasoner, and applications could be successfully based on the minimal language, which makes all reflection relations obvious by inspection.

In Kyburg's favor, the system copes with the traditional problems as advertised. In his disfavor, the system does not have much locality; bits of knowledge in all sorts of a knowledge base's corners can be relevant, and are not easily pre-processed.

The probability intervals produced are intuitively appealing. The next step is to see how well these ideas fare in applications.

```
-> (setq KBASE '(
      (% (Home Victory) (.6 .8))
      (% ((I D-Gooden Home) Victory) (.65 .95))
      (% ((I D-Gooden K-Hernandez Home) Victory) (.4 .99))
      (% (K-Hernandez Victory) (.7 .75))
      (MEMBER m-game (I K-Hernandez D-Gooden Home))))
t
-> (prob 'm-game 'Victory)
      K-Hernandez (I D-Gooden Home)
          (0 2) add; (.81 .98)
      K-Hernandez Home
          (0 3) add; (.78 .92)

<       new candidate  K-Hernandez (.70 .75)
failed > (XP (Home) (K-Hernandez)) (.78 .92)

<       new candidate  Home (.60 .80)
failed > (XP (Home) (K-Hernandez)) (.78 .92)

<       new candidate  (XP (Home) (K-Hernandez)) (.78 .92)
failed > (XP (D-Gooden Home) (K-Hernandez)) (.81 .98)

<       new candidate  (I D-Gooden Home) (.65 .95)
failed > (XP (D-Gooden Home) (K-Hernandez)) (.81 .98)

<       new candidate  (XP (D-Gooden Home) (K-Hernandez)) (.81 .98)
reflect > (XP (Home) (K-Hernandez)) (.78 .92)
no dis > (XP (D-Gooden Home) (K-Hernandez)) (.81 .98)
reflect > K-Hernandez (.70 .75)
no dis > (I D-Gooden K-Hernandez Home) (.40 .99)
reflect > (I D-Gooden Home) (.65 .95)
reflect > Home (.60 .80)

      Prob (MEMBER m-game Victory) = (.81 .98)
      w.r.c. (XP (D-Gooden Home) (K-Hernandez))
```

Figure 6. A short trace showing use of ISXB classes.

"(XP (Home) (K-Hernandez))" is [Home,K-Hernandez], i.e., the ISXB-style product of the class "Home" with the class "K-Hernandez". Two product classes are added, prior to sorting through the inference structure to find IS*.

The reference class turns out to be the ISXB-style product of the class "K-Hernandez" with the intersection of "D-Gooden" and "Home". Note that the positive evidence in each class has been reinforced in the product class; the intervals [.7, .75] and [.65, .95] yielded the interval [.81, .98].

Acknowledgements.

This research is dedicated to my early mentor, the late Gene Nathan Johnson.

Henry Kyburg was indispensable in this study; ISXB-style products are basically his idea. A smaller implementation by Matt Miller was useful for comparison. This work was supported by a grant from the U.S. Army Signals Warfare Laboratory.

References.

[1] Brown, F. M. "Towards the Automation of Set Theory and its Logic," AI 10, 1978.
[2] Cheeseman, P. "In Defense of Probability," IJCAI 9, 1985.
[3] Kyburg, H. Probability and the Logic of Rational Belief, Wesleyan University Press, 1961.
[4] ----------. The Logical Foundations of Statistical Inference, Reidel, 1974.
[5] ----------. "The Reference Class," Philosophy of Science 50, 1983.
[6] Pastre, D. "Towards the Automation of Set Theory and its Logic," AI 10, 1978.
[7] Pollock, J. "A Theory of Direct Inference," Theory and Decision 15, 1983.
[8] ----------. "Foundations for Direct Inference," Theory and Decision 17, 1984.
[9] Reichenbach, H. The Theory of Probability. U. C. Berkeley Press, 1949.

DISTRIBUTED REVISION OF BELIEF COMMITMENT IN COMPOSITE EXPLANATIONS * †

Judea Pearl

Cognitive Systems Laboratory, UCLA Computer Science Department, Los Angeles, CA. 90024

ABSTRACT

This paper extends the applications of belief-networks to include the revision of belief **commitments**, i.e., the categorical acceptance of a subset of hypotheses which, together, constitute the most satisfactory explanation of the evidence at hand. A coherent model of non-monotonic reasoning is established and distributed algorithms for belief revision are presented. We show that, in singly-connected networks, the most satisfactory explanation can be found in linear time by a message-passing algorithm similar to the one used in belief updating. In multiply-connected networks, the problem may be exponentially hard but, if the network is sparse, topological considerations can be used to render the interpretation task tractable. In general, finding the most probable combination of hypotheses is no more complex than computing the degree of belief for any individual hypothesis. Applications to medical diagnosis are illustrated.

1. INTRODUCTION

People's beliefs are normally cast in categorical terms, often involving not just one, but a composite set of propositions which, stated together, offer a satisfactory account of the observed data. For example, a physician might state, "This patient apparently suffers from two simultaneous disorders A and B which, due to condition C, caused the deterioration of organ D." Except for the hedging term "apparently," such a composite statement conveys a sense of unreserved commitment (of beliefs) to a set of four hypotheses. The individual components in the explanation above are meshed together by mutually enforced cause-effect relationships, forming a cohesive whole; the removal of any one component from the discourse would tarnish the completeness of the entire explanation.

Such a sense of cohesiveness normally suggests that a great amount of refuting evidence would have to be gathered before the current interpretation would undergo a revision. Moreover, once a revision is activated, it will likely change the entire content of the interpretation, not merely its level of plausibility. Another characteristic of coherent explanations is that they do not assign degrees of certainty to any individual hypothesis in the argument; neither do they contain information about alternative, next-to-best combinations of hypotheses.

---

* This work was supported in part by the National Science Foundation, Grant DCR 83-13875 and U.S. Army Center for Signals Warfare, DAAB10-86-C-0603.
† An expanded version of this paper will appear in *Artificial Intelligence*, 1987.

Even the certainty of the accepted composite explanation is only seldom consulted; most everyday activities are predicated upon beliefs which, despite being provisional do not seem to be muddled with varying shades of uncertainty. Consider, for example the sentence: "John decided to have a bowl of cereal but, finding the cupboard empty, he figured out that Mary must have finished it at breakfast." Routine actions such as reaching for the cupboard are normally performed without the slightest hesitation or reservation, thus reflecting adherence to firmly-held beliefs (of finding cereal there). When new facts are observed, refuting current beliefs, a process of belief revision takes place; new beliefs replace old ones, also to be firmly held, until refuted.

These behavioral features are somewhat at variance with past work on belief network models of evidential reasoning [Pearl, 1986a]. Thus far, this work has focussed on the task of *belief updating*, i.e., assigning each hypothesis in a network a degree of belief, $BEL (\cdot)$, consistent with all observations. The function BEL changes smoothly and incrementally with each new item of evidence.

This paper extends the applications of Bayesian analysis and belief networks models to include revision of belief *commitments*, i.e., the tentative categorical acceptance of a subset of hypotheses which, together, constitute the most satisfactory explanation of the evidence at hand. Using probabilistic terminology, that task amounts to finding the most probable instantiation of all hypothesis variables, given the observed data. The resulting output is an optimal list of jointly accepted propositions, that may vary dynamically as more evidence obtains.*

In principle, this optimization task seems intractable because enumerating and rating all possible instantiations is computationally prohibitive and, instead, many heuristic techniques have been developed in various fields of application. In pattern recognition the problem became known as the "multimembership problem" [Ben Bassat 1980]; in medical diagnosis it is known as "multiple disorders" [Ben Bassat et al. 1980; Pople 1982; Reggia, Nau & Wang 1983; Cooper 1984; Peng & Reggia 1986] and in circuit diagnosis as "multiple-faults" [Reiter 1985; deKleer & Williams 1986].

This paper departs from previous work by emphasizing a *distributed* computation approach to belief revision. The impact of each new piece of evidence is viewed as a perturbation that propagates through the network via local communication among neighboring concepts, with minimum external supervision. At equilibrium, each variable will be bound to a definite value which, together with all other value assignments, is the best interpretation of the evidence. The main reason for adopting this distributed message-passing paradigm is that it provides a natural mechanism for exploiting the independencies embodied in sparsely-constrained systems and translating them, by subtask decomposition, into substantial reduction in complexity. Additionally, distributed propagation is inherently "transparent," namely, the intermediate steps, by virtue of their reflecting interactions only among semantically related variables, are conceptually meaningful. This facilitates the use of natural, object-oriented programming tools and helps establish confidence in the final result.

We show that, in singly-connected networks, the most satisfactory explanation can be found in linear time by a message-passing algorithm similar to the one used in belief updating. In multiply-connected networks, the problem may be exponentially hard but, if the network is sparse, topological considerations can be used to render the interpretation task tractable. In general, assembling the most believable combination of hypotheses is no more complex than com-

---

* Note that this list cannot be computed from the belief assigned to individual variables. For example, in diagnosing malfunctioning systems, each component is individually more likely to be operational, while the optimal list should identify at least one faulty component.

puting the degree of belief for any individual hypothesis.

This paper comprises five sections. Section 2 provides a brief summary of belief updating in Bayesian networks, as described in [Pearl 1986a]. It defines the semantics of network representations, describes the task of belief updating and summarizes the propagation rules which lead to coherent updating in singly connected networks. Section 3 develops the propagation rules for belief revision in singly connected networks and compares them to those governing belief updating. Section 4 extends the propagation scheme to multiply-connected networks using two methods, clustering and conditioning. Section 5 illustrates the method of conditioning on a simple medical-diagnosis example, involving four diseases and four symptoms.

2. REVIEW OF BELIEF UPDATING IN BAYESIAN BELIEF NETWORKS

Bayesian belief networks [Pearl, 1986a] are directed acyclic graphs (DAGS) in which the nodes represent propositional variables, the arcs signify the existence of direct causal influences between the linked propositions and the strength of these influences are quantified by the conditional probabilities of each variable given the state of its parents. Thus, if the nodes in the graph represent the ordered variables $X_1, X_2, \cdots, X_n$, then each variable X_i draws arrows from a subset S_i of variables perceived to be "direct causes" of X_i, i.e., S_i is a set of X_i's predecessors satisfying $P(x_i \mid s_i) = P(x_i \mid x_1, x_2, \cdots x_{i-1})$. A complete and consistent parametrization of the model can be obtained by specifying, for each X_i, an assessment of $P(x_i \mid s_i)$. The product of all these local assessments,

$$P(x_1, x_2, \cdots x_n) = \Pi_i P(x_i \mid s_i),$$

constitutes a joint-probability model consistent with the assessed quantities. Thus, for example, the distribution corresponding to the network of Figure 1 can be written by inspection:[1]

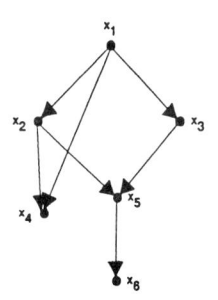

$$P(x_1, \cdots, x_6) = P(x_6 \mid x_5) P(x_5 \mid x_2, x_3) P(x_4 \mid x_1, x_2) P(x_3 \mid x_1) P(x_2 \mid x_1) P(x_1)$$

Figure 1. A typical Bayesian network representing the distribution
$P(x_6 \mid x_5) P(x_5 \mid x_2, x_3) P(x_4 \mid x_1, x_2) P(x_3 \mid x_1) P(x_2 \mid x_1) P(x_1)$.

A Bayesian network provides a clear graphical representation for the essential independence relationships embedded in the underlying causal model. These independencies can be detected by the following *DAG-separation* criterion: if all paths between X_i and X_j are "blocked" by a subset S of variables, then X_i is independent of X_j, given the values of the vari-

---

[1] Probabilistic formulae of this kind are shorthand notation for the statement that for any instantiation $x_1, x_2, \cdots, x_n$ of the variables $X_1, X_2, \cdots, X_n$, the probability of the joint event $(X_1 = x_1) \& \cdots \& (X_n = x_n)$ is equal to the product of the probabilities of the corresponding conditional events
$(X_1 = x_1), (X_2 = x_2 \text{ if } X_1 = x_1), (X_3 = x_3 \text{ if } X_2 = x_2 \& X_1 = x_1) \cdots$

ables in S. A path is "blocked" by S if it contains a member of S between two diverging or two cascaded arrows or, alternatively, if it contains two arrows converging at node X_k, and neither X_k nor any of its descendants is in S. In particular, each variable X_i is independent of both its grandparents and its non-descendant siblings, given the values of the variables in its parent set S_i. In Figure 1, for example, X_2 and X_3 are independent, given either $\{X_1\}$ or $\{X_1, X_4\}$, because the two paths between X_2 and X_3 are blocked by either one of these sets. However, X_2 and X_3 may not be independent given $\{X_1, X_6\}$ because X_6, as a descendant of X_5, "unblocks" the head-to-head connection at X_5, thus opening a pathway between X_2 and X_3.

Once a Bayesian network is constructed, it can be used as an interpretation engine, namely, newly arriving information will set up a parallel constraint-propagation process which ripples multidirectionally through the networks until, at equilibrium, every variable is assigned a measure of belief consistent with the axioms of probability calculus. Incoming information may be of two types: *specific evidence* and *virtual evidence*. Specific evidence corresponds to direct observations which validate, with certainty, the values of some variables already in the network. Virtual evidence corresponds to judgment based on undisclosed observations which affect the belief of some variables in the network. Such evidence is modeled by dummy nodes representing the undisclosed observations connected to the variables affected by the observations.

The objective of updating beliefs coherently by purely local computations can be fully realized if the network is singly-connected, namely, if there is only one undirected path between any pair of nodes. These include causal trees, where each node has a single parent, as well as networks with multi-parent nodes, representing events with several causal factors. We shall first review the propagation scheme in singly-connected networks and then discuss (in Section 5) how it can be extended to multiply-connected networks.

Let variable names be denoted by capital letters, e.g., U, V, X, Y, Z and their associated values by lower case letters, e.g., u, v, x, y, z. All incoming information, both specific and virtual, will be denoted by e to connote *evidence* and will be represented by nodes whose values are held constant. For the sake of clarity, we will distinguish between the fixed conditional probabilities that label the links, e.g., $P(x|u, v)$, and the dynamic values of the updated node probabilities. The latter will be denoted by $BEL(x)$, which reflects the overall belief accorded to the proposition $X = x$ by all evidence so far received. Thus,

$$BEL(x) \overset{\Delta}{=} P(x|e), \qquad (1)$$

where e is the value combination of all instantiated variables.

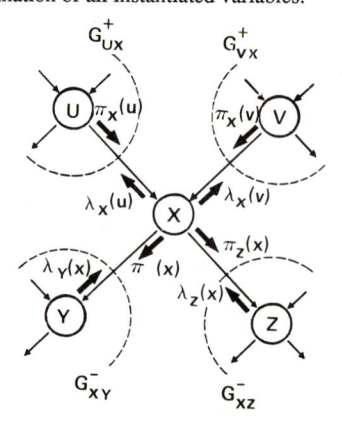

Figure 2. Fragment of a singly connected network with multiple parents, illustrating graph partitioning and message parameters.

Consider a fragment of a singly-connected Bayesian network, as depicted in Figure 2. The link $U \to X$ partitions the graph into two: a *tail* sub-graph, G_{UX}^+, and a *head* sub-graph, G_{UX}^-, the complement of G_{UX}^+. Each of these two sub-graphs may contain a set of evidence, which we shall call respectively e_{UX}^+ and e_{UX}^-. Likewise, the links $V \to X$, $X \to Y$ and $X \to Z$ respectively define the sub-graphs G_{VX}^+, G_{XY}^-, and G_{XZ}^-, which may contain the respective evidence sets e_{VX}^+, e_{XY}^- and e_{XZ}^-.

The belief distribution of each variable X in the network can be computed if three types of parameters are made available:

(1) the current strength of the *causal* support, π, contributed by each incoming link to X:

$$\pi_X(u) = P(u \mid e_{UX}^+) \tag{2}$$

(2) the current strength of the *diagnostic* support, λ, contributed by each outgoing link from X:

$$\lambda_Y(x) = P(e_{XY}^- \mid x) \tag{3}$$

(3) the fixed conditional probability matrix, $P(x \mid u, v)$, which relates the variable X to its immediate parents.

Using these parameters, local belief updating can be accomplished by the following three steps, to be executed in any order:

Step 1 - Belief Updating: When node X is activated to update its parameters, it simultaneously inspects the $\pi_X(u)$ and $\pi_X(v)$ communicated by its parents and the messages $\lambda_Y(x), \lambda_Z(x) \cdots$ communicated by each of its sons. Using this input, it then updates its belief measure as follows:

$$BEL(x) = \alpha \, \lambda_Y(x) \, \lambda_Z(x) \sum_{u,v} P(x \mid u, v) \, \pi_X(u) \, \pi_X(v), \tag{4}$$

where α is a normalizing constant, rendering $\sum_x BEL(x) = 1$.

Step 2 - Updating λ: Using the messages received, each node computes new λ messages to be sent to its parents. For example, the new message $\lambda_X(u)$ that X sends to its parent U is computed by:

$$\lambda_X(u) = \alpha \sum_v [\pi_X(v) \sum_x \lambda_Y(x) \, \lambda_Z(x) \, P(x \mid u, v)] \tag{5}$$

Step 3 - Updating π: Each node computes new π messages to be sent to its children. For example, the new $\pi_Y(x)$ message that X sends to its child Y is computed by:

$$\pi_Y(x) = \alpha \, \lambda_Z(x) \, [\sum_{u,v} P(x \mid u, v) \, \pi_X(u) \, \pi_X(v)] \tag{6}$$

These three steps summarize the six steps described in [Pearl 1986] and can be executed in any order (Step 1 can be skipped when $BEL(x)$ is of no interest.) An alternative way of calculating $BEL(x)$ would be to multiply the incoming and outgoing messages on some link from X to any of its children, e.g.,

$$BEL(x) = \alpha \, \pi_Y(x) \, \lambda_Y(x), \tag{7}$$

where $\pi_Y(x)$ is calculated via (6).

This concurrent message-passing process is both initiated and terminated at the peripheral nodes of the network, subject to the following boundary conditions:

1. **Anticipatory Node:** representing an uninstantiated variable with no successors. For such a node, X, we set $\lambda_Y(x) = (1, 1 \cdots, 1)$.

2. **Evidence Node:** representing a variable with instantiated value. If variable X assumes the value x', we introduce a dummy child Z with

$$\lambda_Z(x) = \begin{cases} 1 & \text{if } x = x' \\ 0 & \text{otherwise} \end{cases}$$

This implies that, if X has children, $Y_1, \cdots, Y_m$, each child should receive the same message $\pi_{Y_j}(x) = \lambda_Z(x)$ from X.

3. **Root Node:** representing a variable with no parents. For each root variable X, we introduce a dummy parent U, permanently instantiated to $U = 1$, and set the conditional probability on the link $U \rightarrow X$ equal to the prior probability of X, i.e., $P(x \mid u) = P(x)$.

In [Pearl 1986a], it is shown that, in singly connected networks, the semantics of the messages produced via Eqs.(4), (5) and (6) are preserved, namely,

$$\lambda_X(u) = P(e^-_{UX} \mid u), \quad \pi_Y(x) = P(x \mid e^+_{XY}), \tag{8}$$

and

$$BEL(x) = P(x \mid e) \tag{9}$$

3. BELIEF REVISION IN SINGLY-CONNECTED NETWORKS

Let W stand for the set of all variables considered, including those in e. Any assignment of values to the variables in W consistent with e will be called an *extension, explanation* or *interpretation* of e. Our problem is to find an extension w^* which maximizes the conditional probability $P(w \mid e)$. In other words, $W = w^*$ is the *most probable explanation (MPE)* of the evidence at hand if

$$P(w^* \mid e) = \max_w P(w \mid e) \tag{10}$$

The task of finding w^* will be executed locally, by letting each variable X compute the function

$$BEL^*(x) = \max_{w'_X} P(x, w'_X \mid e) \tag{11}$$

where $W'_X = W - X$. Thus, $BEL^*(x)$ stands for the probability of the most probable extension of e which is also consistent with the hypothetical assignment $X = x$. Unlike $BEL(x)$, Eq.(1), $BEL^*(x)$ need not sum to unity over x.

The propagation scheme presented below is based on the following philosophy: For every value x of a singleton variable X, there is a best extension of the complementary variables W'_X. Due to the many independence relationships embedded in the network, the problem of finding the best extension of $X = x$ can be decomposed into that of finding the best complementary extension to each of the neighboring variables, then using this information to choose the best value of X. This process of decomposition (resembling the principle of optimality in dynamic programming) can be applied recursively until, at the network's periphery, we meet evidence variables whose values are predetermined, and the process halts.

3.1 Deriving the Propagation Rules

We consider again the fragment of a singly-connected network in Figure 2 and denote by W_{XY}^+ and W_{XY}^- the subset of variables contained in the respective sub-graphs G_{XY}^+ and G_{XY}^-. Removing any node X would partition the network into the sub-graphs G_X^+ and G_X^- containing two sets of variables, W_X^+ and W_X^-, and (possibly) two sets of evidence, e_X^+ and e_X^-, respectively.

Using this notation, we can write

$$P(w^* | e) = \max_{x, w_X^+, w_X^-} P(w_X^+, w_X^-, x | e_X^+, e_X^-) \qquad (12)$$

The conditional independence of W_X^+ and W_X^-, given X, and the entailments $e_X^+ \subseteq W_X^+$ and $e_X^- \subseteq W_X^-$ yield:

$$P(w^* | e) = \max_{x, w_X^+, w_X^-} \frac{P(w_X^+, w_X^-, x)}{P(e_X^+, e_X^-)}$$

$$= \alpha \max_{x, w_X^+, w_X^-} P(w_X^- | x) P(x | w_X^+) P(w_X^+) \qquad (13)$$

where $\alpha = [P(e_X^+, e_X^-)]^{-1}$ is a constant, independent of the uninstantiated variables in W and would have no influence on the maximization in (13). From here on we will use the symbol α to represent any constant which need not be computed in practice, because it does not affect the choice of w^*.

Equation (13) can be rewritten as a maximum, over x, of two factors:

$$P(w^* | e) = \alpha \max_x [\max_{w_X^-} P(w_X^- | x)] [\max_{w_X^+} P(x | w_X^+) P(w_X^+)]$$

$$= \alpha \max_x \lambda^*(x) \pi^*(x) \qquad (14)$$

where

$$\lambda^*(x) = \max_{w_X^-} P(w_X^- | x) \qquad (15)$$

$$\pi^*(x) = \max_{w_X^+} P(x, w_X^+) \qquad (16)$$

Thus, if, for each x an oracle were to provide us the MPE values of the variables in W_X^-, together with the MPE values of the variables in W_X^+, we would be able to determine the best value of X by computing $\lambda^*(x)$, and $\pi^*(x)$ and then maximize their product, $\lambda^*(x) \pi^*(x)$.

We now express $\lambda^*(x)$ and $\pi^*(x)$ in such a way that they can be computed at node X from similar parameters available at X's neighbors. Writing

$$W_X^- = W_{XY}^- \cup W_{XZ}^- \quad W_X^+ = W_{UX}^+ \cup W_{VZ}^+$$
$$W_{U'X}^+ = W_{UX}^+ - U \quad W_{V'X}^+ = W_{VX}^+ - U,$$

we obtain

$$\lambda^*(x) = \max_{w_{\bar{X}Y}} P(w_{\bar{X}Y}|x) \max_{w_{\bar{X}Z}} P(w_{\bar{X}Z}|x) = \lambda_Y^*(x)\lambda_Z^*(x) \tag{17}$$

and

$$\pi^*(x) = \max_{u,v,w_{\dot{U}}^+,w_{\dot{V}}^+} [P(x|u,v) P(u,v,w_{\dot{U}}^+,w_{\dot{V}}^+)]$$

$$= \max_{u,v}[P(x|u,v) \max_{w_{\dot{U}'x}} P(u, w_{\dot{U}'x}^+) \max_{w_{\dot{V}'x}} P(v, w_{\dot{V}'x}^+)]$$

$$= \max_{u,v} P(x|u,v) \pi_X^*(u)\pi_X^*(v), \tag{18}$$

where $\lambda_Y^*(x)$ (and, correspondingly, $\lambda_Z^*(x)$) can be regarded as a message that a child, Y, sends to its parent, X:

$$\lambda_Y^*(x) = \max_{w_{\bar{X}Y}} P(w_{\bar{X}Y}|x) \tag{19}$$

Similarly,

$$\pi_X^*(u) = \max_{w_{\dot{U}'x}} P(u, w_{\dot{U}'x}^+) \tag{20}$$

can be regarded as a message that a parent U sends to its child X. Note the similarities between λ^*-π^* and λ-π in Eqs. (2) and (3).

Clearly, if these λ^* and π^* messages are available to X, it can compute its best value x^* using Eqs. (14-16). What we must show now is that, upon receiving these messages, it can send back to its neighbors the appropriate $\lambda_X^*(u)$, $\lambda_X^*(v)$, $\pi_Y^*(x)$ and $\pi_Z^*(x)$ messages, while preserving their probabilistic definitions according to Eqs. (19) and (20).

Updating π^*

Rewriting Eq. (11) as

$$BEL^*(x) = P(x, w_X^{+^*}, w_X^{-^*}|e) \tag{21}$$

and using Eqs.(15-20), we have

$$BEL^*(x) = \alpha \lambda^*(x) \pi^*(x)$$

$$= \alpha \lambda_Y^*(x)\lambda_Z^*(x) \max_{u,v} P(x|u,v)\pi_X^*(u)\pi_X^*(v) \tag{22}$$

Comparing this expression to the definition of $\pi_Y^*(x)$, we get

$$\pi_Y^*(x) = \max_{w_{\dot{X}Y}} P(x, w_{\dot{X}Y}^+) = \max_{w_{\dot{X}},w_{\bar{X}Z}} P(x, w_{\dot{X}}^+, w_{\bar{X}Z})$$

$$= \lambda_Z^*(x) \max_{u,v} P(x|u,v) \pi_X^*(u) \pi_X^*(v) \tag{23}$$

Alternatively, $\pi_Y^*(x)$ can be obtained from $BEL^*(x)$ by setting $\lambda_Y^*(x) = 1$ for all x. Thus,

$$\pi_Y^*(x) = \alpha\, BEL^*(x)\bigg|_{\lambda_Y^*(x)=1} = \alpha \frac{BEL^*(x)}{\lambda_Y^*(x)} \tag{24}$$

The division by $\lambda_Y^*(x)$ in Eq.(24) amounts to discounting the contribution of all variables in $G_{\bar{X}Y}^-$. Note that $\pi_Y^*(x)$, unlike $\pi_Y(x)$, need not sum to unity over x.

Updating λ^*

Starting with the definition

$$\lambda_X^*(u) = \max_{w_{\bar{U}X}} P(w_{\bar{U}X} | u) \qquad (25)$$

we partition $W_{\bar{U}X}$ into its constituents

$$W_{\bar{U}X} = X \cup W_{\bar{X}Y} \cup W_{\bar{X}Z}^+ \cup W_{\bar{V}'X}^+ \cup V$$

and obtain

$$\lambda_X^*(u) = \max_{x, w_{\bar{X}Y}, w_{\bar{X}Z}^+, w_{\bar{V}'X}^+, v} P(x, w_{\bar{X}Y}, w_{\bar{X}Z}^+, v, w_{\bar{V}'X}^+)$$

$$= \max_{x, v, w's} P(w_{\bar{X}Y}, w_{\bar{X}Z}^+ | w_{\bar{V}'X}^+ x, v, u) P(x, v, w_{\bar{V}'X}^+ | u)$$

$$= \max_{x, v} [\lambda_Y^*(x) \lambda_Z^*(x) P(x | u, v) \max_{w_{\bar{V}'X}^+} P(v, w_{\bar{V}'X}^+ | u)]$$

Finally, using the marginal independence of U and W_{VX}^+, we have

$$\lambda_X^*(u) = \max_{x, v} [\lambda_Y^*(x) \lambda_Z^*(x) P(x | u, v) \pi_X^*(v)] \qquad (26)$$

3.2 Summary of Propagation Rules

In general, if X has n parents, $U_1, U_2, ..., U_n$, and m children, $Y_1, Y_2, ..., Y_m$, node X receives the messages $\pi_X^*(u_i)$, $i=1,...,n$, from its parents and $\lambda_{Y_j}^*(x)$, $j=1,...,m$, from its children.

$\pi_X^*(u_i)$ stands for the probability of the most probable tail-extension of the proposition $U_i = u_i$ relative the link $U_i \to X$. This subextension is sometimes called an "explanation," or a "causal argument."

$\lambda_{Y_j}^*(x)$ stands for the conditional probability of the most probable head-extension of the proposition $X = x$ relative of the link $X \to Y_j$. This subextension is sometimes called a "prognosis" or a "forecast."

Using these $n+m$ messages together with the fixed probability $P(x | u_1, ..., u_n)$, X can identify its best value and further propagate these messages using the following three steps:

Step 1 - Updating BEL*: When node X is activated to update its parameters, it simultaneously inspects the $\pi_X^*(u_i)$ and $\lambda_{Y_j}^*(x)$ messages communicated by each of its parents and children and forms the product

$$F(x, u_1, ..., u_n) = \qquad (27)$$

$$\prod_{j=1}^{m} \lambda_{Y_j}^*(x) P(x | u_1, ..., u_n) \prod_{i=1}^{n} \pi_X^*(u_i).$$

This F function enables X to compute its $BEL^*(x)$ function and, simultaneously, identify the best value x^* from the domain of X:

where
$$x^* = \max_{x}^{-1} BEL^*(x) \tag{28}$$

$$BEL^*(x) = \alpha \max_{u_k : 1 \leq k \leq n} F(x, u_1, ..., u_n) \tag{29}$$

and α is a constant, independent of x, which need not be computed in practice.

Step 2 - Updating λ^*: Using the F function computed in step 1, node X computes the parent-bound messages by performing n vector maximizations, one for each parent:

$$\lambda_X^*(u_i) = \max_{x, u_k : k \neq i} [F(x, u_1, ..., u_n) / \pi_X^*(u_i)] \quad i = 1, ..., n \tag{30}$$

Step 3 - Updating π^*: Using the $BEL^*(x)$ function computed in step 1, node X computes the children-bound messages:

$$\pi_{Y_j}^*(x) = \alpha \frac{BEL^*(x)}{\lambda_{Y_j}^*(x)} \tag{31}$$

and posts these on the links to $Y_1, ..., Y_m$.

These steps are identical to those governing belief updating (Eqs. (4)-(6) with maximization replacing the summation. They can be viewed as tensor operations, using max for inner-product, i.e., $<AB>_{ik} = \max_{j} A_{ij} B_{jk}$ (Booker, 1987); each outgoing message is computed by taking the max-inner-products of the tensor $P(x | u_1, \cdots, u_n)$ with all incoming messages posted on the other links.

The boundary conditions are identical to those of belief updating and are summarized below for completeness:

1. **Anticipatory Node:** representing an uninstantiated variable with no successors. For such a node, X, we set $\lambda_{Y_j}^*(x) = (1, 1, ..., 1)$.

2. **Evidence Node:** representing a variable with instantiated value. If variable X assumes the value x', we introduce a dummy child z with

$$\lambda_Z^*(x) = \begin{cases} 1 & \text{if } x = x' \\ 0 & \text{otherwise} \end{cases}$$

This implies that, if X has children, $Y_1, ..., Y_m$, each child should receive the same message $\pi_{Y_j}^*(x) = \lambda_Z^*(x)$ from X.

3. **Root Node:** representing a variable with no parents. For each root variable X, we introduce a dummy parent U, permanently instantiated to $U = 1$, and set the conditional probability on the link $U \rightarrow X$ equal to the prior probability of X, i.e., $P(x | u) = P(x)$.

These boundary conditions ensure that the messages defined in Eqs.(19) and (20) retain their semantics on peripheral nodes.

It is instructive, however, to highlight the major differences in the two schemes. First, belief updating involves *summation*, whereas in belief revision, *maximization* is the dominant operation. Second, belief updating involves more absorption centers than belief revision. In the former, every anticipatory node acts as an absorption barrier in the sense that it does not permit the passage of messages between its parents. This is clearly shown in Eq. (5); substituting $\lambda_Y(x) = \lambda_Z(x) = 1$ yields $\lambda_X(u) = 1$, which means that evidence in favor of one parent (V) has no bearing on another parent (U) as long as their common child (X) receives no evidential support ($\lambda(x) = 1$). This matches our intuition about how frames should interact; data about one frame (e.g., seismic data indicating the occurrence of an earthquake) should not evoke a change of belief about another unrelated frame (say, the possibility of a burglary in my home) just because the two may give rise to a common consequence sometimes in the future (e.g., triggering the alarm system). This frame-to-frame isolation no longer holds for belief revision, as can be seen from Eq. (26). Setting $\lambda_Y^*(x) = \lambda_Z^*(x) = 1$ still renders $\lambda_X^*(u)$ sensitive to $\pi_X^*(v)$.

Such endless frame-to-frame propagation raises both psychological and computational issues. Psychologically, in an attempt to explain a given phenomenon, the mere mental act of imagining the likely consequences of the hypotheses at hand will activate other, remotely related, hypotheses just because the latter could also cause the imagined consequence. We simply *do not encounter* that mode of behavior in ordinary reasoning; in trying to explain the cause of a car accident, we do not interject the possibility of lung cancer just because the two (accidents and lung cancer) could lead to the same eventual consequence -- death.

Computationally, it appears that, in large systems, the task of finding the most satisfactory explanation would require an excessive amount of computation; the propagation process would spread across loosely-coupled frames until every variable in the system reexamines its selected value x^*.

These considerations, together with other epistemological issues (see Pearl 1987b), require that the set of variables, w, over which P is maximized be *circumscribed* in advanced to a previledged set called *explanation corpus*. In addition to the evidence e, W should contain only those variables which both stand in clear causal relation to e (i.e., ancestors of e) and have significant impact on pending decisions. For example, if X_6 were the only observed variable in Figure 1, then the explanation corpus would consist of $W = \{X_1, X_2, X_3, X_5, X_6\}$, excluding X_4. If, in addition, there is no practical utility in finding which value of X_1 prevails, than X_1, too, should be excluded from W.

Circumscribing an explanation corpus paritions the variables in the system into two groups, W and its complement W'. The computation of w^* now involves mixed operations; maximization over W and summation over W':

$$P(w^* | e) = \max_w P(w | e) = \max_w \sum_{w'} P(w | w', e) P(w' | e)$$

The propagation rules, likewise, should be mixed; variables in W should follow the revision rules of Eqs.(27) - (31), while those in W' the updating rules of Eqs.(5)-(6). The interaction between the $\lambda^* - \pi^*$ messages produced by the former and the $\lambda - \pi$ messages produced by the latter should conform to their probabilistic semantics and will not be elaborated here.

3.3 Reaching Equilibrium and Assembling a Composite Solution

To prove that the propagation process terminates, consider a parallel and autonomous control scheme whereby each processor is activated whenever any of its incoming messages changes value. Note that, since the network is singly-connected, every path must eventually end at either a root node having a single child or a leaf node having a single parent. Such single-port nodes act as absorption barriers; updating messages received through these ports get absorbed and do not cause subsequent updating of the outgoing messages. Thus, the effect of each new piece of evidence would subside in time proportional to the longest path in the network.

To prove that, at equilibrium, the selected x^* values do, indeed, represent the most likely interpretation of the evidence at hand, we can reason by induction on the depth of the underlying tree, taking an arbitrary node X as a root. The λ^* or π^* messages emanating from any leaf node of such a tree certainly comply with the definitions of Eqs. (19) and (20). Assuming that the λ^* (or π^*) messages at any node of depth k of the tree comply with their intended definitions of Eqs. (19 & 20), the derivation of Eqs. (21-26) guarantees that they continue to comply at depth $k-1$, and so on. Finally, at the root node, $\alpha \, BEL^*(x^*)$ actually coincides with $P(w^*|e)$, as in Eq.(12), which means that $BEL^*(x)$ computed from (29) must induce the same rating on x as does $\max_{w_x'} P(x, w_x'|e)$ (see (11)). This proves that each local choice of x^* is part of some optimal extension w^*.

Had the choice of each x^* value been unique, this would also guarantee that the assembly of x^* values consitutes the (unique) most-probable extension w^*. However, when several assignments $X = x$ yield the same optimal $BEL^*(x)$, a pointer system must be consulted to ensure that the ties are not broken arbitrarily but cohere with choices made at neighboring nodes. This can be accomplished by having each node mark and save the neighbors' values at which the maximization is achieved. The relevant neighborhood consists of parents, children and spouses, i.e., parents of common children (Pearl 1986a)). For example, node X_5 in Figure 1 should maintain pointers from X_2 to X_3 to indicate which value pairs are compatible members in the same optimal extension. These compatible combinations are found during the local maximization required for calculating λ^* and π^*, as in Eq.(26) or (31).

Theaving these pointers available at each node provides a simple mechanism for retrieving the overall optimal extension; we solve for x^* at some arbitrary node X and then recursively follow the pointers attached to x^*. Additionally, we can retrieve an optimal extension compatible with *any* instantiation (say second best) of some chosen variable X and, comparing the merits of several such extensions, the globally second-best explanation can be identified (Geffner & Pearl, 1987). Another use of this mechanism is facilitating sensitivity analysis; to analyze the merit of testing an unknown variable, we can simply follow the links attached to each of its possible instantiations and examine its impact on other propositions in the system.

3.4 Comparison to Belief Updating

The propagation scheme described in this section bears many similarities to that used in belief updating (Eqs. (4-6)). In both cases, coherent global equilibria are obtained by local computations in time proportional to the network's diameter. Additionally, the messages π^* and λ^* bear both formal and semantic similarities to their π and λ counterparts, and the local computations required for updating them involve, roughly, the same order of complexity.

4. COPING WITH LOOPS

Loops are undirected cycles in the underlying network, i.e., the Bayesian network without the arrows. When loops are present, the network is no longer singly-connected, and local propagation schemes invariably run into trouble. The two major methods for handling loops while still retaining some of the flavor of local computation are: *clustering* and *conditioning* (also called *assumption-based* reasoning).

4.1 Clustering Methods

Clustering involves forming compound variables in such a way that the topology of the resulting network is singly-connected. For example, if in the network of Fig. 1 we define the compound variables:

$$Y_1 = \{X_1, X_2\} \qquad Y_2 = \{X_2, X_3\}$$

the following tree ensues: $X_4 \leftarrow Y_1 \rightarrow Y_2 \rightarrow X_5 \rightarrow X_6$. In the network of Figure 4, Section 5, defining the variables $D_{234} = \{D_2, D_3, D_4\}$ and $M_{123} = \{M_1, M_2, M_3\}$, we obtain a singly-connected network of the form:

$$D_1 \rightarrow M_{123} \leftarrow D_{234} \rightarrow M_4$$

The most popular method of selecting clusters is to form *clique-trees* (Tarjan 1984, Spiegelhalter 1986). If the clusters are allowed to overlap each other until they cover all the links of the original network, then the interdependencies between any two clusters are mediated solely by the variables which they share. If we further insist that these clusters grow until their interdependencies form a tree-structure then the tree-propagation scheme of section 4 will be applicable. For example, in the network of Fig. 1, if we define $Z_1 = \{X_1, X_2, X_4\}$, $Z_2 = \{X_1, X_2, X_3\}$, $Z_3 = \{X_2, X_3, X_5\}$ and $Z_4 = \{X_5, X_6\}$, the dependencies among the Z variables will be described by the chain

$$Z_1 - \{X_1, X_2\} - Z_2 - \{X_2, X_3\} - Z_3 - \{X_5\} - Z_4$$

where the X symbols on the links identify the set of elementary variables common to any pair of adjacent Z clusters.

These clustered networks can be easily processed with the propagation techniques of Section 3, except that the multiplicity of each compound variable increases exponentially with the number of elementary variables it contains. Consequently, the size of either the link matrices or the messages transmitted may become prohibitively large.

An extreme case of clustering would be to represent all ancestors of the observed findings by *one* compound variable. For example, if X_6 and X_4 are the observed variables in the network of Figure 1, we can define the compound variable $Z = \{X_1, X_2, X_3, X_5\}$ and obtain the tree $X_4 \leftarrow Z \rightarrow X_6$. Assigning a definite value to the compound variable Z would constitute an explanation for the findings observed. Indeed, this is the approach taken by Cooper [1984] and Peng & Reggia [1986]. To search for the best explanation through the vast number of possible values associated with the explanation variable, admissible heuristic strategies had to be devised, similar to that of the A^* algorithm (Hart et al., [1968]). Yet the complexity of these algorithms is still exponential [Pearl, 1984] since they do not exploit the interdependencies among the variables in Z. Another disadvantage of this technique is the loss of conceptual flavor; the optimization procedure does not reflect familiar mental processes and, consequently, it is hard to con-

4.2 The Method of Conditioning (Reasoning by Assumptions)

Conditioning is an attempt to both reduce complexity by exploiting the structural independencies embodied in the network and preserve, as much as possible, the conceptual nature of the interpretation process. This is accomplished by performing the major portion of the optimization using local computations *at the knowledge level itself*, i.e., using the links provided by the network as communication channels between simple, autonomous and semantically related processors.

The basic idea behind conditioning can be illustrated using Figure 1. It is based on our ability to change the connectivity of a network and render it singly connected by instantiating a selected group of variables, called a cycle-cutset. For example, instantiating node X_1 to some value would block all pathways through X_1 and would render the rest of the network singly connected, amiable to the propagation technique of Section 3. Thus, if we wish to find the most likely interpretation of some evidence e, say $e = \{X_6 = 1\}$, we first assume $X_1 = 0$ (as in Figure 3(a)), propagate λ^* and π^* to find the best interpretation, I_0, under this assumption, repeat the propagation to find the best interpretation, I_1, under the assumption $X_1 = 1$ (as in Figure 3(b)) and, finally, compare the two interpretations and choose the one with the highest probability. For example, if I_0 and I_1 are realized by the vectors

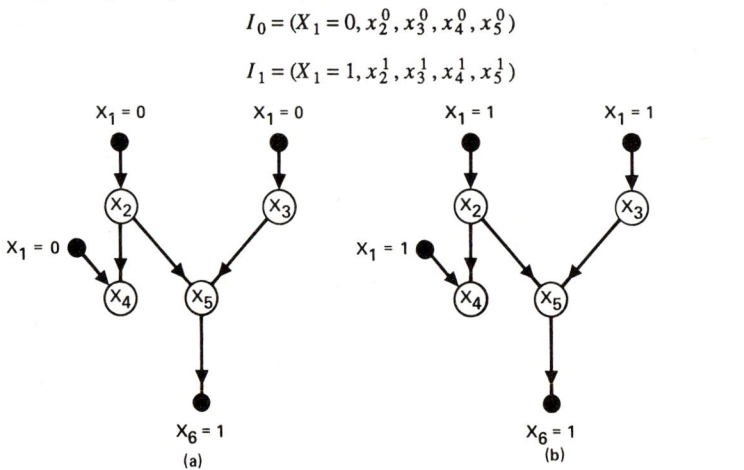

$$I_0 = (X_1 = 0, x_2^0, x_3^0, x_4^0, x_5^0) \tag{32}$$

$$I_1 = (X_1 = 1, x_2^1, x_3^1, x_4^1, x_5^1)$$

Figure 3. Instantiating variable X_1 renders the network of Figure 1 singly connected.

then the best overall interpretation is determined by comparing the two products

$$P(I_0|e) = \alpha P(X_6 = 1|x_5^0) P(x_5^0|x_2^0, x_3^0) P(x_4^0|X_1 = 0, x_2^0) P(x_3^0|X_1 = 0) P(x_2^0|X_1 = 0) P(X_1 = 0)$$

$$P(I_1|e) = \alpha P(X_6 = 1|x_5^1) P(x_5^1|x_2^1, x_3^1) P(x_4^1|X_1 = 1, x_2^1) P(x_3^1|X_1 = 1) P(x_2^1|X_1 = 1) P(X_1 = 1)$$

where $\alpha = [P(e)]^{-1}$ is a constant. Since, all the factors in the products above are available from the initial specification of the links probabilities, the comparison can be conducted by simple computations.

Such globally-supervised comparisons of products are the basic computational steps used in the diagnostic method of Peng & Reggia [1986]. However, we use them to compare only two candidates from the space of 2^5 possible value combinations. Most of the interpretation work was conducted by local propagation, selecting the appropriate match for each of the two assumptions $X_1 = 0$ and $X_1 = 1$. Thus, we see that, even in multiply-connected networks, local propagation provides computationally effective and conceptually meaningful method of trimming the space of interpretations down to a manageable size.

The effectiveness of conditioning depends heavily on the topological properties of the network. In general, a set of several nodes (a cycle cutset) must be instantiated before the network becomes singly-connected. This means that 2^c candidate interpretations will be generated by local propagation, where c is the size of the cycle cutset chosen for conditioning. Since each propagation phase takes only time linear with the number of variables in the system (n), the overall complexity of the optimal interpretation problem is exponential with the size of the cycle cutset that we can identify. If the network is sparse, topological considerations can be used to find a small cycle-cutset and render the interpretation task tractable. Although the problem of finding the minimal cycle cutset is NP hard, simple heuristics exist for finding close-to-minimal sets [Levy & Low, 1983]. Identical complexity considerations apply to the task of belief updating [Pearl 1986b], so, finding the globally best explanation is no more complex than finding the degree of belief for any individual proposition.

4.3 Other Methods

A third method of sidestepping the loop problem is that of stochastic simulation (Pearl, 1987). It amounts to generating a random population of scenarios agreeing with the evidence, then selecting the most probable scenario from that population. This is accomplished distributedly by having each processor inspect the current state of its neighbors, compute the belief distribution of its host variables, then randomly select one value from the computed distribution. The most-likely-interpretation is then found by identifying either the global-state which has been selected most frequently or the one possessing the highest probability (computed by taking the product of n conditional probabilities).

It is important to note that the difficulties associated with the presence of loops are not unique to probabilistic formulations but are inherent to any problem where globally defined solutions are produced by local computations, be it probabilistic, deterministic, logical, numerical or hybrids thereof. Identical computational issues arise in Dempster-Shafer's formalism (Shenoy and Shafer, 1986), constraint-satisfaction problems (Dechter and Pearl, 1985), truth maintenance systems (McAllester, 1978, Doyle, 1979) diagnostic reasoning (de Kleer, 1986) database management (Beeri et al., 1983) matrix inversion (Tarjan, 1976) distributed optimization (Gafni and Barbosa, 1986) and logical deduction.

The importance of network representation, though, is that it uncovers the core of these difficulties, and provides a unifying abstraction that encourages the exchange of solution strategies across domains. The cycle-cutset conditioning method, for example, has been used successfully in non-probabilistic circuit diagnostics (Geffner and Pearl, 1986) and for improving the efficiency of backtracking in constraint-satisfaction problems (Dechter and Pearl, 1987).

5. A MEDICAL DIAGNOSIS EXAMPLE

5.1 The Model

To illustrate the mechanics of the propagation scheme described in section 3, let us consider the diagnosis network of Fig. 4 [after Peng & Reggia, 1986], where the nodes at the top row, $\{D_1, D_2, D_3, D_4\}$, represent four hypothetical diseases and the nodes at the bottom row, $\{M_1, M_2, M_3, M_4\}$, four manifestations (or symptoms) of these diseases. The parameters c_{ij}, shown on the links of Fig. 4, represent the strength of causal connection between disease D_i and symptom M_j,

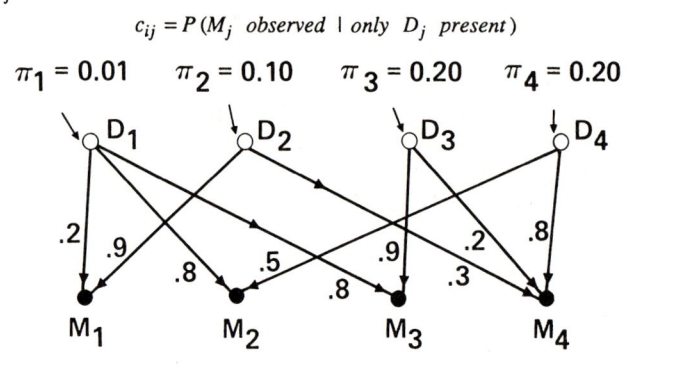

$$c_{ij} = P(M_j \text{ observed } | \text{ only } D_j \text{ present}) \tag{33}$$

$\pi_1 = 0.01 \quad \pi_2 = 0.10 \quad \pi_3 = 0.20 \quad \pi_4 = 0.20$

$D_1 \quad D_2 \quad D_3 \quad D_4$

.2 .9 .8 .5 .9 .2 .8 .8 .3

$M_1 \quad M_2 \quad M_3 \quad M_4$
 T   F   T   F

Figure 4. Network representing causal relations between four diseases and four manifestations. The link parameters, c_{ij}, measure the strength of causal connection.

All four diseases are assumed to be independent and their prior probabilities, $\pi_i = P(D_i = TRUE)$, are shown in Figure 4. When several diseases give rise to the same symptom, their combined effect is assumed to be of the "noisy OR-gate" type [Pearl 1986a], i.e.,

1. A symptom can be triggered only if at least one of its causes is present (Mandatory Causation).

2. The mechanism capable of masking a symptom in the presence of one disease is assumed to be independent of that masking it in the presence of another (Exception Independence).

Given this causal model, we imagine a patient showing symptoms $\{M_1, M_2\}$ but *not* $\{M_2, M_4\}$. Our task is to find that disease *combination* which best explains the observed findings, namely, to find a TRUE-FALSE assignment to variables $\{D_1, D_2, D_3, D_4\}$ which constitutes the most probable extension of the evidence

$$e = \{M_1 = TRUE, M_2 = FALSE, M_3 = TRUE, M_4 = FALSE\}.$$

Let D_i and M_j denote the propositional variables associated with disease D_i and manifestation M_j, respectively; each may assume a *TRUE* or *FALSE* value. Additionally, for each propositional variable X, we let $+x$ and $\neg x$ denote the propositions $X = TRUE$ and $X = FALSE$, respectively. Thus, for example,

$$P(\neg m_j | +d_i) = P(M_j = FALSE | D_i = TRUE)$$

would stand for the probability that a patient definitely having disease D_i will *not* develop symptom M_j.

Let X stand for some manifestation variable and $\{U_1, \cdots, U_n\}$ its parents set. The OR-gate interaction assumed above permits us to construct the combined parents-child relationship $P(x|u_1 \cdots u_n)$ from the individual parent-child relations parametrized by c_{iX} (Eq.(33)). If I_T stands for the set of (indices of) parents with value TRUE,

$$I_T = \{i : U_i = TRUE\}, \tag{34}$$

then X is *FALSE* iff all its *TRUE* parents simultaneously fail to trigger the manifestation corresponding to X. Thus,

$$P(\neg x|u_1, \cdots, u_n) = \prod_{i \in I_T} q_{iX} \tag{35}$$

and

$$P(+x|u_1, \cdots, u_n) = 1 - \prod_{i \in I_T} q_{iX} \tag{36}$$

where

$$q_{iX} = 1 - c_{iX} \tag{37}$$

Substituting in Eq.(27), the function $F(x, u_1 \cdots u_n)$ obtains the form:

$$F(+x, u_1, \cdots, u_n) = \left[1 - \prod_{i \in I_T} q_{iX}\right] \prod_{j=1}^{m} \lambda_{Y_j}^*(+x) \prod_{i=1}^{n} \pi_X^*(u_i) \tag{38}$$

$$F(\neg x, u_1, \cdots, u_n) = \prod_{i \in I_T} q_{iX} \prod_{j=1}^{m} \lambda_{Y_j}^*(\neg x) \prod_{i=1}^{n} \pi_X^*(u_i) \tag{39}$$

These product forms would permit the calculation of the $\pi^*-\lambda^*$ messages according to Eqs.(28)-(31). In particular, for every negatively instantiated symptom node X we have

$$\frac{\lambda_X^*(+u_i)}{\lambda_X^*(\neg u_i)} = q_{iX} \tag{40}$$

independently of $\pi_X^*(u_k)$, $k \neq i$. For every disease node X, setting $P(x|u_1, \cdots, u_n)$ to the prior probability $\pi(x)$, Eq.(23) yields

$$\pi_{Y_j}^*(x) = \pi(x) \prod_{k \neq j} \lambda_{Y_k}^*(x) \tag{41}$$

5.2 Message Propagation

For convenience, let us adopt the following notation:

$$\lambda_{ji} = \lambda_{M_j}^*(+d_i) / \lambda_{M_j}^*(\neg d_i) \tag{42}$$

$$\pi_{ij} = \pi_{M_j}^*(+d_i) / \pi_{M_j}^*(\neg d_i) \tag{43}$$

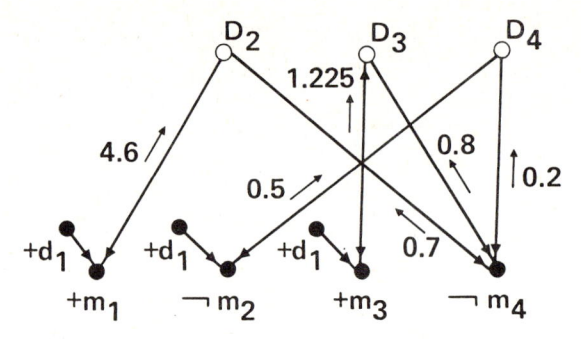

Figure 5(a). λ^* messages after instantiating D_1 and all four symptoms.

The network in Fig.4 becomes singly-connected upon instantiating D_1. We shall first instantiate D_1 to TRUE, find its best extension, then repeat the process under the assumption $D_1 = FALSE$. Fig.5(a) shows the network's message-passing topology, together with the initial messages posted by the instantiated variables $\{+d_1, e\}$:

$$\lambda_{12} = (1 - q_{11}q_{12}) / (1 - q_{11}) = (1 - 0.8\ 0.1) / (1 - 0.8) = 4.600$$

$$\lambda_{33} = (1 - q_{13}q_{33}) / (1 - q_{13}) = (1 - 0.2\ 0.1) / (1 - 0.2) = 1.225$$

$$\lambda_{24} = q_{42} = 0.5 \qquad \lambda_{43} = q_{34} = 0.8$$

$$\lambda_{44} = q_{44} = 0.2 \qquad \lambda_{42} = q_{24} = 0.7$$

The last four values are direct consequence of Eq.(40).

At the second phase, each D_i processor inspects the λ^* messages posted on its links and performs the operation specified in Eq.(41). This leads to the message distribution shown in Fig.5(b), with:

$$\pi_{24} = \pi_2\lambda_{12} / (1 - \pi_2) = 0.510 \quad \pi_{21} = \pi_2\lambda_{42} / (1 - \pi_2) = 0.077$$

$$\pi_{34} = \pi_3\lambda_{33} / (1 - \pi_3) = 0.305 \quad \pi_{33} = \pi_3\lambda_{43} / (1 - \pi_3) = 0.200$$

$$\pi_{44} = \pi_4\lambda_{24} / (1 - \pi_4) = 0.125 \quad \pi_{42} = \pi_4\lambda_{44} / (1 - \pi_4) = 0.050$$

Figure 5(b). π^* messages after activating all D nodes.

The x^* value chosen by each of the D_i processors is $FALSE$, (See Eq.(28)) because, for each $i = 2, 3, 4$, we have

$$\frac{BEL^*(+d_i)}{BEL^*(\neg d_i)} = \prod_{j=1}^{4} \lambda_{ji} \frac{\pi_i}{1-\pi_i} < \frac{1}{2}$$

For example, processor D_2 receives: $\lambda_{12} = 4.6$, $\lambda_{42} = 0.7$; so,

$$\frac{BEL^*(+d_2)}{BEL^*(\neg d_2)} = \frac{\lambda_{12} \cdot \lambda_{42} \cdot \pi_2}{1 \cdot 1 \cdot (1-\pi_2)} = \frac{4.6 \cdot 0.7 \cdot 0.1}{1 \cdot 1 \cdot 0.9} = 0.358 < \frac{1}{2}. \qquad (44)$$

The messages π_{21}, π_{33} and π_{42} will eventually get absorbed at node D_1, while π_{24}, π_{34} and π_{44} are now posted on the ports entering node M_4. Again, since M_4 is instantiated to $\neg m_4$, the λ^* messages generated by M_4 on the next activation phase remain unchanged (Fig.5(c)), and the process halts with the current w^* values: $D_2 = D_3 = D_4 = FALSE$.

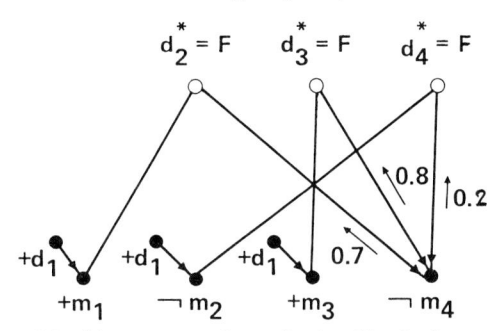

Figure 5(c). λ^* messages after activating M_4; the best explanation is $d_2^* = d_3^* = d_4^* = FALSE$.

Let us now retract the assumption $D_1 = TRUE$ and posit the converse: $D_1 = FALSE$. This results in the messages $\pi_{11} = \pi_{12} = \pi_{13} = \infty$ being posted on all those links emanating from node D_1 which get translated to $\lambda_{12} = \infty$, $\lambda_{13} = \infty$, and $\lambda_{24} = q_{42} = .5$. This means that D_2 and D_3 will switch simultaneously and permanently to state $TRUE$ while D_4, by virtue of

$$\frac{BEL^*(+d_4)}{BEL^*(\neg d_4)} = \lambda_{24} \cdot \lambda_{44} \cdot \pi_4 / (1-\pi_4) = 0.50 \cdot 0.20 \cdot 0.20 / 0.80 = .025 < \frac{1}{2}$$

tentatively remains at the state $FALSE$, as illustrated in Fig.6(a).

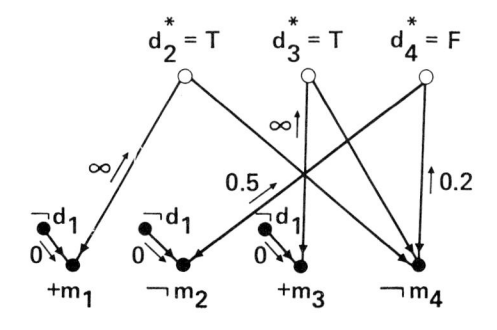

Figure 6(a). Message profile after instantiating D_1 to FALSE; the best explanation switches to $\{d_2^* = d_3^* = TRUE, d_4^* = FALSE\}$

During the next activation phase (Fig.6(b)), D_2 and D_3 post the messages $\pi_{24} = \pi_{34} = \infty$, which M_4 inspects for possible updating of λ_{44}. However, these new messages will not cause any change in λ_{44} because, according to Eqs.(30) and (35), the ratio λ_{44} remains

$$\lambda_{44} = \frac{P(\neg m_4 \mid +d_4, d_2, d_3)}{P(\neg m_4 \mid \neg d_4, d_2, d_3)} = q_{44},$$

independently of π_{24} and π_{34}.

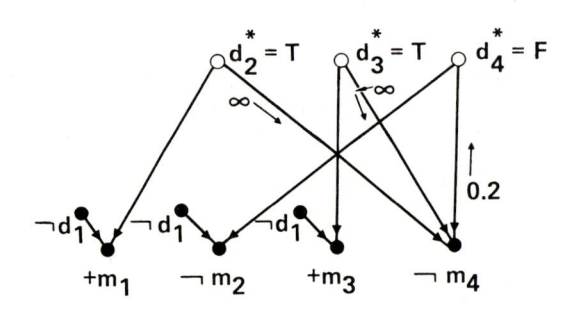

Figure 6(b). Message profile after activating M_4; the best explanation remains $\{dusb\, 2^* = d_3^* = TRUE, d_4^* = FALSE\}$.

Thus, under the current premise $\neg d_1$, the best interpretation of the four symptoms is $\{+d_2, +d_3, \neg d_4\}$, which is to be expected, in view of the network topology.

5.3 Choosing the Best Interpretation

We see that the assumption $+d_1$ yields the interpretation $\{\neg d_2, \neg d_3, \neg d_4\}$, while $\neg d_1$ yields $\{+d_2, +d_3, \neg d_4\}$. The question now is to decide which of the two interpretations is more plausible or, in other words, which has the highest posterior probability given the evidence $e = \{+m_1, \neg m_2, +m_3, \neg m_4\}$ at hand. A direct way to decide between the two candidates is to calculate the two posterior probabilities, $P(I^+ \mid e)$ and $P(I^- \mid e)$, where

$$I^+ = \{+d_1, \neg d_2, \neg d_3, \neg d_4\}$$

and

$$I^- = \{\neg d_1, +d_2, +d_3, \neg d_4\}.$$

These calculations are quite simple, because instantiating the D variables *separates* the M variables from each other, so that the posterior probabilities involve only products of $P(m_j \mid parents\ of\ M_j)$ over the individual symptoms and a product of the prior probabilities over the individual diseases. For example,

$$P(I^+ \mid e) = \alpha P(I^+) P(e \mid I^+)$$

$$= \alpha\, \pi_1 (1 - \pi_2)(1 - \pi_3)(1 - \pi_4)(1 - q_{11})\, q_{12}(1 - q_{13})$$

$$= \alpha\, 0.01 \cdot 0.90 \cdot 0.80 \cdot 0.80 \cdot 0.20 \cdot 0.90 \cdot 0.80$$

$$= \alpha\, 8.2944 \times 10^{-4}$$

$$P(I^- \mid e) = \alpha P(I^-) P(e \mid I^-)$$

$$= \alpha (1 - \pi_1) \pi_2 \pi_3 (1 - \pi_4) (1 - q_{21}) (1 - q_{33}) q_{24} q_{34}$$

$$= \alpha \, 0.99 \cdot 0.10 \cdot 0.20 \cdot 0.80 \cdot 0.90 \cdot 0.90 \cdot 0.70 \cdot 0.80$$

$$= \alpha \, 7.18 \times 10^{-3}$$

Since $\alpha = [P(e)]^{-1}$ is a constant, we conclude that I^- is the most plausible interpretation of the evidence e.

5.4 Generating Explanations

The propagation pattern of the λ^* and π^* messages can also be instrumental in mechanically generating verbal explanations. When belief in a certain proposition is supported (or undermined) from several directions, the π^* and λ^* messages can be consulted to determine the factors most influential in the current selection of x^*. Tracing the most influential π^*–λ^* messages back to the generating evidence would yield a skeleton subgraph from which verbal explanation can be structured. For example, the messages loading the graphs of Figures 6(a)-6(b) should be summarized by:

> "Since we have ruled out disease D_1, the only possible explanation for observing symptoms M_1 and M_3 is that the patient suffers, simultaneously, from D_2 and D_3. The fact that M_2 and M_4 both came out negative indicates that disease D_4 is absent. Moreover, even if M_4 were positive, it would be completely explained away by D_2 and D_3."

The last sentence is a result of running a hypothetical positive instantiation of M_4 and realizing that, due to the strong (∞) π^* messages from D_2 and D_3, M_4 cannot deliver a λ_{42} high enough to switch D_4 to TRUE.

Conflicting evidence is identified by the presence of strongly supportive and strongly opposing messages, simultaneously impinging on the same propostition. For example, the proposition $D_2 = TRUE$ in Figure 5(a) receives a strong support from $\lambda_{12}^* = 4.6$ and a strong denial from $\pi_2 = .2$. The two balance each other out and yield $BEL^*(+d_2)$ very close to $BEL^*(\neg d_2)$ (see Eq.(74)). The following explanation would then be appropriate:

> "Although symptom M_1 strongly suggests D_2, it is partly explained by D_1 (which we assumed TRUE) and, in view of the rarity of D_2, this patient probably does not suffer from D_2."

5.5 Reversibility vs. Perseverance

It is interesting to note that there is a definite threshold value for π_1, $\pi_1 = 0.0804$, at which the two interpretations, I^+ and I^-, are equiprobable. That means that, as evidence in favor of $+d_1$ accumulates and π_1 increases beyond the value 0.0804, the system will switch abruptly from interpretation I^- to interpretation I^+. This abrupt "change of view" is a collective phenomenon, characteristic of massively parallel systems, and is reminiscent of the way people's beliefs undergo complete reversal in response to a minor clue. Note, though, that the transition is *reversible*, i.e., as $\pi_1 = 0.0804$. No hysteresis occurs because, although the computations are done locally, w^* is globally optimal and is, therefore, a unique function of all systems' parameters.

This reversibility differs from human behavior in that, once we commit our belief to a particular interpretation, it often takes more convincing evidence to make us change our mind than the evidence which got us there in the first place. Simply discrediting a piece of evidence would not, in itself, make us abandon the beliefs which that evidence induced [Ross & Anderson, 1982; Harman, 1986]. The phenomena is very pronounced in perceptual tasks; once we adopt one view of Necker's cube or an Escher sketch, it takes a real effort to break ourselves loose and adopt alternative interpretations. Irreversibility (or hysteresis) of that kind is characteristic of systems with local feedback, similar to the one responsible for magnetic hysteresis in metals. If the magnetic spin of one atom heads north, it sets up a magnetic field which encourages its neighbors to follow suit; when the neighbors' spins eventually turn north, they generate a magnetic field which further "locks" the original atom in tis north-pointing orientation.

The hysteresis characteristic of human belief revision may have several sources. One possibility is that local feedback loops are triggered between evoked neighboring concepts; e.g., if I suspect fire, I expect smoke, and that very expectation of smoke reinforces my suspicion of fire -- as if I actually saw smoke. This is a rather unlikely possibility because it would mean that even in simple cases (e.g., the fire and smoke example), people are likely to confuse internal thinking with genuine evidence. A more reasonable explanation is that, by-and-large, the message-passing process used in feedback-free and resembles that of Section 3, where the π^* and λ^* on the same link are orthogonal to each other. However, in complex situations, where loops are rampant, people simply cannot afford the overhead computations required by conditioning or clustering. As an approximation, then, they delegate the optimization task to local processes and continue to pass messages as if the belief network were singly-connected. The resultant interpretation, under these conditions, is locally, not globally, optimal, and this accounts for the irreversibility of belief revision.

Another source of belief perseverance may lie in the difficulty of keeping track of all justifications of ones beliefs and tracing them back to all evidence, past and present, upon which beliefs are founded (Harman, 1986). For computational reasons people simply forget the evidence and retain its conclusion. More formally, propositional networks such as those treated in this paper, are not maintained as stable mental constructs but, rather, are created and destroyed dynamically, to meet pragmatic needs. For example, connections may be formed for the immediate purpose of explaining some strange piece of evidence or for supporting a hypothesis of high immediate importance. Once the evidence imparts its impact onto other propositions, we tend to break the mediating connection, forget the evidence itself and retain only the conclusion. When that evidence is later dicredited, the connection to the induced conclusions is no longer in vivid memory while the discrediting information, in itself, may not be perceived to be of sufficient pragmatic importance for reestablishing old connections.

CONCLUSIONS

This paper develops a distributed scheme for finding the most probable composite explanation of a body of evidence.

We show that, in singly-connected networks, globally optimal explanations can be configured by local and autonomous message passing processes, similar to those used in belief updating; conceptually related propositions communicate with each other via a simple protocol, and the process converges to the correct solution in time proportional to the network diameter. In multiply connected networks,, the propagation method must be assisted either by clustering (i.e., locally supervised groups of variables) or conditioning (i.e., reasoning by assumptions); each exploiting different aspects of the network topology.

The implications of these results are several. First, from a psycho-philosophical viewpoint, they provide a clear demonstration of how cognitive constructs exhibiting global coherence can be assembled by local, neuron-like processors, without external supervision. Second, along a more practical dimension, the message-passing method developed offers substantial reduction in complexity compared with previous optimization techniques, achieving linear complexity in singly connected networks and exp($|cyclecutset|$) in general networks. This is accomplished by subtask decomposition, supervised solely by the network topology. Third, the paper establishes a clear paradigmatic link between probabilistic and logical formalisms of non-monotonic reasoning. It demonstrates how numerical probabilities can be used as a concealed inferencing fuel for performing coherent transformations between evidence sentences and conclusion sentences. It also identifies the kind of structures where such transformations can be executed by autonomous production rules and those that invite problems of intractability and/or instability, unless treated with care.

ACKNOWLEDGMENT

I thank Hector Geffner for a thorough review of the manuscript, for pointing out the importance of treating multiple MPE's and for adopting and expanding the proposed scheme to perform circuit diagnosis [Geffner and Pearl, 1987].

REFERENCES

Ben Bassat, M., Carlson, R. W., Puri, V. K., Lipnick, E., Portigal, L. D. & Weil, M. H. [1980]. "Pattern-Based Interactive Diagnosis of Multiple Disorders: The MEDAS System," *IEEE Transactions on Pattern Analysis & Machine Intelligence,* PAMI-2:148-160.

Ben Bassat, M., [1980]. "Multimembership and Multiperspective Classification: Introduction, Applications and a Bayesian Model," *IEEE Trans. SMC,* Vol. 10:331-336.

Beeri, C., R. Fagin, D. Maier and M. Yannakakis. "On the Desirability of Acyclic Database Schemes," *J. Assoc. Comput.,* 30 (1983), pp.479-513.

Booker, L., [1987]. Personal Communication.

Cooper, G. F., [1984]. "NESTOR: a Computer-Based Medical Diagnostic Aid that Integrates Causal and Probabilistic Knowledge," Ph.D. Dissertation, Department of Computer Science, Stanford University, Stanford, CA.

deKleer, J. & Williams, B., [1986]. "Reasoning about Multiple-Faults," *Proceedings, AAAI-86,* 5th Nat'l. Conf. on AI, Phila., PA., pp.132-139.

Dechter, R. and J. Pearl, [1985]. "The Anatomy of Easy Problems: A Constraint-Satisfaction Formulation," in *Proceedings Ninth International Conference on Artificial Intelligence,* Los Angeles, California, pp.1066-1072.

Dechter R. and J. Pearl, [1987]. "The Cycle-Cutset Method for Improving Search Performance in AI Applications," *Proc. of the Third IEEE Conf. on AI Applications,* Orlando, FL.

Doyle, J. [1979]. "A Truth Maintenance System," *Artificial Intelligence,* 12(3), pp.231-272.

Gafni, E. and Barbosa, V. C. "Optimal Snapshots and the Maximum Flow in Precedence Graphs." *Proc. 24th Allerton Conference,* October, 1986.

Geffner, H. and J. Pearl, [1986]. "An improved Constraint Propagation Algorithm for Diagnosis," UCLA, CS Department, Cognitive System Lab., Los Angeles, California, Tech. Rep. R-73.

Geffner, H. and J. Pearl, [1987]. "A Distributed Approach to Diagnosis," UCLA, CS Department, Cognitive Systems Laboratory, Los Angeles, Ca. Tech. Rep. R-66, Short Version in *Proc. of the Third IEEE Conf. of AI Applications,* Orlando, FL.

Harman, G., [1986]. *Change in View,* MIT Press, Cambridge, Mass.

Hart, P. E., Nilsson, J. J. and Raphael, B. "A Formal Basis for the Heuristic Determination of Minimum Cost Paths." *IEEE Trans. Syst. Science and Cyber,* SSC-4(2): pp.100-107.

Levy, H. & Low, D. W. [1983]. "A New Algorithm for Finding Small Cycle Cutsets," *Report G 320-2721,* IBM Los Angeles Scientific Center.

Pearl, J., [1984] *Heuristics: Intelligent Search Strategies for Computer Problem Solving,* Addison-Wesley, Reading, MA.

Pearl, J., [1986a]. "Fusion, Propagation and Structuring in Belief Networks," *Artificial Intelligence,* September 1986, Vol. 29, No. 3, 241-288.

Pearl, J., [1986b], "A Constraint-Propagation Approach to Probabilistic Reasoning," in Kanal, L. N. & Lemmer, J. (Eds.), *Uncertainty in Artificial Intelligence,* North-Holland, Amsterdam, pp.357-370.

Pearl, J. [1987a], "Evidential Reasoning Using Stochastic Simulation of Causal Models," to appear in *Artificial Intelligence.*

Pearl, J. [1987b], "Distributed Revision of Composite Beliefs" to appear in *Artificial Intelligence,* 1987.

Peng, Y. & Reggia, J., [1986]. "Plausibility of Diagnostic Hypotheses," *Proceedings, AAAI-86,* 5th Nat'l. Conf. on AI, Philadelphia, PA., Aug. 11-15, 1986, pp.140-145.

Pople, H. [1982]. "Heuristic Methods for Imposing Structures on Ill-Structured Problems," in Solovits, P. (Ed.), *AI in Medicine,* Westview Press, Boulder, Colorado.

Reggia, J. A., Nau, D. S. & Wang, Y. [1983]. "Diagnostic Expert Systems Based on a Set-Covering Model," *Int'l. Journal of Man-Machine Studies,* 19, pp. 437-460.

Reiter, R., [1985]. "A Theory of Diagnosis from First Principles," *Technical Report TR-187/86,* Computer Science Department, University of Toronto.

Ross, L. & Anderson, C. A., [1982]. "Shortcomings in the Attribution Process: On the Origins and Maintenance of Erroneous Social Assessments" in *Judgement under Certainty: Heuristics and Biases,* Kahneman, Slovic, Tversky (Eds.) (Cambridge: Cambridge Univ. Press) 129-152. No. 6, pp. 331-336.

Shenoy, P. and G. Shafer, "Propagating Belief Functions with Local Computations," *IEEE Expert 1, (3),* pp.43-52.

Spiegelhalter, D. J., [1985]. "Probabilistic Reasoning in Predictive Expert Systems," in Kanal, L. N. & Lemmer, J., (Eds.), *Uncertainty in Artificial Intelligence,* North-Holland, Amsterdam, 1986, pp.47-68.

Tarjan, R. E. [1976]. "Graph Theory and Gaussian Elimination," in *Sparse Matrix Computations,* J. R. Bunch and D. J. Rose, eds., Academic Press, New York, pp.3-22.

Tarjan, R. E. and Yannakakis, M. [1984]. "Simple Linear-Time Algorithms to Test Chordality of Graphs, Test Acyclicity of Hypergraphs, and Selectively Reduce Acyclic Hypergraphs," *SIAM J. Comput. 13,* 566-579.

A BACKWARDS VIEW FOR ASSESSMENT

Ross D. Shachter and David E. Heckerman

Stanford University
Stanford, California 94305-4025

1. INTRODUCTION

Much artificial intelligence research focuses on the problem of deducing the validity of unobservable propositions or *hypotheses* from observable *evidence*.[1] Many of the knowledge representation techniques designed for this problem encode the relationship between evidence and hypothesis in a directed manner. Moreover, the direction in which evidence is stored is typically *from evidence to hypothesis*. For example, in the rule-based approach, knowledge is represented as rules of the form:

IF ⟨evidence⟩ THEN ⟨hypothesis⟩

In this scheme, observable propositions are most often found in the antecedent of rules while unobservable propositions are usually found in the consequent.

In early applications of these methodologies, the relationship between evidence and hypothesis was assumed to be categorical. However, as artificial intelligence researchers began to address real-world problems, they recognized that the relationship between evidence and hypothesis is often uncertain and developed methods for reasoning under uncertainty. For example, the creators of one of the earliest expert systems, MYCIN, augmented the rule-based approach to knowledge representation and manipulation with a method for managing uncertainty known as the certainty factor (CF) model [Shortliffe75]. In this and other approaches [1, 2], the direction of knowledge representation was carried over from their categorical counterparts. In the MYCIN certainty factor model, for example, knowledge is stored in rules of the form:

IF ⟨evidence⟩ THEN ⟨hypothesis⟩, CF

where CF is a measure of the change in belief in the hypothesis given the evidence.

That knowledge is encoded in the direction from evidence to hypothesis in such popular approaches is not accidental. This direction corresponds to the direction in which knowledge is *used* by the program to deduce or infer the validity of unobservable propositions. This appears to be convenient for problem solving. However, in this paper, we argue that in most real-world applications there are advantages to representing knowledge in the direction *opposite* to the usage direction. In particular, we argue that representing knowledge in the direction from unobservable hypothesis to observable evidence is often cognitively simpler and more efficient.

The argument is based on three observations. The first is that many real-world problems involve *causal* interactions. In this paper, we make no attempt to define causality in terms of more basic concepts; we take it to be a primitive notion. The second observation is that the direction of causality is most often opposite to that of the direction of usage. That is, *hypotheses tend to cause evidence*. There are many examples of this in medicine in which the unobservable hypothesis is the true cause of an illness and the observable evidence is the illness' effect in the form of symptoms. Of course, there are exceptions. In trauma cases such as such as automobile accidents, for example, the cause is observable and some of the effects are difficult to observe. However, tests then performed to determine the hidden effects of the accident fit the more usual model of unobservable cause and observable effect. The final observation is that people are more comfortable when their beliefs are elicited in the causal direction. It appears that it is cognitively simpler to construct assessments in that direction [3]. Furthermore, models are often less complex in the causal direction. Thus, these three observations suggest that there may be advantages to representing knowledge in the direction opposite to the direction of usage. This is summarized in Figure 1.

```
   OBSERVABLE  ─────────▶  UNOBSERVABLE
                 usage
    (usually)                (usually)
               assessment
      EFFECT  ◀─────────     CAUSE
```

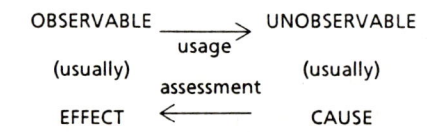

Figure 1: The two directions of representation

2. INFLUENCE DIAGRAMS

In this paper, we will examine these issues in the context of probability theory. Nonetheless, we believe that the distinction between direction of usage and direction of natural assessment is a fundamental issue, independent of the language in which belief is represented.

Within the theory of probability, there are several graphical representations for uncertainty featuring both directed graphs [4, 5, 6, 7]and undirected graphs [8, 9]. The different representations all share the basic concept of the factorization of an underlying joint distribution, and the explicit revelation of conditional independence. We will use a directed graph representation method since directionality is central to our discussion. In particular, will use the influence diagram representation scheme [5].

Each of the oval nodes in an influence diagram represents a random variable or uncertain quantity. The arcs indicate *conditional dependence* with the successor's probability distribution conditioned on the outcomes of its predecessors. For example, there are three possible influence diagrams for the two random variables X and Y shown in Figure 2. In the first case, X has no predecessors so we assess a marginal (unconditional) distribution for X and a conditional distribution for Y given X. In the next case, with the arc reversed, we assess a marginal distribution for Y and a conditional distribution for X given Y. Both correspond to the same fundamental model, at the underlying joint distribution, but the two diagrams represent two different ways of factoring the model. The transformation between them, which involves reversing the direction of conditioning and hence the reversal of the arc, is simply Bayes' Theorem. Finally, in the third case, neither node has any predecessors so X and Y are independent. Therefore, we can obtain the joint by assessing marginal distributions for both X and Y. When the two variables are independent, we are free to use any of the three forms, but we prefer the last one which explicitly reveals that independence in the graph.

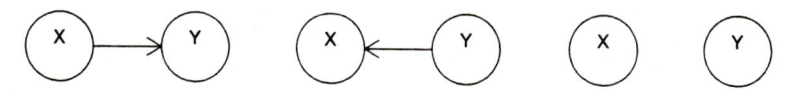

```
  (X) ──▶ (Y)      (X) ◀── (Y)      (X)    (Y)
```

Figure 2: An influence diagram with two nodes

In Figure 3, we see four possible influence diagrams for the random variables, X, Y and Z. In the first case, the general situation, the three variables appear to be completely dependent. We assess a marginal distribution for X, and conditional distributions for Y given X and for Z given X and Y. In general there are $n!$ factorizations of a joint distribution among n variables. Each possible permutation leads to a different influence diagram. In the second case in the figure, the three variables are completely independent; in the third case, X and Y are dependent but Z is independent of both of them. In the fourth case, we see *conditional independence*. The absence of an arc from X to Z, indicates that while X and Z are dependent, they are independent given Y. This type of conditional independence is an important simplifying assumption for the construction and assessment of models of uncertainty.

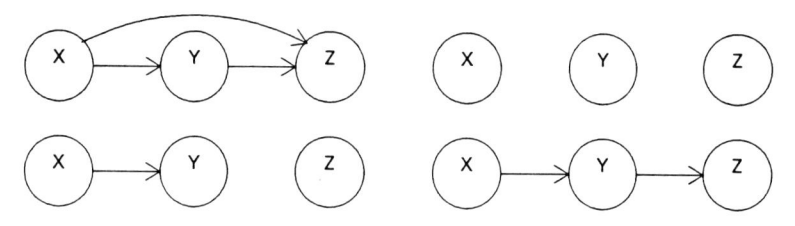

Figure 3: An influence diagram with three nodes

In the influence diagram we always require that there be no directed cycles. By doing so, there is always an ordering among the variables so that we can recover the underlying joint distribution. While there are some anomalous cases with cycles where the joint is still recoverable, we will require that the diagram remain acyclic.

There is one other type of influence diagram node relevant to our discussion, a deterministic node, drawn as a double oval (as opposed to the probabilistic node which we have shown as a single oval). The deterministic variable is a function of its predecessors, so its outcome is known with certainty if we observe the outcomes of those predecessors. In general, we can not observe all of those predecessors, so there can be uncertainty in the outcome of a deterministic variable.

An operation central to our discussion is the transformation of an influence diagram in the assessment direction to one in the usage direction. This is accomplished by *reversing the arcs* in the influence diagram which corresponds to the general version of Bayes' Theorem [5, 10, 11]. This is shown in Figure 4. As long as there is no other path between chance nodes (either probabilistic or deterministic node) X and Y, we can reverse the arc from X to Y. If there were another path, the newly reversed arc would create a cycle. In the process of the reversal, both chance nodes inherit each other's predecessors. This may add a considerable number of arcs to the influence diagram. We shall be concerned in later sections about the relative complexity of the model before and after reversals. Sometimes, not all of the arcs are needed after reversals, but in general they may be. If multiple reversals are needed, then the order in which they are performed may affect this arc structure.[2]

3. DETERMINISTIC MODELS

The importance of distinction between direction of assessment and direction of usage appears even in the simplest categorical models. Suppose, for example, that we have an error in the output from a small computer program. If we knew the source of the error, then we would know with certainty the type of output error to expect. Thus we could use the model shown in Figure 5 in which the programming error is represented by a probabilistic node conditioning the computer output represented by a deterministic node. When we observe the output and

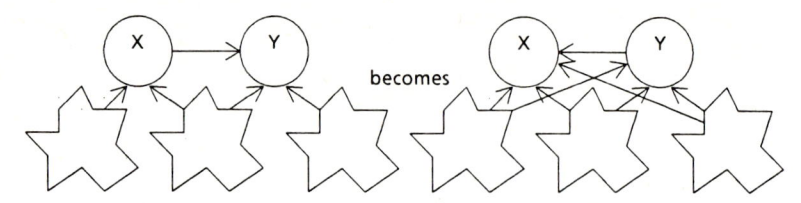

Figure 4: Arc reversal in an influence diagram

wish to learn about the source of the error, we reverse the arc using Bayes' Theorem and find that, after the reversal, both nodes have become probabilistic. Given the output, we do not necessarily know what type of error caused it, but we are able to update our previous beliefs about the possible errors in the light of this new evidence. Our direction of usage is clearly in the more complex, reverse direction, but the model is much more easily constructed in the original direction, which exploits the categorical behavior of our man-made computer system.

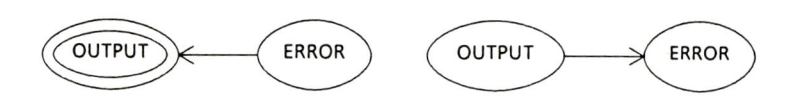

Figure 5: An influence diagram for diagnosing computer programming errors

Suppose now that we have a much larger computer system. If it were written with a modular design, we may have the influence diagram shown in Figure 6. Again this model is relatively easy to construct because of the categorical nature and the independence among subsystems. If however, we observe the output and wish to update our knowledge about those subsystems, we find that they are no longer categorical, nor are they independent, in light of the new information.[3] This newer, more complex model is the correct one to use to update our beliefs as we observe evidence, but it is less convenient for assessment.

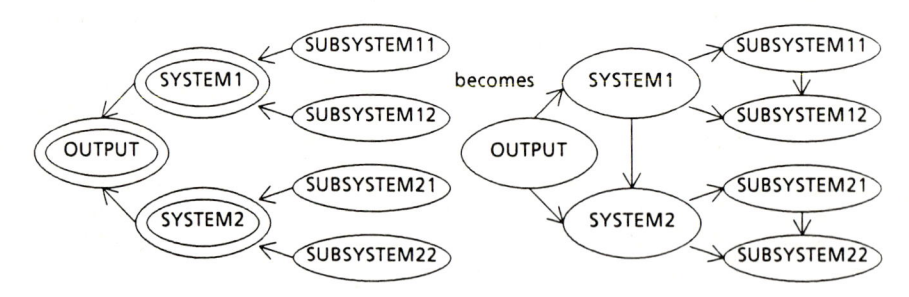

Figure 6: An influence diagram for a modular computer program

4. PROBABILISTIC MODELS

In most real-world domains, we do not have a categorical model to assess, but there is still considerable advantage to thinking about a problem in the causal direction. Often, basic and straightforward probabilistic models become much more complex when viewed in the direction of usage.

Consider the case of two effects with a single common cause. Even when the effects are conditionally independent given the cause as in Figure 7, they are, in general, dependent when the problem is reversed. Similarly, when there are two independent causes and a single common effect as in Figure 8, we see complete dependency when the problem is reversed. Clearly as the number of causes and effects increase, the problem stays straightforward in the causal direction, but becomes even more complex in the direction of usage.

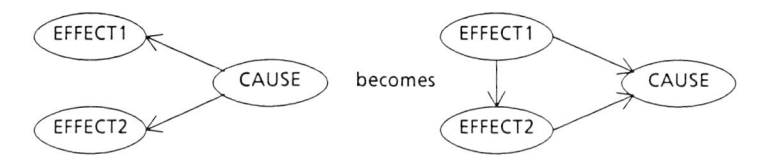

Figure 7: A single cause with multiple effects

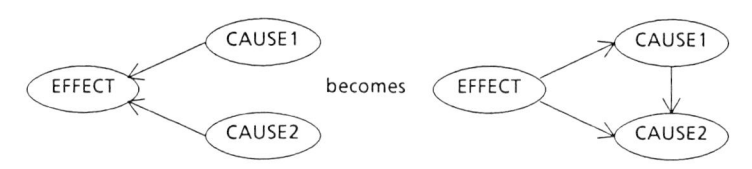

Figure 8: A single effect with multiple causes

As an example, consider two disorders, congestive heart failure and nephrotic syndrome (a kidney disease), which essentially arise independently. Congestive heart failure often results in an enlarged heart (cardiomegaly) and accumulation of fluid in the ankles (pitting edema), while nephrotic syndrome often leads to protein in the urine and pitting edema as well. A simple test for protein in the urine is whether the urine is frothy, and an x-ray is used to detect cardiomegaly. The model corresponding to this is shown on the upper half of Figure 9. If we turn the model around to show how the unobservable events of interest, heart failure and nephrotic syndrome, depend on the observables, x-ray, pitting edema, and frothy urine, then the model becomes the one shown on the lower half of Figure 9. The original model was not only simpler, but more natural to assess, going in the causal direction. The reversed model would be intolerably confusing to assess, but it has all of the dependencies one needs for proper usage.

One other major advantage of viewing a problem in different directions for construction and solution is that parts of the assessment may not vary much from case to case. Consider the simple model in Figure 10, in which a probabilistic effect depends on a probabilistic cause. Often in medicine and other domains, the likelihood distribution for the effect given the cause is independent of patient-specific factors; e.g., a particular disorder will have a distribution over possible symptoms. On the other hand, the probability distribution for the cause, e.g., the distribution of possible disorders, may vary widely between cases, on the basis of age, occupation, climate and so on. When the model is reversed to the direction of usage, e.g., diagnosis for disorder given symptoms, both probabilities have become patient-specific. This suggests considerable time-saving in the construction of models by building them in the direction of natural assessment to exploit any constant likelihoods.

Finally, it is often useful to add new variables which simplify the construction process. Consider the medical example in Figure 9. If we are interested in the probability distribution for pitting edema given congestive heart failure, it is much easier to assess with nephrotic syndrome present in the model. We can then take expectation over nephrotic syndrome to

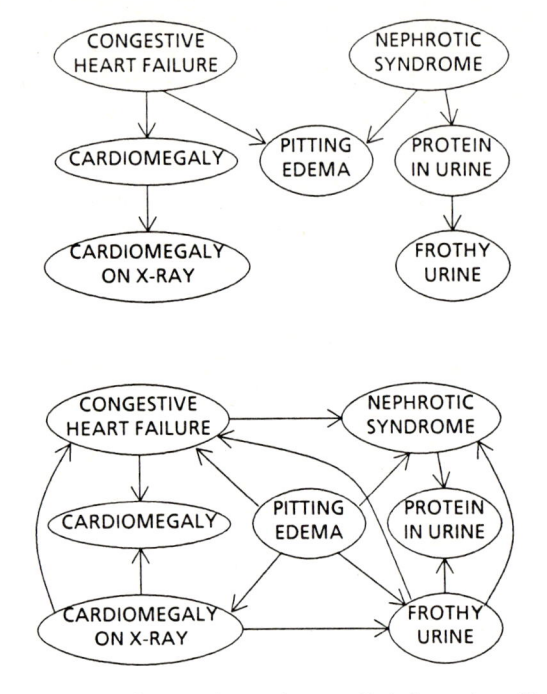

Figure 9: An influence diagram for a medical diagnosis problem

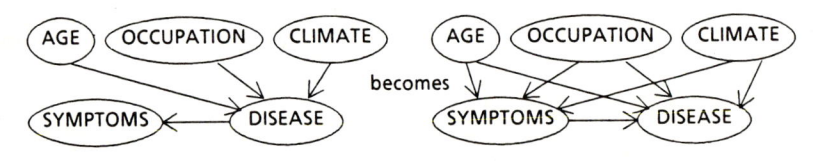

Figure 10: Taking advantage of constant likelihood

arrive at our desired conditional distribution. If we did not explicitly consider nephrotic syndrome, then we would be forced to perform the integration mentally instead. The addition of variables can be of considerable cognitive aid when trying to assess the probability distributions. This process is what Tribus [12] calls "the law of the extension of the conversation." We get little benefit from this technique unless we first build our model in the causal direction.

5. CONCLUSIONS

We believe it is important to distinguish between the direction in which a model is constructed and the direction in which it will be applied. Models which capture the richness of the interactions among their variables can become impossible to assess in the usage direction, even though they may be simple and natural to think about and assess in the opposite direction.

Artificial intelligence researchers have argued that various methods for reasoning with uncertainty are impractical because of the complexity of knowledge assessment and belief revision [13, 14]. Indeed, many AI researchers have sacrificed self-consistency of the reasoning mechanism in order to facilitate simplicity in the knowledge representation process [15]. We contend that the desired simplicity can be found often by constructing models in the direction opposite that of usage without having to sacrifice fundamentals.

ACKNOWLEDGEMENTS

This work was supported in part by Decision Focus, Inc., the Josiah Macy, Jr. Foundation, the Henry J. Kaiser Family Foundation, and the Ford Aerospace Corporation. Computing facilities were provided by the SUMEX-AIM resource under NIH grant RR-00785.

NOTES

[1] Although different meanings have been attached to the terms "evidence" and "hypothesis," we will take "hypothesis" to mean an unobservable proposition and a item of "evidence" to mean an observable proposition.

[2] It is interesting to note that the reversal operation simplifies considerably when the predecessor X is a deterministic node. It does not simplify, however, when the successor Y is the deterministic node.

[3] Notice that the newer model does show some conditional independence which can be exploited at the time of usage.

REFERENCES

[1] Duda, R.O., "Alternative forms of Bayes rule for diagnosis," Tech. report, SRI, 1975, Project file 3805
[2] Miller, R. A., Pople, H. E., and Myers, J. D., INTERNIST-1, An Experimental Computer-Based Diagnostic Consultant for General Internal Medicine, *New England Journal of Medicine*, 307 (8), (1982), pp. 468-476.
[3] Kuipers, B. and Kassirer, J. P., Causal Reasoning in Medicine: Analysis of a Protocol, *Cognitive Science*, 8 (1984), pp. 363-385.
[4] Wright, S., Correlation and causation, *J. Agric. Research*, 20 (1921), pp. 557-585.
[5] Howard, R. A., Matheson, J. E., Influence Diagrams, in "Readings on the Principles and Applications of Decision Analysis", (Howard, R. A., Matheson, J. E., eds.), Strategic Decisions Group, Menlo Park, CA, 1981, pp. 721-762, ch. 37.
[6] Kim, J.H., and Pearl, J., A computational model for causal and diagnostic reasoning in inference engines, *In* "Proceedings 8th international joint conference on artificial intelligence", Karlsruhe, West Germany, IJCAI, 1983, pp. 190-193.
[7] Cooper, G. F., "NESTOR: A Computer-based Medical Diagnostic Aid that Integrates Causal and Probabilistic Knowledge," PhD dissertation, Computer Science Department, Stanford University, November 1984, Rep. No. STAN-CS-84-48. Also numbered HPP-84-48.

[8] Speed, T.P., "Graphical methods in the analysis of data", Lecture notes issued at the University of Copenhagen Institute of Mathematical Statistics

[9] Spiegelhalter, D. J., "A Statistical View of Uncertainty in Expert Systems", Presented at Workshop on AI and Statistics, Bell Laboratories, April 11-12

[10] Olmsted, S.M., "On Representing and Solving Decision Problems," PhD dissertation, Stanford, December 1983.

[11] Shachter, R.D., Intelligent probabilistic inference, in "Uncertainty in Artificial Intelligence", (Kanal, L. and Lemmer, J., eds.), North Holland, 1986.

[12] Tribus, M., What do we mean by rational?, in "Rational Descriptions, Decisions and Designs", Pergamon Press, New York, 1969.

[13] Shortliffe, E. H., "Computer-Based Medical Consultations: MYCIN", Elsevier/North Holland, New York, 1976.

[14] Rich, E., "Artificial Intelligence", McGraw-Hill, 1983.

[15] Heckerman, D.E., Probabilistic Interpretations for MYCIN's Certainty Factors, in "Uncertainty in Artificial Intelligence", (Kanal, L. and Lemmer, J., eds.), North Holland, 1986.

PROPAGATION OF BELIEF FUNCTIONS:
A DISTRIBUTED APPROACH

Prakash P. Shenoy, Glenn Shafer and Khaled Mellouli

School of Business, University of Kansas, Lawrence, Kansas 66045-2003, USA

I. Abstract and Introduction

In this paper, we describe a scheme for propagating belief functions in certain kinds of trees using only local computations. This scheme generalizes the computational scheme proposed by Shafer and Logan[1] for diagnostic trees of the type studied by Gordon and Shortliffe[2,3] and the slightly more general scheme given by Shafer[4] for hierarchical evidence. It also generalizes the scheme proposed by Pearl[5] for Bayesian causal trees (see Shenoy and Shafer[6]).

Pearl's causal trees and Gordon and Shortliffe's diagnostic trees are both ways of breaking the evidence that bears on a large problem down into smaller items of evidence that bear on smaller parts of the problem so that these smaller problems can be dealt with one at a time. This localization of effort is often essential in order to make the process of probability judgment feasible, both for the person who is making probability judgments and for the machine that is combining them. The basic structure for our scheme is a type of tree that generalizes both Pearl's and Gordon and Shortliffe's trees. Trees of this general type permit localized computation in Pearl's sense. They are based on qualitative judgments of conditional independence.

We believe that the scheme we describe here will prove useful in expert systems. It is now clear that the successful propagation of probabilities or certainty factors in expert systems requires much more structure than can be provided in a pure production-system framework. Bayesian schemes, on the other hand, often make unrealistic demands for structure. The propagation of belief functions in trees and more general networks stands on a middle ground where some sensible and useful things can be done.

We would like to emphasize that the basic idea of local computation for propagating probabilities is due to Judea Pearl. It is a very innovative idea; we do not believe that it can be found in the Bayesian literature prior to Pearl's work. We see our contribution as extending the usefulness of Pearl's idea by generalizing it from Bayesian probabilities to belief functions.

In the next section, we give a brief introduction to belief functions. The notions of qualitative independence for partitions and a qualitative Markov tree are introduced in Section III. Finally, in Section IV, we describe a scheme for propagating belief functions in qualitative Markov trees.

II. Belief Functions

Suppose Θ denotes a set of possible answers to some question, one and only one of which is correct. We call Θ a *frame of discernment*. A function Bel that assigns a degree of belief Bel(A) to every subset A of Θ is called a *belief function* if there is a random nonempty subset S of Θ such that Bel(A) = Pr$[S \subseteq A]$ for all A.

Dempster's rule of combination is a rule for calculating a new belief function from two or more belief functions. Consider two random non-empty subsets S_1 and S_2. Suppose S_1 and S_2 are probabilistically independent, and suppose Pr$[S_1 \cap S_2 \neq \emptyset] > 0$. Let S be a random non-empty subset that has the probability distribution of $S_1 \cap S_2$ conditional on $S_1 \cap S_2 \neq \emptyset$. If Bel$_1$ and Bel$_2$ are the belief functions corresponding to S_1 and S_2 then we denote the belief function corresponding to S by Bel$_1 \oplus$ Bel$_2$, and we call Bel$_1 \oplus$ Bel$_2$ the *orthogonal sum* of Bel$_1$ and Bel$_2$. The rule for forming Bel$_1 \oplus$ Bel$_2$ is called *Dempster's rule of combination*. Intuitively, Bel$_1 \oplus$ Bel$_2$ represents the result of pooling the evidence represented by the separate belief functions whenever these items of evidence are independent.

A subset S of Θ is called a *focal element* of Bel if Pr$[S = S]$ is positive. In general, combination by Dempster's rule involves the intersection of focal elements. The focal elements for Bel$_1 \oplus ... \oplus$Bel$_n$ will consist of all non-empty intersections of the form $S_1 \cap ... \cap S_n$, where S_i is a focal element of Bel$_i$. The computations involved in combining belief functions by Dempster's rule may become prohibitively complex when Θ is large since the number of subsets increases exponentially with the size of the frame. Hence it is important to exploit any special structure in the belief functions being combined that may help us reduce the computational burden.

One case where computational complexity of Dempster's rule can be reduced is the case where the belief functions being combined are "carried" by a partition $\wp$ of the frame Θ. The complexity can be reduced in this case because $\wp$, which has fewer elements than Θ, can in effect be used in the place of Θ when the computations are carried out.

Recall that a set $\wp$ of subsets of Θ is a *partition* of Θ if the sets in $\wp$ are all non-empty and disjoint, and their union is Θ. Given a partition $\wp$ of Θ, we denote by $\wp^*$ the set consisting of all unions of elements of $\wp$; $\wp^*$ is a field of subsets of Θ generated by $\wp$. We say that a belief function Bel over Θ is *carried* by $\wp$ if the random subset S corresponding to Bel satisfies

$\Pr[S \in \wp^*] = 1$. It is evident that a belief function Bel is carried by the partition $\wp$ generated by taking intersections of the belief function's focal elements. We can think of such a partition $\wp$ as a qualitative description of the belief function Bel and will refer to $\wp$ as the partition *associated* with Bel.

A partition $\wp$ of a frame Θ can itself be regarded as a frame. If Bel is a belief function on Θ, then the *coarsening* of Bel to $\wp$ is the belief function $\text{Bel}_\wp$ on $\wp$ given by

$\text{Bel}_\wp(\{P_1, ..., P_k\}) = \text{Bel}(P_1 \cup ... \cup P_k)$ for every subset $\{P_1, ..., P_k\}$ of $\wp$. If Bel is a belief function on $\wp$, then the *vacuous extension* of Bel to Θ is the belief function Bel^Θ given by $\text{Bel}^\Theta(A) = \text{Bel}(\cup\{P \mid P \subseteq A, P \in \wp\})$. If a belief function is carried by $\wp$, then $\text{Bel}_\wp$ contains all the information about Bel. In fact, in this case, Bel can be recovered from $\text{Bel}_\wp$ by vacuous extension: $(\text{Bel}_\wp)^\Theta = \text{Bel}$. If $\wp_1$ and $\wp_2$ are two partitions, and Bel is a belief function on $\wp_1$, then the *projection* of Bel to $\wp_2$ is the result of vacuously extending Bel to Θ and then coarsening to $\wp_2$.

III. Qualitative Markov Trees

The concept of conditional independence is familiar from probability theory, and it leads within probability theory to many other concepts, including Markov chains and Markov networks. In this section, we introduce a purely qualitative (non-probabilistic) concept of conditional independence and the corresponding concept of a qualitative Markov tree. Qualitative Markov trees are the setting for our computational scheme for propagating belief functions.

Let $\wp_1$ and $\wp_2$ be two distinct partitions. We say that $\wp_1$ is *coarser* than $\wp_2$ (or equivalently that $\wp_2$ is *finer* than $\wp_1$), written as $\wp_1 > \wp_2$, if for each $P_2 \in \wp_2$, there exists $P_1 \in \wp_1$ such that $P_1 \supseteq P_2$. We call $\wp_1$ a *coarsening* of $\wp_2$ and $\wp_2$ a *refinement* of $\wp_1$. We write $\wp_1 \geq \wp_2$ to indicate that $\wp_1$ is coarser than or equal to $\wp_2$. The relation $\geq$ is a partial order and the set of all partitions is a lattice with respect to this partial order (Birkhoff[7]). The *coarsest common refinement* of $\wp_1, ..., \wp_n$ or the greatest lower bound of $\wp_1, ..., \wp_n$ with respect to $\geq$, denoted by $\wedge\{\wp_j \mid j = 1, ..., n\}$ or by $\wp_1 \wedge ... \wedge \wp_n$, is the partition $\{P_1 \cap ... \cap P_n \mid P_j \in \wp_j, \text{ for } j = 1, ..., n, \text{ and } P_1 \cap ... \cap P_n \neq \emptyset\}$.

We say that $\wp_1, ..., \wp_n$ are **qualitatively independent**, written as

$[\wp_1, ..., \wp_n]\dashv$, if for any $P_j \in \wp_j$ for $j = 1, ..., n$, we have $P_1 \cap ... \cap P_n \neq \emptyset$. Furthermore,

we say that $\wp_1, ..., \wp_n$ are **qualitatively conditionally independent** given $\wp$, written as

$[\wp_1, ..., \wp_n]\dashv\wp$, if whenever we select $P \in \wp$, $P_i \in \wp_i$ for $i = 1, ..., n$ such that

$P \cap P_i \neq \emptyset$ for $i = 1, ..., n$, then $P \cap P_1 \cap ... \cap P_n \neq \emptyset$. These definitions do not involve probabilities; just logical relations. But (stochastic) conditional independence for random variables does imply qualitative conditional independence for associated partitions (see Shafer, Shenoy and Mellouli[9] for details).

Qualitative conditional independence is important for belief functions because it is used in defining the circumstances under which we get the right answer when we implement Dempster's rule on a partition rather than on a finer frame (see Shafer[8], p. 177).

Theorem 3.1 If Bel_1 and Bel_2 are carried by $\wp_1$ and $\wp_2$ respectively, and $[\wp_1, \wp_2]\dashv\wp$, then $(\text{Bel}_1 \oplus \text{Bel}_2)_\wp = (\text{Bel}_1)_\wp \oplus (\text{Bel}_2)_\wp$.

Another consequence of qualitative conditional independence is as follows (see Shafer, Shenoy and Mellouli[9] for details and a proof of this result).

Theorem 3.2 Suppose that $[\wp_1, \wp_2]\dashv\wp$. Let Bel_2 be carried by $\wp_2$. Then

$(\text{Bel}_2)\wp_1 = ((\text{Bel}_2)\wp)\wp_1$.

We now consider networks where the nodes represents partitions and the edges represent certain qualitative conditional independence restrictions on the partitions. An (undirected) **network** is a pair (J, E), where J, the **nodes** of the network, is a finite set, and E, the **edges** of the network, is a set of unordered pairs of distinct elements of J. We say that $i \in J$ and $j \in J$ are **adjacent** or **neighbors** if $\{i, j\} \in E$. A node is said to be a *leaf* node if it has exactly one neighbor. A network is a *tree* if it is connected and there are no cycles.

A **qualitative Markov network** for $\{\wp_j \mid j \in J\}$ is a network (J, E) such that given any three mutually disjoint subsets J_1, J_2, and J_3 of J, if J_1 and J_2 are *separated* by J_3 (in the sense that any path from a node in J_1 to a node in J_2 goes via some node in J_3), then

$[\wedge\{\wp_j \mid j \in J_1\}, \wedge\{\wp_j \mid j \in J_2\}]\dashv \wedge\{\wp_j \mid j \in J_3\}$.

If (J, E) is a qualitative markov network for $\{\wp_j \mid j \in J\}$ and the network (J, E) is a tree, then we say that (J, E) is a *qualitative Markov tree* for $\{\wp_j \mid j \in J\}$. A characterization of qualitative Markov trees is as follows (see Shafer, Shenoy and Mellouli[9] for a proof of this characterization).

Theorem 3.3 Let $\{\wp_j \mid j \in J\}$ be a finite collection of partitions and let (J, E) be a tree. Given any node n in J, deletion of n from J and deletion of all edges incident to n from E results in a forest of m subtrees. Let the collection of nodes in the kth subtree be denoted by $J_{k,n}$. Then (J, E) is a qualitative Markov tree for $\{\wp_j \mid j \in J\}$ if and only if for every $n \in J$,

$$[\wedge\{\wp_i \mid i \in J_{1,n}\}, ..., \wedge\{\wp_i \mid i \in J_{m,n}\}] \dashv \wp_n.$$

IV. Propagating Belief Functions in Qualitative Markov Trees

Suppose T = (J, E) is a qualitative Markov tree for $\{\wp_i \mid i \in J\}$, and suppose that for every node i in J we have a belief function Bel_i carried by $\wp_i$. We are interested in the orthogonal sum of all these belief functions, for which we use the symbol Bel^T:

$$Bel^T = \oplus\{Bel_i \mid i \in J\}.$$

We do not, however, need to know $Bel^T(A)$ for all subsets A of the frame Θ. We need to know only $Bel^T(A)$ for certain A that are in the various fields $\wp_i*$. This means that we will be satisfied if we can compute the coarsening $Bel^T \wp_i$ for every node i.

The coarsening $Bel^T \wp_i$ can in fact be computed efficiently by a simple recursive scheme that begins at the leaf nodes of T and moves towards node i while computing belief functions analogous to $Bel^T \wp_i$ for successively larger subtrees of T. This recursive scheme gains its efficiency from the fact that the computations it requires are local relative to the tree T. In place of a single global application of Dempster's rule, using Θ or $\wedge\{\wp_i \mid i \in J\}$ as our frame, we make many local applications of the rule, using the partitions $\wp_i$ as frames. Since the computational cost of the rule increases exponentially with the size of the frame, these numerous local applications can be inexpensive relative to a global application, provided the $\wp_i$ are all fairly small.

Given a subtree $U = \{J_U, E_U\}$ of T, let Bel^U denote the orthogonal sum $\oplus\{Bel_i \mid i \in J_U\}$. Removal of node n (and all edges incident to node n) from T results in a set of subtrees, one for each neighbor k of n. Let V_n denote the neighbors of n, and for each k in V_n, let $T_{k,n} = (J_{k,n}, E_{k,n})$ denote the subtree containing k (that results when n is removed from T). The basic relation that allows recursive computation of $Bel^T \wp_n$ is stated in Theorem 4.1 below.

Theorem 4.1. Let $T = \{J, E\}$ be a qualitative markov tree for $\{\wp_i \mid i \in J\}$ and let Bel_i be carried by $\wp_i$ for each i in J. Then

$$Bel^T \wp_n = Bel_n \oplus (\oplus\{(Bel^{T_{k,n}} \wp_k) \wp_n \mid k \in V_n\}) \tag{4.1}$$

Proof: Since

$$Bel^T = Bel_n \oplus (\oplus\{Bel^{T_{k,n}} \mid k \in V_n\}),$$

Bel_n is carried by $\wp_n$, $Bel^{T_{k,n}}$ is carried by $\wedge\{\wp_j \mid j \in J_{k,n}\}$, and

$$[\wedge\{\wp_j \mid j \in J_{k,n}\}]_{k \in V_n} \dashv \wp_n,$$

it follows from Theorem 3.1 that

$$Bel^T \wp_n = Bel_n \oplus (\oplus\{Bel^{T_{k,n}} \wp_n \mid k \in V_n\}).$$

Since

$$[\wp_n, \wedge\{\wp_j \mid j \in J_{k,n}\}] \dashv \wp_k$$

for every $k \in V_n$, it follows from Theorem 3.2 that

$$Bel^{T_{k,n}} \wp_n = (Bel^{T_{k,n}} \wp_k) \wp_n. \qquad \text{Q.E.D.}$$

The belief functions in the right hand side of (4.1), Bel_n and $(Bel^{T_{k,n}} \wp_k) \wp_n$ for $k \in V_n$, are all carried by $\wp_n$, and hence their orthogonal sum can be computed using $\wp_n$ as a frame. The computation is recursive because $Bel^{T_{k,n}} \wp_k$ is the same type of object as $Bel^T \wp_n$, except that it is based on the smaller tree $T_{k,n}$. We need, of course, to get the recursion started; we need to be able to compute $Bel^U \wp_j$ when U is a tree containing only the node j, or perhaps j and some of its neighbors. But this is easy. If U consists of the single node j, then (4.1) tells us that

$$Bel^U \wp_j = Bel_j, \tag{4.2}$$

and if U consists of j and some of its neighbors, say in V_j', then (4.1) tells us that

$$\text{Bel}^U \wp_j = \text{Bel}_j \oplus (\oplus \{(\text{Bel}_k) \wp_j \mid k \in V_j'\}). \tag{4.3}$$

We can take either (4.2) or (4.3) as the starting point of the recursion.

In order to see more clearly how to direct the recursion, let us introduce some further notation. Given two neighboring nodes i and j in the tree T, set

$$\text{Bel}_{j \to i} = (\text{Bel}^{T_{j,i}} \wp_j) \wp_i$$

where, as noted before, $T_{j,i}$ denotes the subtree containing j that results when i is removed from T. With this notation, (4.1) can be written as

$$\text{Bel}^T \wp_n = \text{Bel}_n \oplus (\oplus \{\text{Bel}_{k \to n} \mid k \in V_n\}). \tag{4.4}$$

Moreover, Theorem 4.1 applied to $T_{j,i}$ tells us that

$$\text{Bel}_{j \to i} = \left(\text{Bel}_j \oplus (\oplus \{\text{Bel}_{k \to j} \mid k \in (V_j - \{i\})\})\right) \wp_i \tag{4.5}$$

for any neighboring nodes i and j. If j is a leaf node and i is its only neighbor, then the set $V_j - \{i\}$ is empty, and then (4.5) says simply that $\text{Bel}_{j \to i} = (\text{Bel}_j) \wp_i$.

Formulae (4.4) and (4.5) suggest a very simple way to program our recursive computations of $\text{Bel}^T \wp_i$ in a forward chaining production system. We begin with a working memory that contains Bel_i for each node i in J, and we use just two rules:

Rule 1:

If $j \in J, i \in V_j$, $\text{Bel}_{k \to j}$ is present in working memory for every k in $V_j - \{i\}$, and Bel_j is present in working memory,

then use (4.5) to compute $\text{Bel}_{j \to i}$ and place it in working memory.

Rule 2:

If $i \in J$, $\text{Bel}_{k \to i}$ is present in working memory for every k in V_i, and Bel_i is present in working memory,

then use (4.4) to compute $\text{Bel}^T \wp_i$, and then print it.

Notice that Rule 1 will fire initially only for leaf nodes, since initially no $\text{Bel}_{k \to j}$ are in working memory. Rule 1 will eventually fire in both directions for every edge (i, j) producing both $\text{Bel}_{j \to i}$ and $\text{Bel}_{i \to j}$. We assume that repetitions of these firings are prevented by a refractory principle that prevents a rule from firing again for the same instantiation of the antecedent. Rule 2 will eventually fire for every i. Thus the total number of firings is equal to $2(|J| - 1) + |J| = 3|J| - 2$.

The potential efficiency of this computational scheme is enhanced by the fact that many of the applications of Dempster's rule on different $\wp_i$ can be carried out in parallel. We can make this potential parallelism graphic by imagining that a separate processor is assigned to each $\wp_i$. The processor assigned to $\wp_i$ computes $Bel^T \wp_i$ and $Bel_{i \to k}$ using (4.4) and (4.5) respectively. This means that it combines belief functions using $\wp_i$ as a frame. It also projects belief functions from $\wp_i$ to $\wp_k$, where k is a neighbor of i.

Since the processor assigned to $\wp_i$ communicates directly with the processor devoted to $\wp_k$ only when k is a neighbor of i, the Markov tree itself can be thought of as a picture of the architecture of the parallel machine; the nodes are processors and the links are communication lines. In this parallel machine, the "working memory" of the production system implementation is replaced by local memory registers at the links. We may assume that every link, there are two sets of memory registers -- one for communication in each direction. Thus at the link between i and k, say, there will be one set of registers where i writes $Bel_{i \to k}$ for k to read, and another where k writes $Bel_{k \to i}$ for i to read. Each processor i also has an input register, where Bel_i is written from outside the machine, and an output register, where it writes $Bel^T \wp_i$. Figure 1 shows a typical processor, with three neighbors.

We may assume that the processor at i begins work on the computations it is authorized to perform as soon as it receives the necessary inputs. In other words, it computes $Bel_{i \to j}$ as soon as it receives Bel_i and $Bel_{k \to i}$ for all $k \in V_i - \{j\}$, and it computes $Bel^T \wp_i$ as soon as it receives Bel_i and $Bel_{k \to i}$ for all $k \in V_i$. If we further assume that the processor does not repeat computations for the same inputs, and if we input all the Bel_i before turning the processors on, then our parallel machine will operate in fundamentally the same way as the production system we described above.

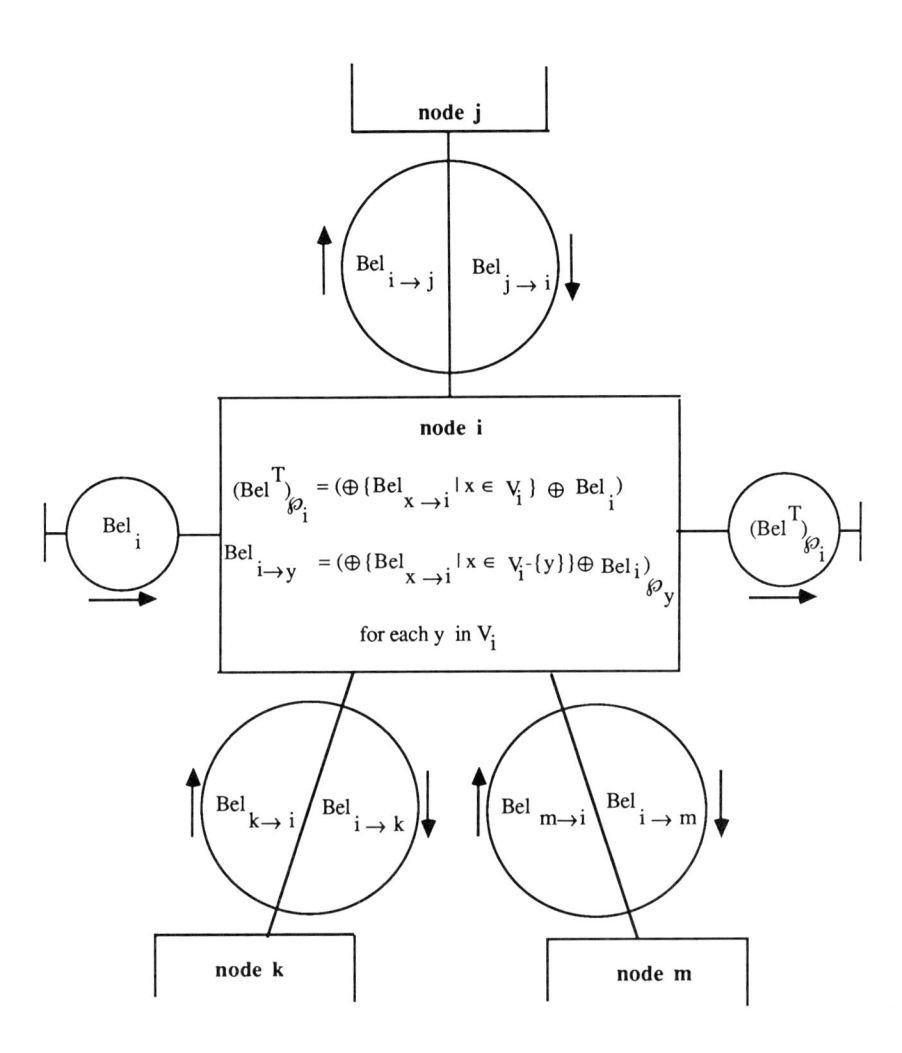

Figure 1 A typical node processor (with three neighbors).

The parallel machine could also be operated in a more dynamic way. Instead of entering all Bel_i before starting the computations, the Bel_i could be entered at any time. Initially, to get the computations started, we let all the belief functions Bel_i to be vacuous. Then as we accumulate independent pieces of evidence, we enter these (non-vacuous) belief functions reprsenting the evidence at the appropriate nodes in the tree. Note that if we have two or more independent pieces of evidence that is represented by belief functions carried by the same node $\wp_i$, and these belief functions are all entered at $\wp_i$, then the processor at $\wp_i$ combines all the belief functions input to it to form a belief function Bel_i. Also note that the refractory principle does not prevent the two rules from firing again for the same edges and nodes if the instantiation is different (as a result of entering a new belief function at a node).

V. Conclusion

The scheme described above is not an algorithm. It does not specify how the coarsenings from one partition to its neighbors are to be carried out, since the most efficient way to do this will depend on the particular nature of the relations between these partitions. The details of the implementation of Dempster's rule at the level of each partition may also depend on the nature of the belief functions being combined there. The general scheme is useful, however, because of its conceptual clarity and its unifying role. In particular, it unifies two computational schemes that had previously seemed rather disparate: Pearl's scheme for propagation of probabilities in Bayesian causal trees (Pearl[5]) and Shafer and Logan's scheme for combining belief functions in diagnostic trees (Shafer and Logan[1]). Both these schemes are special cases of the general scheme for propagation in qualitative Markov trees, and they derive most of their computational power from this fact though they also exploit special features of the problem they solve. Pearl's scheme derives some computational power from the simplicity of Bayesian probability measures relative to general belief functions, and Shafer and Logan's scheme derives some computational power from Barnett's technique (Barnett[10]) which it is able to exploit because the belief functions being combined are "simple support functions" (i.e., have atmost two focal elements one of which is the frame Θ). A comparison of Pearl's and Shafer and Logan's schemes with the general scheme presented here is sketched in Shenoy and Shafer[6].

VI. Acknowledgements

Research for this paper has been partially supported by NSF grants IST-8405210, IST-8610293, and by ONR grant N00014-85-K-0490.

VII. References

1. G. Shafer, and R. Logan, "Implementing Dempster's Rule For Hierarchical Evidence," *Working Paper* No. 174, 1985, School of Business, University of Kansas.

2. J. Gordon, and E. H. Shortliffe, "A Method For Managing Evidential Reasoning In Hierarchical Hypothesis Spaces," *Artificial Intelligence*, Vol. 26, 1985, pp. 323-358.

3. J. Gordon, and E. H. Shortliffe, "The Dempster-Shafer Theory of Evidence," in *Rule-Based Expert Systems: The MYCIN Experiments of The Stanford Heuristic Programming Project*, eds. B. G. Buchanan and E. H. Shortliffe, Addison-Wesley, 1985.

4. G. Shafer, "Hierarchical Evidence," in *The Second Conference on Artificial Intelligence Applications - The Engineering of Knowledge-Based Systems*, IEEE Computer Society Press, 1985, pp. 16-25.

5. J. Pearl, "Fusion, Propagation, And Structuring In Bayesian Networks," *Artificial Intelligence*, Vol. 29, 1986, pp. 241-288.

6. P. P. Shenoy and G. Shafer, "Propagating Belief Functions with Local Computations," *IEEE Expert*, Vol. 1, No. 3, 1985, pp. 43-52.

7. G. Birkhoff, *Lattice Theory*, American Mathematical Society Colloquium Publications, Vol. XXV, 1967.

8. G. Shafer, *A Mathematical Theory of Evidence*, Princeton University Press, 1976.

9. G. Shafer, P. P. Shenoy, and K. Mellouli, "Propagating Belief Functions in Qualitative Markov Trees," *Working Paper* No. 186, 1986, School of Business, University of Kansas.

10. J. A. Barnett, "Computational Methods for A Mathematical Theory of Evidence," in *Proceedings of the 7th International Joint Conference on Artificial Intelligence*, 1981, pp. 868-875.

GENERALIZING FUZZY LOGIC PROBABILISTIC INFERENCES

Silvio URSIC

Ursic Computing
810 Ziegler Rd.
Madison, Wisconsin 53714

Linear representations for a subclass of boolean symmetric functions selected by a parity condition are shown to constitute a generalization of the linear constraints on probabilities introduced by Boole. These linear constraints are necessary to compute probabilities of events with relations between them arbitrarily specified with propositional calculus boolean formulas.

1. INTRODUCTION

Given the probabilities of some events, we wish to compute the probabilities of some other events. The terms "event" and "probability" are to be understood as having the meaning assigned to them in statistics. The following example is representative of the problems and of the type of solution we seek for the problem. Let A and B be two events from a sample space U, and let $P(x)$ indicate a probability measure on events in U. Given $P(A)$ and $P(B)$, without any additional information about possible relations between A and B, what can we say about $P(A\&B)$? From Boole [7], page 299, we have:

$$\max(\ 0,\ P(A) + P(B) - 1\ ) \leq P(A\&B) \leq \min(\ P(A),\ P(B)\ ). \tag{1}$$

For example, for $P(A) = 0.4$ and $P(B) = 0.8$, we conclude $0.2 \leq P(A \& B) \leq 0.4$. The constraints on $P(A\&B)$ in (1) represent the worst case when nothing at all is known about A and B. For example, if A and B are known to be statistically independent, we then have $P(A\&B) = P(A) \cdot P(B) = 0.32$, and $0.2 \leq 0.32 \leq 0.4$. Quoting Boole [7] page 304 verbatim:

> "Given the respective numbers of individuals comprised in any classes, s, t, & c, logically defined, to deduce a system of numerical limits of any other class w, also logically defined.".

Given the number of elements present in each set of a collection of subsets of U, Boole general method intends to compute lower and upper bounds on the number of elements in any other subset described with what we today know as a "Boolean formula". In equating the computation of probabilities with counting, Boole assumed an equally likely probability measure on the elements, or members, or objects, constituting the sample space U. Counting and computing probabilities are intimately connected. For additional information on the topic, from a complexity theory point of view, consult [16, 27, 35, 38, 48, 49].

The first sentence of George Boole 1854 book " AN INVESTIGATION OF THE LAWS OF THOUGHT ON WHICH ARE FOUNDED THE MATHEMATICAL THEORIES OF LOGIC AND PROBABILITIES" is: "The design of the following treatise is to investigate the fundamental laws of those operations of the mind by which reasoning is performed". The simulation of human reasoning, for Boole, was a probablistic problem. Boole then explained how this would entail blending Calculus, Logic and Probability. Since then, the problem studied by Boole has assumed a variety of identities. It is variously known as discrete probability, probability logic, probabilistic logic, fuzzy logic, reasoning with uncertainty, uncertain inference, approximate deduction, evidential reasoning, probabilistic reasoning and many others. Under all those labels we find, with no exception, Boole's min-max formulas (1). In using formulas (1) we tacitly assume the validity of his probabilistic approach and of the many ramifications it entails. As repeatedly pointed out by Boole, formulas (1) are definitely not all there is. When our events are "logically defined" with what we today know as a (propositional calculus) boolean formula, many other inequalities become also necessary.

Conceptually, we will follow Boole's plan for the problem. To find out more precisely what the plan is, the reader is invited to acquire a copy of [7] and read its first chapter (23 pages), titled "Nature and design of this work". A very thorough appraisal of these ideas, with contemporary notation, can be found in Hailperin [20]. Some further developments can be found in [11, 13, 14]. We will use tools and techniques totally unknown to Boole. One hundred and thirty years of continuous mathematical development have produced substantial advances. Besides much improved linear algebra tools, what follows owes its existence to a collection of ideas and techniques developed mostly in the last fifteen years and known as (computability) complexity theory, in particular NP-completeness theory [9, 23]. NP-completeness, while not providing directly any specific algorithms, has had the very beneficial effect of helping us better understand what truly needs to be done.

1.1. The product partition

We will introduce with an example the techniques to be utilized to generalize (1) for any collection of events with arbitrary relationships between them. We will use standard probability theory language and concepts. Consult, for example, the book by Gangolli & Ylvisaker [15]. We start with the product partition probability simplex. It describes the fact that the probability of each event in the product partition generated by the collection of events under consideration is nonnegative and, being disjoint and covering the whole universe, their probabilities must add up to one. We have (we indicate event complementation with an overbar and a logical "AND", that is set intersection, with "&"):

$P(A\&B) \geq 0$, $P(\bar{A}\&B) \geq 0$, $P(A\&\bar{B}) \geq 0$, $P(\bar{A}\&\bar{B}) \geq 0$,

$P(A\&B) + P(\bar{A}\&B) + P(A\&\bar{B}) + P(\bar{A}\&\bar{B}) = 1$. (2)

We now describe the events A and B as a union of events from the product partition. Any event can be so described. We have (we indicate a logical "OR", that is set union with "v", Peano's "vel" [30]):

$A = A\&B \vee A\&\bar{B}$, $B = A\&B \vee \bar{A}\&B$. (3)

Converting to probabilities we have:

$P(A) = P(A\&B) + P(A\&\bar{B})$, $P(B) = P(A\&B) + P(\bar{A}\&B)$. (4)

The system of linear equations and inequalities in (2) and (4) has six variables, namely $P(A)$, $P(B)$, $P(A\&B)$, $P(\bar{A}\&B)$, $P(A\&\bar{B})$ and $P(\bar{A}\&\bar{B})$. We eliminate the variables that do not interest us with a projection of the probability simplex on the linear subspace defined by $P(A)$, $P(B)$ and $P(A\&B)$. We obtain:

$$0 \leq P(A\&B)$$
$$0 \leq P(A) - P(A\&B)$$
$$0 \leq P(B) - P(A\&B)$$
$$0 \leq 1 - P(A) - P(B) + P(A\&B). \tag{5}$$

All the probabilities for events that do not interest us, namely $P(\bar{A}\&B)$, $P(A\&\bar{B})$ and $P(\bar{A}\&\bar{B})$, are thus eliminated. Each inequality in (5) provides an upper or a lower bound for $P(A\&B)$, as a function of $P(A)$ and $P(B)$, and we have Boole's inequalities (1).

In our example the reduction in the number of variables achieved with the projection of the product partition probability simplex on the events subspace is not significant. We reduced the number of variables from six to three. With a larger number of events, the exponential growth in the number of elements in the product partition will be overwhelming. Without some method of elimination of unwanted events the entire procedure outlined in the example can be classified as a "thought experiment". We can apply it to ten events, but not one hundred.

1.2. Choice of a programming language for event description

By "event description" we mean here an algorithm able to recognize the objects constituting the event we wish to describe. Perhaps a more precise characterization would be "event recognition". In some sense, the vernacular we use every day is such a programming language. When we say "I understand what you are saying" what we truly mean is that we have acquired an algorithm (an algorithm has been downloaded to our brain, translated to our own machine language, so we can run it in our hardware) capable of recognizing the same set of objects recognized by the originator of the communication. From this point of view, understanding is algorithm transfer. One may identify the set of objects constituting the event with a table (a data base). The recognition algorithm then is simply a table lookup. This data base approach is a valid way of expressing the effect of a recognition algorithm, but does not lead very far. Over the data base approach an algorithm, as represented by a boolean formula, offers the advantage of being able to recognize events with a number of objects which can be exponential in relation to the size of the describing boolean formula.

The need for a programming language to describe events is therefore essential. Human (and programming languages) communicate recognition algorithms for events of interest. The choice made here is to describe events with boolean formulas in conjunctive normal form with a bounded number of literals per clause. The significance of this normal form was made clear by Blake [6]. Such propositional calculus formulas are to be understood as representing recognition algorithms, see [2, 8]. From NP-completeness theory, we know that it is possible to transform to this form, in polynomial time, any algorithm able to recognize the objects in an event in polynomial time. In our context, this choice limits the kind of linear subspaces in which we must project the probability simplex. The limitation is drastic and simplifies matters consideraby. The computation of the projection of the partition simplex becomes much easier as only subspaces of a specific form have to be manipulated.

1.3. A second example

The next example introduces the notation we will use and illustrates that other forms of inequalities arise besides the ones in (5). We will project the partition simplex defined by the three events x, y, and z onto the subspace defined by events defined by all the clauses of a boolean formula in conjunctive normal form with exactly two literals per clause. The following matrix defines the events of interest. Its rows are labeled with boolean clauses. Its colums are labeled with all the events of the product partition. We omit the logical "&" and write, for example, $x\bar{y}$ for $x\&\bar{y}$. We also omit the functional notation for probabilities. Each column of the matrix defines the event that labels it in terms of events in the product partition. For example, from the first column of this matrix we have $xy = xyz + xy\bar{z}$, or expanding the notation, we have $P(x\&y) = P(x\&y\&z) + P(x\&y\&\bar{z})$. We have:

$$
\begin{array}{ccccccccccccl}
xy & x\bar{y} & \bar{x}y & \bar{x}\bar{y} & xz & x\bar{z} & \bar{x}z & \bar{x}\bar{z} & yz & y\bar{z} & \bar{y}z & \bar{y}\bar{z} & \\
|\ 1 & 0 & 0 & 0 & 1 & 0 & 0 & 0 & 1 & 0 & 0 & 0 & |\ xyz \\
|\ 1 & 0 & 0 & 0 & 0 & 1 & 0 & 0 & 0 & 1 & 0 & 0 & |\ xy\bar{z} \\
|\ 0 & 1 & 0 & 0 & 1 & 0 & 0 & 0 & 0 & 0 & 1 & 0 & |\ x\bar{y}z \\
|\ 0 & 1 & 0 & 0 & 0 & 1 & 0 & 0 & 0 & 0 & 0 & 1 & |\ x\bar{y}\bar{z} \\
|\ 0 & 0 & 1 & 0 & 0 & 0 & 1 & 0 & 1 & 0 & 0 & 0 & |\ \bar{x}yz \\
|\ 0 & 0 & 1 & 0 & 0 & 0 & 0 & 1 & 0 & 1 & 0 & 0 & |\ \bar{x}y\bar{z} \\
|\ 0 & 0 & 0 & 1 & 0 & 1 & 0 & 0 & 0 & 0 & 1 & 0 & |\ \bar{x}\bar{y}z \\
|\ 0 & 0 & 0 & 1 & 0 & 0 & 0 & 1 & 0 & 0 & 0 & 1 & |\ \bar{x}\bar{y}\bar{z}
\end{array}
\qquad (6)
$$

The columns of this matrix are linearly dependent. We choose as a basis for its column space the collection of events corresponding to clauses with no negation. Other useful choices are possible. With our choice we obtain the following matrix as a basis for this linear subspace:

$$
\begin{array}{ccccccc|l}
\emptyset & x & y & z & xy & xz & yz & \\
|\ 1 & 1 & 1 & 1 & 1 & 1 & 1 & |\ xyz \\
|\ 1 & 1 & 1 & 0 & 1 & 0 & 0 & |\ xy\bar{z} \\
|\ 1 & 1 & 0 & 1 & 0 & 1 & 0 & |\ x\bar{y}z \\
|\ 1 & 1 & 0 & 0 & 0 & 0 & 0 & |\ x\bar{y}\bar{z} \\
|\ 1 & 0 & 1 & 1 & 0 & 0 & 1 & |\ \bar{x}yz \\
|\ 1 & 0 & 1 & 0 & 0 & 0 & 0 & |\ \bar{x}y\bar{z} \\
|\ 1 & 0 & 0 & 1 & 0 & 0 & 0 & |\ \bar{x}\bar{y}z \\
|\ 1 & 0 & 0 & 0 & 0 & 0 & 0 & |\ \bar{x}\bar{y}\bar{z}
\end{array}
\qquad (7)
$$

The label $\emptyset$ corresponds to the empty clause, and hence corresponds to the sample space. We wish to project the product partition probability simplex on the linear subspace defined by the events $\emptyset$, x, y, z, xy, xz and yz. As the vertices of the product partition probability simplex form an identity matrix this projection is simply the convex hull of the points whose coordinates are given by the rows of matrix (7). This convex hull is the polytope described by the inequalities:

$$
\begin{aligned}
1 - x - y + xy &\geq 0 & 1 - x - z + xz &\geq 0 & 1 - y - z + yz &\geq 0 \\
x - xy &\geq 0 & x - xz &\geq 0 & y - yz &\geq 0 \\
y - xy &\geq 0 & z - xz &\geq 0 & z - yz &\geq 0 \\
xy &\geq 0 & xz &\geq 0 & yz &\geq 0
\end{aligned}
\qquad (8)
$$

$$
\begin{aligned}
1 - x - y - z + xy + xz + yz &\geq 0 \\
x - xy - xz + yz &\geq 0 \\
y - xy + xz - yz &\geq 0 \\
z + xy - xz - yz &\geq 0
\end{aligned}
\qquad (9)
$$

The first group of inequalities (8) corresponds to Boole's inequalities (1). The second group (9) does not.

2. GENERATING FUNCTIONS FOR BOOLEAN FORMULAS

This section presents an algebraic description for the clauses of boolean formulas in conjunctive normal form in terms of generating functions. Our goal consists in giving algebraic descriptions for the family of matrices represented by matrix (6).

2.1. Generating functions in matrix form

At their inception, generating functions list the objects on some set. See, for example, how they are introduced in Riordan [34]. The paper by Polya [32] is a very interesting and explicit presentation of this fact. This basic idea of listing objects with generating functions will be developed here. We will consider matrices with labeled rows and columns. We will indicate by <+> the joining by columns of two matrices with identically labeled rows. The dual operator <+>^{T} will indicate the joining by rows of two matrices with identically labeled columns. We will indicate by <*> the standard tensor, or Kronecker, product of two matrices. For basic linear algebra information consult, for example, Pease [31] and Stoer & Witzgall [41]. Row and column labels of the tensor product will be sets, unions of the corresponding row and column labels of the factors. In small examples we will use x, y, z and w as row and column labels for the matrices. In recursive definitions we will use $x_1, x_2, \ldots, x_N$. The empty set, or the empty label, will be indicated with ∅. The starting point is the following matrix:

$$A_x = \begin{array}{c|ccc|c} & \emptyset & x & \bar{x} & \\ & 1 & 1 & 0 & x \\ & 1 & 0 & 1 & \bar{x} \end{array} \quad (1)$$

The labels x and $\bar{x}$ represent a boolean variable (or a statistical event) and its negation (its complement). We will call literals boolean variables or their negations. The row labels $\bar{x}$ and x represent the two events in the product partition defined by the single event x. The column labels ∅, x, and $\bar{x}$ represent the three events defined by all the clauses of a boolean formula in conjunctive normal form in a single variable, namely x. Matrix A_x can be interpreted as defining three characteristic functions, its three columns defining three sets on the two elements x and $\bar{x}$ of the product partition generated by the event x. The event corresponding to clause ∅ has as elements both $\bar{x}$ and x. A logical "AND", that is set intersection, will be performed with tensor products. This is possible because the multiplication table for zeros and ones over the reals mimics an intersection. As an example, consider:

$$A_x <*> A_y = \begin{array}{c|ccc|c} & \emptyset & x & \bar{x} & \\ & 1 & 1 & 0 & x \\ & 1 & 0 & 1 & \bar{x} \end{array} <*> \begin{array}{c|ccc|c} & \emptyset & y & \bar{y} & \\ & 1 & 1 & 0 & y \\ & 1 & 0 & 1 & \bar{y} \end{array} \quad (2)$$

$$= \begin{array}{c|ccc|ccc|ccc|c} & \emptyset & x & \bar{x} & y & xy & \bar{x}y & \bar{y} & x\bar{y} & \bar{x}\bar{y} & \\ & 1 & 1 & 0 & 1 & 1 & 0 & 0 & 0 & 0 & xy \\ & 1 & 0 & 1 & 1 & 0 & 1 & 0 & 0 & 0 & \bar{x}y \\ & 1 & 1 & 0 & 0 & 0 & 0 & 1 & 1 & 0 & x\bar{y} \\ & 1 & 0 & 1 & 0 & 0 & 0 & 1 & 0 & 1 & \bar{x}\bar{y} \end{array} \quad (3)$$

Row and column labels for matrix (3) are sets whose elements are the row and column labels of A_x and A_y. The column labeled xy defines the characteristic function for x v y. Similar matrix products have had a decisive role in the development of the fast Fourier transform, see [1, 18]. They have also been found useful in [1, 12, 18, 26, 28, 42]. Let us sort the columns of this matrix by the size of its column labels. Using a standard generating functions technique, we add a parameter t to sort the columns of matrix (3) by the size of their labels. First define two additional matrices E_x (Empty label) and L_x (Literal x).

$$E_x = \begin{array}{c|c} \emptyset & x \\ \hline 1 & x \\ 1 & \bar{x} \end{array} \quad ; \quad L_x = \begin{array}{c|cc|c} & x & \bar{x} & \\ \hline 1 & 0 & x \\ 0 & 1 & \bar{x} \end{array} . \tag{4}$$

We now have $A_x = E_x \text{<+>} L_x$, and the product in (2) can be rewritten with the t added. We obtain:

$$(E_x \text{<+>} L_x \text{<*>} t) \text{<*>} (E_y \text{<+>} L_y \text{<*>} t) =$$

$$\begin{array}{c|c} \emptyset & \\ \hline 1 & xx \\ 1 & \bar{x}y \\ 1 & x\bar{y} \\ 1 & \bar{x}\bar{y} \end{array} \text{<+>} \begin{array}{c|cccc|c} & x & \bar{x} & y & \bar{y} & \\ \hline 1 & 0 & 1 & 0 & xy \\ 0 & 1 & 1 & 0 & \bar{x}y \\ 1 & 0 & 0 & 1 & x\bar{y} \\ 0 & 1 & 0 & 1 & \bar{x}\bar{y} \end{array} \text{<*>} t \text{<+>} \begin{array}{c|cccc|c} & xy & \bar{x}y & x\bar{y} & \bar{x}\bar{y} & \\ \hline 1 & 0 & 0 & 0 & xy \\ 0 & 1 & 0 & 0 & \bar{x}y \\ 0 & 0 & 1 & 0 & x\bar{y} \\ 0 & 0 & 0 & 1 & \bar{x}\bar{y} \end{array} \text{<*>} t^2. \tag{5}$$

To obtain the generating function for the clauses of a boolean formula in conjunctive normal form in N variables and exactly i literals per clause, indicated with $C_{N,i}$, we write:

$$\underset{1 \leq i \leq N}{\text{<*>}} (E_i \text{<+>} L_i \text{<*>} t) = \underset{0 \leq i \leq N}{\text{<+>}} C_{N,i} \text{<*>} t^i \tag{6}$$

where L_i and E_i are the matrices L and E indexed with x_i. Formula (6) defines a matrix with 3^N columns and 2^N rows. The terms with t^i select the matrices $C_{N,i}$, whose columns correspond to clauses with exactly i literals. As a consequence of (6) it is possible to use the binomial recursion to obtain an alternate definition for the matrices $C_{N,i}$. We have:

$$C_{0,0} = \begin{array}{c|c} \emptyset & \\ \hline 1 & \emptyset \end{array}; \quad \text{for } i \neq 0, \ C_{0,i} = \emptyset;$$

$$C_{N,i} = C_{N-1,i} \text{<*>} \begin{array}{c|c} \emptyset & \\ \hline 1 & x_N \\ 1 & \bar{x}_N \end{array} \text{<+>} C_{N-1,i-1} \text{<*>} \begin{array}{c|cc|c} & x_N & \bar{x}_N & \\ \hline 1 & 0 & x_N \\ 0 & 1 & \bar{x}_N \end{array} \tag{7}$$

Recursion (7) closely mimics the binomial recursion. It generates matrices which define the logical meaning of the clauses of a boolean formula in conjunctive normal form in N variables and with exactly i literals per clause. The first few matrices generated by (7) are:

$C_{0,0} = 1; \ C_{0,1} = \emptyset; \ C_{0,2} = \emptyset; \ C_{0,2} = \emptyset;$

$$C_{1,0} = \begin{array}{c|c} \emptyset & \\ \hline 1 & x_1 \\ 1 & \bar{x}_1 \end{array} \ ; \quad C_{1,1} = \begin{array}{c|cc|c} & x_1 & \bar{x}_1 & \\ \hline 1 & 0 & x_1 \\ 0 & 1 & \bar{x}_1 \end{array} \ ; \quad C_{1,2} = \emptyset; \ C_{1,3} = \emptyset;$$

$$C_{2,0} = \begin{array}{c|c} \emptyset & \\ \hline 1 & x_1 x_2 \\ 1 & x_1 \bar{x}_2 \\ 1 & \bar{x}_1 x_2 \\ 1 & \bar{x}_1 \bar{x}_2 \end{array}; \quad C_{2,1} = \begin{array}{c|cccc|c} & x_1 & \bar{x}_1 & x_2 & \bar{x}_2 & \\ \hline 1 & 0 & 1 & 0 & x_1 x_2 \\ 1 & 0 & 0 & 1 & x_1 \bar{x}_2 \\ 0 & 1 & 1 & 0 & \bar{x}_1 x_2 \\ 0 & 1 & 0 & 1 & \bar{x}_1 \bar{x}_2 \end{array}; \quad C_{2,2} = \begin{array}{c|cccc|c} & x_1 x_2 & \bar{x}_1 x_2 & x_1 \bar{x}_2 & \bar{x}_1 \bar{x}_2 & \\ \hline 1 & 0 & 0 & 0 & x_1 x_2 \\ 0 & 1 & 0 & 0 & \bar{x}_1 x_2 \\ 0 & 0 & 1 & 0 & x_1 \bar{x}_2 \\ 0 & 0 & 0 & 1 & \bar{x}_1 \bar{x}_2 \end{array} .$$

Recursion (7) defines matrices with 2^N rows, labeled with all the distinct truth assignments to N variables, and $2^p C_{N,p}$ columns, labeled with all the clauses in exactly p literals. Many identities involving binomial coefficients that have been collected as a byproduct of research on some combinatorial problem are usable here. For example, compare and contrast the following identity pairs, $c_{N,p}$ for binomial coefficients and $C_{N,p}$ for binomial matrices:

$$c_{N+M,p} = \sum_i c_{N,i} \cdot c_{M,p-i}; \qquad C_{N+M,p} = \underset{i}{<+>} C_{N,i} <*> C_{M,p-i}; \qquad (8)$$

$$\sum_i c_{N,i} = 2^N; \qquad \underset{i}{<+>} C_{N,i} = \underset{1 \leq i \leq N}{<*>} A_i. \qquad (9)$$

2.2. The binomial matrices

We will call with the general name of BINOMIAL MATRICES various families of matrices defined with matrix recursions similar to the binomial recursion. This section presents some of their properties.

The matrices $C_{N,i}$ usually do not have linearly independent columns. We will select a suitable basis for their column space in Theorem B. We start by subdividing the matrix L_x (literal x) in two to obtain the two matrices V_x (variable x) and $\bar{V}_x$ (variable $\bar{x}$), with $L_x = V_x <+> \bar{V}_x$. We have:

$$V_x = \begin{array}{c|c|c} & x & \\ \hline 1 & x \\ \hline 0 & \bar{x} \end{array} \quad ; \quad \bar{V}_x = \begin{array}{c|c|c} & \bar{x} & \\ \hline 0 & x \\ \hline 1 & \bar{x} \end{array} \qquad (10)$$

The two vectors in (10) are two of the columns of A_x in (1). We choose as a basis for the column space of A_x the two vectors labeled $\emptyset$ and x. This in turn leads to bases for the matrices $C_{N,i}$ whose column labels do not have negations. With (10) we define two additional families of matrices, which provide us with the wanted bases. They are the families of matrices, for $0 \leq i \leq N$, $R_{N,i}$ and $B_{N,i}$. As the two vectors V_x and E_x are a subset of the columns of A_x, the matrices $R_{N,i}$ and $B_{N,i}$ will be formed with a subset of the columns of $C_{N,i}$. Let us define:

$$R_{0,0} = 1, \quad \text{for } i \neq 0, \ R_{0,i} = \emptyset;$$

$$R_{N,i} = R_{N-1,i-1} <*> V_N <+> R_{N-1,i} <*> E_N; \qquad (11)$$

$$B_{N,p} = \underset{0 \leq i \leq p}{<+>} R_{N,i}. \qquad (12)$$

The matrices $R_{N,i}$ correspond to clauses whose literals have no negation, that is monotone clauses, with exactly i variables. The matrices $B_{N,i}$ correspond to monotone clauses with up to i variables. Starting with definitions (11) and (12) we obtain a recursive definition for the matrices $B_{N,i}$ similar to the ones for $C_{N,i}$ and $R_{N,i}$. We proceed as follows:

[Use definition (12)]
$$B_{N,p} = \underset{0 \leq i \leq p}{<+>} R_{N,i}$$

[Use definition (11)]
$$= \underset{0 \leq i \leq p}{<+>} (R_{N-1,i-1} <*> V_N <+> R_{N-1,i} <*> E_N)$$

[Separate sums]
$$= (\underset{0 \leq i \leq p}{<+>} R_{N-1,i-1}) <*> V_N <+> (\underset{0 \leq i \leq p}{<+>} R_{N-1,i}) <*> E_N$$

[Use definition (11)]
$$= B_{N-1,p-1} <*> V_N <+> B_{N-1,p} <*> E_N. \tag{13}$$

We have a recurrence relation for $B_{N,p}$. The start up for it is given by

$$B_{0,p} = \underset{0 \leq i \leq p}{<+>} R_{0,i}, \quad \text{and hence, using (11), is:}$$

for $i < 0$, $B_{0,i} = \emptyset$; for $i \geq 0$, $B_{0,i} = 1$.

Notice that this start up is different from the one used in (7) for the matrices $C_{N,i}$, or the one in (11) for the matrices $R_{N,i}$. In identities, the matrices $B_{N,i}$ behave like the binomial coefficients sum

$$\underset{0 \leq i \leq p}{\Sigma} c_{N,i} = c_{N,0} + c_{N,1} + \ldots + c_{N,p}. \tag{14}$$

Knuth [25] on page 64 mentions that there seems to be no simple formula for (14), meaning it does not seem possible to obtain identities for it without the explicit summation sign. It is nevertheless possible to derive meaningful identities involving (14). As the columns of matrices $B_{N,i}$ will be proven, in theorem B, to be a basis for the column space of matrices $C_{N,i}$, the sum (14) assumes a special status here. Riordan [34], pp. 128-130, reports some results with binomial identities involving (14). We have, for example, the following matrix identity:

$$B_{N+M,p} = \underset{0 \leq i \leq N}{<+>} (R_{N,i} <*> B_{M,p-i}) = \underset{0 \leq i+j \leq p}{<+>} (R_{N,i} <*> R_{M,j}). \tag{15}$$

2.3. The basis theorem

We are now ready to choose a basis for the column space of the matrices $C_{N,i}$. This choice is performed in the next theorem.

<u>Theorem B</u> (Computation of the Basis). The columns of $B_{N,p}$ are a basis for the column space of $C_{N,p}$.

<u>Proof.</u> The matrices $B_{N,p}$ were defined so that this would be true. We show that the columns of $B_{N,p}$ are the wanted basis in two steps. First we show that they are a spanning set for the column space of $C_{N,p}$. We then show that they are linearly independent. We proceed as follows:

[Use definition of the matrices $C_{N,i}$]
$$\underset{0 \leq i \leq p}{<+>} C_{N,i} = \underset{0 \leq i \leq p}{<+>} (C_{N-1,i-1} <*> L_N <+> C_{N-1,i} <*> E_N)$$

[Separate the sum in two parts]
$$= (\underset{0 \leq i \leq p}{<+>} C_{N-1,i-1} <*> L_N) <+> (\underset{0 \leq i \leq p}{<+>} C_{N-1,i} <*> E_N)$$

[Shift indices of first sum, separate last term of the second sum]
$$= (\underset{0 \leq i \leq p-1}{<+>} C_{N-1,i} <*> L_N) <+>$$

$$(\underset{0 \leq i \leq p-1}{<+>} C_{N-1,i} <*> E_N) <+> (C_{N-1,p} <*> E_N)$$

[Merge sums]
$$= (\underset{0 \leq i \leq p-1}{<+>} C_{N-1,i} <*> (L_N <+> E_N)) <+> (C_{N-1,p} <*> E_N). \tag{16}$$

But, by definition

$$L_N <+> E_N = V_N <+> \bar{V}_N <+> E_N. \tag{17}$$

We choose as a basis for the two by three matrix in (17) the two column vectors V_N and E_N. Hence a spanning set of vectors for the column space of (1) is given by:

[Discard $\bar{V}_N$ by substituting ($L_N <+> E_N$) with ($V_N <+> E_N$)]

$$(\underset{0 \leq i \leq p-1}{<+>} C_{N-1,i} <*> (V_N <+> E_N)) <+> (C_{N,p} <*> E_N). \tag{18}$$

[Rearrange terms]

$$= (\underset{0 \leq i \leq p-1}{<+>} C_{N-1,i} <*> V_N) <+> (\underset{0 \leq i \leq p}{<+>} C_{N-1,i} <*> E_N) \tag{19}$$

We can now use relations (12) to show that the columns of $B_{N,p}$ are indeed our spanning set. We proceed by induction on N. In fact, for any p, the columns of $B_{0,p}$ are a spanning set for the column space of

$$\underset{0 \leq i \leq p}{<+>} C_{0,i}$$

This follows immediately from definition (7). Hence the property is true for N = 0. Let us suppose that the columns of $B_{N-1,p}$, for any p, are a spanning set for the column space of

$$\underset{0 \leq i \leq p}{<+>} C_{N-1,i} .$$

Substituting in (19) we obtain the following spanning set for it:

$$B_{N-1,p-1} <*> V_N <+> B_{N-1,p} <*> E_N$$

[Use definition of $B_{N,p-1}$ and $B_{N,p}$]

$$= (\underset{0 \leq i \leq p-1}{<+>} (R_{N-1,i-1} <*> V_N <+> R_{N-1,i} <*> E_N)$$

[Use definition of $R_{N,i}$]

$$= \underset{0 \leq i \leq p}{<+>} R_{N,i} = B_{N,p} .$$

The first part of our proof is now complete. We showed that the columns of $B_{N,p}$ are the required spanning set. For the second part we have:

$$B_{N,N} = \underset{0 \leq i \leq N}{<+>} R_{N,i}$$

[Use definition for $R_{N,i}$]

$$= \underset{0 \leq i \leq N}{<+>} (R_{N-1,i-1} <*> V_N <+> R_{N-1,i} <*> E_N)$$

[Split sum and use the fact that $R_{N-1,N} = \emptyset$]

$$= (\underset{0 \leq i \leq N-1}{<+>} R_{N-1,i} <*> V_N) <+> (\underset{0 \leq i \leq N-1}{<+>} R_{N-1,i} <*> E_N)$$

[Merge sums]

$$= (\underset{0 \leq i \leq N-1}{<+>} R_{N-1,i}) <*> (V_N <+> E_N)$$

[Use definition for $B_{N-1,N-1}$]
$$= B_{N-1,N-1} <*> (V_N <+> E_N)$$

As $B_{1,1}$ is $(V_1 <+> E_1)$, by induction we have an alternate definition for the matrix $B_{N,N}$:

$$B_{N,N} = \underset{1 \leq i \leq N}{<*>} (V_i <+> E_i). \tag{20}$$

The matrices $(V_i <+> E_i)$, for $1 \leq i \leq N$, are two by two matrices of rank two. Hence $B_{N,N}$ is a 2^N by 2^N matrix of rank 2^N. In particular, the columns of $B_{N,p}$, as they are a subset of the columns of $B_{N,N}$, are linearly independent./-/

2.4. Binomial identities in matrix form

The families $B_{N,i}$ and $R_{N,i}$ have been defined with subsets of the columns of $C_{N,i}$. A further subdivision of their entries into smaller submatrices is necessary. The building blocks for the recursive definitions of these smaller submatrices are given by the following two by two matrix, with labeled rows and columns, defined with the entries of the matrices V_x and E_x.

$$G_x = \begin{array}{c|cc|c} & \emptyset & x & \\ \hline \emptyset & 1 & 0 & \bar{x} \\ x & 1 & 1 & x \end{array} = \begin{array}{c|cc|c} & \emptyset & x & \\ \hline & a_x & b_x & \bar{x} \\ & c_x & d_x & x \end{array}. \tag{21}$$

The four entries in matrix G_x can be considered one by one labeled matrices. We have:

$$a_x = \begin{array}{c|c} \emptyset \\ \hline 1 \end{array} \bar{x}; \quad b_x = \begin{array}{c|c} x \\ \hline 0 \end{array} \bar{x}; \quad c_x = \begin{array}{c|c} \emptyset \\ \hline 1 \end{array} x; \quad d_x = \begin{array}{c|c} x \\ \hline 1 \end{array} x; \tag{22}$$

Our main family of matrices is recursively defined as follows:

$$r_{0,0,0} = \begin{array}{c|c} & \emptyset \\ \hline & 1 \end{array} \emptyset; \quad \text{for } i, j \neq 0, \; r_{0,i,j} = \emptyset; \tag{23}$$

$$r_{N,i,j} = \begin{pmatrix} r_{N-1,i,j} <*> a_N & <+> & r_{N-1,i,j-1} <*> b_N \\ r_{N-1,i-1,j} <*> c_N & <+> & r_{N-1,i-1,j-1} <*> d_N \end{pmatrix}^T$$

$$= \begin{vmatrix} r_{N-1,i,j} <*> a_N & r_{N-1,i,j-1} <*> b_N \\ r_{N-1,i-1,j} <*> c_N & r_{N-1,i-1,j-1} <*> d_N \end{vmatrix}. \tag{24}$$

Definition (24) closely mirrors a recursive definition for binomial coefficients, applied twice to the indices i and j of $r_{N,i,j}$. We can describe it as a doubly binomial recursion. The family of matrices $r_{N,i,j}$ are defined for $N \geq 0$ and are non-void in the range $0 \leq i, j \leq N$. For example:

$$r_{1,0,0} = \begin{vmatrix} a_1<*>r_{0,0,0} & b_1<*>r_{0,0,-1} \\ c_1<*>r_{0,-1,0} & d_1<*>r_{0,-1,-1} \end{vmatrix} = \begin{array}{c|c|c} & \emptyset & \emptyset \\ \hline \emptyset & 1 & \emptyset \\ \hline & \emptyset & \emptyset \end{array} \bar{x}_1 = \begin{array}{c|c} \emptyset \\ \hline 1 \end{array} \bar{x}_1;$$

$$r_{5,3,2} = \begin{vmatrix} a_5<*>r_{4,3,2} & b_5<*>r_{4,3,1} \\ c_5<*>r_{4,2,2} & d_5<*>r_{4,2,1} \end{vmatrix}$$

	x_1x_2	x_1x_3	x_1x_4	x_2x_3	x_2x_4	x_3x_4	x_1x_5	x_2x_5	x_3x_5	x_4x_5		
|	1	1	0	1	0	0 |	0	0	0	0	|	$x_1x_2x_3\bar{x}_4\bar{x}_5$
|	1	0	1	0	1	0 |	0	0	0	0	|	$x_1\bar{x}_2x_3x_4\bar{x}_5$
|	0	1	1	0	0	1 |	0	0	0	0	|	$x_1\bar{x}_2x_3x_4\bar{x}_5$
|	0	0	0	1	1	1 |	0	0	0	0	|	$\bar{x}_1x_2x_3x_4\bar{x}_5$
= |	1	0	0	0	0	0 |	1	1	0	0	|	$x_1x_2\bar{x}_3\bar{x}_4x_5$
|	0	1	0	0	0	0 |	1	0	1	0	|	$x_1\bar{x}_2x_3\bar{x}_4x_5$
|	0	0	1	0	0	0 |	1	0	0	1	|	$x_1\bar{x}_2\bar{x}_3x_4x_5$
|	0	0	0	1	0	0 |	0	1	1	0	|	$\bar{x}_1x_2x_3\bar{x}_4x_5$
|	0	0	0	0	1	0 |	0	1	0	1	|	$\bar{x}_1x_2\bar{x}_3x_4x_5$
|	0	0	0	0	0	1 |	0	0	1	1	|	$\bar{x}_1\bar{x}_2x_3x_4x_5$

The next identity, theorem E is the counterpart of the binomial identity (9). The matrices G_i assume the role of the constant "two" and the matrices $r_{N,i,j}$ are doubly binomial, either by the row index i or by the column index j.

Theorem E (The exponential identity for binomial coefficients in matrix form). The following is a matrix identity:

$$\underset{1 \leq i \leq N}{<*>} G_i = \underset{0 \leq i \leq N}{<+>^T} \left(\underset{0 \leq j \leq N}{<+>} r_{N,i,j} \right). \tag{25}$$

<u>Proof</u>. By induction on N. In relation to the similar proof for binomial coefficients, we have the additional complication of having to take care of two indices, for the rows and columns.

Formula (25) is true for N = 1. In this case it reduces to

$$G_1 = (a_1 <+> b_1) <+>^T (c_1 <+> d_1),$$

which is true by definition. The proof of the induction step develops as follows:

[Separate G_N from the product.]

$$\underset{1 \leq i \leq N}{<*>} G_i = \left(\underset{1 \leq i \leq N-1}{<*>} G_i \right) <*> G_N$$

[Use induction hypothesis for N-1 and definition of matrix G_N.]

$$= \underset{0 \leq i \leq N-1}{<+>^T} \left(\underset{0 \leq j \leq N-1}{<+>} r_{N-1,i,j} \right) <*> ((a_N <+> b_N) <+>^T (c_N <+> d_N))$$

[Perform tensor product.]

$$= \underset{0 \leq i \leq N-1}{<+>^T} \left(\underset{0 \leq j \leq N-1}{<+>} ((r_{N-1,i,j} <*> a_N <+> r_{N-1,i,j} <*> b_N) <+>^T \right.$$
$$\left. (r_{N-1,i,j} <*> c_N <+> r_{N-1,i,j} <*> d_N))\right)$$

[Extend summation ranges using $r_{N,i,j} = \emptyset$ for i, j not in $0 \leq i, j \leq N$.]

$$= \left(\underset{0 \leq i \leq N}{<+>^T} \left(\underset{0 \leq j \leq N}{<+>} r_{N-1,i,j} <*> a_N \right) <+> \right.$$

$$\underset{0 \leq i \leq N}{<+>^T} \left(\underset{-1 \leq j \leq N-1}{<+>} r_{N-1,i,j} <*> b_N \right) <+>^T$$

$$\left(\underset{-1 \leq i \leq N-1}{<+>^T} \left(\underset{0 \leq j \leq N}{<+>} r_{N-1,i,j} <*> c_N \right) <+> \right.$$

$$\underset{-1 \leq i \leq N-1}{<+>^T} \left(\underset{-1 \leq j \leq N-1}{<+>} r_{N-1,i,j} <*> d_N \right) \right)$$

[Shift the indices and merge sums.]
$$= \underset{0 \leq i \leq N}{<+>^T} (\underset{0 \leq j \leq N}{<+>} ((r_{N-1,i,j} <*> a_N <+> r_{N-1,i,j-1} <*> b_N) <+>^T$$
$$(r_{N-1,i-1,j} <*> c_N <+> r_{N-1,i-1,j-1} <*> d_N))$$

[Use defining recurrence relation for $r_{N,i,j}$.]
$$= \underset{0 \leq i \leq N}{<+>^T} (\underset{0 \leq j \leq N}{<+>} r_{N,i,j}).$$

We conclude that (25) is indeed an identity. /-/

The following example, with N = 3, illustrates the effect of Theorem E. We have:

$$\underset{0 \leq i \leq 3}{<+>^T} (\underset{0 \leq j \leq 3}{<+>} r_{3,i,j}) = \begin{vmatrix} r_{3,0,0} & r_{3,0,1} & r_{3,0,2} & r_{3,0,3} \\ r_{3,1,0} & r_{3,1,1} & r_{3,1,2} & r_{3,1,3} \\ r_{3,2,0} & r_{3,2,1} & r_{3,2,2} & r_{3,2,3} \\ r_{3,3,0} & r_{3,3,1} & r_{3,3,2} & r_{3,3,3} \end{vmatrix}$$

	∅	x_1	x_2	x_3	x_1x_2	x_1x_3	x_2x_3	$x_1x_2x_3$	
	1	0	0	0	0	0	0	0	$\bar{x}_1\bar{x}_2\bar{x}_3$
	1	1	0	0	0	0	0	0	$x_1\bar{x}_2\bar{x}_3$
	1	0	1	0	0	0	0	0	$\bar{x}_1x_2\bar{x}_3$
	1	0	0	1	0	0	0	0	$\bar{x}_1\bar{x}_2x_3$
=	1	1	1	0	1	0	0	0	$x_1x_2\bar{x}_3$
	1	1	0	1	0	1	0	0	$x_1\bar{x}_2x_3$
	1	0	1	1	0	0	1	0	$\bar{x}_1x_2x_3$
	1	1	1	1	1	1	1	1	$x_1x_2x_3$

$$\underset{1 \leq i \leq 3}{<*>} G_i =$$

	∅	x_1	x_2	x_1x_2	x_3	x_1x_3	x_2x_3	$x_1x_2x_3$	
	1	0	0	0	0	0	0	0	$\bar{x}_1\bar{x}_2\bar{x}_3$
	1	1	0	0	0	0	0	0	$x_1\bar{x}_2\bar{x}_3$
	1	0	1	0	0	0	0	0	$\bar{x}_1x_2\bar{x}_3$
	1	1	1	1	0	0	0	0	$x_1x_2\bar{x}_3$
	1	0	0	0	1	0	0	0	$\bar{x}_1\bar{x}_2x_3$
	1	1	0	0	1	1	0	0	$x_1\bar{x}_2x_3$
	1	0	1	0	1	0	1	0	$\bar{x}_1x_2x_3$
	1	1	1	1	1	1	1	1	$x_1x_2x_3$

From Theorem E, with the definitions for $R_{N,j}$ and $B_{N,p}$ we obtain the identities:

$$R_{N,j} = \underset{0 \leq i \leq N}{<+>^T} r_{N,i,j};$$

$$B_{N,p} = \underset{0 \leq j \leq p}{<+>} R_{N,j} = \underset{0 \leq j \leq p}{<+>} (\underset{0 \leq i \leq N}{<+>^T} r_{N,i,j}).$$

It should be emphasized that the identity (25) is an identity among matrix entries on the right and the left hand side of the equality sign having identical row and column labels. All that is truly achieved with Theorem E is to show that two matrices, defined in two different ways, are a row and column permutation of each other. Each step in the proof can be interpreted as performing some row and column permutations on some matrix.

The next theorem presents essential information about the entries and rank of the matrices $r_{N,i,j}$. This information will be used later in theorems V and R.

In it we perform various matrix products with the matrices $r_{N,i,j}$. As their row and column labels are different, to perform the products we need to define an association among these two sets of labels. Associate the column labels with the row labels, ignoring the negated variables in the row labels. For example, with variables x, y, z and w: column label xy corresponds to row label $xy\bar{z}\bar{w}$; column label ∅ corresponds to row label $\bar{x}\bar{y}\bar{z}\bar{w}$; column label xyw corresponds to row label $xy\bar{z}w$.

<u>Theorem P</u> (Properties of the binomial matrices). The following is true:

(A) Matrix $r_{N,i,j}$ has $c_{N,i}$ rows and $c_{N,j}$ columns;
(B) Matrix $r_{N,i,j}$ is a matrix of zeros and ones with exactly $c_{i,j}$ ones in each row and $c_{N-j,N-i}$ ones in each column;
(C) For $N \geq p \geq q \geq s \geq 0$ we have

$$r_{N,p,q} \cdot r_{N,q,s} = r_{N,p,s} <*> c_{p-s,q-s} \qquad (26)$$

where the binomial coefficient $c_{p-s,q-s}$ is considered a one by one unlabeled matrix;

(D) For $i \geq j$, matrix $r_{N,i,j}$ has full rank. If $c_{N,i} \leq c_{N,j}$ then its rows are linearly independent. If $c_{N,i} \geq c_{N,j}$ then its columns are linearly independent. If $c_{N,i} = c_{N,j}$ we have a full rank square matrix.

<u>Proof.</u> All four properties are proven by induction using the defining recursion, namely (25). The proof of properties (A) and (B) is uncomplicated. Property (C), that is identity (26), is trivially true for $N = 0$. The proof of the induction step is as follows:

[use defining recurrence (24) for $r_{N,p,q}$ and $r_{N,q,s}$]
$r_{N,p,q} \cdot r_{N,q,s}$ = { ($r_{N-1,p,q}$ <*> a_N <+> $r_{N-1,p,q-1}$ <*> b_N) <+>^{T}
    ($r_{N-1,p-1,q}$ <*> c_N <+> $r_{N-1,p-1,q-1}$ <*> d_N) } ·
{ ($r_{N-1,q,s}$ <*> a_N <+> $r_{N-1,q,s-1}$ <*> b_N) <+>^{T}
    ($r_{N-1,q-1,s}$ <*> c_N <+> $r_{N-1,q-1,s-1}$ <*> d_N) }

[perform the products using the matrix identity (A.B)<*>(C.D) = (A<*>C).(B<*>D)]
= { [($r_{N-1,p,q}$ · $r_{N-1,q,s}$) <*> (a_N · a_N) +
      ($r_{N-1,p,q-1}$ · $r_{N-1,q-1,s}$) <*> (b_N · c_N)] <+>
    [($r_{N-1,p,q}$ · $r_{N-1,q,s-1}$) <*> (a_N · b_N) +
      ($r_{N-1,p,q-1}$ · $r_{N-1,q-1,s-1}$) <*> (b_N · d_N)] } <+>^{T}
  { [($r_{N-1,p-1,q}$ · $r_{N-1,q,s}$) <*> (c_N · a_N) +
      ($r_{N-1,p-1,q-1}$ · $r_{N-1,q-1,s}$) <*> (d_N · c_N)] <+>
    [($r_{N-1,p-1,q}$ · $r_{N-1,q,s-1}$) <*> (c_N · b_N) +
      ($r_{N-1,p-1,q-1}$ · $r_{N-1,q-1,s-1}$) <*> (d_N · d_N)] }

[use induction hypothesis for $r_{N-1,x,x}$ and use the fact that b_N is zero]
= { ($r_{N-1,p,s}$ <*> $c_{p-s,p-q}$)   <*> a_N <+>
    ($r_{N-1,p,s-1}$ <*> $c_{p-s+1,q-s+1}$)   <*> b_N } <+>^{T}
  { ($r_{N-1,p-1,s}$ <*> $c_{p-s-1,p-q-1}$ + $r_{N-1,p,s}$ <*> $c_{p-s-1,p-q}$) <*> c_N <+>
    ($r_{N-1,p-1,s-1}$ <*> $c_{p-s,p-q}$)   <*> d_N }

[use defining recurrence (24)]
= $c_{p-s,q-s}$ <*> $r_{N,p,s}$

We thus have property (C).

Property (D) follows, also by induction, from the fact that the entry in b_i is zero. As a consequence, the matrices $r_{N,i,j}$ are block triangular. The two blocks on the diagonal, matrices $r_{N-1,i,j}$ and $r_{N-1,i-1,j-1}$, either both have row or column full rank and by induction on N we are done, or are mismatched, one full rank by rows and the other full rank by columns. In these two mismatched cases, case (D1) and case (D2), we have:

(D1) $c_{N-1,i} < c_{N-1,j}$ and $c_{N-1,i-1} > c_{N-1,j-1}$;
(D2) $c_{N-1,i} > c_{N-1,j}$ and $c_{N-1,i-1} < c_{N-1,j-1}$.

The two systems of inequalities (D1) and (D2) can be solved in the unknowns i and j. The additional condition $i \geq j$ discards indices corresponding to submatrices above the main diagonal of $B_{N,N}$, which are all zero. With this additional constraint, the inequalities in (D2) have no feasible solution. The inequalities in (D1) have as the only feasible solutions $N = i + j$. Hence we only have to consider case (D1). We have $c_{N,i} = c_{N,j}$ and the two matrices

$r_{N-1,i-1,j}$ and $r_{N-1,i,j-1}$

are square matrices and, by induction on N, full rank. Full rank for the square matrix $r_{N,i,j}$ follows from the following linear combination of its columns. Multiply the matrices $r_{N-1,i,j}$ and $r_{N-1,i-1,j}$ in (24) by

$r_{N-1,j,j-1}$ <*> $(1/c_{i-j,1})$

and subtract them from the other two matrices in (24). Use property (C). We obtain the matrix

$\begin{vmatrix} r_{N-1,i,j} & r_{N-1,i,j-1} \text{ <*> } (c_{i-j+1,1}/c_{i-j,1}) \\ r_{N-1,i-1,j} & 0 \end{vmatrix}$

which is block triangular and, by induction, is of full rank. /-/

Theorem P established basic information about the matrices generated by recursion (24). The next theorem makes critical use of them.

<u>Theorem V</u> (Generalized Vandermonde). Let a_i, $1 \leq i \leq k \leq N$, be distinct positive integers such that $c_{N,i} \leq c_{N,a_i}$. Then the matrix

$\underset{1 \leq i \leq k}{<+>^T} \underset{1 \leq j \leq k}{<+>} r_{N,a_i,j} = \begin{vmatrix} r_{N,a_1,1} & r_{N,a_1,2} & r_{N,a_1,3} & \cdots & r_{N,a_1,k} \\ r_{N,a_2,1} & r_{N,a_2,2} & r_{N,a_2,3} & \cdots & r_{N,a_2,k} \\ \vdots & \vdots & \vdots & & \vdots \\ r_{N,a_k,1} & r_{N,a_k,2} & r_{N,a_k,3} & \cdots & r_{N,a_k,k} \end{vmatrix}$ (27)

has linearly independent columns.

<u>Proof.</u> We will reduce it to block triangular form, with each matrix in the diagonal having full column rank. The technique is similar to the one normally employed to compute the determinant of Vandermonde matrix. See, for example, exercise 1.2.3-37 (Second set) of [25]. Knuth grades the exercise of difficulty [M24]. On Knuth scale, theorem V is probably an [M30], once we know what we are supposed to look for. The reader is invited to compare the proof that follows with the proof of exercise 1.2.3-37 on page 472 of [25].

For $j = 2, 3, \ldots, k$, in this order, subtract from column j-1 of (27) the product of column j with $r_{N-1,j,j-1}$ <*> $1/(a_k-j+1)$. By column of index j we mean here the submatrix of (27) given by

$\underset{1 \leq i \leq k}{<+>^T} r_{N,a_i,j}$.

Use the identity

$r_{N,a_i,j} \cdot r_{N,j,j-1} = r_{N,a_i,j-1}$ <*> $c_{a_i-j+1,1}$,

that is property (C) of theorem P. Use also $c_{a_i-j+1,1} = a_i-j+1$.

Generalizing Fuzzy Logic Probabilistic Inferences 351

For $j = 1, 2, \ldots, k-1$ the submatrices $r_{N, a_k, j}$ will be zeroed.

Factor $(a_k - a_j)$ from the columns of the result and continue the block triangularization on a matrix of the same kind of order k-1. Theorem V follows from the fact that, for $1 \leq i \leq k$, the matrices $r_{N, a_i, i}$ have linearly independent columns, by property (D) of theorem P. /-/

In this section we have defined four families of zero-one matrices. With the exception of the matrices $r_{N, i, j}$, their rows are in correspondence with all the 2^N events in the product partition. The families are:

$C_{N, i}$ -- columns correspond to all the $2^i c_{N, i}$ clauses with exactly i literals of a boolean formula in N variables;

$B_{N, i}$ -- columns correspond all to the $c_{N, 0} + c_{N, 1} + \ldots + c_{N, i}$ clauses of up to i literals with no negations (the monotone clauses) in N variables;

$R_{N, i}$ -- columns correspond to all the $c_{N, i}$ monotone clauses with exactly i literals in N variables;

$r_{N, i, j}$ -- rows correspond to labels with exactly i non-negated variables; columns correspond to monotone clauses with exactly j literals.

This concludes our study of "BINOMIAL MATRIXOLOGY" (My dictionary informs me that "matrix", in latin times, meant "pregnant animal" with further connections to the Indo-European root "mater", that is "mother").

It should be noted that not all binomial identities become binomial **MATRIX** identities. For example, the basic binomial identity $c_{N, i} = c_{N, N-i}$ has no counterpart here. To fix the discrepancy, it is possible to pursue binomial matrix identities for their own sake and define an operator <->, analogously to <+>, which removes columns from a matrix, instead of joining more columns to it, with some interesting results.

3. COMPUTING PROJECTIONS

We are now ready to compute faces of the projection of the product partition probability simplex on the events subspace. Computing faces of polytopes given by their vertices is the basic problem of polyhedral combinatorics. This is exactly our problem here. References [4, 5, 19, 22, 24, 29, 33] will provide information on the scope and breadth of the subject. In Ursic [48] we develop the related problem of counting exactly the number of satisfying truth assignments to a boolean formula, a #P-complete problem. Instead of projecting a simplex, as with probabilities, counting entails projecting the unit cube. Each event in the product partition in this exact counting case is constituted of a single object. The constraints for a partition event e become $0 \leq e \leq 1$, instead of simply $0 \leq e$. The problem of counting the number of solutions to #P-complete problems can also be expressed as a linear program in a polynomial number of variables.

It is convenient to explicitly list the boolean variables used to generate $B_{N, N}$ and $B_{N, p}$. We will write: $B_{3, 3} = G_x$ <*> G_y <*> $G_z = B_{3, 3}(x, y, z)$. We will call polytope $B_{N, p}$, the polytope that results form the projection of the probability simplex on the subspace specified by matrix $B_{N, p}$. We will indicate a face of $B_{N, p}$ with $f_{N, p}$. We will also write, for example $f_{4, 3}(x, y, z, w)$ for a face of $B_{4, 3}(x, y, z, w)$. Each matrix $B_{N, p}$ can be completed to the square and full rank matrix $B_{N, N}$ by joining suitable columns to it. We have:

$$B_{N, N} = B_{N, p} \text{ <+> } (\underset{p+1 \leq i \leq N}{\text{<+>}} R_{N, i}).$$

To obtain all the faces of polytope $B_{N, N}$, we have to compute the inverse of matrix $B_{N,N}$. This inverse is easy (formally) to compute. We have (using the matrix identity A^{-1} <*> B^{-1} = $(A$ <*> $B)^{-1}$):

$$(B_{N,N})^{-1} = (\underset{1 \leq i \leq N}{<*>} G_i)^{-1} = \underset{1 \leq i \leq N}{<*>} (G_i)^{-1} = \underset{1 \leq i \leq N}{<*>} \begin{array}{|cc|c} \bar{x}_i & x_i & \\ 1 & 0 & \emptyset \\ -1 & 1 & x_i \end{array}.$$

Each column of $(B_{N,N})^{-1}$ describes a face of $B_{N,N}$. For example, for N = 2 we have:

$$(B_{2,2})^{-1} = (G_1)^{-1} <*> (G_2)^{-1} = \begin{array}{|cc|cc|c} \bar{x}\bar{y} & x\bar{y} & \bar{x}y & xy & \\ 1 & 0 & 0 & 0 & \emptyset \\ -1 & 1 & 0 & 0 & x \\ \hline -1 & 0 & 1 & 0 & y \\ 1 & -1 & -1 & 1 & xy \end{array}.$$

From the column $\bar{x}\bar{y}$ we obtain $0 \leq 1 - x - y + xy$, a face of $B_{2,2}(x, y)$, with:

$$f_{2,2}(x, y) = \begin{array}{|c|c} 1 & \emptyset \\ -1 & x \\ -1 & y \\ 1 & xy \end{array}$$

As the columns of matrices $B_{N,p}$ are subsets of the columns of $B_{N,N}$, each face of polytope $B_{N,p}$ will be a positive linear combination of some of the faces of $B_{N,N}$. The Fourier multipliers used to obtain the projection form a column vector $h_{N,p}$ so that

$$\begin{aligned} f_{N,p} &= (B_{N,N})^{-1} \cdot h_{N,p}, \quad \text{or} \\ h_{N,p} &= B_{N,N} \cdot f_{N,p}. \end{aligned} \quad (1)$$

As $f_{N,p}$ is a face of $B_{N,p}$, and $B_{N,p}$ is a projection of $B_{N,N}$, we can also write

$$h_{N,p} = B_{N,p} \cdot f_{N,p}$$

with the understanding that all the zero entries in $f_{N,p}$ corresponding to columns of $B_{N,N}$ missing from $B_{N,p}$ will be disregarded. We say that $f_{N,p}$ defines a face, or is a face, of $B_{N,p}$ if the collection of vertices of $B_{N,p}$ touched by it defines a submatrix of maximum rank. Otherwise $f_{N,p}$ defines, or is, a facet of $B_{N,p}$ (facets are small faces).

3.1. Boolean symmetric functions

Symmetric functions have been appearing with some regularity in connections with methods to obtain solutions to boolean formulas. Our $s_{N,i}$ are exactly the the boolean functions defined by Whitehead in [50]. The many interesting properties of boolean symmetric functions have continued to direct attention to them from an algebraic and combinatorial point of view, as in [3, 10, 36, 37, 39]. For our purpose here we need a linear algebraic representation for boolean symmetric functions. We will indicate $s_{N,i}$, the elementary boolean symmetric function of index i in N variables, with a column vector with $c_{N,i}$ components, all equal to one, and with the row labels constructed with all the $c_{N,i}$ combinations of the N boolean variables. With this definition, the first few of the vectors defining the elementary symmetric functions are given by:

$$s_{0,0} = \begin{array}{|c|} 1 \mid \emptyset \end{array}; \quad s_{1,0}(x) = \begin{array}{|c|} 1 \mid \emptyset \end{array}; \quad s_{1,1}(x) = \begin{array}{|c|} 1 \mid x \end{array};$$

$$s_{2,0}(x,y) = \begin{vmatrix} 1 \\ 1 \end{vmatrix} \emptyset; \quad s_{2,1}(x,y) = \begin{vmatrix} 1 \\ 1 \end{vmatrix} \begin{vmatrix} x \\ y \end{vmatrix}; \quad s_{2,2} = \begin{vmatrix} 1 \\ 1 \end{vmatrix} xy;$$

$$s_{3,0}(x,y,z) = \begin{vmatrix} 1 \\ 1 \\ 1 \end{vmatrix} \emptyset; \quad s_{3,1}(x,y,z) = \begin{vmatrix} 1 \\ 1 \\ 1 \end{vmatrix} \begin{vmatrix} x \\ y \\ z \end{vmatrix}; \quad s_{3,2}(x,y,z) = \begin{vmatrix} 1 \\ 1 \\ 1 \end{vmatrix} \begin{vmatrix} xy \\ xz \\ yz \end{vmatrix}.$$

We are now ready to define some faces for $B_{N,p}$.

Theorem R (Representative faces). Let $a_1, \ldots, a_p$ be the constants used in theorem V, such that the product

$$\prod_{1 \leq k \leq p} (a_k - i) = (a_1 - i) \cdot (a_2 - i) \cdot \ldots \cdot (a_p - i). \tag{2}$$

is either non-negative or non-positive for $0 \leq i \leq N$. Compute the constants $b_0, b_1, \ldots, b_p$, by solving the homogeneous linear system

$$\text{for } 1 \leq j \leq p, \quad \sum_{0 \leq k \leq p} c_{a_j,k} \cdot b_k = 0. \tag{3}$$

Then
$$f_{N,p} = f_{N,(a_1, a_2, \ldots, a_p)} = \sum_{0 \leq k \leq p}^{<+>T} s_{N,k} \cdot b_k \tag{4}$$

defines a face of $B_{N,p}$, with the direction of the inequality given by the sign of (2).

Proof. We show how to locate a plane that touches all the points defined by the rows of the submatrix of $B_{N,p}$ forming the matrix (27) in theorem V. Most of our matrix manipulations so far had the next few lines as their objective. We have:

$$B_{N,p} \cdot f_{N,p} =$$

[use definition of $B_{N,p}$ and (4)]

$$= (\sum_{0 \leq i \leq N}^{<+>T} \sum_{0 \leq j \leq p}^{<+>} r_{N,i,j}) \cdot (\sum_{0 \leq j \leq p}^{<+>T} (s_{N,j} \cdot b_j))$$

[use the identity $r_{N,i,j} \cdot s_{N,j} = s_{N,i} \cdot c_{i,j}$ from property (B) of theorem P]

$$= \sum_{0 \leq i \leq N}^{<+>T} (s_{N,i} \cdot \sum_{0 \leq j \leq p} b_j \cdot c_{i,j}).$$

But, for $i = a_1, a_2, \ldots, a_p$, condition (3) applies. Hence, by theorem V, hyperplane $f_{N,p}$ as defined by (4), touches a subset of the rows of $B_{N,p}$ defining a matrix of maximum rank. To verify the position of all the other vertices of $B_{N,p}$ not touched by $f_{N,p}$ we must check the sign of the sums in (3) for all the other values that i can assume, besides $a_1, a_2, \ldots, a_p$. To this respect, add to the linear system (3) the linear equation

$$\sum_{0 \leq j \leq p} b_j \cdot c_{i,j} = t_i \tag{5}$$

in order to determine the sign of t_i. The quantity t_i will be a function of $a_1, a_2, \ldots, a_p$ and i. To compute t_i we have to evaluate two determinants of matrices whose entries are binomial coefficients. The entries in such matrices are rational polynomials. Its numerators are polynomials in a_j, and hence can be obtained as linear combinations of the columns of Vandermonde matrix. The denominators are factorials and can be ignored as they will not influence the sign of the determinant. We conclude that the sign of t_i is determined by the ratio of two determinants of Vandermonde matrices. The numerator is defined by the constants a_1, a_2, ... , a_p, and the denominator by the constants a_1, a_2, ... , a_p and i. Hence the sign of t_i is determined by the product (2). As i goes from zero to N, (5) will change sign every time i crosses one of the a_j. Equation (5) is zero whenever i is equal to one of the a_j. Hence condition (2) is satisfied by the constants a_1, a_2, ... ,a_p used in equation (4). /-/

The linear system (3) is homogeneous. We can use this fact to obtain its solutions, that is the constants b_0, b_1, ... , b_p, in a denominator free form, as a function of the constants a_j. We obtain

for $p = 1$, $b_0 = a_1$,
               $b_1 = -1$,

for $p = 2$, $b_0 = a_1 a_2$,
               $b_1 = 1 - a_1 - a_2$,
               $b_2 = 2$,

for $p = 3$, $b_0 = a_1 a_2 a_3$,
               $b_1 = -1 + a_1 + a_2 + a_3 - a_1 a_2 - a_1 a_3 - a_2 a_3$,
               $b_2 = -6 + 2a_1 + 2a_2 + 2a_3$,
               $b_3 = -6$.

The b_i are symmetric functions of the a_j. A particular permutation of the a_j does not influence the value of the b_i. For example, with $N = 1$, $p = 1$ and $a_1 = 1$ we obtain a face of $B_{1,1}(x)$:

$$f_{1,(1)}(x) = s_{1,0} <*> b_0 <+>^T s_{1,1}(x) <*> b_1 = \begin{vmatrix} 1 & \emptyset \\ -1 & x \end{vmatrix}.$$

Additional examples are given by:

$f_{2,(1,2)}(x, y) = 1-x-y+xy$;
$f_{3,(1,2)}(x, y, z) = 1-x-y-z+xy+xz+yz$;
$f_{3,(1,2,3)}(x, y, z) = 1-x-y-z+xy+xz+yz-xyz$;
$f_{5,(1,2)}(x, y, z, w, t) = 3-2x-2y-2z-2w-2t+xy+xz+xw+xt+yz+yw+yt+zw+zt+wt$.

3.2. Using minus-one-plus-one instead of zero-one

Our matrices of zeros and ones arise from the fact that we have chosen to write boolean formulas in conjunctive normal form. Despite of all the advantages of this zero-one formulation, we have found that to describe the symmetries of $B_{N,p}$ it is sometimes more convenient to use -1 and +1 instead of 0 and 1. As the multipication table for +1 and -1 mimics an "EXCLUSIVE OR", the (-1,+1) formulation is equivalent to using an exclusive-or normal form. We will use primed matrices to refer to the (-1, +1) case. In this (-1, +1) setting, the matrices G_x and $B_{N,N}$ become G'_x and $B'_{N,N}$:

$$G'_x = \begin{matrix} & \emptyset & x \\ & | 1 & 1 | & \bar{x} \\ & | & | \\ & | 1 & -1 | & x \end{matrix} \quad ; \quad B'_{N,N} = \underset{1 \leq i \leq N}{<*>} G'_i. \quad (6)$$

The changes of basis from zero-one variables to minus-one-plus-one variables are given by the matrix T_x and its inverse, computed as follows:

$$T_X = (G_X)^{-1} \cdot G'_X = \begin{array}{c} \emptyset \quad x \\ \begin{array}{|cc|} \hline 1 & 1 \\ 0 & -2 \\ \hline \end{array} \end{array} \begin{array}{c} \emptyset \\ x \end{array} \quad ; \quad (T_X)^{-1} = \begin{array}{c} \emptyset \quad x \\ \begin{array}{|cc|} \hline 1 & 1/2 \\ 0 & -1/2 \\ \hline \end{array} \end{array} \begin{array}{c} \emptyset \\ x \end{array} . \qquad (7)$$

With (7) we define the linear transformations:

$$(T_{N,N})^{-1} = \underset{1 \leq i \leq N}{<*>} (T_i)^{-1}; \quad T_{N,N} = \underset{1 \leq i \leq N}{<*>} T_i .$$

Hence the $(-1,+1)$ face corresponding to $_{N,p}$ is

$$f'_{N,p} = (T_{N,N})^{-1} \cdot f_{N,p} . \qquad (8)$$

In this $(-1, +1)$ form, the product partition probability simplex becomes a REGULAR SIMPLEX. This is a consequence of the fact that matrix $B'_{N,N}$ is an ORTHOGONAL matrix (the matrix $G'_{X,X}$ defined in (6) is orthogonal and as a consequence so is the matrix $B'_{N,N}$). Triangularity of the matrix $B_{N,N}$ has been transformed to orthogonality of the matrix $B'_{N,N}$. The $(-1, +1)$ formulation leads to simpler forms for the symmetries appearing with the linearized descriptions of boolean functions we are using. Ortogonality of $B'_{N,N}$ has also been found of help with numerical properties of the iterative algorithms currently being used to obtain feasible points in the projections $B'_{N,p}$.

3.3. Polyhedral symmetries

Propositional calculus boolean formulas exhibit two well known symmetries, see for example Slepian [40]. We can permute, or interchange, variables and we can negate them, without altering in any essential way the properties of the formula. It is reasonable to suppose that the binomial polytopes will inherit these two symmetries. This is indeed so. In addition, a third symmetry has been found to be present. All three symmetries are constructed by permuting in all the 4! = 24 ways the four rows of $B_{2,2}$. A symmetry of $B_{N,p}$ is given by a permutation matrix P for which there exists a matrix Q which satisfies

$$P \cdot B_{N,p} \cdot Q = B_{N,p} . \qquad (9)$$

Matrix $P \cdot B_{N,p}$ is a permutation of the rows of $B_{N,p}$. The transformation given by matrix Q reverses the effect of this row permutation with a linear combination of its columns. As P and $B_{N,p}$ are full rank, Q must also be full rank. We would like to find all the matrices P for which the matrix Q, satisfying (9), exists. If $p = N$, $B_{N,N}$ is square and full rank. Any permutation matrix will do. In this case we have

$$Q = (B_{N,N})^{-1} \cdot P^{-1} \cdot B_{N,N} . \qquad (10)$$

The new equations of faces and the corresponding Fourier multipliers resulting after performing the permutation of the vertices given by the matrix P are computed as follows. Start with $h_{N,p} = B_{N,p} \cdot f_{N,p}$. From it we have

$$P \cdot h_{N,p} = P \cdot B_{N,p} \cdot (Q \cdot Q^{-1}) \cdot f_{N,p} \quad \text{or} \quad P \cdot h_{N,p} = (P \cdot B_{N,p} \cdot Q) \cdot (Q^{-1} \cdot f_{N,p}) .$$

Using (9) we obtain $P \cdot h_{N,p} = B_{N,p} \cdot (Q^{-1} \cdot f_{N,p})$. The new face, made to correspond to $f_{N,p}$ by the symmetry defined by P is $(Q^{-1} \cdot f_{N,p})$. The new Fourier multipliers of the transformed face are $(P \cdot h_{N,p})$, just a permutation of the original ones. It is interesting to notice that it is possible to find symmetries of polytopes without explicitly knowing any of their faces. Our three symmetries will be described with elementary matrices, padded to their full size of 2^N rows and 2^N columns, with identity matrices. The symmetries are: negate a variable; permute two variables; flip a variable (on all the other variables). We will give the transformations for both the (0,1) formulation and the (-1,+1) formulation (with primed matrices). The first item to consider is the elementary identity matrix (the padding matrix):

$$I_x = \begin{array}{c|cc|c} & \emptyset & x & \\ \hline 1 & 0 & \emptyset \\ 0 & 1 & x \end{array}.$$

The other elementary matrices that define the symmetries follow.

<u>Negate a variable</u> (Matrices PN_x, QN_x, QN'_x).

$$PN_x = \begin{array}{c|cc|c} & \bar{x} & x & \\ \hline 0 & 1 & \emptyset \\ 1 & 0 & x \end{array} ; \quad QN_x = \begin{array}{c|cc|c} & \emptyset & x & \\ \hline 1 & 1 & \emptyset \\ 0 & -1 & x \end{array} ; \quad QN'_x = \begin{array}{c|cc|c} & \emptyset & x & \\ \hline 1 & 0 & \emptyset \\ 0 & -1 & x \end{array}. \qquad (12)$$

These matrices have the following interpretations. The matrix PN_x permutes the truth assignments for x. The matrix QN_x expresses the transformation $\bar{x} = 1 - x$. The matrix QN'_x performs the same function in a (-1, +1) setting, namely it negates a variable with the transformation $\bar{x} = -x$. The fact that QN'_x is a diagonal matrix and QN_x is not is the source of the convenience in using QN'_x over QN_x.

<u>Interchange two variables</u> (Matrices $PI_{x,y}$, $QI_{x,y}$, $QI'_{x,y}$).

$$PI_{x,y} = \begin{array}{c|cccc|c} & \bar{x}\bar{y} & x\bar{y} & \bar{x}y & xy & \\ \hline 1 & 0 & 0 & 0 & \emptyset \\ 0 & 0 & 1 & 0 & x \\ 0 & 1 & 0 & 0 & y \\ 0 & 0 & 0 & 1 & xy \end{array}; \quad QI_{x,y} = \begin{array}{c|cccc|c} & \emptyset & x & y & xy & \\ \hline 1 & 0 & 0 & 0 & \emptyset \\ 0 & 0 & 1 & 0 & x \\ 0 & 1 & 0 & 0 & y \\ 0 & 0 & 0 & 1 & xy \end{array}; \quad QI'_{x,y} = \begin{array}{c|cccc|c} & \emptyset & x & y & xy & \\ \hline 1 & 0 & 0 & 0 & \emptyset \\ 0 & 0 & 1 & 0 & x \\ 0 & 1 & 0 & 0 & y \\ 0 & 0 & 0 & 1 & xy \end{array} \qquad (13)$$

A permutation of two boolean variables has the same effect on the face equations in both the (0, 1) and the (-1, +1) setting. We have $QI_{x,y} = QI'_{x,y}$.

<u>Flip a variable</u> (Matrices $PF_{x,y}$, $QF_{x,y}$, $QF'_{x,y}$).

$$PF_{x,y} = \begin{array}{c|cccc|c} & \bar{x}\bar{y} & x\bar{y} & \bar{x}y & xy & \\ \hline 1 & 0 & 0 & 0 & \emptyset \\ 0 & 0 & 0 & 1 & x \\ 0 & 0 & 1 & 0 & y \\ 0 & 1 & 0 & 0 & xy \end{array}; \quad QF_{x,y} = \begin{array}{c|cccc|c} & \emptyset & x & y & xy & \\ \hline 1 & 0 & 0 & 0 & \emptyset \\ 0 & 1 & 1 & 1 & x \\ 0 & 0 & 1 & 0 & y \\ 0 & 0 & -2 & -1 & xy \end{array}; \quad QF'_{x,y} = \begin{array}{c|cccc|c} & \emptyset & x & y & xy & \\ \hline 1 & 0 & 0 & 0 & \emptyset \\ 0 & 1 & 0 & 0 & x \\ 0 & 0 & 0 & 1 & y \\ 0 & 0 & 1 & 0 & xy \end{array} \qquad (14)$$

QN'_x and $QF'_{x,y}$ are both simpler than QN_x and $QF_{x,y}$. Using (-1, +1) instead of (0, 1) leads to polytopes with more apparent symmetries. We also have

$$QN_x = (QN_x)^{-1}; \quad QI_{x,y} = (QI_{x,y})^{-1}; \quad QF_{x,y} = (QF_{x,y})^{-1}.$$

One erases the effect of a transformation by applying it again. We are now ready to define the symmetries for $B_{N,p}$. The next theorem pads the matrices in (12), (13) and (14) to full size with identity matrices labeled with all the untransformed variables.

<u>Theorem S</u> (Symmetries). If $f_{N,p}$ is a face of $B_{N,p}$ then so are:

[Negate x_i] for any p, $f_{N,p}(x_1, x_2, \ldots, \bar{x}_i, \ldots, x_N)$

$$= (\ QN_{x_i} \ <*> \ (\ <*> \atop {1 \leq j \leq N \atop j \neq i}} I_j)\ ) \cdot f_{N,p}(x_1, x_2, \ldots, x_i, \ldots, x_N); \qquad (15)$$

[Interchange x_i with x_j] for any p, $f_{N,p}(x_1, \ldots, x_j, \ldots, x_i, \ldots, x_N)$

$$= (QI_{x_i,x_j} <*> (\underset{\substack{1 \leq k \leq N \\ k \neq i, k \neq j}}{<*>} I_k)) \cdot f_{N,p}(x_1, \ldots, x_i, \ldots, x_j, \ldots, x_N); \quad (16)$$

[Flip x_i] for p even, $f_{N,p}(x_1, x_2, \ldots, x^*_i, \ldots, x_N)$

$$= (\underset{\substack{1 \leq j \leq N \\ j \neq i}}{\prod} (QF_{x_i,x_j} <*> (\underset{\substack{1 \leq k \leq N \\ k \neq i, k \neq j}}{<*>} I_k))) \cdot f_{N,p}(x_1, x_2, \ldots, x_N). \quad (17)$$

Proof. To perform these matrix-vector products we pad with zeros the column vectors $f_{N,p}$ for all the coordinates of the matrices Q not present in it. We have to verify that the submatrices of the matrices in (15), (16) and (17) whose rows and columns are labeled with the row labels of $f_{N,p}$, are of full rank. We will check each of the three cases separately. The checks are easier to perform in the (-1, +1) case. In each case the elementary symmetries are padded with identities for all the variables not involved in the transformation. Notice that the flip symmetry first pads the elementary transformation with identities and then further compounds them with standard matrix products. It "flips" x_i in relation to all the other variables.

Negation Symmetry. The effect of the matrix in (15) consists in changing the sign of all the terms in the face equation having in its label x_i. The corresponding matrix is an identity matrix with some of its elements changed from +1 to -1.

Interchange Symmetry. The effect of the matrix in (16) consists in the interchange of x_i with x_j whenever they occur in the labels. The interchange does not alter the number of variables in each label. Hence the matrix in question is a full rank permutation matrix.

Flip Symmetry. The effect of the matrix specified in (17) can be described as follows:

(A) Add x_i to all the labels of <u>odd</u> length not having x_i. If the label contains x_i, do nothing to it;
(B) Remove x_i from all the labels of <u>even</u> length having x_i. If the label does not contain x_i, do nothing to it.

If p is even, labels with no more than p variables will stay that way. Hence (A) and (B) describe a permutation matrix of full rank. /-/

For example, let us compute the matrix that flips x for the faces of $B_{3,2}(x, y, z)$. We have:

$$f_{3,2}(x^*, y, z) = (QF_{x,y} <*> I_z) \cdot (QF_{x,z} <*> I_y) \cdot f_{3,2}(x, y, z);$$

$$QF_{x,y} <*> I_z = \begin{array}{c} \\ \\ \emptyset \\ x \\ y \\ xy \end{array} \begin{array}{|cccc|} \emptyset & x & y & xy \\ \hline 1 & 0 & 0 & 0 \\ 0 & 1 & 1 & 1 \\ 0 & 0 & 1 & 0 \\ 0 & 0 & -2 & -1 \end{array} \begin{array}{c} \\ \emptyset \\ x \\ y \\ xy \end{array} <*> \begin{array}{c} \\ \emptyset \\ z \end{array} \begin{array}{|cc|} \emptyset & z \\ \hline 1 & 0 \\ 0 & 1 \end{array} \begin{array}{c} \\ \emptyset \\ z \end{array} = \begin{array}{c} \\ \emptyset \\ x \\ y \\ xy \\ z \\ xz \\ yz \\ xyz \end{array} \begin{array}{|cccccccc|} \emptyset & x & y & xy & z & xz & yz & xyz \\ \hline 1 & 0 & 0 & 0 & 0 & 0 & 0 & 0 \\ 0 & 1 & 1 & 1 & 0 & 0 & 0 & 0 \\ 0 & 0 & 1 & 0 & 0 & 0 & 0 & 0 \\ 0 & 0 & -2 & -1 & 0 & 0 & 0 & 0 \\ 0 & 0 & 0 & 0 & 1 & 0 & 0 & 0 \\ 0 & 0 & 0 & 0 & 0 & 1 & 1 & 1 \\ 0 & 0 & 0 & 0 & 0 & 0 & 1 & 0 \\ 0 & 0 & 0 & 0 & 0 & 0 & -2 & -1 \end{array} \begin{array}{c} \\ \emptyset \\ x \\ y \\ xy \\ z \\ xz \\ yz \\ xyz \end{array}$$

$$QF_{x,z} <*> I_y = \begin{array}{c|cccc|c} & \emptyset & x & z & xz \\ \hline 1 & 0 & 0 & 0 & \emptyset \\ 0 & 1 & 1 & 1 & x \\ 0 & 0 & 1 & 0 & z \\ 0 & 0 & -2 & -1 & xz \end{array} <*> \begin{array}{c|cc|c} & \emptyset & y \\ \hline 1 & 0 & \emptyset \\ 0 & 1 & y \end{array} = \begin{array}{c|cccccccc|c} & \emptyset & x & y & xy & z & xz & yz & xyz \\ \hline 1 & 0 & 0 & 0 & 0 & 0 & 0 & 0 & \emptyset \\ 0 & 1 & 0 & 0 & 1 & 1 & 0 & 0 & x \\ 0 & 0 & 1 & 0 & 0 & 0 & 0 & 0 & y \\ 0 & 0 & 0 & 1 & 0 & 0 & 1 & 1 & xy; \\ 0 & 0 & 0 & 0 & 1 & 0 & 0 & 0 & z \\ 0 & 0 & 0 & 0 & -2 & -1 & 0 & 0 & xz \\ 0 & 0 & 0 & 0 & 0 & 0 & 1 & 0 & yz \\ 0 & 0 & 0 & 0 & 0 & 0 & -2 & -1 & xyz \end{array}$$

$$f_{3,2}(x^*, y, z) = \begin{array}{c|cccccccc|c} & \emptyset & x & y & xy & z & xz & yz & xyz \\ \hline 1 & 0 & 0 & 0 & 0 & 0 & 0 & 0 & \emptyset \\ 0 & 1 & 1 & 1 & 1 & 1 & 1 & 1 & x \\ 0 & 0 & 1 & 0 & 0 & 0 & 0 & 0 & y \\ 0 & 0 & -2 & -1 & 0 & 0 & -1 & -1 & xy \\ 0 & 0 & 0 & 0 & 1 & 0 & 0 & 0 & z \\ 0 & 0 & 0 & 0 & -2 & -1 & -1 & -1 & xz \\ 0 & 0 & 0 & 0 & 0 & 0 & 1 & 0 & yz \\ 0 & 0 & 0 & 0 & 0 & 0 & 0 & 1 & xyz \end{array} \cdot \begin{array}{c|c} 1 & \emptyset \\ 0 & x \\ -1 & y \\ 0 & xy \\ -1 & z \\ 0 & xz \\ 1 & yz \\ 0 & xyz \end{array} = \begin{array}{c|c} 1 & \emptyset \\ -1 & x \\ -1 & y \\ 1 & xy \\ -1 & z \\ 1 & xz \\ 1 & yz \\ 0 & xyz \end{array}$$

By applying the transformation to the face $1 - y - z + yz \geq 0$ of $B_{3,2}(x, y, z)$ we obtain the face $1 - x - y - z + xy + xz + yz \geq 0$.

It is also interesting to analize the three symmetries from the point of view of the vertices of polytopes $B_{N,p}$. To do so, consider the entries in the permutation matrices PN, PI and PF. The negation symmetry, for a given i, interchanges x_i and $\bar{x}_i$ whenever they occur in the vertex labels. The permutation symmetry, for i and j, interchanges these two indices whenever they occur in the vertex labels. The flip symmetry, for a given i, has the following effect: do nothing to a label that contains x_i; if the label contains $\bar{x}_i$, interchange x_j with $\bar{x}_j$ for all $j \neq i$. If we interchange odd with even and even with odd in the description of the effect of the flip symmetry on a label we obtain another interesting symmetry, which <u>does not</u> correspond to a permutation of the rows of $B_{N,p}$. To this respect, see references [12, 26, 28].

4. COMPOSITION OF FACES

The next result expands considerably the number of inequalities available to us. It has been known for quite some time that polytopes associated with hard combinatorial problems have relatively few vertices in relation to their very large number of faces. In other words, they are strongly degenerated. At the end of Gomory [17] we find an interesting discussion of some of the earlier work on a related subject. A small polytope associated with the traveling salesman problem is characterized by H. W. Kuhn as a "miserable polyhedron". How can a polytope with so few vertices have so many faces? In the next page J. Edmonds remarks that as the vertices have a simple description, so might its faces. The next theorem gives some support to this view.

<u>Theorem C</u> (Composition of supporting hyperplanes). Let $g_{M,q}$ be a supporting hyperplane of $B_{M,q}$ and let $f_{N,p}$ be a supporting hyperplane to $B_{N,p}$. Then

$$g_{M,q} <*> f_{N,p} = f_{N+M, p+q} \tag{1}$$

is a supporting hyperplane of $B_{N+M, p+q}$.

<u>Proof</u>. We have $(B_{N,N} \cdot f_{N,p}) <*> (B_{M,M} \cdot g_{M,q})$

$= (B_{N,N} <*> B_{M,M}) \cdot (f_{N,p} <*> g_{M,q}) = B_{N+M, p+q} \cdot f_{N+M, p+q}$.

But $B_{N,N} \cdot f_{N,p} \geq 0$ and $B_{M,M} \cdot g_{M,q} \geq 0$, hence $B_{N+M, p+q} \cdot f_{N+M, p+q} \geq 0$. /-/

The next theorem shows that a face of $B_{N,p}$ is also a face of $B_{N+1,p}$ and, by induction, of $B_{N+M,p}$ for any M. As we add variables to build larger polytopes, all the faces of the smaller ones are preserved.

Theorem I (Face inclusion). For q = 0 and q = 1 theorem C transforms faces into faces.

Proof. We have:

$$B_{N+1,p} = B_{N,p-1} <*> V_{N+1} <+> B_{N,p} <*> E_{N+1} \qquad (2)$$

$$= \begin{vmatrix} B_{N,p} <*> a_{N+1} & 0 \\ B_{N,p} <*> b_{N+1} & B_{N,p-1} <*> d_{N+1} \end{vmatrix}$$

For the first case, we must determine the rank of the subset of rows of (1), whose scalar product with $f_{N,p} <*> f_{1,0}(x_{N+1})$ is zero. We will check that the row subsets corresponding to the two diagonal blocks

$$(B_{N,p} <*> a_{N+1}) \quad \text{and} \quad (B_{N,p-1} <*> d_{N+1})$$

of matrix (2) are both of maximum rank. For the block $B_{N,p} <*> a_{N+1}$ this is true, as $f_{N,p}$ is a face of $F_{N,p}$. For the block $B_{N,p-1} <*> d_{N+1}$ this is also true, as none of the entries in $f_{N,p}$ have in their labels the variable x_{N+1}, and hence this row subset of $B_{N,p-1} <*> d_{N+1}$ is the same as for the block $B_{N,p} <*> a_{N+1}$. Full rank for this row subset follows from the fact that the columns of $B_{N,p-1}$ are a subset of the columns of $B_{N,p}$.

Now consider the second case. We must determine the rank of the subset of rows of (24) whose scalar product with $f_{N,p} <*> f_{1,1}(x_{N+1})$ is zero. The vector $f_{1,1}(x_{N+1})$ is either

$$\begin{vmatrix} 0 & \emptyset \\ 1 & x_{N+1} \end{vmatrix} \quad \text{or} \quad \begin{vmatrix} 1 & \emptyset \\ -1 & x_{N+1} \end{vmatrix} \qquad (3)$$

In this second case, (2) becomes:

$$B_{N+1,p+1} = B_{N,p} <*> V_{N+1} <+> B_{N,p+1} <*> E_{N+1} \qquad (4)$$

$$= \begin{vmatrix} B_{N,p+1} <*> a_{N+1} & 0 \\ B_{N,p+1} <*> b_{N+1} & B_{N,p} <*> d_{N+1} \end{vmatrix}$$

We check the subset of vertices touched by the face for each of the two diagonal blocks of (5), namely:

$$(B_{N,p+1} <*> a_{N+1}) \quad \text{and} \quad (B_{N,p} <*> d_{N+1}).$$

Choose as the face of $f_{1,1}(x_{N+1})$ to be considered the first vector in (3). The whole diagonal block $B_{N,p+1} <*> a_{N+1}$ is in the touched set, as none of its labels contains x_{N+1}. The diagonal block $B_{N,p} <*> d_{N+1}$ contains a subset of maximum rank, as $f_{N,p}$ is a face of $B_{N,p}$. /-/

For example, as $0 \leq x$ is a face of $B_{1,1}(x)$ it will also be a face of $B_{2,1}(x,y)$. Theorem I shows the importance of complete analyses of (small) subproblems. For every N, <u>all</u> the combinatorial structure of $B_{N,p}$ is preserved untouched in $B_{N+1,p}$.

5. A TRANSFORMATION OF ANY BOOLEAN FORMULA TO A FACET OF $B_{N,2}$

Polytope $B_{N,p}$ is in a space of dimension $O(N^p)$. Is is well known how to reduce a boolean formula to an equivalent one in conjunctive normal form and with only three literals per clause. As a consequence, without loss of generality, we can take p = 3. The transformation presented in the next theorem shows that in our linear case a further reduction to p = 2 is possible. Polytopes $B_{N,2}$ are all we have to consider.

<u>Theorem T</u> (Transformation of any boolean formula to a facet of $B_{N,2}$). The satisfying truth assignments of any boolean formula in conjunctive normal form can be reduced to correspond to a facet of $B_{N,p}$.

<u>Proof</u>. The two boolean functions

$$c = (a \vee b) \quad \text{and} \quad (\bar{a} \vee c) \,\&\, (\bar{b} \vee c) \,\&\, f_{3,(1,2)}(a,b,\bar{c})$$

have the same truth table. As the three boolean functions $\bar{a} \vee c$, $\bar{b} \vee c$ and $f_{3,(1,2)}(a, b, \bar{c})$ correspond to faces of $B_{3,2}(a, b, c)$, it follows that the corresponding event probabilites can be expressed linearly with the variables present in a $B_{N,2}$. Hence clauses of any length of a boolean formula in conjunctive normal form can be reduced to a facet of $B_{N,2}$. To do so, use the same technique employed to reduce a clause with an arbitrary number of literals to a clause with three literals. /-/

6. CONCLUSIONS

Boole min-max relations for a logical "AND" correspond, in our development, to the faces of polytope $B_{2,2}$. Many other inequalities become necessary when the relations between statistical events are more complicated than a single "AND" (or a single "OR"). For N statistical events, we would like to use polytope $B_{N,N}$. Unfortunately, to define $B_{N,N}$ we need 2^N real variables, and hence this polytope is, for all computational purposes, inaccessible. By projecting the polytopes $B_{N,N}$ on the event subspaces we obtain the polytopes $B_{N,p}$. These polytopes are in subspaces of dimension of $O(N^p)$. We showed that $p = 2$ is all what we need to consider. In trading $B_{N,N}$ for $B_{N,2}$, we trade variables with linear inequalities. We also acquire mechanisms to exchange precision with which we wish to compute probabilites with computing time. If the faces corresponding to $B_{2,2}$ prove insufficient for some desired precision, we can consider the faces of $B_{3,2}$, $B_{4,2}$, $B_{5,2}$, etc. as successive approximations to $B_{N,2}$, until we have an approximation to the event probabilities acceptable for the purpose at hand. In general, the faces of $B_{i,j}$ will provide a better approximation to the problem of computing event probabilities than the faces of $B_{i,j-1}$ or $B_{i-1,j}$.

At this time we can only speculate about the precision practically necessary for event probabilities, and hence about how many of these inequalities we will actually have to use. Available code using these inequalities suggests that we do not need very many for a level of performance that at the moment is considered acceptable. Just the inequalities corresponding to $B_{2,2}$ have proven adequate in many situations. These inequalities corresponding to $B_{2,2}$, that is Boole's original inequalities, are the only ones being used in many currently operational codes for approximate reasoning. Is seems likely, however, that as the required level of performance increases, so will the necessity of using additional inequalities, besides the ones given by $B_{2,2}$.

REFERENCES

[1] H. C. Andrews and J. Kane, Kroneker matrices, computer implementation, and generalized spectra, J. of the ACM, 17 (1970), pp. 260-268.
[2] P. R. H. Anonymous, Summer institute for symbolic logic, Cornell University 1957, Conference Proceedings pp. 432. Second edition 1960

(Institute for Defense Analysis) pp. 427.
[3] R. F. Arnold, M. A. Harrison, Algebraic properties of symmetric and partially symmetric boolean functions, IEEE Trans. on Electr. Comp. 12:244-251 (1963).
[4] M. L. Balinski, Integer programming: methods, uses, computation, Management Science, 12 (1965), pp. 253-313.
[5] M. L. Balinski, On recent developments in integer programming, Proceedings of the Princeton Symposium on Mathematical Programming, ed., H. W. Kuhn, Princeton Univ. Press, New Jersey, 1970, pp. 267-302.
[6] A. Blake, Canonical expressions in boolean algebra, Ph. D. Thesis, Dept. of Mathematics, University of Chicago, August 1937.
[7] G. Boole, An investigation of the laws of thought on which are founded the mathematical theories of logic and probabilities, MacMillan, 1854. Dover reprint 1958 (Consult also his Collected Logical Works).
[8] J. R. Buchi, Turing-machines and the Entscheidungsproblem, Math. Annalen 148:201-213 (1962).
[9] S. A. Cook, The complexity of theorem-proving procedures, Third ACM Symposium on Theory of Computing 3:151-158 (1971).
[10] C. H. Cunkle, Symmetric boolean functions, American Math. Monthly 70:833-836 (1963).
[11] A. P. Dempster, Upper and lower probabilities induced by a multivalued mapping, Annals of Math. Stat. 38:325-339 (1967).
[12] M. L. Dertouzos, Threshold logic: a synthesis approach, Research monograph No. 32, The MIT Press, Cambridge, Ma, 1965.
[13] D. Hunter, An upper bound on the probability of a union, J. Appl. Prob. 13:597-603 (1976).
[14] J. Galambos, Methods for proving Bonferroni type inequalities, J. London Math. Soc. 9:561-564 (1975).
[15] R. A. Gangolli & D. Ylvisaker, Discrete probability, Harbrace College Mathematics Series.
[16] J. T. Gill, Computational complexity of probabilistic turing machines, SIAM J. Comp. 6:675-695 (1977).
[17] R. E. Gomory, The traveling salesman problem, Proc. IBM Scientific Computing Symposium on Combinatorial Problems, 1964, pp. 93-121.
[18] I. J. Good, The interaction algorithm and practical Fourier analysis, J. Royal Stat. Soc. Ser. B, (1958), pp. 361-372, ibid. (1960) pp. 372-375.
[19] M. Grötschel, Approaches to hard combinatorial optimization problems, Modern Applied Mathematics, Optimization and Operations Research, ed., B. Korte, 1982, pp. 437-515.
[20] T. Hailperin, Boole's logic and probability, North Holland 1976.
[21] J. van Heijenoort, From Frege to Godel, a source book in mathematical logic, 1879-1931, Harvard University Press 1967.
[22] T. C. Hu, Integer programming and network flows, Addison-Wesley Publ. Co., 1969.
[23] R. M. Karp, Reducibility among combinatorial problems, Complexity of Computer Computations, eds., R. E. Miller and J. W. Thacher, 1972, pp. 85-103.
[24] R. M. Karp and C. H. Papadimitriou, On linear characterizations of combinatorial optimization problems, SIAM J. Computing 11:620-632 (1982).
[25] D. E. Knuth, The art of computer programming, Volume 1, Addison-Wesley, 1968.
[26] R. J. Lechner, Harmonic analysis of switching functions, in: Recent developments in switching theory, A. Mukhopadhyay, editor, Academic press, 1971, pp. 121-228.
[27] K. de Leeuw, E. F. Moore, C. E. Shannon, N. Shapiro, Computability by probabilistic machines, Annals of mathematics studies, Automata studies, Princeton 34:183-212 (1956).
[28] I. Ninomiya, A theory of the coordinate representation of switching functions, Memoirs of the faculty of engineering, Nagoya University 10: 175-190 (1958) (See also 13:149-363 (1961)).
[29] M. W. Padberg, ed., Combinatorial Optimization, Mathematical Programming

Study 12:1-221, North-Holland, (1980).
[30] I. Peano, Arithmetices Principia Nova Methodo Exposita, Augustae Taurinorum Typis Vincentii Bona 1889 (A translation from the original "latino sine flexione" appears in [Heijenoort 67] pp. 83-97).
[31] M. C. Pease III, Methods of matrix algebra, Academic Press, 1965.
[32] G. Polya, On picture writing, American Math. Montly 63:689-697 (1956).
[33] W. R. Pulleyblank, Polyhedral combinatorics, Mathematical Programming, The State of the Art, Springer-Verlag, 1983, pp. 312-345.
[34] J. Riordan, An introduction to combinatorial analysis (1958), Combinatorial Identities (1968), John Wiley and Sons.
[35] E. S. Santos, Computability by probabilistic turing machines, Trans. Amer. Math. Soc. 159:165-184 (1971).
[36] W. Semon, E-algebras in switching theory, Trans. AIEE 80:265-269 (1961).
[37] S. Seshu, F. E. Hohn, Symmetric polynomials in boolean algebras, Proceedings of an international symposium on the theory of switching, part II, The annals of the computation laboratory of Harvard University, 30:225-234 (1959).
[38] J. Simon, On the difference between one and many, Proc. 4th ICALP, Springer-Verlag lecture notes in computer science: automata, languages and programming 52:480-491 (1977).
[39] T. Skolem, Über die symmetrisch allgemeinen Lösungen im Klassenkalkul, Fundamenta Mathematicae 18:61-76 (1932).
[40] D. Slepian, On the number of symmetry types of boolean functions of N variables, Canadian J. of Math. 5:185-193 (1953).
[41] J. Stoer and C. Witzgall, Convexity and Optimization in Finite Dimensions I, Springer-Verlag, 1970.
[42] J. J. Sylvester, Thoughts on the inverse orthogonal matrices, simultaneous sign-successions, tesselated pavements in two or more colours, with applications to Newton's rule, ornamental tile-work, and the theory of numbers, Philosophical Magazine 34:461-475 (1867)
[43] S. Ursic, A discrete optimization algorithm based on binomial polytopes, Ph. D. Thesis, University of Wisconsin, Madison, 1975.
[44] S. Ursic, Binomial polytopes and NP-complete problems, in: Algorithms and Complexity, New Directions and Recent Results, ed., J. F. Traub, Academic Press, 1976.
[45] S. Ursic, The ellipsoid algorithm for linear inequalities in exact arithmetic, IEEE Foundations of Computer Science, 23 (1982) 321-326.
[46] S. Ursic, A linear characterization of NP-complete problems, Proceedings of the Twenty-first Allerton Conference on Communication, Control and Computing, 1982, pp. 100-109.
[47] S. Ursic, A linear characterization of NP-complete problems, Seventh International Conference on Automated Deduction, Springer-Verlag Lecture Notes in Computer Science 170:80-100 (1984).
[48] S. Ursic, A linear characterization of counting problems, Linear Algebra and Applications, Submitted June 1985.
[49] L. G. Valiant, The complexity of enumeration and reliability problems, SIAM Journal of Computing 8:410-421 (1979).
[50] A. N. Whitehead, Memoir on the algebra of symbolic logic, American J. of Math. 23:139-165 (1901), ibid. Part II 23:297-316 (1901).
[51] L. A. Zadeh, Fuzzy sets, Information and Control 8:338-353 (1965).

IV

APPLICATIONS

THE SUM-AND-LATTICE-POINTS METHOD BASED ON AN EVIDENTIAL-REASONING
SYSTEM APPLIED TO THE REAL-TIME VEHICLE GUIDANCE PROBLEM

Dr. Shoshana ABEL

640 Taylor Court, #504
Mountain View, California 94043

1. INTRODUCTION

This paper presents a methodology for research and development of the
inferencing and knowledge representation aspects of an Expert System approach
for performing reasoning under uncertainty in support of a real time vehicle
guidance and navigation system. Such a system could be of major benefit for
non-terrain following low altitude flight systems operating in foreign hos-
tile environments such as might be experienced by NOE helicopter or similar
mission craft. An innovative extension of the evidential reasoning methodology, termed the Sum-and-Lattice-Points Method, has been developed. The research and development effort presented in this paper consists of a formal
mathematical development of the Sum-and-Lattice-Points Method, its formulation and representation in a parallel environment, prototype software development of the method within an expert system, and initial testing of the
system within the confines of the vehicle guidance system.

2. PROBLEM

The desired goal of the work described in this paper is to perform the basic
research, development, and conceptual design of a prototype based on numerical algorithms and an evidential-reasoning expert system for effective real-
time flight guidance and navigation. The heart of the expert system, and
that item which distinguishes this effort is the Sum-and-Lattice-Points Method
based on Evidential Reasoning for performing a decision function. As envi-
sioned, the vehicle guidance and navigation system would employ, in a real
time environment, both real time and static data such as image based sensors
and DMA maps, as the basic information. This data may then be processed by
pattern recognition, data fusion, feature extraction, etc.,--technologies
that yield processed information which the expert system would use to perform
decision processing. The decision process would not only be driven by the
incoming data, but also by the potential action, i.e., be goal driven. Thus
system critical functions, such as collision avoidance, would be treated
differently from feature identification function.

The primary function of the expert system is, at a minimum, to provide the
pilot with guidance or possibly to perform autonomous navigation and response.
This response would be based on the perceived situation in conjunction with
the mission and basic operational guidelines. As an additional function, the
expert system would provide feedback type control to the entire vehicle guidance system including both the sensor information acquisition and data processing resource allocation to ensure optimal performance of the system.

3. RELEVANCE

The information combination and usage of artificial intelligence techniques
for real-time flight guidance system yield the real-time displays, recommendations to the pilot, and the automated computer commands to the flight

vehicle. Both the human pilot command and the automated command serve as the guidance command to the vehicle. Often, the speed at which decisions are made and the order in which decisions are addressed can signify the difference between mission success or mission failure, vehicle safety or vehicle loss. Thus the driving needs of real-time guidance and navigation are the following:
  a) quick object (or object class) identification
  b) rapid system response-time

It is these issues that the research into Sum-and-Lattice-Points Method based on Evidential Reasoning applied to real-time vehicle guidance should address.

Since uncertainty is involved in both of these issues, the best performance that either a human or a computer can do under these circumstances is to formulate hypotheses and gradually confirm or reject them by accumulating the incoming evidence. The source of these hypotheses, whether they are generated by a human or an intelligent system, is a knowledge acquisition task. The hypothesis generated is a result of a broad base of experience. The degree of attention yielding any hypothesis depends on the mission and its consequences. The nature of the hypothesis is that it is the goal that serves as the statement about the identification of the object or the object class, e.g., "the object in view is a lake," when such a goal is reached, it induces appropriate action, such as climbing over or going around, to destruct or not to destruct, etc. The evidence-pool contains raw data that are often used for numerical programs, as well as for extracting higher-level abstraction as features yielding a set of hypotheses. The hypotheses themselves can be viewed as the consequent of if-then rules, whose antecedents are observed features. An example of a low altitude vehicle that can utilize obstacle avoidance methods is a helicopter. Object identification is important for helicopter-flight, since it is likely to encounter several obstacles. The active hypotheses are then gradually confirmed or rejected in real-time by the reasoning-system, which invokes the proper response at each time-interval.

An example of a short-range guidance rule for helicopters might be the following:

IF: 1) An object consisting of a bounded area covers a number of pixels on the optical range.
  2) Its shape is approximately triangular.
  3) It is a certain number of feet from the helicopter.
  4) That I-R color of the object is approximately red.
  5) The current helicopter position is approximately at a certain location according to the reference-frame.

THEN: The object right in front is a tree.

RESPONSE FOR GUIDANCE: The pilot should perform avoidance maneuver.

4. THE NECESSITY OF INTRODUCING GENERAL EVIDENTIAL REASONING

Consider the following rule:

1) If x, y, and z attributes of the object are clearly in view or can be exactly computerized, then the object in view is clearly a lake.

In this case, a "rule" is more or less a direct conclusion from some numerical data-readings to a conclusion about an object. Even then, the attributes like blueness of the color cannot be represented numerically. Clear vision of the blueness (if possible) can be our implementation of exact reasoning using first-order predicate logic. But the matter is more complicated because the evidence in each of these if-clauses has uncertainty associated with it. Since evidence is typically uncertain, it is clear that a method exceeding a purely logical approach is necessary.

Partial beliefs are frequently represented by probabilities. A Bayesian probability model would thus seem a likely candidate for representing evidential information. In fact, the Bayesian probability model is the basis for much of the work in expert systems [1] [2]. However, this approach has some inherent limitations -- most significantly, its inability to capture the incompleteness of evidence.

The problem with this approach is that the system has to determine a precise probability for every proposition in the space no matter how impoverished the evidence. This would not be such a problem if there were a rich source of statistical date for NOE navigation from which these probabilities could be estimated. However, in a domain as expansive and dynamic as this one, the appropriate statistical data are not only unavailable, but unobtainable.

5. THE GENERAL EVIDENTIAL REASONING MODEL

The general evidential reasoning model based on [3] used in the research is described in this section. The problem is posed in the following paragraphs.

Suppose there is a finite set of statements about hypotheses and decisions, Θ, which can be interpreted as a set of possibilities, exactly one subset of which corresponds to the truth or to a decision. For each subset of this set, the belief-function can be interpreted as the degree of belief that the truth or the decision lies in that hypothesis. Conceptually, the subset is any statement about the normal object (e.g., a lake) or an obstacle (e.g., a tower) in view.

One type of belief-function is a simple support function. This is the original function that goes from the domain of the set of all subsets of the original set of statements about hypotheses and decisions to the range of [0,1], if there exists a non-empty subset (of the original set) called the focus, F, and a number, S, $0 \leqslant S \leqslant 1$, which is the degree of support of the focus. The value to this simple support function is 0 if the statement being examined does not contain the focus F. Its value is S (the degree of support of the focus), if the statement itself is not equal to the entire original set of statements. Its value is 1 if the statement is equal to the original set (i.e., we have to __totally__ support this statement; there are no other alternative member of subsets of the original set). This simple support function corresponds to a body of evidence whose effect is to support the focus to the degree S.

There are total accumulation of evidences in favor and against a statement. The measure of support for (__pro__) that statement is a function of the total evidence in favor applied to the focus of that statement; the measure of support against (__con__) that statement is a function applying the total evidence against that statement, to the focus of that statement. The simple support function focused of F is the representation of the evidence in favor and against that statement. There is also a measure, the residue, which accounts for evidence which is neither in favor nor against the statement.

After gathering the evidence, performed in an incremental fashion, one obtains the combination of all the evidence directly for and against that statement in the form of the evidence-function. The evidence-function that is currently used by researchers in this field [4] is an orthogonal sum of the two sets that yield the degree of belief on the basis of the combined evidence. Next, the measure of support -- pro and con -- from the previous stage plus the measure of the uncommitted residual evidence is combined with evidence of the present frame. The measure of belief in the uncommitted evidence is compensated for by a constant of proportionality in the formal representations of the measures of support pro and con. This is a characteristic feature of the evidence-reasoning model.

It is the evidential-reasoning model where the belief in a proposition A is represented by an interval [lower bound, upper bound]. Each such "evidential interval" is a subinterval of the closed real interval [0,1]. The lower bound represents the degree to which the evidence <u>supports</u> the proposition; the upper bound represents the degree to which it <u>remains</u> plausible; and the difference between them represents the residual ignorance. When this technique is used, complete ignorance is represented by the "interval" collapsed about that point. Other degrees of ignorance are captured by evidential intervals with widths greater than 0 and less than 1.

These intervals are induced by a "mass distribution," which differs only slightly from a Bayesian distribution. A Bayesian distribution distributes a unit of belief across a set of mutually exclusive and exhaustive propositions. Then the probability of any given proposition A is just the sum of the belief attributed to those propositions that imply A. The probability of A plus the probability of -A is constrained to equal one. A mass distribution also distributes a unit of belief over a set of propositions, but these focal propositions need not be mutually exclusive.

This technique of using mass distribution helps the "near field" problem and "far field" problem of low altitude flight vehicle guidance and navigation. Whether we are concerned with the flight over the next several seconds (on the order of 10's of seconds at most) or over a longer time-horizon the <u>real-time computation</u> will require a combination of shifting and changing evidence. Mass is attributed to the most precise propositions a body of evidence supports. If a portion of mass is attributed to a proposition, it represents a minimal commitment to that proposition as well as to all the propositions it implies. Additional mass suspended "above" that proposition, i.e., at propositions that neither imply it or it imply its negation -- represents a <u>potential commitment</u>. This mass can shift either way on the basis of additional information. The amount of mass so suspended above a proposition accounts for the relative ignorance remaining about it, that is, the residual latitude is its probability according to all considered evidence.

6. APPROACH: SUM-AND-LATTICE-POINTS METHOD

Recent surveys of evidential reasoning applications show that one of the important aspects of evidential reasoning is the computation of mass, which is represented by the following function:

$$m_1:\{A_j \ / \ A_j \subseteq \Theta\}[0,1] \qquad m_1(\Theta) = 0, \qquad \text{and}$$

$$\sum_{A_j \subseteq \Theta} m_1(A_j) = 1$$

Here $m_1(A_j)$ represents the portion of belief that knowledge-source has committed exactly to proposition A_j, termed its "basic probability mass." m_1 can be duplicated as a partitioned unit line segment, the length of each subsegment corresponding to the mass attributed to one of its focal elements. Once mass has been assigned to a set of propositions, the evidential interval can be determined directly. In general, the relation between mass and interval is the following: support for a proposition A is the total mass ascribed to A and to the subsets of -A. The uncertainty of A is equal to the mass remaining, i.e., that attributed to supersets of A, including Θ.

In short, $m_1(A_j)$ committed by knowledge-source 1 is an ordered n-tuple, e.g., $<.4, .2, .3, .1>$. The problem is to combine the information provided by the several knowledge-sources. The method proposed is the method of direct sum of ordered n-tuples and lattice-point information. The progress of hypotheses confirmation can be viewed as a state-transition graph, with the internal nodes forming the partial solutions (confirmation or rejection) of each hypothesis according to the accumulation of evidence. The leaves represent the final decisions. This reasoning graph corresponds to the successful flight vehicle (e.g., helicopter) response geometry. The proof of their equivalence, in brief, is provided in the following discussion.

7. THE EQUIVALENCE PROOF AND THE TRANSITION GRAPH

The successive real-time flight vehicle response is authentically represented as a sequence of information from knowledge-sources. For $n>0$, an ordered n-tuple with i_{th} component a_i is a sequence of n pieces of evidence denoted by $<a_1, a_2, a_3, a_n>$. Two ordered n-tuples are equal if and only if their i_{th} components are equal for all $1 \leqslant i \leqslant n$.

The sum of n-tuples is a method that puts fast bounds on the state transition graph and helps achieve partial solutions. The criterion of determining whether a hypothesis is better than the other is the method of not only noting the lower bound and the upper bound of the interval induced by the mass computation, but also by the additional knowledge of the lower-level geometry at each response-stage. This is the geometry of 1) heading, 2) airspeed, and 3) altitude of the flight vehicle, in response to which the location of the object is to be determined. Even though 1, 2, and 3 can be determined with certainty for the flight vehicle itself, the location of the object in view can be determined only relative to the location of the flight vehicle. This can be accomplished by generating lattice-points. An n-dimensional lattice-point is an n-tuple $<x_1, x_2, x_3, x_n>$ of numbers (in our case, these reflect the location of the object) satisfying the condition: $l_i \leqslant x_i \leqslant u_i$, for some vectors $<l_1, l_2, l_3, l_n>$ and $<u_1, u_2, u_3, u_n>$ which are, in our case, the ordered n-tuples of the previous evidence and the incoming evidence. Thus, a lattice-point of $<.4, .3, .2, .1>$ and $<.5, .6, .7, .8>$ can be $<.2, .3, .5>$.

8. PARALLEL IMPLEMENTATION

A significant advantage of direct sum or ordered n-tuples and lattice-point generation method is that it is well suited for parallel computation. A number of distinct processes can be simultaneously performed. While the parallel sum is being performed, the active hypotheses are being determined by the accumulation of evidence in conjunction with goal demands, and the lattice-point describing the object-location is being generated by the algorithm operating on the previous lattice-points and incoming lattice-points. The proof of the parallel implementation of the operation involved (sum and lattice-point generation) and the inference-rules based on the operation, will be elucidated in the further development of this work.

9. ADVANTAGES

A significant advantage of employing lattice-points for this application is that the location of the object may carry different weights of the evidence, and hence though it is computed from the mass assignment, it can affect the bounds of the evidential internal. Thus, an <u>example</u> of an inference-rule involving the direct sum and the lattice-point computation method can be the following:

IF: The evaluated lattice-point at time t_1 is <set of values>

THEN: The lower bound of the evidential interval associated with that hypothesis at time t_1 is <u>number</u>.

Usage of such inference-rules leads to fine discrimination of objects in view.

An augmentation of this approach can include a set of decision-rules associated with the reasoning-system that helps activate several predefined lattice-points simultaneously, or alternative lattice-points serving different purposes (i.e., describing different types of situational geometry) during the real-time process.

The impact of lattice-points on the bounds of the evidential interval shows further justification as to why evidence should be regarded as interval-valued. The change of the interval-bounds induced by lattice-points, as illustrated by the rule incorporating the lattice-points given above, adds to the flexibility in the manipulation of the inference-rules.

10. CONCLUSION

The sum-and-lattice-points method as an extension of evidential reasoning is a promising approach for real-time information processing and decision making in flight vehicle guidance and navigation systems. The potential benefits as indicated by very preliminary investigations supports the prototypic implementation of the system. The computations and data designs of the sum-and-lattice-points methods should be the focal point of this prototype research and development effort.

REFERENCES

[1] Duda, R.O., Hart, P.E., Nilsson, Subjective Bayesian Methods for Rule-Based Inference Systems, Proceedings of National Computer Conference, 1976, pp. 1075-1082.
[2] Pearl, J., Fusion Propagation and Structure in Bayesian Networks, Technical Report Number CSD-850022, UCLA, 1985.
[3] Shafer, G., A Mathematical Theory of Evidence, Princeton Press, 1976.
[4] Garvey, T.D., Lowrance, J.D., Fischler, M.A., An Inference Technique for Integrating Knowledge from Disparate Sources, in Readings in Knowledge Representation, R.J. Brachman and H.J. Levesque (eds.), Morgan Kaufman Publishers, 1985.

Probabilistic Reasoning About Ship Images

Lashon B. BOOKER
Naveen HOTA†

Navy Center for Applied Research in AI
Code 5510
Naval Research Laboratory
Washington, D.C. 20375

One of the most important aspects of current expert systems technology is the ability to make causal inferences about the impact of new evidence. When the domain knowledge and problem knowledge are uncertain and incomplete, Bayesian reasoning has proven to be an effective way of forming such inferences [3,4,8]. While several reasoning schemes have been developed based on Bayes Rule, there has been very little work examining the comparative effectiveness of these schemes in a real application. This paper describes a knowledge based system for ship classification [1], originally developed using the PROSPECTOR updating method [2], that has been reimplemented to use the inference procedure developed by Pearl and Kim [4,5]. We discuss our reasons for making this change, the implementation of the new inference engine, and the comparative performance of the two versions of the system.

1. INTRODUCTION

Classifying images is extremely difficult whenever the feature information available is incomplete or uncertain. Under such circumstances, identification of an object requires some kind of reasoning mechanism to help resolve ambiguous interpretations within the constraints of the available domain knowledge. The need for a reasoning mechanism becomes even more acute if the interpretation process is also constrained by limited resources. When there is not enough time or memory for an exhaustive feature analysis, intelligent decisions must be made about how to use the resources available to maximum advantage. This means that the reasoning mechanism must be involved in the control of the information extraction activities, as well as the interpretation of the results. Ship classification is an example of one practical application in which all of these problems arise.

Classification of ships in an operational environment is a difficult task regardless of what kind of images are used. This is not always obvious to those who are only familiar with the detailed views of a ship one finds in a reference book. Observers in the field rarely have the luxury of an abundance of clear details to work with. Images are most often obtained during a *brief* observation interval from a distance that makes high resolution difficult to achieve. The viewing angle is usually a matter of opportunity rather than choice, and the observer must make do with the prevailing visibility, weather, and lighting conditions at sea. Another factor degrading image quality is the fact that sensor platforms are often buffeted by turbulence in the air or the ocean. The quality of images produced in this way is likely to be lower than that attainable using sophisticated enhancement techniques and powerful computing resources. These difficulties are of course exacerbated when the classification must be done in real time.

---

† Author is employed by JAYCOR, 1608 Spring Hill Road, Vienna, VA 22180

All of this is in addition to the complexity faced when distinguishing among hundreds of classes of vessels, some of which differ only in fine feature details.

Having this task performed well is obviously important to the Navy, which has invested heavily in training personnel to analyze and interpret images under operational conditions. The human observer-sensor operator must be highly trained and experienced. He/she must know which features are related to which ship classes, and make a judgement as to how well various features are manifested in the image. Moreover, the observer must keep track of the implications of all these judgements — both with respect to their uncertainty and consistency, and with respect to an eventual classification. A decision aid must also cope with these problems, but in a way that acknowledges the meager computational resources available on most military platforms — an important constraint now and in the near future. The most useful kind of system is one that can distinguish *similar* ship types. Most trained personnel can easily tell the difference between an aircraft carrier and a cruiser. It is much more difficult to make decisions about several types of cruisers whose images are similar.

Real-time ship classification is a demanding application. It is a task requiring that complex inferences, based on incomplete and uncertain information, be made reliably under stringent computational constraints. In devising a system that meets this challenge, two of the most important research issues are control and inference. Given that time constraints often preclude an exhaustive feature analysis, which features should be sought after in the time available? Given an uncertain and incomplete feature description, what kind of heuristic reasoning tools provide reliable and computationally inexpensive ship classifications? This paper describes a knowledge-based system for reasoning about ship images that successfully manages many of these issues. A prototype developed at the Navy Center for Applied Research in AI (NCARAI) has convincingly demonstrated that a heuristic approach to this problem is effective and practical. Our current research effort builds on this work, and is developing a 2nd generation expert system to help solve this classification problem.

2. REASONING ABOUT SHIP IMAGES

The focus of this research is on how to use incomplete and uncertain feature information to make plausible inferences about Naval Class.[1]

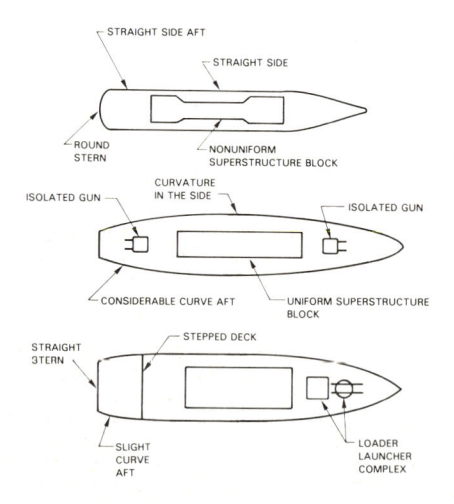

Figure 1 Examples of plan view features

Reasoning about plausible classifications for a ship image requires knowledge about the features needed to describe various Naval Classes; and, knowledge about how the presence or absence of these features in an image implies one class versus another. Feature details might be observable from either a *profile* (or side) view, a *plan* (or top down) view, or both.

Figure 1 shows the kinds of features that are important in analyzing a plan view image. The primary items of interest are the shape of the stern, curvature of the sides, superstructure configuration, etc. Needless to say, not all of this detail is likely to be available in every image, and an analyst often has to make uncertain judgements about whether or not they are really there.

This knowledge can be organized into a simple hierarchy having four levels: Naval Class, major structural components, features, and observations. At the top of the hierarchy are the hypotheses about how to classify a particular image. This presumably cannot be directly determined, so at the next level are hypotheses about the gross structural components of the ship — the stern, deck, superstructure blocks, etc. Sometimes evidence is available that directly bears on knowledge at this level. For instance, the stern of the Sverdlov class is very distinctive and can often be recognized immediately. In most cases, though, components have to be determined from lower level attributes. These lower level structural attributes, in turn, are usually established based on knowledge about what is manifested in the imagery.

TABLE 1 — PLAN VIEW STERN DESCRIPTIONS

Shape Attribute	Stern Type				
	Virginia	Belknap Leahy	Sverdlov	Bainbridge California Coontz Long Beach Truxtun	Forrest Sherman
Square	10	0	1	0	1
Round	0	10	0	5	2
Tapered	0	0	10	0	0

More specifically, consider the following example from a real Navy problem. Table 1 summarizes an expert analyst's description of the stern component for plan views of 10 classes. There is an implicit knowledge hierarchy in this description. At the component level, 5 types of stern components are represented here. The description of each type includes a subjective weight for each shape attribute. This number indicates an expectation about whether that attribute will be manifested in the imagery. The weights are given on a scale of 0 to 10, with 0 meaning the attribute should never be detected and 10 meaning it should always be detected. Two structures with the same weight for a given attribute cannot be distinguished on that basis alone. So, for example, the sterns of Sverdlov and Forrest Sherman are square in the same way. Such knowledge about the specific nature of the attributes resides at the level directly below the component level in the hierarchy. For this set of ships, there are two ways for a stern to be square, three ways to be round, and one way to be tapered. In practice, it is often difficult even to obtain evidence at this level. A poor quality image or non-expert observer might only be able to provide evidence that the stern in the image is somewhat rounded, period. The lowest level in the hierarchy represents these very simple assertions.

The hierarchical organization of knowledge corresponds to the reasoning steps involved in classifying an image: image analysis or user observations provide data about features; feature information can be used to infer higher order ship components; and, the higher-order components provide a much simpler basis for determining Naval Class. The process does not proceed in only a "bottom-up" fashion however. At each stage, the features extracted so far designate a set of likely candidate classes. Each such class can be used as a source of prediction about additional features that should be in the image, thus directing the feature extraction process in a "top-down" manner. One AI framework made to order for this hierarchical reasoning task is the *inference network*, which directly represents the causal influences among propositions or variables of interest. Each node in such a network represents a proposition (or variable) describing some aspect of the domain. Each link signifies a direct dependency between two propositions. The network not only can be used as a knowledge structure in which facts about the domain are stored, but it can also provide a computational framework for reasoning about that knowledge. If some measure of belief is associated with each node, and the dependencies between nodes are summarized by constraints on beliefs, then the network structure indicates which beliefs need to be updated when new information is available. In this way, an integrated summary can be maintained of what is known directly about each hypothesis and what can be inferred from their inter-relationships.

3. A SIMPLE PROTOTYPE

In order to demonstrate that the inference network approach is an effective way to deal with the ship classification problem, a prototype decision aid was developed and tested [1]. The knowledge for this system was provided by an expert analyst who picked 10 Naval Classes that have similar imagery and are often difficult to distinguish from one another. Feature descriptions for the plan and profile views of each class were given in the manner shown in Table 1. Because the number of ships belonging to each class is known in advance, simple counting arguments can be used to quantify the relative beliefs and constraints on beliefs associated with this knowledge. Probabilities are therefore a very natural measure of belief to use in the system. Several probabilistic reasoning schemes have been devised for updating beliefs in inference networks [8]. A version of the PROSPECTOR updating method [2] was developed at NCARAI to solve a resource allocation problem [10], and was available for the ship classification work. Consequently, a PROSPECTOR-style inference engine was used to implement the prototype.

In our version of the PROSPECTOR scheme, the relation between evidence and hypothesis is a rule of inference of the following type:

If P1 then (to extent $\lambda 1$, $\lambda 2$) conclude P.

P1 and P are both propositions. P1 is the antecedent of the rule and P is the consequent. The strength of the implication is attenuated by the two numbers $\lambda 1$ and $\lambda 2$: $\lambda 1$ is the conditional probability of P given that P1 is true; and, $\lambda 2$ is the conditional probability of P given that P1 is false. This information, together with the prior probability of P and P1, is used to compute a posterior probability for P when the truth of P1 is uncertain. When several independent propositions have an evidential relationship with P, the posterior probability of P is computed using a heuristic generalization of Bayes rule. See Duda *et al.* [2] for more details.[2] Reasoning is accomplished in this framework by *propagating* changes through the inference network. A change in the probability of a proposition causes the probabilities of its consequents to be updated as described above. The procedure is then recursively applied starting at each consequent. In this way, the effects of the initial change spread throughout the network to all propositions that are directly or indirectly related.

As a simplification, the prototype system was implemented to rely exclusively on operator input. This allows the reasoning issues to be examined without having to worry at all about feature extraction issues. The system interacts with the operator to get the feature information in a mixed-initiative fashion. At any point during the session the operator can volunteer information about the presence or absence of certain features in the image. In this way, the operator can direct the program's chain of reasoning in a manner he deems appropriate. When the operator is not volunteering information, the program asks a series of questions about the image. The questioning sequence is dynamically ordered so as to maximize the effectiveness of the evidence in determining a classification.

A global control strategy is used to select which question to ask. Each proposition is assigned a weight — called a *merit* value — proportional to its ability to alter the value of a top-level proposition. More specifically, the merit of a proposition H is the ratio $\delta P/\delta C$ where δP is the expected change in the value of the top-level proposition if a value for H is obtained; and, δC is the expected cost of obtaining a value for H. With this information, an efficient algorithm can be used that finds the proposition with the highest merit[3] in a network. See Slagle [9] for a complete discussion of how merit values are dynamically calculated and updated. Details about how these ideas were implemented in the prototype can be found in [1].

Probabilistic Reasoning About Ship Images   375

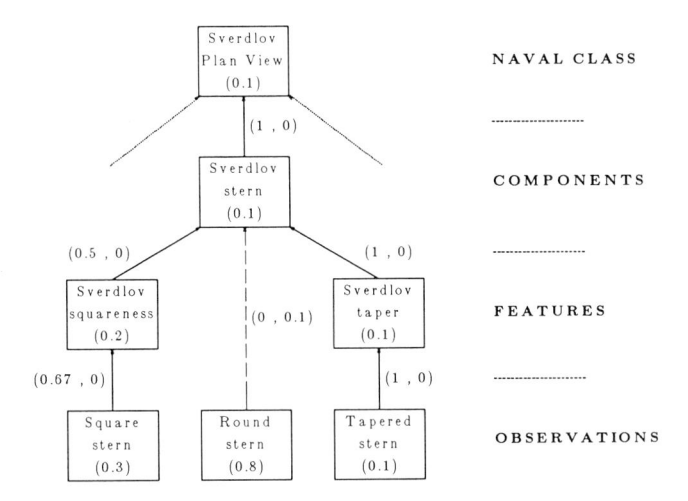

```
                    ┌──────────┐
                    │ Sverdlov │
                    │Plan View │                    NAVAL CLASS
                    │  (0.1)   │
                    └──────────┘
                   /  (1 , 0)  \
                  /             \
                    ┌──────────┐
                    │ Sverdlov │
                    │  stern   │                    COMPONENTS
                    │  (0.1)   │
                    └──────────┘
            (0.5,0) /    |    \ (1,0)
                   /     |     \
         ┌──────────┐    |    ┌──────────┐
         │ Sverdlov │    |    │ Sverdlov │
         │squareness│ (0,0.1) │  taper   │          FEATURES
         │  (0.2)   │    |    │  (0.1)   │
         └──────────┘    |    └──────────┘
        (0.67,0) |       |         | (1,0)
                 |       |         |
         ┌────────┐ ┌────────┐ ┌────────┐
         │ Square │ │ Round  │ │Tapered │
         │ stern  │ │ stern  │ │ stern  │          OBSERVATIONS
         │ (0.3)  │ │ (0.8)  │ │ (0.1)  │
         └────────┘ └────────┘ └────────┘
```

Figure 2. An excerpt from the hierarchical network used to determine how well a plan view image fits the Sverdlov class. Each rectangle designates a proposition along with its prior probability (the number in parentheses). The conditional probabilities $\lambda 1$ and $\lambda 2$ needed to do evidential updating are given as an ordered pair adjacent to each arc.

The structure of the inference networks derived from the feature descriptions is illustrated in Figure 2. This excerpt is a portion of the network for evaluating the hypothesis that a plan view image belongs to the Sverdlov class. It shows how the shape of the stern influences the top-level hypothesis. The bottom nodes correspond to the three relevant observations about the shape of the stern in the image. There are two propositions at the feature level, corresponding to the fact that the Sverdlov class is described as both square and tapered in Table 1. At the third level in the hierarchy, belief is computed about whether the overall stern shape fits Sverdlov. An observation that the stern is round is evidence that the stern does not fit Sverdlov, so its influence comes in at this point. It is also at this level that the feature weights are explicitly factored into the computation. The impact of evidence not sure to be detected (ie. with a weight less than 10) is modeled by changing the link parameters by the ratio weight/10. Networks of this type were constructed for all 10 Naval Classes, one set for plan views and another set for profiles. Overall, they contained 598 propositions and over 1000 links.

The prototype system has been extensively tested on 101 images of the 10 classes. These images were photographs of sensor data from various sources, chosen because they are typical of the mediocre quality available from most operational systems. In 85 of the 101 trials, the ship class ranked first by the program was the correct classification. For profile images, the correct ship class was never ranked lower than second. The correct ship class was not as easily singled out for plan views. This is to be expected, however, given the relatively small amount of information available in a plan view image. Overall, the prototype reliably ranked the correct class at or near the top of the list. Navy experts have reviewed these results and judged them to be excellent given the quality of the test images.

4. SCALING UP TO MORE REALISTIC PROBLEMS

Because of the interest generated by the performance of the prototype, work on this problem has now moved into a second phase in which a more realistic system is being developed. A system suitable for the operational Navy must have the capacity to represent and reason about any of the approximately 640 military Naval Classes that might be encountered at sea. The information available for making classification decisions will come from several sources. In many situations, human judgement and pattern recognition capabilities will continue to be an important source of information. Increasingly, however, information is becoming available from machine-generated feature analysis of raw sensor signals and imagery. Eventually, much of the classification process will be completely automated.

The research issues associated with this larger problem are considerably more complex than those dealt with in the feasibility study. For example, the knowledge base used in the prototype is much too shallow. It is clear that more extensive feature descriptions will be needed to resolve ambiguities in a larger set of ships. More important, though, is the fact that more *kinds* of knowledge will be needed. At the very least, the system will have to know something about the reliability of the sensor being used, the physical relationships among ship components, and the many taxonomic relations among concepts related to the structure and function of ships. Knowledge about the classification process itself would also be useful, so that classification decisions can be made at a level of specificity commensurate with prevailing resource constraints. Moreover, an interface with signal and image processing modules sometimes requires the capability to represent knowledge about continuous-valued variables.

The increased complexity of the problem also has implications for the kinds of reasoning that will be necessary. Effective interaction with feature extraction modules will involve decisions about the order to acquire data, the number of image frames to process before making a judgement about some feature, etc. This means that inferences must flow from hypotheses to evidence as well as from evidence to hypotheses. Non-causal inferences will also be required. For instance, geometric reasoning about aspect angle and hidden features is extremely important. Clearly, the causal inference mechanism will have to interact smoothly with the other methods used for inference and control.

Taking all of these requirements into account, the PROSPECTOR inference scheme does not appear to be well suited for the larger problem. It only provides for data-driven inferences and works best with data driven control strategies. Because of the stringent independence assumptions made in this framework, sets of mutually exclusive and exhaustive multi-valued variables cannot be adequately modeled [3]. Consequently, only true-false propositions were used in the prototype system and the networks only encoded a selected subset of the dependencies among propositions. Even with these simplifications, however, the networks were difficult to maintain. The entire system used 2726 inter-related probabilities. As the domain expert refined the feature descriptions, managing the changes in so many probabilities became extremely difficult. A spreadsheet calculator database was constructed to alleviate some of the computational burden. An annoying conceptual burden still remained though. The network structure simply did not correspond closely enough to the intuitive picture of how the evidence interacts. These difficulties would of course be compounded in a larger, more complex classification problem.

5. THE BMS APPROACH

After examining several alternatives, we have chosen the Belief Maintenance System (BMS) developed by Pearl and Kim [4,5] as the point of departure for this work. The BMS approach has several properties that fit nicely with the requirements of the ship classification problem:

- Both goal driven and data driven inferences are allowed.
- Updating is done with local computations that are independent of the control mechanism that initiates the process.
- Network nodes can represent discrete or continuous valued variables [6].
- A related mechanism can be used to maintain beliefs in object/class hierarchies [7].

These properties, together with the fact that beliefs are updated in a manner consistent with the axioms of probability theory, make BMS a good choice for this application.

The BMS procedure is a Bayesian updating scheme that keeps track of two sources of support for belief at each node: the diagnostic support of the data gathered by descendants of the node and the causal support of the data gathered by ancestors of the node. Each source of support is summarized by a separate local parameter. These two parameters, together with a matrix of conditional probabilities relating the node to its parents, are all that is required to update beliefs. Incoming evidence perturbates one or both of the support parameters for a node. This serves as an activation signal, causing belief at that node to be recomputed and support for neighboring nodes to be revised. The revised support is transmitted to the neighboring nodes, thereby propagating the impact of the evidence. Propagation continues until the network reaches equilibrium. See [4] for a more detailed description.

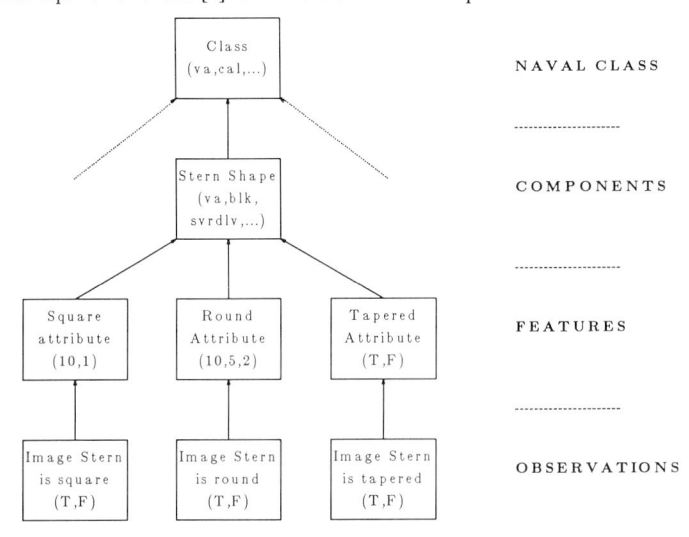

```
            Class
           (va,cal,...)              NAVAL CLASS

                                     ----------------------

          Stern Shape
           (va,blk,                  COMPONENTS
           svrdlv,...)

                                     ----------------------

  Square      Round       Tapered
 attribute   Attribute   Attribute   FEATURES
  (10,1)     (10,5,2)     (T,F)

                                     ----------------------

Image Stern  Image Stern  Image Stern
 is square   is round    is tapered  OBSERVATIONS
  (T,F)       (T,F)        (T,F)
```

Figure 3. An excerpt from the BMS network used to determine how to classify a plan view image. Each rectangle designates a variable along with its mutually exclusive and exhaustive values (given in parentheses).

We have completed an object-oriented implementation of this procedure and tested it on the problem formulated for the original classification prototype. Starting with the same feature descriptions, an inference network was constructed for the BMS system to reason about plan view images of the 10 Naval Classes. A portion of the network is shown in Figure 3. Because the nodes can represent multi-valued variables, the evidential interactions among the features can be specified directly in a manner that is intuitively meaningful. The result is a more compact and more easily understood model. This network required only 36 nodes and 35 links, as compared to the 181 nodes and 297 links used in the original version. Since the links in the network point from cause to effect, the conditional probabilities for the links do not depend on the proportion of ships of each type. This means that a spreadsheet database is no longer needed to manage changes in the model parameters.

When tested on the 52 plan view images, the BMS version produced results nearly identical to those obtained with the PROSPECTOR version. The correct class was ranked first on exactly the same set of images (39 out of 52). In fact, the two versions assigned slightly different rankings to the correct class on just 4 occasions. Overall, the average rank assigned to the correct class was the same for both systems. This is not too surprising, given that the PROSPECTOR version was supplied with a consistent set of probabilities and the network was really a tree. Under those circumstances, the PROSPECTOR method complies with the axioms of probability and the weight of diagnostic evidence is properly distributed.

One interesting implementation issue that emerged from this exercise relates to the order in which nodes are updated. Any sequential implementation of the BMS computation has to keep track of which nodes need to be activated for belief revision. Our original implementation used a stack for this purpose, and it worked well as long as only one piece of evidence was offered to the network at a time. When several perturbations were made at the same time, however, the efficiency of the propagation scheme deteriorated. There are two reasons for this. First, using a stack causes the system to bring small parts of the network into equilibrium before considering the effects of other perturbed nodes.

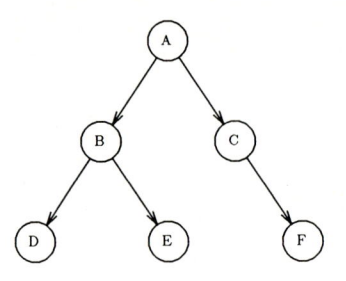

Figure 4

For example, if nodes E and F in Figure 4 are both activated, the impact from E does not propagate to C until A, B and E are in equilibrium. Achieving equilibrium here is a waste of time, however, since the effects from F will disrupt it. This can be avoided by processing activated nodes in a first-in, first-out (FIFO) order, which is more in keeping with the distributed processing spirit of the BMS computation. Second, the number of updates needed to reach equilibrium can be substantially reduced by avoiding duplicate entries in the list. If a node already on the list is moved to the end whenever it receives another activation signal, updating that node is postponed until the information from its neighbors is more complete. These alternatives have been tested on a simple network consisting of 24 nodes and 23 links. Given 8 pieces of evidence simultaneously, the stack implementation reached equilibrium after 195 node updates, the FIFO version needed 108 updates, and the FIFO version with duplicates removed needed only 71 updates.

6. CONCLUSIONS

For our purposes, the BMS updating method provides a flexibility, robustness and conceptual clarity that was not available with the PROSPECTOR approach. It has the additional advantage of being amenable to a straightforward hardware implementation, an important consideration in a real-time application. There was no significant difference in the performance of the two versions of the classification system on a simple task reasoning from evidence to hypothesis. However, the BMS version was much easier to understand and maintain.

Acknowledgements

This research would not have been possible without the cooperation of NRL's image interpretation experts.

Footnotes

[1] A Naval Class is a group of ships built to the same design and known by the lead ship's name.

[2] The scheme also allows belief to be inferred between propositions related by logical AND, OR and NOT. However, only evidential relations were needed for the classification prototype.

[3] Since merit is a signed quantity, what is intended here is the merit with highest absolute value.

REFERENCES

[1] Booker, L. B., An Artificial Intelligence (AI) Approach to Ship Classification. In *Intelligent Systems: Their Development and Application*. Proceedings of the 24th Annual Technical Symposium, Washington D.C. Chapter of the ACM. Gaithersburg, MD., June, 1985, p. 29-35.

[2] Duda, R.O., Hart, P.E., and Nilsson, N.J., Subjective Bayesian Methods for Rule-Based Inference Systems. Technical Note 124, SRI International, Menlo Park, CA, January 1976.

[3] Duda, R.O., Hart, P.E., Konolige, K., and Reboh, R., A Computer-Based Consultant for Mineral Exploration. Final Report, SRI Project 6415, SRI International, Menlo Park, CA, September 1979.

[4] Kim, J. and Pearl, J., A Computational Model for Combined Causal and Diagnostic Reasoning in Inference Systems, *Proceedings of IJCAI-83*, Los Angeles, CA., August, 1985, p. 190-193.

[5] Pearl, J., How To Do With Probabilities What People Say You Can't. Technical Report CSD-850031, Computer Science Department, University of California, Los Angeles, CA, September 1985.

[6] Pearl, J., Distributed Diagnosis in Causal Models with Continuous Variables. Technical Report CSD-860051, Computer Science Department, University of California, Los Angeles, CA, December 1985.

[7] Pearl, J., On Evidential Reasoning in a Hierarchy of Hypotheses. *Artificial Intelligence* , Vol. 28, No. 1 (1986), p. 9-15.

[8] Quinlan, J., Inferno: A Cautious Approach to Uncertain Inference. *The Computer Journal*, Vol. 26, No. 3 (1983), p. 255-269

[9] Slagle, J., Gaynor, M., and Halpern, E., An Intelligent Control Strategy for Computer Consultation. *IEEE Trans. Pattern Anal. Machine Intell.* PAMI-6, (March 1984), p. 129-136.

[10] Slagle, J. and Hamburger, H., An Expert System for a Resource Allocation Problem. *Communications of the ACM*, Vol. 28, No. 9 (Sept. 1985), p. 994-1004.

Information and Multi-Sensor Coordination

Greg Hager* and Hugh F. Durrant-Whyte†

General Robotics and Active Sensory Processing Laboratory
Department of Computer and Information Science
University of Pennsylvania
Philadelphia, PA 19104-6389
USA

The control and integration of distributed, multi-sensor perceptual systems is a complex and challenging problem. The observations or opinions of different sensors are often disparate, incomparable and are usually only partial views. Sensor information is inherently uncertain, and in addition the individual sensors may themselves be in error with respect to the system as a whole. The successful operation of a multi-sensor system must account for this uncertainty and provide for the aggregation of disparate information in an intelligent and robust manner.
We consider the sensors of a multi-sensor system to be members or agents of a team, able to offer opinions and bargain in group decisions. We will analyze the coordination and control of this structure using a theory of team decision-making. We present some new analytic results on multi-sensor aggregation and detail a simulation which we use to investigate our ideas. This simulation provides a basis for the analysis of complex agent structures cooperating in the presence of uncertainty. The results of this study are discussed with reference to multi-sensor robot systems, distributed AI and decision making under uncertainty.

1 Introduction

The general problem of seeking, sensing, and using perceptual information is a complex and, as yet, unsolved problem. Complications arise due to the inherent uncertainty of information from perceptual sources, incompleteness of information from partial views, and questions of deployment, coordination and fusion of multiple data sources. Yet another dimension of complexity results from organizational and computational considerations. We feel that these three topics – information, control, and organization – are fundamental for understanding and constructing complex, intelligent robotics systems. In this paper, we are concerned with developing useful analytic methods for describing, analyzing and comparing the behavior of robotic systems based on these criteria.

We assume from the outset that the behavior of such a system is determined entirely by the goal it is working toward and the information it has about its environment. At any point in time, such an agent should use the available information to select some feasible action. The most preferable action should be that which is expected to lead the system closest to the current goal. In short, we will consider the question of driving robotics systems as a large and complex problem in estimation and control. To adopt the nomenclature of decision theory [1], at any point in time an agent has a local *information structure* reflecting the state of the world, a set of *feasible actions* to choose from, and a *utility* which supplies a preference ordering of actions with respect to states of the world. We generally assume that a *rational* decision-maker is one which, at any point in time, takes that action which maximizes his utility. Our commitment, as a result of casting the problem in a decision theoretic perspective, is to provide principled means for specifying information structures, actions, and (perhaps most crucially) determination of utility.

---

*This material is based on work supported under a National Science Foundation Graduate Fellowship and by the National Science Foundation under Grants DMC-8411879 and DMC-12838. Any opinions, findings, and conclusions or recommendations expressed in this publication are those of the authors and do not necessarily reflect the views of the National Science Foundation. This work was also partially funded by US Air Force F49620-85-K-0018, US Air Force F33615-83-C-3000, US Air Force F33615-86-C-3610, DARPA/ONR, ARMY/DAAG-29-84-K-0061, and NSF-CER DCR82-19196 A02.
†This author's current address is Department of Engineering Science, Oxford University, Parks Road, Oxford OX1 3PJ, U.K.

This monolithic formulation is certainly too naive and general to successfully attack the problem. The state of the system is a complex entity which must be decomposed and analyzed to be understood. The resulting procedures for control will undoubtedly be computationally complex. Computer resources, like human problem solvers, have resource limitations which bound the complexity of problems that can be solved by a single agent – otherwise known as *bounded rationality* [27]. Such computational considerations suggest distributing the workload to increase the problem solving potential of the system. From a practical standpoint, the system itself is composed of physically distinct devices, each with its own special characteristics. Software and hardware modules should be designed so that information and control local to subtasks is kept locally, and only information germane to other subtasks is made available. Ultimately, sensors and subtasks should be independent modules which can be added or removed from a system without catastrophic results [23]. In this case we desire each subtask to have the ability to cooperate and coordinate its actions with a group while maintaining its own local processing intelligence, local control variables, and possibly some local autonomy.

Our approach is to view the systems as decomposed into several distinct decision-makers. These modules are to be organized and communicate in such a manner as to achieve the common goal of the system. Organizations of this type of are often referred to as teams [7,18]. We propose to consider a team-theoretic formulation formulation of multi-sensor systems in the following sense: the agents are considered as members of the team, each observing the environment and making local decisions based on the information available to them. A manager (executive or coordinator) makes use of utility considerations to converge the opinions of the sensor systems. Section 2 will be devoted to a review of team decision theory and present some new analytic results [6].

One criticism of decision theory is that optimal solutions are often difficult or impossible to find. In order to aid in analysis of these problems, we have built a simulation environment. We use the simulation to examine various non-optimal and heuristic solutions to otherwise intractable problems, and experiment with different loss functions to determine the character of the resultant decision method. The simulation is a generalization of classic pursuit and evasion games [16] to teams of pursuers and evaders. Each team member has local sensors and state variables. They are coordinated through a team executive. Section 3 will be devoted to a detailed look at the simulation and our results to date.

We feel that the team formulation of sensory systems has implications for the broader study of Artificial Intelligence. AI is relevant to this work in at least two respects:

- First, it is certainly possible to consider the agents of the system as performing some reasoning process. Considering AI systems as decision-makers seems a plausible approach to the construction of intelligent distributed systems. Thus, this work has commonalities with Distributed AI in that both are interested in questions of structuring information and communication between intelligent systems.

- Second, we often want to *interpret* the information available to the system, and to communicate information as interpretations rather than simple signals. This is primarily a problem in representation of information. Again, AI has focussed on the interpretation of information, and the representation of that interpretation.

More generally, we would like to discover when systems like this can be profitably posed as decision problems. Section 4 will be devoted to an in depth discussion of the general merits and shortcomings of the organizational view, and attempt to define when it is most appropriate or useful.

2 A Team-Theoretic Formulation of Multi-Sensor Systems

Team theory originated from problems in game theory [28] and multi-person control. The basis for the analysis of cooperation among structures with different opinions or interests was formulated by Nash [22] in the well known bargaining problem. Nash's solution for the two person cooperative game was developed into the concepts of information, group rationality and multi-person decisions by Savage [26]. Team theory has since been extensively used by economists to analyze structure [18], information [20] and communication. Section 2.1 introduces the team structure and defines the function of the team members and manager. Different team organizations are discussed and the concepts of information structure, team decision, team utility and cooperation are defined in Section 2.2. Section 2.3 applies these techniques to the multi-sensor team and a method for aggregating opinions is derived. In the sequel, we will assume some familiarity with probability and decision theory.

2.1 Team Preliminaries

A sensor or member of a team of sensors is characterized by its information structure and its decision function. Consider a team comprising of n members or sensors each making observations of the state of the environment. The information structure of the ith team member is a function η_i which describes the character of the sensor observations $z_i \in \mathcal{H}_i$ in terms of the state of the environment $\theta \in \Theta$, and the actions of other team members, $a_j \in \mathcal{A}_j$, $j = 1, \cdots, n$.

$$z_i = \eta_i(\theta, a_1, \cdots, a_n)$$

Collectively the n-tuple $\eta = (\eta_i, \cdots, \eta_n)$ is called the information structure of the team. The action a_i of the ith team member is related to its information z_i by a decision function $\delta_i \in \mathcal{D}_i$ as $a_i = \delta_i(z_i)$. We may also allow randomized rules, in which case δ associates information with a *distribution* over the set of feasible actions. Collectively the n-tuple $\delta = (\delta_1, \cdots, \delta_n)$ is called the team decision function. For an estimation problem, the action space $\mathcal{A}_i$ is the same as the space of possible states of nature Θ: our action is to choose an estimate $\hat{\theta}_i \in \Theta$.

There are a number of different forms that the information structure can take which in turn characterizes the type of problem to be solved. If, for all team members, η_i is defined *only* on Θ ($\eta_i: \Theta \longrightarrow \mathcal{H}$) the resulting structure is called a *static* team [18]. When η_i also depends on the other team members' actions, then the structure is called a *dynamic team* [15]. Clearly as each team member can not make decisions and be aware of the result simultaneously, the general form of information structure for a dynamic team must induce a causal relation on the team member actions a_j. We can apply a precedence structure on the time instant a member makes a decision, so that if member i makes a decision prior to member j then the information structure η_i will not be a function of a_j. Indexing the team members by their decision-making precedence order we can rewrite the information structure as:

$$z_i = \eta_i(\theta, a_1 \cdots, a_{i-1})$$

A sensor or member of a team will be considered rational if it can place a preference ordering on its actions that admits a utility function $u_i : \mathcal{A} \times \Theta \longrightarrow \Re$. One possible set of rationality axioms can be found in [1, p. 43] and the proof that these axioms admit a utility function can be found in [4]. A utility function can be used to evaluate a decision rule $\delta(\cdot)$ in terms of its payoff:

$$U_i(\delta, \theta) = E[u_i(\delta(z_i), \theta)] = \int_{\mathcal{H}_i} u_i(\delta(z_i), \theta) f(z_i|\theta) \, dz_i$$

We assume that a rational team member is attempting to maximize its gains and hence will attempt to choose the rule δ^* with maximum payoff.

2.2 Team Organizations

The extension of individual rationality to group rationality requires the comparison of individual preferences. Any such comparison incorporates a number of assumptions about the nature of the group or team. For example, each team member must assume some subjective knowledge of other players rationality, interpersonal comparisons of utility require preferences to be congruent, and assumptions must be made about indifference, dominance and dictatorship. Nash first introduced a set of group rationality axioms [22]. There has been considerable disagreement about these axioms [30], and a number of other definitions have been suggested *e.g.* [12].

A group preference is expressed in terms of a team utility function, G. Since there is no universally accepted foundation for group utilities, the actual form of G can vary considerably depending on the desired relationship between individual and team preferences. To gain some intuition about the effect G has on a group, we will discuss its consequences in terms of a hypothetical team "manager." The manager makes group decisions based on maximizing G.

Most generally, G may combine local and global objectives by considering team member utilities and joint team actions as in $G(a_1, a_2, \cdots, a_n, u_1, u_2, \ldots, u_n, \theta)$. In this case, the manager considers both the opinions of members and the actual state of affairs at hand. Alternatively G may disregard individual preferences and take the form $G(a_1, a_2, \cdots, a_n, \theta)$. The interpretation of team action in this case, due to Ho, Chu, Marschak and Radnor [15,18], is that the goal of the manager is to maximize G regardless of personal loss to the team members (in fact, personal loss is not even defined). This is the formulation most often found in control theory.

Finally, the team utility may be restricted to some combination of member utilities: $G(u_1, u_2, \cdots, u_n)$. In this case, G is referred to as an *opinion pool*. This formulation may be interpreted in two ways. If the team member's utility structures are of the form $u_i(a, \theta)$, G can be considered as $G(a_1, a_2, \ldots, a_n, \theta)$. The manager disregards personal objectives and attempts to maximize the group pool. An alternative formulation is to allow individual team members to retain personal utility as well as an interest in the team. For example a team member may agree to cooperate with a team decision and be subject to the utility G, or to disagree with the other team members and be subject to a personal utility. In this case a rational team member will agree to cooperate *only* if it will gain by doing so: when the team utility exceeds its personal utility.

A number of utility pools have been studied [1,30]. Two common examples of are the generalized Nash product:

$$G(a_1, \cdots, a_n, \theta) = c \prod_{i=1}^{n} u_i^{\alpha_i}(a_i, \theta) \quad \alpha_i \geq 0$$

and the linear opinion pool:

$$G(a_1, \cdots, a_n, \theta) = \sum_{i=1}^{n} \lambda_i u_i(a_i, \theta), \quad \lambda_i \geq 0, \quad \sum_{i=1}^{n} \lambda_i = 1$$

The value of the generalized Nash product can be seen by noting that, if the $u_i(a_i, \theta)$ take the form of probability distributions and the α_i are unit valued, then G takes the form of a joint density function. A criticism leveled at the generalized Nash product is that it assumes independence of opinions, though this may be accounted for through the weights α_i. A criticism of the linear opinion pool is that there is no reinforcement of opinion.

The team utility G is in turn used to derive a team decision rule. In the case where there is a single decision-maker, it is intuitively appealing that maximizing payoff is the proper definition of optimality. However, team members may weigh the consequences of their actions in many ways depending on the team structure. We will adopt an evaluation of decision rules based strictly on team preferences [15]:

Definition 2.1 A decision, $\mathbf{a}^* = [a_1^*, \cdots, a_n^*]^T \in \mathcal{A}$, is called *person-by-person* optimal if, for all team members $i = 1, \cdots, n$, this team action satisfies

$$E[G(a_1^*, \cdots, a_i, \cdots, a_n^*)] \leq E[G(a_1^*, \cdots, a_i^*, \cdots, a_n^*)] \quad (1)$$

If the payoff function of the team, $G(a_1, \cdots, a_n)$ is unimodal and concave in all a_i, then it can be shown that there is a single group decision, $\mathbf{a}^*$, which is person-by-person optimal [15]. Thus, if G is concave and unimodal in all a_i there is a single team action which is incontestably the best choice.

If G is not of this form, randomized decisions may be called for. A randomized decision can be thought of as picking a team action based on a lottery. When observations are made, the lottery is played and the result of this lottery is the team action. The actual form of this lottery may vary considerably depending on the degree of independence or coupling between the components of group actions. In general, if $\mathcal{A}$, includes all jointly randomized rules then the expected value of G considered as a function defined on $\mathcal{A}$ will *always* be concave. If we really believed in complete team agreement, we must use this class and be subject to these results. Considerable work has been done on finding solutions to equation 1 under these conditions [13,14,15,18], particularly as regards the effect of information structure on distributed control problems. Our analysis will be based on the observation that if randomization is required, there is no longer a *single* action which is person-by-person optimal. This provides a basis for disagreement within the team – different team choices may be preferred by different team members based on local utility considerations.

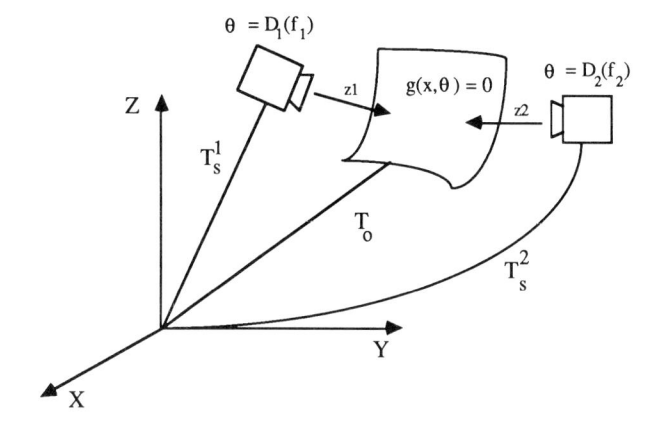

Figure 1: An example configuration of two sensors observing different features of a parametric surface.

2.3 Multi-Sensor Teams

We are primarily interested in teams of observers — sensors making observations of the state of the environment. In this case the team members can be considered as Bayesian estimators, and the team decision is to come to a consensus view of the observed state of nature. The static team of estimators is often called a Multi-Bayesian system [30]. These systems have many of the same characteristics as more general team decision problems. Weerahandi [29] has shown that the set of non-randomized decision rules is not always complete in these systems. These cases can be thought of as situations where individual team members would choose to disagree in a single point estimate.

Our results are based on considering each sensor as an estimation expert. This allows us to pose the fusion of diverse sensor observations in terms of a comparison of opinions toward a consensus decision. Each sensor comes up with uncertain partial views of the state of the environment, and the goal of the team is to integrate the various sensor opinions. We will adopt a team structure which allows members to disagree if for some reason they have made a mistake or cannot reconcile their views with those of the other team members. Since we are now speaking of *opinions* toward a team decision rather than classical utilities, we will write $o_i(\cdot, \theta)$, instead of $u_i(\cdot, \theta)$.

Figure 1 depicts a typical multisensor estimation problem. We have two sensors, S_1 and S_2, taking observations z_1 and z_2 of features f_1 and f_2 of a surface parameterized as $g(x, \theta) = 0$. We will assume that these observations are described by some transformation $h(\cdot)$ contaminated by additive, zero-mean, gaussian noise *e.g.*, $z_i = h_i(f_i) + V_i$ where $V_i \sim N(0, \Lambda_i)$. Each sensor returns an estimate based on observations as $\hat{f}_i = \delta_i(z_i)$, where δ_i is the local sensor estimation procedure. These features in turn depend on θ, the parameter we are estimating. If the observations from different sensors are incomparable – for example, when the sensors are in different locations – they must be interpreted in some common framework. Let D_i interpret S_i's estimates in some common description framework as $D_1(f_1) = \theta$ and $D_2(f_2) = \theta$.[1] Clearly, any *consistent* estimate $\hat{f}_1$ and $\hat{f}_2$ of the features f_1 and f_2 based on the uncertain sensor observations z_1 and z_2 *must* satisfy

$$D_1(\hat{f}_1) = \hat{\theta} = D_2(\hat{f}_2)$$

This means that we cannot estimate $\hat{f}_1$ and $\hat{f}_2$ independently. Rather, we must base the decision on a consensus interpretation of the surface $\hat{\theta}$. In order to simplify the notation, we will henceforth require that δ_i both estimates f_i and transforms it into the proper description frame. Thus, f_i will depend on and be directly comparable to θ.

---

[1] Realistically, features underdetermine a surface interpretation so our functional notation is not entirely correct. However, this can be handled by assuming that a sensor returns infinite uncertainty in those aspects of θ which it cannot determine from its observations. See [6] for details.

A sensor's opinion towards a team estimate θ given an observation z_i will be based on the probability density $\pi_i(\cdot|f_i)$. If the sensor estimation procedures are of the form $\delta_i(z_i) = A_i z_i$ and z_i is gaussian, then the distribution of $\hat{f}_i$ is given by $\pi_i(\cdot|f_i) = N(A_i h_i(f_i), \Sigma_i^{-1})$ where $\Sigma_i = (A \Lambda_i A^T)^{-1}$. If δ_i is not linear, we can approximate it by the linear procedure $\delta'_i(z_i) = J_i z_i$ where J_i is the Jacobian of the nonlinear function δ_i. We can then construct the distribution of f_i based on this approximation in the manner described above. In the sequel, we will assume that $\delta_i(z_i) = A_i z_i$ is linear or a linearized version of the true procedure and $\hat{f}_i$ will represent the corresponding estimate.

A sensor's opinion will be that its estimate, $\hat{f}_i = A_i z_i$ is the correct value for the team estimate. Its confidence in that estimate will depend on Σ_i, the inverse of the variance. Large variance will cause it to have little confidence, and small variance will lead to a high degree of belief in the estimate. Therefore, we will define o_i to take the form of a gaussian with mean $\hat{f}_i$ and variance Σ_i^{-1}. If θ is of dimension k, we have

$$o_i(\hat{f}_i, \theta) = \frac{1}{2\pi^{k/2} |\Sigma_i^{-1/2}|} \exp\left(-\frac{1}{2}(\hat{f}_i - \theta)^T \Sigma_i (\hat{f}_i - \theta)\right) \quad (2)$$

Fix G to be an opinion pool of the form $G(\hat{\mathbf{f}}, \theta) = G(o_1(\hat{f}_1, \theta), \ldots, o_n(\hat{f}_n, \theta))$, and restrict group actions $\hat{\theta}$ to non-randomized decisions, i.e., $\hat{\theta} \in \Theta$. Then the consensus surface parameter estimate, $\hat{\theta}$, is found from:

$$\hat{\theta} = \arg\max_{\theta \in \Theta} G(o_1(\hat{f}_1, \theta), o_2(\hat{f}_2, \theta), \ldots, o_n(\hat{f}_n, \theta))$$

This expression finds the surface parameter (if it exists) which simultaneously tries to provide the best explanation for both sensor observations. As decisions are made in a common framework, this equation automatically finds the estimate which maintains a consistent environment model. Intuitively, the manager proposes a surface and the sensors (based on their observations) tell the manager what they think of the suggestion.

When o_i takes the form of a gaussian, it is simple to show that the generalized Nash product is *always* concave about a unique optimal point so that a team using this pool would never disagree. This is not surprising since the Nash product team estimate is essentially the maximum likelihood estimate which is always unique. Thus, the Nash product is not desirable since it does not allow for any discrimination between opinions which are closely aligned and those which are highly separated. The linear opinion pool *does* allow for disagreement – if all the o_i are concave functions, then G will always be concave on the class of non-randomized decisions. However, if some o_i is not concave, then G is not concave and there will be a basis for disagreement. Our sensor fusion method is based on determining what conditions cause this to occur.

Fix G to be a linear pool with unit weights and fix sensor opinions as defined by equation 2. Then the function G will be concave on a convex set, Θ, if its matrix of second order derivatives (the Hessian $\nabla^2 G$) is negative semi-definite [1, pg. 39]. However, since G is linear in the o_i, this is equivalent to requiring that each of the o_i be negative semi-definite in θ. Differentiating o_i gives

$$\nabla^2_\theta o_i = \left(\Sigma_i (\theta - \hat{f}_i)(\theta - \hat{f}_i)^T \Sigma_i - \Sigma_i\right) \cdot o_i(\hat{f}_i, \theta) \leq 0 \quad (3)$$

Since o_i is a positive function it has no effect on the sign of this expression. We can omit it and invert the sense of the expression to obtain, for each sensor, a matrix expression which must be nonnegative-definite for each i.

$$\Sigma_i - \Sigma_i (\theta - \hat{f}_i)(\theta - \hat{f}_i)^T \Sigma_i \geq 0 \quad (4)$$

We can show, via the Cauchy-Schwartz-Buniakowsky inequality, that equation 4 will be satisfied (and hence G concave) if there is a θ which satisfies:

$$(\theta - \hat{f}_i)^T \Sigma_i (\theta - \hat{f}_i) \leq 1 \quad \text{for } i = 1, \cdots, n \quad (5)$$

Consider any two estimates $\hat{f}_i$ and $\hat{f}_j$. They will form a consensus if we can find a θ that satisfies equation 5 for both $\hat{f}_i$ and $\hat{f}_j$. Since the left hand side of equation 5 is always positive, we must find a θ which satisfies

$$\frac{1}{2}(\theta - \hat{f}_i)^T \Sigma_i (\theta - \hat{f}_i) + \frac{1}{2}(\theta - \hat{f}_j)^T \Sigma_j (\theta - \hat{f}_j) \leq 1 \quad (6)$$

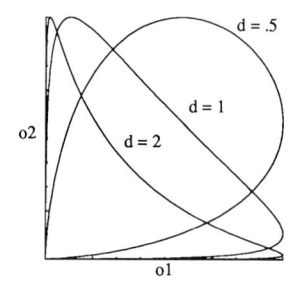

Figure 2: Plots of individual opinions toward an estimate for three values of the Mahalanobis distance.

The value of θ which makes the left hand side of this equation a minimum (and which is also the consensus when it exists) is given by the usual combination of normal observations [1]:

$$\hat{\theta} = (\Sigma_i + \Sigma_j)^{-1}(\Sigma_i \hat{f}_j + \Sigma_j \hat{f}_i)$$

Substituting this into equation 6 gives:

$$\frac{1}{2}(\hat{f}_i - \hat{f}_j)^T \Sigma_i (\Sigma_i + \Sigma_j)^{-1} \Sigma_j (\hat{f}_i - \hat{f}_j) = d_{ij} \leq 1 \qquad (7)$$

We will say that $\hat{f}_i$ and $\hat{f}_j$ admit a Bayesian (non-randomized) consensus if and only if they satisfy equation 7. The left side of Equation 7, which we have denoted d_{ij}, is called the generalized Mahalanobis distance (a restricted form of this is derived in [29]) and is a measure of disagreement between two observations. Figure 2 shows plots of o_i against o_j for various values of d_{ij} which clearly demonstrate that the concavity of G corresponds to requiring that $d_{ij} \leq 1$. For $d_{ij} = .5$, there is clearly a single optimal θ. As d_{ij} increases past 1, the curve flattens and then dips so that there are now two team choices.

In most real situations, it is unlikely that we will know the variance-covariance matrices exactly. In this case, any estimates of the Λ_i act as if they were thresholds in the sense that the larger the Λ_i that is used, the more disagreement will be tolerated.

3 Simulation Studies

To this point, we have discussed the theoretical aspects of estimation in the team framework. Our goal is to eventually pose problems of multi-sensor control in coordination and solve them in a similar manner. However, finding and analyzing solutions to decision, control, or game problems – especially in the face of anything less than perfect information – can be extremely difficult. From a technical perspective, solutions under even relatively simple losses are complex optimization problems. Other heuristic or *ad hoc* approaches must often be considered. Methodologically, there is a question as to what proper loss functions are for different problems. Ideally, the loss function should reflect the actual state of affairs under consideration since it reflects the preferences of the decision-maker. Whereas in the economics literature, losses are usually derived from utility considerations based on monetary rewards, we have a much wider set of competing criteria to consider. This complicates matters to the point that we need to gain intuition about the issues involved before hypothesizing a solution.

In order to deal with these issues, we have constructed a simulation on a Symbolics Lisp Machine. The simulation takes the form of a game of pursuit and evasion similar in character to the differential game known as the *homicidal chauffeur* [16]. That classical form of this game consists of a pursuer and evader moving at constant velocity in a plane. Both players have perfect information about the

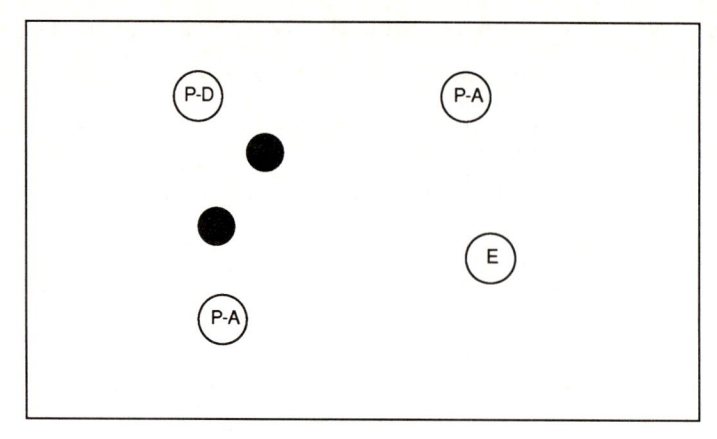

Figure 3: The Pursuit-Evasion Game.

other's state, and attempt use this information to intercept or evade their opponent respectively. The payoff structure of the game is the time until capture. The major changes we have made are that we have equipped the players with imperfect sensing devices (i.e., the players use imperfect state information), and we allow multiple pursuers and evaders grouped into teams coordinated by a team executive. It is important to note that the motivation for using the pursuit-evasion framework is primarily to provide each team with a well-defined method for comparing structures and control policies. The game is not of intrinsic value by itself, but forms a structured, flexible, closed system in which sensor models, organizational structures and decision methods may be implemented and easily evaluated

The simulation is constructed so that we can vary the structure of team members, as well as overall team structure, and quickly evaluate the effects of the change based on the character of the simulated game that ensues. We have in mind to allow variation in such factors as dynamics, sensors, information integration policies, incentive structures, and uncertainty of information, and observe what types of policies lead to the adequate performance in these circumstances. We imagine a situation where this simulation provides an environment in which distributed expert coordination and control problems can be investigated before implementation and conversely that applications of the sensor systems under development will suggest what directions, sensor models and dynamics would most fruitful to explore in the simulation. The remainder of this section details the current structure of the simulation environment, and outlines our initial experiences with it.

3.1 The Game Environment

The simulation takes place on a planar field possibly littered with obstacles. The basic execution cycle involves team members taking sensor readings, executives integrating information and offering incentives, and finally team members making decisions. The state variables are updated and the game moves to a new step. A game terminates if and when the pursuit robots, which are equipped with a simple ballistics system, capture all the evaders. This is a medium level of granularity with emphasis on the general behavior of teams, not the precise performance issues of team members. Some time-constraint issues can be investigated by including time parameters in the payoff functions, but computational complexity issues and investigations of asynchronous behavior are outside the scope of our considerations. For instance, if some decision policy is computationally more complex than another, differences in performance will not reflect that complexity.

3.2 The Structure of Team Members

The character of individual team members is determined by three modules: the kinematics and dynamics of motion on the plane; the sensors that are available, the noise characteristics of those sensors, and their kinematics and dynamics; and, the ballistics which determine the termination of the game.

The team members are constant velocity, variable direction units operating in a plane with state variables x, y, and θ. Since the robots move with constant velocity, the only directly controlled variable is θ. The only dynamical consideration involved is how we allow the robot to change its current heading to some new desired heading θ_d – the single control. Currently, we assume that when reorienting, each agent can move with some fixed (possibly infinite) velocity, ω. This has the effect of defining a minimal turning radius. Pursuers generally have some finite ω, while evaders have infinite ω – i.e., they turn instantaneously.

The sensor model we are currently using is a range and direction sensor. The sensor has a limited cone of data gathering, and a limited range. It has a single control variable α which the robot can select to point the sensor. We assume that sensors typically return noisy data, so we have different noise models which we "wrap around" the sensor to make it more closely approximate real data gathering devices. This induces decision problems in dealing with both the noise and range limitations of devices. The fact that the sensors are distributed introduces issues in integrating noisy observations from different frames of reference [5]. Finally, since sensors are transported by the robot, there are issues involved in resolving the conflicts between action for pursuit or evasion, and actions which will allow more efficient gathering of information [9,11,10].

Termination of the game occurs when all evaders are eliminated. We define a *capture region* which delineates how close a pursuer must come to eliminate an evader. However, when information is noisy, the area in which the evader can be located will have an associated uncertainty. We sometimes equip each pursuer with some mechanism to "shoot" evaders, allowing the possibility of uncertainty in observation to make it "miss". Part of the payoff structure of the game can include costs for using projectiles and missing; thereby adding incentive to localize the evader to the best degree possible.

3.3 Information Structures, Organization, and Control

The intesting issues are how the robot systems are controlled, and how team members interact. Each team member must make decisions, based on available information, about the best setting of its control variables. Thus, each team member has a local information structure and a utility function or decision rule as outlined in Section 2. The type of information available – its completeness and fidelity – along with the utility function determine how an agent behaves for a fixed set of controls. We have specifically modularized information structure and decision processes so that variations are easily compared.

The information structure can consist of only local information, or can contain information communicated from other team members, as well as computed information based on observation history. The team executive provides the basic organizational structure of the team. It is equipped with the team information structure, and computes the team utility which is offered as the incentives for a team member to cooperate with the team. The issues here involve integrating the team information, and the exact nature of the team utility. In our experiments, we either use the executive as an information integrator and team blackboard, or restrict robots to their own local information.

Our experiments to date have been in controlling the direction of travel of robots. Three decision methods have been used: purely local information and decisions; completely global information and a linear pool team utility; and, a mix of global and local information with a non-concave utility structure.

The first of these is the obvious strategy of chasing whatever is within the viewing radius and avoiding any obstacles. The second amounts to the executive choosing an evader to follow, and the team members agreeing at all costs. This has the undesirable property of the pursuers being destroyed while attempting purely global objectives. The first method disregards centralized control, possibly missing an opportunity for team members to cooperate for common benefit. The latter disregards individual concerns for global objectives, possibly disregarding important local objectives.

The final method uses the executive to integrate information about evaders, and to offer a team incentive to chase a particular evader. But, it also lets team members compute an incentive to avoid obstacles which fall on their path. Figure 3 shows a team configuration where one pursuit team member (labeled "P-D") is disagreeing with the team in order to avoid an obstacle, while the rest of the team (labeled "P-A") are following the executive's order to chase an evader.

Our next objective in the simulation is to consider noisy observations and develop sensor control algorithms. Our idea for this project is the following: recall that sensors return distance and direction. We henceforth assume both quantities are distributed according to some probability distribution. The information structure of the team will consist of the current best estimate and the information matrix of measurements integrated as in Section 2. The utility for an angle α_i of a sensor i will be the expected change in the information for the closest evader within the cone of vision. This means that individual members will choose that evader for which they can contribute the "maximum" information. We have not yet developed any team policies for this scenario

4 Evaluation and Speculation

We have considered a very basic, static, non-recursive team structure for the sensors and cues of a robot system. The results obtained for the aggregation of agent opinions are intuitively appealing and computationally very simple. Similarly, the initial simulation experiments with distributed control seem promising. However, it is clearly the case that the methods presented thus far could easily be developed without recourse to the concepts of team and information structure. We have chosen to introduce these ideas for two main reasons: first as a device through which the interactions between sensor agents may be easily explained, and second because we feel that team-theoretic methodology has great potential for understanding and implementing more complex organizational structures in a systematic manner. Our main point is that team theory is neither a completely abstract non-computational formalization of the problem, nor a computational technique or algorithm with no theoretical potential, but is in fact our analog of a *computational theory* [17]. We assert that the inherent elements of cooperation and uncertainty make team theory the appropriate tool for this class of problems [13]. This section discusses the advantages of team theory and suggests issues which need to be explored more fully.

4.1 Information and Structure

Many of the advantages of team-theoretic descriptions lie in the ability to analyze the effects of different agent (team member) information structures on the overall system capabilities. Recall that in the general case, the ith team member's information structure may well depend on the other team member's actions and information, either as a preference ordering (non-recursive) or in the form of a dialogue (recursive) structure. For example, consider a stereo camera and a tactile sensor acting together in a team. It is often the case that the stereo matching algorithm is incapable of finding disparities and three dimensional locations that are horizontal in the view plane, whereas a tactile sensor mounted on a gripper jaw is *best* at finding just such horizontal features. In addition it is reasonable to assume that, while a vision system is good at finding global locations, a touch sensor is better for refining observations and resolving local ambiguities. What is required is a sharing of information between these two sensors: their respective information structures should be made dependent on each other's actions. We can imagine specifying the problem so that the solution is anything from a simple optimal control to an extended dialogue taking place between the two sensors, resolving each other's observations and actions, arriving at a consensus decision about the environment. This example clearly shows the advantages of a team-theoretic analysis. We can postulate alternative information structures for the sensors and the dynamics of the exchange of opinions can be analyzed: Is a consensus obtained? When is a decision made? Should communication bandwidth be increased or decreased?

Another aspect of this scenario is that the use of information structures automatically partition the sensors into a kind of "who knows what" structure. In general, not all the information about a robotics system is relevant to the construction of specific portions of the system. Analogously, all the information available via sensor is not relevant to the performance of all parts of the system. In the example above, the spatial characteristics of the camera image are of interest only to the camera agent, and the response characteristics of the tactile sensor are only relevant to the tactile controller. The ambient illumination as measured by the camera has no relevance to a decision made by the tactile sensor even though they may cooperate in disambiguating edges. Team theory allows information and control to reside *where it is appropriate*, and thereby reduces problem complexity and increases performance potential. We believe that this is a crucial principle for the construction of intelligent robotics systems.

To this point, we have not discussed uncertainty of information. However, information from perceptual sources is sure to have some associated uncertainty. Uncertainty adds an entire dimension to any discussion of information – we must consider some grade of belief in information [3] and how that should influence the choice of action. In the case of perfect sensing, information is either adequate or inadequate; and new information can be derived by using the constraints of the problem at hand. Hence, new facts will either lead to more information, or be redundant. On the other hand, if information is uncertain, adding more *unrelated* observations may not really increase the available information. Multiple correlated observations may, in fact, be a better strategy since that is likely to reduce uncertainty. Encoding considerations such as this presents no problem in team theory, as information structures are perfectly capable of modeling uncertain information sources. The hard questions that arise are how to structure the pooling of information between sensors with dependent information, how to take action in the face of uncertainty, and what control methods are most appropriate for directing the gathering of information. We are currently exploring these issues.

4.2 Loss Considerations and Control

The loss function associated with an agent or a team determines the essential nature of the decision-maker. In the standard optimal control formulation, specification of information structures and loss provide the criteria for selection of the *optimal control law or decision rule*. However, optimal rules are often difficult to derive, and have a computationally complex nature. General results are known only for a restricted class of information structure/loss function formulations. One way of reducing complexity is to restrict consideration to a smaller class of *admissible controls*, and choose the member of this class which minimizes the loss. For instance, linear controls are mathematically and computationally simple. Lastly, we can consider constructing decision rules *ad hoc* and evaluating their performance relative to an objective based on simulation studies. In any case, the character of the loss function is crucial in determining the resultant decision rule or control law.

One area which needs more exploration is a methodology for the specification of loss functions. Ideally, the loss function should be justifiable in terms of objective criteria related to the problem. Pragmatically, it is often dictated by mathematical convenience. From the team perspective, more work needs to be done on the interaction of team and local loss characterizations. Section 2 presented some results in this direction, but more work is surely needed, particularly in the case where the team objectives are not expressible as some combination of members' objectives.

To illustrate what we have in mind, consider formulating loss functions for controlling a system based on a desired state of information [9]. That is, if the team has as its goal some state of information (for example, to move an arm this information is needed), what action is most appropriate for progressing from the current information state toward the desired information state. Should it select an action which will change the uncertainty associated with current information, or go ahead with an action that adds uncorrelated evidence? How should it decide that it has enough information? More concretely, should the executive take another picture with the camera, or perhaps take a different view, or maybe use another sensor altogether? Maybe the sensors themselves should decide individually what to do. These are all issues dealing with the interaction of information and action. By using team theory, we can easily formulate the problem, specify loss functions or decision methods based on, for example, the parameters of a probability distribution associated with some information source, and examine the results via simulation or by analytic methods.

4.3 Decision Theory and AI

As we stated at the outset, we consider our work relevant to AI in that we may want to consider information as interpreted, and would like to consider parts of a system as intelligent reasoning agents. In related work dealing with the interaction of intelligent agents, Rosenschein and Genesereth in [24] and Ginsburg in [8] have investigated variations on game theoretical definitions of rationality for coordinating intelligent agents. These efforts are an attempt to analyze the interaction of intelligent agents with *no a priori structure* and investigate the consequence of various rationality assumptions. We, on the other hand, postulate a given team structure and are interested in discovering its properties. This is an important fundamental distinction to keep in mind.

It is our view that knowledge-based reasoning agents can be used effectively in the team-theoretic framework; but, we must be able to describe them in terms of the other system elements — that is, as decision-makers with information structures and preferences toward action. In order to achieve this objective, we must develop information structures to be compatible with AI conceptions of information as discrete (usually logical) tokens, and somehow connect control structures and loss formulations. At this point, we can sketch at least one possibility. First, view such reasoning agents as consisting of two phases: computing the information structure, and selecting an optimal action in the face of available information. This is similar to the classic separation of estimation in control theory literature [2]. Computation of the information structure amounts to using furnished information and making implicit information explicit relative to a given model [25]. That is, some part of the information in the knowledge base is used to infer new facts from given information. The complete set of such facts form (in a limiting sense) the information structure. Some of the theoretical analyses of (logical) knowledge have detailed methods for describing this process of inference using variants of modal logic [25].

Loss formulations for the preference of actions can be specified using a conception of action similar to the situation calculus [19,21]. In this system, action is a mapping between world states, where each state represents a configuration of the world. Moore [21] has shown how both information and action can be represented and related within the conceptual framework of world states, making loss formulations based on information possible. The actual details of this procedure are beyond the scope of this paper, but we can show that several problems in the planning domain can, in fact, be reduced to decision problems posed in this manner. As a further example, consider building a decision-maker who attempts to fill in gaps in an incomplete, discrete knowledge base. The specification of information and loss functions can be done in terms of world states as presented above, and the actual implementation of the system done as a rule-based system.

Finally, we may attempt to combine this agent with agents which attempt to reduce uncertainty in the probabilistic sense outlined in the previous subsection. For instance, a camera and a tactile sensor which have local probabilistic uncertainty reduction methods, and a global executive which is building models of the environment. Using team theory, we can analyze possible methods for control and cooperation of these disparate agents and offer a coherent explanation of the full system's behavior.

5 Conclusions and Future Research

Analysis of the general team organization with respect to team members' information structures provides a systematic framework for addressing a number of important questions concerning the effect of sensor agent capabilities on overall system performance. We summarize some of the more important issues:

1. Could a sensor benefit by guidance from another team member? Should communication between members be increased?

2. Should the sensor's ability to make observations be enhanced by changing hardware or finding algorithmic bottlenecks?

3. When should an exchange of opinions and dynamic consensus be attempted?

4. What overall system structure (as described by the information structures of the team members) is best (or better) for different tasks?

Similarly, there are a number of important questions that can be addressed by analyzing the effect of individual team members' utility and decision functions, including:

1. Communication and time costs in the decision process to provide for real time action.

2. Inclusion of decisions to take new observations of the environment if previous opinions are rejected by other team members, or if insufficient information was obtained on a first pass.

3. Effects of new decision heuristics on overall system performance.

Of course all these ideas may well be difficult to consider analytically, though this formalism does reduce the search space of alternatives and provides a framework within which these issues may be evaluated. The team-theoretic organization is a powerful method for analyzing multi-agent systems, but it is certainly not the complete answer.

Acknowledgment: The Authors would like to thank Dr. Max Mintz for many valuable discussions about this subject.

References

[1] J. O. Berger. *Statistical Decision Theory and Bayesian Analysis*. Springer-Verlag, New York, 1985.

[2] D. P. Bertsekas. *Dynamic Progamming and Stochastic Control*. Volume 125 of *Mathematics in Science and Engineering*, Acacdemic Press, Inc., New York, first edition edition, 1976.

[3] P. Cheeseman. In defense of probability. In *Proceedings of IJCAI-85*, pages 1002–1007, Los Angelos, August 1985.

[4] M. DeGroot. *Optimal Statistical Decisions*. McGraw-Hill, 1970.

[5] H. Durrant-Whyte. Concerning uncertain geometry in robotics. Presented at *The International Workshop on Geometric Reasoning*, Oxford U.K. July 1986.

[6] H. Durrant-Whyte. *Integration and Coordination of Multisensor Robot Systems*. PhD thesis, University of Pennsylvania, Philadelphia, Pa, August 1986.

[7] M. Fox. An organizational view of distributed systems. *IEEE Transactions on Systems, Man, and Cybernetics*, 11(1):70–80, January 1981.

[8] M. Ginsburg. Decision procedures. In *Proc. Workshop on Distributed Problem Solving*, page 42, 1985.

[9] G. Hager. *Active Reduction of Uncertainty in Multi-Sensor Systems*. Grasp Lab 79, University of Pennsylvania, Philadelphia, PA, September 1986. Author's Dissertation Proposal, also MS-CIS-86-76.

[10] G. Hager. *Estimation Procedures for Robust Sensor Control*. Technical Report MS-CIS-87-09, University of Pennsylvania, Philadelphia, PA, February 1987.

[11] G. Hager. *Information Maps for Active Sensor Control*. Technical Report MS-CIS-87-07, University of Pennsylvania, Philadelphia, PA, February 1987.

[12] P. Harsanyi. *Cooperation in Games of Social Systems*. Cambridge University Press, Cambridge, 1975.

[13] Y. Ho. Team decision theory and information structures. *Proceedings of the IEEE*, 68(6):644–654, June 1980.

[14] Y. Ho, I. Blau, and T. Basar. *A Tale of Four Information Structures*. Technical Report 657, Harvard University, 1974. Part 1.

[15] Y. Ho and K. Chu. Team decision theory and information structures in optimal control. *IEEE Trans. on Automatic Control*, 17:15–28, 1972.

[16] R. Isaacs. *Differential Games*. Robert E. Kreiger Publishing Co., Huntington, New York, 1975.

[17] D. Marr. *Vision*. Freeman, San Fransisco, 1982.

[18] J. Marschak and R. Radner. *Economic Theory of Teams*. Yale University Press, New Haven, 1972.

[19] J. McCarthy and P. Hayes. Some philosophical problems from the standpoint of artificial intelligence. In B. Meltzer and D. Michie, editors, *Machine Intelligence*, Edinburgh University Press, Edinburgh, 1969.

[20] C. McGuire. Comparisons of information structures. In C. McGuire and R. Radner, editors, *Decision and Organization*, chapter 5, pages 101–130, North-Holland Publishing Co., Amsterdam, 1972.

[21] R. C. Moore. *Knowledge and Action.* Technical Report 191, SRI International, Menlo Park, October 1980.

[22] J. Nash. The bargaining problem. *Econometrica*, 18:155–162, 1950.

[23] R. Paul, H. Durrant-Whyte, and M. Mintz. A robust, distributed multi-sensor robot control system. In *Proc. Third Int. Symposium of Robotic Research*, Gouvieaux, France, 1985.

[24] J. S. Rosenschein and M. R. Genesereth. Deals among rational agents. In *Proceedings of the Ninth IJCAI*, pages 91–99, Los Angelos, August 1985.

[25] S. Rosenschein. *Formal Theories of Knowledge in AI and Robotics.* Technical Report 362, SRI International, Menlo Park, CA., September 1985.

[26] L. Savage. *The Foundations of Statistics.* John Wiley, 1954.

[27] H. Simon. Theories of bounded rationality. In C. McGuire and R. Radner, editors, *Decision and Organization*, chapter 8, pages 161–176, North-Holland Publishing Co., Amsterdam, 1972.

[28] J. Von Neumann and O. Morgenstern. *Theory of Games and Economic Behavior.* Princeton University Press, Princeton, N.J., 1944.

[29] S. Weerahandi and J. Zidek. Elements of multi-bayesian decision theory. *The Annals of Statistics*, 11:1032, 1983.

[30] S. Weerahandi and J. Zidek. Multi-bayesian statistical decision theory. *J. Royal Statistical Society*, 144:85, 1981.

Planning, Scheduling, and Uncertainty in the Sequence of Future Events*

B.R. Fox[1] and K.G. Kempf[2]

McDonnell Douglas Research Laboratories[1]
Artificial Intelligence Group
Dept 225, Bldg 305, Level 2E
P.O. Box 516, St. Louis, Missouri, USA 63166

FMC Corporation[2]
Central Engineering Laboratory
Artificial Intelligence Center
1205 Coleman Avenue
P.O.Box 580, Santa Clara, California, USA 95052

Abstract: *Scheduling in the factory setting is compounded by computational complexity and temporal uncertainty. Together, these two factors guarantee that the process of constructing an optimal schedule will be costly and the chances of executing that schedule will be slight. Temporal uncertainty in the task execution time can be offset by several methods: eliminate uncertainty by careful engineering, restore certainty whenever it is lost, reduce the uncertainty by using more accurate sensors, and quantify and circumscribe the remaining uncertainty. Unfortunately, these methods focus exclusively on the sources of uncertainty and fail to apply knowledge of the tasks which are to be scheduled. A complete solution must adapt the schedule of activities to be performed according to the evolving state of the production world. The example of vision-directed assembly is presented to illustrate that the principle of least commitment, in the creation of a plan, in the representation of a schedule, and in the execution of a schedule, enables a robot to operate intelligently and efficiently, even in the presence of considerable uncertainty in the sequence of future events.*

1. Statement of the Problem

The problem of sequencing and scheduling is to determine, in advance, when some set of events and activities should occur. The events and activities may be subject to some ordering constraints; the time of occurrence or the duration of some activities may be fixed; there may be some cost associated with the time that an activity is performed or with the rate at which it progresses. The times selected for these events and activities must conform to the constraints, expected times and durations, and must generally minimize the associated costs. In problems which are over-constrained, the selected times must at least conform to a rational relaxation of the given constraints.

Scheduling in the factory setting is compounded by two factors[1]; the first is *complexity*. Most scheduling problems are NP-hard. The number of potential schedules grows exponentially with the number of activities to be scheduled and the number of resources to be utilized. It is simply impossible to itemize and evaluate every possible schedule to find the best schedule. At the same time, there is no known method for finding the best

---

*Research conducted under the McDonnell Douglas Independent Research and Development Program.

schedule which does not exhaustively consider, at least implicitly, every possible schedule. The second factor is *uncertainty*. Any schedule constructed in advance is based solely upon assumptions about the ordering, the times of occurrence, and the durations of the activities. The execution time environment rarely conforms to those assumptions. A schedule may be optimal with respect to some set of assumptions, but it may be very costly to force the execution of the given tasks according to that schedule in the context of the actual execution times and durations. Together, these two factors guarantee that the process of constructing an optimal schedule will be very costly and the chances of actually executing that schedule are very slight.

A simple assembly task can be used to illustate one aspect of temporal uncertainty. The task is to assemble a small gearbox consisting of the 10 parts shown in Figure 1. (For brevity the part names are reduced to just the first 2 letters in the remaining figures and tables.) Those parts are randomly packed into a small bin and delivered to a vision-equipped robot which must acquire the parts from the bin and perform the assembly. This is identical to an assembly task which has been developed for the US Air Force as a joint venture by SRI, Honeywell, and Adept Technology[2], and is similar to experimental assembly systems studied at Carnegie-Mellon[3] and Edinburgh[4] universities. The characteristic feature of this task is that it is impossible to predict or control the order in which the parts will be recognized. Clearly, this task can be best categorized as a Markov Process. Unfortunately, with even a few parts, it is impossible to itemize all of the possible states of the process and the relative probabilities of the state transitions. (Hence, this problem illustrates two kinds of uncertainty: uncertainty about the ordering of parts, and uncertainty about the statistical properties of the orderings.) The problem is to produce a working system that can perform this task efficiently, intelligently, and in a cost-effective fashion.

2. Candidate Solutions

2.1 Eliminate Uncertainty

The most frequently proposed solution to this problem is to eliminate the uncertainty in the availability of the parts by re-engineering the task. Instead of delivering the parts in a bin, deliver the parts affixed to a pallet with specific locations and orientations. The robot can then be programmed to perform the task according to a fixed sequence of operations based upon the fixed locations of the parts. Of course, the cost of this solution is determined by the cost of engineering the pallets and transport. The cost may be justifiable in large volume applications but it is unacceptable in the aerospace industry, for instance, where millions of parts are produced in quantities of 100 or less per year. The inventory of pallets and fixtures would exceed the value of the parts to be produced. Moreover, in many circumstances human labor would be required to prepare the pallets. The motive for introducing vision in such applications is to automate the production without introducing the added expense of custom fixtures, pallets, and transport.

2.2 Reduce Uncertainty

A second solution is to apply more powerful sensors to extract more information from the production world. This is the approach employed by SRI, Honeywell, and Adept Technology, in the project cited above. Their goal was to develop sophisticated vision hardware and software so that the robot could find exactly the part required at each step of the assembly. While such efforts might reduce the uncertainty in the process, they can never completely remove the uncertainty. Hence, the proposed system included an escape mechanism. If the required part could not be located, the robot was programmed to shake the bin or stir the parts to reveal the necessary part. Unfortunately, there is no way to predict how many shakes are necessary to reveal an obscured part and the execution time for the assembly can vary widely [5]. The cost of this solution is the cost of the most sophisticated and probably the most expensive vision system available, yet this solution still involves a high degree of uncertainty.

2.3 Restore Certainty

A third solution is to restore certainty whenever it is lost. For example, in the system developed at Edinburgh, the parts were made available in a loose heap. The parts were separated from the heap one at a time and moved, according to their identity, to fixed locations in the workspace. After all of the parts were identified and laid out, the actual process of assembly proceeded according to a fixed sequence of operations. Although the parts would most certainly be acquired from the heap in a random order, the process of placing the parts in fixed locations restored the order necessary to perform the assembly in a fixed order. The cost of this solution is determined by the added execution time required to lay out the parts. Although the number of motions required to perform the assembly is fixed (one motion to acquire and buffer each part, and one motion to install each part) on the average, many of the intermediate motions are extraneous [5]. An intelligent solution would be to move a part to a buffer location *only if* if cannot be immediately installed in the assembly.

2.4 Quantify Uncertainty

Yet another solution might be to gather statistics over hundreds of trials and to program the robot to perform the assembly over the sequence of parts most likely to occur. When the sequence of parts deviates from the programmed order, the robot could resort to some other strategy such as shaking or buffering. This solution carries much of the same costs as the previous solutions and incurs the added cost of performing the experiments and gathering the statistics. Such costs are unjustifiable in small volume productions.

3. The Proposed Solution

It is unlikely that a single strategy or methodology is sufficient in a multifaceted problem such as this. Instead, a good strategy would be to form a composite of the best available hardware and software technologies, incorporating each to the degree that it is useful and cost effective. Unfortunately, there is a common weakness in the candidate solutions which must be addressed: they focus exclusively on the process of acquiring the parts and they fail to apply knowledge of the assembly task itself. While there is no way to precisely predict or completely control the sequence of parts as they are acquired from the bin, there may be many feasible sequences for installing the parts in the assembly. The intelligent solution is to exploit this inherent flexiblibity and to *opportunistically schedule* the sequence of assembly operations at execution time, according to the availability of parts and according to the constraints on the assembly operations.

The implementation of an opportunistic scheduling strategy depends upon consistent application of the principle of least commitment. It is not unusual for a planner to determine the steps of a task and also a single fixed sequence for their execution. However, most tasks can be executed according to many different sequences. It is very unlikely that one sequence, chosen before execution time, will be the best. It is certain, however, that if only one sequence is passed to the robot, it will have no flexibility in the excution of that task. To maximize flexibility, a plan should consist of a set of steps and a *minimum* set of ordering constraints. Likewise, a schedule should consist of the sequence of steps that have been completed plus the set of *all possible* sequences for completing the remaining steps. Given such a schedule, the execution time sequencer can capitalize on opportunities presented in the execution environment, sidestepping difficulties with a given ordering by following a different but equally valid sequence.

These concepts, however, lead to a unique problem of representation. It has been argued in a previous paper[6] that a representation for plans and schedules based upon simple partial orders is inherently inadequate and that a state-space representation is not sufficiently compact. The principle of least commitment dictates that the plan for a task encompass every feasible strategy and that a schedule incorporate every admissible sequence of steps. This in turn dictates a representation which completely and compactly encodes those sequences. A sufficient representation, based upon a language of temporal constraints, is outlined in the paper cited above, but a new style of planning, suitable for problems with a high degree of temporal uncertainty, remains to be explored.

Application of the principle of least commitment also influences the specific sequence of operations chosen at execution time. When several parts are recognized and accessible in the bin, and when more than one of those parts can be immediately included in the assembly, the robot must pick one. The robot may consider the difficulty of acquiring a specific part, or the difficulty of installing that part, but it must give some preference to the operation which preserves the most options in sequencing the remainder of the assembly.

Consistent application of the principle of least commitment, in the creation of the plan, in the representation of the plan and schedule, and in the execution of the schedule, increases the likelihood that each time the robot consults the vision system, at least one of the parts currently visible in the bin can be immediately installed in the assembly. Given this flexibility, the robot can determine the actual sequence of operations at execution time, according to the sequence of parts acquired from the bin and according to the constraints on the assembly operations. Of course, there will be some circumstances when none of the visible parts can be immediately installed. In that case, one of the visible parts can be buffered, thereby introducing some certainty into a later stage of the process. As a whole, the strategy of opportunistically selecting parts to be installed or buffered enables the robot to operate efficiently and intelligently in spite of the considerable uncertainty in the sequence in which parts are acquired from the bin.

4. Empirical Results

Assume that the gearbox shown in Figure 1 is to be assembled as described above. The parts are packed randomly into a small bin and delivered to a vision-equipped robot which must acquire the parts from the bin, one at a time, and perform the assembly. Assume also that the robot will perform the assembly according to the strategy diagrammed in Figure 2. (In fact, the plan for the assembly may consist of several distinct strategies, but for the sake of simplicity, only one strategy will be considered in this example.) Within that diagram, each node denotes the operation of installing a part and each directed arc denotes an ordering constraint. For instance, the arc from ri to co denotes the constraint that the **ring gear** must be installed before the **cover**. Whenever multiple arcs converge at a single node, all of the predecessor steps must be completed before the operation denoted by that node can be executed.

Suppose that the robot has been programmed to perform the assembly in an opportunistic fashion. At each step of the assembly at least one part is visible and available in the bin and there may also be some parts available which have been previously moved from the bin to fixed layout locations. The robot will always install any part which is presently available and can be immediately included in the assembly. If none of the available parts can be immediately installed, the robot will choose one of the parts in the bin and move it to a fixed location for later use. If more than one part can be installed the robot should choose the one which preserves the most future sequence options, and if none can be installed the robot should choose to buffer the part which will be needed earliest in the assembly. The sequence of operations shown in Table 1 might be typical of the course of action generated by an opportunistic scheduling strategy.

To objectively consider the effect of sequencing options, every distinct strategy for the execution of tasks over six steps was generated. That set of 318 strategies then served as the database for an exhaustive set of simulations according to the narrative above. If only one sequence is admissible under a given strategy then the execution of the task is comparable to the expected behavior of the SRI, Honeywell, and Adept Technology system. Under this set of simulations, strategies which defined only one sequence of operations required, on the average, 22.1 motions. Strategies which admit more than one sequence show dramatically improved execution times as shown in Figure 3. Of course, if a strategy allows any of the 720 possible sequences, the expected execution time is exactly six motions. All of the values shown are subject to certain assumptions and parameter settings and it would be a mistake to draw specific numeric conclusions from these data. These results clearly indicate, however, that the capabilities of a robot, performing vision directed part acquisition and assembly, are significantly improved when the robot is given the ability to determine its own sequence of actions according to the state of the world and the constraints on the assembly task.

5. Conclusion

Several different techniques can be applied in problems which involve task execution in the presence of temporal uncertainty. Wherever possible, uncertainty should be eliminated or reduced, certainty should be restored whenever it is lost, the remaining uncertainty should be quantified and circumscribed, but an invaluable technique is to exploit the inherrent flexibility in the tasks to be performed and to implement a strategy of opportunistic scheduling. This requires consistent application of the principle of least commitement in the creation of the plan, in the representation of the plan and schedule, and in the execution of the schedule. A hybrid of these techniques enables a robot to operate intelligently and efficiently in the presence of considerable uncertainty in the sequence of future events.

References

[1] Fox, B.R. and Kempf, K.G., Complexity uncertainty, and opportunistic scheduling, *Proceedings Second Conference on Artificial Intelligence Applications*, Miami, Florida, Dec. 1985.

[2] Interim Report number 3, Research for Intelligent Task Automation, US Air Force Contract F33615-82-C-5092. July 15, 1983.

[3] deMello, L.S.H. and Sanderson, A., AND/OR graph repesentation of assembly plans, *Proceedings Fifth National Conference on Artificial Intelligence*, Philadelphia, Pennsylvania, Aug. 1986.

[4] Ambler, A.P., Barrow, H.G., Brown, C.M., Burstall, R.M., and Popplestone, R.J., A versatile system for computer controlled assembly, *Artificial Intelligence*, v6, pp. 129-156, 1975.

[5] Fox, B.R. and Kempf, K.G., Opportunistic scheduling for robotic assembly, *Proceedings IEEE International Conference on Robotics and Automation*, St. Louis, Missouri, Mar. 1985.

[6] Fox, B.R. and Kempf, K.G., A representation for opportunistic scheduling, *Proceedings Third International Symposium on Robotics Research*, Paris, France, Oct. 1985.

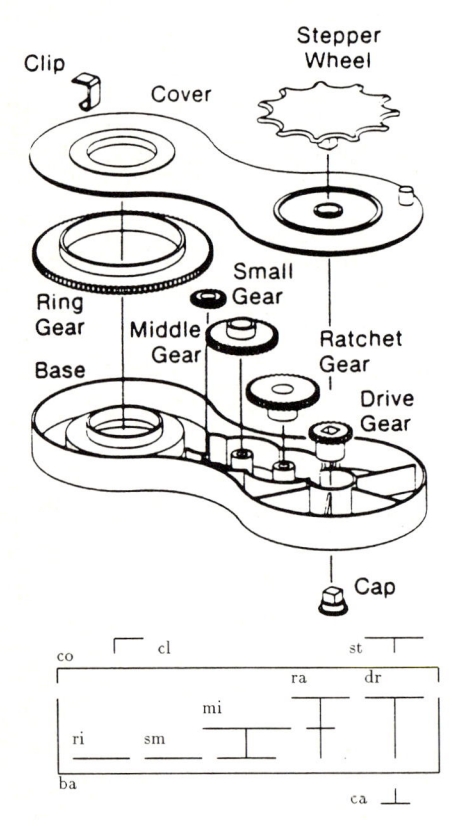

Figure 1.

The gearbox assembly problem.
Exploded view and schematic side view.

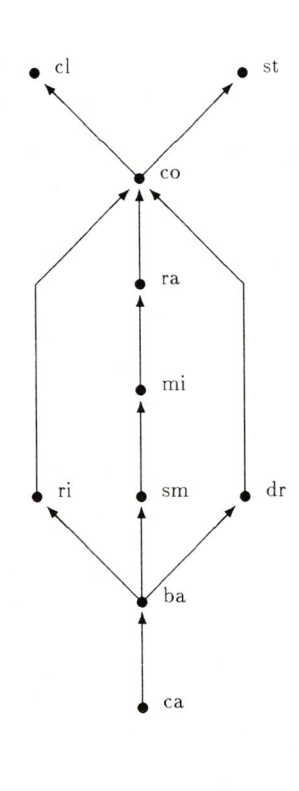

Figure 2.

The strategy for the gearbox assembly.
Parts and their precedence constraints.

Step	Visible	Buffered	Installed	Action
1.	ri,ra			buffer ri
2.	ca,co	ri		install ca
3.	co,mi	ri	ca	buffer mi
4.	st,dr	ri,mi	ca	buffer dr
5.	cl,ba	ri,mi,dr	ca	install ba
6.	cl,co	ri,mi,dr	ca,ba	install ri
7.	cl,co	mi,dr	ca,ba,ri	install dr
8.	cl,co	mi	ca,ba,ri,dr	buffer co
9.	cl,sm	mi,co	ca,ba,ri,dr	install sm
10.	cl,st	mi,co	ca,ba,ri,dr,sm	install mi
11.	cl,st	co	ca,ba,ri,dr,sm,mi	buffer cl
12.	ra,st	co,cl	ca,ba,ri,dr,sm,mi	install ra
13.	st	co,cl	ca,ba,ri,dr,sm,mi,ra	install co
14.	st	cl	ca,ba,ri,dr,sm,mi,ra,co	install st
15.		cl	ca,ba,ri,dr,sm,mi,ra,co,st	install cl
			ca,ba,ri,dr,sm,mi,ra,co,st,cl	

Table 1.

Typical course of action under an opportunistic scheduling stragegy.

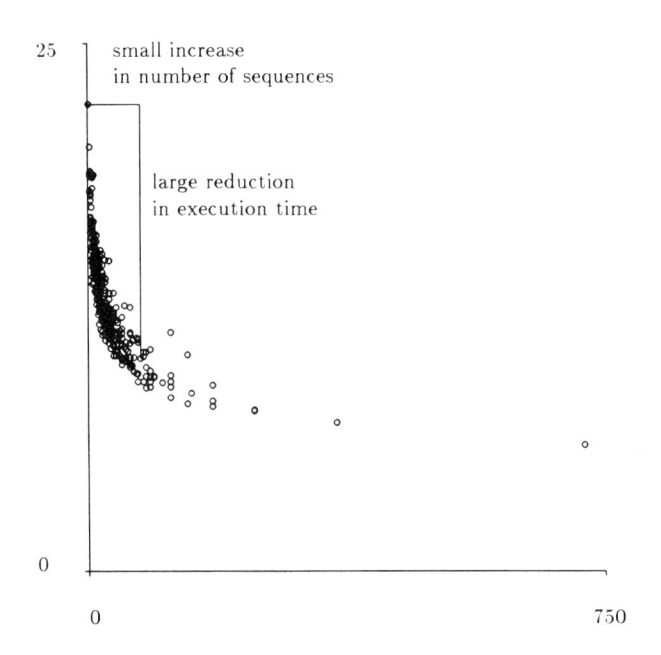

Figure 3.

Simulation results of 318 strategies over 6 steps.
Execution time as a function of number of sequences.

EVIDENTIAL REASONING IN A COMPUTER VISION SYSTEM

Ze-Nian Li

Department of Electrical Engineering and Computer Science
University of Wisconsin-Milwaukee

Leonard Uhr

Department of Computer Sciences
University of Wisconsin-Madison

ABSTRACT *This paper presents an efficient adaptation and application of the Dempster-Shafer theory of evidence, one that can be used effectively in a massively parallel hierarchical system for visual pattern perception. It describes the techniques used, and shows in an extended example how they serve to improve the system's performance as it applies a multiple-level set of processes.*

1. INTRODUCTION

We have been developing a computer vision system which can be implemented in a pyramid-like structure that consists of many thousands of computers. The hierarchy of micro-modular transforms executed by this parallel network of processors has been effective for analyzing images containing complex objects like houses and neurons [1-3]. This paper describes a new evidential reasoning mechanism based on the Dempster-Shafer theory of evidence that we have recently developed for and incorporated into the pyramid vision programs.

The vision program uses *key features* and *evidential reasoning*. Initially, low level local features are assessed in parallel by low level processors, and then used to compute more global and abstract features at consecutively higher levels in the pyramid. Once certain important 'key' features are extracted, a hypothesis will be generated. Typically the program will then move, in a top-down manner, to lower levels in order to search for more evidence that might verify or deny the hypothesis. The reasoning processes can thus be executed in a parallel and hierarchical manner within different nodes and different levels in the pyramid.

Basically, the evidential reasoning is attempting two tasks: *evidence accumulation* and *hypothesis verification*. Uncertainty and *incompleteness* are inevitable in both phases. As is the case with many computer vision systems, our programs are compelled to make decisions on uncertain and incomplete evidence and knowledge. This is especially true whenever factors such as the achievable quality of the image data, the complexity of the domain, and the computational cost, are taken into account.

The new evidential reasoning mechanism is designed to achieve the following goals:

(a) Accommodating uncertainty and incompleteness, both in the evidence and in the world knowledge.
(b) Making the knowledge representation scheme flexible, and easy to update.
(c) Emphasizing the role of some key features and, when desirable, conjunctions of features that are important for the object's recognition.
(d) Embedding the reasoning mechanisms into the basic format of the micro-modular transforms, so they can be executed in parallel in the pyramid.

Section 2 presents a set-theoretical evidential reasoning approach. The method for evidence accumulation is illustrated. A new knowledge representation technique is introduced, and hence a new mechanism for hypothesis verification. In section 3, a program for window recognition is described. The results obtained suggest that the evidential reasoning mechanism has good performance. Section 4 concludes the paper.

2. A SET-THEORETICAL EVIDENTIAL REASONING APPROACH TO COMPUTER VISION

This paper introduces a set-theoretical approach based on the Dempster-Shafer mathematical theory of evidence. The description of the Dempster-Shafer theory can be found in [4, 5]. Here, the notation in [5] is adopted.

Let Θ be a set of propositions about the mutually exclusive and exhaustive possibilities in a domain. Θ is called the *frame of discernment* and 2^Θ is the set of all possible subsets of Θ.

A function $m : 2^\Theta \rightarrow [0, 1]$ is called a *basic probability assignment* if it satisfies $m(\emptyset) = 0$ and $\sum_{A \subseteq \Theta} m(A) = 1$.

If m is a basic probability assignment, then a *belief function* is defined by
$$Bel(A) = \sum_{B \subseteq A} m(B), \quad \text{for } A \subseteq \Theta.$$

2.1. Evidence Accumulation

The accumulation of evidence is conducted in two steps, for single feature assessment and for multi-feature combination.

Single Feature Assessment

At this step, probability values are assigned to the extracted features to represent their uncertainty and incompleteness. The following factors are taken into account:

(1) The quality of the input data, and the weights of the extracted features.

(2) The 'goodness' of feature values. A feature value is compared to the typical feature value of a hypothesized object to answer questions like "How good is the shape of this *long* region, if it is compared to the shape of a typical window shutter". As suggested by Ragade and Gupta [6], many functions $0 \leq \mu(v, M) \leq 1$ can be used to evaluate the feature values, where v denotes the extracted feature value, M is the typical feature value of a hypothesized object and M_1, M_2 and t are constants. The following is the step function that is used in our program. (Many alternatives and variations of these functions can be invented.)

Step Function: $\mu(v) = 1$ $M - M_1 \leqslant v \leqslant M + M_1$
               $\mu(v) = t \;(0 < t < 1)$ $M - M_2 \leqslant v < M - M_1$ or
                                    $M + M_1 < v \leqslant M + M_2$
               $\mu(v) = 0$ otherwise.

The factors in (1) and (2) are combined into a single probability value. As a result, each feature f gets a probability mass $0 \leqslant m(f) \leqslant 1$. In most cases, $m(f)$ is less than 1, and the remainder of the unit mass $1 - m(f)$ is assigned to Θ to represent the uncertainty. Therefore, for single feature assessment *simple belief functions* are used, where $Bel(f) = m(f)$, and $Bel(\Theta) = m(\Theta)$.

Multi-feature Combination

If each extracted feature is viewed as a piece of evidence, then the independent observations on multi-features can be combined to serve as accumulated evidence. Belief functions of independently extracted features are combined using Dempster's combination rule.

Suppose m_1 is the basic probability assignment for a belief function Bel_1 over a frame Θ, with focal elements A_i ($i = 1, \cdots, k$); and similarly m_2 is the basic probability assignment for a belief function Bel_2 over the same frame Θ, with focal elements B_j ($j = 1, \cdots, l$).

If $\;\; K = \sum_{A_i \cap B_j = \emptyset} m_1(A_i) m_2(B_j) < 1$, then the function $m: 2^\Theta \to [0,1]$ is a basic probability assignment, defined by:

(1) $m(\emptyset) = 0$, and

(2) $m(C) = (1 - K)^{-1} \sum_{A_i \cap B_j = C} m_1(A_i) m_2(B_j)$.

The belief function, m, that combines Bel_1 and Bel_2, is called the *orthogonal sum* of Bel_1 and Bel_2, denoted $Bel_1 \oplus Bel_2$. Since Dempster's combination rule is associative and commutative, features can be combined in any order.

2.2 A New Knowledge Representation Technique

In the past few years, the Dempster-Shafer theory has been proposed in several application domains. Some works are described in [7-10]. In AI systems, a sound knowledge representation scheme is crucial to the success of such reasoning systems.

In the field of computer vision, one of the popular knowledge representation schemes used in evidential reasoning is the Dependency-Graph Model [8]. The assumption is that the domains of interest can be modeled in a propositional framework. The frame of discernment is represented by dependency-graphs, in which the nodes represent propositions and the arcs represent relationships, such as *and*, *or*, $\to$, *not*, etc., between the propositions. Based on Dempster-Shafer's evidential reasoning theory, Lowrance claimed that a formal system capable of pooling and extending evidential information could be built, while maintaining internal consistency.

The dependency-graph model approach has been successfully demonstrated in several domains that contain small sets of objects. It has the merit of being formal and sound. However it has drawbacks. The success of the dependency-graph model relies on the construction of a complete graph. Due to the complexity of the graph, the world model would take potentially very large amounts of space to store, and time to process, and it would be difficult to update. As stated in [8], "as these graphs become larger and more complex, it becomes increasingly difficult to guarantee their logical consistency."

The essential point is that a knowledge representation scheme should be able to utilize incomplete knowledge. There should be a way to emphasize the important subset of the world knowledge. Truth should be expressed relative to portions of the environment, responsive to the context. Although the initial model will probably generate poor results, it should be flexible and easy to improve.

Our new knowledge representation technique is characterized by associating probability values with the expected feature components of the hypothesized objects. Probability values are used to answer questions like "If it has a typical elongated shape for a window shutter, how much should this feature of shape contribute to the belief for a shutter?"

To discriminate different objects in a vision system, it is often important to consider beliefs about multiple features, especially those key features of the hypothesized object. If the knowledge about window shutters is that "Window shutters are usually elongated rectangular regions, with a low 'edgeness' measure, next to windows," then the following probability mass assignments m_s (shutter) may be given to the window shutter:

$$m(long) = 0.25, \ m(low) = 0.15, \ m(long \ \& \ low) = 0.15,$$
$$m(next-to) = 0.25, \ m(\Theta) = 0.2.$$

The importance of the feature is represented by the amount of the mass assigned to it. The numbers initially assigned are more or less subjective and 'arbitrary'. But they can be adjusted later on, either by the programmer or by a learning program.

If the current task is to discriminate shutters from a chimney, and the system's knowledge about chimneys is that "Chimneys are usually elongated rectangular regions, not next-to windows," and the system has no knowledge about the importance of the texture, then a mass assignment m_s (chimney) may be given at the same time,

$$m(long) = 0.25, \ m(\overline{next-to}) = 0.35, \ m(\Theta) = 0.4.$$

In this way, the knowledge representation technique allows the invocation of the subsets of the world knowledge that are most closely related to the current context of the objects being recognized, and have the most discriminative power for the current hypotheses.

2.3. Hypothesis Verification

The mechanism of hypothesis verification can be viewed as a set of mappings between two spaces. The first is the evidence space E, and the second the object space O. A mapping

$$e \rightarrow o, Bel(o)$$

defines a belief function $Bel(o)$ over the object space O, where $e \subset E$ is the set of accumulated evidence, $o \subset O$ is the hypothetical object, and $0 \leqslant Bel(o) \leqslant 1$ is the belief committed to o. While conducting this mapping, the knowledge sources are consulted.

As described in sections 2.1 and 2.2, the accumulated evidence can be represented by a belief function whose mass distribution is m_e, whereas the system's knowledge of the hypothetical object can be represented by another belief function whose mass distribution is m_s. Here a third belief function $Bel(o)$ is introduced to represent the result of the hypothesis verification.

(a) $Bel(o) = \sum\limits_{\substack{A_i \subseteq B_j \\ B_j \neq \Theta}} m_e(A_i) m_s(B_j),$

(b) $Bel(\Theta) = 1 - Bel(o).$

Evidential Reasoning in a Computer Vision System   407

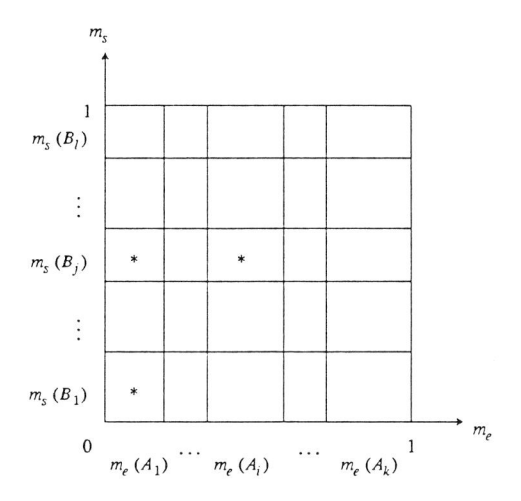

Fig. 1 Belief Function $Bel(o)$

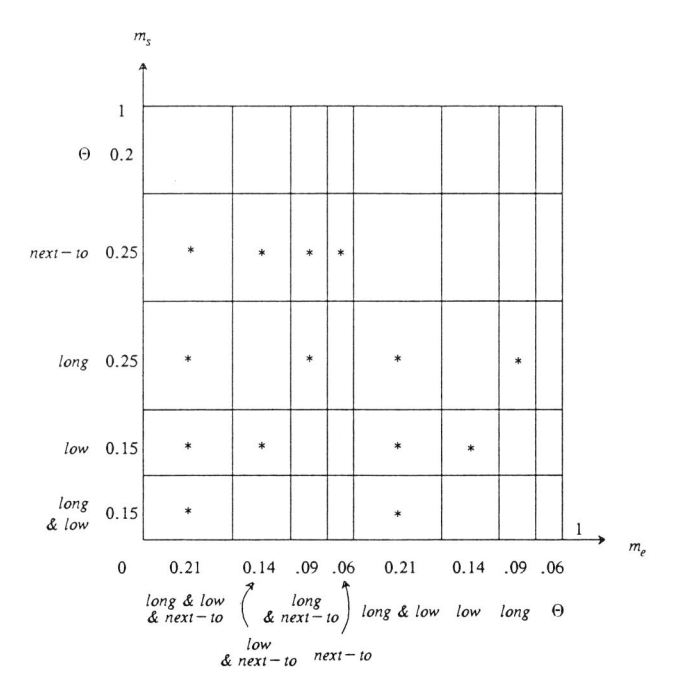

Fig. 2 Hypothesis Verification

This belief function is graphically depicted in Fig. 1. The areas whose masses are committed to the hypothetical object o are marked with *'s. The value of $Bel(o)$ is the sum of these areas. The use of the set inclusion operator in the definition of $Bel(o)$ performs the consistency check between the system's knowledge and the evidence accumulated so far. The creation of this new belief function has extended the notations of the belief functions and the Dempster combination rule. The belief function thus generated is a simple belief function. When the evidential reasoning is applied hierarchically, $Bel(o)$ can be used together with other pieces of evidence for the higher level object it implies.

Figure 2 illustrates this type of hypothesis verification. The knowledge of window shutters (m_s (shutter)) described in section 2.2 is used. Some accumulated evidence m_e is assumed. The new generated belief function of this hypothesis verification is

$$Bel(shutter) = 0.21 \times (0.15 + 0.15 + 0.25 + 0.25) + 0.14 \times (0.15 + 0.25) +$$
$$0.09 \times (0.25 + 0.25) + 0.06 \times 0.25 + 0.21 \times (0.15 + 0.15 + 0.25) +$$
$$0.14 \times 0.15 + 0.09 \times 0.25 = 0.44.$$
$$Bel(\Theta) = 1 - 0.44 = 0.56.$$

3. PROGRAMMING RESULTS

Experimental evaluations have given satisfactory results with four images of houses and office buildings. The window shutter example in the previous section actually comes from Fig. 3(a). In this section, Fig. 3(b), the image of an office building, will be used as an example to illustrate how a program that is capable of recognizing windows of buildings uses our evidential reasoning mechanism. The original digitized image has a resolution of 512×512 pixels. The pyramidal median filtering method is applied [3]. As a result, a filtered image with a reduced resolution 128×128 is obtained. It is stored at level 7 of the pyramid.

The algorithms for recognizing houses can be found in [2]. Briefly, the program first locates micro-edges with eight possible directions at level 7. Next, short edges are extracted by level 6 nodes, and long edges by level 5 nodes. Pairs of parallel long edges with opposite directions (e.g., long edges with $0°$ and $180°$, or $90°$ and $270°$) have been found to be good clues for windows with rectangular shapes. Thus such pairs of horizontal long edges are used to locate the possible window areas. Figure 4 shows all the possible window areas located in the office building image. (Forty six possible window areas are hypothesized by the program. For ease of demonstration, the real window areas are labeled W1 - W12, other (false) areas are labeled by number, 1 - 34. Since the procedure being examined looks for only horizontal long edges, six narrow windows in Fig. 3(b) are not located in this step.)

Apparently additional evidence is needed and should be accumulated, to better distinguish the true window areas from others. The following are illustrations of how multiple features (evidence) can be employed to help the process of evidential reasoning.

Evidence of Shapes and Textures

Several features of the possible window areas are assessed at level 5.

(1) The elongation of the area. The *elongation* of the rectangular areas is defined as *length* / *width*, if *length* $\geq$ *width*; *width* / *length*, otherwise. Under this definition, the elongation values of typical windows are likely to be small positive numbers larger than one. Thus the following belief values are given for the measured elongation.

(a) A House Image

(b) An Office Building Image

Fig. 3 Images of a House and an Office Building

Fig. 4 Possible Window Areas

$$Bel\ (elong\ ) = \begin{cases} 0.5, & \text{if } elongation \leq 3; \\ 0.3, & \text{if } 3 < elongation \leq 5; \\ 0, & \text{otherwise.} \end{cases}$$

(2) The texture of the area. The interior texture of window areas can often be measured by the number of micro-edges. For opened windows or big glass windows, there are very few micro-edges inside the areas. In case of windows with a few panes or half-closed window shades, there will be overwhelmingly more horizontal and vertical edges (micro-edge 0, 2, 4, 6) than diagonal edges (micro-edge 1, 3, 5, 7). Hence the belief value for the texture measure is

$$Bel\ (text\ ) = \begin{cases} 0.4, & \text{if } edgedness < 0.1; \\ 0.4, & \text{if } hv/d \geq 4; \\ 0.2, & \text{if } 2 \leq hv/d < 4; \\ 0, & \text{otherwise.} \end{cases}$$

where $edgedness$ = number-of-edges / area-of-region, and hv/d is the ratio of the total number of the horizontal and vertical edges to the number of diagonal edges. The micro-edges are extracted at level 7. The statistical measures are implemented by pyramid operations.

(3) The vertical edges that serve as the left and right boundaries of the windows. Perfect boundaries cannot always be extracted. $Bel\ (left-bound)$ and $Bel\ (right-bound)$ are thus used in a similar way to assess the evidence of the existence of boundaries.

The belief functions initially assigned to the single features are all 'simple belief functions'. While Bel is assigned to the proposition (e.g., $elong$) supporting the window hypothesis, the value of $1 - Bel$ is assigned to Θ to represent the uncertainty.

After all four features have been assessed individually, these simple belief functions are combined to derive a new belief function:

$$Bel\ (elong\ ) \oplus Bel\ (text\ ) \oplus Bel\ (left-bound\ ) \oplus Bel\ (right-bound\ ),$$

whose mass distribution is denoted by m_e in section 2.2. For verifying window hypotheses, the combined evidence is compared to the knowledge source, having the following probability mass distribution, m_{s_1}:

$$m\ (elong) = 0.15,\ m\ (text) = 0.20,\ m\ (bound) = 0.35,\ m\ (\Theta) = 0.3.$$

The existence of boundaries is thought to be the most convincing evidence, thus a big portion of the total mass is assigned to the proposition $bound$. A certain amount of the mass is attributed to Θ to reflect the incompleteness of this knowledge source.

The results of this verification are the belief functions $Bel\ (window)$ for the hypothesized window areas. The belief values for single features and $Bel\ (window)$ are shown in Table 1. The 18 possible window areas in Table 1 are the ones that obtain higher $Bel\ (window)$ values. The remaining 28 (less possible) areas are not shown.

Evidence about the Geometrical Relations of Windows

The operations just described succeed in yielding higher belief values for the 12 real windows than for any of the false windows. At this step, the geometrical relations between windows are used to further enhance the results. Usually the windows of a building are arranged in a horizontal or vertical alignment. To carry out the necessary 'lateral search' for appropriately positioned neighboring windows, higher level nodes in the

pyramid are used. Belief values $Bel\ (window)$ at level 5 are passed one level up to the nodes at level 4. All the surviving nodes will search for possible sibling window areas vertically and horizontally. In case a vertical sibling is found, the $Bel\ (v-sibl)$ will be set to 0.6. In the same way, $Bel\ (h-sibl)$ will be set. Consequently, the combined belief function $Bel\ (window) \oplus Bel\ (v-sibl) \oplus Bel\ (h-sibl)$ is checked with the knowledge source for verifying the hypothesis that the window area in question is one of the windows in a building. The knowledge source is represented by m_{s_2}:
$m\ (window) = 0.4$, $m\ (v-sibl) = 0.2$, $m\ (h-sibl) = 0.2$, $m\ (v-sibl\ \&\ h-sibl) = 0.2$. A part of the mass values is assigned to the conjunction of $v-sibl$ and $h-sibl$ to emphasize the chance of the coexistence of both siblings. Because this piece of knowledge is judged to be very certain, no mass is assigned to Θ.

Table 1 Belief Values for Possible Windows

	Possible window areas											
	W1-6	W7	W8	W9	W10	W11	W12	4	5	9	15	17	18
$Bel\ (elong)$	0.5	0.5	0.5	0.5	0.5	0.5	0.5	0.3	0.5	0.5	0.3	0.5	0.5
$Bel\ (text)$	0.4	0.2	0.4	0.4	0.4	0.4	0.4	0.4	0	0.4	0.4	0	0
$Bel\ (lt-bound)$	0.6	0.6	0.6	0.6	0.6	0.6	0.6	0	0.1	0	0	0.6	0.3
$Bel\ (rt-bound)$	0.6	0.6	0.6	0.3	0.1	0.6	0.6	0.6	0.3	0.3	0.6	0	0.1
$Bel\ (wnd)$	.449	.409	.449	.407	.379	.449	.449	.335	.205	.262	.335	.285	.205
$Bel\ (v-sibl)$	0.6	0.6	0.6	0.6	0.6	0.6	0.6	0	0	0.6	0	0.6	0.6
$Bel\ (h-sibl)$	0.6	0.6	0.6	0.6	0.6	0.6	0.6	0	0.6	0	0	0	0
$Bel\ '(wnd)$	.492	.475	.492	.475	.462	.492	.492	.134	.203	.225	.134	.234	.203
$Bel\ (non-wnd)$	0	0	0	0	0	0	0	0.5	0.5	0	0	0	0.5
$Bel\ ''(wnd)$	.492	.475	.492	.475	.462	.492	.492	.080	.166	.225	.134	.234	.166

The resulting belief values are $Bel\ '(window)$ in Table 1. The previous results have been enhanced by the usage of the geometrical relations between expected windows. While the belief values for non-window areas decrease (from 0.335 to 0.134 for area 4 and 15), the values for all the real window areas get increased. Thus the contrast between the window and non-window areas becomes better.

Handling of Conflicting Evidence

One of the advantages of the Dempster-Shafer set-theoretical theory of evidence is the ability to accommodate conflicting evidence. The last part of our example will illustrate this capability, by applying the reasoning mechanism to independent observations of conflicting evidence.

The simplicity of the image of a building being used, e.g., the flat roof and the clear outline, makes it possible for the program to find the building's boundaries. Any areas falling outside the boundaries could hardly be windows of the building. Therefore a proposition $non-window$ is introduced as the negation of the proposition $window$. Areas outside of the building boundaries are assigned $Bel\ (non-window) = 0.5$, other areas will be assigned $Bel\ (non-window) = 0$. The remainder of the unit mass is assigned to Θ. The new belief about $non-window$ is combined with the belief about $window$, $v-sibl$ and $h-sibl$ to derive
$$Bel\ (non-window) \oplus Bel\ (window) \oplus Bel\ (v-sibl) \oplus Bel\ (h-sibl).$$
Finally, the same knowledge source with m_{s_2} is utilized to verify the $windows$ hypothesis.

As expected, the belief values for those 'outside' nodes are further decreased (See *Bel " (window)* in Table 1).

The final values *Bel " (wnd)* show that the program is very confident about the existence of the 12 real windows. Because the program found strong evidence as to the number and the arrangement of the windows at this level, it combined this with other evidence (e.g., the shape and outline of the building), and succeeded in recognizing the object in the building scene as an office or apartment building.

4. CONCLUSION

This paper describes how the Dempster-Shafer theory of evidence is used in a massively parallel hierarchical pyramid structure for computer vision. The program used was originally designed to recognize complex real-world objects (e.g., houses, office buildings, neurons) using a structure of micro-modular production rule-like transforms that are applied in a combined bottom-up top-down flow. Evidential reasoning was embedded at several stages in this program's processes. As shown by our examples, it serves to disambiguate and enhance the program's judgments about objects. Preliminary tests indicate that it improved the program's performance. The knowledge representation scheme described in this paper uses incomplete world knowledge. It is modular, flexible, and easy to update. Its reasoning mechanism extends the applications of the belief functions and Dempster's combination rule in a relatively efficient and powerful manner.

ACKNOWLEDGEMENTS

This work was partially supported by NSF Grant DCR-8302397 to L. Uhr.

REFERENCES

[1] Uhr, L. and Douglass, R.J., "A parallel-serial recognition cone system for perception: some test results," *Pattern Recognition* **11**, pp. 29-39 (1979).

[2] Li, Z.N., *Pyramid vision using key features and evidential reasoning*, Ph.D. Thesis, University of Wisconsin-Madison (1986a).

[3] Li, Z.N. and Uhr, L., "A pyramidal approach for the recognition of neurons using key features," *Pattern Recognition* **19**(1) pp. 55-62 (1986b).

[4] Dempster, A.P., "Upper and lower probabilities induced by a multivalued mapping," *Annals of Mathematical Statistics* **38**, pp. 325-339 (1967).

[5] Shafer, G., *A mathematical theory of evidence*, Princeton University Press (1976).

[6] Ragade, R.K. and Gupta, M.M., "Fuzzy set theory: Introduction," pp. 105-132 in *Fuzzy Automata and Decision Processes*, ed. M.M. Gupta, et al., (1977).

[7] Garvey, T.D., Lowrance, J.D., and Fischler, M.A., "An inference technique for integrating knowledge from disparate sources," *Proc. 7th IJCAI*, pp. 319-325 (1981).

[8] Lowrance, J.D., *Dependency-graph models of evidential support*, Ph.D. Thesis, University of Massachusetts at Amherst (1982).

[9] Lu, S.Y. and Stephanou, H.E., "A set-theoretic framework for the processing of uncertain knowledge," *Proc. The National Conf. on Artificial Intelligence*, pp. 216-221 (1984).

[10] Wesley, L.P., Lowrance, J.D., and Garvey, T.D., "Reasoning about control: an evidential approach," SRI Technical Note 324 (1984).

BAYESIAN INFERENCE FOR RADAR IMAGERY BASED SURVEILLANCE

Tod S. Levitt

Advanced Decision Systems
201 San Antonio Circle, Suite 286
Mountain View, California 94040

1. INTRODUCTION

We are interested in creating an automated or semi-automated system with the capability of taking a set of radar imagery, collection parameters and a priori map and other tactical data, and producing likely interpretations of the possible military situations given the available evidence. This paper is concerned with the problem of the interpretation and computation of certainty or belief in the conclusions reached by such a system. For example, if we consider the problem of confirming or denying the presence of a battalion in a given area, we should include in our decision making process the prior likelihood of military presence based on tactical objectives, the evidence of military vehicles in radar image data, the spatial and tactical clustering and patterns of the vehicles extracted from the imagery, etc. Furthermore, if the user of the system has particular interests such as knowing specific deployments, location of battalion headquarters, etc., then these interests should also be responded to in certainty computations.

In this report, we begin by briefly summarizing these functions from the point of view of outlining the inference processes that such a system must perform. Inference is performed over a space of hierarchically linked hypotheses. The hypotheses typically (although not solely) represent statements of the form "There is a military force of type F in deployment D at world location L at time T". The hierarchy in the hypothesis space corresponds to the hierarchy inherent in military doctrine of force structuring. Thus, "array-level" hypotheses of military units such as companies, artillery batteries, and missile sites, are linked to their component unit hypotheses of vehicles batteries and missile launchers. Similarly, companies are grouped to form battalion hypotheses, battalions to form regiments, etc.

The hypotheses are formed by (hierarchical and partial) matching of military force models to evidence available in radar imagery. Thus, we are actually concerned with a model-based radar vision system. Evidence of the truth (or denial) of a hypothesis is accrued numerically from probabilistic estimates about the sub-hypotheses that comprise their parent hypothesis according to the hierarchical military force models in which the vehicle level hypotheses correspond to the leaf-nodes of the hierarchy. In this report, we only address the symbolic inference problem, under the assumption that probabilities of vehicle level hypotheses have already been computed. The vehicle level hypotheses are inferred from evidence supplied by radar image understanding algorithms applied to the radar data. These computations require radar modeling and development of a probabilistic certainty calculus, but these issues are not addressed here. See [Levitt et al., - 86a] for an example of certainty calculus design at the vehicle level.
Summarizing so far, the proposed certainty calculus is a computational method for associating numerical probabilities to conclusions reached by a model-based radar vision sys-

tem applied to problems of military situation assessment. A fundamental concept here is that, while vision system processing may be complex, with numerous feedback loops, multiple levels of resolution, recursion, etc., in the end we should be able to associate a deductive chain of evidence to a system output, along with an associated numerical belief that supports that result. The system concept is pictured in Figure 1.

We selected probability theory as the underlying technology for this numerical accrual of evidence. This approach requires us to lay out, a priori, the links between evidence and hypotheses in the models over which the system will reason. Having laid out these links, we then need a numerical interpretation of the conditional belief (i.e., probability) in a hypothesis given chains of evidence that support it through links. This is similar to the propagation networks of Pearl [Pearl - 85], to influence diagrams [Howard and Matheson - 80], and other probabilistic accrual models such as those of [Kelly and Barclay - 73], [Schum - 77, 80], and [Schum and Martin - 82]. Besides explicit declaration of evidence/hypothesis links, these approaches also require development of numerical accrual formula to capture the semantics of the links, and elicitation of a priori probabilities. However, a certainty calculus for perceptually based military situation assessment addresses additional issues not directly faced in these approaches.

In the aforementioned schemes, the network, influence diagram, etc. typically represents exactly one model at a single level of abstraction. (Pearl has extended his work to hierarchies [Pearl - 86], however, previous applications of his theory have not been hierarchical in nature. Schum's work is also hierarchical, but both are still concerned with a single model.) For example, a model might represent the chains of evidence from symptoms to disease for a diagnosis system. The model is "instantiated" for a single patient; the evidence flows through, and (numerical) conclusions are inferred. Conceptually we perform exactly one pattern match of a single model against a data set known to represent a unique instance (i.e., one person).

In this application there are multiple models linked hierarchically in multiple levels of abstraction. We have a basic (ascending) "part-of" hierarchy of military forces: "vehicle, part-of, company, part-of, battalion, part-of, regiment, part-of, division." Further, at each level of this hierarchy there is an "is-a" hierarchy of military force type refinements. For example, at the vehicle level we have: "T-72-tank, is-a, tank, is-a, tracked-vehicle, is-a, vehicle." Similarly, at the array level we have: tank-company-in-defensive deployment, is-a, tank-company, is-a, company, is-a, array." Thus, the model space represents multiple partial orderings at multiple resolution in both part-of and is-a hierarchies. (N.B. This is a well-known issue in knowledge representation in artificial intelligence. See, for example, [Brachman - 85].)

The second major difference is that we dynamically (i.e., at system runtime) generate multiple matches of models to instances in the radar image data. This corresponds to a hypothesis space with many hypotheses, more than one of which can be correct at the same time, e.g., there may be two divisions on the battlefield, each of which matches an instance of the same division model. This second difference is especially significant. The generation of multiple hypotheses at runtime gives rise to:

- the distribution of a finite amount of belief over a consistent set of hypotheses, and

- the problem of distinguishing conflicting interpretation of links of evidence to hypotheses (i.e., bad pattern matches) from consistent sets of multiple hypotheses.

The first issue is equivalent to not having a single "top level" model in the part-of hierarchy that bounds the number of parts (i.e., evidence) that can (consistently) occur below it. This problem can be finessed by deciding, a priori, that no more than a single division (for example) can be present in the data. In practice this sort of assumption is very reasonable, however, if we want to extend this approach to more general vision, to adapting to changing spatial tactics by commanders, or to any sort of learning system, the requirement for a top level model must be removed.

The second issue is central in the current design. Conflict resolution between sets of hypotheses must be performed to attempt to improve the results of imperfect pattern matching. Matching models to the data is necessarily imperfect because, in general,

- only part of the forces actually present will be imaged in collected imagery.
- detection/recognition algorithms will miss some imaged vehicles, add in false alarms, and mis-classify some observed vehicles.
- models are not perfect and forces do not always follow precise doctrine, so incorrect matches will be made even when large parts of forces are observed.

Thus, the numerical accrual of evidence through the part-of and is-a hierarchies must not only account for accrual through consistent chains of inference, but also aid in disambiguating conflicting chains.

Multiple, possibly conflicting, model matches in a large data space give rise to combinatorial nightmares. We note, however, that the calculus only specifies how accrual should be performed over both conflicting and consistent sets of hypotheses. The control of the accrual process is technically a separable issue. Multiple control schemes could, in principle, be exercised over the same calculus, with radically different combinatorial results. This point is the springboard for the introduction of a technique for performing approximate hierarchical inference, while avoiding exponential processes. The technique presented is complementary to the (potentially expensive) conflict resolution procedures presented in [Levitt - 85] and [Levitt et al. - 86a].

Elicitation of highly conditional prior probabilities and likelihoods is another major research area necessary to design of the probability calculus. Priors combine domain expertise with background information beyond the knowledge boundaries (time, area, types of information) for which the automated system is responsible. We do not address this problem here. For a technical approach, see [Levitt et al. - 86b].

The structure of inference follows a pattern based on the models that are matched to generate hypotheses of the presence of military forces on the battlefield. These models consist purely of force types (i.e., names) and spatial-geometric deployment data relating force types. Modeling of the appearance of vehicles in SAR imagery, sensor models, terrain models, etc. are not addressed here. As depicted in Figure 1, each hypothesis passes on its posterior probabilities to become a priori (evidential) probabilities and hypotheses for hypotheses at the next level of hierarchical inference. Thus, certainties of vehicle detections are passed to inferences of vehicle classification, which in turn passes certainties of vehicle classifications to array-level military unit inference processes, etc. In general, posteriors at one force level become priors for their parent forces in the military hierarchy. Contextual analysis provides prior probabilities concerning a priori terrain evidence, likelihood of force presence based on a priori tactical considerations, as well as runtime estimates of accuracy of image-to-map registration that are necessary to account for the relative locations of forces which are observed in different sets of imagery.

In the following, we address the general problem of symbolic hierarchical Bayesian inference for military force inference. The key technical issue we address is the need to resolve conflicts between multiple incompatible hypotheses. The need to derive mutually consistent sets of (hierarchical) hypotheses gives rise to the exponential process of

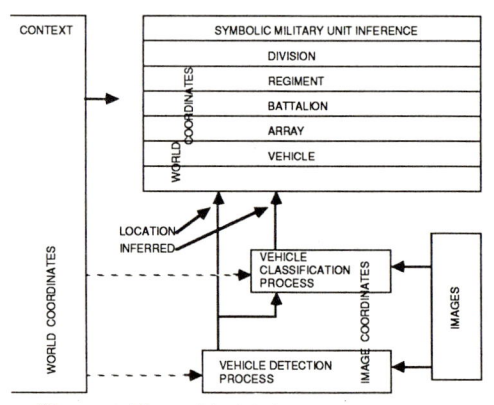

Figure 1: Hierarchical Inference Structure

creating these sets. In this report, we present a method for approximate hierarchical accrual that can be used to selectively avoid unnecessary conflict resolution depending on the system's focus of attention in processing tasks.

2. EVIDENTIAL ACCRUAL

The vehicle classification process provides a hierarchy of probabilities concerning the hypothesis that a chip of synthetic aperture radar (SAR) imagery contains some vehicle from a well defined world, W, of vehicles. All probabilities are explicitly conditioned on contextual information including terrain, and radar dependent measurements, t, m, provided with the chip, and upon evidence, e, extracted from the chip. The vehicle classification process apportions the probability that a vehicle is present among the nodes of its is-a hierarchy. This process ends at the leaf nodes of the tree that represent specific vehicle types. The fundamental problem is to estimate the probability that V occurs given evidence e and context m and t; that is, to compute $P(V \mid e,t,m)$. This is a deep radar modeling issue and we do not address it in this report. In the following we assume this computation has been performed.

We now address evidence accrual up the hierarchy of military force hypotheses. For each hypothesis, H, which is based on a model that has components, C_i, we first find the components which match the component portions of the model and their corresponding evidence, e_i, that supports each component hypothesis C_i. There is also a set of spatial pattern matching evidence associated with H that is specific to the geometric, spatial constraints that are given by the model for H. This set of evidence is denoted f. A hypothesis with components is then defined from the model as the existence of a force that is composed of the listed components C_i. The evidence that supports the hypothesis H is defined as the and of the evidence, e_i, for all of the component hypotheses, C_i, and the new evidence, f, for the hypothesis H. Initially, the e_i are the image data and processing results and H corresponds to a vehicle hypothesis based on that evidence. At the next level of the part-of hierarchy, the array level matches of vehicle sets give rise to array level hypotheses, H, the vehicle hypotheses play the role of components of H in the part-of hierarchy, i.e., the C_i, and the image evidence represents the e_i. With this recursive definition the new set of evidence for the hypothesis H will become the evidence that supports this hypothesis as it is used as a component of a yet higher level hypothesis that matches a yet higher level force model. We use as notation for the conjunction of the component hypotheses, $\wedge_i C_i$. This represents the statement that all of the component forces, C_i, exist. This does not necessarily imply that the hypothesis H exists.

In numerical accrual of evidence, we make several independence assumptions. The first is the standard hierarchical inference assumption that deals with evidence about an intermediate level hypothesis, C, where there is a higher level hypothesis, H, that uses C on the part-of hierarchy. That is, there exists evidence that infers C and then C infers H. The assumption is that given that C is true, the evidence, e supporting C and H are conditionally independent. That is $P(H,e \mid C) = P(H \mid C) \cdot P(e \mid C)$.

The second assumption concerns the independence of evidence at various levels in a consistent hierarchy. If there is a hypothesis that is supported both by components and by inter-relations between those components, and if we assume that the hypothesis is true, then the evidence of the relations among the components is independent of the evidence for each component. This can be written as a single statement as follows. Let the e_i's be the evidence supporting each component for a hypothesis H; then

$$P(\wedge_i e_i \mid H, \wedge_i C_i) = \prod_i P(e_i \mid H, C_i)$$

Here "$\wedge_i e_i$" means the conjunction of the evidence supporting the components.

We also assume that if C is a part-of the hypothesis H, then $P(C \mid H) = 1$.

The next independence assumption concerns conflict recognition between hypotheses. If C_1, C_2 are hypotheses supported by disjoint sets of evidence e_1 and e_2 respectively and, furthermore, C_1 and C_2 are not in military doctrinal conflict (e.g., by being situated too close together, facing opposite directions, etc.), then:

$$P(C_1 \mid e_1, e_2, C_2) = P(C_1 \mid e_1).$$

Now, if $\bigwedge_i C_i$ are parts-of H, and the $\bigwedge_i C_i$ are supported by non-conflicting evidence $\bigwedge_i e_i$, then the value we need to accrue is $P(H \mid \bigwedge_i C_i, \bigwedge_i e_i, f, \bigwedge_i t_i)$. Where t_i is the terrain under C_i, and f is a measure of the fit to formation of the C_i to the parent hypothesis H. In doing so, we also assume that $P(t_i) = 1$, that is, we know the world terrain with absolute certainty, and also that terrain is a local issue so that $P(\bigwedge_i t_i \mid H, \bigwedge_i C_i, \bigwedge_i e_i, f) = \prod_i (t_i \mid C_i)$. Using Bayes rule under these assumptions, we can show that:

$$P(H \mid \bigwedge_i C_i, \bigwedge_i e_i, t_i, f) = \frac{P(f \mid H, \bigwedge_i C_i)}{P(f \mid \bigwedge_i e_i, \bigwedge_i t_i)}$$

$$\cdot \prod_i \left[\frac{P(C_i \mid e_i) P(C_i \mid t_i)}{P(C_i \mid e_i, t_i)} \cdot \frac{P(H)}{P^2(C_i)} \right]$$

3. APPROXIMATE CONFLICT RESOLUTION

The assumption in the previous section that $P(C_1 \mid e_1, e_2, C_2) = P(C_1 \mid e_1)$ is clearly unacceptable if either e_1 and e_2 are not disjoint, or if the truth of C_2 conflicts for any reason with that of C_1. A methodology for handling conflicts was presented in Levitt - 85]. The concept was to accrue non-conflicted evidence up to the highest level of the hierarchy, and then to form a mutually exclusive, exhaustive hypothesis space of maximal consistent sets of hypotheses. Results of disambiguation at the highest level could be passed down the hierarchy with high probability of correct inference. An alternative approach is presented in [Levitt et al. - 86a] where conflict resolution is performed bottom-up in the accrual process by factoring in the negation of each hypothesis in the accrual. Both approaches suffer from an inherently worst-case exponential step in forming sets of consistent hypotheses.

Here, we present a method for analyzing a conflict in polynomial time, and provide a metric, based on the analysis, to determine if conflict is worth dis-ambiguating. If it is not, then accrual must be able to "jump" over the conflicted level in the hierarchy by specifying how to accrue evidence at lower levels as support for higher level hypotheses.

The concept of conflict analysis is embodied in the case for two hypotheses. Let $e = e_1 \cup e_2 \cup e_{12}$ where e_1 is a set of evidence supporting only C_1, e_2 supports only C_2 and e_{12} is shared, conflicted evidence associated to both. Then we approximate

$$P(C_1, C_2, e) = P(C_1 \mid C_2, e) P(C_2 \mid e) P(e)$$
$$\approx P(C_1 \mid e_1) P(C_2 \mid e_2 \cup e_{12}) P(e)$$

$$\approx P(C_2 \mid e_2) P(C_1 \mid e_1 \cup e_{12}) P(e).$$

The underlying independence assumptions are that $P(C_1 \mid e_2) = P(C_1)$ and $P(C_2 \mid e_1) = P(C_2)$. During control of inference, we use this in the following way. Let $\{C_i\}$ be a set of conflicted hypotheses, and let $e = \cup e_i$ be the total set of supporting evidence for the C_i. Use heuristics (e.g., most matches, highest total a priori probability, etc.) to order the C_i. Then form the evidence sets $\{e - \bigcup_{k=i}^{n} e_k\}$ for $i = 2$ to n. This is a polynomial time operation. Then approximate

$$P(\wedge_i C_i \mid e) \approx \prod_{i=1}^{n} P(C_i \mid e - \bigcup_{k=i+1}^{n} e_i) = k.$$

k is interpreted as a measure of how likely the $\{C_i\}$ are all to be true, despite the conflict in evidence association. We use $\frac{1-k}{k}$ as the measure of conflict. If it is small, then the error in not dis-ambiguating the conflict (i.e., accrual skipping the conflicted level in the hierarchy) will be small.

To see this, let $\wedge_i C_i$ be associated to H, supported by e, in which, for convenience, we have included $\wedge e_i, f$ and $\wedge t_i$. Then $P(H \mid \wedge_i C_i, e) = P(e \mid H) P(H) / P(\wedge_i C_i \mid e) P(e)$ because $P(\wedge_i C_i \mid H.e) = 1$. We have the error in "skipping" the level of the C_i as

$$\mid P(H \mid \wedge_i C_i, e) - P(H \mid e) \mid$$

$$= \left| \frac{P(e \mid H) P(H)}{P(\wedge_i C_i \mid e) P(e)} - \frac{P(e \mid H) P(H)}{P(e)} \right|$$

$$= \frac{P(e \mid H) P(H)}{P(e)} \left| \frac{1}{P(\wedge_i C_i \mid e)} - 1 \right|$$

$$= \frac{P(e \mid H) P(H)}{P(e)} \left| \frac{1 - P(\wedge_i C_i \mid e)}{P(\wedge_i C_i \mid e)} \right|$$

$$\approx \frac{P(e \mid H) P(H)}{P(e)} \left(\frac{1-k}{k} \right)$$

which is small if $\frac{1-k}{k}$ is small.

4. ISSUES

Approximate hierarchical accrual provides a tool for choosing to ignore local conflicts in hierarchical inference. There are considerable issues in how to utilize it in the framework of system control. In this report we have presented a partial design for a probabilistic certainty calculus to support inference for military force inference. In the course of performing such inference, the step of exact conflict resolution will often be necessary. The inference control issue is how to decide when, in the face of conflict, to test for the use of approximate accrual and how to threshold the outcome of the test.

The current design of a certainty calculus requires considerable effort in refinement and implementation. Large grain work chunks include:

- Development of a control methodology to address computational combinatorics in the hierarchical inference evidence propagation and (approximate) conflict resolution.
- Elicitation and verification of distributions characterizing the relative occurrence of military forces versus terrain and military contextual knowledge.

ACKNOWLEDGEMENTS

I am indebted to Ward Edwards, Bob Kirby, and Larry Winter for extended discussions that helped clarify many of the points in this paper. Dubious semantic interpretations or errors are, of course, the author's sole responsibility.

This work was supported by Defense Advanced Research Projects Agency and U.S. Army Engineer Topographic Laboratories under U.S. Government Contract No. DACA76-86-C-0010, ADS Contract No. 1131.

REFERENCES

[Brachman - 85] - R.J. Brachman, "I Lied About the Trees, or Defaults and Definitions in Knowledge Representation", AI Magazine, Vol. 6, No. 3, Fall, 1985.

[Howard and Matheson - 80] - R.A. Howard and J.E. Matheson, "Influence Diagrams", SRI Technical Memo, Menlo Park, California, 1980.

[Kelly and Barclay - 73] - C.W. Kelly III and S. Barclay, "A General Bayesian Model for Hierarchical Inference", in Organizational Behavior and Human Performance, Vol. 10, 1973.

[Levitt - 85] - T. Levitt, "Probabilistic Conflict Resolution in Hierarchical Hypothesis Spaces", Proc. AAAI Workshop on Uncertainty in Artificial Intelligence, Los Angeles, California, August, 1985.

[Levitt et al., - 86a] - T. Levitt, W. Edwards, R. Kirby, L. Winter, D. Morgan, S. Mori, S. Simmes, and F. Smith, "Design of A Probabilistic Certainty Calculus for ADRIES", Advanced Decision Systems, TR-1040, May, 1986.

[Levitt, et al., - 86b] - T. Levitt, W. Edwards, and L. Winters, "Elicitation of Terrain Analysis Knowledge in ADRIES", Advanced Decision Systems, TR-1131, August, 1986.

[Pearl - 85] - J. Pearl, "A Constraint-Propagation Approach to Probabilistic Reasoning", Proc. AAAI Workshop on Uncertainty and Probability in Artificial Intelligence, Los Angeles, California, August, 1985.

[Pearl - 86] - J. Pearl, "On Evidential Reasoning in a Hierarchy of Hypotheses", Artificial Intelligence, Vol. 28, No. 1, February, 1986.

[Schum - 77] - D.A. Schum, "The Behavioral Richness of Cumulative and Corroborative Testimonial Evidence", In Castellan, N. J., Jr., Pisoni, & Pitts (Eds.) Cognitive Theory, Vol. 2. Hillsdale, N. J.: Lawrence Erlbaum Press, 1977.

[Schum - 80] - D.A. Schum, "Current Developments in Research on Cascaded Inference", In T. S. Wallsten (Ed.), Cognitive Processes in Decision and Choice Behavior. Hillsdale, N. J.: Lawrence Erlbaum Press, 1980.

[Schum and Martin - 82] - D.A. Schum and A.W. Martin, "Formal and Empirical Research on Cascaded Inference in Jurisprudence", Law and Society Review, 1982, 17, 105-157.

A CAUSAL BAYESIAN MODEL FOR THE DIAGNOSIS OF APPENDICITIS

Stanley M. Schwartz, Jonathan Baron, and John R. Clarke

Department of Psychology, University of Pennsylvania, Philadelphia, PA 19104
Department of Surgery, Medical College of Pennsylvania, Philadelphia, PA 19129

The causal Bayesian approach is based on the assumption that effects (e.g., symptoms) that are not conditionally independent with respect to some causal agent (e.g., a disease) are conditionally independent with respect to some intermediate state caused by the agent, (e.g., a pathological condition). This paper describes the development of a causal Bayesian model for the diagnosis of appendicitis. The paper begins with a description of the standard Bayesian approach to reasoning about uncertainty and the major critiques it faces. The paper then lays the theoretical groundwork for the causal extension of the Bayesian approach, and details specific improvements we have developed. The paper then goes on to describe our knowledge engineering and implementation and the results of a test of the system. The paper concludes with a discussion of how the causal Bayesian approach deals with the criticisms of the standard Bayesian model and why it is superior to alternative approaches to reasoning about uncertainty popular in the AI community.

1. INTRODUCTION AND OVERVIEW

Medical diagnosis is one of the major foci of work on reasoning about uncertainty in artificial intelligence. It is the problem of how optimally to combine evidence from outwardly visible patient symptoms and signs to make the best inference about underlying or invisible disease causes, by using expert knowledge of the relative strengths of the links between causes and effects. The situation is complicated because each cause has multiple effects and several causes may produce the same effect. Also, certain effects are highly intercorrelated, so that treating them as independent may lead to diagnostic errors. Finally, the utility of treatment decisions varies among possible diseases, so that the most rational treatment decision does not necessarily treat the most probable disease. Effective methods of diagnosis should provide enough information to allow the best treatment choice for a given patient.

It may take a physician a lifetime to develop advanced diagnostic expertise in a particular medical specialty. Expert diagnosticians perform well because they have learned much about the placement and strengths of the links between causes and effects in the disease process (Clarke, 1982; Elstein, Shulman, & Sprafka, 1978). However, this does not imply that they have a superior calculus or set of production rules for reasoning about uncertainty. A large body of psychological research (recent reviews are Baron, 1985; Kahneman, Slovic, & Tversky, 1982; Nisbett & Ross, 1980) suggests that people reason about uncertainty using simplifying heuristics and strategies, which commonly lead to biased judgements. Physicians, as people, are subject to the same reasoning biases (Berwick, Fineberg, & Weinstein, 1981; Christensen-Szalanski & Bushyhead, 1981; Detmer, Fryback, & Gassner, 1978; Eddy, 1982).

If a physician's probabilistic knowledge is extracted and combined using a normative calculus, it can result in a diagnostic accuracy better than that of the physician (Clarke, 1984). (This "bootstrapping" phenomenon has a long tradition in psychology, see, for example, Slovic & Lichtenstein, 1971). Our goal as applied scientists, in designing an expert system, should be to use our best theories about normative reasoning to design an inference engine, which can be combined with a knowledge base obtained from an expert who has extended experience observing a domain. The purpose of this paper is:

1) to show why we think the causal Bayesian approach provides the most normative basis for an inference engine for reasoning about uncertainty.
2) to give an example of an implementation.

2. STANDARD BAYESIAN ASSUMPTIONS AND CRITIQUES

Bayes theorem provides a good starting point for the design of an ideal inference engine because it has a firm foundation in the axioms of subjective probability (Savage, 1954). The standard form of Bayes theorem calculates the conditional probability of a cause (disease) given effects (symptoms) in terms of the probabilities of the diseases (priors) and the probabilities of the symptoms given the diseases (likelihoods). The formula, as applied to a single symptom, is as follows:

$$p(D_j/s) = \frac{p(s/D_j)\,p(D_j)}{\sum_{i=1}^{i=n} p(s/D_i)\,p(D_i)}$$

Here the D's refer to diseases, s is a particular symptom, and D_j is the disease of interest.

The formula becomes more complicated for the conditional probability of a disease given more than one symptom. For example, the equation to find the posterior probability of disease D_j when symptom s_k is added to the k-1 known symptoms is:

$$p(D_j/s_1 \& s_2 \cdots \& s_k) = \frac{p(s_k/D_j \& s_1 \& s_2 \cdots \& s_{k-1})\,p(D_j/s_1 \& s_2 \cdots \& s_{k-1})}{\sum_{i=1}^{i=n} p(s_k/D_i \& s_1 \& s_2 \cdots \& s_{k-1})\,p(D_i/s_1 \& s_2 \cdots \& s_{k-1})}$$

This means that to build a complete Bayesian system containing k symptoms and n diseases, it would be necessary to store likelihoods of each symptom given all combinations of from one to k-1 other symptoms with each of the n diseases. Therefore, traditional Bayesian diagnostic systems of sufficient scope to be useful in multiple disease situations are quite often difficult to implement, as has been repeatedly pointed out in reviews of the literature on computer-based diagnostic systems (Charniak & McDermott, 1985; Hayes-Roth, Waterman, & Lenat, 1983; Kleinmuntz, 1984; Schaffner, 1981).

2.1. Assumption Of Symptom Independence

The practicality of Bayesian systems can be improved by assuming symptom independence, thereby reducing the size of the set of symptom likelihoods that need to be known beforehand. Symptom independence is expressed through the following two assumptions:

$$p(s_i/s_j) = p(s_i)$$
$$p(s_i/D \& s_j) = p(s_i/D)$$

The first says that the probability of observing symptom s_i in the subpopulation of individuals with symptom s_j is the same as the probability of observing symptom s_i in the whole universe. The second says that the probability of observing symptom s_i in the subpopulation of individuals with disease D and symptom s_j is the same as the probability of observing symptom s_i among all individuals with disease D. The upshot is these assumptions is that it is necessary to store likelihoods of only individual symptoms given diseases because the likelihood of two or more symptoms occurring together given a disease can be obtained by multiplying the individual likelihoods as follows:

$$p(D_j/s_1 \& s_2 \cdots \& s_k) = \frac{p(D_j) \prod_{l=1}^{l=k} p(s_l/D_j)}{\prod_{l=1}^{l=k} \sum_{i=1}^{i=n} p(s_l/D_i) p(D_i)}$$

The justification for these independence assumptions is questionable. Although the medical AI literature reports examples of independence-assuming Bayesian medical systems (reviewed in deDombal, 1979; Wardle & Wardle, 1978) having diagnostic accuracies of over 90%, it is apparent that symptoms are not usually independent of each other in the real world, because the probability of two symptoms of the same disease occurring together, given that one has the disease, is often much higher than the product of the individual probabilities of the symptoms. If someone has a headache, knowing that it was caused by a cold makes a simultaneous sore throat more likely. Monte Carlo studies by Russek, Kronmal, and Fisher (1983) imply that the assumption of symptom independence does not change the rank ordering of diseases, but it does effect the posterior probability distribution, so that the probabilities of diseases with p's over 0.5 are overestimated, and those with p's under 0.5 are underestimated. Similarly, the work of Fryback (1978) suggests that the reduction of discriminating power caused by assuming independence in situations when it does not apply worsens as the number of symptoms increases. These results would not be problematic for most computer medical diagnostic systems that just come up with lists of likely diseases, but has serious implications if one is trying to perform patient management by weighting utilities with accurate disease probabilities to find an optimum treatment.

2.2. Assumption Of Single Symptom Causes

In Bayes theorem causes of effects are held to be mutually exclusive. Each cause is assigned a prior probability or degree of belief, and when evidence is presented the degree of belief in a cause is incremented or decremented based on the ability of that cause to uniquely account for that evidence. When applied in the medical domain, the usual practice is to map causes onto single diseases. Single, rather than multiple (or single and multiple), diseases are chosen as causes because: people have a better understanding of the mechanisms, and hence probabilities, of symptoms being produced by single diseases; the necessity of keeping track of the probability of all symptom combinations given all disease combinations would make the combinatorial explosion even worse; and people have an understanding of the treatments that should be applied in the event of single, but not multiple, diseases. The problem with this assumption, like with the assumption of symptom independence, is that it violates real-world experience. Having two or more diseases co-occur in the same person is common, and treating one while ignoring the other may have serious medical consequences.

3. THE CAUSAL BAYESIAN MODEL

The causal Bayesian approach allows most of the computational simplicity obtained from assuming symptom independence, while providing a sensible way to model symptom interdependence. Symptoms of a disease that are intercorrelated are assumed to have an additional shared cause, besides the disease, which independent symptoms of the disease do not have. For example, anorexia (loss of appetite) and nausea, two symptoms of appendicitis, co-occur more frequently than would be expected by chance, because they both result from gastrointestinal disturbance. This additional cause, named a pathstate by Charniak (1983), has itself a certain likelihood of being caused by the disease. (Our notion is derived from Charniak, but similar ideas have also been proposed by Pearl, 1986.) The symptoms of gastrointestinal disturbance, anorexia and nausea, cannot appear until appendicitis has produced the disturbance, but after it is present, one or both symptoms may occur, relatively independently of the other. This is modeled by assuming that symptoms are independent with respect to proximal causes, which can be expressed computationally as follows:

p(anorexia & nausea/appendicitis) =
p(anorexia/gi disturbance) p(nausea/gi disturbance)
p(gi disturbance/appendicitis)

In other words, the likelihood of a set of symptoms given a disease is equal to the product of the likelihoods of the symptoms given the pathstate directly causing them times the likelihood of the pathstate given the disease. (The same principle applies, mutatis mutandis, if additional pathstates and symptoms are added.)

```
       append                         append
        /\                              |p
       /  \                             gl
    pq/    \pr                         /  \
     /      \                        q/    \r
    /        \                       /      \
   an        na                     an      na
```

(a) Causal Bayesian Model   (b) Independent Symptom Model

Figure 1

The contrast of the causal Bayesian approach with complete symptom independence is demonstrated by comparing Figures 1(a) and 1(b). In both figures, the likelihood of a gi disturbance given appendicitis is represented by p, the likelihood of anorexia given gi disturbance is represented by q, and the likelihood of nausea given gi disturbance is represented by r. According to the causal Bayesian approach the probability of anorexia and nausea both occurring given appendicitis would be pqr, while according to complete symptom independence it would be pqpr, making this unrealistically infrequent.

In our implementation a disease is represented by a hierarchical graph of a tree, expanding downwards, with the top node representing the disease, middle nodes representing pathstates, and bottom nodes representing symptoms. Figure 2 shows the representation we used for appendicitis. Links between nodes, which are only in a vertical direction, represent the probability of an child node being caused by its direct parent. All the child nodes which are direct descendants of the same parent are treated as probabilistically independent with respect to that parent. The likelihood of the vector of symptom nodes, $\vec{z}_j$, that are direct or indirect descendants of a node x having any particular configuration of values, given x, is evaluated by the function "lhood" as follows:

If (x is a symptom node)

$\quad$ Then $\mathrm{lhood}(\vec{z}_j/x) := 1$

$\quad$ Else $\mathrm{lhood}(\vec{z}_j/x) := \prod_{i=1}^{i=n} p(y_i/x)\, \mathrm{lhood}(\vec{z}_k/y_i)$

Here, y_i is a direct descendent of x, and $\vec{z}_k$ is the symptom vector of direct and indirect descendents of y_i. Individual symptoms can have values of present, absent, or unknown. Other than this new method for calculating likelihoods, the rest of Bayes theorem is used in the way described in the previous section.

A Causal Bayesian Model for the Diagnosis of Appendicitis 427

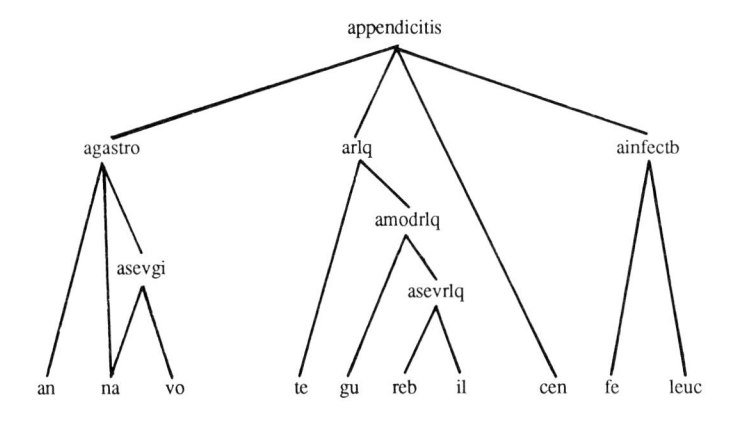

Figure 2

4. THE KNOWLEDGE ENGINEERING

We started the project by locating an expert notable both for his medical knowledge and his sympathetic attitude towards attempts to quantify the medical decision-making process. We decided to work on the problem of the differential diagnosis of appendicitis because it was circumscribed, had hard data available, and the large differences in utilities for the possible treatment options would put a premium on the correct assessment of disease probabilities. The first author spent several weeks reading the literature of the domain, and after extended discussion we chose to limit the modeling process to the six diseases with prior probabilities higher than one percent that would be considered when diagnosing appendicitis. The final model also included 19 symptoms and 32 intermediate pathstates. (The hierarchical structures of the diseases were defined in PROLOG by the first author.)

We developed the pathstate structure for the various diseases by deciding which symptoms were causally related because they all were manifestations of a stress produced by the disease on a particular system, or organ, or at a particular location. In general, similar symptoms were interrelated in the same way for different diseases, simplifying the modeling process.

Although the diseases that are commonly confused with appendicitis may cause the same symptoms with the same probabilities, they can be diagnostically differentiated because they characteristically produce these symptoms at different times after the onset of the disease. Therefore, we needed to modify the pathstate models to allow diseases to evolve over time. We solved this problem by making the likelihood links between nodes conditional on the time since disease onset. This was done by having the expert graph the probability strength of each link as a function of time, from 0 to 132 hours. Even though drawing a line on a graph does not create a much larger time demand on the expert than making a point estimate, it provides much more information. In this way, we could generate likelihoods for symptoms being produced by the various diseases at whatever time since onset that the symptoms were reported. (Time since disease onset was defined as time since first observed symptom.)

Pathstates emerge from the expert's causal understanding of the disease process, but there is no independent evidence of their existence. As scientists, we include them as hypothetical constructs in our models because they improve the quality of our explanations and predictions. However we were posing our expert the difficult question of assigning probabilities to the likelihood of diseases causing theoretical entities or the theoretical entities causing symptoms. To reassure ourselves that he wasn't pulling these numbers from a hat, we devised a coherency check. We asked our expert to graph the direct likelihood of each symptom given appendicitis. These likelihoods should be both more reliable and better calibrated, because they are based on the empirical observation of symptoms and are consistent with the way our expert is used to thinking about diseases. We could then compare these likelihoods with the likelihood of a symptom given a disease obtained from the model and correct large discrepancies. (The model defines the likelihood of a symptom given a disease as equal to the products of the likehoods linking all the nodes on a direct path from the symptom to the disease.) There was substantial overlap, although the model estimates tended to be lower than the direct ones (perhaps because the expert underestimated the effect of multiplying several likelihoods less than one when providing the original pathstate probabilities).

The knowledge engineering also involved obtaining estimates for disease priors and treatment utilities from our expert. We found the priors to be conditional upon age and sex, so we repeated the technique of having the expert draw graphs to show the change in disease probability with age. Some of the prior probabilities of the gynecological diseases also varied according to time of the month, so we also made a graph of these changes and used them to weight the age-based priors. (Afterwards, the prior probabilities across diseases were normalized.) Entering treatment utilities involved the related problems of finding one standard to measure utility and defining the treatment options. The eventual options used were symptomatic treatment until recovery or an intraperitoneal operation (symptomatic treatment implies that an operation may be performed if the patient's condition declines). Utility was estimated in terms of morbidity, specifically, number of days in the hospital expected for a particular disease-treatment combination (mortality was not used as a measure of utility, because it is typically below one percent for all cases).

5. IMPLEMENTING THE MODEL

The rest of this section describes several complications that emerged when we tried to implement the model and the solutions we arrived at to resolve them.

5.1. Modeling Different Levels Of Severity

One problem we encountered was that symptoms could be related without being simply independent with respect to one another, because they reflected different degrees of severity of the same stress. We solved this problem by adding an additional pathstate below the main one to represent each increasing level of severity that we wanted to model. Each pathstate had some probability of causing a direct descendant pathstate reflecting the next higher degree of severity. Pathstates at both levels could also directly cause symptoms, though not usually the same ones. For example, in Figure 2, the pathstate *arlq* reflects the presence of any right lower quadrant peritoneal signs including the most minor, tenderness. If the peritoneal signs reach moderate intensity, reflected by *amodrlq* being caused, then there should also be a high probability of observing guarding. Finally, if the right lower quadrant peritoneal signs reached their most severe, shown by *asevrlq,* then rebound tenderness and ileus should appear as well. The advantage of this kind of structure is that it is impossible for the severe signs of a stress to occur without the mild ones, because the mild ones are caused by a pathstate directly caused by the disease. (We would also expect the low severity pathstates and their symptoms to be present earlier than the high severity pathstates and theirs, because increasing severity evolves over time. This is relatively easy for us to model, because, as stated in the previous section, the likelihood links between pathstate nodes are conditioned on time.)

5.2. Compensating For Single Causes Of Symptoms

Another serious problem to emerge was that not all symptoms we were looking at were caused by all the diseases in the hypothesis pool. Theoretically, the observation of a symptom uniquely caused by one of the diseases should categorically rule out the others. No doctor would perform a diagnosis on this basis. We might try to deal with this problem by relaxing the condition that diseases be mutually exclusive and by adding other diseases thought to cause the symptoms, e.g., colds. We resisted this approach, taken by other recent Bayesian or causal Bayesian diagnostic systems, such as those of Cooper (1986) and Peng and Reggia (1986).

Our choice was not merely based on the desire to simplify computation (perhaps at the patient's expense), but in the sincere belief that it leads to more accurate modeling and hence better decision-making. It is reasonable to consider our six diseases to be mutually exclusive for the practical purpose of differentially diagnosing *appendicitis*. Although any one of the symptoms we were considering might be caused by many different diseases, the co-occurrence of several of these symptoms in the patient would strongly suggest that the relevant disease was from the pool. And since the pool was so small, we felt that the chance of two diseases from within it occurring simultaneously to cause acute symptoms to be vanishingly small.

The solution was to allow the possibility that symptoms could be independently caused by individual diseases from outside the pool and were co-occurring with the diseases from within it. Accordingly, we had our expert graph a "base-rate" external-cause probability for each symptom by sex and age. The numerator of Bayes theorem would now become:

$$p(D_i) \text{ lhood}(\vec{z}_j/D_i) \prod_{l=1}^{l=n} p(z_l)$$

i.e., the prior probability of the disease times the likelihood of the symptoms caused by the disease having a particular set of values, given the disease, times the independent probability of each symptom not caused by the disease having its particular value. D_i represents any disease from the hypothesis pool, and z_l stands for any symptom included in the model not directly or indirectly caused by D_i. The denominator becomes the sum of these expressions across diseases.

Outside Cause	Disease A
of	Disease B
Symptoms	caused by B

Figure 3

There are two ways that "base-rate" symptoms could co-occur with the diseases of the hypothesis pool and their symptoms, as shown in Figure 3. The entire upper rectangle in Figure 3 represents the probability of Disease A, and the entire lower rectangle represents the probability of Disease B. Disease B causes a symptom with a certain likelihood, represented by the lower half of Disease B, while Disease A does not cause it. There is also a certain probability of this symptom co-occurring independently with each disease from outside causes, represented by the vertical rectangle to the left that overlaps the rectangles of both A and B. The probability of this symptom given Disease A is simply equal to the symptom's overall "base-rate" probability, because Disease A and the symptom are independent. The probability of the symptom given Disease B involves two contributions, one from inside the disease and one from outside it. Because they are independent contributions, the total probability of the symptom given Disease B is equal to the probability of the symptom being caused by the disease, plus the probability of its being caused externally, minus the overlap.

The same principle can be extended for each symptom that either is caused or not caused by a particular disease. However, for a symptom to be caused by a disease, there is a long causal chain to follow, any of whose links could break. In other words, a symptom could be absent just as easily from a pathstate not being caused by a disease as from a symptom not being caused by a pathstate. Conversely, any time there is a break in the causal chain, there is some probability that a given symptom could be independently caused. Therefore the revised "lhood" function should include a probability for an independent symptom to be observed given all possible outcomes for the causal chain, either being intact or breaking at any given link. It is as follows:

If (x is a symptom node)

Then $\text{lhood}(\vec{z}_j/x) := 1$

Else $\text{lhood}(\vec{z}_j/x) := \prod_{i=1}^{i=n} [(p(y_i/x) \, \text{lhood}(\vec{z}_k/y_i)) + ((1 - p(y_i/x)) \prod_{k=1}^{k=m} p(z_k))]$

Here $p(z_k)$ is the externally caused probability of a symptom descendant of node y_i having a value of present, absent, or unknown. The "base-rate" probability assigned for a symptom z_k being absent is one minus the probability $p(z_k)$ of that symptom being present, and the value assigned for unknown status is one (so that the product in the numerator of Bayes theorem depends only on known symptoms). The term on the left side of the definition of "lhood" for disease and pathstate nodes remains unchanged from the previous definition. The term on the right side represents the probability of the set of descendant symptoms being observed in the absence of node y_i being caused.

Theoretically, as pointed out by G. Cooper, there is some probability of any given pathstate in the model having an outside cause as well. In this case $p(y_i/x)$ should be expanded as follows:

$$p(y_i/x) := p(y_i/x) + (1-p(y_i/x))p(y)$$

where p(y) is the probability of pathstate y being independently caused.

6. TESTING THE MODEL

We tested the ability of the model to distinguish the symptoms of 100 recorded cases of appendicitis from those of 100 recorded cases of nonspecific abdominal pain. The cases were chosen to present a wide range of diagnostic difficulty, with some causing high probabilities of error for human diagnosticians and previous (Bayesian) diagnostic systems. For the test, we constructed a comparison independent Bayesian model which had the same likelihoods for individual symptoms being caused by a disease, but in which the probabilities of combinations of symptoms given a disease were obtained by multiplying their separate likelihoods, as in Figure 1(b). The probabilities of individual symptoms for the independent model were found by multiplying all the likehoods linking all the nodes on a direct path from the symptom to the disease in the pathstate model. This would provide a fair comparison; any difference in the performance of the models could not be attributed to the accuracy of the likelihoods of individual symptoms and must therefore depend on how the data about symptoms were combined.

To accurately describe the test sample, we set the prior probabilities of appendicitis and non-specific abdominal pain to 0.5 in both models. We entered the symptoms of the cases into both models and obtained posterior probabilities of appendicitis for each case. An appropriate measure of performance is calibration, also known as "reliability in the small" (Yates, 1982). A person or decision-system is well calibrated if the probability she or it assigns to a given outcome occurs that with that frequency; for example, if 9 out of 10 abdominal cases that were assigned a 90% probability of of being appendicitis actually were appendicitis. (We are more interested in calibration than in maximizing discrimination between appendicitis and non-appendicitis because good calibration allows maximum accuracy in placing diseases above or below the probability threshold for switching treatment options based on utility considerations. This threshold is rarely 0.5).

The result, obtained using the jackknife statistical technique (Mosteller & Tukey, 1977), was that the calibration of the causal Bayesian model (.0735) was superior to the independent model (.0785). The probability of this difference being due to chance was <.001. An alternative comparison using a measure of the area of error between a quadratic regression function fitted on the probabilities of the cases assigned by a particular model and the perfect calibration function also showed the causal model to be significantly superior.

We were concerned that for the data sample we tested, our causal Bayesian model was not as well calibrated as an independent Bayesian model constructed from our expert's direct estimates of the likelihoods of symptoms given diseases. The model based on direct estimates was also a better discriminator. (Neither difference was significant.) It appeared that our expert was able to describe the causal structure of a disease, but was less able to generate robust estimates to the strengths of the probabilistic links between hypothetical pathstates. This is understandable, since the pathstates were unobservable and could not always be inferred from the presence of their symptoms, which were observable. Therefore, to be sure of the model, we felt it necessary to find some way to externally correct the link estimates.

We faced four constraints, two hard and two soft. The first hard constraint was that we wanted the likelihoods obtained by multiplying links on the path from a symptom to a disease to be equal to some external or objective criterion of the likelihood of symptoms given diseases. The second hard constraint was that we wanted the links to be probabilities, so that they had to remain between 0 and 1. The first soft constraint was that we wanted the link probabilities to reproduce the true causal association among symptoms, at least to the extent that our causal model performed reliably better than a comparable independent model. The second soft constraint was that we wanted to retain as much of our expert's model as we could, given that the goal of the enterprise was to use causal understanding as a heuristic to improve upon the performance given by blindly assuming independence while not having to turn to the unpalatable alternative of a complete Bayesian analysis with its excessive demands for data.

These constraints were contradictory to a certain extent, and they imposed limitations on the types of symptom associations we could model. After several attempts, we found a method for setting link probabilities so that our causal Bayesian model could be both better calibrated and a better discriminator than a comparable independent model for the differential diagnosis of appendicitis. (A detailed discussion of the implications of the constraints, our attempts to meet them, and the technique we came up with are provided in Schwartz, Clarke, Baron, & deDombal, 1987.) A conceptually similar variation of the model using objective probabilities to define the links between pathstates also showed a considerable improvement in calibration over an independent comparison model (Clarke, Schwartz, Baron, & deDombal, 1986). These results suggest that the causal Bayesian approach can provide a viable solution to the interdependence problem.

7. WORK IN PROGRESS

Another problem that we have been considering is how to take advantage of symptom information from two different times. For example, a doctor learns about a first set of symptoms, noticed by the patient when he contracts a disease, and a second set of symptoms when the patient is examined. Between the two measurements, symptom values may change in either direction. Given that one has a model of how various diseases evolve over time, these changing symptoms should be very diagnostic in distinguishing among diseases.

Suppose the likelihood of a symptom given a disease increases over time. Four symptom patterns may be observed: yes-yes, yes-no, no-yes, or no-no. The two temporal measurements are not independent, because they reflect the operation of a single disease process. Probabilities may be assigned to these patterns by assuming a relationship of implication between likelihoods. If a symptom is caused by a disease at a time when it is less likely to do so, then we must also expect it to occur when it is more likely. However, a symptom occurring when it is more likely does not necessarily imply that it will occur when it is less likely. Therefore, the probability of the yes-yes pattern may be defined as probability of the symptom at the less likely time. The yes-no pattern, with a symptom being observed at the less likely, but not more likely, time, is impossible and could only be produced by some outside cause. The no-yes pattern, with the symptom being observed only at the more likely time, has a probability equal to the difference between the likelihoods of the symptom at the more and less likely times. The probability of the no-no pattern is equal to one minus the likelihood of the symptom being caused at the more likely time.

This logic can easily be extended to describe the temporal changes in the likelihood of any child node given its parent. A parallel representation describes how the four patterns can be accounted for by independently caused symptoms. However, a major problem emerges in defining disease onset. What are thought to be early symptoms of a disease, may in fact be independently caused. Therefore, it may be necessary to compare the posterior probabilities of having each disease start at many different times, leading to a combinatoric explosion. This problem remains as yet unsolved.

In other research, the first author is using the causal pathstate model of appendicitis described in the previous sections of this paper to compare the diagnostic reasoning of expert and novice surgeons, as part of his doctoral dissertation in Psychology at the University of Pennsylvania.

8. CONCLUSIONS

There are several conclusions we would like to draw about the work we have described. We have tried to show that a Bayesian diagnostic system using subjective causal links between intermediate states is feasible. Above that, the calibration results show that causal modeling is consequential, that is, it visibly improves performance over a Bayesian system based on the conventional assumption of symptom independence. Once again, the lesson of Artificial Intelligence research is that a simple theoretical analysis of a problem does not reveal all the difficulties that arise during implementation. We have found additional difficulties, not foreseen by Charniak (1983), specifically:

1) that symptoms take on different meanings because diseases evolve over time.
2) that symptoms can be indirectly related, because they reveal different levels of severity of a pathological condition.
3) that not all the diseases in an hypothesis pool cause the same symptoms, so that it is necessary to allow symptoms to have external causes.

Fortunately, these problems are soluble.

The main advantage of this approach that we would like to emphasize is that unlike the current "hot" approaches for dealing with uncertainty in AI, MYCIN's certainty factors and Dempster-Shafer (Buchanan & Shortliffe, 1984; Shafer, 1976; Shortliffe, 1976), the output of this system is real probabilities that can be used to weigh the utilities of teatment options for patient management. Other advantages are that it solves the interdependence problem in a palatable way, is computationally simple, and does not place an excessive demand for probability estimates on the expert. Given the theoretical justification for the Bayesian approach, there now seems to be no further excuse for neglecting it in the design of expert systems.

Acknowledgements: Thanks to Ruzena Bajcsy for her generosity in the use of the use of the University of Pennsylvania GRASP Lab computer facilities without which this work would not have been possible. Thanks also to F. T. deDombal for permitting us access to some very necessary data.

REFERENCES

Baron, J. *Rationality and intelligence.* New York: Cambridge University Press, 1985.

Berwick, D. M., Fineberg, H. V., & Weinstein, M. C. When doctors meet numbers. *The American Journal of Medicine,* 1981, *71,* 991-998.

Buchanan, B. G., & Shortliffe, E. H. (Eds.). *Rule-based expert systems: The MYCIN experiments of the Stanford heuristic programming project.* Reading: Addison-Wesley, 1984.

Charniak, E. The Bayesian basis of common sense medical diagnosis. *Proceedings of the National Conference on Artificial Intelligence*, 1983, *3*, 70-73.

Charniak, E., & McDermott, D. *Introduction to artificial intelligence.* Massachusetts: Addison-Wesley, 1985.

Christensen-Szalanski, J. J. J., & Bushyhead, J. B. Physicians' use of probabilistic information in a real clinical setting. *Journal of Experimental Psychology: Human Perception and Performance*, 1981, *7*, 928-935.

Clarke, J. R. The role of decision skills and medical knowledge in the clinical judgement of surgical residents. *Surgery*, 1982, *39*, 153-158.

Clarke, J. R. *Surgical judgement using decision sciences.* New York: Prager, 1984.

Clarke, J. R., Schwartz, S. M., Baron, J., & deDombal, F. T. *Intermediate states of pathology: A solution to interdependence in Bayesian databases.* Manuscript submitted for publication, 1986.

Cooper, G. F. A diagnostic method that uses causal knowledge and linear programming in the application of Bayes' formula. *Computer Methods and Programs in Biomedicine*, 1986, *22*, 223-237.

deDombal, F. T. Computers and the surgeon: A matter of decision. *Surgery Annual*, 1979, *11*, 33-57.

Detmer, D. E., Fryback, D. G. & Gassner, K. Heuristics and biases in medical education. *Journal of Medical Education*, 1978, *53*, 682-683.

Eddy, D. M. Probabilistic reasoning in clinical medicine: Problems and opportunities. in D. Kahneman, P. Slovic, & Tversky, A. (Eds.). *Judgement under uncertainty: Heuristics and biases.* New York: Cambridge University Press, 1982.

Elstein, A. S., Shulamn, L. S., & Sprafka, S. A. *Medical problem solving: An analysis of clinical reasoning.* Cambridge: Harvard University Press, 1978.

Fryback, D. G. Bayes' theorem and conditional nonindependence of data in medical diagnosis. *Computers and Biomedical Research*, 1978, *11*, 423-434.

Hayes-Roth, F., Waterman, D. A., & Lenat, D. B. (Eds.). *Building expert systems* Reading: Addison-Wesley, 1983.

Kahneman, D., Slovic, P., & Tversky, A. (Eds.). *Judgement under uncertainty: Heuristics and biases.* New York: Cambridge University Press, 1982.

Kleinmuntz, B. Diagnostic problem solving by computer: A historical review and the current state of the science. *Computers in Biology and Medicine*, 1984, *14*, 255-270.

Mosteller, F., & Tukey, J. W. *Data analysis and regression: A second course in statistics.* Massachusetts: Addison-Wesly, 1977.

Nisbett, R., & Ross, L. *Human inference: Strategies and shortcomings of social judgement*. New Jersey: Prentice-Hall, 1980.

Pearl, J. *Fusion, propagation, and structuring in Bayesian networks* (Tech. Rep. CSD-850022 R-42-VII-12). U.C.L.A., June, 1986.

Peng, Y., & Reggia, J. Plausabilty of diagnostic hypotheses: The nature of simplicity. *Proceedings of the National Conference on Artificial Intelligence*, 1986, *5*, 140-146.

Russek, E., Kronmal, R. A., & Fisher, L. D. The effects of assuming independence in applying Bayes' theorem to risk estimation and classification in diagnosis. *Computers and Biomedical Research*, 1983, *16*, 537-552.

Savage, L. J. *The foundations of statistics*. New York: Wiley, 1954.

Schaffner, K. A. Modeling medical diagnosis: Logical and computer approaches. *Synthese*, 1981, *47*, 163-199.

Schwartz, S. M., Clarke, J. R., Baron, J., & deDombal, F. T. *Fitting a causal Bayesian diagnostic model using objective data*. Manuscript in preparation, 1987.

Shafer, G. *A mathematical theory of evidence*. New Jersey: Princeton University Press, 1976.

Shortliffe, E. H. *Computer-based medical consultations: MYCIN*. New York: American Elsvier, 1976.

Slovic, P., & Lichtenstein, S. Comparison of Bayesian and regression approaches to the study of information processing in judgement. *Organizational Behavior and Human Performance*, 1971, *6*, 649-744.

Wardle, A., & Wardle, L. Computer aided diagnosis: A review of research. *Methods of Information in Medicine*, 1978, *17*, 15-28.

Yates, J. F. External correspondence: Decompositions of the mean probability score. *Organization Behavior and Human Performance*, 1982, *30*, 132-156.

Estimating Uncertain Spatial Relationships in Robotics*

Randall Smith[†] Matthew Self[‡] Peter Cheeseman[§]

SRI International
333 Ravenswood Avenue
Menlo Park, California 94025

In this paper, we describe a representation for spatial information, called the *stochastic map*, and associated procedures for building it, reading information from it, and revising it incrementally as new information is obtained. The map contains the estimates of relationships among objects in the map, and their uncertainties, given all the available information. The procedures provide a general solution to the problem of estimating uncertain relative spatial relationships. The estimates are probabilistic in nature, an advance over the previous, very conservative, worst-case approaches to the problem. Finally, the procedures are developed in the context of state-estimation and filtering theory, which provides a solid basis for numerous extensions.

1 Introduction

In many applications of robotics, such as industrial automation, and autonomous mobility, there is a need to represent and reason about spatial uncertainty. In the past, this need has been circumvented by special purpose methods such as precision engineering, very accurate sensors and the use of fixtures and calibration points. While these methods sometimes supply sufficient accuracy to avoid the need to represent uncertainty explicitly, they are usually costly. An alternative approach is to use multiple, overlapping, lower resolution sensors and to combine the spatial information (including the uncertainty) from all sources to obtain the best spatial estimate. This integrated information can often supply sufficient accuracy to avoid the need for the hard engineered approach.

In addition to lower hardware cost, the explicit estimation of uncertain spatial information makes it possible to decide *in advance* whether proposed operations are likely to

---

*The research reported in this paper was supported by the National Science Foundation under Grant ECS-8200615, the Air Force Office of Scientific Research under Contract F49620-84-K-0007, and by General Motors Research Laboratories.

[†]Currently at General Motors Research Laboratories
Warren, Michigan.

[‡]Currently at UC Berkeley.

[§]Currently at NASA Ames Research Center,
Moffett Field, California.

fail because of accumulated uncertainty, and whether proposed sensor information will be sufficient to reduce the uncertainty to tolerable limits. In situations utilizing inexpensive mobile robots, perhaps the *only* way to obtain sufficient accuracy is to combine the (uncertain) information from many sensors. However, a difficulty in combining uncertain spatial information arises because it often occurs in the form of uncertain *relative* information. This is particularly true where many different frames of reference are used, and the uncertain spatial information must be propagated between these frames. This paper presents a general solution to the problem of estimating uncertain spatial relationships, regardless of which frame the information is presented in, or in which frame the answer is required.

Previous methods for representing spatial uncertainty in typical robotic applications (e.g. [Taylor, 1976]) numerically computed min-max bounds on the errors. Brooks developed other methods for computing min-max bounds symbolically[Brooks, 1982]. These min-max approachs are very conservative compared to the probabilistic approach in this paper, because they combine many pieces of information, each with worst case bounds on the errors. More recently, a probabilistic representation of uncertainty was utilized by the HILARE mobile robot [Chatila, 1985] that is similar to the one presented here, except that it uses only a scalar representation of positional uncertainty instead of a multivariate representation of position and orientation. Smith and Cheeseman ([Smith, 1984], [Smith, 1985]), working on problems in off-line programming of industrial automation tasks, proposed operations that could reduce graphs of uncertain relationships (represented by multivariate probability distributions) to a single, best estimate of some relationship of interest. The current paper extends that work, but in the formal setting of estimation theory, and does not utilize graph transformations.

In summary, many important applications require a representation of spatial uncertainty. In addition, methods for combining uncertain spatial information and transforming such information from one frame to another are required. This paper presents a representation that makes explicit the uncertainty of each degree of freedom in the spatial relationships of interest. A method is given for combining uncertain information regardless of which frame it is presented in, and it allows the description of the spatial uncertainty of one frame relative to any other frame. The necessary procedures are presented in matrix form, suitable for efficient implementation. In particular, methods are given for incrementally building the best estimate "map" and its uncertainty as new pieces of uncertain spatial information are added.

2 The Stochastic Map

Our knowledge of the spatial relationships among objects is inherently uncertain. A manmade object does not match its geometric model *exactly* because of manufacturing tolerances. *Even if it did*, a sensor could not measure the geometric features, and thus locate the object *exactly*, because of measurement errors. And *even if it could*, a robot using the sensor cannot manipulate the object *exactly* as intended, because of hand positioning errors. These errors can be reduced to neglible limits for some tasks, by "pre-enginerring" the solution — structuring the working environment and using specially-suited high–precision equipment — but at great cost of time and expense. However, rather than treat spatial uncertainty as a side issue in geometrical reasoning, we believe it must be treated as an intrinsic part of spatial representations. In this paper, uncertain spatial relationships will be tied together in a representation called the *stochastic map*. It contains estimates of the spatial relationships, their uncertainties, and their inter-dependencies.

First, the map structure will be described, followed by methods for extracting information from it. Finally, a procedure will be given for building the map *incrementally*, as new spatial information is obtained. To illustrate the theory, we will present an example of a mobile robot acquiring knowledge about its location and the organization of its environment by making sensor observations at different times and in different places.

2.1 Representation

In order to formalize the above ideas, we will define the following terms. A *spatial relationship* will be represented by the vector of its *spatial variables*, **x**. For example, the position and orientation of a mobile robot can be described by its coordinates, x and y, in a two dimensional cartesian reference frame and by its orientation, ϕ, given as a rotation about the z axis:

$$\mathbf{x} = \begin{bmatrix} x \\ y \\ \phi \end{bmatrix}.$$

An *uncertain* spatial relationship, moreover, can be represented by a *probability distribution* over its spatial variables — i.e., by a probability density function that assigns a probability to each particular combination of the spatial variables, **x**:

$$P(\mathbf{x}) = f(\mathbf{x})d\mathbf{x}.$$

Such detailed knowledge of the probability distribution is usually unneccesary for making decisions, such as whether the robot will be able to complete a given task (e.g. passing through a doorway). Furthermore, most measuring devices provide only a nominal value of the measured relationship, and we can estimate the average error from the sensor specifications. For these reasons, we choose to model an uncertain spatial relationship by estimating the first two moments of its probability distribution—the *mean*, $\hat{\mathbf{x}}$ and the *covariance*, $\mathbf{C}(\mathbf{x})$, defined as:

$$\begin{aligned} \hat{\mathbf{x}} &\triangleq E(\mathbf{x}), \\ \tilde{\mathbf{x}} &\triangleq \mathbf{x} - \hat{\mathbf{x}}, \\ \mathbf{C}(\mathbf{x}) &\triangleq E(\tilde{\mathbf{x}}\tilde{\mathbf{x}}^T). \end{aligned} \quad (1)$$

where E is the expectation operator, and $\tilde{\mathbf{x}}$ is the deviation from the mean. For our mobile robot example, these are:

$$\hat{\mathbf{x}} = \begin{bmatrix} \hat{x} \\ \hat{y} \\ \hat{\phi} \end{bmatrix}, \quad \mathbf{C}(\mathbf{x}) = \begin{bmatrix} \sigma_x^2 & \sigma_{xy} & \sigma_{x\phi} \\ \sigma_{xy} & \sigma_y^2 & \sigma_{y\phi} \\ \sigma_{x\phi} & \sigma_{y\phi} & \sigma_\phi^2 \end{bmatrix}.$$

The diagonal elements of the covariance matrix are just the variances of the spatial variables, while the off-diagonal elements are the covariances between the spatial variables. It is useful to think of the covariances in terms of their correlation coefficients, ρ_{ij}:

$$\rho_{ij} \triangleq \frac{\sigma_{ij}}{\sigma_i \sigma_j} = \frac{E(\tilde{x}_i \tilde{x}_j)}{\sqrt{E(\tilde{x}_i^2) E(\tilde{x}_j^2)}}, \quad -1 \leq \rho_{ij} \leq 1.$$

Similarly, to model a system of n uncertain spatial relationships, we construct the vector of *all* the spatial variables, which we call the *system state vector*. As before, we will estimate the mean of the state vector, $\hat{\mathbf{x}}$, and the *system covariance matrix*, $\mathbf{C}(\mathbf{x})$:

$$\mathbf{x} = \begin{bmatrix} \mathbf{x}_1 \\ \mathbf{x}_2 \\ \vdots \\ \mathbf{x}_n \end{bmatrix}, \quad \hat{\mathbf{x}} = \begin{bmatrix} \hat{\mathbf{x}}_1 \\ \hat{\mathbf{x}}_2 \\ \vdots \\ \hat{\mathbf{x}}_n \end{bmatrix},$$

$$\mathbf{C}(\mathbf{x}) = \begin{bmatrix} \mathbf{C}(\mathbf{x}_1) & \mathbf{C}(\mathbf{x}_1, \mathbf{x}_2) & \cdots & \mathbf{C}(\mathbf{x}_1, \mathbf{x}_n) \\ \mathbf{C}(\mathbf{x}_2, \mathbf{x}_1) & \mathbf{C}(\mathbf{x}_2) & \cdots & \mathbf{C}(\mathbf{x}_2, \mathbf{x}_n) \\ \vdots & \vdots & \ddots & \vdots \\ \mathbf{C}(\mathbf{x}_n, \mathbf{x}_1) & \mathbf{C}(\mathbf{x}_n, \mathbf{x}_2) & \cdots & \mathbf{C}(\mathbf{x}_n) \end{bmatrix} \quad (2)$$

where:

$$\begin{aligned} \mathbf{C}(\mathbf{x}_i, \mathbf{x}_j) &\triangleq E(\tilde{\mathbf{x}}_i \tilde{\mathbf{x}}_j^T), \\ \mathbf{C}(\mathbf{x}_j, \mathbf{x}_i) &= \mathbf{C}(\mathbf{x}_i, \mathbf{x}_j)^T. \end{aligned} \quad (3)$$

Here, the $\mathbf{x}_i$'s are the vectors of the spatial variables of the individual uncertain spatial relationships, and the $\mathbf{C}(\mathbf{x}_i)$'s are the associated covariance matrices, as discussed earlier. The $\mathbf{C}(\mathbf{x}_i, \mathbf{x}_j)$'s are the cross-covariance matrices between the uncertain spatial relationships. These off-diagonal sub-matrices encode the dependencies between the estimates of the different spatial relationships, and provide the mechanism for updating all the relational estimates that depend on those that are changed.

In our example, each uncertain spatial relationship is of the same form, so $\mathbf{x}$ has $m = 3n$ elements, and we may write:

$$\mathbf{x}_i = \begin{bmatrix} x_i \\ y_i \\ \phi_i \end{bmatrix}, \quad \hat{\mathbf{x}}_i = \begin{bmatrix} \hat{x}_i \\ \hat{y}_i \\ \hat{\phi}_i \end{bmatrix}, \quad \mathbf{C}(\mathbf{x}_i, \mathbf{x}_j) = \begin{bmatrix} \sigma_{x_i x_j} & \sigma_{x_i y_j} & \sigma_{x_i \phi_j} \\ \sigma_{x_i y_j} & \sigma_{y_i y_j} & \sigma_{y_i \phi_j} \\ \sigma_{x_i \phi_j} & \sigma_{y_i \phi_j} & \sigma_{\phi_i \phi_j} \end{bmatrix}.$$

Thus our "map" consists of the current estimate of the mean of the system state vector, which gives the nominal locations of objects in the map with respect to the world reference frame, and the associated system covariance matrix, which gives the uncertainty of each point in the map and the inter-dependencies of these uncertainties.

2.2 Interpretation

For some decisions based on uncertain spatial relationships, we must assume a particular distribution that fits the estimated moments. For example, a robot might need to be able to calculate the probability that a certain object will be in its field of view, or the probability that it will succeed in passing through a doorway.

Given only the mean, $\mathbf{x}$, and covariance matrix, $\mathbf{C(x)}$, of a multivariate probability distribution, the principle of maximum entropy indicates that the distribution which assumes the least information is the normal distribution. Furthermore if the spatial relationship is calculated by combining many different pieces of information the central limit theorem indicates that the resulting distribution will tend to a normal distribution:

$$P(\mathbf{x}) = \frac{\exp\left[-\frac{1}{2}(\mathbf{x}-\hat{\mathbf{x}})^T \mathbf{C}^{-1}(\mathbf{x})(\mathbf{x}-\hat{\mathbf{x}})\right]}{\sqrt{(2\pi)^m |\mathbf{C(x)}|}} d\mathbf{x}. \qquad (4)$$

We will graph uncertain spatial relationships by plotting contours of constant probability from a normal distribution with the given mean and covariance information. These contours are concentric ellipsoids (ellipses for two dimensions) whose parameters can be calculated from the covariance matrix, $\mathbf{C(x_i)}$ [Nahi, 1976]. It is important to emphasize that we do not assume that the uncertain spatial relationships are described by normal distributions. We estimate the mean and variance of their distributions, and use the normal distribution only when we need to calculate specific probability contours.

In the figures in this paper, the plotted points show the *actual* locations of objects, which are known only by the simulator and displayed for our benefit. The robot's information is shown by the ellipses which are drawn centered on the estimated mean of the relationship and such that they enclose a 99.9% confidence region (about four standard deviations) for the relationships.

2.3 Example

Throughout this paper we will refer to a two dimensional example involving the navigation of a mobile robot with three degrees of freedom. In this example the robot performs the following sequence of actions:

- The robot senses object #1
- The robot moves.
- The robot senses an object (object #2) which it determines cannot be object #1.
- Trying again, the robot succeeds in sensing object #1, thus helping to localize itself, object #1, and object #2.

Figure 1 shows two examples of uncertain spatial relationships — the sensed location of object #1, and the end-point of a planned motion for the robot. The robot is initially sitting at a landmark which will be used as the world reference location. There is enough information in our stochastic map at this point for the robot to be able to decide how likely a collision with the object is, if the motion is made. In this case the probability is vanishingly small. The same figure shows how this spatial knowledge can be presented from the robot's new reference frame after its motion. As expected, the uncertainty in the location of object #1 becomes larger when it is compounded with the uncertainty in the robot's motion.

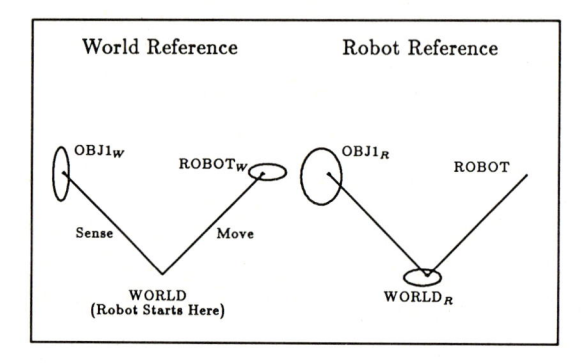

Figure 1: The Robot Senses Object 1 and Moves

From this new location, the robot senses object #2 (Figure 2). The robot is able to determine with the information in its stochastic map that this must be a new object and is not object #1 which it observed earlier.

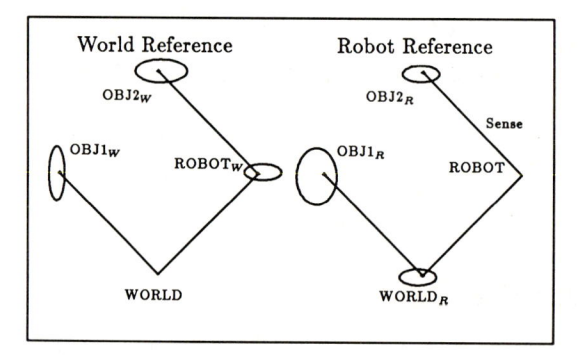

Figure 2: The Robot Senses Object 2

In Figure 3, the robot senses object #1 again. This new sensor measurement acts as a constraint and is incorporated into the map, reducing the uncertainty in the locations of the robot, object #1 *and* Object #2 (Figure 4).

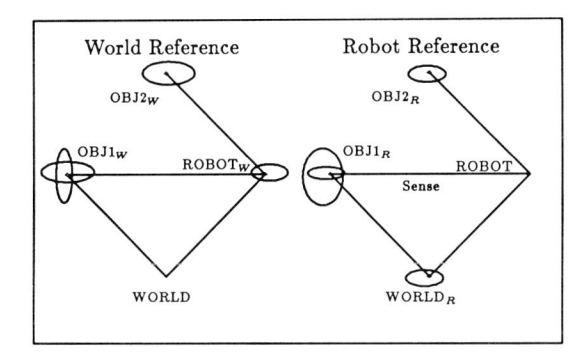

Figure 3: The Robot Senses Object 1 Again

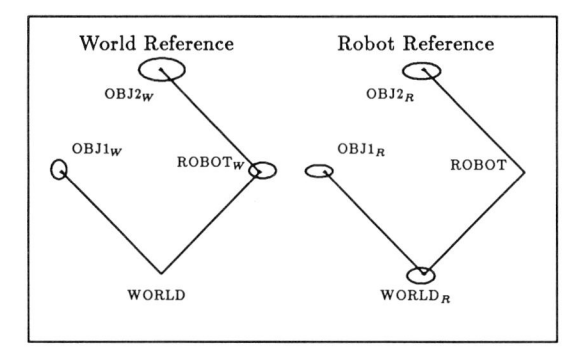

Figure 4: The Updated Estimates After Constraint

3 Reading the Map

3.1 Uncertain Relationships

Having seen how we can represent uncertain spatial relationships by estimates of the mean and covariance of the system state vector, we now discuss methods for estimating the first two moments of unknown multivariate probability distributions. See [Papoulis, 1965] for detailed justifications of the following topics.

3.1.1 Linear Relationships

The simplest case concerns relationships which are linear in the random varables, e.g.:

$$\mathbf{y} = \mathbf{Mx} + \mathbf{b},$$

where, $\mathbf{x}$ ($n \times 1$) is a random vector, $\mathbf{M}$ ($r \times n$) is the *non*-random coefficient matrix, $\mathbf{b}$ ($r \times 1$) is a constant vector, and $\mathbf{y}$ ($r \times 1$) is the resultant random vector. Using the definitions from (1), and the linearity of the expectation operator, E, one can easily verify that the mean of the relationship, $\hat{\mathbf{y}}$, is given by:

$$\hat{\mathbf{y}} = \mathbf{M}\hat{\mathbf{x}} + \mathbf{b}, \tag{5}$$

and the covariance matrix, $\mathbf{C}(\mathbf{y})$, is:

$$\mathbf{C}(\mathbf{y}) = \mathbf{MC}(\mathbf{x})\mathbf{M}^T. \tag{6}$$

We will also need to be able to compute the covariance between $\mathbf{y}$ and some other relationship, $\mathbf{z}$, given the covariance between $\mathbf{x}$ and $\mathbf{z}$:

$$\begin{aligned}\mathbf{C}(\mathbf{y},\mathbf{z}) &= \mathbf{MC}(\mathbf{x},\mathbf{z}), \\ \mathbf{C}(\mathbf{z},\mathbf{y}) &= \mathbf{C}(\mathbf{z},\mathbf{x})\mathbf{M}^T.\end{aligned} \tag{7}$$

The first two moments of the multivariate distribution of $\mathbf{y}$ are computed exactly, given correct moments for $\mathbf{x}$. Further, if $\mathbf{x}$ follows a normal distribution, then so does $\mathbf{y}$.

3.1.2 Non-Linear Relationships

The first two moments computed by the formulae below for non-linear relationships on random variables will be first-order estimates of the true values. To compute the actual values requires knowledge of the *complete* probability density function of the spatial variables, which will not generally be available in our applications. The usual approach is to approximate the non-linear function

$$\mathbf{y} = \mathbf{f}(\mathbf{x})$$

by a Taylor series expansion about the estimated mean, $\hat{\mathbf{x}}$, yielding:

$$\mathbf{y} = \mathbf{f}(\hat{\mathbf{x}}) + \mathbf{F}_\mathbf{x}\tilde{\mathbf{x}} + \cdots,$$

where $\mathbf{F}_\mathbf{x}$ is the matrix of partials, or Jacobian, of $\mathbf{f}$ evaluated at $\hat{\mathbf{x}}$:

$$\mathbf{F}_\mathbf{x} \triangleq \frac{\partial \mathbf{f}(\mathbf{x})}{\partial \mathbf{x}}(\hat{\mathbf{x}}) \triangleq \begin{bmatrix} \frac{\partial f_1}{\partial x_1} & \frac{\partial f_1}{\partial x_2} & \cdots & \frac{\partial f_1}{\partial x_n} \\ \frac{\partial f_2}{\partial x_1} & \frac{\partial f_2}{\partial x_2} & \cdots & \frac{\partial f_2}{\partial x_n} \\ \vdots & \vdots & \ddots & \vdots \\ \frac{\partial f_r}{\partial x_1} & \frac{\partial f_r}{\partial x_2} & \cdots & \frac{\partial f_r}{\partial x_n} \end{bmatrix}_{\mathbf{x}=\hat{\mathbf{x}}}.$$

This terminology is the extension of the f_x terminology from scalar calculus to vectors. The Jacobians are always understood to be evaluated at the estimated mean of the given variables.

Truncating the expansion for **y** after the linear term, and taking the expectation produces the linear estimate of the mean of **y**:

$$\hat{\mathbf{y}} \approx \mathbf{f}(\hat{\mathbf{x}}). \qquad (8)$$

Similarly, the first-order estimate of the covariances are:

$$\begin{aligned} \mathbf{C}(\mathbf{y}) &\approx \mathbf{F_x C(x) F_x^T}, \\ \mathbf{C}(\mathbf{y,z}) &\approx \mathbf{F_x C(x,z)}, \\ \mathbf{C}(\mathbf{z,y}) &\approx \mathbf{C(z,x) F_x^T}. \end{aligned} \qquad (9)$$

Though not utilized in our application, the second order term may be included in the Taylor series expansion to improve the mean estimate:

$$\mathbf{y} = \mathbf{f}(\hat{\mathbf{x}}) + \mathbf{F_x}\tilde{\mathbf{x}} + \frac{1}{2}\mathbf{F_{xx}}(\tilde{\mathbf{x}}\tilde{\mathbf{x}}^T) + \cdots,$$

We denote the (3 dimensional) matrix of second partials of **f** by $\mathbf{F_{xx}}$. To avoid uneccesary complexity, we simply state that the ith element of the vector produced when $\mathbf{F_{xx}}$ is multiplied on the right by a matrix **A** is defined by:

$$(\mathbf{F_{xx} A})_i = trace\left[\left(\left.\frac{\partial^2 f_i}{\partial x_j \partial x_k}\right|_{\mathbf{x}=\hat{\mathbf{x}}}\right)\mathbf{A}\right].$$

The second-order estimate of the mean of **y** is then:

$$\hat{\mathbf{y}} \approx \mathbf{f}(\hat{\mathbf{x}}) + \frac{1}{2}\mathbf{F_{xx} C(x)},$$

and the second-order estimate of the covariance is:

$$\mathbf{C}(\mathbf{y}) \approx \mathbf{F_x C(x) F_x^T} - \frac{1}{4}\mathbf{F_{xx} C(x) C(x)^T F_{xx}^T}.$$

In the remainder of this paper we consider only first order estimates, and the symbol "$\approx$" should read as "linear estimate of."

3.2 Spatial Relationships

We now consider the actual spatial relationships which are most often encountered in robotics applications. We will develop our presentation about the three degree of freedom formulae, since they suit our examples concerning a mobile robot. Formulae for the three dimensional case with six degrees of freedom are given in Appendix A.

We would like to take a chain of relationships, starting at an initial coordinate frame, passing through several intermediate frames to a final frame, and estimate the resultant relationship between initial and final frames. Since frame relationships are directed, we will need the ability to invert the sense of some given relationships during the calculation. The formulae needed for calculating these estimates are given in the following sections.

3.2.1 Compounding

Given two spatial relationships, $\mathbf{x}_{ij}$ and $\mathbf{x}_{jk}$, as in Figure 1 (under Robot Reference), we wish to compute the resultant relationship $\mathbf{x}_{ik}$. The formula for computing $\mathbf{x}_{ik}$ from $\mathbf{x}_{ij}$ and $\mathbf{x}_{jk}$ is:

$$\mathbf{x}_{ik} \triangleq \mathbf{x}_{ij} \oplus \mathbf{x}_{jk} = \begin{bmatrix} x_{jk} \cos \phi_{ij} - y_{jk} \sin \phi_{ij} + x_{ij} \\ x_{jk} \sin \phi_{ij} + y_{jk} \cos \phi_{ij} + y_{ij} \\ \phi_{ij} + \phi_{jk} \end{bmatrix}.$$

We call this operation compounding, and it is used to calculate the resultant relationship from two given relationships which are arranged head-to-tail. It would be used, for instance, to determine the location of a mobile robot after a sequence of relative motions. Remember that these transformations involve rotations, so compounding is not merely vector addition.

Utilizing (8), the first-order estimate of the mean of the compounding operation is:

$$\hat{\mathbf{x}}_{ik} \approx \hat{\mathbf{x}}_{ij} \oplus \hat{\mathbf{x}}_{jk}.$$

Also, from (9), the first-order estimate of the covariance is:

$$\mathbf{C}(\mathbf{x}_{ik}) \approx \mathbf{J}_\oplus \begin{bmatrix} \mathbf{C}(\mathbf{x}_{ij}) & \mathbf{C}(\mathbf{x}_{ij}, \mathbf{x}_{jk}) \\ \mathbf{C}(\mathbf{x}_{jk}, \mathbf{x}_{ij}) & \mathbf{C}(\mathbf{x}_{jk}) \end{bmatrix} \mathbf{J}_\oplus^T.$$

where the Jacobian of the compounding operation, $\mathbf{J}_\oplus$ is given by:

$$\mathbf{J}_\oplus \triangleq \frac{\partial (\mathbf{x}_{ij} \oplus \mathbf{x}_{jk})}{\partial (\mathbf{x}_{ij}, \mathbf{x}_{jk})} = \frac{\partial \mathbf{x}_{ik}}{\partial (\mathbf{x}_{ij}, \mathbf{x}_{jk})} = \begin{bmatrix} 1 & 0 & -(y_{ik} - y_{ij}) & \cos \phi_{ij} & -\sin \phi_{ij} & 0 \\ 0 & 1 & (x_{ik} - x_{ij}) & \sin \phi_{ij} & \cos \phi_{ij} & 0 \\ 0 & 0 & 1 & 0 & 0 & 1 \end{bmatrix}.$$

Note how we have utilized the resultant relationship $\mathbf{x}_{ik}$ in expressing the Jacobian. This results in greater computational efficiency than expressing the Jacobian only in terms of the compounded relationships $\mathbf{x}_{ij}$ and $\mathbf{x}_{jk}$. We can always estimate the mean of an uncertain relationship and then use this result when evaluating the Jacobian to estimate the covariance of the relationship.

If the two relationships being compounded are independent ($\mathbf{C}(\mathbf{x}_{ij}, \mathbf{x}_{jk}) = \mathbf{0}$), we can rewrite the first-order estimate of the covariance as:

$$\mathbf{C}(\mathbf{x}_{ik}) \approx \mathbf{J}_{1\oplus} \mathbf{C}(\mathbf{x}_{ij}) \mathbf{J}_{1\oplus}^T + \mathbf{J}_{2\oplus} \mathbf{C}(\mathbf{x}_{jk}) \mathbf{J}_{2\oplus}^T$$

where $\mathbf{J}_{1\oplus}$ and $\mathbf{J}_{2\oplus}$ are the left and right halves (3×3) of the compounding Jacobian (3×6):

$$\mathbf{J}_\oplus = \begin{bmatrix} \mathbf{J}_{1\oplus} & \mathbf{J}_{2\oplus} \end{bmatrix}.$$

3.2.2 The Inverse Relationship

Given a relationship $\mathbf{x}_{ij}$, the formula for the coordinates of the inverse relationship $\mathbf{x}_{ji}$, as a function of $\mathbf{x}_{ij}$ is:

$$\mathbf{x}_{ji} \stackrel{\triangle}{=} \ominus \mathbf{x}_{ij} \stackrel{\triangle}{=} \begin{bmatrix} -x_{ij} \cos \phi_{ij} - y_{ij} \sin \phi_{ij} \\ x_{ij} \sin \phi_{ij} - y_{ij} \cos \phi_{ij} \\ -\phi_{ij} \end{bmatrix}.$$

We call this the reverse relationship. Using (8) we get the first-order mean estimate:

$$\hat{\mathbf{x}}_{ji} \approx \ominus \hat{\mathbf{x}}_{ij}.$$

From (9) the first-order covariance estimate is:

$$\mathbf{C}(\mathbf{x}_{ji}) \approx \mathbf{J}_\ominus \mathbf{C}(\mathbf{x}_{ij}) \mathbf{J}_\ominus^T,$$

where the Jacobian for the reversal operation, $\mathbf{J}_\ominus$ is:

$$\mathbf{J}_\ominus \stackrel{\triangle}{=} \frac{\partial \mathbf{x}_{ji}}{\partial \mathbf{x}_{ij}} = \begin{bmatrix} -\cos \phi_{ij} & -\sin \phi_{ij} & y_{ji} \\ \sin \phi_{ij} & -\cos \phi_{ij} & -x_{ji} \\ 0 & 0 & -1 \end{bmatrix}.$$

Note that the uncertainty is not inverted, but rather expressed from the opposite (reverse) point of view.

3.2.3 Composite Relationships

We have shown how to compute the resultant of two relationships which are arranged head-to-tail, and also how to reverse a relationship. With these two operations we can calculate the resultant of any sequence of relationships. For example, the resultant of a chain of relationships arranged head-to-tail can be computed recursively by:

$$\begin{aligned} \mathbf{x}_{il} &= \mathbf{x}_{ij} \oplus \mathbf{x}_{jl} = \mathbf{x}_{ij} \oplus (\mathbf{x}_{jk} \oplus \mathbf{x}_{kl}) \\ &= \mathbf{x}_{ik} \oplus \mathbf{x}_{kl} = (\mathbf{x}_{ij} \oplus \mathbf{x}_{jk}) \oplus \mathbf{x}_{kl} \end{aligned}$$

Note, the compounding operation is associative, but not commutative. We have denoted the reversal operation by $\ominus$ so that by analogy to conventional $+$ and $-$ we may write:

$$\mathbf{x}_{ij} \ominus \mathbf{x}_{kj} \stackrel{\triangle}{=} \mathbf{x}_{ij} \oplus (\ominus \mathbf{x}_{kj}).$$

This is the head-to-head combination of two relationships. The tail-to-tail combination arises quite often (as in Figure 1, under World Reference), and is given by:

$$\mathbf{x}_{jk} = \ominus \mathbf{x}_{ij} \oplus \mathbf{x}_{ik}$$

To estimate the mean of a complex relationship, such as the tail-to-tail combination, we merely solve the estimate equations recursively:

$$\hat{\mathbf{x}}_{jk} = \hat{\mathbf{x}}_{ji} \oplus \hat{\mathbf{x}}_{ik} = \ominus \hat{\mathbf{x}}_{ij} \oplus \hat{\mathbf{x}}_{ik}.$$

The covariance can be estimated in a similar way:

$$\begin{aligned}C(x_{jk}) &\approx J_\oplus \begin{bmatrix} C(x_{ji}) & C(x_{ji}, x_{ik}) \\ C(x_{ik}, x_{ji}) & C(x_{ik}) \end{bmatrix} J_\oplus^T \\ &\approx J_\oplus \begin{bmatrix} J_\ominus C(x_{ij}) J_\ominus^T & J_\ominus C(x_{ij}, x_{ik}) \\ C(x_{ik}, x_{ij}) J_\ominus^T & C(x_{ik}) \end{bmatrix} J_\oplus^T. \end{aligned}$$

This method is easy to implement as a recursive algorithm. An equivalent method is to precompute the Jacobians of useful combinations of relationships such as the tail-to-tail combination by using the chain rule. Thus, the Jacobian of the tail-to-tail relationship, $_\ominus J_\oplus$, is given by:

$$_\ominus J_\oplus \triangleq \frac{\partial x_{jk}}{\partial(x_{ij}, x_{ik})} = \frac{\partial x_{jk}}{\partial(x_{ji}, x_{ik})} \frac{\partial(x_{ji}, x_{ik})}{\partial(x_{ij}, x_{ik})} = J_\oplus \begin{bmatrix} J_\ominus & 0 \\ 0 & I \end{bmatrix} = \begin{bmatrix} J_{1\oplus} J_\ominus & J_{2\oplus} \end{bmatrix}.$$

Comparison will show that these two methods are symbolically equivalent, but the recursive method is easier to program, while pre-computing the composite Jacobians is more computationally efficient. Even greater computational efficiency can be achieved by making a change of variables such that the already computed mean estimate is used to evaluate the Jacobian, much as described earlier and in Appendix A.

It may appear that we are calculating first-order estimates of first-order estimates of ..., but actually this recursive procedure produces *precisely* the same result as calculating the first-order estimate of the composite relationship. This is in contrast to min-max methods which make conservative estimates at each step and thus produce *very* conservative estimates of a composite relationship.

If we now assume that the cross-covariance terms in the estimate of the covariance of the tail-to-tail relationship are zero, we get:

$$C(x_{jk}) \approx J_{1\oplus} J_\ominus C(x_{ij}) J_\ominus^T J_{1\oplus}^T + J_{2\oplus} C(x_{ik}) J_{2\oplus}^T$$

The Jacobians for six degree-of-freedom compounding and reversal relationships are given in Appendix A.

3.2.4 Extracting Relationships

We have now developed enough machinery to describe the procedure for estimating the relationships between objects which are in our map. The map contains, by definition, estimates of the locations of objects with respect to the world frame; these relations can be extracted directly. Other relationships are implicit, and must be extracted, using methods developed in the previous sections. For any general spatial relationship among world locations we can write:

$$y = g(x).$$

The estimated mean and covariance of the relationship are given by:

$$\begin{aligned} \hat{y} &\approx g(\hat{x}), \\ C(y) &\approx G_x C(x) G_x^T. \end{aligned}$$

In our mobile robot example we will need to be able to estimate the relative location of one object with respect to the coordinate frame of another object in our map. In this case, we would simply substitute the tail-to-tail operation previously discussed for $\mathbf{g}()$,

$$\mathbf{y} = \mathbf{x}_{ij} = \ominus \mathbf{x}_i \oplus \mathbf{x}_j.$$

4 Building the Map

Our map represents uncertain spatial relationships among objects referenced to a common world frame. Entries in the map may change for two reasons:

- An object moves.
- New spatial information is obtained.

To change the map, we must change the two components that define it — the (mean) estimate of the system state vector, $\hat{\mathbf{x}}$, and the estimate of the system variance matrix, $\mathbf{C}(\mathbf{x})$. Figure 5 shows the changes in the system due to moving objects, or the addition of new spatial information (from sensing).

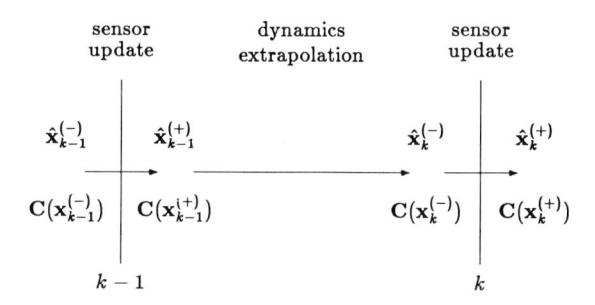

Figure 5: The Changing Map

We will assume that new spatial information is obtained at discrete moments, marked by states k. The update of the estimates at state k, based on new information, is considered to be instantaneous. The estimates, at state k, *prior* to the integration of the new information are denoted by $\hat{\mathbf{x}}_k^{(-)}$ and $\mathbf{C}(\mathbf{x}_k^{(-)})$, and *after* the integration by $\hat{\mathbf{x}}_k^{(+)}$ and $\mathbf{C}(\mathbf{x}_k^{(+)})$.

In the interval between states the system may be changing dynamically — for instance, the robot may be moving. When an object moves, we must define a process to extrapolate the estimate of the state vector and uncertainty at state $k-1$, to state k to reflect the changing relationships.

4.1 Moving Objects

Before describing how the map changes as the mobile robot moves, we will present the general case, which treats any processes that change the state of the system.

The *system dynamics model*, or process model, describes how components of the system state vector change (as a function of time in a continuous system, or by discrete transitions). Between state $k-1$ and k, no measurements of external objects are made. The new state is determined only by the process model, $\mathbf{f}$, as a function of the old state, and any control variables applied in the process (such as relative motion commands sent to our mobile robot). The process model is thus:

$$\mathbf{x}_k^{(-)} = \mathbf{f}\left(\mathbf{x}_{k-1}^{(+)}, \mathbf{y}_{k-1}\right), \tag{10}$$

where $\mathbf{y}$ is a vector comprised of control variables, $\mathbf{u}$, corrupted by mean-zero process noise, $\mathbf{w}$, with covariance $\mathbf{C}(\mathbf{w})$. That is, $\mathbf{y}$ is a noisy control input to the process, given by:

$$\mathbf{y} = \mathbf{u} + \mathbf{w}. \tag{11}$$

$$\hat{\mathbf{y}} = \mathbf{u}, \quad \mathbf{C}(\mathbf{y}) = \mathbf{C}(\mathbf{w}).$$

Given the estimates of the state vector and variance matrix at state $k-1$, the estimates are extrapolated to state k by:

$$\hat{\mathbf{x}}_k^{(-)} \approx \mathbf{f}\left(\hat{\mathbf{x}}_{k-1}^{(+)}, \hat{\mathbf{y}}_{k-1}\right), \tag{12}$$

$$\mathbf{C}(\mathbf{x}_k^{(-)}) \approx \mathbf{F}_{(\mathbf{x},\mathbf{y})} \begin{bmatrix} \mathbf{C}(\mathbf{x}_{k-1}^{(+)}) & \mathbf{C}(\mathbf{x}_{k-1}^{(+)}, \mathbf{y}_{k-1}) \\ \mathbf{C}(\mathbf{y}_{k-1}, \mathbf{x}_{k-1}^{(+)}) & \mathbf{C}(\mathbf{y}_{k-1}) \end{bmatrix} \mathbf{F}_{(\mathbf{x},\mathbf{y})}^T.$$

where,

$$\mathbf{F}_{(\mathbf{x},\mathbf{y})} = \begin{bmatrix} \mathbf{F}_\mathbf{x} & \mathbf{F}_\mathbf{y} \end{bmatrix} \triangleq \frac{\partial \mathbf{f}(\mathbf{x},\mathbf{y})}{\partial (\mathbf{x},\mathbf{y})}\left(\hat{\mathbf{x}}_{k-1}^{(+)}, \hat{\mathbf{y}}_{k-1}\right)$$

If the process noise is uncorrelated with the state, then the off-diagonal sub-matrices in the matrix above are $\mathbf{0}$ and the covariance estimate simplifies to:

$$\mathbf{C}(\mathbf{x}_k^{(-)}) \approx \mathbf{F}_\mathbf{x} \mathbf{C}(\mathbf{x}_{k-1}^{(+)}) \mathbf{F}_\mathbf{x}^T + \mathbf{F}_\mathbf{y} \mathbf{C}(\mathbf{y}_{k-1}) \mathbf{F}_\mathbf{y}^T.$$

The new state estimates become the current estimates to be extrapolated to the next state, and so on.

In our example, only the robot moves, so the process model need only describe its motion. A continuous dynamics model can be developed given *a particular robot*, and the above equations can be reformulated as functions of time (see [Gelb, 1984]). However, if the robot only makes sensor observations at discrete times, then the discrete motion approximation is quite adequate. When the robot moves, it changes its relationship, $\mathbf{x}_R$, with the world. The robot makes an uncertain relative motion, $\mathbf{y}_R = \mathbf{u}_R + \mathbf{w}_R$, to reach a final world location $\mathbf{x}'_R$. Thus,

$$\mathbf{x}'_R = \mathbf{x}_R \oplus \mathbf{y}_R.$$

Only a small portion of the map needs to be changed due to the change in the robot's location from state to state — specifically, the Rth element of the estimated mean of the state vector, and the Rth row and column of the estimated variance matrix. Thus, $\hat{\mathbf{x}}_{k-1}^{(+)}$ becomes $\hat{\mathbf{x}}_k^{(-)}$ and $\mathbf{C}(\mathbf{x}_{k-1}^{(+)})$ becomes $\mathbf{C}(\mathbf{x}_k^{(-)})$, as shown below:

$$\hat{\mathbf{x}}_{k-1}^{(+)} = \begin{bmatrix} \hat{\mathbf{x}}_R \\ \hline \\ \end{bmatrix}, \quad \hat{\mathbf{x}}_k^{(-)} = \begin{bmatrix} \hat{\mathbf{x}}_R' \\ \hline \\ \end{bmatrix}, \quad \mathbf{C}(\mathbf{x}_k^{(-)}) = \begin{bmatrix} & & \mathbf{B}'^T & \\ \hline & \mathbf{B}' & \mathbf{A}' & \\ \hline & & & \\ \end{bmatrix}$$

where

$$\hat{\mathbf{x}}_R' \approx \hat{\mathbf{x}}_R \oplus \hat{\mathbf{y}}_R,$$

$$\mathbf{A}' = \mathbf{C}(\mathbf{x}_R') \approx \mathbf{J}_{1\oplus} \mathbf{C}(\mathbf{x}_R) \mathbf{J}_{1\oplus}^T + \mathbf{J}_{2\oplus} \mathbf{C}(\mathbf{y}_R) \mathbf{J}_{2\oplus}^T,$$

$$\mathbf{B}_i' = \mathbf{C}(\mathbf{x}_R', \mathbf{x}_i) \approx \mathbf{J}_{1\oplus} \mathbf{C}(\mathbf{x}_R, \mathbf{x}_i).$$

$\mathbf{A}'$ is the covariance matrix representing the uncertainty in the new location of the robot. $\mathbf{B}'$ is a row in the system variance matrix. The ith element is a sub-matrix — the cross-covariance of the robot's estimated location and the estimated location of the ith object, as given above. If the estimates of the two locations were not dependent, then that sub-matrix was, and remains $\mathbf{0}$. The newly estimated cross-covariance matrices are transposed, and written into the Rth column of the system variance matrix, marked by $\mathbf{B}'^T$.

4.2 New Spatial Information

The second process which changes the map is the update that occurs when new information about the system state is incorporated. New spatial information might be given, determined by sensor measurements, or even deduced as the consequence of applying a geometrical constraint. For example, placing a box on a table reduces the degrees of freedom of the box and eliminates the uncertainties in the lost degrees of freedom (with respect to the table coordinate frame). In our example, state information is obtained as prior knowledge, or through measurement.

There are two cases which arise when adding new spatial information about objects to our map:

- I: A new object is added to the map,

- II: A (stochastic) constraint is added between objects already in the map.

We will consider each of these cases in turn.

4.2.1 Case I: Adding New Objects

When a new object is added to the map, a new entry must be made in the system state vector to describe the object's *world* location. A new row and column are also added to the system variance matrix to describe the uncertainty in the object's estimated location, and the inter-dependencies of this estimate with estimated locations of other objects. The expanded system is:

$$\hat{x}^{(+)} = \begin{bmatrix} \hat{x}^{(-)} \\ \hline \hat{x}_{n+1} \end{bmatrix}, \quad C(x^{(+)}) = \begin{bmatrix} C(x^{(-)}) & B^T \\ \hline B & A \end{bmatrix},$$

where $\hat{x}_{n+1}$, A, and B will be defined below.

We divide Case I into two sub-cases: I-a, the estimate of the new object's location is *independent* of the estimates of other object locations described in the map; or I-b, it is *dependent* on them.

Case I-a occurs when the estimated location of the object is given directly in world coordinates — i.e., $\hat{x}_{new}$ and $C(x_{new})$ — perhaps as prior information. Since the estimate is independent of other location estimates:

$$x_{n+1} = x_{new},$$

$$\hat{x}_{n+1} = \hat{x}_{new},$$

$$A = C(x_{n+1}) = C(x_{new}), \quad (13)$$

$$B_i = C(x_{n+1}, x_i) = C(x_{new}, x_i) = 0.$$

where A is a covariance matrix, and B is a row of cross-covariance matrices, as before. B is identically 0, since the new estimate is independent of the previous estimates, by definition.

Case I-b occurs when the *world* location of the new object is determined as a function, g, of its spatial relation, z, to other object locations estimated in the map. The relation might be measured or given as prior information. For example, the robot measures the location of a new object relative to itself. Clearly, the uncertainty in the object's *world* location is correlated with the uncertainty in the robot's (world) location. For Case I-b:

$$x_{n+1} = g(x, z),$$

$$\hat{x}_{n+1} = g(\hat{x}, \hat{z}),$$

$$A = C(x_{n+1}) = G_x C(x) G_x^T + G_y C(z) G_y, \quad (14)$$

$$B_i = C(x_{n+1}, x_i),$$

$$B = G_x C(x).$$

We see that Case I-a is the special case of Case I-b, where estimates of the world locations of new objects are independent of the old state estimates and are given exactly by the measured information. That is, when:

$$g(\mathbf{x}, \mathbf{z}) = \mathbf{z}.$$

4.2.2 Case II: Adding Constraints

When new information is obtained relating objects *already in the map*, the system state vector and variance matrix do not increase in size; i.e., no new elements are introduced. However, the old elements are *constrained* by the new relation, and their values will be changed. Constraints can arise in a number of ways:

- A robot measures the relationship of a *known* landmark to itself (i.e., estimates of the world locations of robot and landmark already exist).

- A geometric relationship, such as colinearity, coplanarity, etc., is given for some set of the object location variables.

In the first example the constraint is noisy (because of an imperfect measurement). In the second example, the constraint could be absolute, but could also be given with a tolerance. The two cases are mathematically similar, in that they have to do with uncertain relationships on a number of variables — either measured, or hypothesized. A "rectangularity" constraint is discussed later in the example.

When a constraint is introduced, there are two estimates of the geometric relationship in question — our current best estimate of the relation, which can be extracted from the map, and the new information. The two estimates can be compared (in the same reference frame), and together should allow some improved estimate to be formed (as by averaging, for instance).

For each sensor, we have a *sensor model* that describes how the sensor maps the spatial variables in the state vector into sensor variables. Generally, the measurement, $\mathbf{z}$, is described as a function, $\mathbf{h}$, of the state vector, corrupted by mean-zero, additive noise $\mathbf{v}$. The covariance of the noise, $\mathbf{C}(\mathbf{v})$, is given as part of the model.

$$\mathbf{z} = \mathbf{h}(\mathbf{x}) + \mathbf{v}. \tag{15}$$

The *conditional* sensor value, given the state, and the *conditional covariance* are easily estimated from (15) as:

$$\hat{\mathbf{z}} \approx \mathbf{h}(\hat{\mathbf{x}}).$$
$$\mathbf{C}(\mathbf{z}) \approx \mathbf{H}_\mathbf{x} \mathbf{C}(\mathbf{x}) \mathbf{H}_\mathbf{x}^T + \mathbf{C}(\mathbf{v}),$$

where:

$$\mathbf{H}_\mathbf{x} \triangleq \frac{\partial \mathbf{h}_k(\mathbf{x})}{\partial \mathbf{x}} \left(\hat{\mathbf{x}}_k^{(-)} \right)$$

The formulae describe what values we *expect* from the sensor under the circumstances, and the likely variation; it is our current best estimate of the relationship to be measured.

The actual sensor values returned are usually assumed to be conditionally independent of the state, meaning that the noise is assumed to be independent in each measurement, even when measuring the same relation with the same sensor. The actual sensor values, corrupted by the noise, are the second estimate of the relationship.

For simplicity, in our example we assume that the sensor measures the relative location of the observed object in Cartesian coordinates. Thus the sensor function becomes the tail-to-tail relation of the location of the sensor and the sensed object, described in Section 3.2.3. (Formally, the sensor function is a function of all the variables in the state vector, but the unused variables are not shown below):

$$\mathbf{z} = \mathbf{x}_{ij} = \ominus \mathbf{x}_i \oplus \mathbf{x}_j.$$

$$\hat{\mathbf{z}} = \hat{\mathbf{x}}_{ij} = \ominus \hat{\mathbf{x}}_i \oplus \hat{\mathbf{x}}_j.$$

$$\mathbf{C}(\mathbf{z}) = {}_\ominus \mathbf{J}_\oplus \begin{bmatrix} \mathbf{C}(\mathbf{x}_i) & \mathbf{C}(\mathbf{x}_i, \mathbf{x}_j) \\ \mathbf{C}(\mathbf{x}_j, \mathbf{x}_i) & \mathbf{C}(\mathbf{x}_j) \end{bmatrix} {}_\ominus \mathbf{J}_\oplus^T + \mathbf{C}(\mathbf{v}).$$

Given the sensor model, the conditional estimates of the sensor values and their uncertainties, and an actual sensor measurement, we can update the state estimate using the Kalman Filter equations [Gelb, 1984] given below, and described in the next section:

$$\hat{\mathbf{x}}_k^{(+)} = \hat{\mathbf{x}}_k^{(-)} + \mathbf{K}_k \left[\mathbf{z}_k - \mathbf{h}_k(\hat{\mathbf{x}}_k^{(-)}) \right],$$

$$\mathbf{C}(\mathbf{x}_k^{(+)}) = \mathbf{C}(\mathbf{x}_k^{(-)}) - \mathbf{K}_k \mathbf{H}_\mathbf{x} \mathbf{C}(\mathbf{x}_k^{(-)}), \qquad (16)$$

$$\mathbf{K}_k = \mathbf{C}(\mathbf{x}_k^{(-)}) \mathbf{H}_\mathbf{x}^T \left[\mathbf{H}_\mathbf{x} \mathbf{C}(\mathbf{x}_k^{(-)}) \mathbf{H}_\mathbf{x}^T + \mathbf{C}(\mathbf{v})_k \right]^{-1}.$$

4.2.3 Kalman Filter

The updated estimate is a weighted average of the two estimates, where the weighting factor (computed in the weight matrix $\mathbf{K}$) is proportional to the prior covariance in the state estimate, and inversely proportional to the conditional covariance of the measurement. Thus, if the measurement covariance is large, compared to the state covariance, then $\mathbf{K} \to \mathbf{0}$, and the measurement has little impact in revising the state estimate. Conversely, when the prior state covariance is large compared to the noise covariance, then $\mathbf{K} \to \mathbf{I}$, and nearly the entire difference between the measurement and its expected value is used in updating the state.

The Kalman Filter generally contains a system dynamics model defined less generally than presented in (10); in the standard filter equations the process noise is additive:

$$\mathbf{x}_k^{(-)} = \mathbf{f}\left(\mathbf{x}_{k-1}^{(+)}, \mathbf{u}_{k-1}\right) + \mathbf{w}_{k-1} \qquad (17)$$

in that case $\mathbf{F_y}$ of (10) is the identity matrix, and the estimated mean and covariance take the form:

$$\hat{\mathbf{x}}_k^{(-)} \approx \mathbf{f}\left(\hat{\mathbf{x}}_{k-1}^{(+)}, \mathbf{u}_{k-1}\right), \qquad (18)$$

$$\mathbf{C}(\mathbf{x}_k^{(-)}) \approx \mathbf{F_x} \mathbf{C}(\mathbf{x}_{k-1}^{(+)}) \mathbf{F_x}^T + \mathbf{C}(\mathbf{w}_{k-1}).$$

If the functions **f** in (17) and **h** in (15) are *linear* in the state vector variables, then the partial derivative matrices **F** and **H** are simply constants, and the update formulae (16) with (17), (15), and (18), represent the Kalman Filter [Gelb, 1984].

If, in addition, the noise variables are drawn from normal distributions, then the Kalman Filter produces the *optimal minimum-variance Bayesian estimate*, which is equal to the mean of the *a posteriori conditional density function* of **x**, given the prior statistics of **x**, and the statistics of the measurement **z**. No non-linear estimator can produce estimates with smaller mean-square errors. If the noise does not have a normal distribution, then the Kalman Filter is not optimal, but produces the optimal *linear* estimate.

If the functions **f** and **h** are *non-linear* in the state variables, then **F** and **H** will have to be evaluated (they are not constant matrices). The given formulae then represent the Extended Kalman Filter, a sub-optimal non-linear estimator. It is one of the most widely used non-linear estimators because of its similarity to the optimal linear filter, its simplicity of implementation, and its ability to provide accurate estimates in practice. The error in the estimation due to the non-linearities in **h** can be greatly reduced by iteration, using the Iterated Extended Kalman Filter equations [Gelb, 1984]:

$$\hat{\mathbf{x}}_{k,i+1}^{(+)} = \hat{\mathbf{x}}_k^{(-)} + \mathbf{K}_{k,i} \left[\mathbf{z}_k - \left(\mathbf{h}_k(\hat{\mathbf{x}}_{k,i}^{(+)}) + \mathbf{H}_\mathbf{x}(\hat{\mathbf{x}}_k^{(-)} - \hat{\mathbf{x}}_{k,i}^{(+)}) \right) \right],$$

$$\mathbf{C}(\mathbf{x}_{k,i+1}^{(+)}) = \mathbf{C}(\mathbf{x}_k^{(-)}) - \mathbf{K}_{k,i} \mathbf{H}_\mathbf{x} \mathbf{C}(\mathbf{x}_k^{(-)}),$$

$$\mathbf{K}_{k,i} = \mathbf{C}(\mathbf{x}_k^{(-)}) \mathbf{H}_\mathbf{x}^T \left[\mathbf{H}_\mathbf{x} \mathbf{C}(\mathbf{x}_k^{(-)}) \mathbf{H}_\mathbf{x}^T + \mathbf{C}(\mathbf{v}_k) \right]^{-1},$$

where:

$$\mathbf{H}_\mathbf{x} \triangleq \frac{\partial \mathbf{h}_k(\mathbf{x})}{\partial \mathbf{x}} \left(\hat{\mathbf{x}}_{k,i}^{(-)} \right)$$

$$\hat{\mathbf{x}}_{k,0}^{(+)} \triangleq \hat{\mathbf{x}}_k^{(-)}.$$

Note that the original measurement value, **z**, and the prior estimates of the mean and covariance of the state, are used in each step of the iteration. The ith estimate of the state is used to evaluate the weight matrix, **K**, and is the argument to the non-linear sensor function, **h**. Iteration can be carried out until there is little further improvement in the estimate. The final estimate of the covariance need only be computed at the end of iteration, rather than at each step, since the intermediate system covariance estimates are not used.

5 Developed Example

The methods developed in this paper will now be applied to the mobile robot example in detail. We choose the world reference frame to be the initial location of the robot, without loss of generality. The robot's initial location with respect to the world frame is then the identity relationship (of the compounding operation), with no uncertainty.

$$\hat{\mathbf{x}} = [\hat{\mathbf{x}}_R] = [\mathbf{0}],$$

$$\mathbf{C}(\mathbf{x}) = [\mathbf{C}(\mathbf{x}_R)] = [\mathbf{0}].$$

Note, that the normal distribution corresponding to this covariance matrix (from (4)) is singular, but the limiting case as the covariance goes to zero is a dirac delta function centered on the mean estimate. This agrees with the intuitive interpretation of zero covariance implying no uncertainty.

Step 1: When the robot senses object #1, the new information must be added into the map. Normally, adding new information relative to the robot's position would fall under case I-b, but since the robot's frame is the same as the world frame, it falls under case I-a. The sensor returns the mean location and variance of object #1 ($\hat{z}_1$ and $\mathbf{C}(\mathbf{z}_1)$). The new system state vector and variance matrix are:

$$\hat{\mathbf{x}} = \begin{bmatrix} \hat{\mathbf{x}}_R \\ \hat{\mathbf{x}}_1 \end{bmatrix} = \begin{bmatrix} \mathbf{0} \\ \hat{\mathbf{z}}_1 \end{bmatrix},$$

$$\mathbf{C}(\mathbf{x}) = \begin{bmatrix} \mathbf{C}(\mathbf{x}_R) & \mathbf{C}(\mathbf{x}_R, \mathbf{x}_1) \\ \mathbf{C}(\mathbf{x}_1, \mathbf{x}_R) & \mathbf{C}(\mathbf{x}_1) \end{bmatrix} = \begin{bmatrix} \mathbf{0} & \mathbf{0} \\ \mathbf{0} & \mathbf{C}(\mathbf{z}_1) \end{bmatrix}.$$

where $\mathbf{x}_1$ is the location of object #1 with respect to the world frame.

Step 2: The robot moves from its current location to a new location, where the relative motion is given by $\mathbf{y}_R$. Since this motion is also from the world frame, it is a special case of the dynamics extrapolation.

$$\hat{\mathbf{x}} = \begin{bmatrix} \hat{\mathbf{x}}_R \\ \hat{\mathbf{x}}_1 \end{bmatrix} = \begin{bmatrix} \hat{\mathbf{y}}_R \\ \hat{\mathbf{z}}_1 \end{bmatrix},$$

$$\mathbf{C}(\mathbf{x}) = \begin{bmatrix} \mathbf{C}(\mathbf{x}_R) & \mathbf{C}(\mathbf{x}_R, \mathbf{x}_1) \\ \mathbf{C}(\mathbf{x}_1, \mathbf{x}_R) & \mathbf{C}(\mathbf{x}_1) \end{bmatrix} = \begin{bmatrix} \mathbf{C}(\mathbf{y}_R) & \mathbf{0} \\ \mathbf{0} & \mathbf{C}(\mathbf{z}_1) \end{bmatrix}.$$

We can now transform the information in our map from the world frame to the robot's new frame to see how the world looks from the robot's point of view:

$$\hat{\mathbf{x}}_{RW} = \ominus \hat{\mathbf{x}}_R,$$
$$\mathbf{C}(\mathbf{x}_{RW}) \approx \mathbf{J}_\ominus \mathbf{C}(\mathbf{x}_R) \mathbf{J}_\ominus^T,$$
$$\hat{\mathbf{x}}_{R1} = \ominus \hat{\mathbf{x}}_R \oplus \hat{\mathbf{x}}_1,$$
$$\mathbf{C}(\mathbf{x}_{R1}) \approx \mathbf{J}_{1\oplus} \mathbf{J}_\ominus \mathbf{C}(\mathbf{x}_R) \mathbf{J}_\ominus^T \mathbf{J}_{1\oplus}^T + \mathbf{J}_{2\oplus} \mathbf{C}(\mathbf{x}_1) \mathbf{J}_{2\oplus}^T.$$

Step 3: The robot now senses an object from its new location. The new measurement, $\mathbf{z}_2$, is of course, relative to the robot's location, $\mathbf{x}_R$.

$$\hat{\mathbf{x}} = \begin{bmatrix} \hat{\mathbf{x}}_R \\ \hat{\mathbf{x}}_1 \\ \hat{\mathbf{x}}_2 \end{bmatrix} = \begin{bmatrix} \hat{\mathbf{y}}_R \\ \hat{\mathbf{z}}_1 \\ \hat{\mathbf{y}}_R \oplus \hat{\mathbf{z}}_2 \end{bmatrix},$$

$$\mathbf{C}(\mathbf{x}) = \begin{bmatrix} \mathbf{C}(\mathbf{x}_R) & \mathbf{C}(\mathbf{x}_R, \mathbf{x}_1) & \mathbf{C}(\mathbf{x}_R, \mathbf{x}_2) \\ \mathbf{C}(\mathbf{x}_1, \mathbf{x}_R) & \mathbf{C}(\mathbf{x}_1) & \mathbf{C}(\mathbf{x}_1, \mathbf{x}_2) \\ \mathbf{C}(\mathbf{x}_2, \mathbf{x}_R) & \mathbf{C}(\mathbf{x}_2, \mathbf{x}_1) & \mathbf{C}(\mathbf{x}_2) \end{bmatrix}$$

$$= \begin{bmatrix} \mathbf{C}(\mathbf{y}_R) & \mathbf{0} & \mathbf{C}(\mathbf{y}_R)\mathbf{J}_{1\oplus}^T \\ \mathbf{0} & \mathbf{C}(\mathbf{z}_1) & \mathbf{0} \\ \mathbf{J}_{1\oplus}\mathbf{C}(\mathbf{y}_R) & \mathbf{0} & \mathbf{C}(\mathbf{x}_2) \end{bmatrix}.$$

where:
$$\mathbf{C}(\mathbf{x}_2) = \mathbf{J}_{1\oplus}\mathbf{C}(\mathbf{y}_R)\mathbf{J}_{1\oplus}^T + \mathbf{J}_{2\oplus}\mathbf{C}(\mathbf{z}_2)\mathbf{J}_{2\oplus}^T.$$

Step 4: Now, the robot senses object #1 again. In practice one would probably calculate the world location of a new object, and only after comparing the new object to the old ones could the robot decide that they are likely to be the same object. For this example, however, we will assume that the sensor is able to identify the object as being object #1 and we don't need to map this new measurement into the world frame before performing the update. The symbolic expressions for the estimates of the mean and covariance of the state vector become too complex to reproduce as we have done for the previous steps. Also, if the iterated methods are being used, there is no symbolic expression for the results.

Notice that the formulae presented in this section are correct for *any* network of relationships which has the same topology as this example. This procedure can be completely automated, and is very suitable for use in off-line robot planning.

As a further example of some of the possibilities of this stochastic map method, we will present an example of a geometric constraint — four points known to be arranged in a rectangle. Figure 6 shows the estimated locations of the four points with respect to the world frame, before and after introduction of the information that they are the vertices of a rectangle. The improved estimates are overlayed on the original estimates in the "after" diagram. One way to specify the "rectangularity" of four points — $\mathbf{x}_i, \mathbf{x}_j, \mathbf{x}_k, \mathbf{x}_l$ is as follows:

$$\mathbf{h} = \begin{bmatrix} x_i - x_j + x_k - x_l \\ y_i - y_j + y_k - y_l \\ (x_i - x_j)(x_k - x_j) + (y_i - y_j)(y_k - y_j) \end{bmatrix}.$$

The first two elements of **h** are zero when opposite sides of the closed planar figure represented by the four vertices are parallel; the last element of **h** is zero when the two sides forming the upper-right corner are perpendicular.

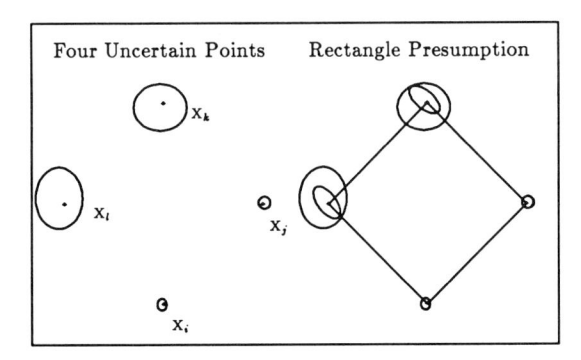

Figure 6: Application of a Rectangular Shape Constraint

We model the rectangle constraint similarly to a sensor, except that we hypothesize rather than measure the relationship. Just as the sensor model included measurement noise, this shape constraint could be "noisy", but here the "noise" describes random tolerances in the shape parameters, possibly given in the geometric model of the object:

$$\mathbf{z} = \mathbf{h}(\mathbf{x}) + v.$$

Given four estimated points, their nominal rectangularity ($\hat{\mathbf{z}}$) and the estimated covariance can be computed. The new information — the presumed shape — is chosen with shape parameters from a distribution with mean $\mathbf{0}$ and covariance $\mathbf{C}(\mathbf{v})$. We might as well choose the most likely a priori value, $\mathbf{0}$.

If we are going to impose the constraint that the four points are precisely in a rectangle — i.e., there is no shape uncertainty, and $\mathbf{C}(\mathbf{v}) = \mathbf{0}$ — then we can choose $\mathbf{h}$ to be *any* function which is zero only when the four points are in a rectangle. If, however, we wish to impose a *loose* rectangle constraint, we must formulate the function $\mathbf{h}$ such that $\mathbf{z}$ is a useful measure of *how* the four points fail to be rectangular.

6 Discussion and Conclusions

This paper presents a general theory for estimating uncertain relative spatial relationships between reference frames in a network of uncertain spatial relationships. Such networks arise, for example, in industrial robotics and navigation for mobile robots, because the system is given spatial information in the form of sensed relationships, prior constraints, relative motions, and so on. The theory presented in this paper allows the efficient estimation of these uncertain spatial relations. This theory can be used, for example, to compute *in advance* whether a proposed sequence of actions (each with known uncertainty) is likely to fail due to too much accumulated uncertainty; whether a proposed sensor observation will reduce the uncertainty to a tolerable level; whether a sensor result is so unlikely given its expected value and its prior probability of failure that it should be ignored, and so on. This paper applies state estimation theory to the problem of estimating parameters of an entire spatial configuration of objects, with the ability to transform estimates into any frame of interest.

The estimation procedure makes a number of assumptions that are normally met in practice. These assumptions are detailed in the text, but the main assumptions can be summarized as follows:

- The angular errors are "small". This requirement arises because we linearize inherently nonlinear relationships. In Monte Carlo simulations[Smith, 1985], angular errors with a standard deviation as large as 5° gave estimates of the means and variances to within 1% of the correct values.

- Estimating only two moments of the probability density functions of the uncertain spatial relationships is adequate for decision making. We believe that this is the case since we will most often model a sensor observation by a mean and variance, and the relationships which result from combining many pieces of information become rapidly Gaussian, and thus are accurately modelled by only two moments.

Although the examples presented in this paper have been solely concerned with *spatial* information, there is nothing in the theory that imposes this restriction. Provided that functions are given which describe the relationships among the components to be estimated, those components could be forces, velocities, time intervals, or other quantities in robotic and non-robotic applications.

Appendix A

In this paper we presented formulae for computing the resultant of two spatial relationships in two dimensions (three degrees of freedom). The Jacobians for the three-dimensional transformations are described below. In three dimensions, there are six degrees of freedom: translations in x, y, z and three orientation angles: ϕ, θ, ψ. For computational reasons, orientation is often expressed as a rotation matrix composed of orthogonal column vectors (one per Cartesian axis):

$$\mathbf{R} = \begin{bmatrix} \mathbf{n} & \mathbf{o} & \mathbf{a} \end{bmatrix} = \begin{bmatrix} n_x & o_x & a_x \\ n_y & o_y & a_y \\ n_z & o_z & a_z \end{bmatrix}$$

A primitive rotation is a rotation about one of the axes, and can be represented by a primitive rotation matrix with the above form (see [Paul, 1981] for definitions). For example, $Rot(z, a)$ describes the rotation by a radians about the z axis. Primitive rotation matrices can be multiplied together to produce a rotation matrix describing the final orientation. Orientation will be represented by rotation matrices in the following. There are two common interpretations of the orientation angles—Euler angles and roll, pitch, and yaw.

Relationships Using Euler Angles

Euler angles are defined by:

$$Euler(\phi, \theta, \psi) = Rot(z, \phi) Rot(y', \theta) Rot(z'', \psi) =$$

$$\begin{bmatrix} \cos\phi\cos\theta\cos\psi - \sin\phi\sin\psi & -\cos\phi\cos\theta\sin\psi - \sin\phi\cos\psi & \cos\phi\sin\theta \\ \sin\phi\cos\theta\cos\psi + \cos\phi\sin\psi & -\sin\phi\cos\theta\sin\psi + \cos\phi\cos\psi & \sin\phi\sin\theta \\ -\sin\theta\cos\psi & \sin\theta\sin\psi & \cos\theta \end{bmatrix}.$$

The head to tail relationship, $\mathbf{x}_3 = \mathbf{x}_1 \oplus \mathbf{x}_2$, is then given by:

$$\mathbf{x}_3 = \begin{bmatrix} x_3 \\ y_3 \\ z_3 \\ \phi_3 \\ \theta_3 \\ \psi_3 \end{bmatrix} = \begin{bmatrix} \mathbf{T}_E \\ \mathbf{A}_E \end{bmatrix}$$

where $\mathbf{T}_E$ and $\mathbf{A}_E$ are

$$\mathbf{T}_E = \mathbf{R}_1 \begin{bmatrix} x_2 \\ y_2 \\ z_2 \end{bmatrix} + \begin{bmatrix} x_1 \\ y_1 \\ z_1 \end{bmatrix},$$

$$\mathbf{A}_E = \begin{bmatrix} atan2(a_{y_3}, a_{z_3}) \\ atan2(a_{x_3}\cos\phi_3 + a_{y_3}\sin\phi_3, a_{z_3}) \\ atan2(-n_{z_3}\sin\phi_3 + n_{y_3}\cos\phi_3, -o_{z_3}\sin\phi_3 + o_{y_3}\cos\phi_3) \end{bmatrix}.$$

The matrix $\mathbf{R}_1$, representing the orientation angles of $\mathbf{x}_1$, has the same definition as the Euler rotation matrix defined above (with angles subscripted by 1). The terms a_{z_3} etc. are the elements of the compound rotation matrix $\mathbf{R}_3$, whose values are defined by $\mathbf{R}_3 = \mathbf{R}_1\mathbf{R}_2$. Note that the inverse trignometric function $atan2$ is a function of two arguments, the ordinate y and the abscissa x. This function returns the correct result when either x or y are zero, and gives the correct answer over the entire range of possible inputs [Paul, 1981]. Also note that the solution for ϕ_3 is obtained first, and then used in solving for the other two angles.

The Jacobian of this relationship, $\mathbf{J}_\oplus$, is:

$$\mathbf{J}_\oplus = \frac{\partial \mathbf{x}_3}{\partial(\mathbf{x}_1, \mathbf{x}_2)} = \begin{bmatrix} \mathbf{I}_{3\times3} & \mathbf{M} & \mathbf{R}_1 & \mathbf{0}_{3\times3} \\ \mathbf{0}_{3\times3} & \mathbf{K}_1 & \mathbf{0}_{3\times3} & \mathbf{K}_2 \end{bmatrix}$$

where

$$\mathbf{M} = \begin{bmatrix} -(y_3 - y_1) & (z_3 - z_1)\cos\phi_1 & o_{x_1}x_2 - n_{z_1}y_2 \\ x_3 - x_1 & (z_3 - z_1)\sin\phi_1 & o_{y_1}x_2 - n_{y_1}y_2 \\ 0 & -x_2\cos\theta_1\cos\psi_1 + y_2\cos\theta_1\sin\psi_1 - z_2\sin\theta_1 & o_{z_1}x_2 - n_{z_1}y_2 \end{bmatrix},$$

$$\mathbf{K}_1 = \begin{bmatrix} 1 & [\cos\theta_3\sin(\phi_3 - \phi_1)]/\sin\theta_3 & [\sin\theta_2\cos(\psi_3 - \psi_2)]/\sin\theta_3 \\ 0 & \cos(\phi_3 - \phi_1) & \sin\theta_2\sin(\psi_3 - \psi_2) \\ 0 & \sin(\phi_3 - \phi_1)/\sin\theta_3 & [\sin\theta_1\cos(\phi_3 - \phi_1)]/\sin\theta_3 \end{bmatrix},$$

$$\mathbf{K}_2 = \begin{bmatrix} [\sin\theta_2\cos(\psi_3 - \psi_2)]/\sin\theta_3 & [\sin(\psi_3 - \psi_2)]/\sin\theta_3 & 0 \\ \sin\theta_2\sin(\psi_3 - \psi_2) & \cos(\psi_3 - \psi_2) & 0 \\ [\sin\theta_1\cos(\phi_3 - \phi_1)]/\sin\theta_3 & [\cos\theta_3\sin(\psi_3 - \psi_2)]/\sin\theta_3 & 1 \end{bmatrix}.$$

Note that this Jacobian (and similarly, the one for RPY angles) has been simplified by the use of final terms (e.g. x_3, ψ_3). Since the final terms are computed routinely in determining the mean relationship, they are available to evaluate the Jacobian. Examination of the elements indicates the possibility of a singularity; as the mean values of the angles approach a singular combination, the accuracy of the covariance estimates using this Jacobian will decrease. Methods for avoiding the singularity during calculations are being explored.

The inverse relation, $\mathbf{x}'$, in terms of the elements of the relationship $\mathbf{x}$, using the Euler angle definition, is:

$$\mathbf{x}' = \begin{bmatrix} x' \\ y' \\ z' \\ \phi' \\ \theta' \\ \psi' \end{bmatrix} = \begin{bmatrix} -(n_x x + n_y y + n_z z) \\ -(o_x x + o_y y + o_z z) \\ -(a_x x + a_y y + a_z z) \\ -\psi \\ -\theta \\ -\phi \end{bmatrix}$$

where n_x etc. are the elements of the rotation matrix $\mathbf{R}$ associated with the angles in the given transformation to be inverted, $\mathbf{x}$. The Jacobian of the this relationship, $\mathbf{J}_\ominus$, is:

$$\mathbf{J}_\ominus = \frac{\partial \mathbf{x}'}{\partial \mathbf{x}} = \begin{bmatrix} -\mathbf{R}^T & \mathbf{N} \\ \mathbf{0}_{3\times 3} & \mathbf{Q} \end{bmatrix}, \quad \mathbf{Q} = \begin{bmatrix} 0 & 0 & -1 \\ 0 & -1 & 0 \\ -1 & 0 & 0 \end{bmatrix},$$

$$\mathbf{N} = \begin{bmatrix} n_y x - n_x y & -n_z x \cos\phi - n_z y \sin\phi + z\cos\theta\cos\psi & y' \\ o_y x - o_x y & -o_z x \cos\phi - o_z y \sin\phi - z\cos\theta\sin\psi & -x' \\ a_y x - a_x y & -a_z x \cos\phi - a_z y \sin\phi + z\sin\theta & 0 \end{bmatrix}.$$

Relationships Using Roll, Pitch and Yaw Angles

Roll, pitch, and yaw angles are defined by:

$$RPY(\phi,\theta,\psi) = Rot(z,\phi)Rot(y',\theta)Rot(x'',\psi) =$$

$$\begin{bmatrix} \cos\phi\cos\theta & \cos\phi\sin\theta\sin\psi - \sin\phi\cos\psi & \cos\phi\sin\theta\cos\psi + \sin\phi\sin\psi \\ \sin\phi\cos\theta & \sin\phi\sin\theta\sin\psi + \cos\phi\cos\psi & \sin\phi\sin\theta\cos\psi - \cos\phi\sin\psi \\ -\sin\theta & \cos\theta\sin\psi & \cos\theta\cos\psi \end{bmatrix}$$

The head to tail relationship, $\mathbf{x}_3 = \mathbf{x}_1 \oplus \mathbf{x}_2$, is then given by:

$$\mathbf{x}_3 = \begin{bmatrix} x_3 \\ y_3 \\ z_3 \\ \phi_3 \\ \theta_3 \\ \psi_3 \end{bmatrix} = \begin{bmatrix} \mathbf{T}_{RPY} \\ \mathbf{A}_{RPY} \end{bmatrix}$$

where $\mathbf{T}_{RPY}$ and $\mathbf{A}_{RPY}$ are defined by:

$$\mathbf{T}_{RPY} = \mathbf{R}_1 \begin{bmatrix} x_2 \\ y_2 \\ z_2 \end{bmatrix} + \begin{bmatrix} x_1 \\ y_1 \\ z_1 \end{bmatrix},$$

$$\mathbf{A}_{RPY} = \begin{bmatrix} atan2(n_{y_3}, n_{x_3}) \\ atan2(-n_{z_3}, n_{x_3}\cos\phi_3 + n_{y_3}\sin\phi_3) \\ atan2(a_{x_3}\sin\phi_3 - a_{y_3}\cos\phi_3, -o_{x_3}\sin\phi_3 + o_{y_3}\cos\phi_3) \end{bmatrix}.$$

The matrix $\mathbf{R}_1$ is the rotation matrix for the RPY angles in $\mathbf{x}_1$. The Jacobian of the head-to-tail relationship is given by:

$$\mathbf{J}_\oplus = \frac{\partial \mathbf{x}_3}{\partial(\mathbf{x}_1,\mathbf{x}_2)} = \begin{bmatrix} \mathbf{I}_{3\times 3} & \mathbf{M} & \mathbf{R}_1 & \mathbf{0}_{3\times 3} \\ \mathbf{0}_{3\times 3} & \mathbf{K}_1 & \mathbf{0}_{3\times 3} & \mathbf{K}_2 \end{bmatrix}$$

where

$$\mathbf{M} = \begin{bmatrix} -(y_3 - y_1) & (z_3 - z_1)\cos(\phi_1) & a_{z_1}y_2 - o_{z_1}z_2 \\ x_3 - x_1 & (z_3 - z_1)\sin(\phi_1) & a_{y_1}y_2 - o_{y_1}z_2 \\ 0 & -x_2\cos\theta_1 - y_2\sin\theta_1\sin\psi_1 - z_2\sin\theta_1\cos\psi_1 & a_{z_1}y_2 - o_{z_1}z_2 \end{bmatrix},$$

$$\mathbf{K}_1 = \begin{bmatrix} 1 & [\sin\theta_3 \sin(\phi_3 - \phi_1)]/\cos\theta_3 & [o_{x_2}\sin\psi_3 + a_{x_2}\cos\psi_3]/\cos\theta_3 \\ 0 & \cos(\phi_3 - \phi_1) & \cos\theta_1 \sin(\phi_3 - \phi_1) \\ 0 & [\sin(\phi_3 - \phi_1)]/\cos\theta_3 & [\cos\theta_1 \cos(\phi_3 - \phi_1)]/\cos\theta_3 \end{bmatrix},$$

$$\mathbf{K}_2 = \begin{bmatrix} [\cos\theta_2 \cos(\psi_3 - \psi_2)]/\cos\theta_3 & [\sin(\psi_3 - \psi_2)]/\cos\theta_3 & 0 \\ \cos\theta_2 \sin(\psi_3 - \psi_2) & \cos(\psi_3 - \psi_2) & 0 \\ [a_{x_1}\cos\phi_3 + a_{y_1}\sin\phi_3]/\cos\theta_3 & [\sin\theta_3 \sin(\psi_3 - \psi_2)]/\cos\theta_3 & 1 \end{bmatrix}.$$

The inverse relation, $\mathbf{x}'$, in terms of the elements of $\mathbf{x}$, using the RPY angle definition, is:

$$\mathbf{x}' = \begin{bmatrix} x' \\ y' \\ z' \\ \phi' \\ \theta' \\ \psi' \end{bmatrix} = \begin{bmatrix} -(n_x x + n_y y + n_z z) \\ -(o_x x + o_y y + o_z z) \\ -(a_x x + a_y y + a_z z) \\ atan2(o_z, n_z) \\ atan2(-a_z, n_z \cos\phi + o_z \sin\phi) \\ atan2(n_z \sin\phi - o_z \cos\phi, -n_y \sin\phi + o_y \cos\phi) \end{bmatrix}$$

where n_x etc. are the elements of the rotation matrix, $\mathbf{R}$, for the RPY angles in $\mathbf{x}$. The Jacobian of the inverse relationship is:

$$\mathbf{J}_\ominus = \frac{\partial \mathbf{x}'}{\partial \mathbf{x}} = \begin{bmatrix} -\mathbf{R}^T & \mathbf{N} \\ \mathbf{0}_{3\times 3} & \mathbf{Q} \end{bmatrix}$$

where

$$\mathbf{N} = \begin{bmatrix} n_y x - n_z y & -n_z x \cos\phi - n_z y \sin\phi + z \cos\theta & 0 \\ o_y x - o_z y & -o_z x \cos\phi - o_z y \sin\phi + z \sin\theta \sin\psi & z' \\ a_y x - a_z y & -a_z x \cos\phi - a_z y \sin\phi + z \sin\theta \cos\psi & -y' \end{bmatrix},$$

$$\mathbf{Q} = \begin{bmatrix} -a_z/(1 - a_{z^2}) & -a_y \cos\phi/(1 - a_{z^2}) & n_x a_z/(1 - a_{z^2}) \\ a_y/(1 - a_{z^2})^{1/2} & -a_z \cos\phi/(1 - a_{z^2})^{1/2} & o_x/(1 - a_{z^2})^{1/2} \\ a_z a_x/(1 - a_{z^2}) & -o_z \cos\psi/(1 - a_{z^2}) & -n_x/(1 - a_{z^2}) \end{bmatrix}.$$

References

Brooks, R. A. 1982. Symbolic Error Analysis and Robot Planning. *Int. J. Robotics Res.* 1(4):29-68.

Chatila, R. and Laumond, J-P. 1985. Position Referencing and Consistent World Modeling for Mobile Robots. *Proc. IEEE Int. Conf. Robotics and Automation.* St. Louis: IEEE, pp. 138-145.

Gelb, A. 1984. *Applied Optimal Estimation.* M.I.T. Press

Nahi, N. E. 1976. *Estimation Theory and Applications.* New York: R.E. Krieger.

Papoulis, A. 1965. *Probability, Random Variables, and Stochastic Processes.* McGraw-Hill.

Paul, R. P. 1981. *Robot Manipulators: Mathematics, Programming and Control.* Cambridge: MIT Press.

Smith, R. C., and Cheeseman, P. 1985. On the Representation and Estimation of Spatial Uncertainty. SRI Robotics Lab. Tech. Paper, and to appear *Int. J. Robotics Res.* 5(4): Winter 1987.

Smith, R. C., *et al.* 1984. Test-Bed for Programmable Automation Research. Final Report-Phase 1, SRI International, April 1984.

Taylor, R. H. 1976. A Synthesis of Manipulator Control Programs from Task-Level Specifications. AIM-282. Stanford, Calif.: Stanford University Artificial Intelligence Laboratory.